The College
WRITER

A Guide to Thinking, Writing, and Researching

Fifth Edition

CENGAGE Learning

Australia • Brazil • Mexico • Singapore • United Kingdom • United States

Randall VanderMey
Westmont College

Verne Meyer
Dordt College

John Van Rys
Redeemer University College

Pat Sebranek

The College Writer: A Guide to Thinking, Writing, and Researching, **Fifth Edition**

Randall VanderMey, Verne Meyer, John Van Rys, and Pat Sebranek

Product Director: Monica Eckman

Product Manager: Margaret Leslie

Managing Developer: Leslie Taggart

Content Developer: Stephanie Carpenter

Content Coordinator: Sarah Turner

Product Assistant: Cailin Barrett-Bressack

Media Developer: Janine Tangney

Brand Manager: Lydia LeStar

Market Development Manager: Erin Parkins

Content Project Manager: Rosemary Winfield

Art Director: Hannah Wellman

Manufacturing Planner: Betsy Donaghey

Rights Acquisition Specialist: Ann Hoffman

Design and Production Services: Write Source

Cover Image: Vadim Georgiev/used under license from Shutterstock.com; MrGarry/ used under license from Shutterstock.com; tassel78/used under license from Shutterstock.com

Compositor: Sebranek, Inc.

Printed in the United States of America

1 2 3 4 5 6 7 17 16 15 14 13

Library of Congress Control Number: 2013947896

Student casebound edition:
ISBN-13: 978-1-285-43795-8
ISBN-10: 1-285-43795-0

Student paperbound edition:
ISBN-13: 978-1-285-43801-6
ISBN-10: 1-285-43801-9

Cengage Learning
200 First Stamford Place, 4th floor
Stamford, CT 06902
USA

Cengage Learning is a leading provider of customized learning solutions with office locations around the globe, including Singapore, the United Kingdom, Australia, Mexico, Brazil and Japan. Locate your local office at **international.cengage.com/region**.

Cengage Learning products are represented in Canada by Nelson Education, Ltd.

For your course and learning solutions, visit **www.cengage.com**.

Purchase any of our products at your local college store or at our preferred online store **www.cengagebrain.com**.

Instructors: Please visit **login.cengage.com** and log in to access instructor-specific resources.

Brief Contents

Contents

Thematic Table of Contents for Readings

Character and Conscience

Community and Culture

Environment and Nature

Ethics and Ideology

Ethnicity and Identity

Humor and Humanity

Language and Literature

Memory and Tradition

Science and Health

Terror and Our Time

Work and Play

Preface

The fifth edition of *The College Writer* is a fully updated text in four parts: Rhetoric, Reader, Research, and Handbook. Each section combines purposeful instruction in the writing process with an accessible style to help college students connect effective reading, writing, and thinking. The book's visual format enables students to grasp the big picture and easily locate supporting details. To further help students craft papers for all of their courses, samples of student and professional writing in different disciplines highlight features of effective writing.

New Features

- **NEW Chapter 26, "Building Credibility: Avoiding Plagiarism,"** helps students understand what constitutes plagiarism, why it is a serious ethical and academic problem, and how to avoid plagiarism and other source abuses.

- **ENHANCED Chapter 27, "Drafting Papers with Documented Research,"** includes new instructions for making the transition from research to writing, and it includes two new sample papers, one in the humanities, and one in the sciences. In addition, chapters 28 and 29, which address MLA and APA styles, open with new Quick Guides that present a handy overview of each style, and include new sample papers.

- **NEW Chapter 16, "Reading Literature: A Case Study in Analysis,"** addresses literary analysis as a form of analytical writing that utilizes many of the principles and practices addressed in the "Analytical Writing" chapters (Chapters 11-15). Four key approaches to literary analysis are covered, as are literary terms. Sample writings include an analysis of a poem, a short story, and a novel. To help students understand the first two analyses, the poem and short story are also included in the chapter.

- **NEW instructions on "Common Traits of College Writing"** (in Chapter 2) and new material on key rhetorical issues for writing within each discipline (in Chapter 10) help students develop the range of writing skills that are required in college and are aligned with the "WPA Outcomes Statement for First-Year Composition."

- **NEW consolidated coverage of the rhetorical modes** is offered in each Part 2 chapter, including additional coverage of key principles to keep in mind when dealing with the particular mode.

- **NEW chapter-opening photographs and critical-thinking prompts** engage students in critical thinking and analysis.

- **In Part II, six new essays on current topics** are annotated to illustrate the writer's strategies. In addition, three new research papers are included in Part III.

Key Features

- *The College Writer* **provides students with a concise yet complete overview of the writing process.** The text's unique "at-a-glance" visual format presents each major concept in a one- or two-page spread, with a description of the concept followed by an example, and then the opportunity for hands-on practice, with writing assignments or practice exercises.

- **Consistent attention to the rhetorical situation**—writer, reader, message, medium, context—gives students a tool to analyze the works of others and create their own works. Chapter 1, for instance, begins with an illustration of the rhetorical situation and extended tips for reading actively.

- **"Learning Objectives" at the beginning of each chapter help students focus on key learning points,** and "Learning-Objective Checklists" at the end help students track their performance.

- **Emphasis on thesis and outline creation** encourages students to organize their thinking as they write.

- **High-interest academic writings from students and professionals** help writers understand and create a scholarly tone. Throughout the text, the authors offer examples of writing for different disciplines as well as in different work contexts.

- **"Working with Sources"**—instructions integrated into the writing-process chapters—show students how attention to research-related issues might help them at a given step in the writing process.

- **Each chapter includes group projects or collaborative-learning activities,** in addition to activities for individual thinking and writing.

- **The Handbook covers key points of grammar, mechanics, and punctuation.** These topics are reinforced by exercises in the text.

- **MLA and APA documentation instructions** aid students in finding reliable sources and creating strong research papers.

- **Charts, graphs, and photos** help visual learners grasp concepts.

- **Cutout tabs** make flipping to any of the four sections of the book quick and easy.

New to This Edition

Avoiding Plagiarism: The Research section gives integrated attention to building credibility through ethical research. In particular, a separate chapter highlights ways students can recognize and avoid plagiarism.

Developing Credibility through Source Use

Your credibility—how fully readers trust and believe you—is partly rooted in how well you treat your sources. While abuses such as distorting a source's ideas damage your credibility, good practices enhance it. Contrast the passages below and on the next page.

Writing with Poor Use of Sources

A poor paper might read like a recitation of unconnected facts, unsupported opinions, or undigested quotations. It may contain contradictory information or illogical conclusions. A source's ideas may be distorted or taken out of context. At its worst, poor source use involves plagiarism.

> The writing offers weak generalizations in several spots.

It goes without saying that cell phone usage has really increased a lot, from the beginning of the cell phone's history until now. How many people still don't have a cell—basically, no one! The advantages of cell phones are obvious, but has anyone really thought about the downside of this technological innovation? For example, there's "rinxiety," where people believe that their cell phones are ringing but they're not. Two-thirds of cell users have reported this feeling, which some experts believe to be a rewiring of the nervous system similar to phantom limb pain, while other experts thinks it's about the pitch of cell rings. It's not good.

> Material from sources is clearly borrowed but not referenced through in-text citation.

But the most serious problem with cell phones is without a doubt driving while talking or texting. Due to the increasi[...]
more like mobile computers in their availab[...]
difficulties for law enforcement officials in b[...]

> A passage from an online source is copy-and-pasted into the paper without credit.

as drivers use their devices. This is more app[...]
hand-held and hands-free usage, rather tha[...]
only, as officials cannot easily tell which fun[...]
simply by visually looking at the driver. This[...]
for using their device illegally on a phone ca[...]
using the device for a legal purpose such as [...]
car stereo or satnav usage – either as part of [...]
mobile phone itself.

> The writer uses a visual without indicating the source or effectively discussing its meaning.

The question arises, is the cell phone even being used as a phone? And are these other uses legitimate or just gimmicks? This chart makes the point.

Writing with Strong Use of Sources

A strong paper centers on the writer's ideas, ideas advanced through thoughtful engagement with and crediting of sources. It offers logical analysis or a persuasive argument built on reliable information from quality sources that have been treated with intellectual respect. Note these features at work in the excerpt below from student writer Brandon Jorritsma's essay on cell-phone dependency.

> Facts and ideas are credited through in-text citations, which are linked to full source information on a works-cited page.

This dependency on cells is reflected in the phenomenon that has come to be termed "rinxiety." Frequent cell phone users are reporting numerous instances of either hearing their phones ring or feeling them vibrate, even if their phones are not around. Two thirds of cell phone users in a recent survey report having experienced this ("Phantom Ringing"), which is thought by some to be a rewiring of the nervous system similar to phantom limb pain (Lynch). Others theorize that it is a result of the pitch of typical cell rings being similar to elements of commonplace sounds, such as running water, music, traffic, and television (Lynch, Goodman). Regardless of the particular explanation, the experience of rinxiety is more common among young, frequent users of cell phones, which seems to indicate a constant expectation of calls ("Phantom Ringing"). This expectation is damaging to relationships because someone expecting a phone call or email to arrive at any moment is not mentally present in other interactions he or she may be involved in. We've all experienced being around someone who was waiting on a phone call. How much more distracted would that person be if he or she were subconsciously expecting a phone call every hour of the day?

> The writer builds on and reasons with source material.

> Direct quotations from sources are indicated with quotation marks.

The corollary of constantly expecting incoming cell communication is the constant impulse to send out messages. Fifty-two percent of respondents to an informal survey at CSU, Fresno, admitted to being "preoccupied with the next time they could text message," and forty-six percent of students "reported irritability when unable to use their cell phones" (Lui). In a study of an international sample of cell phone users, some respondents recounted how they felt anxiety if they forgot to take their phone out of the house with them (Jarvenpaa 12). Even when the phone was not anywhere near them, they couldn't escape its demands on their attention. The phone has moved from being an object of utility to being one of psychological necessity, which constantly demands attention from its user regardless of its proximity or restrictions on its use.

> A case study from a source makes a concept concrete through cause-effect reasoning.

Lauren Hawn, a student at Pennsylvania State University, reports that when she is near her cell, she does the following: "I seem to look at it a lot and check the time [on the phone's digital display] even when I don't need to" (qtd. in Lynch). Hawn does not consciously think that there is a phone call or text message . . . .

"Weak Signals: How Cellular Phones Inhibit Communication" by Brandon Jorritsma. Reprinted by permission of the author.

Enhanced Research Models: In addition to fully-updated sections on MLA and APA documentation styles, the fifth edition includes new sample research papers, including MLA and APA papers as well as one in the humanities and one in the sciences.

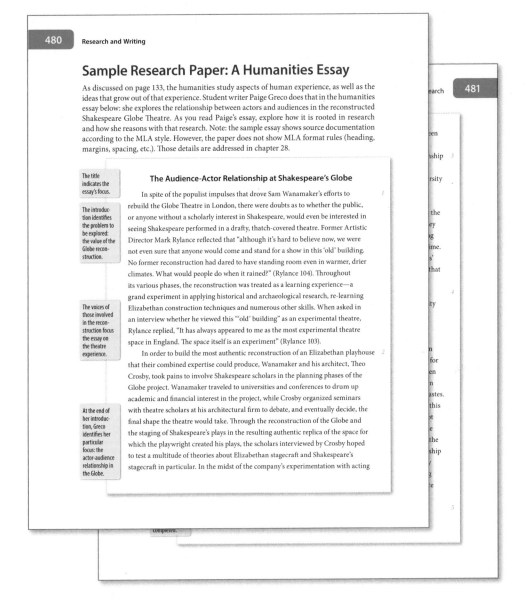

480   **Research and Writing**

Sample Research Paper: A Humanities Essay

As discussed on page 133, the humanities study aspects of human experience, as well as the ideas that grow out of that experience. Student writer Paige Greco does that in the humanities essay below: she explores the relationship between actors and audiences in the reconstructed Shakespeare Globe Theatre. As you read Paige's essay, explore how it is rooted in research and how she reasons with that research. Note: the sample essay shows source documentation according to the MLA style. However, the paper does not show MLA format rules (heading, margins, spacing, etc.). Those details are addressed in chapter 28.

The title indicates the essay's focus.

The introduction identifies the problem to be explored: the value of the Globe reconstruction.

The voices of those involved in the reconstruction focus the essay on the theatre experience.

At the end of her introduction, Greco identifies her particular focus: the actor-audience relationship in the Globe.

The Audience-Actor Relationship at Shakespeare's Globe

In spite of the populist impulses that drove Sam Wanamaker's efforts to rebuild the Globe Theatre in London, there were doubts as to whether the public, or anyone without a scholarly interest in Shakespeare, would even be interested in seeing Shakespeare performed in a drafty, thatch-covered theatre. Former Artistic Director Mark Rylance reflected that "although it's hard to believe now, we were not even sure that anyone would come and stand for a show in this 'old' building. No former reconstruction had dared to have standing room even in warmer, drier climates. What would people do when it rained?" (Rylance 104). Throughout its various phases, the reconstruction was treated as a learning experience—a grand experiment in applying historical and archaeological research, re-learning Elizabethan construction techniques and numerous other skills. When asked in an interview whether he viewed this "'old' building" as an experimental theatre, Rylance replied, "It has always appeared to me as the most experimental theatre space in England. The space itself is an experiment" (Rylance 103).

In order to build the most authentic reconstruction of an Elizabethan playhouse that their combined expertise could produce, Wanamaker and his architect, Theo Crosby, took pains to involve Shakespeare scholars in the planning phases of the Globe project. Wanamaker traveled to universities and conferences to drum up academic and financial interest in the project, while Crosby organized seminars with theatre scholars at his architectural firm to debate, and eventually decide, the final shape the theatre would take. Through the reconstruction of the Globe and the staging of Shakespeare's plays in the resulting authentic replica of the space for which the playwright created his plays, the scholars interviewed by Crosby hoped to test a multitude of theories about Elizabethan stagecraft and Shakespeare's stagecraft in particular. In the midst of the company's experimentation with acting

481

A Case Study in Literary Analysis: In the Reader, a revamped chapter provides a detailed case study of literary analysis, a special form of analytical writing. The chapter covers four key approaches to literary analysis and a glossary of literary terms. In addition, sample literary readings and analyses of those readings serve to model the process of analysis for students.

Chapter 16 | Reading Literature: A Case Study in Analysis   259

Analyzing a Poem

In the essay on the following two pages, student writer Sherry Van Egdom analyzes the form and meaning of the poem below, "Let Evening Come," by American poet Jane Kenyon. Born in 1947 and raised on a farm near Ann Arbor, Michigan, Kenyon settled in New Hampshire at Eagle Pond Farm after she married fellow poet Donald Hall. During her life, Kenyon struggled with her faith, with depression, and with cancer. At the time of her death in 1995 from leukemia, she was the poet laureate of New Hampshire.

Before you read the student writer's analysis, read the poem aloud to enjoy its sounds, rhythm, images, diction, and comparisons. Then read the piece again to grasp more fully how the poem is structured, what it expresses, and how its ideas might relate to your life. Finally, read Van Egdom's analysis and answer the questions that follow it.

Let Evening Come

Let the light of late afternoon
shine through chinks in the barn, moving
up the bales as the sun moves down.

Let the crickets take up chafing
as a woman takes up her needles
and her yarn. Let evening come.

Let dew collect on the hoe aba[...]
in long grass. Let the stars app[...]
and the moon disclose her silv[...]

Let the fox go back to its sand[...]
Let the wind die down. Let the [...]
go black inside. Let evening co[...]

To the bottle in the ditch, to th[...]
in the oats, to air in the lung
let evening come.

Let it come, as it will, and don'[...]
be afraid. God does not leave [...]
comfortless, so let evening co[...]

Jane Kenyon, "Let Evening Come" from Collected Poems. Co[...]
Estate of Jane Kenyon. Reprinted with the permission of The [...]
behalf of Graywolf Press, Minneapolis, Minnesota, www.gra[...]

260   Reader: Strategies and Samples

Analysis of Kenyon's Poem

In the essay below, student writer Sherry Van Egdom Doyle analyzes "Let Evening Come." Watch how she develops the essay by introducing the poem, describing how it unfolds, and then examining its structure, ideas, poetic devices, and theme.

"Let Evening Come": An Invitation to the Inevitable

> The writer introduces the poet and her poetry.

The work of American poet Jane Kenyon is influenced primarily by the circumstances and experiences of her own life. She writes carefully crafted, deceptively simple poems that connect both to her own life and to the lives of her readers. Growing out of her rural roots and her struggles with illness, Kenyon's poetry speaks in a still voice of the ordinary things in life in order to wrestle with issues of faith and mortality (Timmerman 163). One of these poems is "Let Evening Come." In this poem, the poet takes the reader on a journey into the night, but she points to hope in the face of that darkness.

> Narrowing her focus to the specific poem, the writer states her thesis.

> She begins her analysis by explaining the stanza structure and progression.

That movement toward darkness is captured in the stanza form and in the progression of stanzas. Each three-line stanza offers a self-contained moment in the progress of transition from day to night. The first stanza positions the reader in a simple farm setting. Late afternoon fades into evening without the rumble of highways or the gleam of city lights to distract one's senses from nature, the peace emphasized by the alliteration of "l" in "Let the light of late afternoon." As the sun sinks lower on the horizon, light seeps through cracks in the barn wall, moving up the bales of hay. In the second stanza, the crickets get busy with their nighttime noises. Next, a forgotten farm hoe becomes covered with dew drops, and the silvery stars and moon appear in the sky. In the fourth stanza, complete blackness arrives as a fox returns to its empty den and the silent wind rests at close of day. The alliteration of "d" in "den" and "die down" gives a sinking, settling feeling (Timmerman 176). In the fifth stanza, a bottle and scoop keep still, untouched in their respective places, while sleep comes upon the human body. In the final stanza, Kenyon encourages readers to meet this emerging world of darkness without fear.

> The writer shows attention to the poem's fine details and to secondary sources on the poem.

> She advances her reading of the poem by exploring images, comparisons, and symbols; the poem's "imaginative logic."

Within this stanza progression, the journey into the night is intensified by strong images, figures of speech, and symbols. The natural rhythm of work and rest on the farm is symbolized by the light that rises and falls in the first stanza (Timmerman 175). The simile comparing the crickets taking up their song to a woman picking up her knitting suggests a homespun energy and conviction. The moon revealing her "silver horn" implies that the moon does not instantly appear with brightness and beauty but rather reveals her majesty slowly as the night comes on. The den, the wind, and the shed in stanza four stress a kind of internal, hidden darkness. Then stanza five focuses on connected objects: the thoughtlessly discarded bottle resting in the ditch, oats and the scoop for feeding, human lungs and the air that fills them. Kenyon mentions the air in the lung after the bottle, ditch, scoop, and

Common Traits of College Writing: An introduction to the common traits of college writing gives students a common vocabulary to discuss and assess their own writing to ensure it fulfills the standards required of college writers.

Aiming for Writing Excellence

What makes your writing strong enough to engage and enlighten readers? As already suggested on pages 28–29, that depends in part on the rhetorical situation: what your purpose is, who your readers are, and so on. Writing excellence can be measured by the depth of what you learn through writing, as well as by what your reader gains through reading. However, while the world of writing is so diverse that no formula or prescription can state definitively what makes for strong writing, we can point to common traits that describe such writing. Consider the relevance of these traits at the beginning of any writing project.

Common Traits of College Writing

Quality writing shows strengths in the traits below, which range from global issues to local, sentence-level issues.

- **Strong ideas** are what you discover and develop through your writing. They are what make your content substantial and meaningful. These elements include a clear, sharp thesis or theme; strong and balanced reasoning; and accurate, supportive information that is properly credited.

- **Logical organization** creates the structure and flow of your writing. Through organization, reasoning is delivered through a clear chain of ideas, a unified whole. Typically, an engaging opening focuses discussion, the middle effectively develops the main idea, and a closing offers conclusions and points forward—all in paragraphs that are well developed (unified, coherent, and complete).

- **Engaging voice** refers to how your writing "sounds" to readers—the attitude, pacing, and personality that come through. An engaging voice sounds authentic and natural, engaged with the topic. Moreover, the tone—whether serious, playful, or sarcastic—is confident but also sincere and measured, fitting the writing occasion.

- **Clear word choice** carries your meaning. In your writing, the vocabulary should fit the topic, purpose, and audience. Phrasing should be clear throughout—language that readers will understand, precise terminology and plain English whenever possible.

- **Smooth sentences** express complete thoughts in a good blend of sentence lengths (short and punchy, long and thoughtful) and patterns (loose, balanced, and periodic). Such sentences use phrases and clauses in logical and expressive ways—energetically, economically, gracefully.

- **Correct writing** follows the conventions of language (grammar, punctuation, mechanics, usage, and spelling), as well as standards of citation and documentation (e.g., MLA, APA).

- **Professional document design** refers to the appearance of your writing on the page, the screen, and so on. Such design includes the document's format (e.g., essay, lab report, presentation, Web site), its page layout (e.g., margins, headings, bullets, white space), its typography (typefaces, type sizes, and type styles), and its use of tables and visuals.

"The Gullible Family" by Mary Bruins. Used by permission of the author.

Chapter-Opening Photographs and Prompts: New photographs offer visually-engaging and thought-provoking introductions to chapters. Each photograph is accompanied by a "Visually Speaking" prompt that asks students to think critically about how the photograph relates to the subject at hand.

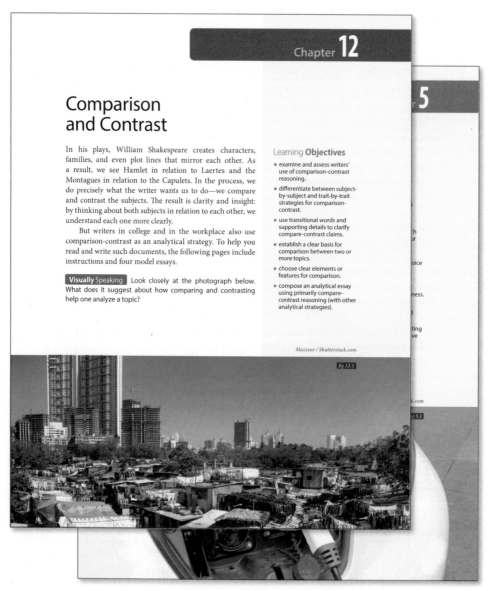

Chapter **12**

Comparison and Contrast

In his plays, William Shakespeare creates characters, families, and even plot lines that mirror each other. As a result, we see Hamlet in relation to Laertes and the Montagues in relation to the Capulets. In the process, we do precisely what the writer wants us to do—we compare and contrast the subjects. The result is clarity and insight: by thinking about both subjects in relation to each other, we understand each one more clearly.

But writers in college and in the workplace also use comparison-contrast as an analytical strategy. To help you read and write such documents, the following pages include instructions and four model essays.

Visually Speaking   Look closely at the photograph below. What does it suggest about how comparing and contrasting help one analyze a topic?

Learning **Objectives**

- examine and assess writers' use of comparison-contrast reasoning.
- differentiate between subject-by-subject and trait-by-trait strategies for comparison-contrast.
- use transitional words and supporting details to clarify compare-contrast claims.
- establish a clear basis for comparison between two or more topics.
- choose clear elements or features for comparison.
- compose an analytical essay using primarily compare-contrast reasoning (with other analytical strategies).

Mazzzur / Shutterstock.com

fig 12.1

Key Principles for Rhetorical Modes: Part 2 of *The College Writer* includes coverage of key principles for each rhetorical mode, followed by models and writing guidelines.

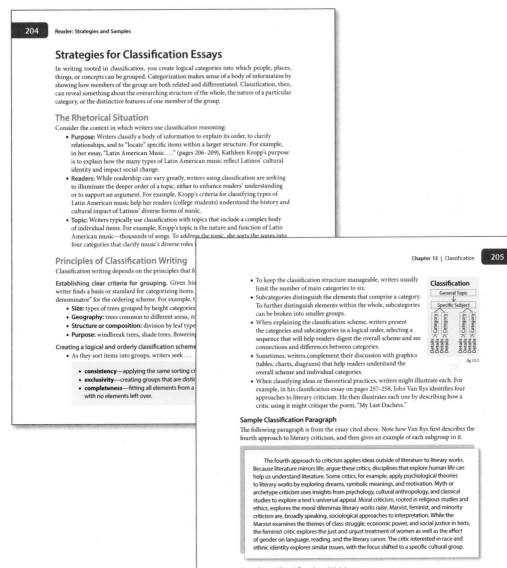

204 Reader: Strategies and Samples

Strategies for Classification Essays

In writing rooted in classification, you create logical categories into which people, places, things, or concepts can be grouped. Categorization makes sense of a body of information by showing how members of the group are both related and differentiated. Classification, then, can reveal something about the overarching structure of the whole, the nature of a particular category, or the distinctive features of one member of the group.

The Rhetorical Situation

Consider the context in which writers use classification reasoning:

- **Purpose:** Writers classify a body of information to explain its order, to clarify relationships, and to "locate" specific items within a larger structure. For example, in her essay, "Latin American Music . . ." (pages 206–209), Kathleen Kropp's purpose is to explain how the many types of Latin American music reflect Latinos' cultural identity and impact social change.
- **Readers:** While readership can vary greatly, writers using classification are seeking to illuminate the deeper order of a topic, either to enhance readers' understanding or to support an argument. For example, Kropp's criteria for classifying types of Latin American music help her readers (college students) understand the history and cultural impact of Latinos' diverse forms of music.
- **Topic:** Writers typically use classification with topics that include a complex body of individual items. For example, Kropp's topic is the nature and function of Latin American music—thousands of songs. To address the topic, she sorts the songs into four categories that clarify music's diverse roles

Principles of Classification Writing

Classification writing depends on the principles that fo

Establishing clear criteria for grouping. Given his writer finds a basis or standard for categorizing items. denominator" for the ordering scheme. For example, t

- **Size:** types of trees grouped by height categories
- **Geography:** trees common to different areas, zc
- **Structure or composition:** division by leaf type
- **Purpose:** windbreak trees, shade trees, flowering

Creating a logical and orderly classification scheme

- As they sort items into groups, writers seek . . .

  - **consistency**—applying the same sorting cr
  - **exclusivity**—creating groups that are distin
  - **completeness**—fitting all elements from a
    with no elements left over.

Chapter 13 | Classification 205

- To keep the classification structure manageable, writers usually limit the number of main categories to six.
- Subcategories distinguish the elements that comprise a category. To further distinguish elements within the whole, subcategories can be broken into smaller groups.
- When explaining the classification scheme, writers present the categories and subcategories in a logical order, selecting a sequence that will help readers digest the overall scheme and see connections and differences between categories.
- Sometimes, writers complement their discussion with graphics (tables, charts, diagrams) that help readers understand the overall scheme and individual categories.
- When classifying ideas or theoretical practices, writers might illustrate each. For example, in his classification essay on pages 257–258, John Van Rys identifies four approaches to literary criticism. He then illustrates each one by describing how a critic using it might critique the poem, "My Last Duchess."

Classification

General Topic
↓
Specific Subject

Details › Category
Details › Category
Details › Category

Details › Category
Details › Category
Details › Category

fig 13.2

Sample Classification Paragraph

The following paragraph is from the essay cited above. Note how Van Rys first describes the fourth approach to literary criticism, and then gives an example of each subgroup in it.

> The fourth approach to criticism applies ideas outside of literature to literary works. Because literature mirrors life, argue these critics, disciplines that explore human life can help us understand literature. Some critics, for example, apply psychological theories to literary works by exploring dreams, symbolic meanings, and motivation. Myth or archetype criticism uses insights from psychology, cultural anthropology, and classical studies to explore a text's universal appeal. Moral criticism, rooted in religious studies and ethics, explores the moral dilemmas literary works raise. Marxist, feminist, and minority criticism are, broadly speaking, sociological approaches to interpretation. While the Marxist examines the themes of class struggle, economic power, and social justice in texts, the feminist critic explores the just and unjust treatment of women as well as the effect of gender on language, reading, and the literary canon. The critic interested in race and ethnic identity explores similar issues, with the focus shifted to a specific cultural group.

Reading Classification Writing

As you read the essays on the following pages, consider these questions:

1. Does the writer explain the classification scheme, and is this reasoning logical, given his or her topic and purpose? Explain.
2. Are the number of categories sufficient, given the size and diversity of the topic?
3. Are the categories consistent, exclusive, and complete? Explain.
4. Are the categories presented in a clear, logical order?

Enhanced Writing Guidelines and Checklists: Writing guidelines and checklists lead students through the writing process for each rhetorical mode.

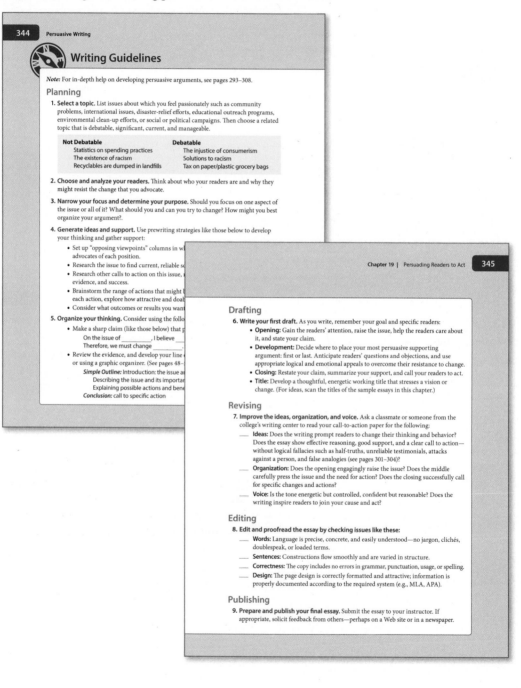

344   Persuasive Writing

Writing Guidelines

Note: For in-depth help on developing persuasive arguments, see pages 293–308.

Planning

1. **Select a topic.** List issues about which you feel passionately such as community problems, international issues, disaster-relief efforts, educational outreach programs, environmental clean-up efforts, or social or political campaigns. Then choose a related topic that is debatable, significant, current, and manageable.

Not Debatable	Debatable
Statistics on spending practices	The injustice of consumerism
The existence of racism	Solutions to racism
Recyclables are dumped in landfills	Tax on paper/plastic grocery bags

2. **Choose and analyze your readers.** Think about who your readers are and why they might resist the change that you advocate.

3. **Narrow your focus and determine your purpose.** Should you focus on one aspect of the issue or all of it? What should you and can you try to change? How might you best organize your argument?.

4. **Generate ideas and support.** Use prewriting strategies like those below to develop your thinking and gather support:
   - Set up "opposing viewpoints" columns in wh[...]
     advocates of each position.
   - Research the issue to find current, reliable s[...]
   - Research other calls to action on this issue, [...]
     evidence, and success.
   - Brainstorm the range of actions that might [...]
     each action, explore how attractive and doab[...]
   - Consider what outcomes or results you want [...]

5. **Organize your thinking.** Consider using the follo[...]
   - Make a sharp claim (like those below) that p[...]
     On the issue of _____, I believe ___
     Therefore, we must change _____.
   - Review the evidence, and develop your line [...]
     or using a graphic organizer. (See pages 48–[...]
     Simple Outline: Introduction: the issue a[...]
          Describing the issue and its importan[...]
          Explaining possible actions and bene[...]
     Conclusion: call to specific action

Drafting

6. **Write your first draft.** As you write, remember your goal and specific readers:
   - **Opening:** Gain the readers' attention, raise the issue, help the readers care about it, and state your claim.
   - **Development:** Decide where to place your most persuasive supporting argument: first or last. Anticipate readers' questions and objections, and use appropriate logical and emotional appeals to overcome their resistance to change.
   - **Closing:** Restate your claim, summarize your support, and call your readers to act.
   - **Title:** Develop a thoughtful, energetic working title that stresses a vision or change. (For ideas, scan the titles of the sample essays in this chapter.)

Revising

7. **Improve the ideas, organization, and voice.** Ask a classmate or someone from the college's writing center to read your call-to-action paper for the following:
   ___ **Ideas:** Does the writing prompt readers to change their thinking and behavior? Does the essay show effective reasoning, good support, and a clear call to action—without logical fallacies such as half-truths, unreliable testimonials, attacks against a person, and false analogies (see pages 301–304)?
   ___ **Organization:** Does the opening engagingly raise the issue? Does the middle carefully press the issue and the need for action? Does the closing successfully call for specific changes and actions?
   ___ **Voice:** Is the tone energetic but controlled, confident but reasonable? Does the writing inspire readers to join your cause and act?

Editing

8. **Edit and proofread the essay by checking issues like these:**
   ___ **Words:** Language is precise, concrete, and easily understood—no jargon, clichés, doublespeak, or loaded terms.
   ___ **Sentences:** Constructions flow smoothly and are varied in structure.
   ___ **Correctness:** The copy includes no errors in grammar, punctuation, usage, or spelling.
   ___ **Design:** The page design is correctly formatted and attractive; information is properly documented according to the required system (e.g., MLA, APA).

Publishing

9. **Prepare and publish your final essay.** Submit the essay to your instructor. If appropriate, solicit feedback from others—perhaps on a Web site or in a newspaper.

More Online Supplementation for the Student

- **MindTap:** *The College Writer* is also available on MindTap. MindTap is a total course solution for English Composition, combining all digital assets—e-Book, writing assignments, multimedia, assessments, and  a gradebook—into a singular customizable learning path designed to improve student skills in grammar, research, citation and, above all, writing. MindTap is well beyond an e-Book or digital supplement. MindTap is the first in a new category—The Personal Learning Experience.

- **Enhanced InSite for *The College Writer*** Insightful writing begins with Enhanced InSite™ for *The College Writer*, 5th Edition. From a single, easy-to-navigate site, you and your instructor can manage the flow of papers online, check for originality, and conduct peer reviews. You'll access a multimedia eBook with text-specific workbook, private tutoring options, and resources for writers that include anti-plagiarism tutorials and downloadable grammar podcasts—all designed to help you become a stronger, more effective writer. Learn more at www.cengage.com/insite.

More Online Supplementation for the Instructor

- ***Online Instructor's Resource Manual*** This manual is available for download or printing on the instructor website. The *Instructor's Resource Manual* includes assessment rubrics, learning objectives, an overview of the course, sample syllabi, chapter summaries, and teaching suggestions. Whether you are just starting out or have been teaching for years, the authors have designed this manual to accommodate you.

- **Instructor Website** This password-protected site, accessed through www.cengagebrain.com, provides a downloadable version of the Instructor's Resource Manual, assessment rubrics, and learning objectives.

- **Enhanced InSite for *The College Writer*** Easily create, assign, and grade writing assignments with Enhanced InSite™ for *The College Writer*, 5th Edition. From a single, easy-to-navigate site, you and your students can manage the flow of papers online, check for originality, and conduct peer reviews. Students can access a multimedia eBook with text-specific workbook, private tutoring options, and resources for writers that include anti-plagiarism tutorials and downloadable grammar podcasts. Enhanced InSite™ provides the tools and resources you and your students need plus the training and support you want. Learn more at www.cengage.com/insite.

Acknowledgements

The authors express their gratitude to the following reviewers of the *The College Writer*, 5th Edition.

Reviewers

Lauryn Angel-Cann, *Collin College*; Marlene Archie, *Cheyney University*; Elizabeth Barnes, *Daytona State College*; Vicki Besaw, *College of Menominee Nation*; Brenda Craven, *Fort Hays State University*; Gabriel Decio, *McHenry County College*; Susan Guzman-Trevino, *Temple College*; Jerri A. Harwell, *Salt Lake Community College*; Dianne Krob, *Rose State College*; Elizabeth Langenfeld, *Crafton Hills College*; Yingqin Liu, *Cameron University*; Anna Maheshwari, *Schoolcraft College*; Andrew Preslar, *Lamar State College-Orange*; Thomas Sanfilip, *Oakton Community College*; John Stevens, *Temple College*; Cynthia VanSickle, *McHenry County College*; Theresa Walther, *Rose State College*

The authors also thank the following instructors who contributed to the development of prior editions and supplements.

Belinda Adams, *Navarro College*; Mary Adams, *Peru State College*; Jim Addison, *Western Carolina University*; Susan Aguila, *Palm Beach Community College*; Cathryn Amdahl, *Harrisburg Area Community College*; Edmund August, *McKendree College*; Alena Balmforth, *Salt Lake Community College*; Richard Baker, *Adams State College*; Cherrie Bergandi, *Chippewa Valley Technical College*; Thomas G. Beverage, *Coastal Carolina Community College*; Patricia Blaine, *Paducah Community College*; Tammie Bob, *College of DuPage*; Candace Boeck, *San Diego State University*; Charley Boyd, *Genesee Community College*; Deborah Bradford, *Bridgewater State College*; Linda Brender, *Macomb Community College*; Colleen M. Burke, *Rasmussen College*; Mary Burkhart, *University of Scranton*; Hugh Burns, *Texas Woman's University*; Vicki Byard, *Northeastern Illinois University*; Susan Callender, *Sinclair Community College*; Sandra Camillo, *Finger Lakes Community College*; Sandy Cavanah, *Hopkinsville Community College*; Annette Cedarholm, *Snead State Community College*; James William Chichetto, *Stonehill College*; Sandra Clark, *Anderson University*; Beth Conomos, *Erie Community College, SUNY*; Michael D. Cook, *Everest College—Phoenix*; Keith Coplin, *Colby Community College*; Sue Cornett, *St. Petersburg College*; Debra Cumberland, *Winona State University*; David Daniel, *Newbury College*; Sarah Dangelantonio, *Franklin Pierce College*; Rachelle L. Darabi, *Indiana University, Purdue University Fort Wayne*; Judy C. Davidson, *University of Texas, Pan American*; Tamera Davis, *Northern Oklahoma College—Stillwater*; Helen Deese, *University of California, Riverside*; Darren DeFrain, *Wichita State University*; Sarah Dengler, *Franklin Pierce College*; Linda Dethloff, *Prairie State College*; Steven Dolgin, *Schoolcraft College*; Carol Jean Dudley, *Eastern Illinois University*; Chris Ellery, *Angelo State University*; Ernest J. Enchelmayer, *Louisiana State University*; Anne K. Erickson, *Atlantic Cape Community College*; Mary Etter, *Davenport University*; Kelly A. Foth, *University of Dubuque*; Julie Foust, *Utah State University*; Lyneé Lewis Gaillet, *Georgia State University*; Gregory R. Glau, *Arizona State University*; Patricia

Glynn, *Middlesex Community College*; Samuel J. Goldstein, *Daytona Beach Community College*; Patrick L. Green, *Aiken Technical College*; Kim Grewe, *Wor-Wic Community College*; Loren C. Gruber, *Missouri Valley College*; Jennifer Haber, *St. Petersburg College*; Michael Hammond, *Northeastern Illinois University*; Katona Hargrave, *Troy State University*; Dick Harrington, *Piedmont Virginia Community College*; Karla Hayashi, *University of Hawaii, Hilo*; Anne Christine Helms, *Alamance Community College*; Julie Hemker, *De Anza, UC Berkeley, University of San Francisco*; Patricia A. Herb, *North Central State College*; Stan Hitron, *Middlesex Community College*; Karen Holleran, *Kaplan College*; Barbara Dondiego Holmes, *University of Charleston*; Elizabeth Huergo, *Montgomery College*; Maurice Hunt, *Baylor University*; David Jacobsen, *Westmont College*; Barbara Jacobskind, *University of Massachusetts, Dartmouth*; Linda G. Johnson, *Southeast Technical Institute*; Alex M. Joncas, *Estrella Mountain Community College*; Nina B. Keery, *Massachusetts Bay Community College*; Sandra Keneda, *Rose State College*; Margo LaGattuta, *University of Michigan, Flint*; Richard Larschan, *University of Massachusetts, Dartmouth*; John L. Liffiton, *Scottsdale Community College*; Molly Luby, *Central Carolina Community College*; Kelly B. McCalla, *Central Lakes College*; Dusty Maddox, *DeVry University*; Bonnie J. Marshall, *Grand Valley State University*; Daphne Matthews, *Mississippi Delta Community College*; Christine A. Miller, *Davenport University*; Claudia Milstead, *Missouri Valley College*; Boyd Minner, *Navarro College*; Kate Mohler, *Mesa Community College*; Meghan Monroe, *Central Michigan University*; Ed Moritz, *Indiana University, Purdue University Fort Wayne*; Linda Morrison, *Niagara University*; Deborah Naquin, *Northern Virginia Community College*; Julie Nichols, *Okaloosa-Walton Community College*; Nancy W. Noel, *Germanna Community College*; Robert H. Nordell, *Des Moines Area Community College*; Julianne Palma, *Monroe Community College*; Christine Pavesic, *University of Wisconsin, Waukesha*; Francie Quaas-Berryman, *Cerritos College*; Christine Sherry Rankin, *Abilene Christian University*; Laura Robbins, *Portland Community College*; Matthew Roudané, *Georgia State University*; Robert E. Rubin, *Wright State University*; Nancy Ruff, *Southern Illinois University, Edwardsville*; Christine M. Ryan, *Middlesex Community College*; A. Saxlid, *Wisconsin Indianhead Technical College*; Vicki Scheurer, *Palm Beach Community College*; Catherine Scudder Wolf, *Susssex County Community College*; Larry W. Severeid, *College of Eastern Utah*; Susan M. Smith, *Tompkins Cortland Community College*; Donna K. Speeker, *Wallace State Community College*; Talbot Spivak, *Edison College*; Donald Stinson, *Northern Oklahoma College*; Joyce Swofford, *Clayton College & State University*; Christine Szymczak, *Erie Community College*; Terry Thacker, *Coastline Community College*; Diane Thompson, *Northern Virginia Community College*; Monica Parrish Trent, *Montgomery College*; Carolyn Towles, *Liberty University*; Dori Wagner, *Austin Community College*; John Williamson, *Thomas More College*; Shonda Wilson, *Suffolk County Community College*; Frances J. Winter, *Massachusetts Bay Community College*; Kelly Wonder, *University of Wisconsin, Eau Claire*; Benjamin Worth, *Bluegrass Community and Technical College*; Deanna L. Yameen, *Quincy College*.

Students

Lindsi Bittner, *St. Petersburg College;* Danielle Brown, *Oakton Community College;* Marie Burns, *University of Tampa;* Will Buttner, *University of Tampa;* Debra Cotton, *St. Petersburg College;* Jessica de Olivera, *Northeastern Illinois University;* Petra Hickman, *St. Petersburg College;* Anne Hsiao, *Oakton Community College;* Cassie Hull, *St. Petersburg College;* Courtney Langford, *St. Petersburg College;* Sandy Lehrke, *Hillsborough Community College;* Michael Pistorio, *Oakton Community College;* Crystal Smuk, *Triton Junior College;* Marc Sordja, *St. Petersburg College;* Johnny Velez, *Hillsborough Community College;* Anthony Zalud, *Harper Community College;* Omar Zamora, *Northeastern Illinois University.*

Special Thanks

A special thanks goes to Sarah Dangelantonio and Sarah Dengler of *Franklin Pierce College* for their work on the *Instructor's Resource Manual.* Also, thanks to Mark Gallaher, Kelly McGuire, Julie Nash, Dee Seligman, and Janet Young.

I. Rhetoric:
A College Student's Guide to Writing

Rhetoric

Chapter 1

Critical Thinking Through Reading, Viewing, and Writing

Every day, we encounter words and images; often, we create them for others to read and view. Exchanging these messages constitutes communication, a complex process that involves several variables: the writer/designer, the message and the medium used, the reader/viewer, and the context.

In college, such communication—whether in reading articles, viewing films, or writing essays—requires critical thinking. Such thinking puts ideas in context, makes connections between them, and tests their meaning and logic. This chapter provides strategies that will help you think critically as you read, view, and write.

Visually Speaking Figure 1.1 shows people viewing art in a museum. What thinking practices does such viewing involve? Consider, as well, other types of images. What viewing do you do, for what reasons, and using what brain power?

Learning **Objectives**

By working through this chapter, you will be able to

- actively read different written texts.
- produce personal responses to texts.
- objectively summarize texts.
- actively view, analyze, and critique visual images.
- implement strategies to think critically about topics.
- practice modes of thinking through writing.

Adriano Castelli / Shutterstock.com

fig. 1.1

Critical Thinking Through Reading

Critical reading involves a kind of mental dialogue with the text. To initiate that dialogue, engage the text smartly by using strategies like these: reading actively, mapping the text, outlining it, responding to it, summarizing it, and evaluating it.

Read Actively

Active reading is reading that is mentally alert. Practically speaking, you can read actively by following techniques like these.

- **Remove distractions.** Engaged reading requires that you disengage from all distractions such as your cell phone, Facebook, or TV.
- **Take your time.** Read in stretches of about forty-five minutes, followed by short breaks. And when you break, think about what you read, what might come next, and why.
- **Assess the rhetorical situation.** Where and when was this text written and published? Who is the author, and why did he or she write the piece? What are the writer's qualifications to address this topic? Why are you reading it?
- **Preview, read, review.** Start by previewing the text: scan the title, opening and closing paragraphs, headings, topic sentences, and graphics. Next, read the text carefully, asking questions such as "What does this mean?" and "Why is this important?" Finally, review what you have learned and what questions remain unanswered.
- **Read aloud.** Do so for especially difficult parts of the text, or take turns reading aloud with a partner.
- **Write while reading.** Take notes, especially when working on research projects. (See page 395). Annotate the text by highlighting main points, writing a "?" beside puzzling parts, or jotting key insights in the margin.

Sample Text

The following article was written by Dan Heath and was first published in the June 2, 2010 edition of the newsletter, *Fast Company*. Read the essay, using the active reading tips above and answering the questions that follow.

Why Change Is So Hard: Self-Control Is Exhaustible

You hear something a lot about change: People won't change because they're too lazy. Well, I'm here to stick up for the lazy people. In fact, I want to argue that what looks like laziness is actually exhaustion. The proof comes from a psychology study that is absolutely fascinating.   *1*

The Study

So picture this: Students come into a lab. It smells amazing—someone has just baked chocolate-chip cookies. On a table in front of them, there are two bowls. One has the   *2*

---

fresh-baked cookies. The other has a bunch of radishes. Some of the students are asked to eat some cookies but no radishes. Others are told to eat radishes but no cookies, and while they sit there, nibbling on rabbit food, the researchers leave the room—which is intended to tempt them and is frankly kind of sadistic. But in the study none of the radish-eaters slipped—they showed admirable self-control. And meanwhile, it probably goes without saying that the people gorging on cookies didn't experience much temptation.

Then, the two groups are asked to do a second, seemingly unrelated task—basically a   3
kind of logic puzzle where they have to trace out a complicated geometric pattern without raising their pencils. Unbeknownst to the group, the puzzle can't be solved. The scientists are curious how long individuals will persist at a difficult task. So the cookie-eaters try again and again, for an average of 19 minutes, before they give up. But the radish-eaters—they only last an average of 8 minutes. What gives?

The Results

The answer may surprise you: The radish-eaters ran out of self-control. Psychologists   4
have discovered that self-control is an exhaustible resource. And I don't mean self-control only in the sense of turning down cookies or alcohol; I mean a broader sense of self-supervision—any time you're paying close attention to your actions, like when you're having a tough conversation or trying to stay focused on a paper you're writing. This helps to explain why, after a long hard day at the office, we're more likely to snap at our spouses or have one drink too many—we've depleted our self-control.

And here's why this matters for change: In almost all change situations, you're   5
substituting new, unfamiliar behaviors for old, comfortable ones, and that burns self-control. Let's say I present a new morning routine to you that specifies how you'll shower and brush your teeth. You'll understand it and you might even agree with my process. But to pull it off, you'll have to supervise yourself very carefully. Every fiber of your being will want to go back to the old way of doing things. Inevitably, you'll slip. And if I were uncharitable, I'd see you going back to the old way and I'd say, "You're so lazy. Why can't you just change?"

This brings us back to the point I promised I'd make: That what looks like laziness is   6
often exhaustion. Change wears people out—even well-intentioned people will simply run out of fuel.

Reading for Better Writing

Working by yourself or with a group, answer these questions:

1. In a single sentence, what is the thesis of this essay?
2. How do the findings of the study explain why change is difficult?
3. Compare your notes and annotations with those of a classmate. Which parts of your notes and annotations are the same? Which parts are different? How does discussing the essay reinforce or otherwise alter your understanding of the essay?
4. Think about your own life. What activities require you to exert a great deal of self-control? How could this information help you avoid temptation?

Map the text.

If you are visually oriented, you may understand a text best by mapping out its important parts. One way to do so is by "clustering." Start by naming the main topic in an oval at the center of the page. Then branch out using lines and "balloons," where each balloon contains a word or phrase for one major subtopic. Branch out in further layers of balloons to show even more sub points, as in Figure 1.2. If you wish, add graphics, arrows, drawings—anything that helps you visualize the relationships among ideas.

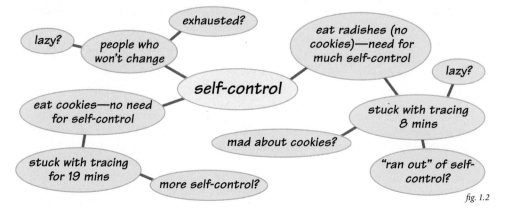

fig. 1.2

Outline the text.

Outlining is the traditional way of showing all the major parts, points, and sub points in a text. An outline uses parallel structure to show main points and subordinate points. See pages 48–50 for more on outlines.

Sample Outline for "Why Change Is So Hard: Self-Control Is Exhaustible"

1. Introduction: Change is hard not because of laziness but because of exhaustion.
2. A study tests self-control.
   a. Some students must eat only cookies—using little self-control.
   b. Some students must eat only radishes—using much self-control.
   c. Both sets of students have to trace a pattern without lifting the pencil—an unsolvable puzzle.
      • Cookie-only students last an average of 19 minutes before quitting.
      • Radish-only students last an average of 8 minutes before quitting.
3. Results show that self-control is exhaustible.
   a. Avoiding temptation and working in a hard, focused way require self-control.
   b. Change requires self-control.
   c. Failure to change often results from exhaustion of self-control.

Evaluate the text.

Critical reading does not mean disproving the text or disapproving of it. It means thoughtfully inspecting, weighing, and evaluating the writer's ideas. To strengthen your reading skills, learn to evaluate texts using the criteria below.

1. **Judge the reading's credibility.** Where was it published? How reliable is the author? How current is the information? How accurate and complete does it seem to be? In addition, consider the author's tone of voice, attitude, and apparent biases.

   > *Discussion:* Dan Heath, the author of "Why Change Is So Hard" is a *New York Times* best-selling author, a consultant to the Aspen Institute, and a monthly columnist for *Fast Company*. How do these credentials affect your reading of the article? How does the article itself build or break credibility?

2. **Put the reading in a larger context.** How do the text's ideas match what you know from other sources? Which details of background, history, and social context help you understand this text's perspective? How have things changed or remained the same since the text's publication? Which allusions (references to people, events, and so on) does the writer use? Why?

   > *Discussion:* "Why Change Is So Hard" centers around a single psychological study and draws from it specific conclusions about self-control. What other studies have attempted to track self-control? Is this a new subdiscipline in psychological research, or a well-established one?

3. **Evaluate the reasoning and support.** Is the reasoning clear and logical? Are the examples and other supporting details appropriate and enlightening? Are inferences (what the text implies) consistent with the tone and message? (Look especially for hidden logic and irony that undercut what is said explicitly.)

   > *Discussion:* In "Why Change Is So Hard," Heath identifies exhaustion of self-control as the reason for the difference between the performance of the two test groups. What other explanations could there be for the difference in performance between the two groups of subjects? Is Heath's reasoning sound and convincing?

4. **Reflect on how the reading challenges you.** Which of your beliefs and values does the reading call into question? What discomfort does it create? Does your own perspective skew your evaluation?

   > *Discussion:* What self-control issues have you faced? What might this article have to say about those who work two jobs, run single-parent households, serve extended terms in war zones, or otherwise must exert superhuman levels of self-control? What social changes could help keep people from "snapping"?

fyi For additional help evaluating texts, see pages 412–415. For information on detecting logical fallacies, which weaken writers' arguments, see pages 301–304.

Responding to a Text

In a sense, when you read a text, you enter into a dialogue with it. Your response expresses your turn in the dialogue. Such a response can take varied forms, from a journal entry to a blog to a posting in an online-comments forum.

Follow these guidelines for response writing.

On the surface, responding to a text seems perfectly natural—just let it happen. But it can be a bit more complicated. A written response typically is not the same as a private diary entry but is instead shared with other readers, who may be in your class or someone else. To develop a fitting response, keep in mind common expectations for this kind of writing, as well as your instructor's requirements, if the response is for a course:

1. **Be honest.** Although you want to remain sensitive to the context in which you will share your response, be bold enough to be honest about your reaction to the text— what it makes you think, feel, and question. To that end, a response usually allows you to express yourself directly using the pronoun "I."

2. **Be fluid.** Let the flow of your thoughts guide you in what you write. Don't stop to worry about grammar, punctuation, mechanics, and spelling. These can be quickly cleaned up before you share or submit your response.

3. **Be reflective.** Generally, the goal of a response is to offer thoughtful reflection as opposed to knee-jerk reaction. Show, then, that you are engaging the text's ideas, relating them to your own experience, looking both inward and outward. Avoid a shallow reaction that comes from skimming the text or misreading it.

4. **Be selective.** By nature, a response must limit its focus; it cannot exhaust all your reactions to the text. So zero in on one or two elements of your response, and run with those to see where they take you in your dialogue with the text.

Sample Response

Here is part of a student's response to Dan Heath's "Why Change Is So Hard" on pages 4–5. Note the informality and explanatory tone.

> Heath's report of the psychological experiment is very vivid, referring to the smell of chocolate-chip cookies and hungry students "gorging" on them. He uses the term "sadistic" to refer to making the radish-eaters sit and watch this go on. I wonder if this mild torment plays into the student's readiness to give up on the later test. If I'd been rewarded with cookies, I'd feel indebted to the testers and would stick with it longer. If I'd been punished with radishes, I might give up sooner just to spite the testers.
>
> Now that I think of it, the digestion of all that sugar and fat in the cookies, as opposed to the digestion of roughage from the radishes, might also affect concentration and performance. Maybe the sugar "high" gives students the focus to keep going?

Summarizing a Text

Writing a summary disciplines you by making you pull only essentials from a reading—the main points, the thread of the argument. By doing so, you create a brief record of the text's contents and exercise your ability to comprehend, analyze, and synthesize.

Use these guidelines for summary writing.

Writing a summary requires sifting out the least important points, sorting the essential ones to show their relationships, and stating those points in your own words. Follow these guidelines:

1. **Skim first; then read closely.** First, get a sense of the whole, including the main idea and strategies for support. Then read carefully, taking notes as you do.

2. **Capture the text's argument.** Review your notes and annotations, looking for main points and clear connections. State these briefly and clearly, in your own words. Include only what is essential, excluding most examples and details. Don't say simply that the text talks about its subject; tell what it says about that subject.

3. **Test your summary.** Aim to objectively provide the heart of the text; avoid interjecting your own opinions and presence as a writer. Don't confuse an objective summary of a text with a response to it (shown on the previous page). Check your summary against the original text for accuracy and consistency.

Sample Summary

Below is a student's summary of Dan Heath's "Why Change Is So Hard," on pages 4–5. Note how the summary writer includes only main points and phrases them in her own words. She departs from the precise order of details, but records them accurately.

> In the article "Why Change Is So Hard," Dan Heath argues that people who have trouble changing are not lazy, but have simply exhausted their self-control. Heath refers to a study in which one group of students was asked to eat cookies and not radishes, while another group in the same room was asked to eat radishes and not cookies. Afterward, both groups of students were asked to trace an endless geometric design without lifting their pencils. The cookie-only group traced on average 19 minutes before giving up, but the radish-only group traced on average only 8 minutes. They had already used up their self-control. Heath says that any behavioral change requires self-control, an exhaustible resource. Reverting to old behavior is what happens due not to laziness but to exhaustion.

INSIGHT Writing formal summaries—whether as part of literature reviews or as abstracts—is an important skill, especially in the social and natural sciences.

Critical Thinking Through Viewing

Images are created to communicate, just as words are. Most images in everyday life are made to communicate very quickly—magazine covers, ads, signs, movie trailers, and so forth. Other images require contemplation, such as the *Mona Lisa*. When you view an image, view actively and critically.

Actively view images.

Survey the image. See the image as a whole so that you can absorb its overall idea. Look for the image's focal point—what your eye is drawn to. Also consider the relationship between the image's foreground and background, its left content and right content, and its various colors.

Inspect the image. Let your sight touch every part of the image, as if you were reading Braille. Hints of its meaning may lurk in the tiny details as well as in the relationship between the image's parts.

Question the image. Think in terms of each part of the rhetorical situation.
- **Designer:** Who created the image? Why did the person create it?
- **Message:** What is the subject of the image? What is the purpose?
- **Medium:** How was the image originally shown? How is it currently shown?
- **Viewer:** Who is the intended viewer? Why are you viewing the image?
- **Context:** When and where did the image first appear? When and where does it appear now? How does the image relate to its context?

Understand the purpose. Different images have different purposes. Ask yourself, "What is this image meant to do?" and then decide on an appropriate response:
- **Arouse curiosity?** Open your imagination, but stay on guard.
- **Entertain?** Look for the pleasure or the joke, but be wary of excess or of ethically questionable material in the image.
- **Inform or educate?** Search for key instruction, noting what's left out.
- **Illustrate?** Relate the image to the words or concept being illustrated: Does the image clarify or distort the meaning?
- **Persuade?** Examine how the image appeals to the viewer's needs, from safety and satisfaction to self-worth. Are the appeals manipulative, clichéd, or fallacious? Do they play on emotions to bypass reason?
- **Summarize?** Look for the essential message in the image: Does that main idea correspond with the written text?

catwalker / Shutterstock.com

View an image.

Chris Krenzke

The use of *minors* as *miners* is no *minor* problem.

fig. 1.3

Discussion ▼

Figure 1.3 by Chris Krenzke and the caption by Verne Meyer effectively combine humor with instruction. Originally published in a high school writing handbook, the image's aim is to teach students about a specific word-usage problem while also entertaining them. The image is line art in the "comic" genre, using a humorous scene to convey a serious message. Here are some thoughts on how you might actively view this image:

1. **Survey.** The image tells a story of heavily burdened children working under the demanding supervision of an authoritarian male. That story moves from left to right, from breaking rocks to loading rocks to carrying rocks toward a likely distant destination, the destination pointed to by the man. The black-and-white medium accentuates the starkness.

2. **Inspect.** In terms of the illustration's details, each figure is striking. The individual children share a thinness in their bodies and a strain in their faces. The four children in the line are pictured as beasts of burden bent over by bags that dwarf them. The repetition of figures emphasizes the trudging repetition of their work, and each child in line is pressed farther toward the ground. As for the man, his back is straight and his posture tall. His enormous chin, large nose, overly long but skinny arm, and sharply pointed finger suggest a negative authority. His stubbly face and his caveman clothing add to this figure's prehistoric character.

3. **Question.** Who is the artist Chris Krenzke? When did he first create this image? In what book was it published? When? Why did Krenzke use this caveman style? Who or what do "minors," "miners," and "minor" refer to in the illustration?

4. **Relate.** The connection between the sentence and the image becomes clear when the viewer realizes that "minors" are children not of a legal age to work, "miners" refers to an occupation, and "minor" means insignificant. But the image prompts other connections: the history of horrific child-labor practices during the Industrial Revolution as well as continuing child-labor issues in today's global economy. With these allusions, Krenzke succeeds in deepening the instruction offered by his art.

Interpreting an Image

Interpreting an image follows naturally from viewing or "reading" the image. Interpreting means figuring out what the image or design is meant to do, say, or show. Interpreting requires you to think more deeply about each element of the rhetorical situation shown in Figure 1.4, and complications with each element.

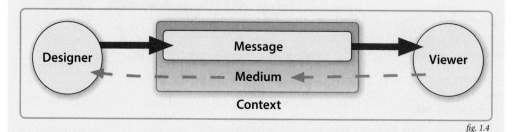

fig. 1.4

- **Designer:** Who created the image—a photographer, a painter, a Web designer, an eyewitness using a smartphone? Why did the person create it? What other people might have been involved—editors, patrons?

    Complications: The designer might be unknown or a group.

- **Message:** What is the subject of the image? How is the subject portrayed? What is the main purpose of the image—to entertain, inform, persuade, entice, or shock?

    Complications: The message might be mixed, implied, ironic, unwelcome, or distorted. The subject might be vague, unfamiliar, complex, or disturbing.

- **Medium:** What is the image—a painting, a cartoon panel, a photo? How might the image have been modified over time? What visual language has the sender used?

    Complications: The medium might be unusual or unfamiliar, or more than one medium may be involved. The visual languages might be literal, stylized, numeric, symbolic, and so on.

- **Viewer:** Whom was the image made for? Are you part of the intended audience? What is your relationship with the designer? Do you agree with the message? How comfortable are you with the medium? What is your overall response to the image?

    Complications: You might be uninterested in, unfamiliar with, or biased toward the message.

- **Context:** What was the context in which the image was first presented? What context surrounds the image now? Does the image fit its context or fight it?

    Complications: The context might be disconnected, ironic, changing, or multilayered.

INSIGHT   Like words, visuals can be clichés—trite, misleading, or worn-out expressions of concepts or ideas. For example, TV ads for weight-loss drugs commonly picture scantily clad, fit young people, deceptively linking use of the drug to beauty, youth, and sex.

Interpret an image.

fig. 1.5

© BAZUKI MUHAMMAD/Reuters/Corbis

Discussion ▼

Figure 1.5 shows a multireligious commemoration of the 229,000 victims of the Indian Ocean tsunami of December 26, 2004.

The symbolism is clearly rooted in the points of light created by the candle balloons, where light itself is a cross-cultural symbol of hope, endurance, the human spirit, and God's presence. The skyward angle of the photograph, with the clusters of candle balloons floating up and the people in the lower right of the frame, creates this sense of vertical longing and release, emphasizing perhaps humanity's longing to solve life's mysteries, including death and disaster. Although the large, just-released candle balloons are most prominent, the viewer's eyes are also drawn upward, where clusters of far-off candles become constellations of starlike lights. The mourners in the right of the frame, forming a loose circle, are all gazing skyward, like the viewer. Ordinary people in ordinary clothes, they appear to be clapping and, for some, the clapping shows their hands virtually in a posture of prayer. In this way, the image both mourns the dead and celebrates life.

Designer: Photographer Bazuki Muhammad; authors of *The College Writer*

Message: Thai people release candle balloons during a mass prayer for victims of the Indian Ocean tsunami. The message is to remember those who died, but move forward with hope.

Medium: Digital color photograph

Viewer: The intended viewer was anyone reading a newspaper, magazine, or Web article. The current viewer is likely a student or an instructor in a composition course.

Context: This photograph was part of a series provided by Reuters for global newspapers. It now is part of a composition text.

Evaluating an Image

As a critical thinker, you must do more than understand and interpret an image you encounter: You must assess its quality, truthfulness, and value. In other words, you must evaluate it. When you have done that well, you can fairly say you have thought it through. The following questions will guide your assessment.

Consider the purpose.

What purpose does the visual image best seem to serve?

- **Ornamentation:** Makes the page more pleasing to the eye
- **Illustration:** Supports points made in the accompanying text
- **Revelation:** Gives an inside look at something or presents new data
- **Explanation:** Uses imagery or graphics to clarify a complex subject
- **Instruction:** Guides the viewer through a complex process
- **Persuasion:** Influences feelings or beliefs
- **Entertainment:** Amuses the viewer

Evaluate the quality.

Essentially, how good is the image?

- Is the image done with skill? A map, for example, should be accurately and attractively drawn, should use color effectively, and should be complete enough to serve its purpose.
- Does the image measure up to standards of quality?
- Is it backed by authority? Does the designer have a good reputation? Does the publication or institution have good credentials?
- How does the image compare to other images like it? Are clearer or more accurate images available?
- What are its shortcomings? Are there gaps in its coverage? Does it twist the evidence? Does it convey clichéd or fallacious information? (See pages 301–304 for a discussion of logical fallacies.)
- Could you think of a better way to approach the image's subject? If you were to produce the visual, what might you improve?

Determine the value.

What is the image's tangible and intangible worth? Its benefits and drawbacks?

- Is the visual worth viewing? Does it enrich the document by clarifying or otherwise enhancing its message?
- Does the visual appeal to you? Listen to authorities and peers, but also consider your own perspective.

Evaluate an image.

Discussion ▼

Evaluating an image such as the WWII poster in Figure 1.6 aimed at U.S. servicemen reveals its strong stereotypes of both men and women, stereotypes related to the historical period. As with all images, evaluation begins with understanding and interpreting the poster.

In the poster's center is a woman in evening dress, her hair done up, wearing jewels and a corsage. She is seated, at ease, looking at us. Perhaps she represents beauty, both sensual attractiveness and sophistication. The colors used to present her are pale and muted, except for her blue eyes and red lips.

Surrounding the woman are three men, individually dressed in the uniforms of Army, Air Force, and Navy. Drinking and smoking, the men seem to be competing for her attention.

The poster implies that all service personnel were male, which was not true even in WWII, when WACs and WAVEs served in the armed forces. It

National Archives, London, Great Britain

fig. 1.6

cautions that these male members of the armed forces should be wary in seemingly innocent social situations, since even a beautiful woman, whom popular stereotypes of the day characterized as "dumb," might not be what she appears. Such a woman might, in fact, be a spy—an idea perhaps inspired by the famous case of WWI spy Mata Hari. The statement that "careless talk costs lives" is a version of another common phrase from the period: "Loose lips sink ships."

Evaluating this poster involves considering its original context while assessing it from our current perspective. In the heat of WWII, this poster could be considered a fair piece of military persuasion. Today, however, what is striking are the gender stereotypes at work in both image and words. Not only are service personnel today both male and female, in every branch of the armed forces, but they fulfill the same roles, including combat positions. With respect to the men, the image implies that in social situations (which are assumed to include smoking and drinking), they are untrustworthy and apt to boast or compete in the presence of an attractive woman. With respect to women, the image both denounces and warns, implying that women, especially attractive women, are cunning and dangerous. Today, such stereotypes press us to question the quality, truthfulness, and value of the image.

Critical Thinking Through Writing

In college, your writing often must show your ability to think critically about topics and issues by analyzing complex processes, synthesizing distinct concepts, weighing the value of opposing perspectives, and practicing new applications of existing principles. The following tips can help you.

Develop sound critical-thinking habits.

Like everything worthwhile, improving your critical thinking skills takes time and practice. But cultivating the habits below will pay off in sound, thoughtful writing.

1. **Be curious.** Ask "Why?" Cultivate your ability to wonder; question what you see, hear, and read—both inside and outside the classroom.

2. **Be creative.** Don't settle for obvious answers. Look at things in a fresh way, asking "what-if" questions such as "What if Ophelia didn't die in *Hamlet*?"

3. **Be open to new ideas.** Approach thinking as you would approach a road trip—looking for the unexpected and musing over mysteries.

4. **Value others' points of view.** Look at issues from another person's perspective and weigh that against your own. Honestly examine how the core of her or his perspective compares to the core of your perspective, and how each basis for thought might lead to different conclusions.

5. **Get involved.** Read books, journals, and newspapers. Watch documentaries. Join book clubs, film clubs, or political and social-action activities.

6. **Focus.** Sharpen your concentration, looking for details that distinguish a topic and reveal key questions related to its nature, function, and impact.

7. **Be rational.** Choose logical thinking patterns like those discussed in this chapter, and then work through the steps to deepen your understanding of a topic.

8. **Make connections.** Use writing to explore how and why topics or issues are related. Use comparisons to identify and name these relationships.

9. **Tolerate ambiguity.** Respectfully analyze issues not readily resolved—and acknowledge when your position requires further research or thought.

10. **Test the evidence.** Be properly skeptical about all claims (see pages 296–297). Look for corroboration (or verification) in other sources.

11. **Develop research-based conclusions.** Focus on understanding issues, assessing their history, development, function, and impact. During the process, gather details that lead to and support a reasonable conclusion.

12. **Assess results.** Consider each paper to be a benchmark that reflects your progress in developing your thinking and writing skills. Save your papers for periodic analyses of your progress and revision of the writing.

Ask probing questions.

Every field uses questions to trigger critical thinking. For example, scientific questions generate hypotheses, sociological questions lead to studies, mathematical questions call for proofs, and literary criticism questions call for interpretations. A good question opens up a problem and guides you all the way to its solution. But not all questions are created equal. Consider the differences:

- **"Rhetorical" questions** aren't meant to be answered. They're asked for effect.

    Example: Who would want to be caught in an earthquake?

- **Closed questions** seek a limited response and can be answered with "yes," "no," or a simple fact.

    Example: Would I feel an earthquake measuring 3.0 on the Richter scale?

- **Open questions** invite brainstorming and discussion.

    Example: How might a major earthquake affect this urban area?

- **Theoretical questions** call for organization and explanation of an entire field of knowledge.

    Example: What might cause a sudden fracturing of Earth's crust along fault lines?

To improve the critical thinking in your writing, ask better questions. The strategies below will help you think freely, respond to reading, study for a test, or collect your thoughts for an essay.

☑ **Ask open questions.** Closed questions sometimes choke off thinking. Use open questions to trigger a flow of ideas.

☑ **Ask "educated" questions.** Compare these questions: (A) What's wrong with television? (B) Does the 16.3 percent rise in televised acts of violence during the past three years signal a rising tolerance for violence in the viewing audience? You have a better chance of expanding the "educated" question—question B—into an essay because the question is clearer and suggests debatable issues.

☑ **Keep a question journal.** Divide a blank notebook page or split a computer screen. On one side, write down any questions that come to mind regarding the topic that you want to explore. On the other side, write down answers and any thoughts that flow from them.

☑ **Write Q & A drafts.** To write a thoughtful first draft, write quickly, then look it over. Turn the main idea into a question and write again, answering your question. For example, if your main idea is that TV viewers watch far more violence than they did ten years ago, ask *Which viewers? Why?* and *What's the result?* Go on that way until you find a key idea to serve as the main point of your next draft.

 For more help with critical thinking skills such as making and supporting claims, recognizing logical fallacies, and dealing with opposition, see "Strategies for Argumentation and Persuasion," pages 293–308.

Practice inductive and deductive logic.

Questions invite thinking; reasoning responds to that challenge in an organized way. Will the organization of your thoughts be inductive or deductive? Inductive logic reasons from specific information toward general conclusions. Deductive logic reasons from general principles toward specific applications. Notice in Figure 1.7 that inductive reasoning starts with specific details or observations (as shown at the base) and then moves "up" to broader ideas and eventually to a concluding generalization. In contrast, deduction starts with general principles at the top and works down, applying the principles to explain particular instances.

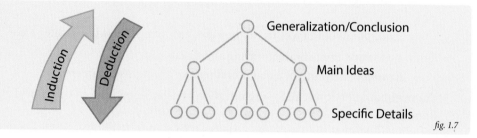

fig. 1.7

Sentences, paragraphs, and entire essays can be organized either inductively or deductively. Use induction when you want to postpone your conclusions. Use deduction for logical clarity, directness, and strength, or to apply what is already agreed on to what is still under dispute. Narrative or personal essays tend toward inductive organization, whereas analytical essays typically use both induction and deduction.

Example: Read through the paragraphs below from the student essay, "Sethe in *Beloved* and Orleanna in *Poisonwood Bible*," by Rachel De Smith. (The complete essay is on pages 184–186.) The first paragraph works inductively, the second paragraph deductively.

Induction: specific details to generalization

Sethe lives in house number 124, a house generally believed to be haunted, "full of a baby's venom" (Morrison 3). The child's ghost inhabiting the house throws things around, makes spots of colored light appear, shakes floors, and stomps up the stairs. The people of the surrounding community—remembering Sethe's past, fearing ghostly retribution, and resenting the long-ago extravagance of Sethe's mother-in-law, Baby Suggs—diligently avoid the house and its residents. Sethe's one remaining daughter, Denver, will not leave the yard (Morrison 205). The two of them live with the ghost, ostracized.

Deduction: generalization to specific details

Orleanna lives in a less malignant but equally isolated situation. When she and her daughters follow her husband on his zealous missionary trip to the Congo, she is the only white woman in a village of people with whom she shares nothing, not even a word of their language. Preoccupied with the troubles in her own house, she remains separated from the villagers by a gulf of cultural misunderstanding—from how to behave in the marketplace to where to get her drinking water (Kingsolver 89, 172). Even when she returns to the United States, Orleanna lives in isolation, hidden among her flower gardens, set apart by the stigma of her past (Kingsolver 407).

Practicing Modes of Thinking in Your Writing

In your various writing assignments, you will need to practice specific modes of thinking. The table below maps out these modes (from elementary to complex) and the tasks each requires. The more complex modes are then fleshed out on the following pages.

When you are asked to . . .

Know
define	memorize
identify	name
list	recall
match	recognize

Understand
comprehend	interpret
connect	restate
explain	summarize
grasp	

Analyze
characterize	contrast
classify	divide
compare	examine

Synthesize
assemble	imagine
combine	invent
construct	link
formulate	

Evaluate
assess	measure
check	monitor
critique	rank
judge	rate

Apply
anticipate	propose
choose	select
generate	

be ready to . . .

Call to mind what you have learned
- Recall information
- List details
- Define key terms
- Identify main points

Show what you have learned
- Connect related examples
- Summarize important details
- Explain how something works
- Interpret what something means

Break down information
- Divide a whole into its parts
- Group things into categories
- Analyze causes and effects
- Examine similarities and differences

Shape information into a new form
- Bring together a body of evidence
- Blend the old with the new
- Predict or hypothesize
- Construct a new way of looking at something

Determine the worth of information
- Point out a subject's strengths and weaknesses
- Evaluate its clarity, accuracy, logic, value, and so on
- Convince others of its value/worth

Use what you have learned
- Propose a better way of doing something
- Generate a plan of action
- Offer solutions to a problem

Think by using analysis.

The word *analyze* literally means "to loosen or undo." When you analyze something, you break it down into parts and examine each part separately. You classify information, compare objects, trace a process, or explain causes.

As you analyze, think about the questions listed below. Note that each type of thinking answers certain kinds of questions. Remember, too, that thinking tasks often require two or more kinds of analysis that support one another.

Composition:	What elements does it contain? What is not part of it?
Categories:	How are things grouped, divided, or classified?
Structures:	What are the parts or elements? How are they related?
Comparisons/ contrasts:	How are things similar? How are they different?
Causes/effects:	Why did this happen? What are the results?
Processes:	How does it work or happen? What are the stages?

Example: Read through the passage below, from "Wayward Cells." In the full essay on pages 220–221, student writer Kerri Mertz explains the process by which healthy body cells become cancerous cells. Note how in this excerpt, the writer develops an overall analysis based on a process but also uses compare-contrast and cause-effect thinking within that structure, as well as informal definition.

> *The writer explains a cellular process and contrasts healthy and cancerous versions.*
>
> Most healthy cells reproduce rather quickly, but their reproduction rate is controlled. For example, your blood cells completely die off and replace themselves within a matter of weeks, but existing cells make only as many new cells as the body needs. The DNA codes in healthy cells tell them how many new cells to produce. However, cancer cells don't have this control, so they reproduce quickly with no stopping point, a characteristic called "autonomy" (Braun 3). What's more, all their "offspring" have the same qualities as their messed-up parent, and the resulting overpopulation produces growths called tumors.   *1*
>
> *The writer explains the three harmful effects of tumor cells (the cause).*
>
> *Examples illustrate the analysis.*
>
> Tumor cells can hurt the body in a number of ways. First, a tumor can grow so big that it takes up space needed by other organs. Second, some cells may detach from the original tumor and spread throughout the body, creating new tumors elsewhere. This happens with lymphatic cancer—a cancer that's hard to control because it spreads so quickly. A third way that tumor cells can hurt the body is by doing work not called for in their DNA. For example, a gland cell's DNA code may tell the cell to produce a necessary hormone in the endocrine system. However, if cancer damages or distorts that code, sick cells may produce more of the hormone than the body can use—or even tolerate (Braun 4). Cancer cells seem to have minds of their own, and this is why cancer is such a serious disease.   *2*

Think by using synthesis.

Synthesis is the opposite of analysis. Where analysis breaks things down into parts, synthesis combines elements into a new whole. In your writing, when you pull together things that are normally separate, you are synthesizing. Common ways of synthesizing include predicting, inventing, redesigning, and imagining a whole new way of looking at something.

Working with synthesis involves both reason and imagination. Start by looking closely at two or more items that you want to synthesize, and then think of fresh ways they can be related. Don't be afraid to see your subjects in a new way. In other words, think "sideways" rather than straight ahead. Ask the following questions:

> **Applying:** What can I do with both? What will be the outcome?
>
> **Bridging:** How can I build a connection between the two?
>
> **Combining:** How can I connect, associate, or blend the two?
>
> **Conflicting:** Which is good, better, or best? What strength does each offer the other?
>
> **Inventing:** What parts could these two play in a drama?
>
> **Proposing:** What do I suggest doing with both?
>
> **Sequencing:** Which comes first? Is one an extension of the other?
>
> **Projecting:** Based on current information, what is the best forecast for what will happen in the near future or the long term?

Example: Read through the passage below, from "In Africa, AIDS Has a Woman's Face," by former United Nations Secretary-General Kofi Annan (see pages 338–339). In the full article, Annan argues that resolving the AIDS crisis in Africa must begin by saving the familial, social, and economic backbones of African cultures—women. In the following passage, Annan synthesizes his discussion by projecting what is necessary for successful solutions.

> Pulling together his discussion of the twin tragedies of AIDS and famine in Africa, the writer calls for imaginative, multifaceted solutions.

> Because this crisis is different from past famines, we must look beyond relief measures of the past. Merely shipping in food is not enough. Our effort will have to combine food assistance and new approaches to farming with treatment and prevention of H.I.V. and AIDS. It will require creating early-warning and analysis systems that monitor both H.I.V. infection rates and famine indicators. It will require new agricultural techniques, appropriate to a depleted work force. It will require a renewed effort to wipe out H.I.V.-related stigma and silence.   *1*
>
> It will require innovative, large-scale ways to care for orphans, with specific measures that enable children in AIDS-affected communities to stay in school. Education and prevention are still the most powerful weapons against the spread of H.I.V. Above all, this new international effort must put women at the center of our strategy to fight AIDS.   *2*

Think by using evaluation.

Movies, proposals, arguments—anything can be evaluated. Evaluation measures the value or worth of things. For example, when you express your judgment about an issue or discuss the weak and strong points of what someone else has said, you are evaluating. Many kinds of writing are evaluative.

To evaluate a topic, start by learning as much about it as possible. Then consider which criteria or standards are appropriate. Next, judge how the topic measures up based on those criteria. Support your judgment with concrete details, examples, illustrations, and comparisons. Ask questions like these:

Aspects:	What elements of the topic will I evaluate?
Vantage point:	What are my experience and my point of view?
Criteria:	On which standards will I base my judgment?
Assessment:	How does the topic measure up by those standards?
Comparison:	How does it compare to and contrast with similar things?
Recommendation:	Based on my evaluation, what do I advise?

Example: The passage below is taken from David Blankenhorn's "Fatherless America," on pages 320–325. In the full essay, Blankenhorn examines the causes and effects of the increased fatherlessness within U.S. families—that is, the absence of fathers in many homes. In the following excerpt, he assesses the failures of a society that is losing a healthy sense of fatherhood.

The writer establishes a criterion for evaluating a culture's fatherhood models and practices.

... Margaret Mead and others have observed that the supreme test of any civilization is whether it can socialize men by teaching them to be fathers—creating a culture in which men acknowledge their paternity and willingly nurture their offspring. Indeed, if we can equate the essence of the antisocial male with violence, we can equate the essence of the socialized male with being a good father. Thus, at the center of our most important cultural imperative, we find the fatherhood script: the story that describes what it ought to mean for a man to have a child. ... 1

After exploring this criterion in depth (not shown), the writer measures U.S. culture and assesses its failures with respect to fatherhood.

The stakes on this issue could hardly be higher. Our society's conspicuous failure to sustain or create compelling norms of fatherhood amounts to a social and personal disaster. Today's story of fatherhood features one-dimensional characters, an unbelievable plot, and an unhappy ending. It reveals in our society both a failure of collective memory and a collapse of moral imagination. It undermines families, neglects children, causes or aggravates our worst social problems, and makes individual adult happiness—both male and female—harder to achieve. 2

Ultimately, this failure reflects nothing less than a culture gone awry: a culture increasingly unable to establish the boundaries, erect the sign-posts, and fashion the stories that can harmonize individual happiness with collective well-being. In short, it reflects a culture that increasingly fails to "enculture" individual men and women, mothers and fathers. 3

Think by using application.

Thinking by using application defines the practical implications of something. It involves using what you know to demonstrate, show, relate, or extend ideas in view of their outcomes. For example, using what you have learned about the ecology of forest fires to examine the effects of a particular fire—that's application in action.

Applying involves moving from ideas to possible action. First, understand the information you have. Second, relate this information to a given situation. Third, select those facts and details that clarify and support the application. Fourth, test the application to see whether it has been reasonable.

When applying ideas, let questions like these guide your writing:

Purpose: What is something designed to be or do?

Benefits: What would this idea make clearer, better, or more complete?

Solutions: What problems are solved by application of this idea?

Outcomes: What results can be expected? Where could we go from there?

Example: Read the paragraphs below, from Anna Quindlen's "Uncle Sam and Aunt Samantha" (pages 351–353). In this essay, Quindlen argues that in the United States, women— as well as men—should be eligible to be drafted for military service. In the passage below, she applies the concept of equal rights to this specific situation.

> *Using the word "egalitarian" to refer to a key principle, the writer points out the real inequality and argues for a change.*
>
> Parents face a series of unique new challenges in this more egalitarian world, not the least of which would be sending a daughter off to war. But parents all over this country are doing that right now, with daughters who enlisted; some have even expressed surprise that young women, in this day and age, are not required to register alongside their brothers and friends. While all involved in this debate over the years have invoked the assumed opposition of the people, even 10 years ago more than half of all Americans polled believed women should be made eligible for the draft. Besides, this is not about comfort but about fairness. My son has to register with the Selective Service this year, and if his sister does not when she turns 18, it makes a mockery not only of the standards of this household but of the standards of this nation.
>
> *She backs up her conclusion with historical context and presses readers to agree.*
>
> It is possible in Afghanistan for women to be treated like little more than fecund pack animals precisely because gender fear and ignorance and hatred have been codified and permitted to hold sway. In this country, largely because of the concerted efforts of those allied with the women's movement over a century of struggle, much of that bigotry has been beaten back, even buried. Yet in improbable places the creaky old ways surface, the ways suggesting that we women were made of finer stuff. The finer stuff was usually porcelain, decorative and on the shelf, suitable for meals and show. Happily, the finer stuff has been transmuted into the right stuff. But with rights come responsibilities, as teachers like to tell their students . . .

1

2

Critical-Thinking and Writing Activities

As directed by your instructor, complete the following critical thinking and writing activities by yourself or with classmates:

1. Northrop Frye has argued that "[n]obody is capable of free speech unless he [or she] knows how to use language, and such knowledge is not a gift: It has to be learned and worked at." How does Frye's claim relate to the discussions of critical reading, viewing, and writing in this chapter?

2. What thinking, reading, viewing, and writing skills are required in your field of study? Reflect on those possibilities.

3. Choose a subject you know something about. Practice thinking about that subject both inductively and deductively. Then write two paragraphs—one developed inductively and the other developed deductively.

4. Select a sample essay from the "Strategies and Models" section. Read the piece carefully and identify where and how the writer uses different thinking modes. Do the same analysis on a recent sample of your own writing, rating your analysis, synthesis, evaluation, and application.

Learning-Objectives Checklist ✓

Have you achieved this chapter's learning objectives? Check your progress with the items below, revisiting topics in the chapter as needed. *I have . . .*

_____ read texts actively by assessing their rhetorical situation (writer, message, medium, reader, context), and practicing techniques such as preview, read, review (4–5).

_____ read texts actively through note-taking, annotating, mapping, and outlining (6–9).

_____ responded to written texts in an honest, fluid, reflective, and selective way (8).

_____ objectively summarized texts in my own words, distinguishing main arguments and key supporting points from secondary content (9).

_____ viewed images actively by surveying and inspecting them (10–11).

_____ carefully interpreted images by deeply analyzing the rhetorical situation and its complications—designer, message, medium, viewer, and context (12–13).

_____ critiqued visual images by assessing their purpose, value, and quality (14–15).

_____ thought critically about topics by practicing sound thinking habits, asking probing questions, and using inductive and deductive patterns strategically (16–18).

_____ produced writing that practices modes of thinking such as analysis, synthesis, evaluation, and application (19–23).

Chapter 2

Beginning the Writing Process

The blank page or screen can be daunting for any writer. That's because writing doesn't go from nothing to a masterpiece in one step. Writing is a process, much like painting.

This chapter focuses on beginning that process. It provides numerous concrete strategies for understanding writing assignments, deciding on a topic, and exploring it. The very act of writing generates ideas and creates new connections that will make it easy to fill the blank page.

Visually Speaking   Painting is the process of converting infinite possibilities into a single image. How is writing similar? How is it different? What is the starting point for painting? For writing? Consider these questions as you examine Figure 2.1.

Learning **Objectives**

By working through this chapter, you will be able to

- outline the writing process and decide how to follow it for different projects.
- analyze the rhetorical situation behind writing tasks.
- summarize seven traits of strong, college-level writing.
- interpret the nature and requirements of specific writing assignments.
- generate and choose topics for writing projects.
- collect, track, and examine information for writing projects.

© Jose Luis Pelaez, Inc./Corbis

fig. 2.1

The Writing Process: From Start to Finish

It's easy to feel overwhelmed by a writing project—especially if the form of writing is new to you, the topic is complex, or the paper must be long. However, using the writing process will relieve some of that pressure by breaking down the task into manageable steps. An overview of those steps is shown below, and key principles are addressed on the next page.

Consider the writing process.

Figure 2.2 maps out the basic steps in the writing process. As you work on your writing project, periodically review this diagram to keep yourself on task.

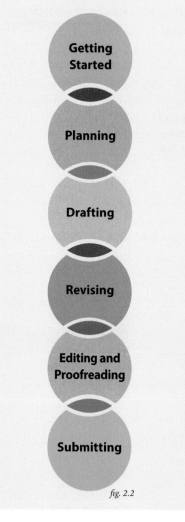

Getting Started
- Understanding the assignment
- Selecting a subject
- Collecting information

Planning
- Forming a thesis
- Using methods of development
- Developing a plan or an outline

Drafting
- Opening your draft
- Developing the middle
- Ending your draft

Revising
- Improving ideas, organization, and voice
- Reviewing with peers

Editing and Proofreading
- Editing for style
- Proofreading for correctness

Submitting
- Preparing a paper for submission
- Checking for page design and documentation

fig. 2.2

Adapt the process to your project.

The writing process shown on the previous page is flexible, not rigid. As a writer, you need to adapt the process to your situation and assignment. To do so, consider these essential principles.

- **Writing tends not to follow a straight path.** While writing begins with an assignment or a need and ends with a reader, the journey in between is often indirect. The steps in the flowchart overlap to show that when you write, you sometimes move back and forth between steps, meaning that the process is recursive. For example, during the revision phase, you may discover that you need to draft a new paragraph or do more research.

- **Each assignment presents distinct challenges.** A personal essay may develop best through clustering or freewriting; a literary analysis through close reading of a story; a lab report through the experimental method; and a position paper through reading of books and journal articles, as well as through careful and balanced reasoning. Moreover, an assignment may or may not involve extensive research and working with sources.

- **Writing can involve collaboration.** From using your roommate as a sounding board for your topic choice to working with a group to produce a major report, college writing is not solitary writing. In fact, many colleges have a writing center to help you refine your writing assignments. (See pages 87–89 for more.)

- **Each writer works differently.** Some writers do extensive prewriting before drafting, while others do not. You might develop a detailed outline, whereas someone else might draft a brief list of topics. Experiment with the strategies introduced in chapters 2–7, adopting those that help you.

- **Good writing can't be rushed.** Although some students regard pulling an all-nighter as a badge of honor, good writing takes time. A steady, disciplined approach will generally produce the best results. For example, by brainstorming or reading early in a project, you stimulate your subconscious mind to mull over issues, identify problems, and project solutions—even while your conscious mind is working on other things. Similarly, completing a first draft early enough gives you time to revise objectively.

- **Different steps call for attention to different writing issues.** As you use the writing process, at each stage keep your focus where it belongs:

    1. While getting started, planning, and drafting, focus on global issues: ideas, structure, voice, format, and design.

    2. During revising, fix big content problems by cutting, adding, and thoroughly reworking material. (Our experience is that students benefit the most from revising—but spend the least time doing it!)

    3. While editing and proofreading, pay attention to small, local issues—word choice, sentence smoothness, and grammatical correctness. Worrying about these issues early in the writing process interrupts the flow of drafting and wastes time on material that may later be deleted.

Understanding the Rhetorical Situation

Rhetoric is the art of using language effectively. As Aristotle, Quintilian, and others have explained, your language is effective when all aspects of your message fit the rhetorical situation (Figure 2.3):

Rhetorical Situation

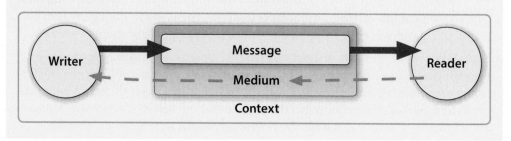

fig. 2.3

Think of your role as the writer.

Are you writing as a concerned citizen, as a student in a class, as a friend relating a story, as a reporter providing news, as a blogger giving an opinion? Your role in writing and otherwise communicating affects the level of language you use, the voice you use, the types of details you include, the evidence you cite to support a claim, and so on.

Understand your subject.

To truly understand your subject, you need to gather and assimilate all relevant details about it, including its history, makeup, function, and impact on people and culture. Knowing those details will help you narrow your focus to a specific thesis and develop it well.

> **Working with Sources** | As you search for information, think about which types of sources are recommended or expected for the assignment. Which should be avoided?

Understand your purpose.

Key words in an assignment—such as *analyze, explain, defend,* or *describe*—tell you what the purpose of the writing is supposed to be. Understanding why you are writing helps you choose an organizational strategy, such as classification, definition, or process. (See pages 62–64.)

> **Working with Sources** | Think of the sources that will most help you achieve your purpose, whether to entertain, compare, inspire, enlighten, and so on.

Understand your audience.

For any writing task, you must understand your audience in order to develop writing that meets their needs. To assess your audience, answer questions like these:

- Who are my readers: instructor? classmates? Web users?
- What do they know about my topic, and what do they need to know?
- How well do they understand the terminology involved?
- What are their attitudes toward the topic and toward me?
- How well do they read written English—or visuals such as graphs and charts?
- How will they use my writing (as entertainment or to complete a task)?

Note: Answers to such questions will help you develop meaningful sentences (pages 93–99), choose appropriate words (pages 100–104), and select relevant visuals (page 392).

Working with Sources | Ask yourself what sources your reader will best understand and most respect. What sources will add to your credibility and authority?

Understand the medium (form).

Many communication options are available for every message. Academic forms include essays, analyses, reports, proposals, research papers, reviews, and so on. It is important to understand the form of the assignment. What works well in a narrative about a past experience would not work as well in a lab report. Also, each of these forms can contain multiple media: written elements, graphics, photos, drawings, videos, audios, links, and so on. Understanding the overall medium and the media within it will help you succeed.

Working with Sources | Make sure you understand the way that sources are to be cited in the form of communication you are using. (See 493–564 for MLA and APA styles.)

Think about the context.

Think about how this assignment relates to others in the course. Consider these issues:

- **Weight:** Is this an everyday assignment, a weekly or biweekly one, or the big one?
- **Assessment:** Find out how the assignment will be graded. What traits will your instructor look for? Will your writing be assessed with a rubric? (See page 30.)
- **Intent:** Make certain that you understand the goals of the assignment and understand what your instructor wants you to get out of it.

Note: If the writing you are doing is not in response to an assignment, think about the environment in which the message will be read. What is the history of this issue? What is the current climate like? What might the future be?

Working with Sources | If you are writing material that will be reviewed and debated by others in your field, think about what sources you would most want your writing to appear in. Make certain you understand the submission guidelines for the source.

Aiming for Writing Excellence

What makes your writing strong enough to engage and enlighten readers? As already suggested on pages 28–29, that depends in part on the rhetorical situation: what your purpose is, who your readers are, and so on. Writing excellence can be measured by the depth of what you learn through writing, as well as by what your reader gains through reading. However, while the world of writing is so diverse that no formula or prescription can state definitively what makes for strong writing, we can point to common traits that describe such writing. Consider the relevance of these traits at the beginning of any writing project.

Common Traits of College Writing

Quality writing shows strengths in the traits below, which range from global issues to local, sentence-level issues.

- **Strong ideas** are what you discover and develop through your writing. They are what make your content substantial and meaningful. These elements include a clear, sharp thesis or theme; strong and balanced reasoning; and accurate, supportive information that is properly credited.

- **Logical organization** creates the structure and flow of your writing. Through organization, reasoning is delivered through a clear chain of ideas, a unified whole. Typically, an engaging opening focuses discussion, the middle effectively develops the main idea, and a closing offers conclusions and points forward—all in paragraphs that are well developed (unified, coherent, and complete).

- **Engaging voice** refers to how your writing "sounds" to readers—the attitude, pacing, and personality that come through. An engaging voice sounds authentic and natural, engaged with the topic. Moreover, the tone—whether serious, playful, or sarcastic—is confident but also sincere and measured, fitting the writing occasion.

- **Clear word choice** carries your meaning. In your writing, the vocabulary should fit the topic, purpose, and audience. Phrasing should be clear throughout—language that readers will understand, precise terminology and plain English whenever possible.

- **Smooth sentences** express complete thoughts in a good blend of sentence lengths (short and punchy, long and thoughtful) and patterns (loose, balanced, and periodic). Such sentences use phrases and clauses in logical and expressive ways—energetically, economically, gracefully.

- **Correct writing** follows the conventions of language (grammar, punctuation, mechanics, usage, and spelling), as well as standards of citation and documentation (e.g., MLA, APA).

- **Professional document design** refers to the appearance of your writing on the page, the screen, and so on. Such design includes the document's format (e.g., essay, lab report, presentation, Web site), its page layout (e.g., margins, headings, bullets, white space), its typography (typefaces, type sizes, and type styles), and its use of tables and visuals.

Common Traits in Action

What do these common traits looks like in a typical piece of college writing such as the definition essay below? Spurred on by a funny experience, student writer Mary Bruins researched the word gullible and wrote this essay. Study the paper to explore why it represents strong freshman-level college writing.

The Gullible Family

Ideas
Clear focus, engaging thesis, and precise content

The other day, my friend Loris fell for the oldest trick in the book: "Hey, somebody wrote *gullible* on the ceiling!" Shortly after mocking "Gullible Loris" for looking up, I swallowed the news that Wal-Mart sells popcorn that pops into the shapes of cartoon characters. And so, as "Gullible Mary," I decided to explore what our name means, and who else belongs to our Gullible family. What I learned is that the family includes both people and birds, related to each other by our willingness to "swallow."

Organization
Lively opening, well-structured middle, and thoughtful closing

A gullible person will swallow an idea or argument without questioning its truth. Similarly, the gull (a long-winged, web-footed bird) will swallow just about anything thrown to it. In fact, the word *gullible* comes from *gull*, and this word can be traced back to the Germanic word *gwel* (to swallow). Both *gull* and *gwel* are linked to the modern word *gulp*, which means "to swallow greedily or rapidly in large amounts." It's not surprising, then, that Loris and I, sisters in the Gullible family, both eagerly gulped (like gulls) the false statements thrown to us.

Voice
Informed and engaging tone

Swallowing things this quickly isn't too bright, and gull (when referring to a bird or person) implies that the swallower is immature and foolish. For example, gull refers to an "unfledged" fowl, which the *Grolier Encyclopedia* describes as either "an immature bird still lacking flight feathers," or something that is "inexperienced, immature, or untried." These words describe someone who is fooled easily, and that's why gull, when referring to a human, means "dupe" or "simpleton." In fact, since 1550, *gullet,* which means "throat," has also meant "fooled."

Words
Precise, lively, clear phrasing

To illustrate this usage, the *Oxford English Dictionary* quotes two authors who use *gull* as a verb meaning to fool. "Nothing is so easy as to gull the public, if you only set up a prodigy," writes Washington Irving. William Dean Howells uses the word similarly when he writes, "You are perfectly safe to go on and gull imbeciles to the end of time, for all I care."

Sentences
Smooth, varied, and graceful constructions

Both of these authors are pretty critical of gullible people, but does *gullible* have only negative connotations? Is there no hope for Gullibles like Loris and me? C. O. Sylvester Marson's comments about *gullible* may give us some comfort. He links *gullible* to "credulous, confiding, and easily deceived." At first, these adjectives also sound negative, but *credulous* does mean "to follow implicitly." And the word credit comes from the Latin word *credo* (meaning "I believe"). So what's bad about that? In other words, isn't wanting to believe other people a good thing? Why shouldn't Loris and I be proud of at least that aspect of our gull blood? We want to be positive—and we don't want to be cynics!

Correctness
Error-free prose

Design
Attractive format, page layout, and typography

"The Gullible Family" by Mary Bruins. Used by permission of the author.

Understanding the Assignment

Each college instructor has a way of personalizing a writing assignment, but most assignments will spell out (1) the objective, (2) the task, (3) the formal requirements, and (4) suggested approaches and topics. Your first step, therefore, is to read the assignment carefully, noting the options and restrictions that are part of it. The suggestions below will help you do that. (Also see pages 112–115 for one writer's approach.)

Read the assignment.

Certain words in the assignment explain what main action you must perform. Here are some words that signal what you are to do:

Key Words

Analyze:	Break down a topic into subparts, showing how those parts relate.
Argue:	Defend a claim with logical arguments.
Classify:	Divide a large group into well-defined subgroups.
Compare/contrast:	Point out similarities and/or differences.
Define:	Give a clear, thoughtful definition or meaning of something.
Describe:	Show in detail what something is like.
Evaluate:	Weigh the truth, quality, or usefulness of something.
Explain:	Give reasons, list steps, or discuss the causes of something.
Interpret:	Tell in your own words what something means.
Reflect:	Share your well-considered thoughts about a subject.
Summarize:	Restate someone else's ideas very briefly in your own words.
Synthesize:	Connect facts or ideas to create something new.

Options and Restrictions

The assignment often gives you some choice of your topic or approach but may restrict your options to suit the instructor's purpose. Note the options and restrictions in the following short sample assignment:

Reflect on the way a natural disaster or major historical event has altered your understanding of the past, the present, or the future.

Options:	(1) You may choose any natural disaster or historical event.
	(2) You may focus on the past, present, or future.
	(3) You may examine any kind of alteration.
Restrictions:	(1) You must reflect on a change in your understanding.
	(2) The disaster must be natural.
	(3) The historical event must be major.

Relate the assignment to the goals of the course.

1. How much value does the instructor give the assignment? (The value is often expressed as a percentage of the course grade.)
2. What benefit does your instructor want you to receive?
    - Strengthen your comprehension?
    - Improve your research skills?
    - Deepen your ability to explain, prove, or persuade?
    - Expand your style?
    - Increase your creativity?
3. How will this assignment contribute to your overall performance in the course? What course goals (often listed in the syllabus) does it address?

Relate the assignment to other assignments.

1. Does it build on previous assignments?
2. Does it prepare you for the next assignment?

Relate the assignment to your own interests.

1. Does it connect with a topic that already interests you?
2. Does it connect with work in your other courses?
3. Does it connect with the work you may do in your chosen field?
4. Does it connect with life outside school?

Reflect on the assignment.

1. **First impulses:** How did you feel when you first read the assignment?
2. **Approaches:** What's the usual approach for an assignment like this? What's a better way of tackling it?
3. **Quality of performance:** What would it take to produce an excellent piece of writing?
4. **Benefits:** What are the benefits to your education? To you personally? To the class? To society?
5. **Features:** Reflect further on four key features of any writing assignment.
    - **Purpose:** What is the overall purpose of the assignment—to inform, to explain, to analyze, to entertain? What is the desired outcome?
    - **Readers:** Should you address your instructor? Your classmates? A general reader? How much does the reader already know about the topic? What type of language should you use?
    - **Form:** What are the requirements concerning length, format, and due date?
    - **Assessment:** How will the assignment be evaluated? Which of the traits discussed on pages 30–31 are important to this assignment? How can you be sure that you are completing the assignment correctly?

Developing a Topic

For some assignments, finding a suitable topic may require little thinking on your part. If an instructor asks you to summarize an article in a professional journal, you know what you will write about—the article in question. But suppose the instructor asks you to analyze a feature of popular culture in terms of its impact on society. You won't be sure of a specific writing topic until you explore the possibilities. Keep the following points in mind when you conduct a topic search. Your topic must . . .

- meet the requirements of the assignment.
- be limited in scope.
- seem reasonable (that is, be within your means to research).
- genuinely interest you.

Limit the subject area.

Many of your writing assignments may relate to general subject areas you are currently studying. Your task, then, is to select a specific topic related to the general area of study—a topic limited enough that you can treat it with sufficient depth in the number of pages and preparation time allowed for the assignment. The following examples show the difference between general subjects and limited topics:

General Subject Area: Popular culture
Limited Topic: *The Simpsons* TV show

General Subject Area: Energy sources
Limited Topic: Using wind power

Conduct your search.

Finding a writing idea that meets the requirements of the assignment should not be difficult, if you know how and where to look. Follow these steps:

1. **Check your class notes and handouts** for ideas related to the assignment.
2. **Search the Internet.** Type in a keyword or phrase (the general subject stated in the assignment) and see what you can find. You could also follow a subject tree to narrow a subject. (See page 448.)
3. **Consult indexes, guides, and other library references.** Subscription databases such as EBSCOhost, for example, list current articles published on specific topics and where to find them. (See pages 440–445.)
4. **Discuss the assignment** with your instructor or an information specialist.
5. **Use one or more of the prewriting strategies** described on the following pages to generate possible writing ideas.

Explore for possible topics.

You can generate possible writing ideas by using the following strategies. These same strategies can be used when you've chosen a topic and want to develop it further.

Journal Writing

Write in a journal on a regular basis. Reflect on your personal feelings, develop your thoughts, and record the happenings of each day. Periodically go back and underline ideas that you would like to explore in writing assignments. In the following journal-writing samples, the writer came up with an idea for a writing assignment about the societal impacts of popular culture.

> I read a really disturbing news story this morning. I've been thinking about it all day. In California a little girl was killed when she was struck by a car driven by a man distracted by a billboard ad for lingerie featuring a scantily clothed woman. Not only is it a horrifying thing to happen, but it also seems to me all too symbolic of the way that sexually charged images in the media are putting children, and especially girls, in danger. That reminds me of another news story I read this week about preteen girls wanting to wear the kinds of revealing outfits that they see in music videos, TV shows, and magazines aimed at teenagers. Too many of today's media images give young people the impression that sexuality should begin at an early age. This is definitely a dangerous message.

Listing

Freely list ideas as they come to mind, beginning with a key concept related to the assignment. (Brainstorming—listing ideas in conjunction with members of a group—is often an effective way to extend your lists.) The following is an example of a student's list of ideas for possible topics on the subject of news reporting:

> **Aspect of popular culture: News reporting**
>
> Sensationalism
> Sound bites rather than in-depth analysis
> Focus on the negative
> Shock radio
> Shouting matches pretending to be debates
> Press leaks that damage national security, etc.
> Lack of observation of people's privacy
> Bias
> Contradictory health news confusing to readers
> Little focus on "unappealing" issues like poverty
> Celebration of "celebrity"

Clustering

To begin the clustering process, write a key word or phrase related to the assignment in the center of your paper. Circle it, and then cluster ideas around it. Circle each idea as you record it, and draw a line connecting it to the closest related idea. Keep going until you run out of ideas and connections. Figure 2.4 is a student's cluster on the subject of sports:

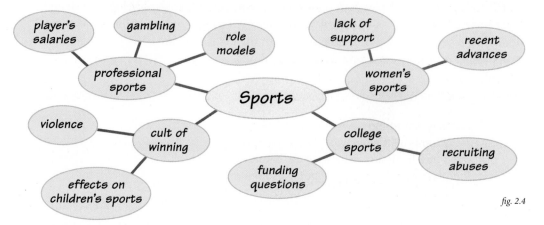

fig. 2.4

> **fyi** After four or five minutes of listing or clustering, scan your work for an idea to explore in a freewriting. A writing idea should begin to emerge during this freewriting session. (See page 37.)

Freewrite to discover and develop a topic.

Freewriting is the writing you do without having a specific outcome in mind. You simply write down whatever pops into your head as you explore your topic. Freewriting can serve as a starting point for your writing, or it can be combined with any of the other prewriting strategies to help you select, explore, focus, or organize your writing. If you get stuck at any point during the composing process, you can return to freewriting as a way of generating new ideas.

Reminders

- **Freewriting helps you get your thoughts down on paper.**
  (Thoughts are constantly passing through your mind.)
- **Freewriting helps you develop and organize these thoughts.**
- **Freewriting helps you make sense out of things that you may be studying or researching.**
- **Freewriting may seem awkward at times, but just stick with it.**

The Process

- **Write nonstop and record whatever comes into your mind.** Follow your thoughts instead of trying to direct them.
- **If you have a particular topic or assignment to complete, use it as a starting point.** Otherwise, begin with anything that comes to mind.
- **Don't stop to judge, edit, or correct your writing;** that will come later.
- **Keep writing even when you think you have exhausted all of your ideas.** Switch to another angle or voice, but keep writing.
- **Watch for a promising writing idea to emerge.** Learn to recognize the beginnings of a good idea, and then expand that idea by recording as many specific details as possible.

The Result

- **Review your writing and underline the ideas you like.** These ideas will often serve as the basis for future writings.
- **Determine exactly what you need to write about.** Once you've figured out what you are required to do, you may then decide to do a second freewriting exercise.
- **Listen to and read the freewriting of others;** learn from your peers.

Freewriting

Write nonstop for ten minutes or longer to discover possible writing ideas. Use a key concept related to the assignment as a starting point. You'll soon discover potential writing ideas that might otherwise have never entered your mind. Note in the following example that the writer doesn't stop writing even when he can't think of anything to say. Note also that he doesn't stop to correct typos and other mistakes.

Popular culture. What does that include? Television obviously but that's a pretty boring subject. What else? Movies, pop music, video games. Is there a connection between playing violent video games and acting out violent behavior? Most video players I know would say no but sometimes news reports suggest a connection. Is this something I'd want to write about? Not really. What then? Maybe I could think about this a different way and focus on the positive effects of playing video games. They release tension for one thing and they can really be challenging. Other benefits? They help to kill time, that's for sure, but maybe that's not such a good thing. I would definitely read more if it weren't for video games, TV, etc. Maybe I could write about how all the electronic entertainment that surrounds us today is creating a generation of nonreaders. Or maybe I could focus on whether people aren't getting much physical exercise because of the time they spend with electronic media. Maybe both. At least I have some possibilities to work with.

Collecting Information

Writer and instructor Donald Murray said that "writers write with information. If there is no information, there will be no effective writing." How true! Before you can develop a thoughtful piece of writing, you must gain a thorough understanding of your topic; to do so, you must carry out the necessary reading, reflecting, and researching. Writing becomes a satisfying experience once you can speak with authority about your topic. Use the following guidelines when you start collecting information. (Also see "Research and Writing" in this book.)

- Determine what you already know about your topic. (Use the strategies below this bulleted list.)
- Consider listing questions you would like to answer during your research. (See page 39.)
- Identify and explore possible sources of information. (See page 40.)
- Carry out your research following a logical plan. (See pages 48–53.)

Find out what you already know.

Use one or more of the following strategies to determine what you already know about a writing topic.

1. **Focused freewriting:** At this point, you can focus your freewriting by (1) exploring your limited topic from different angles or (2) approaching your freewriting as if it were a quick draft of the actual paper. A quick version will tell you how much you know about your topic and what you need to find out.

2. **Clustering:** Try clustering with your topic serving as the nucleus word. Your clustering should focus on what you already know. (See page 36.)

3. **Five W's of writing:** Answer the five W's—Who? What? When? Where? and Why?—to identify basic information on your subject. Add How? to the list for better coverage.

4. **Directed writing:** Write whatever comes to mind about your topic, using one of the modes listed below. (Repeat the process as often as you need to, selecting a different mode each time.)

> **Describe it:** What do you see, hear, feel, smell, and taste?
> **Compare it:** What is it similar to? What is it different from?
> **Associate it:** What connections between this topic and others come to mind?
> **Analyze it:** What parts does it have? How do they work together?
> **Argue it:** What do you like about the topic? What do you not like about it? What are its strengths and weaknesses?
> **Apply it:** What can you do with it? How can you use it?

Ask questions.

To guide your collecting and researching, you may find it helpful to list questions about your topic that you would like to answer. Alternatively, you can use the questions below to guide your research.

	Description	Function	History	Value
PROBLEMS	• What is the problem? • What type of problem is it? • What are its parts? • What are the signs of the problem?	• Who or what is affected by it? • What new problems might it cause in the future?	• What is the current status of the problem? • What or who caused it? • What or who contributed to it?	• What is its significance? Why? • Why is it more (or less) important than other problems? • What does it symbolize or illustrate?
POLICIES	• What is the policy? • How broad is it? • What are its parts? • What are its most important features?	• What is the policy designed to do? • What is needed to make it work? • What are or will be its effects?	• What brought about this policy? • What are the alternatives?	• Is the policy workable? • What are its advantages and disadvantages? • Is it practical? • Is it a good policy? Why or why not?
CONCEPTS	• What is the concept? • What are its parts? • What is its main feature? • Whom or what is it related to?	• Who has been influenced by this concept? • Why is it important? • How does it work?	• When did it originate? • How has it changed over the years? • How might it change in the future?	• What practical value does it have? • Why is it superior (or inferior) to similar concepts? • What is its social worth?

Andrzej Tokarski / Shutterstock.com

Identify possible sources.

Finding meaningful sources is one of the most important steps you will take as you prepare to write. (That's why Part 3 of this text is dedicated to research instruction. See especially chapters 24–26.) Listed below are tips that will help you identify good sources:

1. **Give yourself enough time.** Finding good sources of information may be time-consuming. Books and periodicals you need may be checked out, your computer service may be down, and so on.

2. **Be aware of the limits of your resources.** Print material may be out-of-date. Online information may be more current, but it may not always be reliable. (See pages 412–415 for ways to help you evaluate information.)

3. **Use your existing resources to find additional sources of information.** Pay attention to books, articles, and individuals mentioned in reliable initial sources of information.

4. **Ask for help.** The specialists in your school library can help you find information that is reliable and relevant. These people are trained to find information; don't hesitate to ask for their help.

5. **Bookmark useful Web sites.** Include reference works and academic resources related to your major.

Explore different sources of information.

Of course, books and Web sites are not the only possible sources of information. Primary sources such as interviews, observations, and surveys may lead you to a more thorough and meaningful understanding of a topic. (See pages 427–458.)

Primary Sources	**Secondary Sources**
Interviews	Articles
Observations	Reference book entries
Participation	Books
Surveys	Web sites

Carry out your research.

As you conduct your research, try to use a variety of reliable sources. It's also a good idea to choose an efficient note-taking method before you start. You will want to take good notes on the information you find and record all the publishing details necessary for citing your sources. (See pages 418–421.)

Reserve a special part of a notebook or file on your computer to question, evaluate, and reflect on your research as it develops. Reflection helps you make sense of new ideas, refocus your thinking, and evaluate your progress.

Track sources.

Follow these strategies for tracking sources and taking notes.

- **Track resources in a working bibliography.** Once you find a useful book, journal article, news story, or Web page, record identifying information for the source. For more help, see pages 416–417.

- **Use a note-taking system that respects sources.** Essentially, your note-taking system should help you keep an accurate record of useful information and ideas from sources while also allowing you to engage those sources with your own thinking. For a discussion of possible systems, see pages 418–421.

- **Distinguish summaries, paraphrases, and quotations.** As you read sources, you will find material that answers your questions and helps you achieve your writing purpose. At that point, decide whether to summarize, paraphrase, or quote the material:
    - **A summary** pulls just the main points out of a passage and puts them in your own words: Summarize source material when it contains relevant ideas and information that you can boil down.
    - **A paraphrase** rewrites a passage point by point in your own words: Paraphrase source material when all the information is important but the actual phrasing isn't especially important or memorable.
    - **A quotation** records a passage from the source word for word: Quote when the source states something crucial and says it well. Note: In your notes, always identify quoted material by putting quotation marks around it.

Summarizing, paraphrasing, and quoting are treated more fully on pages 422–424. Here is a brief example, with the original passage coming from Coral Ann Howells' *Alice Munro*, published in 1998 by Manchester University Press as part of its Contemporary World Writers series.

> **Original:** "To read Munro's stories is to discover the delights of seeing two worlds at once: an ordinary everyday world and the shadowy map of another imaginary or secret world laid over the real one, so that in reading we slip from one world into the other in an unassuming domestic sort of way."
>
> **Summary:** Munro's fiction moves readers from recognizable reality into a hidden world.
>
> **Paraphrase:** Reading Munro's fiction gives readers the enjoyment of experiencing a double world: day-to-day reality and on top of that a more mysterious, fantastic world, with the result that readers move smoothly between the worlds in a seamless, ordinary way.
>
> **Quotation:** Munro's fiction takes us into "the shadowy map of another imaginary or secret world laid over the real one."

Critical-Thinking and Writing Activities

As directed by your instructor, complete the following critical-thinking and writing activities by yourself or with classmates.

1. Writer Ralph Fletcher shares, "When I write, I am always struck at how magical and unexpected the process turns out to be." Would you describe the writing process you follow as "magical" and "unexpected"? Why or why not?

2. Reread one of your recent essays. Does the writing show that you thoroughly understood your subject, met the needs of your readers, and achieved your purpose? How does it measure against the traits of strong writing? What traits in your writing are strong? Which need work? Where can you find help on these traits in this book?

3. Below is a list of general subject areas. Select one that interests you and do the following: Using the strategies on pages 34–37, brainstorm possible topics and select one. Then use the strategies on pages 38–40 to explore what you know about that topic and what you need to learn.

   Arts/music   Environment   Health/medicine   Work/occupation

Learning-Objectives Checklist ✓

Have you achieved this chapter's learning objectives? Check your progress with the items below, revisiting topics in the chapter as needed. *I have . . .*

____ outlined the writing process, from getting started to submitting (26).

____ adapted the writing process to a specific writing project, taking into account the assignment challenges and my own writing habits (27).

____ analyzed the rhetorical situation for a specific writing project (including my role as writer, the subject, my purpose, the audience, the form, and the context) so as to make good decisions about my approach, tone, and content (28–29).

____ differentiated seven traits of strong, college-level writing and assessed my relative strengths and weaknesses with respect to these traits (30–31).

____ carefully identified a writing assignment's key words, options, and restrictions, and have related the assignment to course goals, other assignments, and my own interests (32–33).

____ developed and chosen a strong topic for a writing project by limiting the subject, conducting an exploratory search, and using techniques such as journal writing, listing, clustering, and freewriting (34–37).

____ identified what I already know about the topic, generated questions to research, formulated a list of possible resources, and worked with those sources, while carefully tracking my use of these sources (38–41).

Chapter 3

Planning

Some of us are meticulous planners. We organize our lives in advance and formulate strategies for completing every task. Others of us live more in the moment, believing that whatever needs to get done will get done, with or without a plan.

In writing, author and instructor Ken Macrorie calls for a blend of these two approaches: "Good writing," says Macrorie, "is formed partly through plan and partly through accident." In other words, too much early planning can get in the way of the discovery aspect of writing, while not enough planning can harm the focus and coherence of your writing.

Visually Speaking   Consider Figure 3.1. In a paragraph or two, explain how planning might play a role in military life. What might be some of its benefits and drawbacks? Does such planning parallel planning to write in any way?

Learning **Objectives**

By working through this chapter, you will be able to

- re-examine the rhetorical situation with an eye to planning your writing.
- generate a focused, thoughtful working thesis.
- determine the pattern of development suggested by your thesis.
- produce a plan or outline for your writing.

U.S. Air Force photo/Master Sgt. Jack Braden

fig. 3.1

Revisit the Rhetorical Situation

Use the following planning checklist to help you decide whether to move ahead with your planning or reconsider your topic.

Rhetorical Checklist

Writer

_____ Am I interested in this topic?

_____ How much do I know about this topic, and how much do I need to learn?

Subject

_____ Does the topic fit with the subject requirements of the assignment?

_____ Is the topic the right size—not too general or too specific—for the assignment?

_____ What sources can I use to find out more about this topic?

Purpose

_____ What are the specific goals of the assignment?

_____ Am I writing to entertain, inform, explain, analyze, persuade, reflect?

Form

_____ What form should I create: essay, proposal, report, review?

Audience

_____ Will my readers be interested in this topic? How can I interest them?

_____ What do they know and need to know about it? What opinions do they have?

Context

_____ What weight does this assignment have in terms of my grade?

_____ How will the assignment be assessed?

Working with Sources ▎ For projects that involve research, consider how the rhetorical situation can guide your use of sources:

1. **For your subject**, which sources offer reliable information and analysis that has shaped your thinking and pointed toward a working thesis?

2. **To achieve your purpose** (to entertain, inform, analyze, and/or persuade), which resources/sources should be featured in your writing?

3. **Given your audience**, which resources will help you create credibility with the audience and clarify the topic for them?

Forming Your Thesis Statement

After you have completed enough research and collecting, you may begin to develop a more focused interest in your topic. If all goes well, this narrowed focus will give rise to a thesis for your writing. A thesis statement identifies your central idea. It usually highlights a special condition or feature of the topic, expresses a specific claim about it, or takes a stand.

State your thesis in a sentence that effectively expresses what you want to explore or explain in your essay. Sometimes a thesis statement develops early and easily; at other times, the true focus of your writing emerges only after you've written your first draft.

Find a focus.

A general subject area is typically built into your writing assignments. Your task, then, is to find a limited writing topic and examine it from a particular angle or perspective. (You will use this focus to form your thesis statement.) Figure 3.2 shows this process.

General Subject	Limited Topic	Specific Focus
Alternative energy sources	Wind power	Wind power as a viable energy source in the Plains states

fig. 3.2

State your thesis.

You can use the formula in Figure 3.3 to write a thesis statement for your essay. A thesis statement sets the tone and direction for your writing. Keep in mind that at this point you're writing a *working thesis statement*—a statement in progress, so to speak. You may change it as your thinking on the topic evolves.

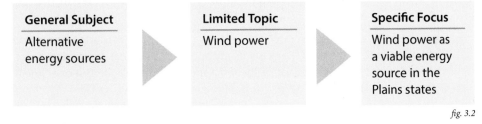

a manageable or limited topic	+	a specific claim or focus	=	an effective thesis statement
wind power		provides a viable energy source in the plains states		Wind power provides a viable energy source in the plains states.

fig. 3.3

Working with Sources | Sometimes your writing can take direction specifically from your sources. You may consider making your thesis a response to a specific source. For example, if one source is especially strong or especially contrary to your own thinking, you could shape your thesis as an affirmation of the strong source's authority or as a rebuttal to the contrary source's claims.

Using a Thesis to Pattern Your Writing

An organizing pattern for your essay may be built into your assignment. For example, you may be asked to develop an argument or to write a process paper. When a pattern is not apparent, one may still evolve naturally during the research and information-collecting steps. If this doesn't happen, take a careful look at your thesis statement.

Let your thesis guide you.

An effective thesis will often suggest an organizing pattern. Notice how the thesis statements below direct and shape the writing to follow. (Also see page 19.)

Thesis (Focus) for a Personal Narrative

Writers of personal narratives do not always state a thesis directly, but they will generally have in mind an implied theme or main idea that governs the way they develop their writing. The thesis below focuses the reader's attention on a less-than-perfect day in the life of a "perfect" flight attendant. (See essay on pages 151–152.)

> From the first day Northwest hired me in Minneapolis in 1969, I tried to be a model flight attendant, to develop the qualities my operations manual demanded: poise, good judgment, initiative, adaptability and a spotless appearance. But one time I slipped up: I fell asleep.

Thesis for a Cause-and-Effect Essay

A cause-and-effect essay usually begins with one or more causes followed by an explanation of the effects, or with a primary effect followed by an explanation of the causes. In the thesis below, the writer credits team sports with helping to advance women into leadership roles in major corporations. (See essay on pages 171–173.)

> While most of America's corporations are still commanded by male chief executives, women are gaining ground, winning vice-presidential and top management slots and, in a few cases, the highest leadership roles. Many of these young female executives say playing team sports helped them get ahead.

Thesis for an Essay of Comparison

Some comparisons treat one subject before the other (subject by subject), others discuss the subjects point by point, and some treat similarities and then differences. The writer of the thesis below introduces her comparison and contrast of two different views of Islamic dress—both of which she holds. (See essay on pages 187–189.)

> To wear *hijab*—Islamic covering—is to invite contradiction. Sometimes I hate it. Sometimes I value it.

Thesis for an Essay of Classification

An essay of classification identifies the main parts or categories of a topic and then examines each one. In the thesis below, the writer identifies four ways to discuss literature, and he examines each one in turn. (See essay on pages 257–258.)

> There are four main perspectives, or approaches, that readers can use to converse about literature.

Thesis for a Process Essay

Process essays are organized chronologically. As indicated in the thesis below, the writer of this essay will explain how cancer cells multiply and affect the body. (See essay on pages 220–221.)

> When a cell begins to function abnormally, it can initiate a process that results in cancer.

Thesis for a Position Essay

A position paper first introduces a topic and then states a position in its thesis. The thesis statement below defines the writer's position on fatherlessness. (See essay on pages 320–325.)

> Fatherlessness is the most harmful demographic trend of this generation. Yet, despite its scale and social consequences, fatherlessness is a problem that is frequently ignored or denied.

Thesis for an Essay of Definition

An essay of definition explores the denotation, connotation, and history of a term. In the following thesis statement, the writer names the two words he will explore—*deft* and *daft*—and provides an overview of the definition essay. (See essay on page 240.)

> Let me see if I can explain the original meaning and also how *daft* and *deft* came to part company.

Thesis for an Essay Proposing a Solution

A problem-solution essay usually begins with a discussion of the problem and its causes and then examines possible solutions. In the following thesis statement, the writer points to a problem in the supposedly gender-equal society of the United States. After explaining the problem, she offers and argues for a specific solution. (See essay on pages 351–353.)

> While women are represented today in virtually all fields, including the armed forces, only men are required to register for the military draft that would be used in the event of a national-security crisis.

Developing a Plan or an Outline

After writing a working thesis and reviewing the methods of development (pages 45–47), you should be ready to organize the information you have collected. Remember, organizing your research and background information *before* you start writing can make the drafting stage less of a hassle. Here are five strategies for effective organizing, starting with the basic list.

- **Quick List:** A brief listing of main points (See below.)
- **Topic Outline:** A more formal plan, including main points and essential details (See page 49.)
- **Sentence Outline:** A formal plan, including main points and essential details, written as complete sentences (See page 50.)
- **Writing Blueprints:** Basic organizational strategies preferred for different forms of writing (See page 51.)
- **Graphic Organizer:** An arrangement of main points and essential details in an appropriate chart or diagram (See pages 52–53.)

Quick Lists

Though listing is the simplest of all the methods of organization, it can help you take stock of your main ideas and get a sense of what further research or planning needs to be done. There is no right or wrong way to go about listing. The key is to come up with a system that works best for you. Here are two examples that you may consider: **the basic bulleted list,** which briefly lists the main points you will discuss, and a **T Chart,** which lists the main points on one side and a supporting detail on the other side.

Sample Basic List

Topic: Different ways to discuss literature ——————— Topic

- Focus on the text itself
- Focus on the text and the reader
- Focus on the author of the text
- Focus on ideas outside of literature

——— Main Points

Sample T Chart

Topic: Different ways to discuss literature ——————— Topic

Approach	Emphasis
Text-centered approach	Emphasizes structure and rules
Audience-centered approach	Relationship between reader and text
Author-centered approach	Emphasizes the writer's life

fig. 3.4

Topic Outline

If you have a good deal of information to sort and arrange, you may want to use a **topic outline** for your planning. In a topic outline, you state each main point and essential detail as a word or phrase. Before you start constructing your outline, write your working thesis statement at the top of your paper to help keep you focused on the subject. (Do not attempt to outline your opening and closing paragraphs unless you are specifically asked to do so.)

An effective topic outline is parallel in structure, meaning the main points (I, II, III) and essential details (A, B, C) are stated in the same way. Notice how the sample outline below uses a parallel structure, making it easy to follow.

Sample Topic Outline

Thesis: There are four main perspectives, or approaches, ——————— Topic
that readers can use to converse about literature.

    I. Text-centered approaches ——————————————— Main Points
       a. Also called formalist criticism
       b. Emphasis on structure of text and rules of genre ——— Supporting
       c. Importance placed on key literary elements   Details

   II. Audience-centered approaches
       a. Also called rhetorical or reader-response criticism
       b. Emphasis on interaction between reader and text

  III. Author-centered approaches
       a. Emphasis on writer's life
       b. Importance placed on historical perspective
       c. Connections made between texts

  IV. Ideological approaches
       a. Psychological analysis of text
       b. Myth or archetype criticism
       c. Moral criticism
       d. Sociological analysis

fig. 3.5

Maxx-Studio / Shutterstock.com

INSIGHT Planning is adaptable. Some writers prefer to generate an outline before they begin writing, while others prefer to make a more detailed outline after having written a draft. In the latter strategy, an outline can serve as a tool for evaluating the logic and completeness of the paper's organization.

Sentence Outline

A **sentence outline** uses complete sentences to explain the main points and essential details in the order that they will be covered in the main part of your essay. Such an outline can help you develop your ideas when writing the paper.

Sample Sentence Outline

Thesis: There are four main perspectives, or approaches, that readers —— Thesis
can use to converse about literature.

I. A text-centered approach focuses on the literary piece itself. —— Main Points
   a. This approach is often called formalist criticism.
   b. This method of criticism examines text structure and the
      rules of the genre. —— Supporting
   c. A formalist critic determines how key literary elements   Details
      reinforce meaning.

II. An audience-centered approach focuses on the "transaction" between text
    and reader.
   a. This approach is often called rhetorical or reader-response criticism.
   b. A rhetorical critic sees the text as an activity that is different for each reader.

III. An author-centered approach focuses on the origin of a text.
   a. An author-centered critic examines the writer's life.
   b. This method of criticism may include a historical look at a text.
   c. Connections may be made between the text and related works.

IV. The ideological approach applies ideas outside of literature.
   a. Some critics apply psychological theories to a literary work.
   b. Myth or archetype criticism applies anthropology and classical studies
      to a text.
   c. Moral criticism explores the moral dilemmas in literature.
   d. Sociological approaches include Marxist, feminist, and minority criticism.

fig. 3.6

Working with Sources | When your writing project involves sources, the planning phase will include a great deal of sorting through material. Outlining can help you organize your primary and secondary sources to best support your thesis. As you organize your research in your outline, ask these questions:

- Where and how should I work with primary sources—interviews, surveys, analyses, observations, experiments, and other data I have collected?
- Where and how should I bring in secondary sources—scholarly books, journal articles, and the like?

Writing Blueprints

The writing blueprints in Figures 3.7–3.10 lay out basic organizational strategies for different forms of writing. The blueprints may help you arrange the details of your essay or even find holes in your research.

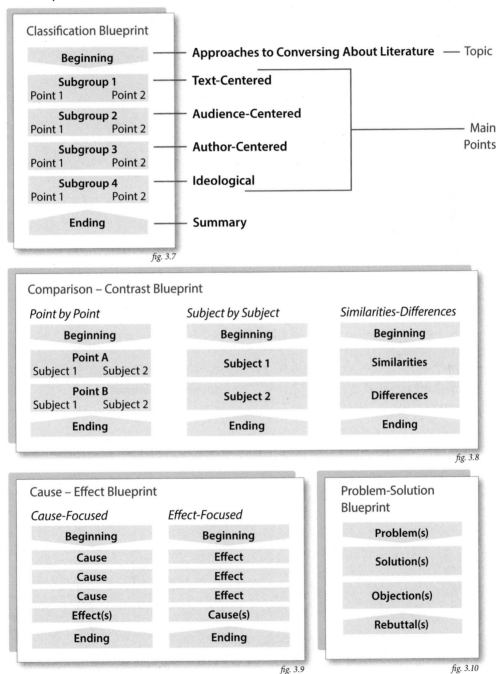

fig. 3.7

fig. 3.8

fig. 3.9

fig. 3.10

Graphic Organizers

If you are a visual person, you might prefer a graphic organizer when it comes to arranging your ideas for an essay or a report. Graphic organizers can help you map out ideas and illustrate relationships among them. The organizers in Figures 3.11–3.17 are related to the methods of development discussed on pages 46–47. Each will help you collect and organize your information. Adapt the organizers as necessary to fit your particular needs or personal style.

▼ Note how the line diagram breaks out the topic, main ideas, and supporting details for use in building an essay of classification.

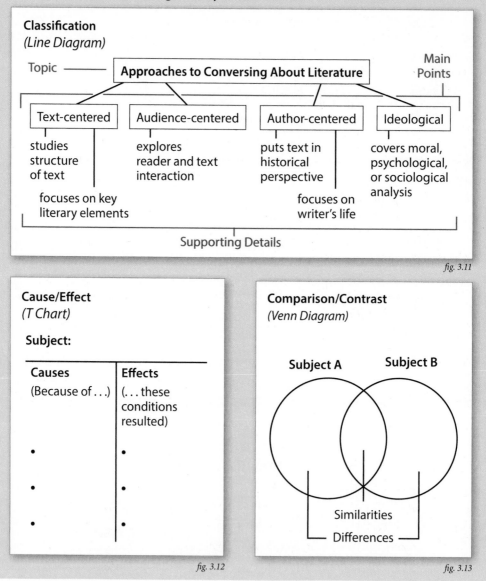

Classification
(Line Diagram)

Topic ——— **Approaches to Conversing About Literature**   Main Points

| Text-centered | Audience-centered | Author-centered | Ideological |

studies structure of text

explores reader and text interaction

puts text in historical perspective

covers moral, psychological, or sociological analysis

focuses on key literary elements

focuses on writer's life

Supporting Details

fig. 3.11

Cause/Effect
(T Chart)

Subject:

Causes	Effects
(Because of . . .)	(. . . these conditions resulted)
•	•
•	•
•	•

fig. 3.12

Comparison/Contrast
(Venn Diagram)

Subject A   Subject B

Similarities

Differences

fig. 3.13

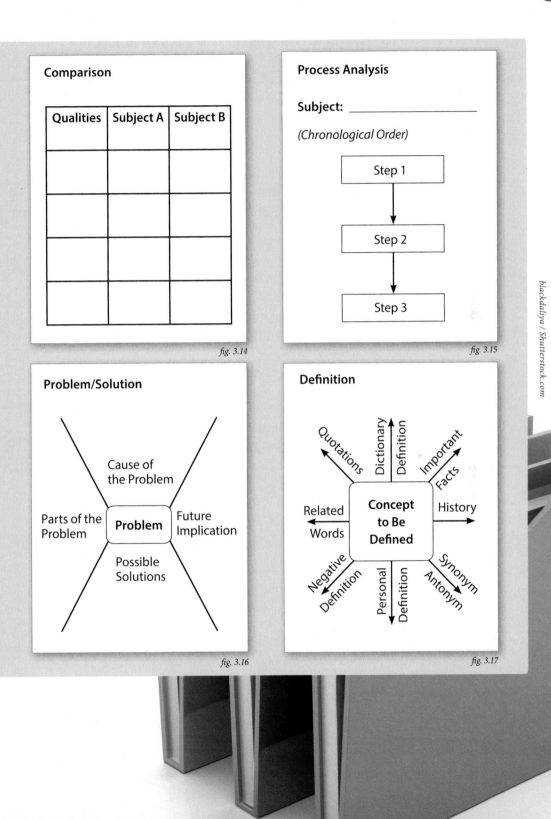

Comparison

Qualities	Subject A	Subject B

fig. 3.14

Process Analysis

Subject: _____

(Chronological Order)

Step 1

↓

Step 2

↓

Step 3

fig. 3.15

Problem/Solution

Cause of the Problem

Parts of the Problem

Problem

Future Implication

Possible Solutions

fig. 3.16

Definition

Quotations

Dictionary Definition

Important Facts

Related Words

Concept to Be Defined

History

Negative Definition

Personal Definition

Synonym Antonym

fig. 3.17

Critical-Thinking and Writing Activities

As directed by your instructor, complete the following activities.

1. Author Ken Macrorie claims that "good writing is formed partly through plan and partly through accident." Do you agree? Why or why not? Relate Macrorie's idea to your own writing experiences. How carefully do you plan? How much do you leave to accident?

2. A number of organizational patterns are discussed on pages 46–47. Choose one of these patterns and select a model essay from chapters 11–20 that follows the pattern. Read the essay, note the thesis, and explain how the writer develops it.

Learning-Objectives Checklist ✓

Have you achieved this chapter's learning objectives? Check your progress with the items below, revisiting topics in the chapter as needed. *I have . . .*

____ re-examined the rhetorical situation of my writing project (my role as writer, the subject, my purpose, the form, my readers, and the context) so that I can confidently move forward with planning my writing (44).

____ formulated a focused, insightful working thesis for my writing (45).

____ analyzed my working thesis so as to determine what pattern of organization it suggests (46–47).

____ generated a plan for my writing, whether a quick list, a topic outline, a formal sentence outline, a blueprint, or a graphic organizer (48–53).

Cross-Curricular Connections

In most disciplines, it is common practice early in the paper to "survey the literature" on the topic. In a literary analysis, you might survey common interpretations of a key issue in the literary work before you relay your view. In the social or natural sciences, you might write a report called a literature review—a report that surveys, summarizes, and synthesizes the studies on a specific topic. (See, for example, Amanda Khoe's "Teaching K-12 English Language Learners in the Mainstream Classroom" on pages 554–563.) To plan a literature review, follow these steps:

1. Identify the studies that should be included in the review.
2. Categorize studies by approach or arrange them chronologically.
3. Summarize and synthesize the studies.

Chapter 4

Drafting

French novelist Anatole France once said that one of his first drafts could have been written by a schoolboy, his next draft by a bright college student, his third draft by a superior graduate, and his final draft "only by Anatole France." Think in those terms as you write your first draft. Your main objective is to get ideas down; you'll have a chance later to improve your writing.

This chapter provides information and advice about drafting a college-level essay. You'll find specific advice for creating the three main parts and arranging information.

Visually Speaking   How is drafting like sketching? Note the blurred hand with the pencil in Figure 4.1. What does it suggest about the process of drafting? Then again, are there important differences between sketching and drafting?

Learning **Objectives**

By working through this chapter, you will be able to

- re-examine the rhetorical situation as preparation for drafting.
- describe and explain the parts or "major moves" of essays.
- compose an effective opening for your writing.
- generate a substantial middle to follow the opening.
- produce a closing that effectively ends your draft.
- effectively integrate source material into your draft.

Jupiterimages

fig. 4.1

Reconsider the Rhetorical Situation

As you prepare to write, think about the parts of the rhetorical situation:

Think about your role.

Are you writing as a student, a citizen, a friend, a member of a scholarly community or discipline? Use a voice that represents you well.

Focus on your subject.

As you develop your first draft, these strategies can help you keep your subject in focus.

- **Use your outline or writing plan** as a general guide. Try to develop your main points, but allow new ideas to emerge naturally.
- **Write freely** without being too concerned about neatness and correctness. Concentrate on developing your ideas, not on producing a final copy.
- **Include as much detail as possible**, continuing until you reach a logical stopping point.
- **Use your writing plan** or any charts, lists, or diagrams you've produced, but don't feel absolutely bound by them.
- **Complete your first draft** in one or two sittings.
- **Use the most natural voice you can** so that the writing will flow smoothly. If your voice is too formal during drafting, you'll be tempted to stop and edit your words.
- **Quote sources accurately** by using your word-processing program's copy-and-paste features or by handwriting or typing quotations carefully.

Reconsider your purpose.

Briefly review (1) what you want your writing to do (your task), (2) what you want it to say (your thesis), and (3) how you want to say it (list of ideas or outline).

Reconsider your audience.

Review who your readers are, including their knowledge of and attitude toward your topic. Then get ready to talk with them, person to person.

Review the form and context.

Make sure you understand the type of writing you should do, the weight of the assignment, and any assessment issues.

Working with Sources Use sources that aid your purpose and connect to your audience. Also, make sure your sources do not crowd out your own reasoning and thinking—your role in the assignment.

Basic Essay Structure: Major Moves

The chart in Figure 4.2 lists the main writing moves that occur during the development of a piece of writing. Use it as a general guide that you adapt as needed for all of your drafting. Remember to keep your purpose and audience in mind throughout the drafting process.

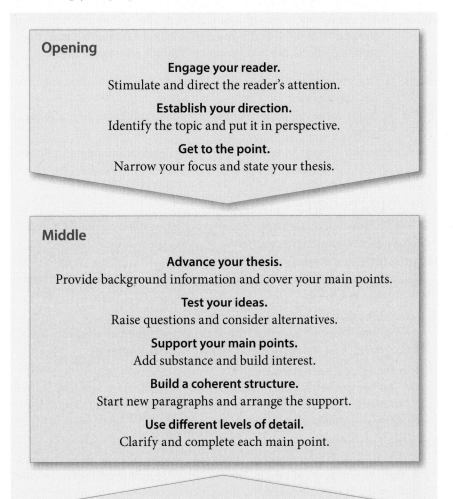

Opening

Engage your reader.
Stimulate and direct the reader's attention.

Establish your direction.
Identify the topic and put it in perspective.

Get to the point.
Narrow your focus and state your thesis.

Middle

Advance your thesis.
Provide background information and cover your main points.

Test your ideas.
Raise questions and consider alternatives.

Support your main points.
Add substance and build interest.

Build a coherent structure.
Start new paragraphs and arrange the support.

Use different levels of detail.
Clarify and complete each main point.

Ending

Reassert the main point.
Remind the reader of the purpose and rephrase the thesis.

Urge the reader.
Gain the reader's acceptance and look ahead.

fig. 4.2

Opening Your Draft

The opening paragraph is one of the most important elements in any composition. It should accomplish at least three essential things: (1) engage the reader; (2) establish your direction, tone, and level of language; and (3) introduce your line of thought.

Advice: • The conventional way of approaching the first paragraph is to view it as a kind of "funnel" that draws a reader in and narrows to a main point. In some situations, the final sentence explicitly states your thesis.

Cautions: • Don't feel bound by the conventional pattern, which may sound stale if not handled well.
• Don't let the importance of the first paragraph paralyze you. Relax and write.

The information on the next two pages will help you develop your opening. For additional ideas, you can refer to the sample essays in part 2 of this text, the Reader. (See page 129.)

Engage your reader.

Your reader will be preoccupied with other thoughts until you seize, stimulate, and direct his or her attention. Here are some effective ways to "hook" the reader:

- **Mention little-known facts about the topic.**

  Beads may have been what separated human ancestors from their Neanderthal cousins. Yes, beads.

- **Pose a challenging question.**

  Why would human ancestors spend days carving something as frivolous as beads while Neanderthals spent days hunting mammoths?

- **Offer a thought-provoking quotation.**

  "The key thing in human evolution is when people start devoting just ridiculous amounts of time to making these [beads]," says archeologist John Shea of Stonybrook University.

- **Tell a brief, illuminating story.**

  When I walked into the room, I had only to show my hand to be accepted in the group of strangers there. The Phi Delta Kappa ring on my finger—and on all of our fingers—bound us across space and time as a group. Our ancestors discovered the power of such ornamentation forty thousand years ago.

Establish your direction.

The direction of your line of thought should become clear in the opening part of your writing. Here are some moves you might make to set the right course:

- **Identify the topic (issue).** Show a problem, a need, or an opportunity.
- **Deepen the issue.** Connect the topic, showing its importance.
- **Acknowledge other views.** Tell what others say or think about the topic.

Get to the point.

You may choose to state your main point up front, or you may wait until later to introduce your thesis. For example, you could work inductively by establishing an issue, a problem, or a question in your opening and then build toward the answer—your thesis—in your conclusion. (See page 18 for more on inductive reasoning.) Sometimes, in fact, your thesis may simply be implied. In any case, the opening should at least hint at the central issue or thesis of your paper. Here are three ways to get to the point:

1. **Narrow your focus.** Point to what interests you about the topic.
2. **Raise a question.** Answer the question in the rest of the essay.
3. **State your thesis.** If appropriate, craft a sentence that boils down your thinking to a central claim. You can use the thesis sentence as a "map" for the organization of the rest of the essay. (See pages 45–47, 112–115, and 400–401.)

Weak Opening

Although the opening below introduces the topic, the writing lacks interesting details and establishes no clear focus for the essay.

> I would like to tell you about the TV show *The Simpsons*. It's about this weird family of five people who look kind of strange and act even stranger. In fact, the characters aren't even real—they're just cartoons.

Strong Opening

In the essay opener below, the writer uses his first paragraph to get his readers' attention and describe his subject. He uses the second paragraph to raise a question that leads him to a statement of his thesis (underlined).

> *The Simpsons,* stars of the TV show by the same name, are a typical American family, or at least a parody of one. Homer, Marge, Bart, Lisa, and Maggie Simpson live in Springfield, U.S.A. Homer, the father, is a boorish, obese oaf who works in a nuclear power plant. Marge is an overprotective, nagging mother with an outrageous blue hairdo. Ten-year-old Bart is an obnoxious, "spiky-haired demon." Lisa is eight and a prodigy on the tenor saxophone and in class. The infant Maggie never speaks but only sucks on her pacifier.
>
> What is the attraction of this yellow-skinned family that stars on a show in which all of the characters have pronounced overbites and only four fingers on each hand? Viewers see a little bit of themselves in everything the Simpsons do. <u>The world of Springfield is a parody of the viewer's world, and Americans can't get enough of it.</u> Viewers experience this parody in the show's explanations of family, education, workplace, and politics.

INSIGHT   After stating the thesis, the writer forecasts the method of supporting that thesis.

Developing the Middle

The middle of an essay is where you do the "heavy lifting." In this part you develop the main points that support your thesis statement.

Advice: • As you write, you will likely make choices that were unforeseen when you began. Use "scratch outlines" (temporary jottings) along the way to show where your new ideas may take you.

Cautions: • Writing that lacks effective detail gives only a vague image of the writer's intent.
• Writing that wanders loses its hold on the essay's purpose.

For both of these reasons, always keep your thesis in mind when you develop the main part of your writing. Refer to the guidelines on the next two pages for help. You can refer to the sample essays in this book for ideas.

Advance your thesis.

If you stated a thesis in the opening, you can advance it in the middle paragraphs by covering your main points and supporting them in these ways.

Explain: Provide important facts, details, and examples.
Narrate: Share a brief story or re-create an experience to illustrate an idea.
Describe: Tell in detail how someone appears or how something works.
Define: Identify or clarify the meaning of a specific term or idea.
Analyze: Examine the parts of something to better understand the whole.
Compare: Provide examples to show how two things are alike or different.
Argue: Use logic and evidence to prove that something is true.
Reflect: Express your thoughts or feelings about something.
Cite authorities: Add expert analysis or personal commentary.

Test your ideas.

When you write a first draft, you're testing your initial thinking about your topic. You're determining whether your thesis is valid and whether you have enough compelling information to support it. Here are ways to test your line of thinking as you write:

• **Raise questions.** Try to anticipate your readers' questions.
• **Consider alternatives.** Look at your ideas from different angles; weigh various options; reevaluate your thesis.
• **Answer objections.** Directly or indirectly deal with possible problems that a skeptical reader might point out.

Build a coherent structure.

Design paragraphs as units of thought that develop and advance your thesis clearly and logically. For example, look at the brief essay below, noting how each body paragraph presents ideas with supporting details that build on and deepen the main idea.

Seeing the Light

The writer introduces the topic and states his thesis.

All lightbulbs make light, so they're all the same, right? Not quite. You have many choices regarding how to light up your life. Two types of bulbs are the traditional incandescent and the newer, more compact fluorescent. By checking out how they're different, you can better choose which one to buy. *1*

The writer starts with a basic explanation of how the two types of lightbulbs function differently.

While either incandescent or compact fluorescent bulbs can help you read or find the bathroom at night, each bulb makes light differently. In an incandescent bulb, electricity heats up a tungsten filament (thin wire) to 450 degrees, causing it to glow with a warm, yellow light. A compact fluorescent is a glass tube filled with mercury vapor and argon gas. Electricity causes the mercury to give off ultraviolet radiation. That radiation then causes phosphors coating the inside of the tube to give off light. *2*

The writer shifts his attention to weaknesses of compact bulbs.

Both types of bulbs come in many shapes, sizes, and brightnesses, but compacts have some restrictions. Because of their odd shape, compacts may not fit in a lamp well. Compacts also may not work well in very cold temperatures, and they can't be used with a dimmer switch.

He next explains the strengths of compacts.

On the other hand, while compact fluorescents are less flexible than incandescents, compacts are four times more efficient. For example, a 15-watt compact produces as many lumens of light as a 60-watt incandescent! Why? Incandescents turn only about 5 percent of electricity into light and give off the other 95 percent as heat. *3*

He acknowledges that compacts cost more, but he justifies the cost.

But are compacts less expensive than incandescents? In the short run, no. Whereas a 60-watt incandescent costs about one dollar, a comparable compact can cost about $5.00. However, because compacts burn less electricity—and last 7 to 10 times longer—in the long run, compacts are less expensive. *4*

The writer rephrases his thesis as a challenge.

Now that you're no longer in the dark about lightbulbs, take a look at the lamp you're using to read this essay. Think about the watts (electricity used), lumens (light produced), efficiency, purchase price, and lamplife. Then decide how to light up your life in the future. *5*

Arrange supporting details.

Organizing information in a logical pattern within a paragraph strengthens its coherence. The following pages explain and illustrate organizational strategies. As you study the paragraphs, pay attention to the transitional words used to create coherence. (For more on paragraph principles, see pages 472–473.)

Definition

A definition provides the denotation (dictionary meaning) and connotation (implied meaning) of a given term. In addition, the definition often includes examples, gives anecdotes, and offers negative definitions—what the thing is not.

> First of all, what is the grotesque—in visual art and in literature? A term originally applied to Roman cave art that distorted the normal, the grotesque presents the body and mind so that they appear abnormal—different from the bodies and minds that we think belong in our world. Both spiritual and physical, bizarre and familiar, ugly and alluring, the grotesque shocks us, and we respond with laughter and fear. We laugh because the grotesque seems bizarre enough to belong only outside our world; we fear because it feels familiar enough to be part of it. Seeing the grotesque version of life as it is portrayed in art stretches our vision of reality. As Bernard McElroy argues, "The grotesque transforms the world from what we 'know' it to be to what we fear it might be. It distorts and exaggerates the surface of reality in order to tell a qualitative truth about it."
>
> —John Van Rys

Illustration

An illustration supports a general idea with specific reasons, facts, and details.

"My Obsession" by Paula Treick DeBoard

> As the years passed, my obsession grew. Every fiber and cell of my body was obsessed with the number on the scale and how much fat I could pinch on my thigh. No matter how thin I was, I thought I could never be thin enough. I fought my sisters for control of the TV and VCR to do my exercise programs and videos. The cupboards were stacked with cans of diet mixes, the refrigerator full of diet drinks. Hidden in my underwear drawer were stacks of diet pills that I popped along with my vitamins. At my worst, I would quietly excuse myself from family activities to turn on the bathroom faucet full blast and vomit into the toilet. Every day I stood in front of the mirror, a ritual not unlike brushing my teeth, and scrutinized my body. My face, arms, stomach, buttocks, hips, and thighs could never be small enough.
>
> —Paula Treick

vipman / Shutterstock.com

Analogy

An analogy is a comparison that a writer uses to explain a complex or unfamiliar phenomenon. For example, in the following paragraph, the writer describes a mall security system in order to explain the human immune system.

> The human body is like a mall, and the immune system is like mall security. Because the mall has hundreds of employees and thousands of customers, security guards must rely on photo IDs, name tags, and uniforms to decide who should be allowed to open cash registers and who should have access to the vault. In the same way, white blood cells and antibodies need to use DNA cues to recognize which cells belong in a body and which do not. Occasionally security guards make mistakes, wrestling Kookie the Klown to the ground while DVD players "walk" out of the service entrance, but these problems amount only to allergic reactions or little infections. If security guards become hypervigilant, detaining every customer and employee, the situation is akin to leukemia, in which white blood cells attack healthy cells. If security guards become corrupt, letting thieves take a "five-finger discount," the situation is akin to AIDS. Both systems—mall security and human immunity—work by correctly differentiating friend from foe.
>
> —Rob King

Cause and Effect

Cause-and-effect organization shows how events are linked to their results. If you start with effects, follow with specific causes; if you begin with causes, follow with specific effects. The example below discusses the effects of hypothermia on the human body.

> Even a slight drop in the normal human body temperature of 98.6 degrees Fahrenheit causes hypothermia. Often produced by accidental or prolonged exposure to cold, the condition forces all bodily functions to slow down. The heart rate and blood pressure decrease. Breathing becomes slower and shallower. As the body temperature drops, these effects become even more dramatic until it reaches somewhere between 86 and 82 degrees Fahrenheit and the person lapses into unconsciousness. When the temperature reaches between 65 and 59 degrees Fahrenheit, heart action, blood flow, and electrical brain activity stop. Normally such a condition would be fatal. However, as the body cools down, the need for oxygen also slows down. A person can survive in a deep hypothermic state for an hour or longer and be revived without serious complications.
>
> —Laura Black

Climax

Climax is a method in which you first present details and then provide a general climactic statement or conclusion drawn from the details.

> As I walked home, I glanced across the road to see a troubling scene unfold. A burly man strode along the curb, shoulders rounded and face clenched in anger or grief. Behind him, a slim little girl sat on her heels on the sidewalk, hands in her lap and tears streaming down white cheeks. I glanced back at that brute, who climbed into his big black truck and started up the engine. I almost ran across the road to stop him, to set right whatever he'd done. But then I spotted the little dog lying very still in the gutter. The man in the truck must have hit the poor creature, stopped to see if he could help, realized he couldn't, apologized, and left the little girl to grieve. There was nothing I could do, either. Face clenched, I looked back to my side of the street and walked on.
>
> —Jamal Kendal

Compare-Contrast

To compare and contrast, show how two or more subjects are similar and different.

> Americans are often thought to take little interest in the world around them, except perhaps when invading it. The paucity of Americans with passports is often held up as an indication of uninterest. Eighty-five percent of American tourism and travel is domestic. If it follows that 15 percent is international, then Americans join the company of the Greeks, Spaniards, and French, among whom, respectively, 12, 13, and 17 percent of holidays are taken abroad. And that does not take into account the distance needed to travel before the Great Abroad begins. That more than 99 percent of Luxembourgeois vacations of four nights or more were enjoyed outside the nation's borders does not surprise; where else could they possibly have been taken? Assuming that for a European to leave Europe is an effort roughly analogous to that of an American leaving the United States, the figures become more comparable. In 2006, 9.7 million Western Europeans visited the United States, and 13 million Americans visited Europe. Thus, in the realm of travel, Americans were proportionally more interested in Europeans than the other way around. The same year, significantly more Americans (30 million) traveled overseas (other than to Mexico and Canada) than overseas visitors came to the United States (22 million).
>
> —Peter Baldwin

Working with Sources ▌ Advance and deepen your thesis with reliable reasons and evidence. A typical supporting paragraph starts with a topic sentence and elaborates it with detailed evidence and careful reasoning. Make sure to smoothly integrate quotations into the flow of the writing. Also, avoid dropping in quotations without setting them up and explaining them.

Ending Your Draft

Closing paragraphs can be important for tying up loose ends, clarifying key points, or signing off with the reader. In a sense, the entire essay is a preparation for an effective ending; the ending helps the reader look back over the essay with new understanding and appreciation. Many endings leave the reader with fresh food for thought.

Advice:
- Because the ending can be so important, draft a variety of possible endings. Choose the one that flows best from a sense of the whole.

Cautions:
- If your thesis is weak or unclear, you will have a difficult time writing a satisfactory ending. To strengthen the ending, strengthen the thesis.
- You may have heard this formula for writing an essay: "Say what you're going to say, say it, then say what you've just said." Remember, though, if you need to "say what you've just said," say it in new words.

The information on the next two pages will help you develop your ending. For ideas, you can refer to the sample essays elsewhere in this book.

Reassert the main point.

If an essay is complicated, the reader may need reclarification at the end. Show that you are fully addressing the issues that you forecast earlier in the essay.

- **Remind the reader.** Recall what you first set out to do; check off the key points you've covered; or answer any questions left unanswered.
- **Rephrase the thesis.** Restate your thesis in light of the most important support you've given. Deepen and expand your original thesis.

Urge the reader.

Your reader may still be reluctant to accept your ideas or argument. The ending is your last chance to gain the reader's acceptance. Here are some possible strategies:

- **Show the implications.** Follow further possibilities raised by your train of thought; be reasonable and convincing.
- **Look ahead.** Suggest other possible connections.
- **List the benefits.** Show the reader the benefits of accepting or applying the things you've said.

INSIGHT   When your writing comes to an effective stopping point, conclude the essay. Don't tack on another idea.

Complete and unify your message.

Your final paragraphs are your last opportunity to refocus, unify, and otherwise reinforce your message. Draft the closing carefully, not merely to finish the essay but to further advance your purpose and thesis.

Weak Ending

The ending below does not focus on and show commitment to the essay's main idea. Rather than reinforcing this idea, the writing leads off in a new direction.

> I realize I've got to catch my bus. I've spent too much time talking to this woman whose life is a wreck. I give her some spare change and then head off. She doesn't follow me. It's kind of a relief. Toronto is a great city, but sometimes you have weird experiences there. Once a street vendor gave me a free falafel. I didn't want to eat it because maybe something was wrong with it. What a weird city!

Strong Endings

Below are final paragraphs from two essays in this book. Listen to their tone, watch how they reconsider the essay's ideas, and note how they offer further food for thought. (The first example is a revision of the weak paragraph above.)

> I tell her I need to get going. She should go, too, or she'll be late for the hearing. Before getting up, I reach into my wallet and give her two TTC passes and some spare change. I walk her to the street and point her toward Old City Hall. She never thanks me, only looks at me one last time with immense vulnerability and helplessness. Then she walks away.
>
> I wonder as I hurry towards the station if she'll be okay, if her boyfriend really will get out of jail, and if her grandmother will ever take her back. Either way, I think as I cross Bay Street, what more can I do? I have a bus to catch.
>
> (See the full essay on pages 148–150.)

> Passion and power permeate all of Latin America's music. The four major types of music—indigenous, Iberian and Mestizo folk, Afro-American, and popular urban—are as diverse as the people of Latin America, and each style serves a valued need or function in Latinos' everyday lives. As a result, those listening to Latin American music—whether it is a Peruvian Indian's chant, a Venezuelan farmer's whistled tune, a Cuban mambo drummer's vivacious beat, or the Bogotá rock concert's compelling rhythms—are hearing much more than music. They are hearing the passion and power of the Latin American people.
>
> (See the full essay on pages 206–209.)

Working with Sources | Save the best for last. Consider using an especially thought-provoking statement, quotation, or detail in your conclusion. Doing so can help you clinch your point.

Working with Sources | If you are using sources, take care not to overwhelm your draft with source material. Keep the focus on your own ideas:

- Avoid strings of references and chunks of source material with no discussion, explanation, or interpretation on your part in between.
- Don't offer entire paragraphs of material from a source (whether paraphrased or quoted) with a single in-text citation at the end. When you do so, your thinking disappears.
- Be careful not to overload your draft with complex information and dense data lacking explanation.
- Resist the urge to simply copy and paste big chunks from sources. Even if you document the sources, your paper will quickly become a patchwork of source material with a few weak stitches (your contribution) holding it together.
- Note the careful use of source material in the following paragraph.

Sample Paragraph Showing Integration of Source Material

Topic sentence: idea elaborating and supporting thesis

Development of idea through reasoning

Support of idea through reference to source material

Concluding statement of idea

Antibiotics are effective only against infections caused by bacteria and should never be used against infections caused by viruses. Using an antibiotic against a viral infection is like throwing water on a grease fire—water may normally put out fires but will only worsen the situation for a grease fire. In the same way, antibiotics fight infections, but they cause the body harm only when they are used to fight infections caused by viruses. Viruses cause the common cold, the flu, and most sore throats, sinus infections, coughs, and bronchitis. Yet antibiotics are commonly prescribed for these viral infections. *The New England Journal of Medicine* reports that 22.7 million kilograms (25,000 tons) of antibiotics is prescribed each year in the United States alone (Wenzel and Edmond, 1962). Meanwhile, the CDC reports that approximately 50 percent of those prescriptions are completely unnecessary ("Antibiotic Overuse" 25). "Every year, tens of millions of prescriptions for antibiotics are written to treat viral illnesses for which these antibiotics offer no benefits," says the CDC's antimicrobial resistance director David Bell, M.D. (qtd. in Bren 30). Such mis-prescribing is simply bad medical practice that contributes to the problem of growing bacterial infection.

Critical-Thinking and Writing Activities

As directed by your instructor, complete the following critical-thinking and writing activities by yourself or with classmates.

1. Patricia T. O'Connor says, "All writing begins life as a first draft, and first drafts are never any good. They're not supposed to be." Is this claim true? Why or why not? What do you hope to accomplish with a first draft?

2. Study the chart on page 57. Based on other material you have read or written, add another writing move for each of the three main parts of the essay: opening, middle, and ending. Name the move, explain it, and tell what types of writing it might appear in.

3. Read the final paragraphs of any three essays included in this book. Write a brief analysis of each ending based on the information on pages 66–67.

4. Imagine that you are a journalist who has been asked to write an article about a wedding, a funeral, or another significant event you have experienced. Choose an event and sketch out a plan for your article. Include the main writing moves and the type of information at each stage of your writing.

Learning-Objectives Checklist ✓

Have you achieved this chapter's learning objectives? Check your progress with the items below, revisiting topics in the chapter as needed. *I have . . .*

____ re-examined the rhetorical situation of my writing project (my role as writer, my subject, my purpose, the audience, the form, and the context) to be better prepared for drafting (56).

____ identified and explained the parts or "major moves" of an essay, including strategies for openings, middles, and closings (57).

____ composed an opening that effectively engages my readers; establishes my direction, tone, and diction level; and introduces my line of thought through a thesis or a theme (58-59).

____ generated a substantial middle that advances my thesis, tests out my ideas, builds a coherent structure, and provides a fitting level of detail (60-64).

____ produced a closing that reasserts my main point in a fresh way, connects with readers, and unifies my writing (65-66).

____ integrated source material so that it supports my thinking rather than encumbers my ideas (67).

Cross-Curricular Connections

The next time you write a paper in one of your content-area classes, use the tips in this chapter. Afterward, indicate which tip was most helpful and why.

Chapter 5

Revising

The word revising means "taking another look," so revising is best done after a brief break. Set aside your writing and return to it later with fresh eyes. Also, enlist the fresh eyes of another reader, whether a roommate, a classmate, or someone at the writing center. Revising is all about getting perspective.

Of course, once you have perspective, you need to figure out how to make improvements. This chapter provides numerous strategies for focusing on the global traits of your writing—ideas, organization, and voice. The changes you make should improve the work significantly, perhaps even reshaping it.

Visually Speaking To effectively revise your draft, you need to first "recharge your writing batteries (Figure 5.1)." Practically speaking, what might this idea mean for your own writing?

Learning **Objectives**

By working through this chapter, you will be able to

- assess the overall approach that you have taken in your draft.

- critique and improve the ideas, organization, and voice of your draft.

- test and strengthen your paragraphs for unity, coherence, and completeness.

- give and receive helpful feedback by collaborating with classmates.

- explain the role of the writing center and use it to improve your own writing.

Alison Hancock / Shutterstock.com

fig. 5.1

Consider Whole-Paper Issues

When revising, first look at the big picture. Take it all in. Determine whether the content is interesting, informative, and worth sharing. Note any gaps or soft spots in your line of thinking. Ask yourself how you can improve what you have done so far. The information that follows will help you address whole-paper issues such as these.

Revisit the rhetorical situation.

Just as the rhetorical situation helped you to set your direction in writing, it can help you make course corrections. Think about each part of the rhetorical situation.

- **Consider your role.** How are you coming across in this draft? Do you sound authoritative, engaged, knowledgeable, confident? How do you want to come across?
- **Think about your subject.** Have you stated a clear focus? Have you supported it with a variety of details? Have you explored the subject fully?
- **Remember your purpose.** Are you trying to analyze, describe, explain, propose? Does the writing succeed? Do the ideas promote your purpose? Does your organization support the purpose? Is your writing voice helpful in achieving your purpose?
- **Check the form.** Have you created writing that matches the form that your instructor requested? Have you taken best advantage of the form, including graphics or other media, if appropriate?
- **Consider your readers.** Have you captured their attention and interest? Have you provided them the information they need to understand your writing? Have you considered their values, needs, and opinions, and used them to connect?
- **Think about the context.** Is this piece of writing the correct length and level of seriousness for the assignment? Is it on schedule? How does it match up to what others are doing?

Working with Sources ▌ Make sure that your sources work well for each part of the rhetorical situation. Verify that the sources you have used:

- reflect well on you, showing that you understand and care about the topic.
- illuminate the subject with accurate, precise, substantial information.
- help you achieve your purpose, whether to inform, persuade, or reflect.
- work well within the form and can be appropriately credited.
- are seen as authoritative by readers.
- are timely and credible in the context.

Consider your overall approach.

Sometimes it's better to start fresh if your writing contains stretches of uninspired ideas. Consider a fresh start if your first draft shows one of these problems:

- **The topic is worn-out.** An essay titled "Lead Poisoning" may not sound very interesting. Unless you can approach it with a new twist ("Get the Lead Out!"), consider cutting your losses and finding a fresh topic.
- **The approach is stale.** If you've been writing primarily to get a good grade, finish the assignment, or sound cool, start again. Try writing to learn something, prompt real thinking in readers, or touch a chord.
- **Your voice is predictable or fake.** Avoid the bland "A good time was had by all" or the phony academic "When one studies this significant problem in considerable depth . . . " Be real. Be honest.
- **The draft sounds boring.** Maybe it's boring because you pay an equal amount of attention to everything and hence stress nothing. Try condensing less important material and expanding what's important.
- **The essay is formulaic.** In other words, it follows the "five-paragraph" format. This handy organizing frame may prevent you from doing justice to your topic and thinking. If your draft is dragged down by rigid adherence to a formula, try a more original approach.

Working with Sources Test the balance of reasoning and sources. Make sure your draft is not thin on source material, but also make sure that the source material does not dominate the conversation. Use these tips for balancing reasoning and sources:

1. Before diving into source material within a paragraph or section of your paper, flesh out your thinking more fully. Offer reasoning that elaborates the claim and effectively leads into the evidence.
2. As you present evidence from source material, build on it by explaining what it means. Evidence doesn't typically speak for itself: through analysis, synthesis, illustration, contrast, and other means, you need to show how or why your sources advance your thesis.
3. After you have presented evidence that elaborates on and supports your idea, extend your thoughts by addressing the reader's "So what?" or "Why does this matter?" skepticism.

Revising Your First Draft

Revising helps you turn your first draft into a more complete, thoughtful piece of writing. The following information will help you do that.

Prepare to revise.

Once you've finished a first draft, set it aside (ideally for a few days) until you can look at the draft objectively and make needed changes. If you drafted on paper, photocopy the draft. If you drafted on a computer, print your paper (double-spaced). Then make changes with a good pencil or colored pen. If you prefer revising on the computer, consider using your software editing program. In all cases, save your first draft for reference.

Think globally.

When revising, focus on the big picture—the overall strength of the ideas, organization, and voice.

Ideas: Check your thesis, focus, or theme. Has your thinking on your topic changed? Also think about your readers' most pressing questions concerning this topic. Have you answered these questions? Finally, consider your reasoning and support. Are both complete and sound?

Organization: Check the overall design of your writing, making sure that ideas move smoothly and logically from one point to the next. Does your essay build effectively? Do you shift directions cleanly? Fix structural problems in one of these ways:

- **Reorder** material to improve the sequence.
- **Cut** information that doesn't support the thesis.
- **Add** details where the draft is thin.
- **Rewrite** parts that seem unclear.
- **Improve** links between points by using transitions.

Voice: Voice is your personal presence on the page, the tone and attitude that others hear when reading your work. In other words, voice is the between-the-lines message your readers get (whether you want them to or not). When revising, make sure that the tone of your message matches your purpose, whether it is serious, playful, or satiric.

INSIGHT Don't pay undue attention to spelling, grammar, and punctuation at this early stage in the process. Otherwise, you may become distracted from the task at hand: improving the content of your writing. Editing and proofreading come later.

Revising for Ideas and Organization

As you review your draft for content, make sure the ideas are fully developed and the organization is clear. From your main claim or thesis to your reasoning and your evidence, strengthen your thinking and sequencing.

Examine your ideas.

Review the ideas in your writing, making sure that each point is logical, complete, and clear. To test the logic in your writing, see pages 301–304.

Complete Thinking

Have you answered readers' basic questions? Have you supported the thesis? The original passage below is too general; the revision is clearly more complete.

> **Original Passage** (Too general)
> As soon as you receive a minor cut, the body's healing process begins to work. Blood from tiny vessels fills the wound and begins to clot. In less than 24 hours, a scab forms.
>
> **Revised Version** (More specific)
> As soon as you receive a minor cut, the body's healing process begins to work. In a simple wound, the first and second layers of skin are severed along with tiny blood vessels called capillaries. As these vessels bleed into the wound, minute structures called platelets help stop the bleeding by sticking to the edges of the cut and to one another, forming a plug. The platelets then release chemicals that react with certain proteins in the blood to form a clot. The blood clot, with its fiber network, begins to join the edges of the wound together. As the clot dries out, a scab forms, usually in less than 24 hours.

Clear Thesis

Make sure that your writing centers on one main issue or thesis. Although this next original passage lacks a thesis, the revision has a clear one.

> **Original Passage** (Lacks a thesis)
> Teen magazines are popular with young girls. These magazines contain a lot of how-to articles about self-image, fashion, and boy-girl relationships. Girls read them to get advice on how to act and how to look. Girls who don't really know what they want are the most eager readers.
>
> **Revised Version** (Identifies a specific thesis statement)
> Adolescent girls often see teen magazines as handbooks on how to be teenagers. These magazines influence the ways they act and the ways they look. For girls who are unsure of themselves, these magazines can exert an enormous amount of influence. Unfortunately, the advice these magazines give about self-image, fashion, and boys may do more harm than good.

Examine your organization.

Good writing has structure. It leads readers logically and clearly from one point to the next. When revising for organization, consider four areas: the overall plan, the opening, the flow of ideas, and the closing.

Overall Plan

Look closely at the sequence of ideas or events that you share. Does that sequence advance your thesis? Do the points build effectively? Are there gaps in the support or points that stray from your original purpose? If you find such problems, consider the following actions:

- **Refine the focus or emphasis** by rearranging material within the text.
- **Fill in the gaps with new material.** Go back to your planning notes.
- **Delete material that wanders** away from your purpose.
- **Use an additional (or different) method of organization.** For example, if you are comparing two subjects, add depth to your analysis by contrasting them as well. If you are describing a complex subject, show the subject more clearly and fully by distinguishing and classifying its parts. (See pages 62–66 for more on organizational methods.)

INSIGHT What is the best method of organization for your essay? The writing you are doing will usually determine the choice. As you know, a personal narrative is often organized by time. Typically, however, you combine and customize methods to develop a writing idea. For example, within a comparison essay you may do some describing or classifying. See pages 46–47 and 115 for more on the common methods of development.

Opening Ideas

Reread your opening paragraph(s). Is the opening organized effectively? Does it engage readers, establish a direction for your writing, and express your thesis or focus? The original opening below doesn't build to a compelling thesis statement, but the revised version engages the reader and leads to the thesis.

Original Opening (Lacks interest and direction)
> The lack of student motivation is a common subject in the news. Educators want to know how to get students to learn. Today's higher standards mean that students will be expected to learn even more. Another problem in urban areas is that large numbers of students are dropping out. How to interest students is a challenge.

Revised Version (Effectively leads readers into the essay)
> How can we motivate students to learn? How can we get them to meet today's rising standards of excellence? How can we, in fact, keep students in school long enough to learn? The answer to these problems is quite simple. Give them money. Pay students to study and learn and stay in school.

Flow of Ideas

Look closely at the beginnings and endings of each paragraph. Have you connected your thoughts clearly? (See page 84 for a list of transition words.) The original opening words of the paragraph sequence below, from an essay of description, offer no links for readers. The revised versions use strong transitions indicating spatial organization (order by location).

Original First Words in the Four Middle Paragraphs
> There was a huge, steep hill . . .
> Buffalo Creek ran . . .
> A dense "jungle" covering . . .
> Within walking distance from my house . . .

Revised Versions (Words and phrases connect ideas)
> Behind the house, there was a huge, steep hill . . .
> Across the road from the house, Buffalo Creek ran . . .
> On the far side of the creek bank was a dense "jungle" covering . . .
> Up the road, within walking distance from my house . . .

INSIGHT Review "Supporting Your Claims" (pages 298–300) and use those strategies to strengthen weak or unconvincing passages.

Closing Ideas

Reread your closing paragraph(s). Do you offer an effective summary, reassert your main point in a fresh way, and provide readers with food for thought as they leave your writing? Or is your ending abrupt, repetitive, or directionless? The original ending below is uninspiring; it adds little to the main part of the writing. The revision summarizes the main points in the essay and then urges the reader to think again about the overall point of writing.

Original Ending (Sketchy and flat)
> Native Son deals with a young man's struggle against racism. It shows the effects of prejudice. Everyone should read this book.

Revised Version (Effectively ends the writing)
> Native Son deals with a young man's struggle in a racist society, but also with so much more. It shows how prejudice affects people, how it closes in on them, and what some people will do to find a way out. Anyone who wants to better understand racism in the United States should read this book.

Tip: To generate fresh ideas for your closing, freewrite answers to questions like these: Why is the topic important to me? What should my readers have learned? Why should this issue matter to readers? What evidence or appeal (pages 306–308) will help readers remember my message and act on it? How does the topic relate to broader issues in society, history, or life?

Revising for Voice and Style

Generally, readers more fully trust writing that speaks in an informed voice and a clear, natural style. To develop an informed voice, make sure that your details are correct and complete; to develop a clear style, make sure that your writing is well organized and unpretentious. Check the issues below. (For a definition of voice, see page 72.)

Check the level of commitment.

Consider how and to what degree your writing shows that you care about the topic and reader. For example, note how the original passage below lacks a personal voice, revealing nothing about the writer's connection to—or interest in—the topic. In contrast, the revision shows that the writer cares about the topic.

Original Passage (Lacks voice)

Cemeteries can teach us a lot about history. They make history seem more real. There is an old grave of a Revolutionary War veteran in the Union Grove Cemetery. . . .

Revised Version (Personal, sincere voice)

I've always had a special feeling for cemeteries. It's hard to explain any further than that, except to say history never seems quite as real as it does when I walk among many old gravestones. One day I discovered the grave of a Revolutionary War veteran. . . .

Check the intensity of your writing.

All writing—including academic writing—is enriched by an appropriate level of intensity, or even passion. In the original passage below, the writer's concern for the topic is unclear because the piece sounds neutral. In contrast, the revised version exudes energy.

Original Passage (Lacks feeling and energy)

The Dream Act could make a difference for people. It just takes a long time to get any bill through Congress. This bill probably will never get approved. Instead of passing the Dream Act, the country will probably just deport high school students from other countries.

Revised Passage (Expresses real feelings)

Given such debates, it might be a long time before the bill becomes law, thereby dashing the dreams of nearly 65,000 high school students like Maria who can't wait another year because they may already be in deportation proceedings. We need to step up and educate our representatives and senators about the importance of passing the Dream Act on its own instead of including the bill along with other resolutions. We need to urge them to debate and approve the Dream Act now, thereby making Maria's dreams—and the dreams of thousands of students like her—a reality!

Develop an academic style.

Most college writing requires an academic style. Such a style isn't stuffy; you're not trying to impress readers with ten-dollar words. Rather, you are using language that facilitates a thoughtful, engaged discussion of the topic. To choose the best words for such a conversation, consider the issues that follow.

Personal Pronouns

In some academic writing, personal pronouns are acceptable. Such is the case in informal writing, such as reading responses, personal essays involving narration, description, and reflection, and opinion-editorial essays written for a broad audience. In addition, *I* is correctly used in academic writing rooted in personal research, sometimes called an I-search paper.

Generally, however, avoid using *I, we,* and *you* in traditional academic writing. The concept, instead, is to focus on the topic itself and let your attitude be revealed indirectly. As E. B. White puts it, "To achieve style, begin by affecting none—that is, begin by placing yourself in the background."

> **No:** I really think that the problem of the homeless in Chicago is serious, given the number of people who are dying, as I know from my experience where I grew up.
>
> **Yes:** Homelessness in Chicago often leads to death. This fact demands the attention of more than lawmakers and social workers; all citizens must address the problems of their suffering neighbors.

Tip: Use the pronoun *one* carefully in academic prose. When it means "a person," *one* can lead to a stilted style if overused. In addition, the pronoun *their* (a plural pronoun) should not be used with *one* (a singular pronoun).

Technical Terms and Jargon

Technical terms and jargon—"insider" words—can be the specialized vocabulary of a subject, a discipline, a profession, or a social group. As such, jargon can be difficult to read for "outsiders." Follow these guidelines:

- **Use technical terms** to communicate with people within the profession or discipline as a kind of shorthand. However, be careful that such jargon doesn't devolve into meaningless buzzwords and catchphrases.
- **Avoid jargon** when writing for readers outside the profession or discipline. Use simpler terms and define technical terms that must be used.

> **Technical:** Bin's Douser power washer delivers 2200 psi p.r., runs off standard a.c. lines, comes with 100 ft. h.d. synthetic-rubber tubing, and features variable pulsation options through three adjustable s.s. tips.
>
> **Simple:** Bin's Douser power washer has a pressure rating of 2200 psi (pounds per square inch), runs off a common 200-volt electrical circuit, comes with 100 feet of hose, and includes three nozzles.

Level of Formality

Most academic writing (especially research papers, literary analyses, lab reports, and argumentative essays) should meet the standards of formal English. Formal English is characterized by a serious tone; careful attention to word choice; longer and more complex sentences reflecting complex thinking; strict adherence to traditional conventions of grammar, mechanics, and punctuation; and avoidance of contractions.

Formal

Formal English, modeled in this sentence, is worded correctly and carefully so that it can withstand repeated readings without seeming tiresome, sloppy, or cute.

You may write other papers (personal essays, commentaries, journals, and reviews) in which informal English is appropriate. Informal English is characterized by a personal tone, the occasional use of popular expressions, shorter sentences with slightly looser syntax, contractions, and personal references (I, we, you), but it still adheres to basic conventions.

Informal

Informal English sounds like one person talking to another person (in a somewhat relaxed setting). It's the type of language that you're reading now. It sounds comfortable and real, not affected or breezy.

Tip: In academic writing, generally avoid slang—words considered outside standard English because they are faddish, familiar to few people, and sometimes insulting.

Unnecessary Qualifiers

Using qualifiers (such as *mostly, often, likely,* or *tends to*) is an appropriate strategy for developing defendable claims in argumentative writing. (See pages 296–297.) However, when you "overqualify" your ideas or add intensifiers (*really, truly*), the result is insecurity—the impression that you lack confidence in your ideas. The cure? Say what you mean, and mean what you say.

Insecure: I totally and completely agree with the new security measures at sporting events, but that's only my opinion.

Secure: I agree with the new security measures at sporting events.

fyi Each academic discipline has its own vocabulary and its own vocabulary resources. Such resources include dictionaries, glossaries, or handbooks. Check your library for the vocabulary resources in your discipline. Use them regularly to deepen your grasp of that vocabulary.

Know when to use the passive voice.

Most verbs can be in either the active or the passive voice. When a verb is active, the sentence's subject performs the action. When the verb is passive, the subject is acted upon.

> **Active:** If you can't attend the meeting, notify Richard by Thursday.
>
> **Passive:** If a meeting can't be attended by you, Richard must be notified by Thursday.

Weaknesses of Passive Voice

The passive voice tends to be wordy and sluggish because the verb's action is directed backward, not ahead. In addition, passive constructions tend to be impersonal, making people disappear.

> **Passive:** The sound system can now be used to listen in on sessions in the therapy room. Parents can be helped by having constructive one-on-one communication methods with children modeled by therapists.
>
> **Active:** Parents can now use the sound system to listen in on sessions in the therapy room. Therapists can help parents by modeling constructive one-on-one communication methods with children.

Strengths of Passive Voice

Using the passive voice isn't wrong. In fact, the passive voice has some important uses: (1) when you need to be tactful (say, in a bad-news letter), (2) if you wish to stress the object or person acted upon, and (3) if the actual actor is understood, unknown, or unimportant.

> **Active:** Our engineers determined that you bent the bar at the midpoint.
>
> **Passive:** Our engineers determined that the bar had been bent at the midpoint. (tactful)
>
> **Active:** Congratulations! We have approved your scholarship for $2,500.
>
> **Passive:** Congratulations! Your scholarship for $2,500 has been approved. (emphasis on receiver; actor understood)

Tip: Avoid using the passive voice unethically to hide responsibility. For example, an instructor who says, "Your assignments could not be graded because of scheduling difficulties," might be trying to evade the truth: "I did not finish grading your assignments because I was watching *CSI*."

Working with Sources Academic writing must be free of plagiarism. Check that you have clearly indicated which material in your draft is summarized, paraphrased, or quoted from another source. (For more help, see pages 422–424.)

Addressing Paragraph Issues

While drafting, you may have constructed paragraphs that are loosely held together, poorly developed, or unclear. When you revise, take a close look at your paragraphs for focus, unity, and coherence (pages 81–83).

Remember the basics.

A paragraph should be a concise unit of thought. Revise a paragraph until it . . .

- is organized around a controlling idea—often stated in a topic sentence.
- consists of supporting sentences that develop the controlling idea.
- concludes with a sentence that summarizes the main point and prepares readers for the next paragraph or main point.
- serves a specific function in a piece of writing—opening, supporting, developing, illustrating, countering, describing, or closing.

Sample Paragraph

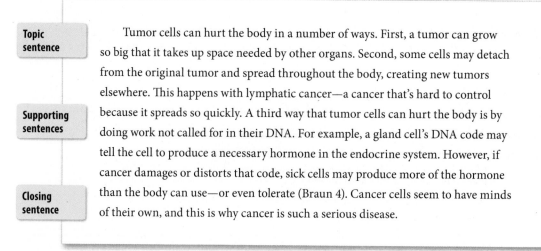

Topic sentence

      Tumor cells can hurt the body in a number of ways. First, a tumor can grow so big that it takes up space needed by other organs. Second, some cells may detach from the original tumor and spread throughout the body, creating new tumors elsewhere. This happens with lymphatic cancer—a cancer that's hard to control

Supporting sentences

because it spreads so quickly. A third way that tumor cells can hurt the body is by doing work not called for in their DNA. For example, a gland cell's DNA code may tell the cell to produce a necessary hormone in the endocrine system. However, if cancer damages or distorts that code, sick cells may produce more of the hormone than the body can use—or even tolerate (Braun 4). Cancer cells seem to have minds

Closing sentence

of their own, and this is why cancer is such a serious disease.

Keep the purpose in mind.

Use these questions to evaluate the purpose and function of each paragraph:

- What function does the paragraph fulfill? How does it add to your line of reasoning or the development of your thesis?
- Would the paragraph work better if it were divided in two—or combined with another paragraph?
- Does the paragraph flow smoothly from the previous paragraph, and does it lead effectively into the next one?

Check for unity.

A unified paragraph is one in which all the details help to develop a single main topic or achieve a single main effect. Test for unity by following these guidelines.

Topic Sentence

Very often the topic of a paragraph is stated in a single sentence called a "topic sentence." Check whether your paragraph needs a topic sentence. If the paragraph has a topic sentence, determine whether it is clear, specific, and well focused. Figure 5.2 presents a formula for writing good topic sentences:

Formula:	A Limited Topic		Specific Feeling or Thought		Topic Sentence
Example:	The fear that Americans feel	+	comes partly from the uncertainty related to this attack	=	The fear that Americans feel comes partly from the uncertainty related to this attack.

fig. 5.2

Placement of the Topic Sentence

Normally the topic sentence is the first sentence in the paragraph. However, it can appear elsewhere in a paragraph.

Middle Placement: Place a topic sentence in the middle when you want to build up to and then lead away from the key idea.

During the making of *Apocalypse Now*, Eleanor Coppola created a documentary about the filming called *Hearts of Darkness:* A Filmmaker's Apocalypse. In the first film, the insane Colonel Kurtz has disappeared into the Cambodian jungle. As Captain Willard searches for Kurtz, the screen fills with horror. **However, as *Hearts of Darkness* relates, the horror portrayed in the fictional movie was being lived out by the production company.** For example, in the documentary, actor Larry Fishburne shockingly says, "War is fun. . . . Vietnam must have been so much fun." Then toward the end of the filming, actor Martin Sheen suffered a heart attack. When an assistant informed investors, the director exploded, "He's not dead unless I say he's dead."

End Placement: Place a topic sentence at the end when you want to build to a climax, as in a passage of narration or persuasion.

When sportsmen stop to reflect on why they find fishing so enjoyable, most realize that what they love is the feel of a fish on the end of the line, not necessarily the weight of the fillets in their coolers. Fishing has undergone a slow evolution over the last century. While fishing used to be a way of putting food on the table, most of today's fishermen do so only for the relaxation that it provides. The barbed hook was invented to increase the quantity of fish a man could land so that he could better feed his family. **This need no longer exists, so barbed hooks are no longer necessary.**

Supporting Sentences

All the sentences in the body of a paragraph should support the topic sentence. The closing sentence, for instance, will often summarize the paragraph's main point or emphasize a key detail. If any sentences shift the focus away from the topic, revise the paragraph in one of the following ways:

- **Delete the material** from the paragraph.
- **Rewrite the material** so that it clearly supports the topic sentence.
- **Create a separate paragraph** based on the odd-man-out material.
- **Revise the topic sentence** so that it relates more closely to the support.

Consistent Focus

Examine the following paragraph about fishing hooks. The original topic sentence focuses on the point that some anglers prefer smooth hooks. However, the writer leaves this initial idea unfinished and turns to the issue of the cost of new hooks. In the revised version, unity is restored: The first paragraph completes the point about anglers who prefer smooth hooks; the second paragraph addresses the issue of replacement costs.

Original Paragraph (Lacks unity)

According to some anglers who do use smooth hooks, their lures perform better than barbed lures as long as they maintain a constant tension on the line. Smooth hooks can bite deeper than barbed hooks, actually providing a stronger hold on the fish. Some people have argued that replacing all of the barbed hooks in their tackle would be a costly operation.

Revised Version (Unified)

According to some anglers who do use smooth hooks, their lures perform better than barbed lures as long as the anglers maintain a constant tension on the line. Smooth hooks can bite deeper than barbed hooks, actually providing a stronger hold on the fish. These anglers testify that switching from barbed hooks has not noticeably reduced the number of fish that they are able to land. In their experience, and in my own, enjoyment of the sport is actually heightened by adding another challenge to playing the fish (maintaining line tension).

Some people have argued that replacing all of the barbed hooks in their tackle would be a costly operation. While this is certainly a concern, barbed hooks do not necessarily require replacement. With a simple set of pliers, the barbs on most conventional hooks can be bent down, providing a cost-free method of modifying one's existing tackle. . . .

fyi Paragraphs that contain unrelated ideas lack unity and are hard to follow. As you review each paragraph for unity, ask yourself these questions: Is the topic of the paragraph clear? Does each sentence relate to the topic? Are the sentences organized in the best possible order?

Check for coherence.

When a paragraph is coherent, the parts stay together. A coherent paragraph flows smoothly because each sentence is connected to others by patterns in the language such as repetition and transitions. To strengthen the coherence in your paragraphs, check for the issues discussed below.

Effective Repetition

To achieve coherence in your paragraphs, consider using repetition—repeating words or synonyms where necessary to remind readers of what you have already said. You can also use parallelism—repeating phrase or sentence structures to show the relationships among ideas. At the same time, you will add a unifying rhythm to your writing.

> **Ineffective:** The floor was littered with discarded soda cans, newspapers that were crumpled, and wrinkled clothes.
>
> **Effective:** The floor was littered with discarded soda cans, crumpled newspapers, and wrinkled clothes. (Three parallel phrases are used.)
>
> **Ineffective:** Reading the book was enjoyable; to write the critique was difficult.
>
> **Effective:** Reading the book was enjoyable; writing the critique was difficult. (Two similar structures are repeated.)

Clear Transitions

Linking words and phrases like "next," "on the other hand," and "in addition" connect ideas by showing the relationship among them. There are transitions that show location and time, compare and contrast things, emphasize a point, conclude or summarize, and add or clarify information. (See page 84 for a list of linking words and phrases.) Note the use of transitions in the following examples:

> **The transition is used to emphasize a point.**
> The paradox of Scotland is that violence had long been the norm in this now-peaceful land. In fact, the country was born, bred, and came of age in war.
>
> **The transition is used to show time or order.**
> The production of cement is a complicated process. First, the mixture of lime, silica, alumina, and gypsum is ground into very fine particles.

INSIGHT Another way to achieve coherence in your paragraphs is to use pronouns effectively. A pronoun forms a link to the noun it replaces and ties that noun (idea) to the ideas that follow. As always, don't overuse pronouns or rely too heavily on them in establishing coherence in your paragraphs.

Transitions and Linking Words

The words and phrases below can help you tie together words, phrases, sentences, and paragraphs.

Words used to **show location:**

above	behind	down	on top of
across	below	in back of	onto
against	beneath	in front of	outside
along	beside	inside	over
among	between	into	throughout
around	beyond	near	to the right
away from	by	off	under

Words used to **show time:**

about	during	next	today
after	finally	next week	tomorrow
afterward	first	second	until
as soon as	immediately	soon	when
at	later	then	yesterday
before	meanwhile	third	

Words used to **compare things (show similarities):**

also	in the same way	likewise
as	like	similarly

Words used to **contrast things (show differences):**

although	even though	on the other hand	still
but	however	otherwise	

Words used to **emphasize a point:**

again	for this reason	particularly	to repeat
even	in fact	to emphasize	truly

Words used to **conclude or summarize:**

all in all	finally	in summary	therefore
as a result	in conclusion	last	to sum up

Words used to **add information:**

additionally	and	equally important	in addition
again	another	finally	likewise
along with	as well	for example	next
also	besides	for instance	second

Words used to **clarify:**

for instance	in other words	put another way	that is

fig. 5.3

Note: Use transitions to link, expand, or intensify an idea, but don't add elements carelessly, creating run-on or rambling sentences.

Check for completeness.

The sentences in a paragraph should support and expand on the main point. If your paragraph does not seem complete, you will need to add information.

Supporting Details

If some of your paragraphs are incomplete, they may lack details. There are numerous kinds of details, including the following:

facts	paraphrases	explanations	definitions
anecdotes	statistics	comparisons	summaries
analyses	quotations	examples	analogies

Add details based on the type of writing you are engaged in.

Describing: Add details that help readers see, smell, taste, touch, or hear it.

Narrating: Add details that help readers understand the events and actions.

Explaining: Add details that help readers understand what it means, how it works, or what it does.

Persuading: Add details that strengthen the logic of your argument.

Specific Details

The original paragraph below fails to answer fully the question posed by the topic sentence. In the revised paragraph, the writer uses an anecdote to answer the question.

Original Paragraph (Lacks completeness)

So what is stress? Actually, the physiological characteristics of stress are some of the body's potentially good self-defense mechanisms. People experience stress when they are in danger. In fact, stress can be healthy.

Revised Version (Full development)

So what is stress? Actually, the physiological characteristics of stress are some of the body's potentially good self-defense mechanisms. Take, for example, a man who is crossing a busy intersection when he spots an oncoming car. Immediately his brain releases a flood of adrenaline into his bloodstream. As a result, his muscles contract, his eyes dilate, his heart pounds faster, his breathing quickens, and his blood clots more readily. Each one of these responses helps the man leap out of the car's path. His muscles contract to give him exceptional strength. His eyes dilate so that he can see more clearly. His heart pumps more blood and his lungs exchange more air—both to increase his metabolism. If the man were injured, his blood would clot faster, ensuring a smaller amount of blood loss. In this situation and many more like it, stress symptoms are good (Curtis 25–26).

INSIGHT▶ If a paragraph is getting long, divide it at a natural stopping point. The topic sentence can then function as the thesis for that part of your essay or paper.

Working with Sources | Test your evidence to make certain that it provides the support you need, support that meets the criteria below.

- **Accurate:** The information is all correct.
- **Precise:** The data are concrete and specific, not vague and general.
- **Substantial:** The amount of evidence reaches a critical mass—enough to convey the idea and convince readers of its validity.
- **Authoritative:** The evidence comes from a reliable source. Moreover, the information is as close to the origin as possible; it is not a report conveying thirdhand information.
- **Representative:** The information fairly represents the range of data on the issue. Your presentation of evidence is balanced.
- **Fitting:** Given your purpose, the topic, and your reader, the evidence is appropriate and relevant for the question or issue you are discussing.

Example: The resources below come from the works-cited list for Paige Louter's essay, "Why the World Deserves Better Than Fair Trade," on pages 525–533. While we would have to go to the sources themselves to test their reliability and Paige's use of them in her essay, we can tell a number of things simply from the source details provided. First, the sources are scholarly— published in respected field-of-study journals and by an academic book publisher. Even the Web resource used is the official site of a recognizable non-profit organization. The articles come from academic databases, and a quick Google search shows that the authors are recognized and respected experts. Furthermore, page spans indicate that the sources are fairly lengthy. Finally, the titles indicate that the sources, though likely coming from a specific argumentative perspective, are likely balanced and thoughtful. In other words, these sources promise to provide information that is accurate and precise (possibly primary data and certainly data that is properly credited), that is substantial and authoritative (given length and authorship), and that is representative and fitting (showing the range of perspectives on the specific issue Paige is exploring).

Fair Trade   12

References

Booth, Philip, and Linda Whetstone. "Half a Cheer for Fair Trade." *Economic Affairs* 27.2
    (2007): 29-36. *Business Source Elite*. Web. 19 Jan. 2012.

Hutchens, Anna. "Empowering Women Through Fair Trade? Lessons from Asia." *Third
    World Quarterly* 31.3 (2010): 449-467. *Academic Search Premier*. Web. 18 Jan. 2012.

Nichols, Alex, and Charlotte Opal. *Fair Trade: Market-Driven Ethical Consumption*.
    London: Sage, 2004. Print.

Walton, Andrew. "What Is Fair Trade?" *Third World Quarterly* 31.3 (2010): 431-47.
    Academic Search Premier. Web. 19 Jan. 2012.

"What is [sic] Fairtrade?" *Fairtrade International*. Fairtrade Labelling Organizations
    International, n.d. Web. 10 Feb. 2012.

Revising Collaboratively

Every writer can benefit from feedback from an interested audience, especially one that offers constructive and honest advice during a writing project. Members of an existing writing group already know how valuable it is for writers to share their work. Others might want to start a writing group to experience the benefits. Your group might collaborate online or in person. In either case, the information on the next two pages will help you get started.

Know your role.

Writers and reviewers should know their roles and fulfill their responsibilities during revising sessions. Essentially, the writer should briefly introduce the draft and solicit honest responses. Reviewers should make constructive comments in response to the writing.

Provide appropriate feedback.

Feedback can take many forms, including the three approaches described here.

- **Basic Description:** In this simple response, the reviewer listens or reads attentively and then simply describes what she or he hears or sees happening in the piece. The reviewer offers no criticism of the writing.

  > **Ineffective:** "That was interesting. The piece was informative."
  >
  > **Effective:** First, the essay introduced the challenge of your birth defect and how you have had to cope with it. Then in the next part you . . .'"

- **Summary Evaluation:** Here the reviewer reads or listens to the piece and then provides a specific evaluation of the draft.

  > **Ineffective:** "Gee, I really liked it!" or "It was boring."
  >
  > **Effective:** "Your story at the beginning really pulled me in, and the middle explained the issue strongly, but the ending felt a bit flat."

- **Thorough Critique:** The reviewer assesses the ideas, organization, and voice in the writing. Feedback should be detailed and constructive. Such a critique may also be completed with the aid of a review sheet or checklist. As a reviewer, be prepared to share specific responses, suggestions, and questions. But also be sure to focus your comments on the writing, rather than the writer.

  > **Ineffective:** "You really need to fix that opening! What were you thinking?"
  >
  > **Effective:** "Let's look closely at the opening. Could you rewrite the first sentence so it grabs the reader's attention? Also, I'm somewhat confused about the thesis statement. Could you rephrase it so it states your position more clearly?"

Respond according to a plan.

Using a specific plan or scheme like the following will help you give clear, helpful, and complete feedback.

- **OAQS Method:** Use this simple four-step scheme—**Observe, Appreciate, Question,** and **Suggest**—to respond to your peers' writing.

  1. **Observe** means to notice what another person's essay is designed to do and say something about its design or purpose. For example, you might say, "Even though you are writing about your boyfriend, it appears that you are trying to get a message across to your parents."

  2. **Appreciate** means to praise something in the writing that impresses or pleases you. You can find something to appreciate in any piece of writing. For example, you might say, "You make a very convincing point" or "With your description, I can actually see his broken tooth."

  3. **Question** means to ask whatever you want to know after you've read the essay. You might ask for background information, a definition, an interpretation, or an explanation. For example, you might say, "Can you tell us what happened when you got to the emergency room?"

  4. **Suggest** means to give helpful advice about possible changes. For example, you might say, "With a little more physical detail—especially more sounds and smells—your third paragraph could be the highlight of the whole essay. What do you think?"

Asking the Writer Questions

Reviewers should ask the following types of questions while reviewing a piece of writing:

- **To help writers reflect on their purpose and audience . . .**
  Why are you writing this?
  Who will read this, and what do they need to know?

- **To help writers focus their thoughts . . .**
  What message are you trying to get across?
  Do you have more than one main point?
  What are the most important examples?

- **To help writers think about their information . . .**
  What do you know about the subject?
  Does this part say enough?
  Does your writing cover all of the basics? (*Who? What? Where? When? Why?* and *How?*)

- **To help writers with their openings and closings . . .**
  What are you trying to say in the opening?
  How else could you start your writing?
  How do you want your readers to feel at the end?

Using the Writing Center

A college writing center or lab is a place where a trained adviser will help you develop and strengthen a piece of writing. You can expect the writing center adviser to do certain things; other things only you can do. For quick reference, refer to the chart below.

Adviser's Job	Your Job
Make you feel at home	Be respectful
Discuss your needs	Be ready to work
Help you choose a topic	Decide on a topic
Discuss your purpose and audience	Know your purpose and audience
Help you generate ideas	Embrace the best ideas
Help you develop your logic	Consider other points of view; stretch your own perspective
Help you understand how to research your material	Do the research
Read your draft	Share your writing
Identify problems in organization, logic, expression, and format	Recognize and fix problems
Teach ways to correct weaknesses	Learn important principles
Help you with grammar, usage, diction, vocabulary, and mechanics	Correct all errors

Tips for getting the most out of the writing center
- Visit the center at least several days before your paper is due.
- Take your assignment sheet with you to each advising session.
- Read your work aloud, slowly.
- Expect to rethink your writing from scratch.
- Do not defend your wording—if it needs defense, it needs revision.
- Ask questions. (No question is "too dumb.")
- Request clarification of anything you don't understand.
- Ask for examples or illustrations of important points.
- Write down all practical suggestions.
- Ask the adviser to summarize his or her remarks.
- Rewrite as soon as possible after—or even during—the advising session.
- Return to the writing center for a response to your revisions.

Critical-Thinking and Writing Activities

As directed by your instructor, complete the following critical-thinking and writing activities by yourself or with classmates.

1. Doris Lessing has stated that when it comes to writing, "The more a thing cooks, the better." In what sense is revision a crucial stage in that cooking process? Using Lessing's cooking metaphor as a starting point, explore how revision should function in your own writing.

2. Review the opening and closing paragraphs of one of your essays. Then come up with fresh and different approaches for those paragraphs using the information on pages 74–75 as a guide.

3. For your current writing assignment, ask a peer to provide detailed feedback using the information in this chapter as a guide. Then take a fresh copy of your paper to the writing center and work through your draft with an adviser. Revise the draft as needed.

Learning-Objectives Checklist ✓

Have you achieved this chapter's learning objectives? Check your progress with the items below, revisiting topics in the chapter as needed. *I have . . .*

____ re-examined the rhetorical situation of my writing project (my role as writer, my subject, my purpose, the audience, the form, and the context) to be better prepared to revise my draft (70).

____ assessed my overall approach to see if it is stale, predicable, boring, or formulaic (71).

____ examined my ideas for a clear thesis and complete development, making necessary improvements (73).

____ evaluated the overall organization of my draft, including whether the opening engages readers and sets a direction, the middle clearly traces a line of reasoning, and the closing effectively ends the draft (74–75).

____ examined and improved the voice in my draft, addressing issues of commitment, intensity, academic style, and active vs. passive voice (76–79).

____ examined each paragraph to ensure that it is an effective unit of thought, unified in its topic or effect, coherent through transitions, and complete in its details (80–86).

____ given and received helpful feedback on a draft by collaborating with classmates through techniques such as the OAQS method (87–88).

____ described the role of the writing center in improving my writing, including my responsibilities and those of the center's tutors (89).

Cross-Curricular Connections

As you write papers for your major, make sure to use types of evidence and methods of analysis that the discipline accepts and values.

Chapter 6

Editing and Proofreading

Editing and proofreading allow you to fine-tune your writing, making it ready to hand in. When you edit, look first for words, phrases, and sentences that sound awkward, uninteresting, or unclear. When you proofread, check your writing for spelling, mechanics, usage, and grammar errors. Ask one of your writing peers to help you.

The guidelines and strategies given in this chapter will help you edit your writing for style and clarity and proofread it for errors.

Visually Speaking   Piano tuning requires special skills and specialized tools (Figure 6.1). What skills and tools do you need to effectively edit and proofread your writing? How are tuning a piano and polishing your writing similar and different?

Learning **Objectives**

By working through this chapter, you will be able to

- assess the overall style of your revised draft.
- combine short, simplistic sentences into more substantial ones.
- expand sparse sentences with meaningful details.
- transform stylistically weak sentences through various techniques.
- replace imprecise, misleading, and biased words.
- identify and correct errors in grammar, punctuation, mechanics, usage, and spelling.

PhotoHouse / Shutterstock.com

fig. 6.1

Editing Your Revised Draft

When you have thoroughly revised your writing, you need to edit it so as to make it clear and concise enough to present to readers. Use the editing guidelines below to check your revised draft.

Review the overall style of your writing.

1. **Read your revised writing aloud.** Better yet, have a writing peer read it aloud to you. Highlight any writing that doesn't read smoothly and naturally.

2. **Check that your style fits the rhetorical situation.**

> **Goal:** Does your writing sound as if you wrote it with a clear aim in mind? Do the sentence style and word choice match the goal?
>
> **Reader:** Is the tone sincere? Does the writing sound authentic and honest?
>
> **Subject:** Does the writing suit the subject and your treatment of it in terms of seriousness or playfulness, complexity or simplicity?

3. **Examine your sentences.** Check them for clarity, conciseness, and variety. Replace sentences that are wordy or rambling; combine or expand sentences that are short and choppy. Also, vary the beginnings of your sentences and avoid sentence patterns that are too predictable. (See pages 93–99.)

Consider word choice.

1. **Avoid redundancy.** Be alert for words or phrases that are used together but mean nearly the same thing.

   ▌ repeat again   red in color   refer back   advance ahead

2. **Watch for repetition.** When used appropriately, repetition can add rhythm and coherence to your writing. When used ineffectively, however, repetition can be distracting.

   ▌ **The man** looked as if he were in his late seventies. **The man** was dressed in an old suit. I soon realized that **the man** was homeless....

3. **Look for general nouns, verbs, and modifiers.** Specific words are much more effective than general ones. (See page 100.)

   ▌ The girl moved on the bench. (general)
   ▌ Rosie slid quietly to the end of the park bench. (specific)

4. **Avoid highly technical terms.** Check for jargon or technical terms that your readers will not know or that you haven't adequately explained. (See page 101.)

   ▌ As the **capillaries** bleed, **platelets** work with **fibrinogens** to form a clot.

5. **Use fair language.** Replace words or phrases that are biased or demeaning. (See pages 102–104.)

Combining Sentences

Effective sentences often contain several basic ideas that work together to show relationships and make connections. Here are five basic ideas followed by seven examples of how the ideas can be combined into effective sentences.

1. The longest and largest construction project in history is the Great Wall of China.
2. The project took 1,700 years to complete.
3. The Great Wall of China is 1,400 miles long.
4. It is between 18 and 30 feet high.
5. It is up to 32 feet wide.

Edit short, simplistic sentences.

Combine your short, simplistic sentences into longer, more detailed sentences. Sentence combining is generally carried out in the following ways:

- Use a **series** to combine three or more similar ideas.

  > The Great Wall of China is **1,400 miles long,** between **18 and 30 feet high,** and up to **32 feet wide**.

- Use a **relative pronoun** (*who, whose, that, which*) to introduce subordinate (less important) ideas.

  > The Great Wall of China, **which is 1,400 miles long and between 18 and 30 feet high,** took 1,700 years to complete.

- Use an **introductory phrase** or **clause**.

  > **Having taken 1,700 years to complete,** the Great Wall of China is the longest construction project in history.

- Use a **semicolon** (and a conjunctive adverb if appropriate).

  > The Great Wall took 1,700 years to complete**;** it is 1,400 miles long and up to 30 feet high and 32 feet wide.

- Repeat a **key word** or phrase to emphasize an idea.

  > The Great Wall of China is the longest construction **project** in history, a **project** that took 1,700 years to complete.

- Use **correlative conjunctions** (*either, or; not only, but also*) to compare or contrast two ideas in a sentence.

  > The Great Wall of China is **not only** up to 30 feet high and 32 feet wide, **but also** 1,400 miles long.

- Use an **appositive** (a word or phrase that renames) to emphasize an idea.

  > The Great Wall of China—**the largest construction project in history**—is 1,400 miles long, 32 feet wide, and up to 30 feet high.

Expanding Sentences

When you edit, expand sentences so as to connect related ideas and make room for new information. Length has no value in and of itself: The best sentence is still the shortest one that says all it has to say. An expanded sentence, however, is capable of saying more—and saying it more expressively.

Use cumulative sentences.

Modern writers often use an expressive sentence form called the cumulative sentence. A cumulative sentence is made of a general "base clause" that is expanded by adding modifying words, phrases, or clauses. In such a sentence, details are added before and after the main clause, creating an image-rich thought. Here's an example of a cumulative sentence, with the base clause or main idea in boldface:

> In preparation for her Spanish exam, **Julie was studying at the kitchen table,** completely focused, memorizing a list of vocabulary words.

Discussion: Notice how each new modifier adds to the richness of the final sentence. Also notice that each of these modifying phrases is set off by a comma. Here's another sample sentence:

> With his hands on his face, **Tony was laughing halfheartedly,** looking puzzled and embarrassed.

Discussion: Such a cumulative sentence provides a way to write description that is rich in detail, without rambling. Notice how each modifier changes the flow or rhythm of the sentence.

Expand with details.

Here are seven basic ways to expand a main idea:

1. with **adjectives and adverbs:** *halfheartedly, once again*
2. with **prepositional phrases:** *with his hands on his face*
3. with **absolute phrases:** *his head tilted to one side*
4. with **participial (-ing or -ed) phrases:** *looking puzzled*
5. with **infinitive phrases:** *to hide his embarrassment*
6. with **subordinate clauses:** *while his friend talks*
7. with **relative clauses:** *who isn't laughing at all*

INSIGHT   To edit sentences for more expressive style, it is best to (1) know your grammar and punctuation (especially commas); (2) practice tightening, combining, and expanding sentences using the guidelines in this chapter; and (3) read good writing carefully, looking for models of well-constructed sentences.

Checking for Sentence Style

Writer E. B. White advised young writers to "approach sentence style by way of simplicity, plainness, orderliness, and sincerity." That's good advice from a writer steeped in style. It's also important to know what to look for when editing your sentences. The information on this page and the following four pages will help you edit your sentences for style and correctness.

Avoid these sentence problems.

Always check for and correct the following types of sentence problems. When attempting to fix problems in your sentences, turn to the pages listed below for guidelines and examples.

Short, Choppy Sentences:	Combine or expand any short, choppy sentences; use the examples and guidelines on page 93.
Flat, Predictable Sentences:	Rewrite any sentences that sound predictable and uninteresting by varying their structures and expanding them with modifying words, phrases, and clauses. (See pages 96–99.)
Incorrect Sentences:	Look carefully for fragments, run-ons, and comma splices and correct them as needed.
Unclear Sentences:	Edit any sentences that contain unclear wording, misplaced modifiers, dangling modifiers, or incomplete comparisons.
Unacceptable Sentences:	Change sentences that include nonstandard language, double negatives, or unparallel constructions.
Unnatural Sentences:	Rewrite sentences that contain jargon, clichés, or flowery language. (See page 101.)

Review your writing for sentence variety.

Use the following strategy to review your writing for variety in terms of sentence beginnings, lengths, and types.

- In one column on a piece of paper, list the opening words in each of your sentences. Then decide if you need to vary some of your sentence beginnings.
- In another column, identify the number of words in each sentence. Then decide if you need to change the lengths of some of your sentences.
- In a third column, list the kinds of sentences used (exclamatory, declarative, interrogative, and so on). Then, based on your analysis, use the instructions on the next two pages to edit your sentences as needed.

Working with Sources When you integrate a quotation into a text, make sure that the quotation works with the material around it. Either make the quotation a grammatical part of the sentence, or introduce the quotation with a complete sentence followed by a colon.

Vary sentence structures.

To energize your sentences, vary their structures using one or more of the methods shown on this page and the next.

1. **Vary sentence openings.** Move a modifying word, phrase, or clause to the front of the sentence to stress that modifier. However, avoid creating dangling or misplaced modifiers.

> **The norm:** We apologize for the inconvenience this may have caused you.
> **Variation:** For the inconvenience this may have caused you, we apologize.

2. **Vary sentence lengths.** Short sentences (ten words or fewer) are ideal for making points crisply. Medium sentences (ten to twenty words) should carry the bulk of your information. When well crafted, occasional long sentences (more than twenty words) can develop and expand your ideas.

> **Short:** Welcome back to Magnolia Suites!
> **Medium:** Unfortunately, your confirmed room was unavailable last night when you arrived. For the inconvenience this may have caused you, we apologize.
> **Long:** Because several guests did not depart as scheduled, we were forced to provide you with accommodations elsewhere; however, for your trouble, we were happy to cover the cost of last night's lodging.

3. **Vary sentence kinds.** The most common sentence is declarative—it states a point. For variety, try exclamatory, imperative, interrogative, and conditional statements.

> **Exclamatory:** Our goal is providing you with outstanding service!
> **Declarative:** To that end, we have upgraded your room at no expense.
> **Imperative:** Please accept, as well, this box of chocolates as a gift to sweeten your stay.
> **Interrogative:** Do you need further assistance?
> **Conditional:** If you do, we are ready to fulfill your requests.

INSIGHT In creative writing (stories, novels, plays), writers occasionally use fragments to vary the rhythm of their prose, emphasize a point, or create dialogue. Avoid fragments in academic or business writing.

4. **Vary sentence arrangements.** Where do you want to place the main point of your sentence? You make that choice by arranging sentence parts into loose, periodic, balanced, or cumulative patterns. Each pattern creates a specific effect.

Loose Sentence

> **The Travel Center offers an attractive flight-reservation plan for students,** one that allows you to collect bonus miles and receive $150,000 in life insurance per flight.

Analysis: This pattern is direct. It states the main point immediately (bold), and then tacks on extra information.

Periodic Sentence

> Although this plan requires that you join the Travel Center's Student-Flight Club and pay the $10 admission fee, **in the long run you will save money!**

Analysis: This pattern postpones the main point (bold) until the end. The sentence builds to the point, creating an indirect, dramatic effect.

Balanced Sentence

> **Joining the club in your freshman year will save you money over your entire college career;** in addition, **accruing bonus miles over four years will earn you a free trip to Europe!**

Analysis: This pattern gives equal weight to complementary or contrasting points (bold); the balance is often signaled by a comma and a conjunction *(and, but)* or by a semicolon. Often a conjunctive adverb *(however, nevertheless)* or a transitional phrase *(in addition, even so)* will follow the semicolon to further clarify the relationship.

Cumulative Sentence

> Because the club membership is in your name, **you can retain its benefits** as long as you are a student, even if you transfer to a different college or go on to graduate school.

Analysis: This pattern puts the main idea (bold) in the middle of the sentence, surrounding it with modifying words, phrases, and clauses.

5. **Use positive repetition.** Although you should avoid needless repetition, you might use emphatic repetition to repeat a key word to stress a point.

Needlessly Repetitive Sentence

> Each year, more than a million young people who read poorly leave high school unable to read well, functionally illiterate.

Emphatic Sentence

> Each year, more than a million young people leave high school functionally illiterate, so **illiterate** that they can't read daily newspapers, job ads, or safety instructions.

Use parallel structure.

Coordinated sentence elements should be parallel—that is, they should be written in the same grammatical forms. Parallel structures save words, clarify relationships, and present the information in the correct sequence. Follow these guidelines.

1. **For words, phrases, or clauses in a series,** keep elements consistent.

> **Not parallel:** I have tutored students in Biology 101, also Chemistry 102, not to mention my familiarity with Physics 200.
> **Parallel:** I have tutored students in *Biology 101, Chemistry 102,* and *Physics 200.*
>
> **Not parallel:** I have volunteered as a hospital receptionist, have been a hospice volunteer, and as an emergency medical technician.
> **Parallel:** I have done volunteer work as *a hospital receptionist, a hospice counselor,* and *an emergency medical technician.*

2. **Use both parts of correlative conjunctions** (*either, or; neither, nor; not only, but also; as, so; whether, so; both, and*) so that both segments of the sentence are balanced.

> **Not parallel:** *Not only* did Blake College turn 20 this year. Its enrollment grew by 16 percent.
> **Parallel:** *Not only* did Blake College turn 20 this year, *but* its enrollment *also* grew by 16 percent.

3. **Place a modifier correctly** so that it clearly indicates the word or words to which it refers.

> **Confusing:** MADD promotes *severely* punishing and eliminating drunk driving because this offense leads to a *great number* of deaths and sorrow.
> **Parallel:** MADD promotes eliminating and *severely* punishing drunk driving because this offense leads to *many* deaths and *untold* sorrow.

4. **Place contrasting details in parallel structures** (words, phrases, or clauses) to stress a contrast.

> **Weak contrast:** The average child watches 24 hours of television a week and reads for 36 minutes.
> **Strong contrast:** Each week, the average child *watches television for 24 hours but reads for only about half an hour.*

Working with Sources | When using sources, smoothly integrate text references to those sources. (For guidelines, see pages 493–534 for MLA and pages 535–564 for APA.)

Avoid weak constructions.

Avoid constructions (like those below) that weaken your writing.

Nominal Constructions

The nominal construction is both sluggish and wordy. Avoid it by changing the noun form of a verb *(description or instructions)* to a verb *(describe or instruct)*. At the same time, delete the weak verb that preceded the noun.

Nominal Constructions (noun form underlined)	**Strong Verbs** (italicized)
Tim gave a <u>description</u> . . .	Lydia provided *instructions* . . .
Tim <u>described</u> . . .	Lydia *instructed* . . .

> **Sluggish:** John *had a discussion* with the tutors regarding the incident. They gave him their *confirmation* that similar developments had occurred before, but they had not *provided* submissions of their reports.
>
> **Energetic:** John *discussed* the incident with the tutors. They *confirmed* that similar problems had developed before, but they hadn't *submitted* their reports.

Expletives

Expletives such as "it is" and "there is" are fillers that serve no purpose in most sentences—except to make them wordy and unnatural.

> **Sluggish:** *It is* likely that Nathan will attend the Communication Department's Honors Banquet. *There is* a journalism scholarship that he might win.
>
> **Energetic:** Nathan will likely attend the Communication Department's Honors Banquet and might win a journalism scholarship.

Negative Constructions

Sentences constructed upon the negatives *no, not, neither/nor* can be wordy and difficult to understand. It's simpler to state what *is* the case.

> **Negative:** During my four years on the newspaper staff, *I have not been* behind in making significant contributions. My editorial skills *have* certainly *not deteriorated,* as I have *never failed* to tackle challenging assignments.
>
> **Positive:** During my four years on the newspaper staff, *I have made* significant contributions. My editorial skills have steadily *developed* as I *have tackled* difficult assignments.

Avoiding Imprecise, Misleading, and Biased Words

As you edit your writing, check your choice of words carefully. The information on the next five pages will help you edit for word choice.

Substitute specific words.

Replace vague nouns and verbs with words that generate clarity and energy.

Specific Nouns

Make it a habit to use specific nouns for subjects. General nouns *(woman, school)* give the reader a vague, uninteresting picture. More specific nouns *(actress, university)* give the reader a better picture. Finally, very specific nouns *(Meryl Streep, Notre Dame)* are the type that can make your writing clear and colorful.

General to Specific Nouns			
Person	**Place**	**Thing**	**Idea**
woman	school	book	theory
actor	university	novel	scientific theory
Meryl Streep	Notre Dame	*Pride and Prejudice*	relativity

Vivid Verbs

Like nouns, verbs can be too general to create a vivid word picture. For example, the verb *looked* does not say the same thing as *stared, glared, glanced,* or *peeked.*

- Whenever possible, use a verb that is strong enough to stand alone without the help of an adverb.

    Verb and adverb: John fell down in the student lounge.
    Vivid verb: John collapsed in the student lounge.

- Avoid overusing the "be" verbs *(is, are, was, were)* and helping verbs. Often a main verb can be made from another word in the same sentence.

    A "be" verb: Cole is someone who follows international news.
    A stronger verb: Cole follows international news.

- Use active rather than passive verbs. (Use passive verbs only if you want to downplay who is performing the action in a sentence. See page 79.)

    Passive verb: Another provocative essay was submitted by Kim.
    Active verb: Kim submitted another provocative essay.

- Use verbs that show rather than tell.

    A verb that tells: Dr. Lewis is very thorough.
    A verb that shows: Dr. Lewis prepares detailed, interactive lectures.

Replace jargon and clichés.

Replace language that is overly technical or difficult to understand. Also replace overused, worn-out words.

Understandable Language

Jargon is language used in a certain profession or by a particular group of people. It may be acceptable to use if your audience is that group of people, but to most ears jargon will sound technical and unnatural.

> **Jargon:** The bottom line is that our output is not within our game plan.
> **Clear:** Production is not on schedule.
>
> **Jargon:** I'm having conceptual difficulty with these academic queries.
> **Clear:** I don't understand these review questions.

Fresh and Original Writing

Clichés are overused words or phrases. They give the reader no fresh view and no concrete picture. Because clichés spring quickly to mind (for both the writer and the reader), they are easy to write and often fail to convey a precise meaning.

an axe to grind	piece of cake
as good as dead	planting the seed
beat around the bush	rearing its ugly head
between a rock and a hard place	stick your neck out
burning bridges	throwing your weight around
easy as pie	up a creek without a paddle

Purpose and Voice

Other aspects of your writing may also be tired and overworked. Be alert to the two types of clichés described below.

Clichés of Purpose:

- Sentimental papers gushing about an ideal friend or family member, or droning on about a moving experience
- Overused topics with recycled information and predictable examples

Clichés of Voice:

- Writing that assumes a false sense of authority: "I have determined that there are three basic types of newspapers. My preference is for the third."
- Writing that speaks with little or no sense of authority: "I flipped when I saw *Viewpoints*."
- Writing that is pretentious: "Because I have researched the topic thoroughly, readers should not question my conclusion."

Change biased words.

When depicting individuals or groups according to their differences, use language that implies equal value and respect for all people.

Words Referring to Ethnicity

Acceptable General Terms	Acceptable Specific Terms
American Indians, Native Americans	**Cherokee people, Inuit people,** and so forth
Asian Americans (not Orientals)	**Chinese Americans, Japanese Americans,** and so forth
Latinos, Latinas	**Mexican Americans, Cubans**
Hispanics	**Americans,** and so forth

African Americans, blacks
"African American" has come into wide acceptance, though the term "black" is preferred by some individuals.

Anglo Americans (English ancestry), European Americans
Use these terms to avoid the notion that "American," used alone, means "white."

Not Recommended	Preferred
Eurasian, mulatto	**person of mixed ancestry**
nonwhite	**person of color**
Caucasian	**white**
American (to mean U.S. citizen)	**U.S. citizen**

fig. 6.2

Words Referring to Age

Age Group	Acceptable Terms
up to age 13 or 14	**boys, girls**
between 13 and 19	**youth, young people, young men, young women**
late teens and 20s	**young adults, young women, young men**
30s to age 60	**adults, men, women**
60 and older	**older adults, older people** (not elderly)
65 and older	**seniors** (senior citizens also acceptable)

fig. 6.3

Words Referring to Disabilities or Impairments

In the recent past, some writers were choosing alternatives to the term *disabled,* including *physically challenged, exceptional,* or *special.* However, it is not generally held that these new terms are precise enough to serve those who live with disabilities. Of course, degrading labels such as *crippled, invalid,* and *maimed,* as well as overly negative terminology, must be avoided.

Not Recommended	Preferred
handicapped	disabled
birth defect	congenital disability
stutter, stammer, lisp	speech impairment
an AIDS victim	person with AIDS
suffering from cancer	person who has cancer
mechanical foot	prosthetic foot
false teeth	dentures

Words Referring to Conditions

People with various disabilities and conditions have sometimes been referred to as though they were their condition (quadriplegics, depressives, epileptics) instead of people who happen to have a particular disability. As much as possible, remember to refer to the person first, the disability second.

Not Recommended	Preferred
the disabled	people with disabilities
cripples	people who have difficulty walking
the retarded	people with a developmental disability
dyslexics	students with dyslexia
neurotics	patients with neuroses
subjects, cases	participants, patients
quadriplegics	people who are quadriplegic
wheelchair users	people who use wheelchairs

Additional Terms

Make sure you understand the following terms that address specific impairments:

hearing impairment	=	partial hearing loss, hard of hearing (not deaf, which is total loss of hearing)
visual impairment	=	partially sighted (not blind, which is total loss of vision)
communicative disorder	=	speech, hearing, and learning disabilities affecting communication

Words Referring to Gender

- Use parallel language for both genders:

  The **men** and the **women** rebuilt the school together.

  Hank and **Marie**

  Mr. Robert Gumble, Mrs. Joy Gumble

Note: The courtesy titles Mr., Ms., Mrs., and Miss ought to be used according to the person's preference.

- Use nonsexist alternatives to words with masculine connotations:

  humanity (not *mankind*)   **synthetic** (not *man-made*)

  artisan (not *craftsman*)

- Do not use masculine-only or feminine-only pronouns *(he, she, his, her)* when you want to refer to a human being in general:

  A politician can kiss privacy good-bye when **he** runs for office.

  (not recommended)

Instead, use *he* or *she*, change the sentence to plural, or eliminate the pronoun:

  A politician can kiss privacy good-bye when **he** or **she** runs for office.

  Politicians can kiss privacy good-bye when **they** run for office.

  A politician can kiss privacy good-bye when running for office.

- Do not use gender-specific references in the salutation of a business letter when you don't know the person's name:

  Dear Sir: Dear Gentlemen: (neither is recommended)

Instead, address a position:

  Dear Personnel Officer:

  Dear Members of the Economic Committee:

Occupational Issues

Not Recommended	Preferred
chairman	chair, presiding officer, moderator
salesman	sales representative, salesperson
clergyman	minister, priest, rabbi
male/female nurse	nurse
male/female doctor	doctor, physician
mailman	mail carrier, postal worker, letter carrier
insurance man	insurance agent
fireman	firefighter
businessman	executive, manager, businessperson
congressman	member of Congress, representative, senator
steward, stewardess	flight attendant
policeman, policewoman	police officer

Proofreading Your Writing

The following guidelines will help you check your revised writing for spelling, mechanics, usage, grammar, and form.

Review punctuation and mechanics.

1. **Check for proper use of commas** before coordinating conjunctions in compound sentences, after introductory clauses and long introductory phrases, between items in a series, and so on.
2. **Look for apostrophes** in contractions, plurals, and possessive nouns.
3. **Examine quotation marks** in quoted information, titles, or dialogue.
4. **Watch for proper use of capital letters** for first words in written conversation and for proper names of people, places, and things.

Look for usage and grammar errors.

1. **Look for words that writers commonly misuse:** *there/their/they're; accept/except.*
2. **Check for verb use.** Subjects and verbs should agree in number: Singular subjects go with singular verbs; plural subjects go with plural verbs. Verb tenses should be consistent throughout.
3. **Review for pronoun/antecedent agreement problems.** A pronoun and its antecedent must agree in number.

Check for spelling errors.

1. **Use a spell checker.** Your spell checker will catch most errors.
2. **Check each spelling you are unsure of.** Especially check those proper names and other special words your spell checker won't know.
3. **Consult a handbook.** Refer to a list of commonly misspelled words, as well as an up-to-date dictionary.

Check the writing for form and presentation.

1. **Note the title.** A title should be appropriate and lead into the writing.
2. **Examine any quoted or cited material.** Are all sources of information properly presented and documented? (See pages 493–534 and 535–564.)
3. **Look over the finished copy of your writing.** Does it meet the requirements for a final manuscript?

Critical-Thinking and Writing Activities

As directed by your instructor, complete the following activities.

1. The nineteenth-century British writer Matthew Arnold offers this advice to writers about refining their writing: "Have something to say and say it as clearly as you can. That is the only secret of style." Does your own writing clearly communicate a meaningful message? Explain why or why not.

2. Choose a writing assignment that you have recently completed. Edit the sentences in this writing for style and correctness using pages 92–99 as a guide. Then use pages 100–104 in this chapter to edit the piece of writing for vague words, jargon, clichés, and biased language.

3. Combine some of the following ideas into longer, more mature sentences. Write at least four sentences, using page 93 as a guide.

   > Dogs can be difficult to train. The necessary supplies include a leash and treats. Patience is also a necessity. Dogs like to please their owners. Training is not a chore for dogs. A well-trained dog is a pleasure to its owner.

Learning-Objectives Checklist ✓

Have you achieved this chapter's learning objectives? Check your progress with the items below, revisiting topics in the chapter as needed. *I have . . .*

____ re-examined the overall style of my revised draft, including how well that style fits the rhetorical situation (92).

____ combined short, simplistic sentences through techniques of coordination and subordination (93).

____ expanded sparse sentences by making them cumulative, building them up with meaningful and rich details (94).

____ transformed weak sentences by varying sentence openings, lengths, types, and arrangements (95–97).

____ re-formulated sentences to strengthen parallel structure of coordinating elements (98).

____ re-written sentences weakened by nominalizations, expletives, and negative constructions (99).

____ replaced vague terms with precise nouns and vivid verbs (100).

____ replaced jargon with understandable language and clichés with fresh, original phrasing (101).

____ replaced any terms showing bias with respect to ethnicity, age, disabilities, health conditions, gender, and occupations (102–104).

Chapter 7

Submitting Writing and Creating Portfolios

Submitting your writing might be as simple as handing it in to your instructor or posting it to a class wiki, or it might be as involved as submitting it to a journal in your area of study or assembling it with your other works to publish in a portfolio. Whatever the case, sharing your writing makes all the work you have done worthwhile. As writer Tom Liner states, "You learn ways to improve your writing by seeing its effect on others."

This chapter will help you prepare your writing for submission and sharing. When you make your writing public—in whatever form—you are *publishing* it.

Visually Speaking   Packages, packaging, packing—how is Figure 7.1 suggestive of what happens at the end of the writing process?

Learning **Objectives**

By working through this chapter, you will be able to

- design the format and layout of your writing.
- choose an appropriate submission method.
- integrate your writing into a portfolio.

Dmitry Kalinovsky / Shutterstock.com

fig. 7.1

Formatting Your Writing

A good page design makes your writing clear and easy to follow. Keep that in mind when you produce a final copy of your writing.

Strive for clarity in page design.

Examine the following design elements, making sure that each is appropriate and clear in your project and in your writing.

Format and Documentation

- **Keep the design clear and uncluttered.** Aim for a sharp, polished look in all your assigned writing.
- **Use the designated documentation form.** Follow all the requirements outlined in the MLA (pages 493–534) or APA (pages 535–564) style guides.

Typography

- **Use an easy-to-read serif font for the main text.** Serif type, **like this**, has "tails" at the tops and bottoms of the letters. For most writing, use a 10- or 12-point type size.
- **Consider using a sans serif font for the title and headings.** In traditional academic writing, typeface and type size should remain consistent throughout (e.g., 12-point Times New Roman.) For other documents, however, consider sans serif type and different sizes for headings. Sans serif type, **like this**, does not have "tails." Use larger, perhaps 18-point, type for your title and 14-point type for any headings. You can also use boldface for headings if they seem to get lost on the page. (Follow your instructor's formatting guidelines.)

 Because most people find a sans serif font easier to read on screen, consider a sans serif font for the body and a serif font for the titles and headings in any writing you publish online.

Spacing

- **Follow all requirements for indents and margins.** This usually means indenting the first line of each paragraph five spaces, maintaining a one-inch margin around each page, and double-spacing throughout the paper.
- **Avoid widows and orphans.** Avoid leaving headings, hyphenated words, or single lines (widows) of new paragraphs alone at the bottom of a page. Also avoid single words (orphans) at the bottom of a page or carried over to the top of a new page.

Graphic Devices

- **Create bulleted or numbered lists to highlight individual items in a list.** But, be selective, using traditional paragraphs when they help you more effectively communicate your message. Writing should not include too many lists.
- **Include charts or other graphics.** Graphics should be neither so small that they get lost on the page, nor so large that they overpower the page.

Submitting Writing and Creating Portfolios

Once you have formatted and proofread your final draft, you should be ready to share your writing. For college assignments, you will often simply turn in your paper to your instructor. However, you should also think about sharing your writing with other audiences, including those who will want to see your writing portfolio.

Consider potential audiences.

You could receive helpful feedback by taking any of the following steps:

- Share your writing with peers or family members.
- Submit your work to a local publication or an online journal.
- Post your writing on an appropriate Web site, including your own.
- Turn in your writing to your instructor.

Select appropriate submission methods.

There are two basic methods for submitting your work.

- **Paper submission:** Print an error-free copy on quality paper.
- **Electronic submission:** If allowed, send your writing as an email attachment.

Use a writing portfolio.

There are two basic types of writing portfolios: (1) *a working portfolio* in which you store documents at various stages of development, and (2) *a showcase portfolio* with which you share appropriate finished work. For example, you could submit a portfolio to complete course requirements or to apply for a scholarship, graduate program, or job. The documents below are commonly included in a showcase portfolio:

- A table of contents listing the pieces included in your portfolio
- An opening essay or letter detailing the story behind your portfolio (how you compiled it and why it features the qualities expected by the intended reader)
- A specified number of—and types of—finished pieces
- A cover sheet attached to each piece of writing, discussing the reason for its selection, the amount of work that went into it, and so on
- Evaluation sheets or checklists charting the progress or experience you want to show related to issues of interest to the reader

Tashatuvango / Shutterstock.com

Critical-Thinking and Writing Activities

As directed by your instructor, complete the following critical-thinking and writing activities by yourself or with classmates.

1. Catherine Drinker Bowen has argued the following: "Writing is not apart from living. Writing is a kind of double living." As you think about sharing your own writing and adding it to your writing portfolio, does this claim ring true? Why or why not?

2. Choose one of your recent writing assignments and use the instructions on page 108 to assess the quality of your formatting and page design. Edit and redesign the paper as needed.

3. For the class in which you are using this book, begin two working portfolios: (1) an electronic portfolio on your computer and (2) a paper portfolio in a sturdy folder or binder. In the electronic portfolio, store all drafts of your assignments, as well as all related electronic correspondence with your instructor. In your paper portfolio, store all printed drafts of your work, including copies that show your instructor's notations and grades.

Learning-Objectives Checklist ✓

Have you achieved this chapter's learning objectives? Check your progress with the items below, revisiting topics in the chapter as needed. *I have*...

_____ produced a clear, reader-friendly page design by developing an overall format that fits the writing assignment and form, following the requirements of a specific style such as MLA or APA, making typographical choices that enhance readability, creating white space as needed, and effectively designing and integrating graphics (108).

_____ chosen a submission method, whether paper or digital, that meets readers' needs and the assignment expectations (109).

_____ integrated my writing into a portfolio, whether a working or showcase portfolio, so as to track and demonstrate my growth as a writer (109).

Cross-Curricular Connections

How does writing a paper in your discipline establish your position in the research community? How does adding a paper to your portfolio establish your position in your writing career?

Chapter 8

One Writer's Process

An essay is an attempt to understand a topic more deeply and clearly. That's one of the reasons this basic form of writing is essential in many college courses. It's a tool for both discovering and communicating.

How do you move from an assignment to a finished, polished essay? The best strategy is to take matters one step at a time, from understanding the assignment to submitting the final draft. Don't try to churn out the essay the night before it's due.

This chapter shows how student writer Angela Franco followed the writing process outlined in chapters 2 through 7.

Visually Speaking A rotary or roundabout (Figure 8.1) effectively controls the flow of traffic. How might writing be thought of as involving a flow of traffic? In what ways does the writing process involve rotaries?

Learning **Objectives**

By working through this chapter, you will be able to

- explain how one writer worked through the writing process to complete an assignment.

- compare this student's process with your own.

- assess how the writing process might help you complete college assignments.

Malota / Shutterstock.com

fig. 8.1

Angela's Assignment and Response

In this chapter, you will follow student Angela Franco as she writes an assigned essay for her Environmental Policies class. Start by carefully reading the assignment and discussion below, noting how she thinks through the rhetorical situation.

Angela examined the assignment.

Angela carefully read her assignment and responded with the notes below.

> "Explain in a two- to three-page essay how a local environmental issue is relevant to the world community. Using *The College Writer* as your guide, format the paper and document sources in MLA style. You may seek revising help from a classmate or from the writing center."

Role
- I'm writing as a student in Environmental Policies, and as a resident of Ontario.

Subject
- The subject is a local environmental issue.

Purpose
- My purpose is to explain how the issue is relevant to all people. That means I must show how this issue affects my audience—both positively and negatively.

Form
- I need to write a two- to three-page essay—that sounds formal.
- I'll need to include a thesis statement, as well as references to my sources using MLA style.

Audience
- My audience will be people like me—neighbors, classmates, and community members.
- I'll need to keep in mind what they already know and what they need to know.

Context
- I'll use the guidelines and checklists in The College Writer to evaluate and revise my writing.
- I'll get editing feedback from Jeannie and from the writing center.

 For each step in the writing process, choose strategies that fit your writing situation. For example, a personal essay in an English class might require significant time getting started, whereas a lab report in a chemistry class might require little or none.

Angela explored and narrowed her assignment.

Angela explored her assignment and narrowed its focus by clustering and freewriting.

Angela's Cluster

When she considered environmental issues, Angela first thought of water pollution as a possible topic for her essay. After writing the phrase in the center of her page, she drew from memories, experiences, and readings to list related ideas and details. Notice how she used three different-colored inks to distinguish the topic (blue) from ideas (red) and details (green) (Figure 8.2).

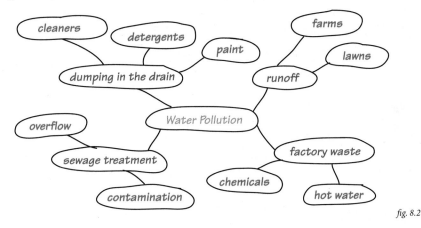

fig. 8.2

Angela's Freewriting

Angela decided to freewrite about the water pollution caused about a decade earlier by improper sewage treatment in a small Canadian town.

> I remember reading an article about problems in Walkerton, a small Ontario town. People actually died. The water they drank was contaminated. This is becoming a problem in developed countries like ours. I thought for a long time this was a problem only in developing countries. So who is responsible for sewage treatment? Who guarantees the safety of our drinking water? How does water get contaminated? Are there solutions for every kind of contamination: mercury, PCBs, sewage?

Angela's Narrowed Assignment

Based on her freewriting, Angela rephrased her assignment to narrow its focus.

> Explain in a two- to three-page essay how a local water pollution problem in a small Ontario town is relevant to the world community.

Angela's Planning

Angela reviewed her narrowed assignment and reassessed her topic.

Narrowed Writing Assignment

Explain in a two- to three-page essay how a recent water pollution problem in a small Ontario town is relevant to the world community.

Angela focused her topic.

To focus her topic, Angela answered the journalistic questions (five Ws and H).

Topic: Water pollution in a small Ontario town

Who?	- Farm operators, wastewater officials, Walkerton residents
What?	- Water supply contaminated
	- Spread bacteria (E. coli)
	- Caused disease
	- Clean, fresh water depleted
Where?	- Walkerton, Ontario
When?	- May 2000
Why?	- Improper regulation; human error
How?	- Groundwater from irrigation, untreated sewage, and runoff

Angela researched the topic.

Angela then did some research to check her information and collect more details for her paper. She recorded all the essential data on each source following MLA format and then listed the specific details related to her topic. Here's one source:

"Inside Walkerton: Canada's worst ever E. coli contamination." CBC News. 17 May 2010. Web. 13 September 2013.
- May 15—water sampled
- May 17—first patients with flu-like symptoms
- May 18—Lab confirms E. coli contamination in water, but Public Utilities Commission (PUC) does not report information.
- May 19—Medical Health Office (MHO) discovers E. coli outbreak, but is assured by the PUC that the water is safe.
- May 20—At least 40 people treated at hospital with bloody diarrhea, but PUC says twice that water is safe.
- May 21—MHO tells people not to drink water, runs their own test.
- May 23—MHO finds E. coli, learns of May 18 memo, and that chlorinator not working for some time.
- May 24—Three adults and a baby die of E. coli.

Angela decided how to organize her writing.

With a focus selected, Angela used the three guidelines below to choose the best organizational pattern for her writing.

Guidelines

1. **Review your assignment** and record your response.

   Assignment:
   Explain in a two- to three-page essay how a recent environmental issue is relevant to the world community.

   Response:
   My assignment clearly states that I need to explain my topic, so I have a general idea of how my paper will be organized.

2. **Decide on your thesis statement** and think about your essay's possible content and organization.

   Thesis Statement:
   The water pollution incident in Walkerton, Ontario, had a devastating effect that every town should learn from.

   Reflection:
   After reading my thesis statement, it's obvious that I'm going to be writing about a problem and its causes.

3. **Choose an overall method** and reflect on its potential effectiveness.

   Reflection:
   Looking at the list of methods, I see that I can use cause/effect or problem/solution. After making two quick lists of my main points using both approaches, I decided to use a problem/ solution approach. I will still talk about causes and effects in my essay—they just won't be front and center.

   With problem/solution, I need to first present the problem clearly so that readers can fully understand it and see why it's important. Then I need to explore solutions to the problem—maybe what they did in Walkerton and what we all need to do to make water safe.

fyi Many essays you write will be organized according to one basic method or approach. However, within that basic structure you may want to include other methods. For example while developing a comparison essay you may do some describing or classifying. In other words, you should choose methods of development that (1) help you understand the topic and (2) help your reader understand your message.

Andreas berheide / Shutterstock.com

Angela's First Draft

After composing her opening, middle, and closing paragraphs, Angela put together her first draft. She then added a working title.

Water Woes

> *The writer uses a series of images to get the reader's attention.*

It's a hot day. Several people just finished mowing their lawns. A group of bicyclists—more than 3,000—have been passing through your picturesque town all afternoon. Dozens of Little Leaguers are batting, running, and sweating. What do all these people have in common? They all drinks lots of tap water, especially on hot summer days. They also take for granted that the water is clean and safe. But in reality, the water they drink could be contaminated and pose a serious health risk. **That's just what happened in Walkerton, Ontario, where a water pollution incident had a devastating effect that every town can learn from.**

> *The thesis statement (boldfaced) introduces the subject.*

> *The writer describes the cause of the problem.*

What happened in Walkerton Ontario? Heavy rains fell on May 12. It wasn't until May 21 that the townspeople were advised to boil their drinking water. The rains washed cattle manure into the town well. The manure contained E coli, a type of bacteria. E coli is harmless to cattle. It can make people sick. Seven days after the heavy rains, people began calling public health officials. The warning came too late. Two people had already died (Wickens).

> *The writer indicates some of her source material with a citation.*

Once Walkerton's problem was identified, the solutions were known. The government acted quickly to help the community and to clean the water supply. One Canadian newspaper reported that a $100,000 emergency fund was set up to help families with expenses. Bottled water for drinking and containers of bleach for sanitizing and cleaning were donated by local businesses.

So what messed up Walkerton? Basically, people screwed up! According to one news story, a flaw in the water treatment system allowed the bacteria-infested water to enter the well. The manure washed into the well, but the chlorine should have killed the deadly bacteria. In Walkerton, the PUC group fell asleep at the wheel.

1

2

3

4

> *The writer covers the solutions that were used to resolve the problem.*

At last, the Provincial Clean Water Agency restored the main water and   5
sewage systems by flushing out all of the town's pipes and wells. The ban on
drinking Walkerton's water was finally lifted seven months after the water became
contaminated.

> *The concluding paragraph stresses the importance of public awareness.*

Could any good come from Walkerton's tragedy? Does it have a silver lining?   6
It is possible that more people are aware that water may be contaminated. Today
people are beginning to take responsibility for the purity of the water they and their
families drink. In the end, more and more people will know about the dangers of
contaminated water—without learning it the hard way.

Angela kept a working bibliography.

As she researched her topic, Angela kept a working bibliography—a list of resources that she thought might offer information helpful to her essay. From the start, she formatted the entries in MLA style. During the writing process, she deleted some resources, added others, and edited the document that became the works-cited list on page 126.

Working Bibliography

Blackwell, Thomas. "Walkerton Doctor Defends Response." *The Edmonton Journal*.

9 Jan. 2001. Web. 13 Sept. 2013.

"Inside Walkerton: Canada's Worst Ever E.coli Contamination." *CBC News*. 17 May

2010. Web. 13 Sept. 2013.

Johnson, Alex. Personal interview. 14 Sept. 2013

Angela's First Revision

After finishing the first draft, Angela set it aside. When she was ready to revise it, she looked carefully at global issues—ideas, organization, and voice. She wrote notes to herself to help keep her thoughts together.

Angela's comments

I need to give my opening more energy.

Does my thesis still fit the paper?— Yes.

Using time sequence, put this paragraph in better order.

Move this paragraph — it interrupts the discussion of causes.

My voice here is too informal.

Water Woes

It's a hot day. *an unusually* *Saturday afternoon* Several people just finished mowing their lawns. A group of bicyclists *pedal up the street* —more than 3,000— have been passing through your picturesque town all afternoon. Dozens of Little Leaguers are batting, running, and sweating. What do all these people have in common? They all drinks lots of tap water, especially on hot summer days. They also take for granted that the water is clean and safe. But in reality, the water they drink could be contaminated and pose a serious health risk. **That's just what happened in Walkerton, Ontario, where a water pollution incident had a devastating effect that every town can learn from.**

What happened in Walkerton Ontario? Heavy rains fell on May 12. It wasn't until May 21 that the townspeople were advised to boil their drinking water. The rains washed cattle manure into the town well. The manure contained E coli, a type of bacteria. E coli is harmless to cattle. It can make people sick. Seven days after the heavy rains, people began calling public health officials. The warning came too late. Two people had already died (Wickens).

Once Walkerton's problem was identified, the solutions were known. The government acted quickly to help the community and to clean the water supply. One Canadian newspaper reported that a $100,000 emergency fund was set up to help families with expenses. Bottled water for drinking and containers of bleach for sanitizing and cleaning were donated by local businesses.

went wrong in *Human error was a critical factor.* *First,* So what messed up Walkerton? Basically, people screwed up. According to one news story, a flaw in the water treatment system allowed the bacteria-infested water *Even after* to enter the well. The manure washed into the well, but the chlorine should have killed the deadly bacteria. In Walkerton, the PUC group fell asleep at the wheel.

1

2

3

4

Explain "fell asleep." Move paragraph three here and combine.

In addition
~~At last,~~ the Provincial Clean Water Agency restored the main water and sewage systems by flushing out all of the town's pipes and wells. The ban on drinking Walkerton's water was finally lifted seven months after the water became contaminated.

5

Cut the clichés.

Could any good come from Walkerton's tragedy? ~~Does it have a silver lining?~~ It is possible that more people are aware that water may be contaminated. Today people are beginning to take responsibility for the purity of the water they and their families drink. In the end, more and more people will know about the dangers of contaminated water—without learning it the hard way.

6

the Public Utilities Commission was responsible for overseeing the testing and treating of the town's water, but they failed to monitor it properly. Apparently, shortcuts were taken when tracking the water's chlorine level, and as a result, some of the water samples were mislabeled. There was also a significant delay between the time that the contamination was identified and the time it was reported.

Angela's Second Revision

Angela revised her draft, taking into account the questions and suggestions she received from a peer. His comments are in the margin, and Angela's changes, including a new opening and closing, are in red.

Reviewer's comments

Angela's Changes

Water Woes

Could you make the opening more relevant and urgent?

WARNING: City tap water is polluted with animal waste. Using the water for drinking, cooking, or bathing could cause sickness or death.   1

According to the Seirra Club, run-off pollutants from farm cites are   2 steadily seeping into our streams, lakes, reservoirs and wells. Because much of our drinking water comes from these resources, warnings like the one above are already posted in a number of U.S. and Canadian communities, and many more postings will be needed ("Water Sentinels").

Could you clarify your focus on the topic?

As the Seirra Club argues, the pollution and related warnings are serious, and failure to take them seriously could be deadly. For example, a few years ago the citizens of Walkerton Ontario learned that the water that they believed to be clean was actually poisoned.

The events   began   , 2000, when heavy rains
~~What happened~~ in Walkerton, ~~Ontario? Heavy rains fell~~ on May 12. ~~The rains~~   3
washed cattle manure into the town well. The manure contained E coli, a type of bacteria. E coli is harmless to cattle. It can make people sick. Seven days after the
                                       to complain of nausea and diarrhea ⊙
heavy rains, people began calling public health officials. It wasn't until May 21 that
the townspeople were advised to boil their drinking water. The warning came too
                     , and more than 2,000 were ill
late. Two people had already died (Wickens).

Add the year and other specific details.

Make sure you document all source material— you have just one citation in your draft.

Several factors contributed to the terrible tragedy in Walkerton, including human error.
∧ ~~So what went wrong in Walkerton? Human error was a~~ critical factor. First,   4
     The Edmonton Journal
according to ~~one news story,~~ a flaw in the water treatment system allowed the
bacteria-infested water to enter the well. Even after the manure washed into the
                                       (Blackwell) ⊙
well, the chlorine should have killed the deadly bacteria. In Walkerton, the Public
Utilities Commission was responsible for overseeing the testing and treating of the
town's water, but it failed to monitor it properly. Apparently, shortcuts were taken
when tracking the water's chlorine level, and as a result, some of the water samples

were mislabeled. There was also a significant delay between the time that the contamination was identified and the time it was reported.

Once Walkerton's problem was identified, ~~the solutions were known.~~ The   5
government acted quickly to help the community~~, and to clean the water supply.~~
The Edmonton Journal
~~One Canadian newspaper~~ reported a $100,000 emergency fund was set up to help
                         Local businesses donated
families with expenses. Bottled water for drinking and containers of bleach for basic sanitizing and cleaning ~~were donated by local businesses.~~ In addition, the Provincial Clean Water Agency restored the main water and sewage systems by flushing out all of the town's pipes and wells. The ban on drinking Walkerton's water was finally lifted seven months after the water became contaminated.

Use active voice.

Consider adding details— maybe an entire paragraph— calling readers to action, and stating your thesis clearly.

As the Sierra Club warned and the citizens of Walkerton learned, water   6
purity is a life-and-death issue. Fortunately, both the United States and Canada have been addressing the problem. For example, since 2001, more states and provinces are tightening their clean-water standards, more communities have begun monitoring their water quality, and more individuals have been using water-filtration systems, bottled water, or boiled tap water. However, a tragedy like that in Walkerton could happen again. To avoid such horror, all of us must get involved by demanding clean tap water in our communities and by promoting the polices and procedures needed to achieve that goal.

Angela's Edited Draft

When Angela began editing, she read each of her sentences aloud to check for clarity and smoothness. **The first page of Angela's edited copy is shown below.**

The writer revises the title.

in Walkerton
Water Woes‸

> **Warning: City tap water is polluted with animal waste. Using the water for drinking, cooking, or bathing could cause sickness or death.**   *1*

According to the Seirra Club, run-off pollutants from farm cites are steadily   *2*

seeping into our streams, lakes, reservoirs‸and wells. Because much of our drinking

She qualifies her statement, replacing "will" with "might."

water comes from these resources, warnings like the one above are already posted

might

in a number of U.S. and Canadian communities, and many more postings ~~will~~ be

in the future

‸~~needed~~("Water Sentinels). As the Seirra Club argues, the pollution and related

warnings are serious, and failure to take them seriously could be deadly. For

example, a few years ago the citizens of Walkerton Ontario learned that the water

tragically

that they believed to be clean was ~~actually~~ poisoned.

The events in Walkerton began on May 12, 2000, when heavy rains washed   *3*

commonly called

She rewrites and combines several choppy sentences.

cattle manure into the town well. The manure contained ~~E. coli~~ a bacteria‸E. coli.

While E. coli

‸is harmless to cattle. ‸It can make people sick. Seven days after the heavy rains,

people began calling public health officials to complain of nausea and diarrhea. It

wasn't until May 21 that the townspeople were advised to boil their drinking water.

The warning came too late. Two people had already died, and more than 2,000 were

ill (Wickens).

Several factors contributed to the ~~terrible~~ tragedy in Walkerton, including   *4*

Angela deletes unnecessary words.

human error. First, according to *The Edmonton Journal*, a flaw in the water

treatment system allowed the ~~bacteria~~ infested water to enter the well (Blackwell).

Even after the manure washed into the well, the chlorine . . .

Angela's Proofread Draft

Angela reviewed her edited copy for punctuation, agreement issues, and spelling. **The first page of Angela's proofread essay is shown below.**

Water Woes in Walkerton

> **Warning: City tap water is polluted with animal waste. Using the water for drinking, cooking, or bathing could cause sickness or death.**

1

The writer corrects errors that the spell checker did not pick up.

According to the Sierra Club, run-off pollutants from farm sites are steadily seeping into our streams, lakes, reservoirs, and wells. Because much of our drinking water comes from these resources, warnings like the one above are already posted in a number of U.S. and Canadian communities, and many more postings might be needed in the future ("Water Sentinels"). As the Sierra Club argues, the pollution and related warnings are serious, and failure to take them seriously could be deadly.

2

She adds a comma between the city and province.

For example, a few years ago the citizens of Walkerton, Ontario, learned that the water that they believed to be clean was tragically poisoned.

She adds periods and italicizes "E. coli" to show that it is a scientific term.

The events in Walkerton began on May 12, 2000, when heavy rains washed cattle manure into the town well. The manure contained bacteria commonly called *E. coli*. While *E. coli* is harmless to cattle, it can make people sick. Seven days after the heavy rains, people began calling public health officials to complain of nausea and diarrhea. It wasn't until May 21 that the townspeople were advised to boil their drinking water. The warning came too late. Two people had already died, and more than 2,000 were ill (Wickens).

3

She adds a word for clarity.

Several factors contributed to the tragedy in Walkerton, including human error. First, according to *The Edmonton Journal*, a flaw in the water treatment system allowed the infested water to enter Walkerton's well (Blackwell). Even after the manure washed into Walkerton's well, the chlorine should have . . .

4

Angela's Finished Essay

After proofreading and formatting her essay, Angela added a heading and page numbers. She also added more documentation and a works-cited list at the end.

Franco 1

Angela Franco

Professor Kim Van Es

English 101

18 October 2013

The writer revises the title.

Clean Water Is Everyone's Business

The warning is emphasized with red print.

> **Warning: City tap water is polluted with animal waste.**
>
> **Using the water for drinking, cooking, or bathing**
>
> **could cause sickness or death.**

An appropriate font and type size are used.

According to the Sierra Club, run-off pollutants from farm sites are steadily   1
seeping into our streams, lakes, reservoirs, and wells. Because much of our drinking
water comes from these resources, warnings like the one above are already posted
in a number of U.S. and Canadian communities, and many more postings might be
needed in the future ("Water Sentinels"). As the Sierra Club argues, the pollution
and related warnings are serious, and failure to take them seriously could be deadly.
For example, a few years ago the citizens of Walkerton, Ontario, learned that the
water that they believed to be clean was tragically poisoned.

The events in Walkerton began on May 12, 2000, when heavy rains washed   2
cattle manure into the town well. The manure contained the bacteria commonly
called *E. coli*. While *E. coli* is harmless to cattle, it can make people sick. Seven days
after the heavy rains, people began calling public health officials to complain of
nausea and diarrhea. It wasn't until May 21 that the townspeople were advised to

Franco 2

Title and page number are cited on each page.

boil their drinking water. The warning came too late. Two people had already died, and more than 2,000 were ill (Wickens).

Several factors contributed to the tragedy in Walkerton, including human error. First, according to *The Edmonton Journal,* a flaw in the water treatment system allowed the infested water to enter Walkerton's well (Blackwell). Even after the manure washed into Walkerton's well, the chlorine should have killed the deadly bacteria. In Walkerton, the Public Utilities Commission was responsible for overseeing the testing and treating of the town's water, but it failed to monitor the procedure properly ("Walkerton's Water-Safety"). Apparently, shortcuts were taken when tracking the water's chlorine level, and as a result, some of the water samples were mislabeled. There was also a significant delay between the time that the contamination was identified and the time it was reported.

Each claim or supporting point is backed up with reasoning and evidence.

Once Walkerton's problem was identified, the government acted quickly to help the community. In its December 7, 2000, edition, *The Edmonton Journal* reported that a $100,000 emergency fund was set up to help families with expenses. Local businesses donated bottled water for drinking and containers of bleach for basic sanitizing and cleaning. In addition, the Provincial Clean Water Agency restored the main water and sewage systems by flushing out all of the town's pipes and wells. Seven months after the water became contaminated, the ban on drinking Walkerton's water was finally lifted.

The writer continues to give credit throughout the essay.

As the Sierra Club warns and the citizens of Walkerton learned, water purity is a life-and-death issue. Fortunately, both the United States and Canada have

3

4

5

Franco 3

been addressing the problem. For example, since 2001, more states and provinces have been tightening their clean-water standards, more communities have been monitoring their water quality, and more individuals have been using water-filtration systems, bottled water, or boiled tap water. However, a tragedy like that in Walkerton could happen again. To avoid such horror, all of us must get involved by demanding clean tap water in our communities and by promoting the policies and procedures needed to achieve that goal.

The writer restates her thesis in the last sentence.

Franco 4

Works Cited

Blackwell, Thomas. "Walkerton Doctor Defends Response." *The Edmonton Journal.* 9 Jan. 2001. Web. 13 Sept. 2013.

"Walkerton's Water-Safety Tests Falsified Regularly, Utility Official Admits." *The Edmonton Journal.* 7 Dec. 2000. Web. 13 Sept. 2013.

"Water Sentinels: Keeping It Clean around the U.S.A." Sierraclub.org. *Sierra Club.* n.d. Web. 15 Sept. 2013.

Wickens, Barbara. "Tragedy in Walkerton." *Maclean's* 5 June 2000. Web. 14 Sept. 2013.

Sources used are listed correctly, in alphabetical order.

Each entry follows MLA rules for content, format, and punctuation.

Critical-Thinking and Writing Activities

Complete these activities by yourself or with classmates.

1. Scott Russell Sanders suggests that "essays are experiments in making sense of things." Does Sanders' statement ring true? What makes such experiments flop or succeed? What kinds of "sense" do essays create?

2. Review Angela's writing process. How does it compare with your own writing process on a recent assignment?

3. Review the peer-editing instructions in "Revising Collaboratively" (pages 87–88). Then reread the reviewer's comments in the margins of Angela's second revision (pages 120–121). Do the comments reflect the instructions? Explain.

Learning-Objectives Checklist ✓

Have you achieved this chapter's learning objectives? Check your progress with the items below, revisiting topics in the chapter as needed. *I have* . . .

____ analyzed how Angela Franco worked through the writing process:
- examining the assignment (112)
- narrowing the topic (113)
- researching her topic and organizing her thoughts (114–115)
- completing her first draft (116–117)
- revising the draft by herself and then through peer review (118–121)
- and editing and proofreading her essay (122–126).

____ compared Angela's process with the process that I normally follow, considering strengths and weaknesses of my own approach.

____ assessed how I might tailor the writing process shown by Angela and outlined in chapters 2–7 to my own writing habits and my college writing assignments.

Cross-Curricular Connections

Angela used MLA style, which is standard for English and the humanities. By contrast, APA is standard for the social sciences: psychology, sociology, political science, and education. Make sure to find out what documentation style your instructor requires.

Traits of College Writing: A Checklist

Early in chapter 2, you learned about the common traits of excellent college writing (pages 30–31). The following checklist is a reminder of those traits. You can use it to check any of your finished writing assignments.

Stimulating Ideas   *The writing . . .*

____ presents interesting and important information.

____ maintains a clear focus or purpose—centered on a thesis, theme, concern, or question.

____ develops the focus through a line of thought or reasoning elaborated with sufficient details or evidence.

____ holds the reader's attention (and answers her or his questions).

Logical Organization

____ includes a clear beginning, middle, and ending.

____ contains specific details, arranged in an order that builds understanding with readers.

____ uses transitions to link sentences and paragraphs.

Engaging Voice

____ speaks in a sincere, natural way that fits the writing situation.

____ shows that the writer really cares about the subject.

Appropriate Word Choice

____ contains specific, clear words.

____ uses a level of language appropriate for the type of writing and the audience.

Overall Sentence Fluency

____ flows smoothly from sentence to sentence.

____ displays varied sentence beginnings and lengths.

____ follows a style that fits the situation (e.g., familiar versus academic).

Correct, Accurate Copy

____ adheres to the rules of grammar, spelling, and punctuation.

____ follows established documentation guidelines.

Reader-Friendly Design

____ exhibits a polished, professional design in terms of overall format, page layout, and typographical choices.

____ makes the document attractive and easy to read.

____ is formatted correctly in MLA or APA style.

II. Reader:
Strategies and Samples

Chapter 9

Forms of College Writing

In college, professors in nearly all fields give writing assignments. Why? Because they know that writing helps you learn course material today and use that knowledge in subsequent college courses and in the workplace. Similarly, college writing develops the thinking skills needed in a field of study and a profession.

This chapter begins by showing the big picture of college writing: the three divisions into which most college curricula are divided, and the academic departments that constitute each division. The chapter then offers instruction in the methods of inquiry and forms of writing typical to each division's disciplines.

Visually Speaking   Consider the analogy suggested by Figure 9.1: different forms of writing are like different modes of transportation. How far can you push the comparison?

Learning **Objectives**

By working through this chapter, you will be able to

- identify and classify fields of study in the college curriculum.
- differentiate and explain writing in the humanities, the social sciences, and the natural and applied sciences.
- analyze the nature of writing in your own field of study or a major that interests you.

Artens / Shutterstock.com

fig. 9.1

Three Curricular Divisions

Based on each department's field of study, the college curriculum is generally divided into three groups: humanities, social sciences, and natural and applied sciences. These groups are then subdivided into specific departments, such as biology, chemistry, and physics. Below you will find an explanation of each division, along with its common departments.

Humanities

Scholars and students within this division study human culture, both past and present. They examine topics such as the history of civilization, cultural institutions and trends, religious beliefs and practices, languages and their use, and artwork and performance skills. Some departments in this division include the following:

Archeology	Ethnic Studies	Modern Languages	Theater Arts
Asian Studies	Film Studies	Music	Theology
Dance	Graphic Design	Philosophy	Visual Arts
English	History	Religion	Women's Studies

Social Sciences

Scholars and students in this division study human behavior and societies using research strategies adapted from the natural sciences. For example, a researcher may develop a hypothesis regarding a topic or phenomenon, and then devise an experiment to test that hypothesis. Students study economic systems, correctional programs, and personality disorders. Departments in this division include the following:

Anthropology	Economics	Geophysics	Psychology
Business	Education	Government	Social Work
Communication	Genetics	Health & Phys. Ed.	Sociology
Criminology	Geography	Political Science	Urban Planning

Natural and Applied Sciences

The natural sciences (such as biology, zoology, and chemistry) focus on specific aspects of nature, such as animal life, plant life, and molecular structures. In contrast, the applied sciences (such as mathematics, computer science, and engineering) consider how to use science-based information to understand concepts and develop artifacts. Here are some of the departments in this division:

Agriculture	Biology	Environment	Physics
Agronomy	Botany	Forestry	Physiology
Anatomy	Chemistry	Mathematics	Public Health
Architecture	Computer Science	Nutrition	Space Science
Astronomy	Engineering	Oceanography	Zoology

Writing in the Humanities

In a humanities class (e.g., English, history, and theater arts), your study and writing likely focus on various types of texts, broadly understood: primary texts, such as poems, novels, historical records, and philosophical essays, as well as secondary sources (books and periodical articles). Such study is largely concerned with the world of ideas, whether creative, historical, or theoretical. Your writing will likely have the character described below.

The Purpose of Inquiry

Humanities study aims to understand more deeply some aspect of human experience and humanity's place in the world, whether that aspect of experience relates to the artistic and imaginative, the historical, the spiritual, the linguistic, or the world of ethics. As a result, writing in the humanities tends to be thesis-driven, focused on a central idea that is explored through coherent analysis and argument.

Forms of Humanities Writing

In humanities courses, you will likely write essays and research papers of this sort: interpretive analyses and arguments on a specific topic, theoretical studies of key concepts in the discipline, and book reviews or broader bibliographic surveys. Here are typical forms:

- **Analysis of a Text or Art Work:** Such a study closely examines a specific work in order to understand more fully what it means, how it communicates, and so on.
- **A Review of the Literature on a Topic:** This form of research writing identifies and synthesizes the studies that have been published on a specific issue or question.
- **A Book, Film, Music, or Performance Review:** Applying general criteria for excellence, reviews evaluate the quality, impact, strengths, and weaknesses of a specific text or art work.

Examples: "Latin American Music: A Diverse and Unifying Force" (page 206), "Wikipedia and the Meaning of Truth" (page 244), "Ah, the Power of Women" (page 283).

Humanities Research Methods

As the forms of writing above suggest, the humanities involve the careful "reading" of primary texts, artifacts, and events. In addition, humanities projects involve a careful investigation of past scholarship on a topic so that the writer can add his or her voice to the ongoing discussion or dialogue. With their focus on "reading," the humanities value skills of interpretation—sensitivity to the primary text, thoughtful use of evidence from the text, attention to the textual context, awareness of theoretical frameworks for understanding texts, insightful theses about texts, and the rhetorical skills involved in analysis and argument. In such research, the following resources may be especially helpful:

- "Analyzing Texts, Documents, Records, and Artifacts" (pages 432–433)
- MLA Documentation (chapter 28, pages 493–534, and www.mla.org)

Writing in the Social Sciences

In a social sciences class (e.g., psychology, sociology, business, education), your writing will likely explore some dimension of the way that people behave, individually or within groups, whether the group is just two people or an entire society. Your writing will likely have the character described below.

The Purpose of Inquiry

Broadly, the social sciences aim to understand through using an adapted version of the natural-science experimental method, the rules and conventions that govern human behavior and societies. As such, social-sciences thinking tends to be hypothesis-driven, seeking not only to describe behavior but also to predict it. To that end, the social sciences involve observing, measuring, and testing various forms of behavior.

Forms of Social-Science Writing

With their focus on behavior and social laws, social scientists typically write reports, often as teams of researchers. Here are specific types of writing that you might do:

- **A Literature Review:** This form of research writing identifies and synthesizes the studies that have been published on a specific behavioral or social issue.
- **An Experiment Report:** Such a report describes a specific experiment designed to test a hypothesis about behavior, and then share and analyze the results.
- **A Field Report:** Whether based on observations, interviews, or surveys, such a report shares insights gathered through such contact with human subjects.
- **A Case Study:** Such a study describes and examines actual individuals and situations so as to understand them more deeply.

Examples: "Dutch Discord" (page 167), "Shades of Prejudice" (page 190), "Saint Cesar of Delano" (page 226), APA model research paper (page 554)

Social-Science Research Methods

Like scholars in the natural sciences, social scientists tend to use the experimental method to test out observation-based hypotheses. Some social-science research, however, is more subjective, involving a speculative approach to the mysteries of human consciousness, emotions, and the like. Because much social-science research is observation-based, much of the thinking is rooted in mathematics, particularly statistical analysis. Focused on testing hypotheses, such research pays careful attention to variables, controls, experiment replication, and case studies. Objective analysis of all the data is valued. The following resources may be especially helpful:

- "Conducting Surveys" (pages 430–431), "Conducting Interviews" (pages 434–435), and "Making Observations" (page 436)
- APA Documentation (chapter 29, pages 535–564, and www.apa.org)

Writing in the Natural and Applied Sciences

In a natural- or applied-science class (e.g., botany, chemistry, engineering, and oceanography), your writing will explore some aspect of the physical, natural world. Such writing seeks to explore and explain the nature of the world that we inhabit and are part of, as well as the natural laws that govern that world. If your major is in the natural or applied sciences, your writing will likely have the character described below.

The Purpose of Inquiry

Broadly, natural science aims to explain observations in the light of current theories, observations that are typically not now explicable. The goal of the scientist—or more likely team of scientists—is to arrive at an explanation, stimulate discussion, and prompt further research. As such, scientific thinking tends to be hypothesis driven: it begins with a possible explanation rooted in current knowledge, makes an experiment-related prediction, observes and measures results, and then accepts, rejects, or modifies the possible explanation.

Forms of Natural-Science Writing

With their focus on natural phenomena, natural scientists typically write research reports. Here are types of writing that you might do:

- **Lab, or Field Reports:** Sometimes called IMRAD reports (introduction, method, results, and discussion), such reports share the results of experiments and measured observations.
- **Literature Reviews:** These reports summarize and synthesize all the current research on a specific topic, perhaps also examining the theories that underlie the topic.
- **Technical Reports:** Applied research might involve writing technical reports aimed at proposing practical solutions to a specific problem or challenge.

Examples: "Wayward Cells" (page 220), "Nuclear Is Not the Answer" (page 311), and "Sample Research Paper: Science IMRAD Report" (page 485)

Natural-Science Research Methods

Natural scientists practice two predominant research methods: laboratory experiments and field work. Both rooted in objective attention to phenomena, laboratory research follows the strict procedures of the experimental method while field work relies on careful, often quantifiable observation. Both forms for research value insightful hypothesizing, carefully collecting and analyzing data (typically in a lab notebook or a field journal), and thoughtfully relating the results to past research and current theories. The following resources might be helpful:

- "Conducting Observations" (page 436)
- Council of Science Editors (councilscienceeditors.org)

Critical-Thinking and Writing Activities

As directed by your instructor, complete the following critical-thinking and writing activities by yourself or with classmates.

1. Using its online or print catalog, review your college's curriculum—its organization into divisions, disciplines, and courses. What does that big picture reveal about knowledge, inquiry, and learning in your school?

2. Using what you have learned about inquiry in the humanities, social sciences, and natural sciences, browse through chapters 10-20, identifying essays and other forms of writing that relate to the different divisions and disciplines. Read closely an essay that interests you, analyzing the thinking and writing strategies the author uses. How does this piece relate to the forms of writing described in this chapter?

3. Consider the major you have chosen, or select a program that interests you. To research the thinking and writing skills practiced in this field, do the following:

   - **In the catalog, study the programs and courses in the department.** What do these reveal about the structure of knowledge, the major issues, and writing practices in the field?

   - **Using library and digital resources, find and study scholarly writing in this field.** What does this writing reveal about the thinking strategies valued, as well as the writing forms used?

   - **How is knowledge from this field presented in writing to the broader culture?** Explore this question by researching an issue in the field as it is discussed in the popular print and digital media.

Learning-Objectives Checklist ✓

Have you achieved this chapter's learning objectives? Check your progress with the items below, revisiting topics in the chapter as needed. *I have . . .*

____ identified the three traditional curricular divisions of the humanities, the social sciences, and the natural sciences—including their area of knowledge and typical disciplines or majors within each (132).

____ differentiated and explained the purpose of inquiry, the forms of writing, and the research methods in the humanities, the social sciences, and the natural and applied sciences (133–135).

____ analyzed how writing works in my field of study or a major that interests me, including in the program itself, in scholarly writing, in popular writing, and in professions to which the major leads.

Chapter 10

Narration, Description, and Reflection

Personal essays often tell stories—not ones that the writers made up, but ones that they lived. Whatever the topics, the stories should help readers see, hear, touch, and taste those details that make the experiences come alive. To do that, writers must carefully describe key aspects of the experience. But they might also reflect on why the experiences are important—exploring their personal and shared meanings.

When reading such personal essays, do so with an open mind—seeking to go where writers guide you, to experience what they carefully describe, and to analyze how they craft their work.

As you prepare to write your own story, get ready to relive it yourself—to reexperience all that you felt, thought, or sensed during the event. In addition, be ready to learn something new about the experience, about others, and even about yourself.

Visually Speaking   Explain how Figure 10.1 is similar to an essay that communicates through narration, description, and reflection.

Learning **Objectives**

By working through this chapter, you will be able to

- critique and create the elements of narrative writing.
- analyze and effectively utilize strategies for descriptive writing.
- evaluate and use reflective-writing strategies such as natural observation and meaningful thesis thinking.
- create and integrate enriching anecdotes in personal and academic writing.
- develop a well-organized personal essay that includes narration, description, and/or reflection.

igor.stevanovic / Shutterstock.com

fig. 10.1

Strategies for Personal Essays

Personal essays typically present and explore some dimension of the writer's experience by blending **narration, description,** and **reflection**. This blending often follows a **fluid organization**. Whether you are reading or writing a personal narrative, start with the **rhetorical situation** and then consider the strategies that follow.

The Rhetorical Situation

To put a personal essay in context, consider the rhetorical situation that gives rise to it:

- **Purpose:** The goal of such writing is to explore topics or issues with which writers have a personal connection. A writer's aim is to deepen his or her own insight while sharing it with readers.
- **Readers:** Most personal essays are written for a general audience, though they may be directed to a specific segment of society. The writer hopes that his or her personal experience will speak universally—that readers will empathize and connect with it.
- **Topic:** Writers address any topic that they find meaningful and worth exploring through the lens of personal experience and reflection—often events, people, and places from their own lives.

Example: In "The Muscle Mystique" (pages 155–157), Barbara Kingsolver focuses on a topic meaningful to her own life, her sense of physical weakness and her attempts to "buff up." Her **purpose** is to gain insight into her own situation, comical as it is, but also to explore more fully the cultural significance of bodybuilding and exercise. Her **readership** would rightly be described as a general public, but the essay may also be directed at fellow "weaklings" and at bodybuilding enthusiasts.

Principles of Narration

Personal essays often center on engaging narratives—stories that focus on meaningful events and people. That's the case, for example, with "Spare Change" (pages 148–150) and "When Dreams Take Flight" (pages 151–152), where the writers tell stories that stand on their own. The following elements are central to a well-crafted narrative:

Action: This refers to the unfolding sequence of events shaped into a meaningful whole, a force that drives narrative forward. Consider these strategies:

- **Handling chronology:** Narrative is time-sensitive, so a good narrative handles time effectively through clear temporal markers, verb tenses, and time transitions. Moreover, the narrative manages temporal pacing by focusing in on key events and compressing or summarizing less significant action. Finally, the narrative may "escape" strict chronology by beginning in the middle of the action before going back to the beginning, as well as by using flashbacks and foreshadowing.
- **Clarifying action:** Narratives move forward energetically when writers use precise, engaging, and suggestive verbs. Example: "I poked my head out and down. The cabin

was packed with businessmen reading the financial papers. I hitched up my skirt—hemmed at precisely one and three-quarter inches above the knee—and lowered my other leg. This snagged the attention of the last 10 rows, as well as my panty hose."

- **Shaping a plot:** A narrative's overall pattern may take many forms, but the traditional structure builds tension and complication toward a climactic moment of decision or discovery, followed by aftermath and resolution.

Character: While events (what happened and why) are often the focus of a narrative, frequently the narrative's focus is character—what the events reveal about people. Characters need to be well-developed and engaging in order to reveal things about life and human nature. Narrative shows people feeling, thinking, acting, and interacting.

Dialogue: Conversations are used in narrative to reveal character, advance the action, and embody the conflict. Typically chosen for significant moments in the action, such dialogue should be natural in word choice, voice, and sentence rhythms (reflecting dialects if needed), with speakers clearly demarcated.

Narrative Perspective: In a personal narrative, the writer is typically the narrator—the voice telling the story. However, the narrative voice might be in the foreground (participating in the action) or the background (observing the action).

Setting: Action happens and people live within specific places and times—the narrative's setting. Settings put events and characters in physical, historical, and cultural context.

Sample Narrative Paragraph

Taken from "When Dreams Take Flight" (pages 151–152), the paragraph below narrates the writer's climactic discovery upon waking up from a nap.

> I opened my eyes and gasped. The passengers and crew had boarded, and no one had checked my overhead bunk. If only someone had tried to store a coat up there or grab a blanket! I should have been down on the cabin floor, on duty and with my one-inch grosgrain ribbon tying my hair in place, my gold logo centered on the front of my hat. Instead, I was up on that rack, breaking into a cold sweat.

Principles of Description

Effective descriptive passages (of places, people, and objects) offer precise, evocative details that help readers thoughtfully experience the essay's topic. Such description may aim for fidelity—objectivity through accurate and complete details, including measurements and so on. Or the description may aim to create a dominant impression, a sense of the person, place, or object that is rooted in carefully selected details that work through imagination, association, and symbolism. For example, "The Entomology of Village Life" (pages 144–147) is filled with vivid descriptions of places and people. Such strong description draws attention to different strategies: naming, detailing, ordering, and comparing (see page 140 for more).

Naming: At its base, description identifies things, and the beginning of such identification is naming—among available terms, choosing words that precisely or suggestively clarify the nature of what is being described.

Detailing: Description appeals to the senses through concrete details, details that may be precise but also rich in connotations and associations. Details that appeal to sight create a mental picture for readers; sounds and smells tend to evoke feelings and memories; taste and touch generate a sense of intimacy.

Ordering: While they may involve a single detail, descriptions are often much fuller. In that case, writers may need to (1) establish a vantage point from which readers will see the object, (2) orient the object in space, and (3) lead readers systematically through the description (e.g., left to right, top to bottom, back to front).

Comparing: Descriptions may be clarified and deepened through comparisons. Here are three common options:

- **Simile** is a comparison of two things in which *like* or *as* is used. Example: "My friends have given me an official item of exercise equipment that looks like a glob of blue putty." (page 157)
- **Metaphor** is a comparison in which one thing is said to be another, establishing an identity. (Neither *like* nor *as is* used.) Example: "Some people were the moths, tied down and struggling; some were the spiders, growing fat on gossip." (page 144)
- **Personification** is a device in which the author speaks of or describes an animal, object, or idea as if it were a person. Example: "I looked at all the little pillows up there, snuggled next to the blankets." (page 151)

Sample Descriptive Paragraph

The paragraph below is the opening paragraph in Teresa Zsuffa's "Spare Change" (pages 148–150). Note how in describing the urban setting she appeals to multiple senses, offers precise details, evokes a feeling of unease, and ends with a metaphor ("starry distance").

    This grime is infectious. The smell of old cigarettes and expired perfume is constricting my throat and turning my stomach. But here I am again on the underground subway platform, changing trains at Bloor-Yonge in Toronto, the weight of my backpack thrusting me forward with the Friday morning rush hour crowd. When the subway doors open I hurry inside and look around frantically, as usual. There is an empty seat to my left, but everyone is keeping a safe four-foot distance, as if the seat will suck them in and destroy them if they sit down. Or at least destroy the facade put on with a Ralph Lauren suit, a Coach handbag, or a pair of authentic Gucci sunglasses. Not like the fake five-dollar ones I picked up from a Chinatown vendor just yesterday. The others keep their starry distance; when I sit down, I see why.

Principles of Reflection

In a personal essay, strong reflective passages—from single sentences to entire paragraphs—relay the writer's observations and insights regarding the nature, impact, and value of the experience. In some personal essays, such reflection is minimal (e.g., essays that are primarily narrative in nature, such as "Spare Change"). However, some essays are rich in reflection, particularly when the writer's purpose is to explore psychological and cultural complexity, as in "Call Me Crazy, But I Have to Be Myself" (pages 153–154) and "The Muscle Mystique" (pages 155–157). Consider these reflection strategies:

Natural Observation: Reflection within a personal essay should have an organic feel—arising naturally out of the material presented, out of the narration and description. That reflection can be thematically implied or openly stated, depending on the writer's purpose. Essentially, however, the reflection should be honest, meaningful, and thought-provoking for readers, pressing them to connect with and universalize the experience. For that reason, reflection is often stated using the pronoun I, but a connection to other people is stated or implied, perhaps through comparison-contrast.

Thesis Thinking: The key idea of a personal essay typically grows out of the writer's questions about the meaning of the experience. More than a simple statement of fact or a clichéd opinion, the thesis should follow these guidelines:

- **The thesis expresses some complexity about the experience**—mixed feelings (ambivalence), tensions, or paradox. The thesis is rarely a blunt, simplistic "This is the moral of the story" statement, as it doesn't do justice to the fullness of the experience or the complications of the narrative. Example: Many marriages demonstrate the notion that opposites attract—with painful consequences for everyone involved.
- **The thesis may be stated openly or simply implied.** If stated, it can be positioned a variety of places in the essay, though toward the middle or end seems best: action and description build inductively toward insight.

Sample Reflective Paragraph

In the paragraph below, from "Call Me Crazy, But I Have to Be Myself" (pages 144–147), Mary Seymour reflects on the impact of bipolar disorder on her life. Note how she relates her personal experience to the experiences of other people.

> Most of the time, I feel lucky to blend in with the crowd. Things that most people grumble about—paying bills, maintaining a car, working 9 to 5—strike me as incredible privileges. I'll never forget gazing through the barred windows of the psychiatric ward into the parking lot, watching people come and go effortlessly, wondering if I'd ever be like them again. There's nothing like a stint in a locked ward to make one grateful for the freedoms and burdens of full citizenship.

Principles of Organization

If a personal essay centers on a narrative, the organization will largely be determined by chronology, arranged according to the logic of the plot. (See, for example, the outline for "The Entomology of Village Life" on page 144.) Generally, the structure of a personal essay tends to be fluid—flowing more freely than a traditional academic essay. Consider these strategies:

Opening: The opening seeks to get readers' attention, usher them into the world of the essay, and orient them to the topic through techniques like these: a memory, an image, an idea, a conflict, a puzzle, a moment from the middle or near the end of the story. Remember that personal essays don't always need to open at the beginning of the story; they can start from the middle or end of the action.

Middle: The body of the essay may weave together elements of narration, description, and reflection to deepen interest, and possibly to build toward a climax—a moment of discovery or decision. This process may involve

- bringing together "strands" of the past and the present
- introducing tensions, complications, and conflicts
- focusing on key moments, episodes, and encounters (including dialogue)
- foreshadowing what is to come or creating a puzzle to be solved
- comparing events, settings, or characters
- moving from a broad view to a narrow focus or vice versa

Closing: Traditional narratives follow the climax with the fallout and resolution (revealing the results of conflict, the outcome). Other narratives, however, aim to be more open-ended. The ending might also focus on authentic reflection (without trite moralism) that leaves readers with food for thought. Finally, it might supply a surprise, a dramatic turn of events, or it might return to the opening in some way.

Reading Personal Writing

On the following pages, you will find personal essays written by both students and professional authors. As you read, consider these questions:

1. Does the essay center on narrative? How is that narrative developed through action, character, dialogue, narrative perspective, and setting? Do you find the narrative engaging?
2. What roles does description play in the essay, and what descriptive techniques are used? Are there descriptions that really jump out at you? Why?
3. What ideas or themes evolve from the story? Is reflection stated or implied? Can you locate a thesis, or is it implied? Can you put it in your own words? Why does the writer care about this topic, and how do you feel about it in the end? What have you learned?
4. How does the essay unfold? How are narrative, description, and reflection blended?

Brief Narratives: Anecdotes

A common narrative is the anecdote—a brief story that enlivens your writing while introducing a topic or illustrating an idea. Read the anecdotes below, along with the essays from which they are taken. Then assess the anecdotes' effectiveness.

Anecdote Introducing a Topic

The other day, my wife, watching our son-in-law with his large hands gracefully tie the shoelaces of his little daughter, remarked, "You really are deft." Ever the cynic, I remarked, "He's not only deft, he's daft." I talk that sort of nonsense frequently, but as I said this, I began to wonder. What if *deft* and *daft* come from the same root and once meant the same thing? A quick trip to the dictionary showed that, indeed, they did once mean the same thing (though my wife thought me daft when I first suggested it).

From "Deft or Daft," page 240

Anecdote Illustrating a Point

LAST week, the Senate majority leader, Harry Reid, found himself in trouble for once suggesting that Barack Obama had a political edge over other African-American candidates because he was "light-skinned" and had "no Negro dialect, unless he wanted to have one." Mr. Reid was not expressing sadness but a gleeful opportunism that Americans were still judging one another by the color of their skin, rather than—as the Rev. Dr. Martin Luther King Jr., whose legacy we commemorated on Monday, dreamed—by the content of their character.

From "Shades of Prejudice," page 190

Anecdote Illustrating a Trait

Jackie Thomas, Nike's associate director of sports marketing, usually spends her lunch hour on the sports-shoe company's basketball courts charging for the basket, always outnumbered by male colleagues. "I hold my own," boasts the 33-year-old executive.

She also does well playing the corporate game back inside the headquarter's offices. Thomas, a former University of California—Berkeley college basketball point guard, says her success is due in large part to the lessons she learned growing up playing competitive team sports. "It's taught me that if you lose a game, you go back afterward and figure out what went wrong and how to overcome it the next time," says the former tomboy from Kingston, Jamaica.

From "If You Let Me Play . . . ," page 171

Sample Personal Essays

Personal essays can focus on a wide range of topics as writers narrate, describe, and reflect upon their experiences. The essays that follow suggest that range as they explore communities, encounters, comic events, illnesses, and cultural trends.

Exploring a Community

In this essay, student writer Robert Minto recalls a series of events through which he learned something about his community, himself, and the nature of life. Note that following his introduction, Minto uses chronological order to organize his narrative.

Essay Outline

Introduction: Setting, key characters, and conflict: moths (such as Ryan) vs. spiders (such as Old Jack)

1. Narrator goes to Ryan's house.
2. They stop at narrator's house, pass church, arrive at cemetery.
3. They explore cemetery and discuss spirits.
4. They hear moaning and move toward it.
5. They see Old Jack's grandson and a girl.
6. They return to bikes and ride past church to Ryan's house.

Closing: Narrator tells Old Jack about grandson and girl and then reflects on the conflict.

The title fore-casts a study of insects.

Introduction: setting, key characters, and conflict: moths (such as Ryan) vs. spiders (such as Old Jack)

Ryan, a moth

The Entomology of Village Life

Buddy didn't know that we were clichés. I knew. I liked it that way. We spent our days together—me too inquisitive and his tail always wagging. My neighbor, Old Jack, who was forever pulling weeds in his garden, self-exiled from a sharp-tongued wife, was a cliché too. So was the grange on the other side of my house. Most of the men in Naymari, Pennsylvania, never missed a grange meeting, mainly to supervise the village's one employee, Pedro, who mowed the grass in the park. Within this small web of places and personalities, life abounded. Some people were the moths, tied down and struggling; some were the spiders, growing fat on gossip.

One of the moths lived across the street. He was my friend Ryan. Ryan lived in the dirtiest house I've ever seen. His mother cared for him and for two younger, mentally disabled boys as well. She had a big heart but too few hands and no husband. In the winter, they all huddled around a kerosene heater, wearing most of the clothing they owned, the two youngest boys often licking the snot that dripped from their cold noses. They couldn't afford oil. Through a government program, Ryan had received an old IBM computer. He spent most of his time playing Tetris on it in his room. Sometimes when Buddy and I got up early in the morning to roam the village, we'd stop outside Ryan's window, and I'd toss pebbles at it. (His mother

1

2

6 They return to bikes and ride past church to Ryan's house.

see the silver flash of the car's antenna between them each time they separated. Me and Ryan froze for a few seconds before comprehension struck. Glancing wildly at each other, we squirmed away.

When we reached the edge of the wood, we stood up and made our way back   *34*
to our bikes. Somehow, waiting for the spirits had lost its appeal. I glanced at the Methodist church and saw the pastor was awake, waving at us through the window. We pedaled quietly back to town. I imagined that even Buddy seemed subdued. When we reached Ryan's house, he stopped and laid his bike on the grass. We could hear his mom inside, talking to his brothers.

Ryan began to walk up the lawn, back to his Tetris. Then he stopped, turned   *35*
around and asked, "What are you gonna do?"

I thought for a moment. Then I told him.   *36*

Closing: Narrator tells Old Jack about grandson and girl and then reflects on the moth/spider conflict.

About an hour later, I finished telling Old Jack what we'd seen. He was watering   *37*
his tomatoes, and as I talked, I noticed that one of the plants was nearly floating even though he was staring right at it. I finished up, and he went right on watering that same plant.

Then he glanced over at me and said, "That's very interesting." He contemplated   *38*
the drowning plant again and added, "But this isn't something to get around town, you know. You wouldn't tell anybody else, would ya?"

I thought for a moment. Then I smiled.   *39*

Somewhere, a spider was about to become a moth.   *40*

Reading for Better Writing

Working by yourself or with a group, answer these questions:

1. Review the title, "The Entomology of Village Life." Then explain what *entomology* is and why it is (or is not) a good choice for this essay.

2. In the opening paragraph, the writer refers to himself and other village residents as *clichés*. Define *cliché* and explain why the writer might use this term. Does the essay show the characters to be clichés? Explain.

3. In the second paragraph, the writer refers to village residents as moths and spiders. Explain what he might mean by these metaphors and the effect of his using them to open and close the essay.

4. Identify a narrative passage, a descriptive passage, and a reflective passage that you consider well written. Explain why.

5. What is the essay's main idea or theme? How does the writer introduce the idea and develop it?

6. Re-read the essay's last sentence and explain why it is (or is not) an effective closing.

"The Entomology of Village Life" by Robert Minto. Used by permission of the author.

Narrating an Encounter

"Spare Change" is the first part of student writer Teresa Zsuffa's "A Diary of Chance Encounters," an essay that explores her experiences of living in Toronto. The piece below recounts a challenging encounter with the face of poverty.

"Spare Change"

The writer describes an urban setting and a common situation.

This grime is infectious. The smell of old cigarettes and expired perfume is constricting my throat and turning my stomach. But here I am again on the underground subway platform, changing trains at Bloor-Yonge in Toronto, the weight of my backpack thrusting me forward with the Friday morning rush hour crowd. When the subway doors open I hurry inside and look around frantically, as usual. There is an empty seat to my left, but everyone is keeping a safe four-foot distance, as if the seat will suck them in and destroy them if they sit down. Or at least destroy the facade put on with a Ralph Lauren suit, a Coach handbag, or a pair of authentic Gucci sunglasses. Not like the fake five-dollar ones I picked up from a Chinatown vendor just yesterday. The others keep their starry distance; when I sit down, I see why.   1

She introduces the central person through concrete details, her words, and the reactions of others (including the writer's own mixed feelings).

She must be about twenty-nine. Her orange track-pants are worn and faded, her T-shirt is far too big, and her powder blue sweatshirt is tied around her waist. Her face and teeth are stained, hair greasy and unkempt. A part of me feels sorry for her. Another part follows the crowd and is careful not to make eye contact.   2

"Excuse me," she says, perching on the edge of her seat, leaning forward and clasping the metal pole with two hands. No one turns. "Excuse me, which stop do I take to the Old City Hall?" One man shrugs and shakes his head while pretending to check his phone. I feel guilt, but it's easily subdued. After all, she wasn't asking me.   3

I am deeply engrossed in my Nicholas Sparks novel by the time the driver announces "Dundas Station." As I stuff the book back into my purse and make my way towards the doorway, I'm irritated to see that she also stands up—one stop early for Old City Hall. Doesn't she know she should stay on until Queen? Oh well, she'll figure it out, I reason. The Toronto Transit Commission officers can help her.   4

I let her off the subway before me. Finally I'm free.   5

The writer narrates the events and dialogue that lead her to offer help.

But then she stops on the platform and turns her head, like a puppy making sure her owner is following close behind. No eye contact, I remind myself, and try to walk past but she falls into step with me.   6

"Can I help you carry your bag?"   7

I may look like a tourist, but I'm smarter. "No, thanks," I reply.   8

"Well it just looks pretty heavy." We reach the escalator and the staircase and I take the left side, where I can climb the steps and go up twice as fast as those just standing there on the right and enjoying the ride. But it doesn't work; the woman is still at my heels.   9

> Details describe the urban setting, and the writer's acclimation to it.

"Are you going somewhere?" she asks.   *10*

"Yeah, I have to get to the Greyhound station, I'm going out of town."   *11*

"Oh." Now we are standing in front of the underground entrance to the Eaton   *12*
Center. The Atrium on Bay is to my right, on the other side of which is the bus
station and my ticket out of this alien city that is now my home. The woman stands
frozen and looks around trying to get her bearings. I start to walk away but hesitate.
Looking back, I see her blinking and flinching as people shove past her. She reminds
me of a small child lost at a summer carnival.

> She refers to the city's cultural "rules."

I check my watch—quarter past eight. I just missed an express shuttle, and   *13*
the next bus to Niagara Falls, where my father lives, won't be leaving for another
forty-five minutes. Something pulls me back to the woman, and against all sworn
Torontonian rules, I ask if she needs help.

Her dull brown eyes light up. "I need to find the Old City Hall."   *14*

> The writer uses dialogue to describe the woman's life and her journey.

"Okay," I nod. "I'll take you." I lead her through the glass doors into the city's   *15*
busiest mall. It's the fastest way from Dundas to Queen Street, and from there she
will need to walk only a few blocks west. As we're walking, I'm aware of the stares
I'm getting from people I'll never see again.

"So where are you from?" I ask.   *16*

"Sudbury." And I'm instantly speechless. What is this woman doing so far from   *17*
home? How did she get here? I ask why she's in the city.

"My boyfriend. He's in jail, and they're letting him go today. I came to take him   *18*
back home with me after his hearing."

While we walk past Mexx, Aritzia, and Abercrombie, I learn that she had   *19*
taken a bus from Sudbury the day before and spent the night on a park bench. Her
boyfriend is forty-two years old and has been in jail for the past ten months. I don't
ask why. She proudly tells me she was a crack addict and that she's been clean for
three months.

> Short quotes create a sharp rhythm.

"I just got out of rehab," she says. "Now maybe my grandma will take me back   *20*
in."

"Back in?"   *21*

> The writer describes her confusion, sympathy, and guilt.

"Yeah, she kicked me out. She told me I wasn't allowed to be a hooker anymore,   *22*
but I got caught bringing someone home once."

I have no idea how to talk to a prostitute, never mind one who is so open about   *23*
everything she's done, but this woman seems to like me and trust me. The next thing
I know, I'm offering to buy her breakfast before she meets up with her boyfriend.

> A dash accents the irony of this unlikely pair sharing personal time and stories.

There's a McDonald's at the southernmost side of the Eaton Centre, overlooking   *24*
the Queen Street entrance. I tell her she can have anything she wants. An Egg
McMuffin? Fruit and yogurt? But all she wants is Coke and a hash-brown. I order
her two.

We sit down at a freshly wiped table by the window. Beside us, two men in   *25*
grey suits sip coffee over an array of files and spreadsheets. They pause in their
conversation to stare at us—the student traveler and the bedraggled prostitute. I tell

the woman a little about my life, and ask more about hers and her grandmother. She says that they used to go to church together, when she was little, but she hasn't been since. She takes another bite of her hash-brown and tells me she's now twenty-one. Only twenty-one, and her boyfriend is forty-two. She talks about the drugs and the providence of God.

The writer acknowledges her own inexperience and confusion.

"I know that he helped me stop," she says. "I've been clean for three months, can you believe that? That's a miracle! It has to be a miracle."   26

At this point all I can do is smile.   27

"I wish I could get my boyfriend to quit," she says, staring off. Then she suddenly leans forward and asks, "Do you know how hard it is? Have you ever done crack?"   28

"No."   29

"Pot, at least?"   30

The writer offers spare change, a gift that is cited in the title and that symbolizes the women's distanced relationship.

"No. Sorry." I'm not sure why I'm apologizing for never having tried drugs, but the way her face drops and she shifts her eyes makes me feel guilty. As though I can never fully understand her because I've never experienced the things she has.   31

"Well you should try it," she urges. "It's really good."   32

"Maybe one day." I glance at my watch. It's now quarter-to, and I still need to stand in line to buy my ticket and get to the right platform. I wonder why I'm not panicking yet.   33

I tell her I need to get going. She should go, too, or she'll be late for the hearing. Before getting up, I reach into my wallet and give her two TTC passes and some spare change. I walk her to the street and point her toward Old City Hall. She never thanks me, only looks at me one last time with immense vulnerability and helplessness. Then she walks away.   34

I wonder as I hurry towards the station if she'll be okay, if her boyfriend really will get out of jail, and if her grandmother will ever take her back. Either way, I think as I cross Bay Street, what more can I do? I have a bus to catch.   35

Reading for Better Writing

Working by yourself or with a group, answer these questions:

1. Teresa's essay focuses on an urban setting. What does she evoke about the city, and what descriptions create that feeling?

2. The central character in the essay is presented primarily through description, comparisons, and dialogue. Identify such passages, exploring what they communicate about the woman and how effectively they work.

3. One focus of the essay is the writer's experience of the city and of her encounter with the prostitute. Describe Teresa's thoughts and feelings about both. How does she communicate these? Identify and analyze specific passages, sentences, and phrases.

"Spare Change" by Teresa Zsuffa. Used by permission of the author.

Narrating a Comic Episode

Elizabeth Fuller writes this essay to describe her one-time experience as a stowaway flight attendant—an experience that she enjoys describing but likely does not want to relive.

When Dreams Take Flight

A playful title forecasts what will happen.

In my 20s I was a flight attendant for Northwest Airlines, and I remember the holiday season as the most exhausting of the year. But I loved my job. From the first day Northwest hired me in Minneapolis in 1969, I tried to be a model flight attendant, to develop the qualities my operations manual demanded: poise, good judgment, initiative, adaptability and a spotless appearance. *1*

The writer describes herself.

A transition and short clause introduce the action.

But one time I slipped up: I fell asleep. It happened one dreary morning around Thanksgiving. We'd just landed in Washington and I was dog-tired. The crew had disembarked for breakfast; the new passengers wouldn't board for two hours. For some reason, my eye drifted toward the overhead racks. Back then, the racks in Boeing 727's had no doors and were used only for storing pillows, blankets and passengers' coats and hats. I looked at all the little pillows up there, snuggled next to the blankets. And then I climbed up. *2*

A dash and short clause at the end of the paragraph forecast trouble.

This was not easy in a pencil skirt and regulation red half-slip. But I did it. And it was heaven. I lay back on the mountain of pillows and pulled a blanket up over my head. Just before I drifted off, the thought crossed my mind that I ought to set my portable alarm clock — but it was too late. *3*

She reflects on and rationalizes her choice.

I certainly wasn't worrying about our operations manual, though I knew, of course, that flight attendants caught sleeping on duty could lose their wings. But I wasn't on duty, not in the strict sense. What's more, I was exhibiting initiative and adaptability, some of those attributes most cherished by Northwest Airlines. *4*

The quotation builds tension and tells what is happening.

It was a sound sleep. Suddenly I woke to a voice on the public address system: "Morning, folks. This is your captain speaking. We're No. 4 for takeoff, up near the end of the runway. So if you'll just sit back and relax, we'll be taking off in a few minutes. The flight attendants will do the best they can for you this morning, even though they are one short in the second cabin." *5*

A series of short sentences suggest her thoughts and fears.

I opened my eyes and gasped. The passengers and crew had boarded, and no one had checked my overhead bunk. If only someone had tried to store a coat up there or grab a blanket! I should have been down on the cabin floor, on duty and with my one-inch grosgrain ribbon tying my hair in place, my gold logo centered on the front of my hat. Instead, I was up on that rack, breaking into a cold sweat. *6*

She describes her cautious and embarrassing descent.

If I ever needed that Northwest Airlines initiative, it was then. I poked my head out and down. The cabin was packed with businessmen reading the financial papers. *7*

I hitched up my skirt — hemmed precisely one and three-quarter inches above the knee — and lowered a leg. This snagged the attention of the last 10 rows, as well as my panty hose. Then I lowered my other leg. By this time, the rows in front had turned around and were watching too. Luckily, no one laughed.

She summarizes her excuse and notes his suspicion.

I swung down and planted my navy blue pump half on a passenger's armrest 8 and half on his pinstriped leg. My hat was in the overhead rack, I told him, and I had been digging around for a long time trying to find it. I pointed out that I had to wear my hat, or I would be fired.

Mention of the captain sets up the conclusion.

He cleared his throat but didn't say anything. I thanked him for his 9 understanding and walked up the aisle toward my two fellow flight attendants, who were howling with laughter. We were sobered only by the realization that somebody had to notify the captain.

The captain responds by quoting Shakespeare.

As the plane rose to cruising altitude, the senior flight attendant went to the 10 cockpit and explained that I was back in the cabin. Meanwhile, I put on my smock and began pouring coffee, trying to avoid the rows near my overhead bunk. As I headed back to the galley to refill my coffeepot, I found the captain waiting for me with a stern and unforgiving look. I was getting ready to try to explain when he snapped the galley curtain closed and doubled over with laughter. "All's well that ends well," he said with a wink.

Reading for Better Writing

Working by yourself or with a group, answer these questions:
1. Review the title and explain why it is (or is not) a good choice.
2. Re-read the opening paragraph and note what the writer says about her age, employer, the season, her employer's expectations, and her desire to excel. Then explain how each of these details helps set up the story, build interest in the action, and create humor.
3. Cite a descriptive passage that you find particularly engaging and explain why.
4. Compare what the captain says in paragraph 5 with what he says in paragraph 10. What does each statement tell you about his personality, role on the plane, and relationship with the crew? Would paraphrasing the captain have been more effective than quoting him? Why?
5. Review paragraphs 7-9 in which the writer describes her descent from the luggage bin, the passenger whom she steps on, her excuse, and his response. Do the details she offers adequately describe her action and his response? Explain.
6. Do you find the story funny? Why or why not?

Reflecting on an Illness

Mary Seymour reflects on her experience with bipolar disorder, which is sometimes called manic depression.

Call Me Crazy, But I Have to Be Myself

The writer labels herself "mentally ill."

Nearly every day, without thinking, I say things like "So-and-so is driving me crazy" or "That's nuts!" Sometimes I catch myself and realize that I'm not being sensitive toward people with mental illness. Then I remember I'm one of the mentally ill. If I can't throw those words around, who can? *1*

An example illustrates the extent of the illness.

Being a functional member of society and having a mental disorder is an intricate balancing act. Every morning I send my son to junior high school, put on professional garb, and drive off to my job as alumni-magazine editor at a prep school, where I've worked for six years. Only a few people at work know I'm manic-depressive, or bipolar, as it's sometimes called. *2*

More examples show the difficulties the writer faces.

Sometimes I'm not sure myself what I am. I blend in easily with "normal" people. You'd never know that seven years ago, fueled by the stress of a failing marriage and fanned by the genetic inheritance of a manic-depressive grandfather, I had a psychotic break. To look at me, you'd never guess I once ran naked through my yard or shuffled down the hallways of a psychiatric ward. To hear me, you'd never guess God channeled messages to me through my computer. After my breakdown at 36, I was diagnosed as bipolar, a condition marked by moods that swing between elation and despair. *3*

It took a second, less-severe psychotic episode in 1997, followed by a period of deep depression, to convince me I truly was bipolar. Admitting I had a disorder that I'd have to manage for life was the hardest thing I've ever done. Since then, a combination of therapy, visits to a psychiatrist, medication, and inner calibration have helped me find an even keel. Now I manage my moods with the vigilance of a mother hen, nudging them back to center whenever they wander too far. Eating wisely, sleeping well, and exercising regularly keep me balanced from day to day. Ironically, my disorder has taught me to be healthier and happier than I was before. *4*

Most of the time, I feel lucky to blend in with the crowd. Things that most people grumble about—paying bills, maintaining a car, working 9 to 5—strike me as incredible privileges. I'll never forget gazing through the barred windows of the psychiatric ward into the parking lot, watching people come and go effortlessly, wondering if I'd ever be like them again. There's nothing like a stint in a locked ward to make one grateful for the freedoms and burdens of full citizenship. *5*

Each sentence begins with a similar phrase that reveals the writer's feelings.

Yet sometimes I feel like an impostor. Sometimes I wish I could sit at the lunch table and talk about lithium and Celexa instead of *Will & Grace*. While everyone talks about her fitness routine, I want to brag how it took five orderlies to hold me *6* down and shoot me full of sedatives when I was admitted to the hospital, and how for a brief moment I knew the answers to every infinite mystery of the blazingly bright universe. I yearn for people to know me—the real me—in all my complexity, but I'm afraid it would scare the bejesus out of them.

An extended example illustrates the point.

Every now and then, I feel like I'm truly being myself. Like the time the school chaplain, in whom I'd confided my past, asked me to help counsel a severely bipolar student. This young woman had tried to commit suicide, had been hospitalized many times, and sometimes locked herself in her dorm room to keep the "voices" from overwhelming her. I walked and talked with her, sharing stories about medication and psychosis. I hoped to show by example that manic-depression did not necessarily mean a diminished life. At commencement, I watched her proudly accept her diploma; despite ongoing struggles with her illness, she's continuing her education.   7

I'm able to be fully myself with my closest friends, all of whom have similar schisms between private and public selves. We didn't set out to befriend each other—we just all speak the same language, of hardship and spiritual discovery and psychological awareness.   8

The final line echoes the title.

What I yearn for most is to integrate both sides of myself. I want to be part of the normal world but I also want to own my identity as bipolar. I want people to know what I've been through so I can help those traveling a similar path. Fear has kept me from telling my story: fear of being stigmatized, of making people uncomfortable, of being reduced to a label. But hiding the truth has become more uncomfortable than letting it out. It's time for me to own up to who I am, complicated psychiatric history and all. Call me crazy, but I think it's the right thing to do.   9

Reading for Better Writing

Working by yourself or with a group, answer these questions:

1. What purpose does Seymour identify for writing the essay? What other purposes might be served by publishing this piece for *Newsweek's* readers?

2. The writer starts with one category label for herself ("mentally ill") and then quickly adds another ("functional member of society"). How does the second label redefine the first?

3. Description is used to support many other kinds of writing, including the types of analytical and persuasive writing outlined here in *The College Writer*. In what other chapters could this essay have been included, and how do you know?

4. Review the "Editing and Proofreading" chapter of this book (pages 91–106), especially the portion on biased words. Why does Seymour use the phrase "call me crazy"? Is her use of the word biased or insulting? Explain.

Reflecting on a Cultural Trend

The following essay by Barbara Kingsolver is taken from her book, *High Tide in Tucson*. In the essay, she describes her brief experience as a bodybuilding wannabe, and she reflects on how she "outgrew" her need to buff up.

The Muscle Mystique

As you read the essay, use this column to record your observations and questions.

The baby-sitter surely thought I was having an affair. Years ago, for a period of three whole months, I would dash in to pick up my daughter after "work" with my cheeks flushed, my heart pounding, my hair damp from a quick shower. I'm loath to admit where I'd really been for that last hour of the afternoon. But it's time to come clean. 1

I joined a health club. 2

I went downtown and sweated with the masses. I rode a bike that goes nowhere at the rate of five hundred calories per hour. I even pumped a little iron. I can't deny the place was a lekking ground: guys stalking around the weight room like prairie chickens, nervously eying each other's pectorals. Over by the abdominal machines I heard some of the frankest pickup lines since eighth grade ("You've got real defined deltoids for a girl"). A truck perpetually parked out front had vanity plates the read: LFT WTS. Another one, PRSS 250, I didn't recognize as a vanity plate until I understood the prestige of bench pressing 250 pounds. 3

I personally couldn't bench press a fully loaded steam iron. I didn't join the health club to lose weight, or to meet the young Adonis who admired my (dubiously defined) deltoids. I am content with my lot in life, save for one irksome affliction: I am what's known in comic-book jargon as the ninety-eight-pound weakling. I finally tipped the scales into three digits my last year of high school, but "weakling" I've remained, pretty much since birth. In polite terminology I'm cerebral; the muscles between my ears are what I get by on. The last great body in my family was my Grandfather Henry. He wore muscle shirts in the days when they were known as BVDs, under his cotton work shirt, and his bronze tan stopped midbiceps. He got those biceps by hauling floor joists and hammering up roof beams every day of his life, including his last. How he would have guffawed to see a roomful of nearly naked bankers and attorneys, pale as plucked geese, heads down, eyes fixed on a horizon beyond the water cooler, pedaling like bats out of hell on bolted-down bicycles. I expect he'd offer us all a job. If we'd pay our thirty dollars a month to *him*, we could come out to the construction site and run up and down ladders bringing him nails. That's why I'm embarrassed about all this. I'm afraid I share his opinion of unproductive sweat. 4

Actually, he'd be more amazed than scornful. His idea of fun was watching Ed Sullivan or snoozing in a recliner, or ideally, both at once. Why work like a maniac on your day off? To keep your heart and lungs in shape. Of course. But I haven't noticed any vanity plates that say GD LNGS. The operative word here is vanity. 5

Standards of beauty in every era are things that advertise, usually falsely: "I'm   *6*
rich and I don't have to work." How could you be a useful farmhand, or even an
efficient clerk-typist, if you have long, painted fingernails? Four-inch high heels,
like the bound feet of Chinese aristocrats, suggest you don't have to do *anything*
efficiently, except maybe put up your tootsies on an ottoman and eat bonbons.
(And I'll point out here that aristocratic *men* wore the first high heels.) In my
grandmother's day, women of all classes lived in dread of getting a tan, since that
betrayed a field worker's station in life. But now that the field hand's station is
occupied by the office worker, a tan, I suppose, advertises that Florida and Maui are
within your reach. Fat is another peculiar cultural flip-flop: in places where food is
scarce, beauty is three inches of subcutaneous fat deep. But here and now, jobs are
sedentary and calories are relatively cheap, while the luxury of time to work them off
is very dear. It still gives me pause to see an ad for a weight-loss program that boldly
enlists: "First ten pounds come off free!" But that is about the size of it, in the strange
food-drenched land of ours. After those first ten, it gets expensive.

As a writer I could probably do my job fine with no deltoids at all, or biceps or   *7*
triceps, so long as you left me those vermicelli-sized muscles that lift the fingers to
the keyboard. (My vermicellis are *very* well defined.) So when I've writ my piece, off
I should merrily go to build a body that says I don't really have a financial obligation
to sit here in video-terminal bondage.

Well, yes. But to tell the truth, the leisure body and even the GD LNGS are   *8*
not really what I was after when I signed up at Pecs-R-Us. What I craved, and long
for still, is to be *strong*. I've never been strong. In childhood, team sports were my
most reliable source of humiliation. I've been knocked breathless to the ground by
softballs, basketballs, volleyballs, and once, during a wildly out-of-hand game of
Red Rover, a sneaker. In every case I knew my teammates were counting on me for a
volley or a double play or anyhow something more than clutching my stomach and
rolling upon the grass. By the time I reached junior high I wasn't even the last one
picked anymore. I'd slunk away long before they got to the bottom of the barrel.

Even now, the great mortification of my life is that visitors to my home   *9*
sometimes screw the mustard and pickle jar lids back on so tightly *I can't get them
open!* (The visitors probably think they are just closing them enough to keep the
bugs out.) Sure, I can use a pipe wrench, but it's embarrassing. Once, my front
gate stuck, and for several days I could only leave home by clambering furtively
through the bougainvilleas and over the garden wall. When a young man knocked
on my door to deliver flowers one sunny morning, I threw my arms around him.
He thought that was pretty emotional, for florists' mums. He had no idea he'd just
casually pushed open the Berlin Wall.

My inspiration down at the health club was a woman fire-fighter who could   *10*
have knocked down my garden gate with a karate chop. I still dream about her

Brittny / Shutterstock.com

triceps. But I've mostly gotten over my brief fit of muscle envy. Oh, I still make my ongoing, creative stabs at bodybuilding: I do "girl pushups," and some of the low-impact things from Jane Fonda's pregnant-lady workout book, even if I'm not. I love to run, because it always seems like there's a chance you might actually get somewhere, so I'll sometimes cover a familiar mile or so of our county road after I see my daughter onto the school bus. (The driver confessed that for weeks he thought I was chasing him; he never stopped.) And finally, my friends have given me an official item of exercise equipment that looks like a glob of blue putty, which you're supposed to squeeze a million times daily to improve your grip. That's my current program. The so-called noncompetitive atmosphere of the health club whipped me, hands down. Realistically, I've always known I was born to be a "before" picture. So I won't be seen driving around with plates that boast: PRSS 250. Maybe: OPN JRS.

11

Reading for Better Writing

Working by yourself or with a group, answer these questions:

1. Kingsolver entitles her essay, "The Muscle Mystique." What does "mystique" mean and in what sense are muscles or bodybuilding a "mystique"?

2. Review the opening few paragraphs and explain how the writer introduces her subject and sets the tone for the essay. Cite words and phrases that you find interesting, engaging, or funny.

3. In the third paragraph, Kingsolver describes the health club as a "lekking ground." What does "lekking" mean, and what does it suggest about the "muscle mystique"?

4. Re-read paragraph four in which the writer compares her own physique with that of her grandfather's. Cite details that help you envision each.

5. Kingsolver contrasts (1) current bodybuilders' focus on playful lekking with (2) her fit grandfather's focus on hard work. What's her point? And how does this point relate to what she says in paragraph 6 about the "standards of beauty" in her time vs. "standards of beauty" in her grandmother's time?

6. Define "self-deprecating humor" and cite examples in paragraphs 7-11. Would these passages be as funny if the writer were describing others' foibles rather than her own?

7. Find two or three passages that you consider reflective writing and explain how they enrich the text.

8. Re-read Kingsolver's last sentence in which she suggests a license-plate inscription that relays her bodybuilding goal. Then work with a classmate to create comic inscriptions that relay your goals.

"The Muscle Mystique" from HIGH TIDE IN TUCSON: ESSAYS FROM NOW OR NEVER by Barbara Kingsolver, pages 80-84. HarperCollins, 1995. Copyright (c) 1995 by Barbara Kingsolver. Reprinted by permission of HarperCollins Publishers Inc. and The Frances Goldin Literary Agency.

Writing Guidelines

Planning

1. **Select a topic.** The most promising topics are experiences that gave you insights into yourself, and possibly into others as well. To identify such topics, consider the categories below and then list whatever experiences come to mind:
   - Times when you felt *secure, hopeful, distraught, appreciated, confident, frightened, exploited,* or *misunderstood.*
   - Times when you made a decision about *lifestyles, careers, education,* or *religion.*
   - Events that tested your *will, patience, self-concept,* or *goals.*
   - Events that changed or confirmed your assessment of *a person, a group,* or *an institution.*

   Tip: List topics in response to the following statement: *Reflect on times when you first discovered that the world was strange, wonderful, complex, frightening, small, full, or empty.* How did these experiences affect you?

2. **Get the big picture.** Once you have chosen a topic, gather your thoughts by brainstorming or freewriting in response to questions like these:
   - Where did the experience take place and what specific sights, sounds, and smells distinguish the place?
   - Who else was involved, and what did they look like, act like, do, and say?
   - What were the key or pivotal points in your experiences and why?
   - What led to these key moments and what resulted from them?
   - How did your or others' comments or actions affect what happened?
   - What did others learn from this experience—and what did you learn?
   - Did the experience end as you had hoped? Why or why not?
   - What themes, conflicts, and insights arose from the experience?
   - How do your feelings now differ from your feelings then? Why?

   Tip: To find out more details about the event or people involved, sort through photo albums and home videos to trigger memories; talk to someone who shared your experiences; consult your journal, old letters, and saved digital communications, such as email.

3. **Probe the topic and reveal what you find.** The mind-searching aspect of writing this essay happens while asking so-why questions: *So why does this picture still make me smile? or Why does his comment still hurt? or Why did I do that when I knew better—or Did I know better?* Your readers need to experience what you experienced, so don't hide what's embarrassing, or painful, or still unclear.

4. **Get organized.** Review your brainstorming or freewriting, and highlight key details, quotations, or episodes. Then list the main events in chronological order, or use a cluster to help you gather details related to your experiences.

Drafting

5. Write the first draft. Rough out the first draft. Then test your narration and description by asking whether the quotations, details, and events are accurate and clear. Test your reflection by asking whether it explains how the experience affected you.

Revising

6. Review the draft. After taking a break, read your essay for truthfulness and completeness. Does it include needed details and questions?

7. Get feedback. Ask a classmate to read your paper and respond to it.

8. Improve the ideas, organization, and voice. Use your own review and peer review to address these issues:

___ **Ideas:** The essay offers readers an engaging, informative look into your life, personality, and perspective.

___ **Organization:** The essay includes (1) an inviting opening that pictures the setting, introduces the characters, and forecasts the themes; (2) a rich middle that develops a clear series of events, nuanced characters, and descriptions; and (3) a satisfying closing that completes the experience and unifies the essay's ideas.

___ **Voice:** The tone is fair, and it fits the experience. The voice is genuine and inviting.

Editing

9. Edit and proofread your essay. Polish your writing by addressing these items:

___ **Words:** The words in descriptive and narrative passages *show* instead of *tell about*; they are precise and rich, helping readers imagine the setting, envision the characters, and vicariously experience the action. The words in reflective passages are insightful and measured.

___ **Sentences:** The sentences in descriptive and reflective passages are clear, varied in structure, and smooth. The sentences in dialogue accurately reflect the characters' personalities, regional diction, and current idioms.

___ **Correctness:** The copy includes no errors in spelling, mechanics, punctuation, or grammar.

___ **Page Design:** The design is attractive and follows assigned guidelines.

Publishing

10. Publish your writing by sharing your essay with friends and family, posting it on a Web site, or submitting it to a journal or newspaper.

Critical-Thinking and Writing Activities

As directed by your instructor, complete the following critical-thinking and writing activities by yourself or with classmates.

1. Review "The Entomology of Village Life," noting how the essay centers on what the writer and his friend witness. Think about what it means to be a witness—to a crime, a tragedy, a triumph, a performance, an encounter, and so on. Then write an essay in which you explore a time that you were a witness.

2. In "Spare Change," Teresa Zsuffa describes her encounter with someone whose qualities, experiences, and values are different from her own. Write a personal essay in which you explore such an encounter in your life.

3. Elizabeth Fuller in "When Dreams Take Flight" and Barbara Kingsolver in "The Muscle Mystique" write about themselves with self-deprecating humor. As readers, we laugh with them because we also have had experiences in which we made mistakes, did something silly, or found that we didn't measure up to our own or others' goals or standards. Choose such an experience that you feel comfortable sharing with others. Then write an essay in which you describe what happened, reflect on its impact, and share the mirth.

Learning-Objectives Checklist ✓

Have you achieved this chapter's learning objectives? Check your progress with the items below, revisiting topics in the chapter as needed. *I have . . .*

____ successfully identified, critiqued, and created these elements of narrative writing: setting, character, plot, dialogue, and theme (138–139).

____ developed engaging, vivid, and well-organized descriptive writing that includes precise words and sensory appeals (139–140).

____ integrated into my personal writing appropriate analytical strategies such as interesting comparisons and contrasts (141).

____ written reflective passages that include honest, relevant, and fitting observations (142).

____ successfully analyzed my writing situation in order to determine when, why, and how to use anecdotes (143).

____ blended techniques of narration, description, and reflection to craft a personal essay that enables readers to share my experience and to understand its broad significance (158–159).

____ developed a well-organized personal essay with an engaging opening, a rich and substantive middle, and a complementary closing (158–159).

Chapter 11

Cause and Effect

Now, why did that happen? We ask this question every day at home, in college, and on the job in order to understand and cope with things that happen in our lives. For example, knowing why a computer crashed will help us avoid that problem, and knowing the causes and effects of a disease such as diabetes can help us control the condition. In other words, cause and effect reasoning helps us deal with everyday issues, whether large or small.

In a cause and effect essay, the writer develops the thesis through cause and effect reasoning. That is, she or he analyzes and explains the causes, the effects, or both the causes and the effects of a phenomenon. In addition, the writer may use other analytical strategies (such as definition or classification) to clarify a concept or further develop a claim. This chapter includes instructions and samples that will help you read and write cause-effect analyses.

Visually Speaking   What cause-effect relationship is implied in Figure 11.1? What research and writing strategies could you use to analyze the phenomenon pictured below?

Learning **Objectives**

By working through this chapter, you will be able to

- understand, interpret, and critique writing that utilizes cause-effect reasoning.
- analyze a phenomenon by identifying and explaining its causes and effects.
- identify and correct related logical fallacies.
- support cause-effect reasoning with detailed, reliable evidence.
- clarify cause-effect relationships by inserting transitional words.
- draft, revise, and edit an essay that uses cause-effect reasoning in conjunction with other relevant analytical modes.

Strahil Dimitrov / Shutterstock.com

fig. 11.1

Strategies for Cause-Effect Essays

Cause-effect thinking can move in two directions. First, it can explore the effects of a particular event, action, or phenomenon—the logical results, actual or anticipated. Second, it can trace backward from a particular result to those forces that created the results—the causes. As writers think through causes and effects, their job is to establish and explain solid cause-effect links, as discussed in the strategies below.

The Rhetorical Situation

To put cause-effect writing in context, consider the situation that gives rise to it:

- **Purpose.** Writers use cause-effect analysis to deepen understanding regarding how specific forces work to bring about particular results. In academia and the workplace, cause-effect logic operates in many forms of writing—from persuasive essays and lab reports to project proposals and market analyses. In each situation, writers use cause-effect thinking to explain a phenomenon or to prove a point.
- **Readers.** The readers of cause-effect writing typically understand the topic at a basic level but want or need a deeper understanding of the forces operating within it so as to make decisions about or take positions on it.
- **Topic.** Cause-effect topics are phenomena—events, occurrences, developments, processes, problems, conditions, and so on—that need to be more fully explained in terms of their operating forces.

Example: In "Dutch Discord" (pages 167–170), Brittany Korver's **topic** is the increasing tension between ethnic Dutch and Muslim immigrants in the Netherlands. Her **purpose** is to help **readers** (classmates and professor) understand how specific historical events and cultural issues have caused this phenomenon.

Principles of Cause-Effect Writing

Cause-effect writing depends upon the logical principles explained below.

Exploring cause-effect links. Such writing tests all possible explanations for a given phenomenon's causes and effects. Consider these options:

- **Causes:** What forces can be designated primary or root causes? What forces are secondary or contributing causes? Which causes are immediate (near), and which are remote (distant)? What cause-effect "evidence" is simply coincidental? What evidence—measurements, testimony, and so on—supports or disproves the causal links? Can the links be tested?
- **Effects:** What are the primary, secondary, and ripple effects? Which are main effects and which are side effects, which immediate and which long-term? What is the seriousness or strength of each effect? What aspects of the cause led to the various effects? Do the effects themselves become causes of a different set of effects in a kind of "chain reaction"?

Establishing a cause-effect thesis. The thesis is an insight growing out of careful study of the topic, often following one of these templates:

- **Focus on causes:** Based on a close examination of the forces at work, we can conclude that A and B are the fundamental causes of C.
- **Focus on effects:** Based on a close examination of the forces at work, we can conclude that the most important results of A have been X, Y, and Z.

Example: When people around the globe watch Hollywood blockbuster films, they absorb a distorted vision of U.S. culture that fuels misunderstanding and, in fact, undermines the government's "war on terror."

Supplying reliable cause-effect evidence. Cause-effect analysis is based on a logical interpretation of the evidence, analysis that avoids these problems: (1) relying extensively on circumstantial evidence, (2) drawing firm conclusions without adequate support, and (3) mistaking sequence for a cause-effect link (see the *false-cause fallacy*, page 303).

Organizing cause-effect analysis to feature the chain of reasoning. The phrasing of the thesis implies a certain method of developing and supporting the thesis—a way of proceeding with and handling the cause-effect evidence. Generally, writers structure their essays according to the direction of analysis (from effect to causes or from cause to effects). It is often necessary to begin by exploring background in order to situate the cause-effect analysis.

Sample Cause-Effect Paragraph:

However, the chief challenges that ethnic Dutch have in relating to their Muslim neighbors have little to do with demographic characteristics or economic standing, and more to do with cultural practices and worldviews. For example, ethnic Dutch have difficulty accepting or respecting traditional Muslim views regarding women's roles in society and homosexual lifestyles, as well as resident Muslims' high crime rate and violent Islamic extremism ("Veils and Wooden Clogs" 230). The ethnic Dutch are repulsed by stories of wife beating, arranged marriages, women forbidden to hold jobs, homosexuals put to death in the immigrants' home countries, terrorist attacks in Western countries, and violent crimes committed by immigrants in the Netherlands (230). This cultural clash has led the Netherlands to re-evaluate and in some ways re-direct its pursuit of a multi-cultural state and return to the nation-state model as the ideal (198 Mamadouh).

Reading Cause-Effect Writing

As you read the essays on the following pages, consider these questions:

1. Is the writer's rationale for writing informed, reasonable, and convincing?
2. Who is the intended audience, and does the essay present all the necessary information?
3. Is the topic clearly identified and explored as a phenomenon?
4. Is the thesis clear, and is the argument free of logical fallacies?
5. Are the writer's claims sufficiently limited, focused, and logical?

Sample Cause-Effect Essays

Cause-effect essays can address a wide range of topics—from phenomena in nature to events in the news. In the following essays, writers address topics as varied as the causes of anorexia, the nature of ethnic conflict in the Netherlands, the effects of sports involvement on careers, and the impacts of new technologies on human intelligence.

Analyzing an Eating Disorder

In the essay below, Trina Rys (a student who attended Humber College and the University of Guelph) makes claims about the causes of anorexia nervosa.

Essay Outline

Introduction: Why do young women practice starvation as a method of weight control?
1. **Cause 1:** the psychological pressures of adolescence
2. **Cause 2:** expectations of family and peers
3. **Cause 3:** potential influence of the media

Conclusion: Cultural values regarding the female body need to change in order for eating disorders to decline.

The Slender Trap

Rys begins with a vivid quotation, powerful questions, and a clear cause-effect thesis.

Starvation is not a pleasant way to expire. In advanced stages of famine, as the body begins to consume itself, the victim suffers muscle pain, heart disturbances, loss of hair, dizziness, shortness of breath, extreme sensitivity to cold, [and] physical and mental exhaustion. The skin becomes discoloured. In the absence of key nutrients, a severe chemical imbalance develops in the brain, inducing convulsions and hallucinations. (Krakauer, 1996, p. 198)   1

Every day, millions die of hunger. The symptoms of starvation are so horrific that it seems unthinkable anyone would choose this way of death. How is it possible that in the Western world, one in two hundred young women from upper- and middle-class families practises starvation as a method of weight control? How do young women become so obsessed with being thin that they develop anorexia nervosa? To cause such a fearsome and potentially fatal condition, the influencing factors must be powerful indeed. And they are powerful: the psychological pressures of adolescence, the inescapable expectations of family and peers, and the potent influence of the media.   2

A tendency to perfectionism, lack of identity, and feelings of helplessness are three aspects of a young woman's psychology that can contribute to the development   3

1 She analyzes the weight of psychological forces on body image.

of anorexia nervosa. Young women who exhibit perfectionism are particularly susceptible to the disease because they often have unrealistic expectations about their physical appearance. These expectations can lead to feelings of helplessness and powerlessness, and some young women with these feelings see starving themselves as a means to empowerment. Their diet is often the only thing they can control, and they control it with a singlemindedness that astonishes and horrifies their families and friends. As well as the need for control, anorexia in young women can be caused by a weak or unformed identity. Confused about who they are, many young women define themselves by how closely they approximate our society's notion of the ideal woman. Unfortunately, for the past half-century, Western society's ideal female image has been that of an unrealistically thin young woman. When women focus on this impossible image as the ideal and strive to starve their bodies into submission, they suffer emotional and physical damage.

2 With a clear transition, the writer turns to the effects of home environment on the desire to be thin.

In addition to an unstable psychological state, family and peer pressure can contribute to a fragile young woman's development of anorexia nervosa. By emphasizing physical appearance, by criticizing physical features, and even by restricting junk food, family members can push a young woman over the cliff edge that separates health from illness. A home environment in which physical appearance is overvalued can be destructive for young women. Surrounded by family members and friends who seem to be concerned primarily about appearance, a young woman can begin to feel insecure about how she looks. This uncertainty can produce the desire—and then the need—to look better. And better means thinner. This flawed logic underlies the disease in many young women. A family or peer group that overvalues physical appearance is often also critical of physical flaws. Critical comments about weight and general appearance, even when spoken jokingly, can be instrumental in a young woman's desire to be thin. Ironically, food restrictions imposed by parents can also contribute to anorexia in young women. Restricting the consumption of junk food, for example, has been known to cause bingeing and purging, a condition associated with anorexia.

3 She argues that media influence is the root cause of an obsession with thinness.

While a young woman's developing psyche and the pressures of those close to her can exert tremendous influence, the root cause of the "thin is beautiful" trap is a media-inspired body image. Television, fashion magazines, and stereotypical Hollywood images of popular stars provide young women with an unrealistic image of the ideal female body. While only 5 percent of North American females are actually underweight, 32 percent of female television and movie personalities are unhealthily thin (ANRED, 2004). The media's unrealistic portrayal of a woman's ideal body can cause a young woman to develop a sense of inadequacy. To be considered attractive, she feels she must be ultra-thin. Television's unrealistic portrayal of the way young women should look is reinforced in the pages of fashion magazines. Magazine ads feature tall, beautiful, thin women. Media images also perpetuate the stereotype that a woman must be thin in order to be successful. Thanks to television and movies, when we think of a successful woman, the image that comes to mind is that of a tall, well-dressed, thin woman. This stereotypical image leads impressionable young women to associate success with body weight and image. When internalized by young women, these artificial standards can result in the development of anorexia nervosa.

> Rys's conclusion calls for the positive changes needed to prevent eating disorders.

If the media do not begin to provide young women with a positive and healthy image of femininity, we will see no lessoning in the numbers of anorexia victims. If our cultural ideal of female beauty does not change to reflect a range of healthy body types, the pressures to realize idealized and unhealthy physical standards will continue, and young women's feelings of helplessness and inadequacy will persist. In order for anorexia to become less prominent among young women, healthier associations must replace the existing connections among beauty, success, and thinness. Young women must realize that self-inflicted starvation is not a means to empowerment, but a process of self-destruction.

6

Note: The Works Cited page is not shown. For examples, see MLA (pages 493–534) and APA (pages 535–564).

Reading for Better Writing

Working by yourself or with a group, answer these questions:

1. Trina Rys's essay follows a careful, traditional structure: an introduction containing a clear thesis, three points that support the thesis, and a conclusion that pulls together the analysis while deepening it. Examine the strategies that she uses in the introduction, middle, and conclusion of her writing (e.g., the opening quotation, the thesis statement, paragraph topic sentences, closing sentences). Does this structure work for her topic and for the cause-effect analysis she is doing? Explain.

2. Rys analyzes three causes behind eating disorders. Why do you think that she ordered them as she did? How convincing do you find her cause-effect claims and the reasoning in support of those claims? Are there other causes she should have considered?

3. How would you characterize the tone and approach of Rys's conclusion? Does it follow logically from her analysis?

"The Slender Trap" by Trina Piscitelli. Used by permission of the author.

Analyzing a Culture Clash

Student writer Brittany Korver wrote the following essay. In the paper, she analyzes how the increasing number of Muslim residents in the Netherlands is impacting Dutch culture and raising tension within a society known for its diversity and tolerance.

Dutch Discord

The title identifies the phenomenon.

Introduction: Dutch symbols and ethnic tensions

When people outside the Netherlands think of the Dutch, what do they envision? Some may picture stoic windmills, grass-covered dykes, and tidy row houses. Others may see barge-filled canals, gay parades, and red-light districts. Still others may envision the Free University in Amsterdam, the harbor in Rotterdam, and the International Court of Justice in The Hague. But when people inside the Netherlands think of common sites in their country, they likely also picture the growing number of domed mosques in Dutch city skylines, veiled faces in the streets, or scarf-covered heads in the classrooms. The fact is, these images are increasingly common in the Netherlands as its Muslim population continues to grow and spread ("One Million Muslims"). More importantly, however, this diffusion appears to have increased tension between the progressive ethnic Dutch—long known for tolerating cultural differences—and their new neighbors.

Social changes brought about by immigration: history.

The first, most notable influx of Muslims was drawn to the Netherlands after World War II by job offers (Shadid 10). The Dutch, looking for cheap labor, recruited large numbers of unskilled laborers from poorer countries (10). These immigrants were typically guest workers who expected to stay temporarily and then return to their homelands, as many of them did (Sunier 318).

By 1973, an economic crisis hit Europe, and the Netherlands no longer needed extra workers (Van Amersfoort 179). Many Muslims, however, decided to stay because the economic conditions in their home countries were even less desirable than conditions in the Netherlands (Ketner 146). Numerous immigrants became permanent residents and were joined by their families. When the Dutch finally tightened restrictions by lowering quotas and raising standards for refugees, marriages continued between Dutch-Muslim citizens and Muslim foreigners. Since family reunification is a Dutch migration priority, these spouses continued to flow into the Netherlands (Van Amersfoort 179). In addition, the Netherlands experienced increased illegal immigration (179).

However, while legal and illegal immigrants increased the Netherlands' Muslim population significantly, the population swelled even more because of Muslims'

1

2

3

4

relatively high fertility rates (Kent). For example, as of 2004, CBS (the Netherlands' statistics bureau) reported 945,000 Muslims living in the country, a jump of over 339,000 from ten years earlier ("One Million Muslims"). They currently account for at least 5.8 percent of the population, which makes Muslims the fourth largest religious group in the Netherlands, trailing just behind Dutch Calvinists ("As many Muslims as Calvinists"). While Muslims are distributed quite sparsely in some provinces (e.g., less than 3 percent in Friesland), they make up as much as one third of the population in cities such as Amsterdam (Rawstome 30).

Impact of Dutch and Muslim cultures on each other

Not surprisingly, this growing minority is both affecting and being affected   5 by Dutch culture. Ethnic foods are increasingly available in stores and restaurants (Wagensveld). New shops and market stands accommodate the demand for folk clothing (Wagensveld). Private Islamic schools are available, and mosques dot the landscape (Landman 1125). Coverage of Turk and Moroccan culture, including their religious festivals, fill many pages in the Netherlands' souvenir books (DeRooi 107). In addition, businesses cater to their new consumers by including dark-haired people in their ads and abandoning potentially offensive practices, such as distributing piggy-banks (Charter 40).

Dutch culture also leaves its mark on this new community. For example, many   6 Muslims find themselves forgetting Islamic holidays because they are too busy or do not know the Arabic calendar ("Time and Migration" 387). Many have adjusted to the Dutch view of time, making their lives faster paced. Some save religious prayers for after work, disrupting the normal prayer schedule (390). In fact, even some mosques encourage change by offering immigrants Dutch language classes, computer courses, and bicycle lessons (Van Amersfoort 185–186).

Secondary differences between Dutch and Muslim cultures

Though assimilation between most cultural groups in the Netherlands is   7 common, the ethnic Dutch and those who trace their roots to Muslim countries retain conspicuous differences, sometimes leading to tensions between them. For example, fertility runs higher among these immigrants, prompting some ethnic Dutch to fear that they will eventually become a minority (Kent). Muslims still have lower education levels, high levels of unemployment, and poorer housing than most other residents. And among second generation Muslims, dropout rates and delinquencies run high (Mamadouh 198).

Major differences: cultural practices and world view

However, the chief challenges that ethnic Dutch have in relating to their   8 Muslim neighbors have little to do with demographic characteristics or economic standing, and more to do with cultural practices and worldviews. For example, ethnic Dutch have difficulty accepting or respecting traditional Muslim views regarding women's roles in society and homosexual lifestyles, as well as resident Muslims' high crime rate and violent Islamic extremism ("Veils and Wooden Clogs" 230). The ethnic Dutch are repulsed by stories of wife beating, arranged marriages, women forbidden to hold jobs, homosexuals put to death in the immigrants' home countries, terrorist attacks in Western countries, and violent crimes committed by immigrants in the Netherlands (230). This cultural clash has led the Netherlands to re-evaluate and in some ways re-direct its pursuit of a multi-cultural state and return to the nation-state model as the ideal (198 Mamadouh).

Us vs. them mentality

In some cases, tensions have evolved into an "us" vs. "them" mentality that   9
includes covert and overt racism and hostility (Shadid 16). In the journal *European Education*, Wasif A. Shadid makes this point by comparing some attitudes in Holland with what appear to be parallel attitudes in South Africa's Apartheid system. Examples of these tensions or attitudes include increasing differentiation between the native Dutch and immigrant groups, politicians speaking negatively of Muslim residents (11-16), and sometimes violent acts between Muslims and non-Muslims (Esman 12).

Fear of extremism, terrorism, and assassinations

Since the turn of the millennium, the ethnic Dutch fear of Islamic extremism   10
has also increased, brought on in part by international events such as the September 11, 2001 attacks in the United States, and the subsequent strikes in Madrid and London. This fear was further intensified when two well-known anti-Islam Dutch politicians were assassinated inside the Netherlands. The first was Pim Fortuyn, who was shot in 2002 (Shadid 17). Fortuyn had his own political party, which called for "stopping all immigration" and a "cold war against Islam" (Esman 12). His assassination created a stir because the Dutch suddenly found their freedom of speech jeopardized, thereby widening the rift between the Dutch and Muslim cultures (Wagensveld).

The second Dutch politician assassinated was Theo Van Gogh in 2004, and this   11
event is often referred to as the September 11 of the Netherlands (Esman 12). Like Fortuyn, Van Gogh was very outspoken. He also used offensive language, gained many young followers (Margaronis 6), and went on to make the movie *Submission* with ex-Muslim and screen writer, Ayaan Hirsi Ali, a film that exposed Dutch-Muslim domestic abuse (6). Van Gogh was shot and stabbed to death, resulting in a martyr-like legacy for his cause (Rawstome 30).

The most recent tension-building event was the March 2008 release of the   12
controversial movie *Fitna* (Arabic for *strife*), directed by Dutch MP Geert Wilders

(Rawstome 30). The short movie displays graphic and disturbing images of terrorism and abuse, and it uses quotes from the Koran and Islamic leaders, suggesting that both sources support these violent actions (*Fitna*). The movie is so controversial that fear of violent repercussions is widespread, and many Netherlanders think that Wilders was irresponsible for releasing it (Rawstome 30). Wilders received six hundred death threats by late March, has six body guards, and at times he and his wife live in prison cells for safety (30).

> Conclusion: Tensions lead to fear and alienation.

As events like these suggest, the growth of the Muslim community in the Netherlands appears to have increased the tension between the ethnic Dutch and Muslims. As a result, many ethnic Dutch feel disconcerted, and many Dutch Muslims feel alienated (Shadid 20). Whether those who built windmills and those who build mosques will ever live together in unity remains unclear. But what is clear is that such unity never will happen until the two groups learn to live with the differences that now separate them.

13

Note: The Works Cited page is not shown. For examples, see MLA (pages 493–534) and APA (pages 535-564).

Reading for Better Writing

Working by yourself or with a group, answer these questions:

1. Do the title and opening paragraph effectively get your attention and introduce the topic? Explain.
2. Brittany Korver wrote this essay expecting that it would be read by other college students and her professor. Review her topic, thesis, and core argument; then explain why they are or are not fitting choices for her readers.
3. In paragraphs 2–4, Brittany uses chronological order to explain how the Muslim population in the Netherlands increased. Review those paragraphs and explain whether her organization and details adequately describe the increase.
4. In the opening sentence of paragraph 5, Brittany says, "[T]his growing minority is both affecting and being affected by Dutch culture." Review paragraphs five and six and explain whether they adequately develop the quotation above.
5. Note how the writer builds paragraphs 7–9 by opening each with a topic sentence and following with documented supporting details. Then explain why these choices do or do not strengthen her argument.
6. In paragraphs 10–12, the writer describes three violent events that transpired since 2002. Explain why she might cite these events and whether she uses them effectively to develop her thesis.

Analyzing the Effects of Sports Participation

In the essay below, Mary Brophy Marcus describes successful businesswomen and argues that the skills they learned from organized sports helped them achieve that success. The essay was first published in *US News & World Report*.

If You Let Me Play . . .

The writer uses an anecdote to introduce the topic and focus the essay.

Jackie Thomas, Nike's associate director of sports marketing, usually spends her lunch hour on the sports-shoe company's basketball courts charging for the basket, always outnumbered by male colleagues. "I hold my own," boasts the 33-year-old executive. *1*

She also does well playing the corporate game back inside the headquarters' offices. Thomas, a former University of California-Berkeley college basketball point guard, says her success is due in large part to the lessons she learned growing up playing competitive team sports. "It's taught me that if you lose a game, you go back afterward and figure out what went wrong and how to overcome it the next time," says the former tomboy from Kingston, Jamaica. *2*

A dependent clause links the second and third paragraphs.

While most of America's corporations are still commanded by male chief executives, women are gaining ground, winning vice-presidential and top management slots and, in a few cases, the highest leadership roles. Many of these young female executives say playing team sports helped them get ahead. A University of Virginia study conducted in the late 1980s showed that 80 percent of key female leaders from *Fortune* 500 companies said they participated in sports and considered themselves tomboys. *3*

The writer describes events (or causes) that helped women gain valuable skills in sports.

A lot of credit, female executives say, has to go to Title IX, part of the Federal Education Amendments Act of 1972. It mandated that federally funded schools give women's sports the same treatment as men's games receive. That meant that in schools and colleges across the United States, for every boy's varsity soccer team, there must be a girl's varsity soccer team; for every male basketball scholarship, there must be a female basketball scholarship of equal dollars. Since the early 1970s, the law has increased money for new equipment, coaches, and travel for women's teams. More college scholarships have translated into more diplomas and better jobs for women. Thomas earned a partial academic scholarship when she applied to Berkeley, one of the country's top universities, but without an additional basketball scholarship awarded in her junior and senior years, she would have had a hard time paying for the education. *4*

Using statistical evidence, she cites effects of the causes described in the previous paragraph.

Girls' participation in high school sports has spiked from about 300,000 in 1971 to 2.4 million in 1996. At the college level, where competition is tougher, the number *5*

Aaron Amat / Shutterstock.com

of female athletes has increased to 123,832 from 80,040 in 1982, says the National Collegiate Athletic Association.

"No other experience I know of can prepare you for the high-level competition of business," says Anh Ngyuen, 25, a former Carnegie Mellon University varsity soccer star. She should know. Now she battles Microsoft as a product manager for Netscape Communications. "My colleagues can't believe how aggressive I am," she says.   6

A quotation supports the writer's thesis: Skills learned in sports help one succeed in business.

Sports helped these women master the interpersonal skills, like teamwork, that many men take for granted. "I've seen firsthand hundreds and hundreds of times that one person can't win a soccer or softball game," says Maria Murnane, a 28-year-old senior account executive for a San Francisco public-relations firm. "Same goes for work. You have to learn to trust the people on your team, let them run with projects," the former Northwestern soccer center midfielder says. Her boss, William Harris, the president of Strategy Associates, agrees: "We don't want Lone Rangers. She's a team player—a captain and cheerleader."   7

Playing team sports helps with the little things, too. Women learn to speak in sports metaphors as many men do. Lisa Delpy, professor of sports management at George Washington University in Washington, D.C., also notes that in many companies a lot of business is conducted on the golf course, at ballgames, or at other sports events. Women who know the difference between a slide tackle and a sweeper at a World Cup soccer match can fit right in.   8

The writer supports her thesis with an anecdote.

Stephanie Delaney, now 31, captained the varsity soccer team at Franklin and Marshall College in Lancaster, Pennsylvania, when it won the Mid-Atlantic Conference championship her senior year. Now the sales manager for the Caribbean and Latin American division of ConAgra's Lamb-Weston, one of the world's largest frozen-french-fry producers, she was the only woman to play a game of basketball with potential clients at a big food conference last year in Jamaica. "I was the high scorer," she notes.   9

A lively quotation offers interesting details.

And yes, it helped sell french fries. "I didn't close the deal on the court, but afterward when we were hanging out drinking water and shooting the breeze, they agreed to test my product. Now we have Kentucky Fried Chicken's business in Jamaica," says Delaney.   10

The dash links the word *power* to the defining clause that follows.

Female executives say that Title IX had another subtle, but important, effect. For the first time, many boys, coaches, and parents opened their eyes to the fact that their sisters and daughters could be just as strong, fast, and nimble on the field as their brothers and sons. Likewise, girls whose talents had formerly gone unnoticed under driveway basketball nets and on back lots began realizing their own power—   11 that they could compete with boys and win. "When my girlfriends and I formed a softball team back in college, we were dreadful—like the Keystone Kops," recalls Penny Cate, 45, now a vice president at Quaker Oats. "There'd be four of us in the outfield and the ball would go through our legs. But after a few years, we became very good. It built my confidence, made me realize I could accomplish anything in sports or out," she says.

> The writer cites an advertisement from which she created the essay's title and with which she advances her thesis.

That point is repeatedly brought home when Nike executives ask schoolgirls what they think of one of the company's TV ads. The ad begins with the voice of a young girl saying, "If you let me play . . . ." The phrase is finished by other little girls saying things like, "I will have greater self-confidence" or "I will be more likely to stay in school."   *12*

The girls often reply, in a tone of genuine befuddlement, "If who lets me play?" They don't see any barriers between themselves and America's playing fields. Twenty years from now, might they say, "*What* glass ceiling?"   *13*

Reading for Better Writing

Working by yourself or with a group, answer these questions:

1. Review the writer's title and her reference to it late in the essay. How does the writer use the title to introduce and advance her thesis?

2. Mary Brophy Marcus is a journalist who wrote this essay and many others for publications such as *US News & World Report* and *USA Today*. Review three or four paragraphs from the essay and explain how her word choice, sentence structure, and use of quotations are or are not appropriate for readers of periodicals like these.

3. Review the qualities of an academic style as discussed on pages 77–78. Then explain why Marcus's essay does or does not reflect this style. Cite specific passages to support your answer.

4. Marcus uses cause-effect reasoning to argue that (1) women's participation in sports produces valuable skills and (2) these skills help women succeed in business. Examine three points, along with the evidence (data, quotations, and other elements), that Marcus uses to support either of these claims. Finally, explain why each supporting point and its related evidence are or are not convincing.

5. Marcus concludes her essay with the question, "What glass ceiling?" Explain why the quotation does or does not (1) advance her thesis and (2) close the essay effectively.

6. Working with a classmate, review the checklist under Step 8, "Revise the essay," found on page 179. Then analyze to what degree Marcus accomplishes each task in this checklist.

Mary Brophy Marcus, "If You Let Me Play…" from U.S. NEWS & WORLD REPORT, October 27, 1997. Copyright 1997 U.S. News & World Report, L.P. Reprinted with permission.

Analyzing the Effects of Technology

Steven Pinker teaches in the Department of Psychology at Harvard University where he also conducts research on language and cognition. He writes regularly for publications such as *Time* and *The New Republic*, and he is the author of seven books, including *The Language Instinct, How the Mind Works, Words and Rules, The Blank Slate*, and *The Stuff of Thought: Language as a Window into Human Nature*. In the essay below, published in the *New York Times*, Pinker analyses how our current use of electronic technologies affects our ability to think deeply and process information.

Mind Over Mass Media

Use a pen to identify Pinker's key points and to record your response.

NEW forms of media have always caused moral panics: the printing press, newspapers, paperbacks and television were all once denounced as threats to their consumers' brainpower and moral fiber. 1

So too with electronic technologies. PowerPoint, we're told, is reducing discourse to bullet points. Search engines lower our intelligence, encouraging us to skim on the surface of knowledge rather than dive to its depths. Twitter is shrinking our attention spans. 2

When comic books were accused of turning juveniles into delinquents in the 1950s, crime was falling to record lows . . .

But such panics often fail basic reality checks. When comic books were accused of turning juveniles into delinquents in the 1950s, crime was falling to record lows, just as the denunciations of video games in the 1990s coincided with the great American crime decline. The decades of television, transistor radios and rock videos were also decades in which I.Q. scores rose continuously. 3

For a reality check today, take the state of science, which demands high levels of brainwork and is measured by clear benchmarks of discovery. These days scientists are never far from their e-mail, rarely touch paper and cannot 4 lecture without PowerPoint. If electronic media were hazardous to intelligence, the quality of science would be plummeting. Yet discoveries are multiplying like fruit flies, and progress is dizzying. Other activities in the life of the mind, like philosophy, history and cultural criticism, are likewise flourishing, as anyone who has lost a morning of work to the Web site *Arts & Letters Daily* can attest.

Critics of new media sometimes use science itself to press their case, citing   5
research that shows how "experience can change the brain." But cognitive neuroscientists roll their eyes at such talk. Yes, every time we learn a fact or skill the wiring of the brain changes; it's not as if the information is stored in the pancreas. But the existence of neural plasticity does not mean the brain is a blob of clay pounded into shape by experience.

Experience does not revamp the basic information-processing capacities   6
of the brain. Speed-reading programs have long claimed to do just that, but the verdict was rendered by Woody Allen after he read *War and Peace* in one sitting: "It was about Russia." Genuine multitasking, too, has been exposed as a myth, not just by laboratory studies but by the familiar sight of an S.U.V. undulating between lanes as the driver cuts deals on his cellphone.

Moreover, as the psychologists Christopher Chabris and Daniel Simons   7
show in their new book *The Invisible Gorilla: And Other Ways Our Intuitions Deceive Us,* the effects of experience are highly specific to the experiences themselves. If you train people to do one thing (recognize shapes, solve math puzzles, find hidden words), they get better at doing that thing, but almost nothing else. Music doesn't make you better

The solution is not to bemoan technology but to develop strategies of self-control, as we do with every other temptation in life.

at math, conjugating Latin doesn't make you more logical, brain-training games don't make you smarter. Accomplished people don't bulk up their brains with intellectual calisthenics; they immerse themselves in their fields. Novelists read lots of novels, scientists read lots of science.

The effects of consuming electronic media are also likely to be far more limited than the panic implies. Media critics write as if the brain takes on the qualities of whatever it consumes, the informational equivalent of "you are what you eat." As with primitive peoples who believe that eating fierce animals will make them fierce, they assume that watching quick cuts in rock videos turns your mental life into quick cuts or that reading bullet points and Twitter postings turns your thoughts into bullet points and Twitter postings.   8

Yes, the constant arrival of information packets can be distracting or addictive, especially to people with attention deficit disorder. But distraction is not a new phenomenon. The solution is not to bemoan technology but to develop strategies of self-control, as we do with every other temptation in life. Turn off e-mail or Twitter when you work, put away your Blackberry at dinner time, ask your spouse to call you to bed at a designated hour.   9

And to encourage intellectual depth, don't rail at PowerPoint or Google. It's not as if habits of deep reflection, thorough research and rigorous reasoning ever came naturally to people. They must be acquired in special institutions, which we call universities, and maintained with constant upkeep, which we call analysis, criticism and debate. They are not granted by propping a heavy encyclopedia on your lap, nor are they taken away by efficient access to information on the Internet.   10

The new media have caught on for a reason. Knowledge is increasing exponentially; human brainpower and waking hours are not.

photovs / Shutterstock.com

The new media have caught on for a reason. Knowledge is increasing *11* exponentially; human brainpower and waking hours are not. Fortunately, the Internet and information technologies are helping us manage, search and retrieve our collective intellectual output at different scales, from Twitter and previews to e-books and online encyclopedias. Far from making us stupid, these technologies are the only things that will keep us smart.

Reading for Better Writing

Working by yourself or with a group, answer these questions:

1. Review Pinker's opening paragraph in which he introduces his topic by suggesting that current allegations regarding the negative impact of electronic technologies are similar to past allegations regarding the impact of the printing press, newspapers, paperbacks, and television. Paraphrase his claim and explain why you do or do not agree.

2. The essay is organized as a series of critics' arguments asserting the negative impact of new media, followed by Pinker's counterarguments. Identify three of these exchanges and explain how the point-counterpoint format clarifies both sides of the argument while also making Pinker's position more convincing.

3. Note that Pinker uses cause-effect logic to identify weaknesses in others' claims and to assert the value of his own claims. Identify an example of each that you find persuasive and explain why.

4. Pinker is a scholar aiming to analyze an academic topic with thoughtful, well-researched arguments in an informed, academic tone. Cite passages that illustrate this voice.

5. However, Pinker is also a writer aiming to engage and inform readers who have likely not studied the topic themselves. Identify passages in which his examples and word choice illustrate his effort to connect with these readers.

6. Review Pinker's opening and closing paragraphs. Then explain why they do or do not effectively frame his argument.

7. Review the boldfaced heading (and following paragraph) on page 163: "Organizing cause-effect analysis to feature the chain of reasoning." Then do the following: (1) explain what the paragraph says about how the phrasing of a thesis may imply a method of developing the thesis; and (2) explain whether the phrasing of Pinker's thesis does or does not forecast the organization of his argument.

Writing Guidelines

Planning

1. **Select a topic.** Begin by thinking about categories such as those listed below and listing phenomena related to each category. From this list, choose a topic and analyze its causes, its effects, or both.

   - **Family Life:** adult children living with parents, more stay-at-home dads, families simplifying their lifestyles, adults squeezed by needs of children and parents
   - **Politics:** fewer student voters, increasing support for green-energy production, increased interest in third-party politics, tension between political-action groups
   - **Society:** nursing shortage, doctor shortage, terrorist threats, increasing immigrant-advocacy efforts, shifting ethnic ratios, decreasing number of newspapers
   - **Environment:** common water pollutants, new water-purification technology, decreasing U.S. space exploration, increasing number of nuclear power plants

2. **Narrow and research the topic.** State your topic and below it, list related causes and effects in two columns. Next, do preliminary research to expand the list and distinguish primary causes and effects from secondary ones. Revise your topic as needed to address only primary causes and/or effects that research links to a specific phenomenon.

Cause-effect Topic:	
Causes (Because of)	**Effects** (this results)
1. _____	1. _____
2. _____	2. _____
3. _____	3. _____

   fig. 11.2

3. **Draft and test your thesis.** Based on your preliminary research, draft a working thesis (you may revise it later) that introduces the topic, along with the causes and/or effects you intend to discuss. Limit your argument to only those points you can prove.

4. **Gather and analyze information.** Research your topic, looking for clear evidence that links specific causes to specific effects. As you study the phenomenon, distinguish between primary and secondary causes (main and contributing), direct and indirect results, short-term and long-term effects, and so on. At the same time, test your analysis to avoid mistaking a coincidence for a cause-effect relationship. Use the list of logical fallacies (see pages 301–304) to weed out common errors in logic. For example, finding chemical pollutants in a stream running beside a chemical plant does not "prove" that the plant caused the pollutants.

5. **Get organized.** Develop an outline that lays out your thesis and argument in a clear pattern. Under each main point asserting a cause-effect connection, list details from your research that support the connection.

Thesis: _____		
Point #1	**Point #2**	**Point #3**
• Supporting details	• Supporting details	• Supporting details
• Supporting details	• Supporting details	• Supporting details

   fig. 11.3

Drafting

6. **Use your outline to draft the essay.** Try to rough out the essay's overall argument before you attempt to revise it. As you write, show how each specific cause led to each specific effect, citing examples as needed. To show those cause-effect relationships, use transitional words like the following:

- accordingly
- as a result
- because
- consequently
- for this purpose
- for this reason
- hence
- just as
- since
- so
- such as
- thereby
- therefore
- thus
- to illustrate
- whereas

Revising

7. **Get feedback.** Ask a peer reviewer or someone from the college's writing center to read your essay for an engaging opening, a thoughtful cause-effect thesis, clear and convincing reasoning that links specific causes to specific effects, and a closing that deepens and extends the cause-effect analysis of the phenomenon.

8. **Revise the essay.** Whether your essay presents causes, effects, or both, use the checklist below to trace and refine your argument.

____ **Ideas:** The essay explains the causes and/or effects of the topic in a clear, well-reasoned analysis. The analysis is supported by credible information and free of logical fallacies.

____ **Organization:** The structure helps clarify the cause-effect relationships through a well traced line of thinking, and the links between the main points, supporting points, and evidence are clear.

____ **Voice:** The tone is informed, polite, logical, and measured.

Editing and Proofreading

9. **Edit the essay for clarity and correctness.** Check for the following:

____ **Words:** The diction is precise and clear, and technical or scientific terms are defined. Causes are linked to effects with transitional words and phrases.

____ **Sentences:** Structures are clear, varied, and smooth.

____ **Correctness:** The grammar, punctuation, mechanics, usage, and spelling are correct.

____ **Design:** The format, layout, and typography adhere to expectation; any visuals used enhance the written analysis and clarify the paper's cause-effect reasoning.

Publishing

12. **Publish your essay.** Share your writing by submitting it to your instructor, posting it on the class's or department's Web site, or turning it into a presentation.

Critical-Thinking and Writing Activities

As directed by your instructor, complete the following critical-thinking and writing activities by yourself or with classmates.

1. In "Dutch Discord," Brittany Korver analyzes the causes and effects of a shift in the Netherlands' immigration practices. Identify a similar shift in the policies or practices of a city, state, or country that interests you. Then write an essay in which you analyze the causes and effects of this shift.

2. In "If You Let Me Play . . . ," Mary Brophy Marcus uses cause-effect reasoning to analyze how Jackie Thomas's experience in college athletics helped her prepare for a successful business career. Identify experiences that will help you prepare for your career. Then write an essay in which you use cause-effect reasoning to prove your claim.

3. While "Dutch Discord" focuses on cultural changes, "Mind Over Mass Media" analyzes changes wrought by technology. Identify a social change or a technological change that has impacted your life; then analyze the causes or effects of that change.

4. Scan editorials in two or three newspapers, looking for arguments based on cause-effect reasoning. Then examine the arguments for logical fallacies such as false-cause or slippery-slope claims (for help, see pages 301–304).

Learning-Objectives Checklist ✓

Have you achieved this chapter's learning objectives? Check your progress with the items below, revisiting topics in the chapter as needed. *I have . . .*

____ examined, interpreted, and critiqued arguments that utilize cause-effect reasoning (162–163).

____ analyzed a phenomenon by identifying and explaining its primary and secondary causes and effects (162–163).

____ developed a credible cause-effect thesis based on my study of the topic (162–163).

____ explained how and why a given cause is linked to one or more logically related effects (178).

____ identified and corrected logical fallacies related to cause-effect thinking (301–304).

____ supported my cause-effect reasoning with current, reliable, and detailed evidence (162–163).

____ clarified cause-effect relationships through the effective use of transitional words and phrases (179).

____ used cause-effect reasoning along with other analytical strategies to effectively plan, draft, revise, and polish a cogent, logical essay (178–179).

Chapter 12

Comparison and Contrast

In his plays, William Shakespeare creates characters, families, and even plot lines that mirror each other. As a result, we see Hamlet in relation to Laertes and the Montagues in relation to the Capulets. In the process, we do precisely what the writer wants us to do—we compare and contrast the subjects. The result is clarity and insight: by thinking about both subjects in relation to each other, we understand each one more clearly.

But writers in college and in the workplace also use comparison-contrast as an analytical strategy. To help you read and write such documents, the following pages include instructions and four model essays.

Visually Speaking   Look closely at Figure 12.1. What does it suggest about how comparing and contrasting help one analyze a topic?

Learning **Objectives**

By working through this chapter, you will be able to

- examine and assess writers' use of comparison-contrast reasoning.

- differentiate between subject-by-subject and trait-by-trait strategies for comparison-contrast.

- use transitional words and supporting details to clarify compare-contrast claims.

- establish a clear basis for comparison between two or more topics.

- choose clear elements or features for comparison.

- compose an analytical essay using primarily compare-contrast reasoning (with other analytical strategies).

Mazzzur / Shutterstock.com

fig. 12.1

Strategies for Comparison-Contrast Essays

Comparison-contrast writing holds two or more things, phenomena, or concepts side by side—with comparison focusing on similarities, and contrast focusing on differences. By looking at subjects side-by-side, we more clearly see their unique and shared traits.

The Rhetorical Situation

Consider the context in which writers use comparison-contrast reasoning:

- **Purpose.** Writers commonly compare and contrast subjects in order to explain how, why, and to what effect their distinguishing features make the subjects similar or different. Depending on their purpose, writers may focus on the similarities between seemingly dissimilar things, or on the differences between things that seem similar.
- **Readers.** A writer using comparison-contrast reasoning may have virtually any reader in mind—the instructor for a student essay or potential clients for a marketing document. Whatever the situation, the writer believes that his or her comparative analysis of the topic will enrich readers' understanding of that topic.
- **Topic.** Writers address a wide range of topics through comparison-contrast: people, events, phenomena, technologies, problems, products, stories, and so on.

Example: In "Sethe in *Beloved* . . ." (pages 184–186), Rachel De Smith's **topics** are two literary characters: Sethe in Toni Morrison's *Beloved* and Orleanna in Barbara Kingsolver's *Poisonwood Bible*. De Smith's **purpose** is to help **readers** (her classmates and professor) understand who the characters are and how they are shaped by different histories, cultures, and personal experiences. To that end, she compares and contrasts the two characters' traits.

Principles of Comparison-Contrast Writing

Comparison-contrast writing should be guided by the principles that follow:

Establishing a solid basis for comparison. Comparable items are types of the same thing (e.g. two rivers, two bodies of water, the atmosphere and oceans). Moreover, the subjects are of the same order—one cannot simply be an example of the other: e.g., all lakes and Lake Michigan. Whereas such a discussion would work as an example or illustration, the topics are not truly comparable.

Developing criteria (standards, features, etc.) on which to base the comparison. For example, a comparison of two characters in a play might focus on their backgrounds, their actions in the play, their psychology, their fate, and so on. Once writers choose the criteria, those criteria must be applied consistently. For help comparing and contrasting subjects, use a Venn Diagram (Figure 12.2), listing the subjects' differences on the left or right, and their similarities in the center.

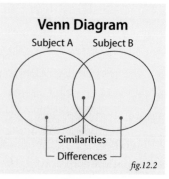

Venn Diagram

Subject A   Subject B

Similarities

Differences

fig.12.2

Considering comparison-contrast. For example, comparison-contrast may be
- the framework for the entire essay, offering a compare-contrast thesis and structuring the discussion around appropriate points of comparison, or as
- a strategy used in a paragraph or a section of an essay, comparing and contrasting details to illuminate an idea.

Phrasing a compare-contrast thesis to clarify relationships. Consider these templates:
- **Emphasizing similarities:** Whereas [subjects A and B] appear quite different in terms of their _____, they show important similarities in that _____ .
- **Emphasizing differences:** Whereas [subjects A and B] appear quite similar in terms of their _____, they are essentially different in that _____ .

Sample thesis: While *Zero Dark Thirty* and *Argo* both dramatize historical events, *Zero's* portrayal of events is more historically accurate than *Argo's*.

Organizing your comparison to clarify similarities and differences for readers. Writers have two choices for organizing comparisons so as to illuminate the topics.
- **Whole vs. whole** discusses items separately, giving a strong overview of each. This pattern works well with short, simple comparisons.
- **Point by point** discusses items together, criterion by criterion. This pattern stresses fine distinctions, making sense for long, complex comparisons.

Sample Comparison-Contrast Paragraph

In the opening paragraph of "Sethe in Beloved . . . " (pages 184–186), Rachel De Smith uses comparison-contrast terms such as *different, one, the other, alike,* and *both.*

> Toni Morrison's Sethe and Barbara Kingsolver's Orleanna Price seem to be vastly different women, living in different times and cultures, descended from different races. One has had a faithful spouse forced away from her by circumstances; the other lives in a devastating marriage. One is a former slave, while the other is a comparatively well-off minister's wife. However, these two women are more alike than they first appear. Both live in isolation and loneliness, both are haunted by the past, both risk everything to get their children out of devastating circumstances—and both reap the consequences of such risks.

Reading Comparison-Contrast Writing

As you read the essays on the following pages, consider these questions:
1. Does the writer compare these topics to stress similarities, differences, or both?
2. What features or traits of the topics are compared? Why?
3. How does the writer present the topics and the criteria for comparison?
4. Is the essay free of logical fallacies (pages 301–304)?
5. What conclusion does the writer develop through compare-contrast analysis?

Sample Comparison-Contrast Essays

Writers compare and contrast topics in order to help readers more fully understand them. For example, in the essays that follow, the writers compare and contrast literary characters, Islamic cultural practices, judicial punishments, and American and European cultures.

Analyzing Two Literary Characters

In the essay below, student writer Rachel De Smith analyzes characters from two novels by comparing and contrasting their history, cultures, experiences, and personalities.

The title identifies the topics compared and the traits examined.

Two seemingly different characters share similar lives.

Both women live in isolation and loneliness.

(a) Sethe

(b) Orleanna

Isolation for both women is rooted in a haunting.

Sethe in *Beloved* and Orleanna in *Poisonwood Bible*: Isolation, Children, and Getting Out

Toni Morrison's Sethe and Barbara Kingsolver's Orleanna Price seem to   1
be vastly different women, living in different times and cultures, descended
from different races. One has had a faithful spouse forced away from her by
circumstances; the other lives in a devastating marriage. One is a former slave, while
the other is a comparatively well-off minister's wife. However, these two women
are more alike than they first appear. Both live in isolation and loneliness, both are
haunted by the past, both risk everything to get their children out of devastating
circumstances—and both reap the consequences of such risks.

Sethe lives in house number 124, a house generally believed to be haunted,   2
"full of a baby's venom" (Morrison 3). The child's ghost inhabiting the house throws
things around, makes spots of colored light appear, shakes floors, and stomps up
the stairs. The people of the surrounding community—remembering Sethe's past,
fearing ghostly retribution, and resenting the long-ago extravagance of Sethe's
mother-in-law, Baby Suggs—diligently avoid the house and its residents. Sethe's one
remaining daughter, Denver, will not leave the yard (Morrison 205). The two of them
live with the ghost, ostracized.

Orleanna lives in a less malignant but equally isolated situation. When she and   3
her daughters follow her husband on his zealous missionary trip to the Congo, she
is the only white woman in a village of people with whom she shares nothing, not
even a word of their language. Preoccupied with the troubles in her own house, she
remains separated from the villagers by a gulf of cultural misunderstanding—from
how to behave in the marketplace to where to get her drinking water (Kingsolver 89,
172). Even when she returns to the United States, Orleanna lives in isolation, hidden
among her flower gardens, set apart by the stigma of her past (Kingsolver 407).

The cause of all this isolation, for both women, is the past. When Sethe saw a   4
slave catcher coming for her, she attempted to kill all four of her young children in

order to prevent them from becoming slaves (Morrison 149, 163). She succeeded in killing only her second-youngest, known as Beloved. No one went back to the plantation; Sethe went to jail instead. Years later, her two oldest children (sons) run off, unable to face the specter of their dead sister knocking over jars and leaving handprints in cakes. Beloved's death is thus the defining moment not only for Sethe's haunted life but also for Denver's, Baby Suggs', and, in many ways, the entire community's.

(a) Sethe

Orleanna, like Sethe, has lost a child, though not by her own hand. Her 5
youngest daughter, Ruth May, died of snakebite after an ugly disagreement (involving much shouting and plenty of voodoo) between the Price family and the rest of the village. Orleanna is not immediately responsible for Ruth May's death—in fact, she has recently brought the girl miraculously through a bout with malaria (Kingsolver 276). However, Orleanna still feels tremendous guilt about Ruth May's death, and even about being in Africa at all. In much of Orleanna's narration, she attempts to move past this guilt, periodically asking her absent daughter's forgiveness. Sethe, also hoping for reconciliation, explains herself in a similar way to Beloved. But Beloved seems to feed off of Sethe's remorse, whereas Ruth May, as portrayed in the final chapter of the novel, bears no such ill-will. Ruth May says, "Mother, you can still hold on but forgive, forgive . . . I forgive you, Mother" (Kingsolver 537, 543). Beloved continually punishes Sethe for leaving her behind, but Ruth May is willing to forgive.

(b) Orleanna

Both Sethe and Orleanna endure grueling journeys of escape, though the 6
journeys begin very differently. Sethe has spent a long time planning an escape with her fellow slaves. When the opportunity finally comes, Sethe sends her children on ahead and then follows, pausing on the way to give birth to Denver. Oddly enough, the final stage of her journey to "freedom" seems to be her time in jail, an episode that kept her from going back to the Sweet Home plantation. However, even after Sethe leaves jail and begins a life free from the degradations of the plantation, she cannot escape the stigma of her past, particularly Beloved's violent death.

Both women take journeys to escape.

(a) Sethe

Orleanna's journey, though also long-anticipated or at least long-desired, is a 7
spontaneous event. Following Ruth May's tragic death (the impetus for her journey), Orleanna simply walks away: her daughter Leah recalls that "Mother never once turned around to look over her shoulder" (Kinsolver 389). Their unplanned journey ends up as a fiasco, culminating in malaria during the rainy season somewhere in the depths of the Congo, but all of Orleanna's remaining daughters survive. Though obvious differences exist between the deaths of Ruth May and Beloved, both deaths allow their families some form of escape. In addition, Orleanna, like Sethe, is willing to give up her children in order for them to escape; she sends Rachel with Eeben

(b) Orleanna

Axelroot and leaves Leah with Anatole when she and Adah leave the country for good. Orleanna's actions parallel Sethe's, as Sethe sends her children ahead of her (in escape or death) in order for them to leave the plantation. Orleanna sees very little of Rachel and Leah for the rest of her life, but they have escaped the devastation of their lives in the Congo, or at least their lives under Nathan Price, and that is—or must be—enough for her.

> These two haunted characters are strong women who eventually move beyond guilt.

Sethe and Orleanna are both haunted women. The deaths of their daughters   8
and estrangement from their remaining children prevent these women from finding peace. Both are haunted by guilt—Sethe for her own actions in the murder of Beloved, and Orleanna for her complicity both in Ruth May's death and in the chaos that enveloped the Congo at the same time. Both women are also isolated and lonely, distanced by distrust and misunderstanding from the people around them. And both women, in the long run, risk everything to gain freedom for their children. Distrust, rage, fear, and bad dreams accompany that risk, but both women keep their children from the evil awaiting them—a plantation, a father's oppression. Paul D. questions Sethe on this point, wondering if other circumstances might be even worse than the plantation. Sethe responds, "It ain't my job to know what's worse. It's my job to know what is and to keep them away from what I know is terrible" (Morrison 165). Sethe is never able to achieve true reconciliation with Beloved, but her relationships with Denver and Paul D. help to make up for this loss, while Orleanna is forgiven by Ruth May and eventually reunited (albeit briefly) with her other children. Despite the attendant circumstances, both Sethe and Orleanna are revealed to be strong women, and both eventually move past their paralyzing guilt in their efforts to "walk forward into the light" (Kingsolver 543).

Note: The Works Cited page is not shown. (See pages 484 and 533 for samples.)

Reading for Better Writing

Working by yourself or with a group, answer these questions:

1. Review the title and opening paragraph, describe how the writer focuses her essay, and explain why you do or do not find that introduction well written.
2. Review the writer's thesis and explain whether she does what she promises.
3. Select two paragraphs and explain why they do or do not clarify the topic and develop the thesis.
4. Based on your reading of this essay, explain why you think that compare-contrast reasoning is or is not an effective strategy for analyzing literature.

"Seth in Beloved and Orleanna in Poisonwood Bible: Isolation, Children, and Getting Out" by Rachel De Smith. *Used by permission of the author.*

Analyzing an Islamic Cultural Practice

Gelareh Asayesh grew up in Iran before moving to Florida. She writes about her experiences in *Saffron Sky: A Life Between Iran and America*. The article below appeared in the *New York Times*.

Shrouded in Contradiction

I grew up wearing the miniskirt to school, the veil to the mosque. In the Tehran of my childhood, women in bright sundresses shared the sidewalk with women swathed in black. The tension between the two ways of life was palpable.
As a schoolgirl, I often cringed when my bare legs got leering or contemptuous glances. Yet, at times, I long for the days when I could walk the streets of my country with the wind in my hair. When clothes were clothes. In today's Iran, whatever I wear sends a message. If it's a chador, it embarrasses my Westernized relatives. If it's a skimpy scarf, I risk being accused of stepping on the blood of the martyrs who died in the war with Iraq. Each time I return to Tehran, I wait until the last possible moment, when my plane lands on the tarmac, to don the scarf and long jacket that many Iranian women wear in lieu of a veil. To wear *hijab*—Islamic covering—is to invite contradiction. Sometimes I hate it. Sometimes I value it.

As a schoolgirl, I often cringed when my bare legs got leering or contemptuous glances.

Most of the time, I don't even notice it. It's annoying, but so is wearing pantyhose to work. It ruins my hair, but so does the humidity in Florida, where I live. For many women, the veil is neither a symbol nor a statement. It's simply what they wear, as their mothers did before them. Something to dry your face with after your ablutions before prayer. A place for a toddler to hide when he's feeling shy. Even for a woman like me, who wears it with a hint of rebellion, hijab is just not that big a deal.

Except when it is.

"Sister, what kind of get-up is this?" a woman in black, one of a pair, asks me one summer day on the Caspian shore. I am standing in line to ride a gondola up a mountain, where I'll savor some ice cream along with vistas of sea and forest. Women in chadors stand wilting in the heat, faces gleaming with sweat. Women in makeup and clunky heels wear knee-length jackets with pants, their hair daringly

1

2

3

4

Two contrasting scenes appear in the first sentence.

Italics distinguish *hijab* as a non-English word.

Notice the one-sentence paragraph.

exposed beneath sheer scarves.

None have been more daring than I. I've wound my scarf into a turban, leaving   5
my neck bare to the breeze. The woman in black is a government employee paid to
police public morals. "Fix your scarf at once!" she snaps.

"But I'm hot," I say.   6

"You're hot?" she exclaims. "Don't you think we all are?"   7

I start unwinding my makeshift turban. "The men aren't hot," I mutter.   8

Her companion looks at me in shocked reproach. "Sister, this isn't about men   9
and women," she says, shaking her head. "This is about Islam."

I want to argue. I feel like a child. Defiant, but   10
powerless. Burning with injustice, but also with
a hint of shame. I do as I am told, feeling acutely
conscious of the bare skin I am covering. In policing
my sexuality, these women have made me more aware
of it.

> Contradictory feelings are pushed together in a compact list.

The veil masks erotic freedom, but its advocates   11
believe *hijab* transcends the erotic—or expands it. In
the West, we think of passion as a fever of the body,
not the soul. In the East, Sufi poets used earthly
passion as a metaphor; the beloved they celebrated
was God. Where I come from, people are more likely
to find delirious passion in the mosque than in the bedroom.

> The writer offers definitions of passion reflecting three different perspectives.

> *The veil masks erotic freedom, but its advocates believe "hijab" transcends the erotic—or expands it.*

There are times when I feel a hint of this passion. A few years after my   12
encounter on the Caspian, I go to the wake of a family friend. Sitting in a mosque
in Mashhad, I grip a slippery black veil with one hand and a prayer book with the
other. In the center of the hall, there's a stack of Koranic texts decorated with green-
and-black calligraphy, a vase of white gladioluses and a large photograph of the
dearly departed. Along the walls, women wait quietly.

From the men's side of the mosque, the mullah's voice rises in lament. His   13
voice is deep and plaintive, oddly compelling. I bow my head, sequestered in my veil
while at my side a community of women pray and weep with increasing abandon.
I remember from girlhood this sense of being exquisitely alone in the company
of others. Sometimes I have cried as well, free to weep without having to offer an
explanation. Perhaps they are right, those mystics who believe that physical love is
an obstacle to spiritual love; those architects of mosques who abstained from images

> The writer uses terms of limited certainty, such as *perhaps* and *all I know*.

of earthly life, decorating their work with geometric shapes that they believed freed the soul to slip from its worldly moorings. I do not aspire to such lofty sentiments. All I know is that such moments of passionate abandon, within the circle of invisibility created by the veil, offer an emotional catharsis every bit as potent as any sexual release.

> The final line summarizes the contradictions described in the essay.

Outside, the rain pours from a sullen sky. I make my farewells and walk toward   *14* the car, where my driver waits. My veil is wicking muddy water from the sidewalk. I gather up the wet and grimy folds with distaste, longing to be home, where I can cast off this curtain of cloth that gives with one hand, takes away with the other.

Note: The Works Cited page is not shown. For examples, see MLA (pages 493–534) and APA (pages 535–564).

Reading for Better Writing

Working by yourself or with a group, answer these questions:

1. Sometimes writers use comparison-contrast organization to take a position on an issue—in some cases to show that one side is better than the other, but in others, to show the difficulty of choosing one side over the other. What do you think is Asayesh's position on *hijab*, and why?

2. Find Asayesh's one-sentence paragraph (paragraph 3). Why might the writer have constructed the paragraph in this way? How would this excerpt differ if that sentence had been part of either the preceding or the following paragraph?

3. What contrasts are listed in paragraph 4? How does the writer use sentence structure and punctuation to mark the contrasts?

4. In paragraph 13, Asayesh uses words that indicate limited certainty, such as *perhaps* and *all I know*. How do these phrases temper her claims?

5. In what ways are the opening and closing sentences alike? How are these similarities significant for readers?

Analyzing the Nature of Prejudice

Shankar Vedantam is a Nieman Fellow at Harvard University, a science reporter for *The Washington Post,* and the author of the book, *The Hidden Brain: How Our Unconscious Minds Elect Presidents, Control Markets, Wage Wars and Save Our Lives.* In this essay, Vedantam analyzes how people judge others based on the shade of their skin. (The essay was published in the *New York Times* on January 18, 2010.)

Shades of Prejudice

The writer uses an anecdote to introduce and illustrate his thesis.	LAST week, the Senate majority leader, Harry Reid, found himself in trouble for once suggesting that Barack Obama had a political edge over other African-American candidates because he was "light-skinned" and had "no Negro dialect, unless he wanted to have one." Mr. Reid was not expressing sadness but a gleeful opportunism that Americans were still judging one another by the color of their skin, rather than—as the Rev. Dr. Martin Luther King Jr., whose legacy we commemorated on Monday, dreamed—by the content of their character. *1*
He asserts that research supports his thesis, but he cites no sources.	The Senate leader's choice of words was flawed, but positing that black candidates who look "less black" have a leg up is hardly more controversial than saying wealthy people have an advantage in elections. Dozens of research studies have shown that skin tone and other racial features play powerful roles in who gets ahead and who does not. These factors regularly determine who gets hired, who gets convicted and who gets elected. *2*
He offers examples.	Consider: Lighter-skinned Latinos in the United States make $5,000 more on average than darker-skinned Latinos. The education test-score gap between light-skinned and dark-skinned African-Americans is nearly as large as the gap between whites and blacks. *3*
He supports his point by referring to his colleague's research.	The Harvard neuroscientist Allen Counter has found that in Arizona, California and Texas, hundreds of Mexican-American women have suffered mercury poisoning as a result of the use of skin-whitening creams. In India, where I was born, a best-selling line of women's cosmetics called Fair and Lovely has recently been supplemented by a product aimed at men called Fair and Handsome. *4*
The writer distinguishes racism and colorism by comparing and contrasting the nature and effects of each.	This isn't racism, per se: it's colorism, an unconscious prejudice that isn't focused on a single group like blacks so much as on blackness itself. Our brains, shaped by culture and history, create intricate caste hierarchies that privilege those who are physically and culturally whiter and punish those who are darker. *5*

Colorism is an intraracial problem as well as an interracial problem. Racial   *6*
minorities who are alert to white-black or white-brown issues often remain silent
about a colorism that asks "how black" or "how brown" someone is within their own
communities.

To support his
claim, he gives
an example and
cites a study.

If colorism lives underground, its effects are very real. Darker-skinned African-   *7*
American defendants are more than twice as likely to receive the death penalty as
lighter-skinned African-American defendants for crimes of equivalent seriousness
involving white victims. This was proven in rigorous, peer-reviewed research into
hundreds of capital punishment-worthy cases by the Stanford psychologist Jennifer
Eberhardt.

Take, for instance, two of Dr. Eberhadt's murder cases, in Philadelphia,   *8*
involving black defendants—one light-skinned, the other dark. The lighter-skinned
defendant, Arthur Hawthorne, ransacked a drug store for money and narcotics. The
pharmacist had complied with every demand, yet Mr. Hawthorne shot him when he
was lying face down. Mr. Hawthorne was independently identified as the killer by
multiple witnesses, a family member and an accomplice.

The writer
compares and
contrasts how
people are
treated by the
legal system.

The darker-skinned defendant, Ernest Porter, pleaded not guilty to the murder   *9*
of a beautician, a crime that he was linked to only through a circuitous chain of
evidence. A central witness later said that prosecutors forced him to finger Mr.
Porter even though he was sure that he was the wrong man. Two people who
provided an alibi for Mr. Porter were mysteriously never called to testify. During his
trial, Mr. Porter revealed that the police had even gotten his name wrong—his real
name was Theodore Wilson—but the court stuck to the wrong name in the interest
of convenience.

He cites a
similarity and a
difference.

Both men were convicted. But the lighter-skinned Mr. Hawthorne was given   *10*
a life sentence, while the dark-skinned Mr. Porter has spent more than a quarter-
century on Pennsylvania's death row.

He compares
colorism in the
legal system
with colorism in
politics.

Colorism also influenced the 2008 presidential race. In an experiment that   *11*
fall, Drew Westen, a psychologist at Emory, and other researchers shot different
versions of a political advertisement in support of Mr. Obama. One version showed a
light-skinned black family. Another version had the same script, but used a darker-
skinned black family. Voters, at an unconscious level, were less inclined to support
Mr. Obama after watching the ad featuring the darker-skinned family than were

To support his
claim, he offers
an example.

those who watched the ad with the lighter-skinned family.

Political operatives are certainly aware of this dynamic. During the campaign, *12* a conservative group created attack ads linking Mr. Obama with Kwame Kilpatrick, the disgraced former mayor of Detroit, which darkened Mr. Kilpatrick's skin to have a more persuasive effect. Though there can be little doubt that as a candidate Mr. Obama faced voters' conscious and unconscious prejudices, it is simultaneously true that unconscious colorism subtly advantaged him over darker-skinned politicians.

In highlighting how Mr. Obama benefited from his links to whiteness, Harry *13* Reid punctured the myth that Mr. Obama's election signaled the completion of the Rev. King's dream. Americans may like to believe that we are now color-blind, that we can consciously choose not to use race when making judgments about other people. It remains a worthy aspiration. But this belief rests on a profound misunderstanding about how our minds work and perversely limits our ability to discuss prejudice honestly.

> To restate his thesis and unify his essay, the writer refers to the anecdote used in the opening.

Reading for Better Writing

Working by yourself or with a group, answer these questions:

1. Describe how Shankar Vedantam uses an anecdote to open and close his essay. Then explain why you do or do not find that strategy effective.
2. The writer asserts that (a) colorism and racism are different and that (b) colorism is both an intraracial problem and an interracial problem. Explain what he means by each assertion and why you do or do not agree.
3. Review paragraphs 7–10 in which the writer compares and contrasts penalties meted out by the legal system. Then explain why these passages do or do not develop his thesis.
4. Note how the writer uses dashes in paragraphs 8 and 9, and then explain why that use is or is not correct.
5. In January 18, 2010, the writer published this essay in the *New York Times*. Cite words or sentences showing that his voice is or is not appropriate for his subject and audience.

Analyzing American and European Cultures

Peter Baldwin, a history professor at the University of California at Los Angeles, has written a number of books, including *The Narcissism of Minor Differences: How America and Europe Are Alike*. In the essay below, adapted from that text, he compares and contrasts Europe and America. As you read the essay, use underlining or highlighting, as well as notes in the margin, to trace and respond to Baldwin's compare-contrast thinking and writing.

The Likeness Across the Atlantic

As you read the essay, use this column to record your observations and questions.

1 The Atlantic gets ever wider. Not just in a physical sense, as oceans rise and coastlines recede, but also in ideological terms. Europe and America appear to be pitted against each other as never before. On one shore, capitalist markets, untempered by proper social policies, allow unbridled competition, poverty, pollution, violence, class divides, and social anomie. On the other side, Europe nurtures a social approach, a regulated labor market, and elaborate welfare networks. Possibly it has a less dynamic economy, but it is a more solidaristic and harmonious society. "Our social model," the voice of British left-liberalism, *The Guardian,* describes the European way, as opposed to "feral capitalism" in the United States.

2 That major differences separate the United States from Europe is scarcely a new idea. But it has become more menacingly Manichaean over the past decade. Foreign-policy disagreements fuel it: Iraq, Iran, Israel, North Korea. So does the more general question of what role the world's one remaining superpower should play while it still remains unchallenged. Robert Kagan, a senior associate at the Carnegie Endowment for International Peace, has famously suggested that, when it comes to foreign policy, Americans and Europeans call different planets home. Americans wield hard power and face the nasty choices that follow. Europeans, sheltered now from most geopolitical strife, enjoy the luxury of approaching conflict in a more conciliatory way: Martian unilateralism confronts Venusian multilateralism. But the dispute goes beyond diplomatic and military strategy. It touches on the nature of these two societies. Does having the

> *But the dispute goes beyond diplomatic and military strategy. It touches on the nature of these two societies.*

strongest battalions change the country that possesses them? After all, America is not just militarily strong. It is also—compared with Europe—harsh, violent, and sharp-elbowed. Or so goes the argument.

The idea that the North Atlantic is socioculturally parted is elaborated in both Europe and America for reasons that are as connected to domestic political needs and tactics as they are to any actual differences. American criticism of Europe, when it can be heard at all, typically concerns foreign policy or trade issues. American conservatives occasionally make the old continent a symbol for what they see as the excesses of the welfare state and statutory regulation. But the longstanding European criticism of America has become more vehement and widespread and is now shared by right and left alike. Europeans are keen to define an alternative to American hegemony, now that Europe no longer needs the protection of the United States in a post-cold-war world. Beset with internal fractures and disagreements, they have rediscovered the truism that nothing unites like a common enemy.

A small library of books has been published over the past few years debating whether a sociocultural chasm separates (continental) Europe from the (Anglo-) American barbarians. America's unregulated capitalism is a danger to Europe, warns the French historian and sociologist Emmanuel Todd. The notion of a unified West has lost whatever meaning it once had, adds Claus Offe, a professor of political sociology at the Hertie School of Governance, in Berlin. A recent letter-writer to the *Financial Times* agrees, although placing Britain on the side of the Continentals. A common language should not, this writer claims, obscure the distance between Britain and the United States: Americans carry guns, execute prisoners, go bankrupt, drive large cars, and live in large houses. Their men are circumcised and their working class is poor. The humanist and secular Europeans, by contrast, enjoy socialist hospitals, schools, and welfare systems. They pay high taxes, live longer, and take the train. One ponders what unspoken motives inspire

> *Americans carry guns, execute prisoners, go bankrupt, drive large cars, and live in large houses. Their men are circumcised and their working class is poor.*

such letters. Andrei S. Markovits, a professor of comparative politics and German studies at the University of Michigan at Ann Arbor and author of one of the most interesting recent books on the subject, *Uncouth Nation: Why Europe Dislikes America* (Princeton University Press, 2007), suggests that anti-Americanism helps fire the engines of pan-European nationalism. Europeans have less in common than the aspiring empire builders of the European Union would like. But at least they can agree on being different from the Americans. Or can they?

Polemic and vituperation abound in the discussion of trans-Atlantic difference;   5
caricature, rather than portrait, is the dominant genre. It is time to examine more closely what it is we do know. It is time, in other words, to bring a little empirical meat to the table.

The evidence shows two things. First, Europe is not a coherent or unified continent. The spectrum of difference within even Western Europe is much broader than normally appreciated. Second, with a few exceptions, the United States fits into the average range of most quantifiable measures that I have been able to find. We may therefore conclude either that there is no coherent European identity, or—if there is one—that the United States is as much a European country as the usual candidates are. We might rephrase this by saying that both Europe and the United States are, in fact, parts of a common, big-tent grouping—call it the West, the Atlantic community, the developed world, or what you will. America is not Sweden, for sure. But nor is Italy Sweden, nor France, nor even Germany. And who says that Sweden is Europe, any more than Vermont is America?

> *We may therefore*   6
> *conclude either*
> *that there is*
> *no coherent*
> *European*
> *identity, or—if*
> *there is one—that*
> *the United States*
> *is as much a*
> *European country*
> *as the usual*
> *candidates are.*

Consider the following examples:

Social welfare: As a portion of the total economy, American public social   7
expenditures narrowly make it into the European norm, sneaking in above Ireland.

But because the American gross domestic product is greater than those of most European nations, the per capita spending is higher than this rank suggests. In terms of how much money is paid out on average for each person, the United States ranks in the lower middle of the European spectrum, above most of the Mediterranean countries and Iceland and in the same league as Britain, the Netherlands, and Finland.

Beyond that, a complete accounting of welfare efforts cannot focus only on what the state does through social policy. Other avenues of redistribution are also important: voluntary efforts, private but legally mandated benefits, and taxes. If we include all those, the American welfare state is more extensive than is often realized. By taking account of all these components of social welfare—public, voluntary, and mandatory—the total effort made in the United States falls into the middle of the European spectrum.   8

Foreign travel: Americans are often thought to take little interest in the world around them, except perhaps when invading it. The paucity of Americans with passports is often held up as an indication of uninterest. Eighty-five percent of American tourism and travel is domestic. If it follows that 15 percent is international, then Americans join the company of the Greeks, Spaniards, and French, among whom, respectively, 12, 13, and 17 percent of holidays are taken abroad. And that does not take into account the distance needed to travel before the Great Abroad begins. That more than 99 percent of Luxembourgeois vacations of four nights or more were enjoyed outside the nation's borders does not surprise; where else could they possibly have been taken? Assuming that for a European to leave Europe is an effort roughly analogous to that of an American leaving the United States, the figures become more comparable. In 2006, 9.7 million Western Europeans visited the United States, and 13 million Americans visited Europe. Thus, in the realm of travel, Americans were proportionally more interested in Europeans than the other way around. The same year, significantly more Americans (30 million) traveled overseas (other than to Mexico and Canada) than overseas visitors came to the United States (22 million).   9

Reading, writing, and culture: Americans do not need to read, Simone de Beauvoir was convinced, because they do not think. Thinking is hard to quantify, reading less so. And read the Americans do. There are more newspapers per head in the United   10

States than anywhere in Europe outside Scandinavia, Switzerland, and Luxembourg. The circulation of American newspapers is higher per capita than in most of the Mediterranean countries and in Ireland and Belgium. The United States is also well equipped with libraries. The long tradition of municipally supported public libraries in the United States means that average American readers are better supplied with library books than their peers in Germany, Britain, France, Holland, Austria, and all the Mediterranean nations. Americans also make better use of those public-library books than most Europeans do. Average Americans borrowed 6.4 books each in 2001, more than their peers in Germany, Austria, Norway, Ireland, Luxembourg, France, and throughout the Mediterranean. And with America's amply endowed universities, it is no surprise that the supply of books per capita in college libraries is higher than in any European country other than Finland, Denmark, and Iceland. Not content with borrowing, Americans also buy more books per head than any European population for which we have numbers. Proportionately more Americans claim to read a book per month than anyone but the Swiss, Swedes, Germans, and Irish. And Americans write more books. Per capita, they come in at the high end of the European spectrum as authors, measured in terms of volumes in print.

> *Average Americans borrowed 6.4 books each in 2001, more than their peers in Germany, Austria, Norway, Ireland, Luxembourg, France, and throughout the Mediterranean.*

It is true that the American government spends less as a percentage of gross domestic product than almost any European government on what the Organization for Economic Cooperation and Development defines as "recreation and culture," though not less than Greece and only a bit less than Britain and Ireland. Those figures, it should be noted, include government payments to Europe's established churches. American households spend more on recreation and culture privately than any Europeans but the Icelanders, the Austrians, and the British. Add state and private money together, and total American outlays on the finer things in life fall in

11

the upper half of the European middle ground.

In short, for most of the quantifiable measures of socioeconomic reality, the   *12*
divergence within Europe is greater than that between Europe and the United
States. Hand on heart, which cities more resemble each other: Stockholm and
Minneapolis or Helsinki and Thessaloniki? And as the European Union widens
eastward—possibly even to accept Turkey, a Muslim country mostly in Asia—the
most recent newcomers (many from regions once called European Turkey, which
were part of the Ottoman Empire) efface many of the issues that do distinguish the
United States from Europe. These new arrivals, along with Europe's many recent
immigrants from Asia and Africa, are very religious,
skeptical of a strong state, unenthusiastic about voting,
and allergic to high taxes. From the vantage of old Europe,
they are, in other words, more like Americans. How odd,
really, that Europeans seek to identify an enemy in a
culture with which they have so much in common, just
at the moment when they are being joined by ones with
whom they actually share even less. How odd to turn
their backs on a country which, like their own continent,
espouses the Reformation, the Scientific Revolution,
the Enlightenment, democracy, liberalism, free but
appropriately regulated markets, and religious toleration.

> *From the vantage of old Europe, they are, in other words, more like Americans.*

Even a few minutes watching the Eurovision Song Contest strengthens both   *13*
a belief in the continued vitality of relations that span the Atlantic and a belief
in a hugely variegated Europe, diverse to the point of incoherence. This must be
the nightmare that keeps the empire builders in Brussels awake at night: a vastly
expanded Europe, stretching from Kamchatka to the Azores, from the North Pole
(now festooned with Danish flags and Russian submarines) to the Dead Sea, with its
pidgin English lingua franca and droning, generic, ritual Europol incantations of
"Hello Europe" even as the voting descends into unabashed tribalism. Imagine now
that Europe's voters were given a choice also between the Australians and the Serbs.
With whom would, say, the Norwegians cast their lot? Place your bets, ladies and
gentlemen.

Of course, this choice will never be on offer. The world is too complicated a   *15*
place for the binary clumpishness of all-or-nothing alternatives between America

and Europe. Both sides of this particular divide would do well to consider how proximate and similar the two slopes of their supposed conceptual chasm in fact are. Whether American conservatives or Europeans, each enamored of their own reflection, unless we break this spell of self-enchantment, we risk suffering the fate of Narcissus. Readers will recall that Ovid's ill-fated hero dies of thirst, for fear that kissing the water's surface will disrupt the image that has so enthralled him.

Reading for Better Writing

Working by yourself or with a group, answer these questions:

1. First describe how Baldwin introduces his topic and thesis, and then explain why the opening is or is not engaging and clear.

2. In the opening 4 paragraphs, the writer focuses on differences between Europe and the U.S; in paragraph 5, he builds a transition; and in the remaining paragraphs, he focuses on similarities. Review these organizational choices and then explain why they do or do not help the writer develop his thesis.

3. Review paragraph 6 and explain how it (a) re-focuses the writer's argument and (b) introduces the claims in the remaining paragraphs.

4. Review paragraphs 8-10, noting how the writer classifies "examples" of similarities into three types, each introduced by a boldfaced title. Then explain why his classification strategy does or does not help him develop his argument.

5. Cite examples from the essay to prove or disprove that Baldwin's document is written in an academic style. (For information about an academic style, see pages 77–78.)

"The Likeness Across the Atlantic" by Peter Baldwin from Chronicle of Higher Education, December 13, 2009. Copyright (c) 2009 by Peter Baldwin. Reprinted with permission from the author.

Writing Guidelines

Planning

1. **Select a topic.** List subjects that are similar and/or different in ways that you find interesting, perplexing, disgusting, infuriating, charming, or informing. Then choose two subjects whose comparison and/or contrast gives the reader some insight into who or what they are. *Note:* Make sure that the items have a solid *basis* for comparison. Comparable items are types of the same thing (e.g., two rivers, two characters, two films, two mental illnesses, two banking regulations, two search engines, two theories).

2. **Get the big picture.** Using a computer or a paper and pen, create three columns as shown below. Brainstorm a list of traits under each heading. (Also see the Venn diagram on page 52.)

Features Peculiar to Subject #1	Shared Features	Features Peculiar to Subject #2

fig. 12.3

3. **Gather information.** Review your list of features, highlighting those that could provide insight into one or both subjects. Research the subjects, using hands-on analysis when possible. Consider writing your research notes in the three-column format shown above.

4. **Draft a working thesis.** Review your expanded list of features and eliminate those that now seem unimportant. Write a sentence stating the core of what you learned about the subjects: what essential insight have you reached about the similarities and/or differences between the topics? If you're stuck, try completing the sentence below. (Switch around the terms "similar" and "different" if you wish to stress similarities.)

> Whereas _____ and _____ seem similar, they are different in several ways, and the differences are important because _____.

5. **Get organized.** Decide how to organize your essay. Generally, *subject by subject* works better for short, simple comparisons. *Trait by trait* works better for longer, more complex comparisons, in that you hold up the topics side by side, trait by trait. Consider, as well, the order in which you will discuss the topics and arrange the traits, choices that depend on what you want to feature and how you want to build and deepen the comparison.

Subject by Subject:
Introduction
Subject #1
- Trait A
- Trait B

Subject #2
- Trait A
- Trait B

Trait by Trait:
Introduction
Trait A
- Subject #1
- Subject #2

Trait B
- Subject #1
- Subject #2

fig. 12.4

Drafting

6. **Write your first draft.** Review your outline and draft the paper.

   Subject-by-subject pattern:
   - **Opening:** get readers' attention, introduce the subjects, and offer a thesis.
   - **Middle:** discuss the first subject, then analyze the second subject, discussing traits parallel to those you addressed with the first subject.
   - **Conclusion:** summarize similarities, differences, and implications.

   Trait-by-trait pattern:
   - **Opening:** get readers' attention, introduce the subjects, and offer a thesis.
   - **Middle:** compare and/or contrast the two subjects trait by trait; include transitions that help readers look back and forth between the two subjects.
   - **Conclusion:** summarize the key relationships and note their significance.

Revising

7. **Get feedback.** Ask someone to read your paper, looking for a clear thesis, an engaging introduction, a middle that compares and/or contrasts parallel traits in a logical order, and a unifying closing.

8. **Rework your draft.** Based on feedback, revise for the following issues:
   - ____ **Ideas:** The points made and conclusions drawn from comparing and contrasting provide insight into both subjects.
   - ____ **Organization:** The structure, whether subject by subject or trait by trait, helps readers grasp the similarities and differences between the subjects.
   - ____ **Voice:** The tone is informed, involved, and genuine.

Editing and Proofreading

9. **Carefully edit your essay.** Look for the following issues:
   - ____ **Words** are precise, clear, and defined as needed.
   - ____ **Sentences** are clear, well reasoned, varied in structure, and smooth.
   - ____ **Correctness:** The writing is clean and properly formatted.
   - ____ **Page design** is attractive and follows MLA or APA guidelines.

Publishing

10. **Publish your essay.** Share your writing by submitting it to your instructor, posting it on a Web site, sharing it with friends and family who might be interested in the topic, crafting a presentation or demonstration, or reshaping your comparison as a blog.

Critical-Thinking and Writing Activities

As directed by your instructor, complete the following activities.

1. Review Rachel De Smith's analysis of Toni Morrison's Sethe and Barbara Kingsolver's Orleanna Price. Then choose two characters from other literary works and write an analysis of them using compare and/or contrast organization.

2. Review Gelareh Asayesh's article "Shrouded in Contradiction," noting how she uses comparison-contrast strategies in order to take a position. Draft or revise an essay in which you use comparison-contrast to develop or support your thesis.

3. Re-examine how Shankar Vedantam opens and closes "Shades of Prejudice" with an anecdote (or a news story) that was current when he wrote the essay. Revise one of your recent essays by selecting a recent news story that you can use to develop your thesis.

4. Re-read Peter Baldwin's "The Likeness Across the Atlantic" in which he analyzes Europeans' and Americans' differences and similarities. Choose two other collectives (e.g., countries, colleges, or groups of people) and write an essay in which you compare and contrast characteristics that distinguish these communities.

5. Write an essay in which you compare and contrast two people, using subject-by-subject organization. Then revise the essay using trait-by-trait organization.

Learning-Objectives Checklist ✓

Have you achieved this chapter's learning objectives? Check your progress with the items below, revisiting topics in the chapter as needed. I have . . .

____ interpreted comparison-contrast essays, ascertaining how the writers' purposes, readers, and topics may have shaped their patterns of reasoning (182–183).

____ examined subject-by-subject and trait-by-trait organizational patterns, identifying their similarities, differences, strengths, and weaknesses (182–183).

____ established a logical basis for a comparison claim by analyzing topics of the same order or type (182–183).

____ developed a reasonable comparison by assessing each subject using the same criteria in the same manner (182–183).

____ supported my comparison-contrast reasoning with precise details, as well as with transitional words that clarify similarities and differences (201).

____ strengthened my compare-contrast writing by using effective revising and editing strategies (200–201).

____ used additional analytical strategies (such as definition) to illustrate a point or develop a claim (200–201).

____ successfully planned, drafted, revised, and polished a logical comparison-contrast essay (200–201).

Chapter 13

Classification

Classification is an organizational strategy that helps writers make sense of large or complex sets of things. A writer using this strategy breaks the topic into individual items or members that can be sorted into clearly distinguishable groups or categories. For example, if writing about the types of residents who live in assisted-care facilities, a nursing student might classify them according to various physical and/or mental limitations.

By sorting residents in this way, the writer can discuss them as individuals, as representatives of a group, or as members of the body as a whole. By using an additional strategy such as comparison-contrast, she or he can show both similarities and differences between individuals within a group, or between one group and another.

Visually Speaking   To learn more about reading and writing classification essays, look again at Figure 13.1 and consider what it suggests about the challenges and benefits of classifying things.

Learning **Objectives**

By working through this chapter, you will be able to

- interpret and critique writers' use of classification reasoning.
- devise a classification plan that aligns with your writing situation.
- create a logical grouping scheme that includes clear criteria for sorting.
- utilize a classification grid to identify your topic's components and to sort them into groups.
- compose an analytical essay using primarily classification reasoning (with other analytical strategies, as needed).

Baloncici / Shutterstock.com

fig. 13.1

Strategies for Classification Essays

In writing rooted in classification, you create logical categories into which people, places, things, or concepts can be grouped. Categorization makes sense of a body of information by showing how members of the group are both related and differentiated. Classification, then, can reveal something about the overarching structure of the whole, the nature of a particular category, or the distinctive features of one member of the group.

The Rhetorical Situation

Consider the context in which writers use classification reasoning:

- **Purpose:** Writers classify a body of information to explain its order, to clarify relationships, and to "locate" specific items within a larger structure. For example, in her essay, "Latin American Music . . ." (pages 206–209), Kathleen Kropp's purpose is to explain how the many types of Latin American music reflect Latinos' cultural identity and impact social change.
- **Readers:** While readership can vary greatly, writers using classification are seeking to illuminate the deeper order of a topic, either to enhance readers' understanding or to support an argument. For example, Kropp's criteria for classifying types of Latin American music help her readers (college students) understand the history and cultural impact of Latinos' diverse forms of music.
- **Topic:** Writers typically use classification with topics that include a complex body of individual items. For example, Kropp's topic is the nature and function of Latin American music—thousands of songs. To address the topic, she sorts the songs into four categories that clarify music's diverse roles in Latino culture.

Principles of Classification Writing

Classification writing depends on the principles that follow.

Establishing clear criteria for grouping. Given his or her purpose for classifying, the writer finds a basis or standard for categorizing items. This standard becomes the "common denominator" for the ordering scheme. For example, trees could be grouped as follows:

- **Size:** types of trees grouped by height categories
- **Geography:** trees common to different areas, zones, or elevations
- **Structure or composition:** division by leaf type (deciduous vs. coniferous)
- **Purpose:** windbreak trees, shade trees, flowering trees, fruit trees, etc.

Creating a logical and orderly classification scheme. These guidelines apply:

- As they sort items into groups, writers seek . . .

  - **consistency**—applying the same sorting criterion in the same way.
  - **exclusivity**—creating groups that are distinct and do not overlap.
  - **completeness**—fitting all elements from a larger group into the subgroups with no elements left over.

- To keep the classification structure manageable, writers usually limit the number of main categories to six.
- Subcategories distinguish the elements that comprise a category. To further distinguish elements within the whole, subcategories can be broken into smaller groups. See Figure 13.2.
- When explaining the classification scheme, writers present the categories and subcategories in a logical order, selecting a sequence that will help readers digest the overall scheme and see connections and differences between categories.
- Sometimes, writers complement their discussion with graphics (tables, charts, diagrams) that help readers understand the overall scheme and individual categories.
- When classifying ideas or theoretical practices, writers might illustrate each. For example, in his classification essay on pages 257–258, John Van Rys identifies four approaches to literary criticism. He then illustrates each one by describing how a critic using it might critique the poem, "My Last Duchess."

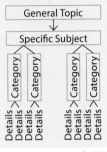

fig. 13.2

Sample Classification Paragraph

The following paragraph is from the essay cited above. Note how Van Rys first describes the fourth approach to literary criticism, and then gives an example of each subgroup in it.

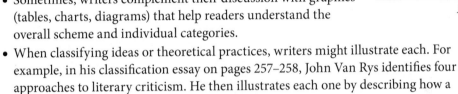

The fourth approach to criticism applies ideas outside of literature to literary works. Because literature mirrors life, argue these critics, disciplines that explore human life can help us understand literature. Some critics, for example, apply psychological theories to literary works by exploring dreams, symbolic meanings, and motivation. Myth or archetype criticism uses insights from psychology, cultural anthropology, and classical studies to explore a text's universal appeal. Moral criticism, rooted in religious studies and ethics, explores the moral dilemmas literary works raise. Marxist, feminist, and minority criticism are, broadly speaking, sociological approaches to interpretation. While the Marxist examines the themes of class struggle, economic power, and social justice in texts, the feminist critic explores the just and unjust treatment of women as well as the effect of gender on language, reading, and the literary canon. The critic interested in race and ethnic identity explores similar issues, with the focus shifted to a specific cultural group.

Reading Classification Writing

As you read the essays on the following pages, consider these questions:

1. Does the writer explain the classification scheme, and is this reasoning logical, given his or her topic and purpose? Explain.
2. Are the number of categories sufficient, given the size and diversity of the topic?
3. Are the categories consistent, exclusive, and complete? Explain.
4. Are the categories presented in a clear, logical order?

Sample Classification Essays

Specialists in a discipline will commonly use classification—along with technical terminology—to analyze a topic for readers familiar with the discipline. However, as shown in the essays in this chapter, writers can also use classification and nontechnical language to communicate with readers.

Analyzing Forms of Music

In the essay below, student writer Kathleen Kropp uses classification strategies to describe the nature of Latin American music and to explain how the music both reflects and affects Latin American culture.

Essay Outline

Introduction: Latin American music's unifying power
  1. **Category 1:** indigenous music
  2. **Category 2:** Iberian and Mestizo folk music
  3. **Category 3:** Afro-American music
  4. **Category 4:** urban popular music

Conclusion: These diverse types together express the passion and power of Latin American people.

Title: the larger topic and the classification theme

Latin American Music: A Diverse and Unifying Force

On September 20, 2009, Latin pop, rock, and salsa rhythms danced through the air in Havana's Plaza de la Revolución as more than one million people gathered to witness Paz Sin Fronteras II (Peace Without Borders II). These benefit concerts brought together performers from Cuba, Puerto Rico, Ecuador, and Venezuela.

Introduction: Latin American music's unifying power

Juanes, a popular Colombian singer who headlined the concerts, explained the event's passion and power like this: "Music becomes an excuse to send a message that we're all here together building peace, that we are here as citizens and this is what we want, and we have to be heard" (Hispanic 17). His statement demonstrates Latinos' belief that their music has the power to unify Latin American people, synthesize their cultural activities, and address their diverse needs. To understand how the music (which is as diverse as Latin America's people) can do this, it is helpful to sort the many forms of music into four major types and consider what each type contributes to Latin American society.

1 Indigenous music

One type is indigenous music, a group of musical forms that connect the human and the spiritual. Archeological evidence indicates that indigenous musical cultures of the Americas began over 30,000 years ago. Over time the first instruments, which were stone and clay sound-producing objects, evolved into wind instruments such as flutes and windpipes. An example of indigenous music connecting the human and spiritual is found among Aymara-speaking musicians in the Lake Titicaca Region of Peru. The people of this region use music to mesh pre-Columbian agricultural rites with current Catholic practices. For instance, during feasts such as the annual Fiesta de la Candelaria (Candlemas Feast), celebrants use Sicus (panpipes), pincullos (vertical duct flutes), cajas (drums), chants, dances, and costumes—in combination with Catholic symbolism—to celebrate the gift of staple crops such as corn and potatoes (Indigenous 328, 330).

2 Iberian and Mestizo (mixed) folk music

A second type, Iberian and Mestizo (mixed) folk music, enrich Latinos' everyday lives in a variety of forms, including liturgical music, working songs, and mariachi tunes. For example, whereas the traditional Catholic mass featured organ music, more recent Catholic services such as the Nicaraguan Peasant Mass use the acoustic guitar along with the colorful sounds of the marimba, maracas, and melodies from popular festivals. As a result, worshipers find the music inviting and the passionate lyrics (which can cite issues of economic or political injustice) socially relevant.

Another form of folk music known as tonadas (or tunes) are used as serenades and working songs. For example, in Venezuela, workers might whistle or sing tonadas while milking, plowing, or fishing (Tonadas). These vocal duets, which also can be accompanied by guitar, have pleasant harmonies, two main melodies, and faster tempos ("Iberian and mestizo folk music" 338, 341).

The mariachi band, a final form of folk music, adds festivity to Mexicans' many celebrations. With its six to eight violins, two trumpets, and a guitar, the band creates a vibrant, engaging sound. During birthdays or feast days, these bands commonly set up on streets and below windows where they awaken the residents above to the sounds of "Las Mañ Anitas," the traditional song for such days. Mariachis are also hired for baptisms, weddings, quinceañeras (the fifteenth birthday for a Mexican girl), patriotic holidays, and funerals (History of the Mariachi).

3 Afro-Ameri-can music

Afro-American music, the third type of Latin American music, infuses 6 passion and power in its percussion-driven dances and complex rhythm structures. These songs and dances, performed throughout the Caribbean, function as an entertaining, unifying force among Latin people ("Afro-American" 345-6). The energy of Afro-American music is clear in genres such as the mambo and the rumba dances. The rumba, an Afro-Caribbean dance, is highly improvisational and exciting. The quinto (a high-pitched drum) establishes a dialogue with a solo voice and challenges the male dancer, while the tumbadora and palitos (sticks on woodblock) provide a contrast with regular, unchanging rhythm patterns.

The mambo, an Afro-Cuban dance, became popular in Havana, Cuba. In the 7 1940s, nightclubs throughout Latin America caught the energy of this fast tempo song and dance. Arsenio Rodríguez' "Bruca Managuá" exemplifies this form. Because of the song's sound and lyrics, many black Cubans consider the piece to be an anthem of Afro-Cuban pride and resistance:

I am Calabrí, black by birth/nation,   8

Without freedom, I can't live,   9

Too much abuse, the body is going to die.   10

(*Oxford Encyclopedia for Latinos and Latinas in the United States.* 218) 11

4 Urban popu-lar music

Urban popular music, the fourth type of Latin American music, combines 12 a dynamic sound with poignant appeals for social change, appeals that resonate with many listeners. The styles of this type of music include rock, heavy metal, punk, hip-hop, jazz, reggae, and R&B. During the September 20, 2009 Paz Sin Fronteras II concerts described earlier, urban popular music was common fare. As U.S. representative Jim McGovern observed, the message of the concerts was to "circumvent politics . . . using the medium of music to speak directly to young people, to change their way of thinking, and leave behind the old politics, hatred, prejudices, and national enmities that have locked too many people in patterns of conflict, violence, poverty, and despair. It is an attempt to break down barriers and ask people to join in common purpose" (Paz Sin Fronteras II). Popular urban musicians such as Juanes utilize music not only to entertain but also to unite Latinos in a universal cause.

Conclusion: passion and power of Latin American music and culture

        Passion and power permeate all of Latin America's music. The four major types *13* of music—indigenous, Iberian and Mestizo folk, Afro-American, and popular urban—are as diverse as the people of Latin America, and each style serves a valued need or function in Latinos' everyday lives. As a result, those listening to Latin American music—whether it is a Peruvian Indian's chant, a Venezuelan farmer's whistled tune, a Cuban mambo drummer's vivacious beat, or the Bogotá rock concert's compelling rhythms—are hearing much more than music. They are hearing the passion and power of the Latin American people.

Note: The Works Cited page is not shown. For examples, see MLA (pages 493–534) and APA (pages 535–564).

Reading for **Better Writing**

Working by yourself or with a group, answer these questions:

1. Review the opening in which Kropp introduces her topic, thesis, and choice to sort the music into four categories. Then explain (a) why the passage is clear or unclear, (b) whether sorting forms into categories seems necessary or helpful, and (c) how Kropp's sorting scheme helps her develop her thesis.
2. Cite three strategies that Kropp uses to distinguish the four types of music and the various forms within those groups. Are the strategies effective? Why?
3. Identify language that Kropp uses to help you imagine the tone and tenor of the music. Is the word choice helpful? Why?
4. Review the instructions at the bottom of page 204 regarding the three guidelines for creating a logical classification scheme: consistency, exclusivity, and completeness. Then Analyze Kropp's classification scheme and explain why it does or does not exemplify the three guidelines.
5. Review the third bulleted instruction on page 205: "[W]riters present the categories and subcategories in a logical order, selecting a sequence that will help readers digest the overall scheme and see connections and differences between categories." Then explain how Kropp's sequence for presenting categories does or does not help readers understand her argument.
6. In the last sentence, Kropp re-states—and re-phrases—her thesis. Review the sentence: Is it an effective closing? Why or why not?

"Latin American Music: A Diverse and Unifying Force" by Kathleen Kropp. Used by permission of the author.

Analyzing Rhetorical Positions on Climate Change

Stewart Brand, author of *Whole Earth Discipline: An Ecopragmatist Manifesto,* published this essay in December 2009. In the piece, he argues that the climate-change debate is better understood as advocating four main perspectives—not two.

Four Sides to Every Story

The writer introduces his topic and thesis.

Climate talks have been going on in Copenhagen for a week now, and it appears to be a two-sided debate between alarmists and skeptics. But there are actually four different views of global warming. A taxonomy of the four: *1*

He distinguishes the four viewpoints with descriptive names.

DENIALISTS They are loud, sure and political. Their view is that climatologists and their fellow travelers are engaged in a vast conspiracy to panic the public into following an agenda that is political and pernicious. Senator James Inhofe of Oklahoma and the columnist George Will wave the banner for the hoax-callers.   *2*

A hyperlink helps readers access the speech.

"The claim that global warming is caused by man-made emissions is simply untrue and not based on sound science," Mr. Inhofe declared in a 2003 speech to the Senate about the Kyoto accord that remains emblematic of his position. "CO2 does not cause catastrophic disasters—actually it would be beneficial to our environment and our economy. . . . The motives for Kyoto are economic, not environmental—that is, proponents favor handicapping the American economy through carbon taxes and more regulations."   *3*

The writer names and describes the second group.

SKEPTICS This group is most interested in the limitations of climate science so far: they like to examine in detail the contradictions and shortcomings in climate data and models, and they are wary about any "consensus" in science. To the skeptics' discomfort, their arguments are frequently quoted by the denialists.   *4*

He offers examples illustrating the group's viewpoint.

In this mode, Roger Pielke, a climate scientist at the University of Colorado, argues that the scenarios presented by the United Nations Intergovernmental Panel on Climate Change are overstated and underpredictive. Another prominent skeptic is the physicist Freeman Dyson, who wrote in 2007: "I am opposing the holy brotherhood of climate model experts and the crowd of deluded citizens who believe the numbers predicted by the computer models. . . . I have studied the climate models and I know what they can do. The models solve the equations of fluid dynamics, and they do a very good job of describing the fluid motions of the atmosphere and the oceans. They do a very poor job of describing the clouds, the dust, the chemistry and the biology of fields and farms and forests."   *5*

The quotation relays the speaker's argument and tone.

WARNERS These are the climatologists who see the trends in climate headed toward planetary disaster, and they blame human production of greenhouse gases as the primary culprit. Leaders in this category are the scientists James Hansen, Stephen Schneider and James Lovelock. (This is the group that most persuades me and whose views I promote.)   *6*

The writer names and describes the third group.

"If humanity wishes to preserve a planet similar to that on which civilization developed and to which life on earth is adapted," Mr. Hansen wrote as the lead author of   *7* an influential 2008 paper, then the concentration of carbon dioxide in the atmosphere would have to be reduced from 395 parts per million to "at most 350 p.p.m."

CALAMATISTS There are many environmentalists who believe that industrial civilization has committed crimes against nature, and retribution is coming. They quote the warners in apocalyptic terms, and they view denialists as deeply evil. The technology critic Jeremy Rifkin speaks in this manner, and the writer-turned-activist Bill McKibben is a (fairly gentle) leader in this category.

8

In his 2006 introduction for The End of Nature, his famed 1989 book, Mr. McKibben wrote of climate change in religious terms: "We are no longer able to think of ourselves as a species tossed about by larger forces—now we are those larger forces. Hurricanes and thunderstorms and tornadoes become not acts of God but acts of man. That was what I meant by the 'end of nature.'"

9

The calamatists and denialists are primarily political figures, with firm ideological loyalties, whereas the warners and skeptics are primarily scientists, guided by ever-changing evidence. That distinction between ideology and science not only helps clarify the strengths and weaknesses of the four stances, it can also be used to predict how they might respond to future climate developments.

10

If climate change were to suddenly reverse itself (because of some yet undiscovered mechanism of balance in our climate system), my guess is that the denialists would be triumphant, the skeptics would be skeptical this time of the apparent good news, the warners would be relieved, and the calamatists would seek out some other doom to proclaim.

11

If climate change keeps getting worse, then I would expect denialists to grasp at stranger straws, many skeptics to become warners, the warners to start pushing geoengineering schemes like sulfur dust in the stratosphere, and the calamatists to push liberal political agendas—just as the denialists said they would.

12

Margin notes (left column):

A hyperlink helps readers access the paper.

The writer identifies the fourth group.

He quotes McKibben and cites the source.

He compares two groups and contrasts them with two others.

The writer distinguishes the groups by projecting how they might respond to good news or bad news.

Reading for Better Writing

Working by yourself or with a group, answer these questions:

1. Identify Brand's thesis. How does his classification thinking make sense of the topic?
2. Cite three strategies that he uses to distinguish the four viewpoints. Do you find these strategies effective? Why or why not?
3. Identify two of Brand's claims, describe how he supports each claim, and then explain why that support is or is not convincing (for information about claims, see pages 296–300).

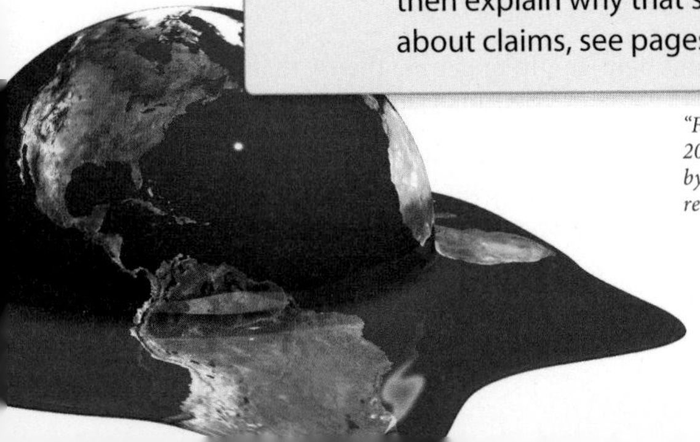

Torian / Shutterstock.com

Analyzing How Readers Read

Jessica Seigel is an award-winning, widely published journalist. In the essay below, she explains how readers should respond to nuanced literary devices such as symbols, themes, and allegories.

The Lion, the Witch and the Metaphor

Use this margin to record your observations regarding how Seigel uses classification to develop her analysis.

THOUGH it's fashionable nowadays to come out of the closet, lately folks are piling in—into the wardrobe, that is, to battle over who owns Narnia: secular or Christian lovers of C. S. Lewis's stories.   *1*

Children, of course, have been slipping through the magic cupboard into the mythical land for 50 years without assistance from pundits or preachers (though fauns and talking badgers have been helpful). But now that the chronicles' first book, *The Lion, the Witch and the Wardrobe,* has been made into a Disney movie, adults are fighting to claim the action. And that means analyzing it. Or not.   *2*

The 7-year-old who sat next to me during a recent showing said, "This is really scary." It was scary when the White Witch kills the lion Aslan, who dies to save the loathsome Edmund before rising to help him and his siblings vanquish evil. But adults reducing the story to one note—their own—are even scarier. One side dismisses the hidden Jesus figure as silly or trivial, while the other insists the lion is Jesus in a story meant to proselytize. They're both wrong.   *3*

As a child, I never knew that Aslan was "Jesus." And that's a good thing. My mother recently remarked that if she'd known the stories were Christian, she wouldn't have given me the books—which are among my dearest childhood memories.   *4*

But parents today will not be innocent of the religious subtext, considering the drumbeat of news coverage and Disney's huge campaign to remind churchgoing audiences of the film's religious themes. The marketing is so intense that the religious Web site HollywoodJesus.com even worried that ham-fisted promotion might ruin it for non-Christians.   *5*

But a brief foray into Criticism 101 shows that the wardrobe is big enough for everyone. Symbolism, for example, is when one thing stands for another but is not the thing itself. Psychoanalysts, for instance, have interpreted "The Wonderful Wizard of Oz" as Dorothy's quest for a penis—that is, retrieving the witch's broomstick. Does that symbolism—if you buy it—make Dorothy a pervert? No, because it's hidden. That's the point. Overt and covert meaning can exist independently.   *6*

Those with a fiduciary, rather than phallic bent, might prefer the theory that L. Frank Baum's Oz stories are a Populist manifesto, with the yellow brick road as the gold standard, the Tin Man as alienated labor, Scarecrow as oppressed farmers, and so on. (And surely some Jungian theory about the collective unconscious explains why both Oz and Narnia are populated by four heroic characters fighting an evil witch.)   *7*

Yes, it's allegory land, a place that strings symbols together to create levels of meaning, which a determined scholar has actually quantified as ranging from two to seven layers. (No word on why not eight.) Allegory, the oldest narrative technique, often involves talking animals, from Aesop's fox with the grapes to Dr. Seuss's Yertle the Turtle, supposedly a Hitler figure. 8

Does that twist the Seuss tale into a political treatise on fascism? No, it adds another level for adults, it teaches morals (even the meekest can unseat the powerful, etc.), and it's fun—when plain little Mack burps, he shakes the bad king Yertle from his throne built on turtles. 9

But which layer is more important—the surface or beneath? Deep thinkers specialize in hidden meanings (building demand, of course, for their interpretive expertise). An Oxford English professor, Lewis himself explored the depths in his scholarly books. But he also defended the literal, lamenting in his essay "On Stories" how modern criticism denigrates the pleasures of a good yarn—and that was 50 years ago. 10

While critics today call it "fallacy" to interpret a work by citing the author's intentions, Lewis left a road map for us marked with special instructions for not annoying children. In his essay "Sometimes Fairy Stories May Say Best What's to Be Said," he denounced as "moonshine" the idea that he wrote the Narnia chronicles to proselytize the young. The lion Aslan, he wrote, bounded into his imagination from his experience as a Christian, coming to him naturally as should all good writing. 11

"Let the pictures tell you their own moral," he advised in "On Three Ways of Writing for Children." "If they don't show you a moral, don't put one in." 12

In keeping with that advice, the Narnia chronicles don't beat you on the head—nor does the faithful movie adaptation. If everyone stays on his own level—the surface for adventurers, and the depths for believers—we can all enjoy, so long as the advertisers stay out of the way. 13

Reading for Better Writing

Working by yourself or with a group, answer these questions:

1. Identify the two conflicting groups (or viewpoints) in this article and describe characteristics of each.

2. Summarize Seigel's thesis and explain why you do or do not agree.

3. In the final paragraph, Seigel differentiates the two categories as "adventurers" and "believers." Are her subgroups **consistent**, **exclusive**, and **distinct**? For example, could a reader be both an adventurer and a believer? How might a third (or fourth) category affect Seigel's argument?

Writing Guidelines

Planning

1. **Select a topic.** Start by writing a few general headings like the academic headings below; then list two or three related topics under each heading. Finally, pick a topic that is characterized by a larger set of items or members that can best be explained by ordering them into categories.

Engineering	Biology	Social Work	Education
Machines	Whales	Child welfare	Learning styles
Bridges	Fruits	Organizations	Testing Methods

fig. 13.3

2. **Look at the big picture.** Do preliminary research to get an overview of your topic. Review your purpose (to explain, persuade, inform, and so on), and consider which classification criteria will help you divide the subject's content into distinct, understandable categories.

3. **Choose and test your criterion.** Choose a criterion for creating categories. Make sure it produces groups that are *consistent* (the same criterion are used throughout the sorting process), *exclusive* (groups are distinct—no member fits into more than one group), and *complete* (each member fits into a subgroup with no member left over).

4. **Gather and organize information.** Gather information from reliable sources. To organize your information, take notes, possibly using a classification grid like the one shown below or the one on page 52. Set up the grid by listing the classification criteria down the left column and listing the groups in the top row of the columns. Then fill in the grid with appropriate details. (The grid below lists the classification criterion and groups discussed in "Latin American Music . . . ," pages 206–209.)

Classification Criteria	Group #1	Group #2	Group #3	Group #4
	Indigenous music	Iberian and Mestizo	Afro-American music	Urban popular music
Historical qualities/functions	• Trait #1 • Trait #2 • Trait #3	• Trait #1 • Trait #2 • Trait #3	• Trait #1 • Trait #2 • Trait #3	• Trait #1 • Trait #2 • Trait #3

fig. 13.4

Note: If you do not use a grid, consider using an outline to organize your thoughts.

5. **Draft a thesis.** Draft a working thesis (you can revise it later as needed) that states your topic and identifies your classification scheme. Include language introducing your criteria for classifying groups.

Drafting

6. Draft the essay. Write your first draft, using organization planned in step 4.

- **Opening:** Get the readers' attention, introduce the subject and thesis, and give your criteria for dividing the subject into categories.
- **Middle:** Develop the thesis by discussing each category, explaining its traits, and showing how it is distinct from the other groups. For example, in the middle section of "Four Ways to Talk About Literature," the writer first shows the unique focus of each of the four approaches to literary criticism, and then illustrates each approach by applying it to the same poem, "My Last Duchess" (see pages 257–258).
- **Closing:** Reflect on and tie together the classification scheme. While the opening and middle of the essay separate the subject into distinct categories, the closing may bring the groups back together. For example, Van Rys closes by identifying characteristics that the four subgroups have in common (see page 257).

Revising

7. Improve the ideas, organization, and voice. Ask a classmate or someone from the writing center to read your essay, looking for the following:

- ____ **Ideas:** Are the classification criteria logical and clear, resulting in categories that are consistent, exclusive, and complete? Does the discussion include appropriate examples that clarify the nature and function of each group?
- ____ **Organization:** Does the essay include (1) an engaging opening that introduces the subject, thesis, and criteria for classification, (2) a well-organized middle that distinguishes groups, shows why each group is unique, and supports these claims with evidence, and (3) a unifying conclusion that restates the main idea and its relevance?
- ____ **Voice:** Is the tone informed, courteous, and rational?

Editing

8. Edit the essay. Polish your writing by addressing these issues:

- ____ **Words:** The words distinguishing classifications are used uniformly.
- ____ **Sentences:** The sentences and paragraphs are complete, varied, and clear.
- ____ **Correctness:** No usage, grammatical, or mechanical errors are present.
- ____ **Page Design:** The design follows MLA, APA, CMS, or CSE formatting rules.

Publishing

9. Publish the essay by sharing it with your instructor and classmates, publishing it on your Web site, or submitting it to a print or online journal.

Critical-Thinking and Writing Activities

As directed by your instructor, complete the following activities.

1. In "Latin American Music: A Diverse and Unifying Force," Kathleen Kropp uses classification to analyze the nature and impact of an art form. Choose an art form that interests you, research the topic, and write an essay that uses classification to explain the art form's historical development and social impact.

2. In "Four Sides to Every Story," Steward Brand uses classification to show that the climate-change debate is more complex than a two-position argument. Select an argument that is erroneously presented as a two-option issue. Then research the topic and write a classification essay that accurately addresses the topic.

3. "Four Ways to Talk About Literature" on pages 257–258 examines four approaches to reading and understanding a piece of literature. Identify a similar group of approaches to analysis or problem solving in your program or major. Write an essay in which you break your topic into categories, sort the groups, and explain the topic to the reader.

4. Find an article in a newspaper or an academic journal that uses classification to develop a thesis. Note the writer's criteria for sorting elements of the topic into categories. Then write a brief essay explaining why the criteria do or do not lead to groups that are consistent, exclusive, and complete. Share your writing with the class.

Learning-Objectives Checklist ✓

Have you achieved this chapter's learning objectives? Check your progress with the items below, revisiting topics in the chapter as needed. *I have...*

____ critically read others' classification essays, assessing their organizational schemes for consistency, exclusivity, and completeness (204–205).

____ examined how these writers craft their analyses in accordance with their purposes, topics, and readers (204–205).

____ evaluated my own writing situation and developed a classification framework that helped me analyze my topic as required in my writing assignment (214–215).

____ devised a logical classification scheme that includes clear criteria for grouping (214–215).

____ created and used a classification grid (1) to logically break down the topic into groups of components, (2) to explain why the groups are unified, complete, and distinct, and (3) to show how the groups together comprise one entity (214–215).

____ used additional analytical strategies such as definition and compare-contrast to clarify similarities and differences between groups (62–64).

____ drafted, revised, and edited an essay that effectively uses classification reasoning to analyze a topic and to present the analysis in clear, logical writing (214–215).

Chapter 14

Process

Process writing helps us understand our world and ourselves by answering interesting questions like these: How does cancer spread? How did Abraham Lincoln come to advocate the "Emancipation Proclamation"? Why did Cesar Chavez's reputation as a labor leader rise or decline?

Writing that answers questions like these analyzes a process by breaking it down into steps, often grouping the steps into stages or phases. In addition to explaining the process, sometimes the writing also examines related causes and effects. Such papers are developed and formatted as essays, and the information in this chapter will help you read and write them.

However, writing that explains how readers can complete a process typically takes the form of technical instructions.

Visually Speaking Figure 14.1 captures a moment in a process. What is the process, and what writing strategies would you use to explain how to do the process?

Learning **Objectives**

By working through this chapter, you will be able to

- examine and assess writers' use of process reasoning.
- investigate a process so as to outline its nature and its workings.
- analyze the process, identifying its steps and related causes and effects.
- sequence the process chronologically, using transitions to link phases or steps.
- compose an analytical essay using primarily process thinking (with other analytical strategies, as needed).

Tyler Olson / Shutterstock.com

fig. 14.1

Strategies for Process Writing

Analyzing a process is an effort to explain how something happens, works, is made, or is done. The process may be natural (a phenomenon that occurs in nature, including human nature), performative (mechanical, something people do), or historical/cultural (events in time and/or within communities or groups).

The Rhetorical Situation

To put process writing in context, consider the situation that gives rise to it:

- **Purpose:** Writers write process essays in order to analyze and explain how an event or other phenomenon transpires. To that end, they first offer an overview of the process and then explain how each step leads logically to the next, and how all the steps together complete the process. (If the writer wants to help readers work through a process themselves, he or she writes instructions.)
- **Readers:** In all process writing, the text should meet the needs of all its readers, including those who know the least about the topic. To do this, writers should (1) include all the information that readers need, (2) use language that they understand, and (3) define unfamiliar or technical terms.
- **Topic:** In academic process writing, the topics are usually course-related phenomena that interest the writer and offer readers insight into the field of study. Topics addressed in professional publications should interest and educate their readers.

Example: In her essay "Wayward Cells" (pages 220–221), Kerry Mertz analyzes her **topic**: the process through which cancer cells overtake and destroy healthy cells. Her **purpose** is to help her **readers** (non-experts—college students and others without detailed technical knowledge) understand how and why the process occurs.

Principles of Process Writing

Analytical process writing should follow these principles:

Being clear and complete. Shape the analysis based on (1) how readers will use it, and (2) what they already know about it. Aim to deepen their current knowledge about how the process unfolds and what principles are at work.

Offering an overview. In order to understand individual parts of or moments in the process, readers generally need the big picture. Start, then, by explaining the process's essential principle, its goal, or its main product and/or result. That overview statement can often serve as the thesis statement. *Example: When a cell begins to function abnormally, it can initiate a process that results in cancer (page 220).*

Making the process manageable. A process essay unfolds effectively and clearly when the process is presented in manageable segments. First identify the process's major phases or stages (perhaps limiting these to three or four). Then break each stage into discrete steps or events, grouping actions in clear, logical ways.

Making the process familiar. To help readers understand the writing, use precise terms, well-chosen adjectives, and clear action verbs. Consider, as well, using comparisons for unfamiliar parts of the process, likening, for example, the growth of hair to the growth of grass. Finally, design graphics such as flowcharts, time lines, or sequential drawings that display the process. (See the sample flowchart in Figure 14.2.)

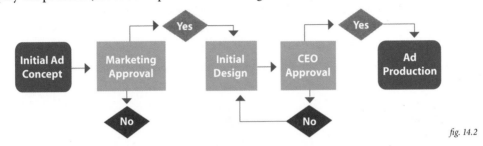

fig. 14.2

Signaling temporal relationships. Because process analysis is time related, readers need clear references to the order of events. Consider using terms such as *step, phase, stage;* transition words such as *first, second, next, finally;* or actual numbering systems (1, 2, 3).

Sample Process Paragraph

In his essay "The Emancipation of Abe Lincoln" (pages 222–225), Eric Foner identifies stages in the development of Lincoln's support for "The Emancipation Proclamation." In the paragraph below, Foner describes a series of events included in one of these stages:

> In the summer of 1862, a combination of events propelled Lincoln in a new direction. Slavery was disintegrating in parts of the South as thousands of slaves ran away to Union lines. With the war a stalemate, more Northerners found themselves agreeing with the abolitionists, who had insisted from the outset that slavery must become a target. Enthusiasm for enlistment was waning in the North. The Army had long refused to accept black volunteers, but the reservoir of black manpower could no longer be ignored. In response, Congress moved ahead of Lincoln, abolishing slavery in the District of Columbia, authorizing the president to enroll blacks in the Army and freeing the slaves of pro-Confederate owners in areas under military control. Lincoln signed all these measures that summer.

Reading Process Writing

As you read process essays, consider these questions:

1. Does the essay identify the process, outline its stages, explain individual steps, and (if appropriate) discuss causes and effects?
2. Does the writer effectively state and support his or her claims?
3. Does the writer use precise language and define unfamiliar terms?
4. Are steps organized chronologically and clearly linked with transitions?

Sample Process Essays

This chapter includes three essays illustrating how writers analyze phenomena related to the topics they write about. One writer explains how cancer develops, another analyzes Abraham Lincoln's shifting response to slavery, and a third writer examines Cesar Chavez's evolution as a labor leader.

Analyzing an Illness

Student writer Kerri Mertz wrote this essay to explain how cancer cells affect the body.

> **The title uses a metaphor for process.**
>
> **The introduction uses a cells-workers analogy.**

Wayward Cells

Imagine a room containing a large group of people all working hard toward the same goal. Each person knows his or her job, does it carefully, and cooperates with other group members. Together, they function smoothly—like a well-oiled machine.

Then something goes wrong. One guy suddenly drops his task, steps into another person's workstation, grabs the material that she's working with, and begins something very different—he uses the material to make little reproductions of himself, thousands of them. These look-alikes imitate him—grabbing material and making reproductions of themselves. Soon the bunch gets so big that they spill into other people's workstations, getting in their way, and interrupting their work. As the number of look-alikes grows, the work group's activity slows, stutters, and finally stops.

A human body is like this room, and the body's cells are like these workers. If the body is healthy, each cell has a necessary job and does it correctly. For example, right now red blood cells are running throughout your body carrying oxygen to each body part. Other cells are digesting that steak sandwich that you had for lunch, and others are patching up that cut on your left hand. Each cell knows what to do because its genetic code—or DNA—tells it what to do. When a cell begins to function abnormally, it can initiate a process that results in cancer.

> **Cancer starts with cell undifferentiating.**

The problem starts when one cell "forgets" what it should do. Scientists call this "undifferentiating"—meaning that the cell loses its identity within the body (Pierce 75). Just like the guy in the group who decided to do his own thing, the cell forgets its job. Why this happens is somewhat unclear.

The problem could be caused by a defect in the cell's DNA code or by something in the environment, such as cigarette smoke or asbestos (German 21). Causes from inside the body are called genetic, whereas causes from outside the body are called carcinogens, meaning "any substance that causes cancer" (Neufeldt and Sparks 90). In either case, an undifferentiated cell can disrupt the function of healthy cells in two ways: by not doing its job as specified in its DNA and by not reproducing at the rate noted in its DNA.

Cancer cells reproduce autonomously.	Most healthy cells reproduce rather quickly, but their reproduction rate is controlled. For example, your blood cells completely die off and replace themselves within a matter of weeks, but existing cells make only as many new cells as the body needs. The DNA codes in healthy cells tell them how many new cells to produce. However, cancer cells don't have this control, so they reproduce quickly with no stopping point, a characteristic called "autonomy" (Braun 3). What's more, all their "offspring" have the same qualities as their messed-up parent, and the resulting overpopulation produces growths called tumors.
Tumors damage the body.	Tumor cells can hurt the body in a number of ways. First, a tumor can grow so big that it takes up space needed by other organs. Second, some cells may detach from the original tumor and spread throughout the body, creating new tumors elsewhere. This happens with lymphatic cancer—a cancer that's hard to control because it spreads so quickly. A third way that tumor cells can hurt the body is by doing work not called for in their DNA. For example, a gland cell's DNA code may tell the cell to produce a necessary hormone in the endocrine system. However, if cancer damages or distorts that code, sick cells may produce more of the hormone than the body can use—or even tolerate (Braun 4). Cancer cells seem to have minds of their own, and this is why cancer is such a serious disease.
Promising treatments offer hope.	Fortunately, there is hope. Scientific research is already helping doctors do amazing things for people suffering with cancer. One treatment that has been used for some time is chemotherapy, or the use of chemicals to kill off all fast-growing cells, including cancer cells. (Unfortunately, chemotherapy can't distinguish between healthy and unhealthy cells, so it may cause negative side effects such as damaging fast-growing hair follicles, resulting in hair loss.) Another common treatment is radiation, or the use of light rays to kill cancer cells. One of the newest and most promising treatments is gene therapy—an effort to identify and treat chromosomes that carry a "wrong code" in their DNA. A treatment like gene therapy is promising because it treats the cause of cancer, not just the effect. Year by year, research is helping doctors better understand what cancer is and how to treat it.
The essay concludes that wayward cells are like wayward workers. **Note:** The Works Cited page is not shown.	Much of life involves dealing with problems like wayward workers, broken machines, or dysfunctional organizations. Dealing with wayward cells is just another problem. While the problem is painful and deadly, there is hope. Medical specialists and other scientists are making progress, and some day they will help us win our battle against wayward cells.

6

7

8

9

"Wayward Cells" by Kerri Mertz. Used by permission of the author.

Reading for Better Writing

Working by yourself or with a group, answer these questions:

1. Explain why the analogy in the opening and closing is or is not effective.
2. Explain how transitions are used to lead into and out of each step.
3. Explain how the essay both describes and analyzes the process.

Analyzing a Policy

Eric Foner is a professor of history at Columbia University and the author of numerous publications, including *The Fiery Trial: Abraham Lincoln and American Slavery* and the essay below. He published the essay on December 31, 2012, one day before the 150th anniversary of Lincoln's signing the "Emancipation Proclamation."

The Emancipation of Abe Lincoln

The opening introduces the topic: Lincoln's signing the "Emancipation Proclamation."

ONE hundred and fifty years ago, on January 1, 1863, Abraham Lincoln presided over the annual White House New Year's reception. Late that afternoon, he retired to his study to sign the "Emancipation Proclamation." When he took up his pen, his hand was shaking from exhaustion. Briefly, he paused—"I do not want it to appear as if I hesitated," he remarked. Then Lincoln affixed a firm signature to the document.   *1*

The writer describes emancipation as a process and offers an overview.

Like all great historical transformations, emancipation was a process, not a single event. It arose from many causes and was the work of many individuals. It began at the outset of the Civil War, when slaves sought refuge behind Union lines. It did not end until December 1865, with the ratification of the 13th Amendment, which irrevocably abolished slavery throughout the nation.   *2*

He explains how the document was a "double emancipation."

But the Emancipation Proclamation was the crucial turning point in this story. In a sense, it embodied a double emancipation: for the slaves, since it ensured that if the Union emerged victorious, slavery would perish, and for Lincoln himself, for whom it marked the abandonment of his previous assumptions about how to abolish slavery and the role blacks would play in post-emancipation American life.   *3*

The first stage in the process is introduced.

There is no reason to doubt the sincerity of Lincoln's statement in 1864 that he had always believed slavery to be wrong. During the first two years of the Civil War, despite insisting that the conflict's aim was preservation of the Union, he devoted considerable energy to a plan for ending slavery inherited from prewar years. Emancipation would be undertaken by state governments, with national financing. It would be gradual, owners would receive monetary compensation and emancipated slaves would be encouraged to find a homeland outside the United States—this last idea known as "colonization."   *4*

Events in this stage are listed.

Lincoln's plan sought to win the cooperation of slave holders in ending slavery. As early as November 1861, he proposed it to political leaders in Delaware, one of the four border states (along with Kentucky, Maryland and Missouri) that remained in the Union. Delaware had only 1,800 slaves; the institution was peripheral to the state's economy. But Lincoln found that even there, slave holders did not wish to surrender their human property. Nonetheless, for most of 1862, he avidly promoted his plan to the border states and any Confederates who might be interested.   *5*

Related events are cited.

Lincoln also took his proposal to black Americans. In August 1862, he met with a group of black leaders from Washington. He seemed to blame the presence   *6* of blacks in America for the conflict: "but for your race among us there could not be war." He issued a powerful indictment of slavery—"the greatest wrong inflicted on any people"—but added that, because of racism, blacks would never achieve equality in America. "It is better for us both, therefore, to be separated," he said. But most blacks refused to contemplate emigration from the land of their birth.

> The phrase "In the summer" signals the second stage in Lincoln's thought process.

In the summer of 1862, a combination of events propelled Lincoln in a new direction. Slavery was disintegrating in parts of the South as thousands of slaves ran away to Union lines. With the war a stalemate, more Northerners found themselves agreeing with the abolitionists, who had insisted from the outset that slavery must become a target. Enthusiasm for enlistment was waning in the North. The Army had long refused to accept black volunteers, but the reservoir of black manpower could no longer be ignored. In response, Congress moved ahead of Lincoln, abolishing slavery in the District of Columbia, authorizing the president to enroll blacks in the Army and freeing the slaves of pro-Confederate owners in areas under military control. Lincoln signed all these measures that summer. *7*

> The writer suggests what Lincoln's transition might imply about his character.

The hallmark of Lincoln's greatness was his combination of bedrock principle with open-mindedness and capacity for growth. That summer, with his preferred approach going nowhere, he moved in the direction of immediate emancipation. He first proposed this to his cabinet on July 22, but Secretary of State William H. Seward persuaded him to wait for a military victory, lest it seem an act of desperation. *8*

> *The hallmark of Lincoln's greatness was his combination of bedrock principle with open-mindedness and capacity for growth.*

> The writer reflects on the implications of stage 1 events.

Soon after the Union victory at Antietam in September, Lincoln issued the Preliminary Emancipation Proclamation, a warning to the Confederacy that if it did not lay down its arms by January 1, he would declare the slaves "forever free." *9*

> He describes the document's limited effects and offers evidence supporting his claim.

Lincoln did not immediately abandon his earlier plan. His annual message to Congress, released on Dec. 1, 1862, devoted a long passage to gradual, compensated abolition and colonization. But in the same document, without mentioning the impending proclamation, he indicated that a new approach was imperative: "The dogmas of the quiet past, are inadequate to the stormy present," he wrote. "We must disenthrall our selves, and then we shall save our country." Lincoln included himself in that "we." On Jan. 1, he proclaimed the freedom of the vast majority of the nation's slaves. *10*

The Emancipation Proclamation is perhaps the most misunderstood of the documents that have shaped American history. Contrary to legend, Lincoln did *11* not free the nearly four million slaves with a stroke of his pen. It had no bearing on slaves in the four border states, since they were not in rebellion. It also exempted certain parts of the Confederacy occupied by the Union. All told, it left perhaps 750,000 slaves in bondage. But the remaining 3.1 million, it declared, "are, and henceforward shall be free."

The proclamation did not end slavery in the United States on the day it was issued. Indeed, it could not even be enforced in most of the areas where it applied, which were under Confederate control. But it ensured the eventual death of slavery—assuming the Union won the war. Were the Confederacy to emerge victorious, slavery, in one form or another, would undoubtedly have lasted a long time.   12

A military order, whose constitutional legitimacy rested on the president's war powers, the proclamation often disappoints those who read it. It is dull and legalistic; it contains no soaring language enunciating the rights of man. Only at the last minute, at the urging of Treasury Secretary Salmon P. Chase, an abolitionist, did Lincoln add a conclusion declaring the proclamation an "act of justice."   13

Nonetheless, the proclamation marked a dramatic transformation in the nature of the Civil War and in Lincoln's own approach to the problem of slavery. No longer did he seek the consent of slave holders. The proclamation was immediate, not gradual, contained no mention of compensation for owners, and made no reference to colonization.   14

In it, Lincoln addressed blacks directly, not as property subject to the will of others but as men and women whose loyalty the Union must earn. For the first time, he welcomed black soldiers into the Union Army; over the next two years some 200,000 black men would serve in the Army and Navy, playing a critical role in achieving Union victory. And Lincoln urged freed slaves to go to work for "reasonable wages"—in the United States. He never again mentioned colonization in public.   15

Having made the decision, Lincoln did not look back. In 1864, with casualties mounting, there was talk of a compromise peace. Some urged Lincoln to rescind the proclamation, in which case, they believed, the South could be persuaded to return to the Union. Lincoln refused. Were he to do so, he told one visitor, "I should be damned in time and eternity."   16

Wartime emancipation may have settled the fate of slavery, but it opened another vexing question: the role of former slaves in American life. Colonization had allowed its proponents to talk about abolition without having to confront this issue; after all, the black population would be gone. After January 1, 1863, Lincoln for the first time began to think seriously of the United States as a biracial society.   17

While not burdened with the visceral racism of many of his white contemporaries, Lincoln shared some of their prejudices. He had long seen blacks as an alien people who had been unjustly uprooted from their homeland and were   18

He contrasts the document's unexceptional diction with the document's exceptional claims and effects.

The phrase "Having made" signals a transition into the final stage of Lincoln's thought process.

 The writer reflects on events distinguishing Lincoln's earlier thinking.	entitled to freedom, but were not an intrinsic part of American society. During his Senate campaign in Illinois, in 1858, he had insisted that blacks should enjoy the same natural rights as whites (life, liberty and the pursuit of happiness), but he opposed granting them legal equality or the right to vote.

The writer claims—and cites evidence—that Lincoln's thinking changed.

By the end of his life, Lincoln's outlook had changed dramatically. In his last public address, delivered in April 1865, he said that in reconstructing Louisiana, and by implication other Southern states, he would "prefer" that limited black suffrage be implemented. He singled out the "very intelligent" (educated free blacks) and "those who serve our cause as soldiers" as most worthy. Though hardly an unambiguous embrace of equality, this was the first time an American president had endorsed any political rights for blacks.   19

And then there was his magnificent second inaugural address of March 4, 1865, in which Lincoln ruminated on the deep meaning of the war. He now identified the institution of slavery—not the presence of blacks, as in 1862—as its fundamental cause. The war, he said, might well be a divine punishment for the evil of slavery. And God might will it to continue until all the wealth the slaves had created had been destroyed, and "until every drop of blood drawn with the lash, shall be paid by another drawn by the sword." Lincoln was reminding Americans that violence did not begin with the firing on Fort Sumter, S.C., in April 1861. What he called "this terrible war" had been preceded by 250 years of the terrible violence of slavery.   20

The writer suggests that in his death, Lincoln left the country to work out its own emancipation.

In essence, Lincoln asked the nation to confront unblinkingly the legacy of slavery. What were the requirements of justice in the face of this reality? What would be necessary to enable former slaves and their descendants to enjoy fully the pursuit of happiness? Lincoln did not live to provide an answer. A century and a half later, we have yet to do so.   21

Reading for Better Writing

Working by yourself or with a group, answer these questions:
1. Describe how the writer introduces his topic and thesis.
2. Review his claim (in paragraph two) that emancipation was a process, not a single event. What does he mean, and how does he support this claim?
3. Cite examples showing how the writer builds transitions that (1) link stages in the process and (2) link specific events within a stage.
4. Identify a passage in which the writer analyzes how specific events caused a shift in Lincoln's thinking. What does this passage contribute to the essay?

Analyzing a Career

Richard Rodriguez is an accomplished writer who has written successfully as a journalist, essayist, and novelist. In the essay that follows, he analyzes the process through which Cesar Chavez's reputation as a successful labor leader developed, and also declined.

Saint Cesar of Delano

> Use this column to record your own observations about the essay.

The funeral for Cesar Chavez took place in an open field near Delano, a small agricultural town at the southern end of California's Central Valley. I remember an amiable Mexican disorder, the crowd listening and not listening to speeches and prayers delivered from a raised platform beneath a canvas tent. I do not remember a crowd numbering 30,000 or 50,000, as some estimates have it—but then I do not remember. Perhaps a cool, perhaps a warm spring sun. Men in white shirts carried forward a pine box. The ease of their movement suggested the lightness of their burden.   *1*

When Cesar Chavez died in his sleep in 1993, not yet a very old man at 66, he died—as he had so often portrayed himself in life—as a loser. The United Farm Workers (UFW) union he had cofounded was in decline; the union had 5,000 members, equivalent to the population of one very small Central Valley town. The labor in California's agricultural fields was largely taken up by Mexican migrant workers—the very workers Chavez had been unable to reconcile to his American union; the workers he had branded "scabs."   *2*

I went to the funeral because I was writing a piece on Chavez for *The Los Angeles Times*. It now occurs to me that I was present at a number of events involving Cesar Chavez. I was at the edge of the crowd in 1966, when Chavez led UFW marchers to the steps of the capitol in Sacramento to rally for a strike against grape growers. I went to hear him speak at Stanford University. I can recall everything about the occasion except why I was there. I remember a light of late afternoon among the oaks beyond the plate-glass windows of Tresidder Union; I remember the Reverend Robert McAfee Brown introducing Cesar Chavez. Something about Chavez embarrassed me—embarrassed me in a way I would be embarrassed if someone from my family had turned up at Stanford to lecture undergraduates on the hardness of a Mexican's life. I did not join in the standing ovation. Well, I was already standing. I wouldn't give him anything. And yet, of course, there was something compelling about his homeliness.   *3*

In her thoroughly researched and thoroughly unsentimental book *The Union of Their Dreams: Power, Hope, and Struggle in Cesar Chavez's Farm Worker Movement*, journalist Miriam Pawel chronicles the lives of a collection of people—farm workers, idealistic college students, young lawyers from the Easy Coast, a Presbyterian minister, and others—who gave years of their lives at subsistence pay to work for the UFW. Every person Pawel profiles has left the union—has been fired or has quit in disgust or frustration. Nevertheless, it is not beside the point to notice that Cesar Chavez inspired such a disparate, devoted company.   *4*

We forget that the era we call "the Sixties" was not only a time of vast civic   5
disaffection; it was also a time of religious idealism. At the forefront of what
amounted to the religious revival of America in those years were the black
Protestant ministers of the civil rights movement, ministers who insisted upon a
moral dimension to the rituals of everyday American life—eating at a lunch counter,
riding a bus, going to school.

Cesar Chavez similarly cast his campaign for better wages and living conditions   6
for farm workers as a religious movement. He became for many Americans,
especially Mexican Americans (my parents among them), a figure of spiritual
authority. I remember a small brown man with an Indian aspect leading labor
protests that were also medieval religious processions of women, children, nuns,
students, burnt old men—under the banner of Our Lady of Guadalupe.

By the time he had become the most famous Mexican American anyone could   7
name—his face on the cover of *Time*—the majority of Mexican Americans lived in
cities, far from the tragic fields of California's Central Valley that John Steinbeck had
made famous a generation before. Mexican Americans were more likely to work in
construction or in service sector jobs than in the fields.

Cesar Chavez was born in Yuma, Arizona, in 1927. During the years of his   8
hardscrabble youth, he put away his ambitions for college. He gave his body to the
fields in order to keep his mother from having to work in the fields. The young farm
worker accumulated an autodidact's library—books on economics, philosophy,
history. (Years later, Chavez was apt to quote Winston Churchill at UFW staff
meetings.) He studied the black civil rights movement, particularly the writings of
Martin Luther King Jr. He studied most intently the lives and precepts of St. Francis
of Assisi and Mohandas Gandhi.

It is heartening to learn about private acts of goodness in notorious lives. It is   9
discouraging to learn of the moral failures of famously good people. The former
console. But to learn that the Reverend Martin Luther King Jr. was a womanizer is to
be confronted with the knowledge that flesh is a complicated medium for grace. To
learn that there were flaws in the character of Cesar Chavez is again to wonder at the
meaning of a good life. During his lifetime, Chavez was considered by many to be a
saint. Pawel is writing outside the hagiography, but while reading her book, I could
not avoid thinking about the nature of sanctity.

Saints? Holiness? I apologize for introducing radiant nouns.   10

Cesar Chavez modeled his life on the lives of saints—an uncommon ambition   11
in a celebrated American life. In America, influence is the point of prominence;
power over history is the point. I think Cesar Chavez would have said striving to
lead a holy life is the point—a life lived in imitation of Jesus Christ, the most famous
loser on a planet spilling over with losers. The question is whether the Mexican saint
survives the tale of the compromised American hero.

The first portrait in *The Union of Their Dreams* is of Eliseo Medina. At the   12
advent of the UFW, Eliseo was a shy teenager, educated only through the eighth

grade. Though he was not confident in English, Medina loved to read *El Malcriado*, the feisty bilingual weekly published by the UFW. Eliseo Medina remembered how his life changed on a Thursday evening when he went to hear Chavez in the social hall of Our Lady of Guadalupe Church in Delano. Medina was initially "disappointed by the leader's unimpressive appearance." But by the end of the meeting, he had determined to join the union.

No Chavez speech I have read or heard approaches the rhetorical brilliance   13
of the Protestant ministers of the black civil rights movement. Chavez was, however, brilliantly theatrical. He seemed to understand, the way Charlie Chaplin understood, how to make an embarrassment of himself—his mulishness, his silence, his witness. His presence at the edge of a field was a blight of beatitude.

Chavez studied the power of abstinence. He internalized his resistance to   14
injustice by refusing to eat. What else can a poor man do? Though Chavez had little success encouraging UFW volunteers to follow his example of fasting, he was able to convince millions of Americans (as many as 20 million, by some estimates) not to buy grapes or lettuce.

Farmers in the Central Valley were bewildered to find themselves roped into a   15
religious parable. Indeed, Valley growers, many of them Catholics, were dismayed when their children came home from parochial schools and reported that Chavez was upheld as a moral exemplum in religion class.

At a time in the history of American business when Avis saw the advantage of   16
advertising itself as "Number Two" and Volkswagen sold itself as "the Bug," Chavez made the smallness of his union, even the haphazardness, a kind of boast. In 1968, during his most publicized fast to support the strike of grape pickers, Chavez issued this statement (he was too weak to read aloud): "Those who oppose our cause are rich and powerful and they have many allies in high places. We are poor. Our allies are few."

Chavez broke his 1968 fast with a public relations tableau that was rich with   17
symbol and irony. Physically diminished (in photographs his body seems unable of sustaining an erect, seated position), Chavez was handed bread (sacramental ministration after his trial in the desert) by Chris Hartmire, the Presbyterian minister who gave so much of his life to serving Chavez and his union. Alongside Chavez sat Robert F. Kennedy, then a U.S. senator from New York. The poor and the meek also have allies in high places.

Here began a conflict between deprivation and success that would bedevil Chavez   18
through three decades. In a way, this was a struggle between the Mexican Cesar Chavez and the American Cesar Chavez. For it was Mexico that taught Chavez to value a life of suffering. It was America that taught him to fight the causes of suffering.

The speech Chavez had written during his hunger strike of 1968 (wherein he   19
likened the UFW to David fighting the Goliath of agribusiness) announced the Mexican theme: "I am convinced that the truest act of courage, the strongest act

Aprilphoto / Shutterstock.com

of manliness is to sacrifice ourselves for others in a totally nonviolent struggle for justice. To be a man is to suffer for others. God help us to be men." (Nearly three decades later, in the program for Chavez's funeral, the wording of his psalm would be revised—"humanity" substituted for "manliness": *To be human is to suffer for others. God help me to be human.*)

Nothing else Chavez would write during his life had such haunting power for me   20
as this public prayer for a life of suffering; no utterance would sound so Mexican. Other cultures in the world assume the reality of suffering as something to be overcome. Mexico assumes the inevitability of suffering. That knowledge informs the folk music of Mexico, the bitter humor of Mexican proverb. To be a man is to suffer for others— your going to suffer anyway. The code of *machismo* (which in American English has translated too crudely to sexual bravado) in Mexico derives from a medieval chivalry whereby a man uses his strength or his resolve or even his foolishness (as did Don Quixote) to protect those less powerful. God help us to be men.

Mexicans believe that in 1531 the Virgin Mary appeared in brown skin, in royal   21
Aztec raiment, to a converted Indian peasant named Juan Diego. The Virgin asked that a church be erected on the site of her four apparitions in order that Mexican Indians could come to her and tell her of their suffering. The image of Our Lady of Guadalupe was an aspect of witness at every UFW demonstration.

Though he grew up during the American Depression, Chavez breathed   22
American optimism and American activism. In the early 1950s, while still a farm worker, he met Fred Ross of the Community Service Organization, a group inspired by the principles of the radical organizer Saul Alinsky. Chavez later became an official in the CSO, and eventually its president. He persuaded notoriously apathetic Mexican Americans to register to vote by encouraging them to believe they could change their lives in America.

If you would understand the tension between Mexico and the United States that   23
is playing out along our mutual border, you must understand the psychic tension between Mexican stoicism—if that is a rich enough word for it—and American optimism. On the one side, Mexican peasants are tantalized by the American possibility of change. On the other side, the tyranny of American optimism has driven Americans to neurosis and depression—when the dream is elusive or less meaningful than the myth promised. This constitutes the great irony of the Mexican-American border: American sadness has transformed the drug lords of Mexico into billionaires, even as the peasants of Mexico scramble through the darkness to find the American dream.

By the late 1960s, as the first UFW contracts were being signed, Chavez began   24
to brood. Had he spent his poor life only to create a middle class? Lionel Steinberg, the first grape grower to sign with the UFW, was drawn by Chavez's charisma but chagrined at the union's disordered operations. He wondered: "Is it a social movement or a trade union?" He urged Chavez to use experienced negotiators from the AFL-CIO.

Chavez paid himself a subsistence annual wage of $5,000. "You can't change   *25*
anything if you want to hold onto a good job, a good way of life, and avoid
suffering." The world-famous labor leader would regularly complain to his poorly
paid staff about the phone bills they ran up and about what he saw as the misuse of a
fleet of second-hand UFW cars. He held the union hostage to the purity of his intent.
Eliseo Medina, who had become one of the union's most effective organizers, could
barely support his young family; ,he asked Chavez about setting up a trust fund
for his infant son. Chavez promised to get back to him but never did. Eventually,
thoroughly discouraged by the mismanagement of the union, Medina resigned.

In 1975, Chavez helped to pass legislation prohibiting the use of the short-   *26*
handled hoe in the fields—its two-foot-long shaft forced farm workers to stoop all
day. That achievement would outlast the decline of his union. By the early 1970s,
California vegetable growers began signing sweetheart contracts with the rival
Teamsters Union. The UFW became mired in scraps with unfriendly politicians
in Sacramento. Chavez's attention wandered. He imagined a "Poor Peoples Union"
that would reach out to senior citizens and people on welfare. He contacted church
officials within the Vatican about the possibility of establishing a lay religious
society devoted to service to the poor. Chavez became interested in the Hutterite
communities of North America and the Israeli kibbutzim as possible models for
such a society.

Chavez visited Synanon, the drug rehabilitation commune headed by Charles   *27*
Dederich, shortly before some Synanon members were implicated in a series of
sexual scandals and criminal assaults. Chavez borrowed from Synanon a version of
a disciplinary practice called the Game, whereby UFW staff members were obliged
to stand in the middle of a circle of peers and submit to fierce criticism. Someone
sympathetic to Chavez might argue that the Game was an inversion of an ancient
monastic discipline meant to teach humility. Someone less sympathetic might conclude
that Chavez was turning into a petty tyrant. I think both estimations are true.

From his reading, Chavez would have known that St. Francis of Assisi desired   *28*
to imitate the life of Jesus. The followers of Francis desired to imitate the life of
Francis. Within 10 years of undertaking his mendicant life, Francis had more than
1,000 followers. Francis realized he could not administer a growing religious order
by personal example. He relinquished the administration of the Franciscans to men
who had some talent for organization. Cesar Chavez never gave up his position as
head of the UFW.

In 1977 Chavez traveled to Manila as a guest of President Ferdinand Marcos.   *29*
He ended up praising the old dictator. There were darker problems within the UFW.
There were rumors that some within the inner circle were responsible for a car crash
that left Cleofas Guzman, an apostate union member, with permanent brain damage.

Chavez spent his last years protesting the use of pesticides in the fields. In April   *30*
of 1993, he died.

After his death, as Cesar Chavez became an American hero, his quarreling   31
family—in the mode of the children of Dr. Martin Luther King Jr.—seemed to want
to profit from the public esteem for their father. The year after his death, Chavez
was awarded the National Medal of Freedom by President Bill Clinton. In 2002, the
U.S. Postal Service unveiled a 37-cent stamp bearing the image of Cesar Chavez.
Politicians throughout the West and the Southwest attached Chavez's name to
parks and schools and streets and civic buildings of every sort. And there began an
effort of mixed success to declare March 31, his birthday, a legal holiday. During the
presidential campaign of 2012, President Barack Obama designated the home and
burial place of Cesar Chavez in Keene, California, a national monument within the
National Park System.

The American hero was also a Mexican saint. In 1997 American painter Robert   32
Lentz, a Franciscan brother, painted an icon of *Cesar Chavez of California*. Chavez
is depicted with a golden halo. He holds in his hand a scrolled broadsheet of the U.S.
Constitution. He wears a pink sweatshirt bearing the UFW insignia.

That same year, executives at the advertising agency TBWA/Chiat/Day came up   33
with a campaign for Apple computers that featured images of some famous dead—
John Lennon, Albert Einstein, Frank Sinatra—alongside a grammar-crunching
motto: *Think different*.

I remember sitting in bad traffic on the San Diego Freeway one day and looking   34
up to see a photograph of Cesar Chavez on a billboard. His eyes were downcast. He
balanced a rake and a shovel over his right shoulder. In the upper-left-hand corner
was the corporate logo of a bitten apple.

Reading for Better Writing

Working by yourself or with a group, answer these questions:

1. In this essay, Richard Rodriguez describes the process through which Cesar Chavez's reputation as a labor leader developed. Summarize that process.
2. Rodriguez opens the essay with three paragraphs that describe Chavez's funeral. What do these paragraphs tell you about (a) Chavez, (b) Rodriguez's purpose for writing, and (c) his assessment of Chavez?
3. Rodriguez claims that Chavez's reputation as the co-founder and leader of a labor union increased over time. Cite evidence that Rodriguez uses to support this claim.
4. What personal qualities does Rodriguez suggest helped Chavez succeed?
5. What evidence appears to mark the peak of his popularity?
6. Which of Chavez's personal traits or actions diminished his success and tainted his reputation?

Writing Guidelines

Planning

1. **Select a topic.** Use prompts like those below to generate a list of topics.
   - A course-related process
   - A process in nature
   - A process in the news
   - A process that helps you get a job
   - A process that would help you achieve a personal goal

2. **Review the process.** Use your knowledge of the topic to fill out an organizer like the one on the right. List the subject at the top, each of the steps in chronological order, and the outcome at the bottom. For a complex process, break it down into stages or phases first; then outline the steps or events within each phase.

   > **Process Analysis**
   > **Subject:**
   > - **Step #1**
   > - **Step #2**
   > - **Step #3**
   > **Outcome:**
   >
   > *fig. 14.3*

3. **Research the process.** Find all the information that you need to fully understand the process yourself and to clearly explain it to your readers. To guide your research, you might list headings and related questions like these:

   - **Context:** When, where, how, and why does the process transpire? How is the context related to the nature of the process?
   - **Content:** What individual steps—or groups of steps—make up the process?
   - **Order:** In what order do the steps take place? Is the order important? Why?
   - **Connections:** What links steps to steps or links stages to stages and how?
   - **Causes:** What causes each individual step or event—or what causes the process as a whole? How can I distinguish between false causes (page 303) and actual causes?
   - **Effects:** What is the outcome of each step or event—and what is the outcome of the whole process? What side effects are associated with the outcome?
   - **Materials:** What materials are used in the process and how do they affect it?
   - **History:** When did this process begin? How has it changed over time and why?
   - **Personnel:** Who is involved in the process? Why? How do they affect the process, and how does it affect them?
   - **Cost:** What is the financial cost? The emotional cost? The environmental cost?
   - **Impact:** How does the process affect my community, my friends, or me?

4. **Organize information.** Revise the organizer as needed. Then develop an outline, including steps listed in the organizer, as well as supporting details from your research.

Drafting

5. **Write the first draft.** Write the document using the guidelines below.
   - **Opening:** Introduce the topic and give an overview of the process, possibly forecasting its main stages. Explain why the process is important: e.g., how it affects a person, community, or country.

- **Middle:** Clearly describe each step in the process, and link steps with transitions such as *first, second, next, finally,* and *while.* Explain the importance of each step, and how it is linked to other steps in the process. If the process is complex and has many steps, consider grouping them into 3-5 phases or stages. Describe the outcomes of steps and phases, as well as the overall outcome and relevance of the process. Depending on your purpose for writing, you might also analyze the causes and effects related to specific steps, or to the entire process.
- **Closing:** Summarize the process and restate key points as needed, such as why understanding the process has value. If appropriate, explain follow-up activity, such as how readers might learn more about the topic.

Revising

6. **Improve the ideas, organization, and voice.** Evaluate the following:

___ **Ideas:** Is the process presented as a unified phenomenon that includes a logical series of stages and steps? Are all claims clear, rational, and supported with reliable evidence? Are assertions regarding causes and effects relevant and explained fully? Does the writing include logical fallacies such as false cause (page 303), broad generalization (page 303), and false analogy (page 304)?

___ **Organization:** Does the essay include an opening that introduces the process, offers an overview, and states the thesis; a middle that describes stages and steps clearly and correctly; and a closing that unifies the essay?

___ **Voice:** Is the tone informed, concerned, and objective? Are sensitive issues well researched, addressed respectfully, and shown to be relevant?

Editing

7. **Edit the essay.** Polish your writing by addressing the following:

___ **Words:** The words are precise, clear, and correct.
   - Technical terms are correct, used uniformly, and defined.

___ **Sentences:** The sentences are smooth, varied in structure, and engaging.

___ **Correctness:** The usage, grammar, punctuation, and spelling are correct.

___ **Page Design:** The page design is attractive and features steps in the process. Essays are correctly formatted in MLA or APA style.

Publishing

8. **Publish the essay** by offering it to instructors, students, and nonprofit agencies working with the process.

Critical-Thinking and Writing Activities

As directed by your instructor, complete the following activities by yourself or in a group.

1. Review "Wayward Cells," the essay that analyzes what cancer is and how it progresses. Then choose another natural or social science process that interests you and write an essay describing and analyzing that process. Conversely, think of a process within the arts and humanities (e.g., a historical movement, a cultural change, a plot pattern in fiction or film, an artistic method).

2. Review Eric Foner's essay, "The Emancipation of Abe Lincoln," noting how Foner analyzes the process through which Lincoln's thinking about slavery developed. Then choose another prominent historical character, research the person's stand on an issue, and write a process essay in which you analyze how and why his or her position changed.

3. Re-read Richard Rodriguez's essay "Saint Cesar of Delano" in which he analyzes how and why Cesar Chavez's reputation as a labor leader changed over time. Then research a prominent person in your discipline, focusing on how his or her reputation changed. Based on your research, write a process essay in which you explain the causes and effects of this change.

4. Think about a time or phase in your own life during which your understanding of—or position on—an issue, event, or other topic changed. Then write an essay in which you analyze the transition, identify related stages and steps, explain possible causes and effects, and address the overall impact of the experience.

Learning-Objectives Checklist ✓

Have you achieved this chapter's learning objectives? Check your progress with the items below, revisiting topics in the chapter as needed. *I have . . .*

___ examined what process essays are, why they are written, and how they are used to analyze and explain phenomena (218–219).

___ analyzed the content and evaluated the quality of process essays (218–219).

___ researched a process, analyzed it, identified steps in the process, and found reliable evidence that distinguishes related causes and effects (232–233).

___ presented this information in a well-crafted essay that introduces the topic, offers an overview of the process, describes the steps clearly in chronological order, links the steps effectively, and explains the overall outcome or impact of the process (232–233).

___ revised the essay for weaknesses in organization and voice, and corrected errors in logic such as false cause, broad generalization, and false analogy (232–233).

___ edited the essay for errors in grammar, punctuation, spelling, and mechanics (232–233).

Chapter 15

Definition

Most forms of academic and workplace writing—from essays and reports to proposals and literature reviews—include brief (one- or two-sentence) definitions of terms, sometimes called formal definitions. Although this chapter will help you read and write those, its main purpose is to help you understand and write longer, essay-length pieces sometimes called extended definitions.

Such definitions clarify and deepen readers' understanding of a term—whether it refers to something concrete or abstract. When reading such essays, consider how the writers "extend" your understanding of their topics, often using examples, illustrations, comparisons, and anecdotes to do so.

Visually Speaking To learn more about reading and writing definition essays, look again at Figure 15.1 and consider what it suggests about why we need definitions, write them, and use them.

Learning **Objectives**

By working through this chapter, you will be able to

- investigate how writers' situations inform their definition writing.
- critically examine and critique both brief and extended definitions.
- research all elements of a word's meaning.
- compose well-researched and well-reasoned brief and extended definitions.
- produce enriching anecdotes, quotations, comparisons, and contrasts, along with smooth transitions.

© Atlantide Phototravel/Corbis

fig. 15.1

Strategies for Definition Essays

Definition clarifies meaning through an equation: **term x = explanation y**. As an analyst, the writer has the task of showing that explanation y on the right amounts to the same thing as the term (or referent) x on the left. Depending on a writer's situation (purpose, readers, and topic), she or he might develop a succinct one-sentence formal definition or a six-page extended definition.

The Rhetorical Situation

To put definition writing in context, consider the situation that gives rise to it:

- **Purpose:** Writers compose definitions for many reasons—to define a misunderstood term, to plumb the meaning of a complex concept, or to entertain readers. Their writing purpose—and readers—affect what form the writing takes. For example, a writer explaining to high school students the classical concept of *catharsis* might begin by offering a one-sentence, formal definition of the term, *tragic hero.*

- **Readers:** People who read definitions also do so for different reasons, which affect the type of definitions they seek. For example, one reader may find a term unclear but want only a brief definition. Another reader may find a term very confusing and want a lengthy analysis of it, including its etymology. A third reader may understand what the term means but want to learn how a writer might expand its meaning.

- **Topic:** For any definition, the topic is a term. But what terms do writers typically focus on, and how does the term itself affect the form and style of the definition? That again depends the writer's purpose and readers. For example, David Shelhaas writes extended definitions for a radio audience. He chooses words that will interest his listeners, and he defines the terms in a playful, narrative style (page 240). In contrast, Shon Bogar writes a lengthy academic essay analyzing the economic roots of a number of serious social abuses. To help readers understand his argument, he first defines one of those abuses, human trafficking (pages 238–239).

Principles of Definition Writing

Definition writing depends on the principles explained on this page and the next.

Examining a term's denotative (or literal) meaning, connotative (or suggested meaning), and etymology (or historical meaning). By studying one or more of these, writers gain a foundational understanding of their topics and commonly find poignant details that lead to fresh insights. For an example, see Schelhaas's essay on page 240.

Seeking accurate, authoritative sources. To write accurate definitions, writers need reliable sources of information. However, as Simon L. Garfinkle explains in his essay, "Wikipedia and the Meaning of Truth" (pages 244–249), not all published sources are equally reliable. For information on how to evaluate the credibility of a source, see pages 412–415.

Using anecdotes, examples, illustrations and comparisons. Writers use strategies such as these to engage readers and help them imagine a situation, visualize details, and discern subtle connotations. For example, in her essay "On Excellence" (241–243), Cynthia Ozick defines excellence in part by sharing numerous, entertaining anecdotes that illustrate how her mother is similar to or different from other members of their family.

Inserting transitions that lead into and out of definitions. When composing a definition within a longer piece of writing, writers typically insert a transition that introduces the definition and explains why it is relevant or needed. After the definition, writers then insert another transition that leads readers back into the discussion that follows. For example, look at how Bogar's opening sentence in the sample paragraph below introduces the term that he is defining and explains why the definition is needed.

Avoiding logical fallacies. Definitions are weakened by logical fallacies such as oversimplification (301), half-truths (303), ambiguity (304), and slanted language (304). Writers need to edit their definitions to correct any poor reasoning.

Sample Definition Paragraph

In his essay analyzing the economic roots of various social and sexual abuses, Shon Bogar writes a two-paragraph definition of the term, *human trafficking* (pages 238–239). In his first paragraph shown below, he states why the definition is needed, and he then defines the term by comparing and contrasting it with two related terms.

> Human trafficking, in particular, is a term that is difficult to define properly, but it must first be clarified if the problem itself is to be addressed. To begin, migration, human smuggling, and human trafficking are distinct but related phenomena, and incorrect definitions would put different groups of people in the wrong category, with potentially dire consequences. For example, the Trafficking Victims Prevention Act (TVPA), which came into law in 2000, requires the U.S. government to ensure that victims of trafficking are not jailed or "otherwise penalized solely for unlawful acts as a direct result of being trafficked" (U.S. Department of State, 2004), whereas illegal immigrants are still subject to deportation and criminal proceedings. The U.S. State Department recognizes the potentially "confusing" difference between smuggling and human trafficking, so it defines human smuggling as "the procurement or transport for profit of a person for illegal entry in a country" (2004). However, even if the smuggling involves "dangerous or degrading conditions," the act is still considered smuggling, not human trafficking, and so smuggling is considered an immigration matter, not necessarily a human rights issue (2004).

Reading Definition Writing

As you read definition essays, consider these questions:

1. What claims are made about the term's denotative and connotative meanings?
2. Is the definition current, relevant, complete, and clear?
3. Does the definition accurately explain the term's past and current usage?
4. Do clear transitions link the definition to the writing that precedes and follows it?

Sample Definition Essays

This chapter includes four sample extended definitions. As you read each piece, consider how the writer's purpose, readers, and topic might have affected how she or he shaped the essay's content, voice, organization, and style.

Defining Key Terms Within an Essay

The excerpt below comes from a research paper by student writer Shon Bogar. The paper focuses on the problems of human trafficking and slavery as phenomena associated with current trends in globalization. After reviewing global economic trends since the end of the Cold War, Bogar defines the key terms that readers must understand if they are to comprehend the problem. The ellipses at beginning and ending of this excerpt indicate that the original essay extends beyond what is shown here. (For more on research writing, see chapters 24–29.)

At the end of the introduction, the writer transitions to the extended definition.

An informal definition of the broader concept of slavery prefaces the extended definition.

The main term is distinguished from related terms using reliable source material.

Economic Disparities Fuel Human Trafficking

. . . . These great economic disparities, from extreme poverty to fabulous wealth, have helped fuel the international trade in human cargo, as those people with nothing seek a better life serving those with excess.   *1*

The buying, selling, and forced exploitation of people—slavery—is not a new phenomenon. Most nations and most cultures have, at one time or another, enslaved others and been themselves enslaved in turn. The pattern continues today; in fact, slavery exists far beyond the developing world and reaches into the comfortable First World of the United States, Europe, Japan, and Australia. However, examining current trends in the trade of human cargo shows that trafficking and slavery are extremely difficult to define and understand, and that they coexist with and are codependent upon each other. These problems, moreover, have a variety of complex causes and too few solutions that offer a realistic possibility of ending this global abomination.   *2*

Human trafficking, in particular, is a term that is difficult to define properly, but it must first be clarified if the problem itself is to be addressed. To begin, migration, human smuggling, and human trafficking are distinct but related phenomena, and incorrect definitions would put different groups of people in the wrong category, with potentially dire consequences. For example, the Trafficking Victims Prevention Act (TVPA), which came into law in 2000, requires the U.S. government to ensure that victims of trafficking are not jailed or "otherwise penalized solely for unlawful acts as a direct result of being trafficked" (U.S. Department of State, 2004), whereas illegal immigrants are still subject to deportation and criminal proceedings. The U.S. State Department recognizes the potentially "confusing" difference between smuggling and human trafficking, so it defines human smuggling as "the procurement or transport for profit of a person for illegal entry in a country" (2004).   *3*

The writer offers a formal definition of the key term "human trafficking" by going to official sources.

However, even if the smuggling involves "dangerous or degrading conditions," the act is still considered smuggling, not human trafficking, and so smuggling is considered an immigration matter, not necessarily a human rights issue (2004).

What distinguishes trafficking from smuggling is the element of exploitation, including but not limited to "fraud, force, or coercion" (U.S. Department of State, 2004). With this distinction in mind, the United Nations Convention Against Transnational Organized Crime has developed this standard definition of human trafficking: "the recruitment, transportation, transfer, harbouring or receipt of persons, by means of the threat or use of force or other forms of coercion, of abduction, of fraud, of deception, of the abuse of power, or of a position of vulnerability or of the giving or receiving of payments or benefits to achieve the consent of a person having control over another person, for the purpose of exploitation" (U.N. Resolution 25, 2001). To unravel the U.N. legalese, human trafficking involves any use of force, coercion, fraud, or deception by those with power so as to exploit people, primarily by moving them into some form of slavery. Under this definition, smuggling can become trafficking if the smugglers have used any means of deception. Unfortunately, the requirement that the smuggler/trafficker be aware of the "victim's final circumstances" makes distinguishing between smuggling and trafficking an inexact science (U.S. Department of State, 2004), and it creates a new set of problems in combating trafficking apart from smuggling. Nevertheless, this definition of human trafficking is a helpful starting point from which the United Nations and governments around the globe can start to fight the trafficking and eventual enslavement of people.

The writer restates a complex legal definition in terms readers will understand.

While admitting a difficulty in the definition, the writer stresses the definition's usefulness.

All difficulties of definition aside, human trafficking and slavery are real problems—historical problems that have taken new shapes due to globalization. In fact, today human trafficking is linked to millions of people experiencing multiple forms of slavery, from traditional "chattel slavery" to sexual slavery to debt bondage. . . .

Reading for Better Writing

Working by yourself or with a group, answer these questions:

1. Without looking back at the model, define "human trafficking" in a sentence or two.
2. Examine each of the three main paragraphs of Bogar's extended definition. What does each paragraph accomplish? How do the paragraphs build on each other?
3. Identify the strategies that the author uses to argue that the definition is necessary. Is the reasoning compelling? Why or why not?
4. Look again at the sources that the writer uses to develop the necessary definitions. Why are these sources appropriate for the terms in question? Which other types of sources might be useful?

"Economic Disparities Fuel Human Trafficking" by Shon Bogar. Used by permission of the author.

Distinguishing Related Terms

Professor David Schelhaas delivered the following definition on his weekly radio program, *What's the Good Word?*

Deft or Daft

The writer introduces the topic with an anecdote.

The other day, my wife, watching our son-in-law with his large hands gracefully tie the shoelaces of his little daughter, remarked, "You really are deft." Ever the cynic, I remarked, "He's not only *deft*, he's *daft*." I talk that sort of nonsense frequently, but as I said this, I began to wonder. What if deft and daft come from the same root and once meant the same thing? A quick trip to the dictionary showed that, indeed, they did once mean the same thing (though my wife thought me daft when I first suggested it).

He describes the history of daft.

Let me see if I can explain the original meaning and also how *daft* and *deft* came to part company. *Daft* originally meant mild or gentle. The Middle English *dafte* comes from the Old English *gadaefte*, which has as its underlying sense fit or suitable. Quite likely, mild or gentle people were seen as behaving in a way that was fit and suitable.

He compares and contrasts the two words.

Gradually, however, the mild, gentle meaning descended in connotation to mean crazy or foolish. First, animals were described as daft—that is, without reason—and eventually people also. The word *silly*, which once meant happy or blessed, slid down the same slope. So that explains where *daft* got its present meaning.

But how does *deft*, meaning skillful or dexterous, fit into the picture? Again, if we start with the Old English meaning of *fit* or *suitable*, we can see a connection to skillful. In fact, the root of *gadaefte*, which is *dhabh*, to fit, carries with it the sense of a joiner or an artisan, someone who skillfully made the ends or corners of a cupboard or piece of furniture fit neatly together. From *fit* to *skillful* to *dexterous*. Thus we see how one root word meaning *fit* or *suitable* went in two different directions—one meaning crazy, the other meaning skillful.

He closes with a reflection and his usual sign-off.

These days it is usually considered much better to be deft than to be daft. But don't be too sure. It is good to remind ourselves that one person's deftness might very well appear as daftness to another.

This is David Schelhaas asking, "What's the Good Word?"

Essay, "Deft or Daft," by David Schelhaas. Reprinted by permission of the author.

Reading for Better Writing

Working by yourself or with a group, answer these questions:

1. Explain how the opening attempts to engage the reader. In what ways does it succeed?
2. Describe how the writer shows that the meanings of the words have changed. Is his explanation clear? Why or why not?
3. Describe the writer's tone. Is it effective for a radio program? Explain.

Defining a Personal Trait

Cynthia Ozick is an American writer known for her fiction, poetry, and essays on Jewish American life. In 2005, she was nominated for the Man Booker International Prize for lifetime achievement in literature.

On *Excellence*

> The writer uses a series of observations and anecdotes to introduce the topic.

In my Depression childhood, whenever I had a new dress, my cousin Sarah would get suspicious. The nicer the dress was, and especially the more expensive it looked, the more suspicious she would get. Finally she would lift the hem and check the seams. This was to see if the dress had been bought or if my mother had sewed it. Sarah could always tell. My mother's sewing had elegant outsides, but there was something catch-as-catch-can about the insides. Sarah's sewing, by contrast, was as impeccably finished inside as out; not one stray thread dangled.

My uncle Jake built meticulous grandfather clocks out of rosewood; he was a perfectionist and sent to England for the clockworks. My mother built serviceable radiator covers and a serviceable cabinet, with hinged doors, for the pantry. She built a pair of bookcases for the living room. Once, after I was grown and in a house of my own, she fixed the sewer pipe. She painted ceilings, and also landscapes; she reupholstered chairs. One summer she planted a whole yard of tall corn. She thought herself capable of doing anything, and did everything she imagined. But nothing was perfect. There was always some clear flaw, never visible head-on. You had to look underneath where the seams were. The corn thrived, though not in rows. The stalks elbowed one another like gossips in a dense little village.

> An inductive organization style begins with details and leads to the definition.

"Miss Brrrrooobaker," my mother used to mock, rolling her Russian r's, whenever I crossed a *t* she had left uncrossed, or corrected a word she had misspelled, or became impatient with a *v* that had tangled itself up in a *w* in her speech. ("Vvventriloquist," I would say. "Vventriloquist," she would obediently repeat. And the next time it would come out "wiolinist.") Miss Brubaker was my high school English teacher, and my mother invoked her name as an emblem of raging finical obsession. "Miss Brrrrooobaker," my mother's voice hoots at me down the years, as I go on casting and recasting sentences in a tiny handwriting on monomaniacally uniform paper. The loops of my mother's handwriting—it was the Palmer Method—were as big as hoops, spilling generous splashy ebullience. She could pull off, at five minutes' notice, a satisfying dinner for ten concocted out of nothing more than originality and panache. But the napkin would be folded a little off-center, and the spoon might be on the wrong side of the knife. She was an optimist who ignored trifles; for her, God was not in the details but in the intent. And all these culinary and agricultural efflorescences were extracurricular,

1

2

3

accomplished in the crevices and niches of a fourteen-hour business day. When she scribbled out her family memoirs, in heaps of dog-eared notebooks or on the backs of old bills or on the margins of last year's calendar, I would resist typing them; in the speed of the chase she often omitted words like "the," "and," "will." The same flashing and bountiful hand fashioned and fired ceramic pots, and painted brilliant autumn views and vases of imaginary flowers and ferns, and decorated ordinary Woolworth platters with lavish enameled gardens. But bits of the painted petals would chip away.

Lavish is introduced as a word that is a synonym of *excellence*.

Lavish: my mother was as lavish as nature. She woke early and saturated the hours with work and inventiveness, and read late into the night. She was all profusion, abundance, fabrication. Angry at her children, she would run after us whirling the cord of the electric iron, like a lasso or a whip; but she never caught us. When, in the seventh grade, I was afraid of failing the Music Appreciation final exam because I could not tell the difference between "To a Wild Rose" and "Barcarolle," she got the idea of sending me to school with a gauze sling rigged up on my writing arm, and an explanatory note that was purest fiction. But the sling kept slipping off. My mother gave advice like mad—she boiled over with so much passion for the predicaments of strangers that they turned into permanent cronies. She told intimate stories about people I had never heard of.

4

One definition of *excellence* is offered.

Despite the gargantuan Palmer loops (or possibly because of them), I have always known that my mother's was a life of—intricately abashing word!—excellence: insofar as excellence means ripe generosity. She burgeoned, she proliferated; she was endlessly leafy and flowering. She wore red hats and called herself a gypsy. In her girlhood she marched with the suffragettes and for Margaret Sanger and called herself a Red. She made me laugh, she was so varied: like a tree on which lemons, pomegranates, and prickly pears absurdly all hang together. She had the comedy of prodigality.

5

The writer offers herself as a contrast to her mother's excellence.

My own way is a thousand times more confined. I am a pinched perfectionist, the ultimate fruition of Miss Brubaker; I attend to crabbed minutiae and am self-trammeled through taking pains. I am a kind of human snail, locked in and condemned by my own nature. The ancients believed that the moist track left by the snail as it crept was the snail's own essence, depleting its body little by little; the farther the snail toiled, the smaller it became, until it finally rubbed itself out. That is how perfectionists are. Say to us "Excellence," and we will show you how we use up our substance and wear ourselves away, while making scarcely any progress at all. The fact that I am an exacting perfectionist in a narrow strait only, and nowhere else, is hardly to the point, since nothing matters to me so much as a comely and muscular sentence. It is my narrow strait, this snail's road: the track of

6

The writer contrasts lavish excellence with the excellence of perfectionism.

the sentence I am writing now; and when I have eked out the wet substance, ink or blood, that is its mark, I will begin the next sentence. Only in reading out sentences am I perfectionist; but then there is nothing else I know how to do, or take much interest in. I miter every pair of abutting sentences as scrupulously as Uncle Jake fitted one strip of rosewood against another. My mother's worldly and bountiful hand has escaped me. The sentence I am writing is my cabin and my shell, compact, self-sufficient. It is the burnished horizon—a merciless planet where flawlessness is the single standard, where even the inmost seams, however hidden from a laxer eye, must meet perfection. Here "excellence" is not strewn casually from a tipped cornucopia, here disorder does not account for charm, here trifles rule like tyrants.

I measure my life in sentences, and my sentences are superior to my mother's, pressed out, line by line, like the lustrous ooze on the underside of the snail, the snail's secret open seam, its wound, leaking attar. My mother was too mettlesome to feel the force of a comma. She scorned minutiae. She measured her life according to what poured from the horn of plenty, which was her ample, cascading, elastic, susceptible, inexact heart. My narrower heart rides between the tiny horns of the snail, dwindling as it goes.

7

A poetic closing sums up the definition.

And out of this thinnest thread, this ink-wet line of words, must rise a visionary fog, a mist, a smoke, forging cities, histories, sorrows, quagmires, entanglements, lives of sinners, even the life of my furnace-hearted mother: so much wilderness, waywardness, plentitude on the head of the precise and impeccable snail, between the horns.

8

Reading for Better Writing

Working by yourself or with a group, answer these questions:

1. What words and phrases does Ozick use to define *excellence*? How does contrasting her mother's life with her own enable Ozick to further define *excellence*? What point(s) is she making about *excellence*?

2. One way to write a definition is to use words and phrases that have similar meanings to the word you wish to define. What other techniques does Ozick use to define *excellence*? What additional strategies could be used to define a term?

3. Writing a good definition is challenging because it requires the use of precise words to shed light on the meaning of another word that has its own precise meaning(s). Find instances where Ozick lists one term or idea after another to build precision into a definition. How would her meaning change if she had used only one word from the list?

4. Find examples of words that have especially positive or negative connotations. How do these connotations help Ozick to make her main point(s)?

Analyzing the Meaning of *Truth*

Simson L. Garfinkle is a contributing editor to *Technology Review;* an associate professor at the Naval Postgraduate School in Monterey, California; and a research associate of the School of Engineering and Applied Sciences at Harvard. In the following essay, he analyzes how the nature and use of Wikipedia affect how we discern what is true.

Wikipedia and the Meaning of *Truth*

Why the online encyclopedia's epistemology should worry those
who care about traditional notions of accuracy.

As you read this essay, annotate it and take notes—identifying strategies the writer uses to develop an extended definition.

With little notice from the outside world, the community-written encyclopedia Wikipedia has redefined the commonly accepted use of the word "truth."   *1*

Why should we care? Because Wikipedia's articles are the first- or second-ranked results for most Internet searches. Type "iron" into Google, and Wikipedia's article on the element is the top-ranked result; likewise, its article on the Iron Cross is first when the search words are "iron cross." Google's search algorithms rank a story in part by how many times it has been linked to; people are linking to Wikipedia articles a lot.   *2*

This means that the content of these articles really matters. Wikipedia's standards of inclusion—what's in and what's not—affect the work of journalists, who routinely read Wikipedia articles and then repeat the wikiclaims as "background" without bothering to cite them. These standards affect students, whose research on many topics starts (and often ends) with Wikipedia. And since I used Wikipedia to research large parts of this article, these standards are affecting you, dear reader, at this very moment.   *3*

Many people, especially academic experts, have argued that Wikipedia's articles can't be trusted, because they are written and edited by volunteers who have never been vetted. Nevertheless, studies have found that the articles are remarkably accurate. The reason is that Wikipedia's community of more than seven million registered users has organically evolved a set of policies and procedures for removing untruths. This also explains Wikipedia's explosive growth: if the stuff in Wikipedia didn't seem "true enough" to most readers, they wouldn't keep coming back to the website.   *4*

These policies have become the social contract for Wikipedia's army of apparently insomniac volunteers. Thanks to them, incorrect information generally disappears quite quickly.   *5*

So how do the Wikipedians decide what's true and what's not? On what is their epistemology based?   *6*

Unlike the laws of mathematics or science, wikitruth isn't based on principles such as consistency or observability. It's not even based on common sense or   *7* firsthand experience. Wikipedia has evolved a radically different set of epistemological standards—standards that aren't especially surprising given that the site is rooted in a Web-based community, but that should concern those of us who are interested in traditional notions of truth and accuracy. On Wikipedia, objective truth isn't all that important, actually. What makes a fact or statement fit for inclusion is that it appeared in some other publication—ideally, one that is in English and is available free online. "The threshold for inclusion in Wikipedia is verifiability, not truth," states Wikipedia's official policy on the subject.

> *On Wikipedia, objective truth isn't all that important, actually. What makes a fact or statement fit for inclusion is that it appeared in some other publication . . .*

Verifiability is one of Wikipedia's three core content policies; it was codified back in August 2003. The two others are "no original research" (December 2003) and "neutral point of view," which the Wikipedia project inherited from Nupedia, an earlier volunteer-written Web-based free encyclopedia that existed from March 2000 to September 2003 (Wikipedia's own NPOV policy was codified in December 2001). These policies have made Wikipedia a kind of academic agora where people on both sides of politically charged subjects can rationally discuss their positions, find common ground, and unemotionally document their differences. Wikipedia is successful because these policies have worked.   8

Unlike Wikipedia's articles, Nupedia's were written and vetted by experts. But few experts were motivated to contribute. Well, some wanted to write about their own research, but Larry Sanger, Nupedia's editor in chief, immediately put an end to that practice.   9

"I said, 'If it hasn't been vetted by the relevant experts, then basically we are setting ourselves up as a frontline source of new, original information, and we aren't set up to do that,'" Sanger (who is himself, ironically or not, a former philosophy instructor and by training an epistemologist) recalls telling his fellow Nupedians.   10

With experts barred from writing about their own work and having no incentive to write about anything else, Nupedia struggled. Then Sanger and Jimmy Wales, Nupedia's founder, decided to try a different policy on a new site, which they launched on January 15, 2001. They adopted the newly invented "wiki" technology, allowing anybody to contribute to any article—or create a new one—on any topic, simply by clicking "Edit this page."   11

Soon the promoters of oddball hypotheses and outlandish ideas were all over   12

Wikipedia, causing the new site's volunteers to spend a good deal of time repairing damage—not all of it the innocent work of the misguided or deluded. (A study recently published in Communications of the Association for Computing Machinery found that 11 percent of Wikipedia articles have been vandalized at least once.) But how could Wikipedia's volunteer editors tell if something was true? The solution was to add references and footnotes to the articles, "not in order to help the reader, but in order to establish a point to the satisfaction of the [other] contributors," says Sanger, who left Wikipedia before the verifiability policy was formally adopted. (Sanger and Wales, now the chairman emeritus of the Wikimedia Foundation, fell out about the scale of Sanger's role in the creation of Wikipedia. Today, Sanger is the creator and editor in chief of Citizendium, an alternative to Wikipedia that is intended to address the inadequacy of its "reliability and quality.")

13   Verifiability is really an appeal to authority—not the authority of truth, but the authority of other publications. Any other publication, really. These days, information that's added to Wikipedia without an appropriate reference is likely to be slapped with a "citation needed" badge by one of Wikipedia's self-appointed editors. Remove the badge and somebody else will put it back. Keep it up and you might find yourself face to face with another kind of authority—one of the English-language Wikipedia's 1,500 administrators, who have the ability to place increasingly restrictive protections on contentious pages when the policies are ignored.

14   To be fair, Wikipedia's verifiability policy states that "articles should rely on reliable, third-party published sources" that themselves adhere to Wikipedia's NPOV policy. Self-published articles should generally be avoided, and non-English sources are discouraged if English articles are available, because many people who read, write, and edit En.Wikipedia (the English-language version) can read only English.

Mob Rules

15   In a May 2006 essay on the technology and culture website Edge.org, futurist Jaron Lanier called Wikipedia an example of "digital Maoism"—the closest humanity has come to a functioning mob rule.

16   Lanier was moved to write about Wikipedia because someone kept editing his Wikipedia entry to say that he was a film director. Lanier describes himself as a "computer scientist, composer, visual artist, and author." He is good at all those things, but he is no director. According to his essay, he made one short experimental film in the 1990s, and it was "awful."

17   "I have attempted to retire from directing films in the alternative universe that is the Wikipedia a number of times, but somebody always overrules me," Lanier

wrote. "Every time my Wikipedia entry is corrected, within a day I'm turned into a film director again."

Since Lanier's attempted edits to his own Wikipedia entry were based on firsthand knowledge of his own career, he was in direct violation of Wikipedia's three core policies. He has a point of view; he was writing on the basis of his own original research; and what he wrote couldn't be verified by following a link to some kind of legitimate, authoritative, and verifiable publication.   *18*

Wikipedia's standard for "truth" makes good technical and legal sense, given that anyone can edit its articles. There was no way for Wikipedia, as a community, to know whether the person revising the article about Jaron Lanier was really Jaron Lanier or a vandal. So it's safer not to take people at their word, and instead to require an appeal to the authority of another publication from everybody who contributes, expert or not.   *19*

An interesting thing happens when you try to understand Wikipedia: the deeper you go, the more convoluted it becomes. Consider the verifiability policy. Wikipedia considers the "most reliable sources" to be "peer-reviewed journals and books published in university presses," followed by "university-level textbooks," then magazines, journals, "books published by respected publishing houses," and finally "mainstream newspapers" (but not the opinion pages of newspapers).   *20*

Once again, this makes sense, given Wikipedia's inability to vet the real-world identities of authors. Lanier's complaints when his Wikipedia page claimed that he was a film director couldn't be taken seriously by Wikipedia's "contributors" until Lanier persuaded the editors at Edge to print his article bemoaning the claim. This Edge article by Lanier was enough to convince the Wikipedians that the Wikipedia article about Lanier was incorrect—after all, there was a clickable link! Presumably the editors at Edge did their fact checking, so the wikiworld could now be corrected.   *21*

> *"Criticism" is actually a mild word for the kind of wikijustice meted out to people who are foolish enough to get caught editing their own Wikipedia entries . . .*   *22*

As fate would have it, Lanier was subsequently criticized for engaging in the wikisin of editing his own wikientry. The same criticism was leveled against me when I corrected a number of obvious errors in my own Wikipedia entry.

"Criticism" is actually a mild word for the kind of wikijustice meted out to people who are foolish enough to get caught editing their own Wikipedia entries: *23* the entries get slapped with a banner headline that says "A major contributor to this article, or its creator, may have a conflict of interest regarding its subject matter." The banner is accompanied by a little picture showing the scales of justice tilted to the left. Wikipedia's "Autobiography" policy explains in great detail how drawing on your own knowledge to edit the Wikipedia entry about yourself violates all three of the site's cornerstone policies—and illustrates the point with yet another appeal to authority, a quotation from The Hitchhiker's Guide to the Galaxy.

But there is a problem with appealing to the authority of other people's written   24
words: many publications don't do any fact checking at all, and many of those that do simply call up the subject of the article and ask if the writer got the facts wrong or right. For instance, Dun and Bradstreet gets the information for its small-business information reports in part by asking those very same small businesses to fill out questionnaires about themselves.

"No Original Research"

What all this means is hard to say. I am infrequently troubled by Wiki's   25
unreliability. (The quality of the writing is a different subject.) As a computer scientist, I find myself using Wikipedia on a daily basis. Its discussions of algorithms, architectures, microprocessors, and other technical subjects are generally excellent. When they aren't excellent and I know better, I just fix them. And when they're wrong and I don't know better—well, I don't know any better, do I?

I've also spent quite a bit of time reviewing Wikipedia's articles about such   26
things as the "Singularity Scalpel," the "Treaty of Algeron," and "Number Six." Search for these terms and you'll be directed to Wikipedia articles with the titles "List of Torchwood items" and "List of treaties in Star Trek," and to one about a Cylon robot played by Canadian actress Tricia Helfer. These articles all hang their wikiexistence upon scholarly references to original episodes of Dr. Who, Torchwood, Star Trek, and Battlestar Galactica—popular television shows that the Wikipedia contributors dignify with the word "canon."

I enjoy using these articles as sticks to poke at Wikipedia, but they represent a   27
tiny percentage of Wikipedia's overall content. On the other hand, they've been an important part of Wikipedia culture from the beginning. Sanger says that early on, Wikipedia made a commitment to having a wide variety of articles: "There's plenty of disk space, and as long as there are people out there who are able to write a decent article about a subject, why not let them? . . . I thought it was kind of funny and cool that people were writing articles about every character in The Lord of the Rings. I didn't regard it as a problem the way some people do now."

What's wrong with the articles about fantastical worlds is that they are at odds   28
with Wikipedia's "no original research" rule, since almost all of them draw their

"references" from the fictions themselves and not from the allegedly more reliable secondary sources. I haven't nominated these articles for speedy deletion because Wikipedia makes an exception for fiction—and because, truth be told, I enjoy reading them. And these days, most such entries are labeled as referring to fictional universes.

So what is Truth? According to Wikipedia's entry on the subject, "the term has no 29 single definition about which the majority of professional philosophers and scholars agree." But in practice, Wikipedia's standard for inclusion has become its de facto standard for truth, and since Wikipedia is the most widely read online reference on the planet, it's the standard of truth that most people are implicitly using when they type a search term into Google or Yahoo. On Wikipedia, truth is received truth: the consensus view of a subject.

That standard is simple: something is true if it was published in a newspaper 30 article, a magazine or journal, or a book published by a university press—or if it appeared on Dr. Who.

Reading for Better Writing

Working by yourself or with a group, answer these questions:

1. What does Garfinkle's subtitle convey about his essay and his purpose?
2. Garfinkle says that wiki readers "repeat the wikiclaims as 'background' without bothering to cite them." Is he correct, and is the practice a problem? Explain.
3. In paragraph 4, Garfinkle writes, "Many people, especially academic experts, have argued that Wikipedia's articles can't be trusted, because they are written and edited by volunteers who have never been vetted." Explain what Garfinkle might mean by this claim—and why he specifies "especially academic experts."
4. Review Garfinkle's subheadings "Mob Rules" and "No Original Research." Then explain what they mean and why they do or do not help readers understand his argument.
5. Review paragraph 29 in which the writer quotes Wikipedia's definition of truth and then says, "On Wikipedia, truth is received truth: the consensus view of a subject." Explain what he means, and whether this issue is a serious one.
6. Describe to the class what professors in your major field of study advise regarding the use of Wikipedia as a source for research and writing. Then discuss why professors in different disciplines might disagree on this issue.

Writing Guidelines

Planning

1. Select a topic. Beneath headings like these, list words that you'd like to explore:

- Words related to an art or sport:
- Words that are (or should be) in the news:
- Words that are overused, un-used, or abused:

- Words that make you laugh or worry:
- Words that do (or don't) describe you:

Tip: The best topics are abstract nouns *(truth, individualism)*, complex terms *(code blue, dementia)*, or words connected to a personal experience *(excellence, deft, daft)*.

2. Identify what you know. To discern what you already know about the topic, write freely about the word, letting your writing go where it chooses. Explore both your personal and your academic connections with the word.

3. Gather information. To find information about the word's history, usage, and grammatical form, use strategies such as these:

- **Consult a general dictionary**, preferably an unabridged dictionary; list both denotative (literal) and connotative (associated) meanings for the word.
- **Consult specialized dictionaries** that define words from specific disciplines or occupations: music, literature, law, medicine, and so on.
- If helpful, **interview experts** on your topic.
- **Check reference books** such as *Bartlett's Familiar Quotations* to see how famous speakers and writers have used the word.
- **Research the word's etymology and usage** by consulting appropriate Web sources such as dictionary.com, m-w.com, or xrefer.com.
- **Do a general search on the Web** to see where the word pops up in titles of songs, books, or films; company names, products, and ads; nonprofit organizations' names, campaigns, and programs; and topics in the news.
- **List synonyms** (words meaning the same—or nearly the same) and antonyms (words meaning the opposite).

4. Compress what you know. Based on your freewriting and research, try writing a formal, one-sentence definition that satisfies the following equation:

Equation: Term = larger class + distinguishing characteristics

Examples: Swedish pimple = fishing lure + silver surface, tubular body, three hooks
melodrama = stage play + flat characters, contrived plot, moralistic theme
Alzheimer's = dementia + increasing loss of memory, hygiene, social skills

5. Get organized. To organize the information that you have, and to identify details that you may want to add, fill out a graphic organizer like the one on page 53.

Drafting

6. Draft the essay. Review your outline as needed to write the first draft.

- **Get the reader's attention and introduce the term.** If you are organizing the essay from general to specific, consider using an anecdote, an illustration, or a quotation to set the context. If you are organizing the essay from specific to general, consider including an interesting detail from the word's history or usage. When using a dictionary definition, avoid the dusty phrase "According to *Webster* . . . "
- **Show your readers precisely what the word means.** Build the definition in paragraphs that address distinct aspects of the word: common definitions, etymology, usage by professional writers, and so on. Link paragraphs so that the essay unfolds the word's meaning layer by layer.
- **Review your main point and close your essay.** (You might, for example, conclude by encouraging readers to use—or not use—the word.)

Revising

7. Improve the ideas, organization, and voice. Ask a classmate or someone from the college's writing center to read your essay for the following:

____ **Ideas:** Is each facet of the definition **clear**, showing precisely what the word does and does not mean? Is the definition **complete**, telling the reader all that she or he needs to know in order to understand and use the word?

____ **Organization:** Does the **opening** identify the word and set the context for what follows? Are the **middle** paragraphs cohesive, each offering a unit of information? Does the **closing** wrap up the message and refocus on the word's core meaning?

____ **Voice:** Is the voice informed, engaging, instructive, and courteous?

Editing

8. Edit the essay by addressing these issues:

____ **Words:** The words are precise and clear to the essay's readers.

____ **Sentences:** The sentences are complete, varied in structure, and readable.

____ **Correctness:** The copy includes no errors in spelling, usage, punctuation, grammar, or mechanics.

____ **Design:** The page design is correctly formatted and attractive.

Publishing

9. Publish the essay. Share your writing with interested readers, including friends, family, and classmates. Submit the essay to your instructor.

Critical-Thinking and Writing Activities

As directed by your instructor, complete the following activities.

1. In the passage excerpted from "Economic Disparities Fuel Human Trafficking" (pages 238–239), student writer Shon Bogar defines terms that readers must grasp in order to understand the rest of his essay. Choose an essay (your own or someone else's) that includes a word or concept needing clarification. Define the topic and insert the definition into the text, along with transitions that smoothly lead the reader into and out of the definition.

2. Review "Deft or Daft" and choose a pair of words that similarly mirror each other's meaning. Research the words, and write an essay comparing and contrasting their etymologies and meanings.

3. In her essay "On *Excellence*," Cynthia Ozick defines *excellence* by comparing and contrasting herself and her mother. Choose two people in your life and select a word or concept that distinguishes how they are similar and different. Then write an essay that defines the word or concept while describing the two people.

4. "Wikipedia and the Meaning of *Truth*" explores how a relatively new phenomenon challenges a traditional concept. Write an extended definition exploring how a similar phenomenon has challenged a traditional term (e.g., reality TV, eBooks, digital natives, smart phones).

5. Write an essay defining a word or phrase that is understood by people in a particular field of study but not by "outsiders." Write for the audience of outsiders.

Learning-Objectives Checklist ✓

Have you achieved this chapter's learning objectives? Check your progress with the items below, revisiting topics in the chapter as needed. *I have* . . .

____ carefully examined the qualities of effective brief and extended definitions (236–237).

____ investigated how writers' consideration of their situations helps them focus and refine their definitions (236–237).

____ researched and analyzed a word's roots, prefix, suffix, denotations, connotations, etymology, and usage (250–251).

____ developed well-reasoned, research-based, brief and extended definitions (250–251).

____ critiqued others' writing and my own for logical fallacies such as oversimplification, half-truths, ambiguity, and slanted language (301–304).

____ utilized enriching anecdotes, quotations, comparisons, and contrasts, along with smooth transitions leading into and out of these passages (250–251).

____ evaluated the quality of my ideas, organization, and voice, revising and editing where needed (250–251).

Chapter 16

Reading Literature:
A Case Study in Analysis

In college, analyzing a literary text is a critical, interpretive process. For that reason, the process must begin with a deep reading of a poem, short story, play, or other literary work. When you research and write the essay, you assume that your readers have also read the text, and your aim is to illuminate some not-fully-understood dimension of the work: the motivations of a particular character, the image patterns of a lyric, the historical context of a Renaissance play, and so on.

In this way, literary analysis is a special form of the analytical writing explained in chapters 11-15. In this application of analysis, your primary research is reading, rereading, and thinking through the literary text itself in order to develop a sound, insightful interpretation; secondary research supplements your primary reading by providing a range of support, from historical background to scholarly criticism.

Visually Speaking   What might Figure 16.1 suggest about the relationship between art and life? Explain.

Learning **Objectives**

By working through this chapter, you will be able to

- examine and assess writers' analyses of literature and the arts.

- investigate how writers' situations inform their analyses.

- use literary terms and concepts to evaluate others' analyses and enrich your own.

- conduct primary and secondary research to analyze a literary text or other artwork.

- develop an analysis with an insightful thesis, clear reasoning, and sound evidence.

© Michael Kim/Corbis

fig. 16.1

Strategies for Analyzing Literature and the Arts

Analyzing the arts is something that most people do (at least informally) every day, whether they're reading reviews of concerts or albums, responding to paintings or photographs in public places, or assessing the value of a film or TV drama. However, this chapter explains a more formal, research-based analysis that is carefully articulated in well-crafted writing. To understand how and why writers produce such analyses, it's helpful to examine the rhetorical situations that give rise to them.

The Rhetorical Situation

Consider the context in which writers analyze literature and the arts:

- **Purpose:** Most writers aim to describe the work's features, to explain how it impacts an audience, and to understand its essential qualities. However, writers reviewing (rather than only analyzing) an artwork focus more on its strengths and weaknesses.
- **Readers:** In college, the primary readers for writing about the arts are students and instructors; outside of the classroom, art news stories and reviews are written for any community members interested in art events, art-related issues, or books.
- **Topic:** The topic might be one artwork (e.g., a sculpture, novel, or film), multiple works created by the same artist (e.g., a series of poems or paintings), a group performance (e.g., a play, an opera, or a symphony), an individual performance (e.g., a pianist, an actor, or a dancer), or critical approaches to an art.

Example: In "'Let Evening Come' An Invitation to the Inevitable"(pages 260–261), Sherry Van Egdom's primary readers are her professor and classmates. Her topic is the poem, "Let Evening Come" (page 259), and her purpose is to explain what and how the poem communicates to her.

Principles of Literary-Analysis Writing

Literary-analysis writing depends on the principles that follow.

Understanding approaches to literary analysis. Literary texts can be interpreted through different critical approaches or schools. Each school, with its specific foci and questions, offers a way of "conversing" about a text. The four basic approaches are as follows:

1. **Formalist criticism** focuses on the literary text itself, especially its structure and genre.
2. **Rhetorical criticism** is audience-centered, focused on the "transaction" between text and reader.
3. **Historical criticism** focuses on the historical context of the literary text, including its author.
4. **Ideological criticism** applies ideas outside of literature (e.g., psychology, mythology, feminism, postcolonialism) to literary texts.

To learn how writers from each school approach literary criticism, read John Van Rys's essay "Four Ways to Talk About Literature" (pages 257–258).

Understanding literary terms that help you read and write about the arts. The terms used to address specific art forms, such as the three examples below, help writers read literature carefully and discuss their topics precisely. To refine your reading skills, learn how the literary elements that these terms identify shape or enrich a literary work. Then when reading a piece of literature, think about how these elements impact what you feel, see, and think. (For definitions of common literary terms, see pages 286–288.)

- **Poetry:** Writers might describe word sounds with terms such as *assonance, consonance,* and *alliteration*; rhythmic effects with words such as *iambic* or *trochaic meter*; and figurative language with words such as *metaphor* and *simile*.
- **Fiction:** Writers might describe diction with terms such as *archaic, colloquial,* or *slang*; narrative method with phrases such as *first person* and *third person*; or genre with terms such as *satire* or *melodrama*.
- **Plays and Films:** To describe characters, writers use terms such as *antagonist, protagonist,* or *tragic hero*; to discuss plots, they use words such as *exposition, rising action,* and *denouement*; or to describe a setting, they might use *stage picture, proscenium arch,* or *thrust stage*.

Understanding primary and secondary research. Writers' reading of a literary text—primary research—is usually the focus of their analyses. However, secondary research can serve many purposes, such as these:

- **Biographical research:** Learning about the author's life may enrich a writer's analysis by helping the person to explore sources of inspiration, personal and literary influences, and modes of thought. Such insights might be gained through learning about the author's childhood, cultural and ethnic background, education, writing apprenticeship, and relationships. Caution: Writers must be careful not to make simplistic connections between biographical details and literary texts (e.g., that the speaker of a poem or the narrator of a story is the author in a direct sense; that because the novelist grew up in the 1960s, the female characters are radical feminists; or that the author's intention must direct an interpretation of the text).
- **Research into historical and cultural context:** Such research illuminates the text by clarifying important contextual issues and historical details. These issues might be the historical realities surrounding the text's writing, its content, and its reception (past and present). Or the issues might be cultural concepts relevant to the text: class, economics, technology, religious institutions and practices, and so on.
- **Research into literary concepts:** This type of secondary research deepens the writer's understanding of literary issues and techniques. For example, he or she might read about methods and theories of irony, or might study the nature of tragedy with the aim of enriching the analysis of the text.
- **Research into theory:** Such research strengthens the writer's understanding of the philosophical and ideological underpinnings of a particular literary school or theorist. Theoretical research—whether into reader-response theory, deconstruction, feminism, or the ideas of a particular theorist such as Mikhail Bakhtin—informs and directs the writer's analysis of the literary text.

- **Research into scholarly interpretations:** In such research, writers join the critical conversation about the text, a conversation that might have been going on for a few years, a few decades, or a few centuries. Many scholarly articles and books will likely offer interpretations of the text—ways of reading, analyzing, and understanding some aspect of the work, typically from a particular point of view. Reading these sources can strengthen a writer's own interpretation in the following ways:

  - She can locate her own reading within the critical conversation, placing her interpretation in context.
  - She can refine her own reading through critical engagement, exploring why different readers interpret the text as they do (comparing their perspectives and values with her own).
  - She can create a critical survey early in her paper, one that reviews the interpretive schools on the issues addressed and makes space for her own reading.
  - Within her essay, she might use the critical comment of a scholar to (a) add expert support to her interpretive argument, (b) create a starting point for further reflection and analysis, or (c) present a claim with which she disagrees.

Focusing on Research Essentials: In a literary analysis project, a writer should use secondary sources carefully and avoid these problems:

- **Substituting his own interpretation** of the text with the readings offered by secondary sources. If he finds himself continually talking about other people's interpretations or simply parroting their interpretations, he needs to get back to his own interpretation in his own voice.
- **Limiting his secondary research** to opinions that he gathers off the free Web (including sites such as Spark Notes and Cliff Notes). Instead, he should rely on substantial sources in academic journals and scholarly books.

Reading Literary-Analysis Writing

As you read the essays on the following pages, consider these questions:

1. Does the writer understand the elements of the art form, what distinguishes a quality artwork, and how to assess those qualities?
2. Does the essay explore nuances such as ironies, motifs, symbols, and allusions?
3. Does the essay have a clear thesis and logical claims, all supported by relevant evidence?
4. Is the tone informed, respectful, and honest?
5. Does the writing sound informed regarding the foci and approaches of schools of literary criticism?
6. Does the writing use literary terms correctly and effectively? (See the list of literary terms on pages 286–288.)
7. Does the writing correctly document both primary and secondary sources?

Approaches to Literary Criticism

In the following essay, Professor John Van Rys describes four schools of (or approaches to) literary criticism. He then illustrates each approach by describing how a critic using it might analyze Robert Browning's poem, "My Last Duchess." The complete text of this poem is available on pages 262–263, along with follow-up ideas for discussing and analyzing it.

The writer introduces the topic and criterion for creating four subgroups.

Four Ways to Talk About Literature

Have you ever been in a conversation in which you suddenly felt lost—out of the loop? Perhaps you feel that way in your literature class. You may think a poem or short story means one thing, and then your instructor suddenly pulls out the "hidden meaning." Joining the conversation about literature—in class or in an essay—may indeed seem daunting, but you can do it if you know what to look for and what to talk about. There are four main perspectives, or approaches, that you can use to converse about literature.   1

He describes the first subgroup and gives an example.

Text-centered approaches focus on the literary piece itself. Often called *formalist criticism*, such approaches claim that the structure of a work and the rules of its genre are crucial to its meaning. The formalist critic determines how various elements (plot, character, language, and so on) reinforce the meaning and unify the work. For example, the formalist may ask the following questions concerning Robert Browning's poem "My Last Duchess": How do the main elements in the poem— irony, symbolism, and verse form—help develop the main theme (deception)? How does Browning use the dramatic monologue genre in this poem?   2

He describes the second subgroup and gives an example.

Audience-centered approaches focus on the "transaction" between text and reader—the dynamic way the reader interacts with the text. Often called *rhetorical* or *reader-response criticism*, these approaches see the text not as an object to be analyzed, but as an activity that is different for each reader. A reader-response critic might ask these questions of "My Last Duchess": How does the reader become aware of the duke's true nature if it's never actually stated? Do men and women read the poem differently? Who were Browning's original readers?   3

He describes the third subgroup and gives examples.

Author-centered approaches focus on the origins of a text (the writer and the historical background). For example, an author-centered study examines the writer's life—showing connections, contrasts, and conflicts between his or her life and the writing. Broader historical studies explore social and intellectual currents, showing links between an author's work and the ideas, events, and institutions of that period. Finally, the literary historian may make connections between the text in question and earlier and later literary works. The author-centered critic might ask these questions of "My Last Duchess": What were Browning's views of marriage, men and women, art, class, and wealth? As an institution, what was marriage like in Victorian England (Browning's era) or Renaissance Italy (the duke's era)? Who was the historical Duke of Ferrara?   4

He describes the fourth approach and gives examples of each sub-group in it.

The fourth approach to criticism applies ideas outside of literature to literary works. Because literature mirrors life, argue these critics, disciplines that explore human life can help us understand literature. Some critics, for example, apply psychological theories to literary works by exploring dreams, symbolic meanings, and motivation. Myth or archetype criticism uses insights from psychology, cultural anthropology, and classical studies to explore a text's universal appeal. Moral criticism, rooted in religious studies and ethics, explores the moral dilemmas literary works raise. Marxist, feminist, minority, and postcolonial criticism are, broadly speaking, sociological approaches to interpretation. While the Marxist examines the themes of class struggle, economic power, and social justice in texts, the feminist critic explores the just and unjust treatment of women as well as the effect of gender on language, reading, and the literary canon. The critic interested in race and ethnic identity explores similar issues, with the focus shifted to a specific cultural group, while the postcolonial critic examines the dynamics of colonialism found in literature of formerly colonized people.   5

He cites sample questions.

Such ideological criticism might ask a wide variety of questions about "My Last Duchess": What does the poem reveal about the duke's psychological state and his personality? How does the reference to Neptune deepen the poem? What does the poem suggest about the nature of evil and injustice? In what ways are the duke's motives class-based and economic? How does the poem present the duke's power and the duchess's weakness? What is the status of women in this society?   6

The closing presents qualities shared by all four approaches.

If you look at the variety of questions critics might ask about "My Last Duchess," you see both the diversity of critical approaches and the common ground between them. In fact, interpretive methods actually share important characteristics: (1) a close attention to literary elements such as character, plot, symbolism, and metaphor; (2) a desire not to distort the work; and (3) a sincere concern for increasing interest in and understanding of a text. In actual practice, critics may develop a hybrid approach to criticism, one that matches their individual questions and concerns about a text. Now that you're familiar with some of the questions defining literary criticism, exercise your own curiosity (and join the ongoing literary dialogue) by discussing a text that genuinely interests you.   7

Reading for Better Writing

Working by yourself or with a group, answer these questions:

1. Explain how the writer introduces the subject and attempts to engage the reader. Is this strategy effective? Why or why not?
2. The writer uses one poem to illustrate how each of the four critical approaches works. Explain why this strategy is or is not effective.
3. Review the last paragraph and explain why it does or does not unify the essay.

Analyzing a Poem

In the essay on the following two pages, student writer Sherry Van Egdom analyzes the form and meaning of the poem below, "Let Evening Come," by American poet Jane Kenyon. Born in 1947 and raised on a farm near Ann Arbor, Michigan, Kenyon settled in New Hampshire at Eagle Pond Farm after she married fellow poet Donald Hall. During her life, Kenyon struggled with her faith, with depression, and with cancer. At the time of her death in 1995 from leukemia, she was the poet laureate of New Hampshire.

Before you read the student writer's analysis, read the poem aloud to enjoy its sounds, rhythm, images, diction, and comparisons. Then read the piece again to grasp more fully how the poem is structured, what it expresses, and how its ideas might relate to your life. Finally, read Van Egdom's analysis and answer the questions that follow it.

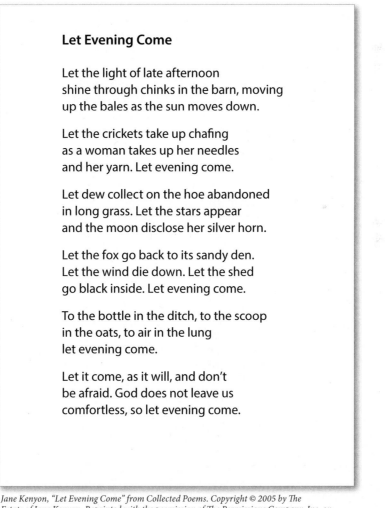

Let Evening Come

Let the light of late afternoon
shine through chinks in the barn, moving
up the bales as the sun moves down.

Let the crickets take up chafing
as a woman takes up her needles
and her yarn. Let evening come.

Let dew collect on the hoe abandoned
in long grass. Let the stars appear
and the moon disclose her silver horn.

Let the fox go back to its sandy den.
Let the wind die down. Let the shed
go black inside. Let evening come.

To the bottle in the ditch, to the scoop
in the oats, to air in the lung
let evening come.

Let it come, as it will, and don't
be afraid. God does not leave us
comfortless, so let evening come.

Analysis of Kenyon's Poem

In the essay below, student writer Sherry Van Egdom Doyle analyzes "Let Evening Come." Watch how she develops the essay by introducing the poem, describing how it unfolds, and then examining its structure, ideas, poetic devices, and theme.

"Let Evening Come": An Invitation to the Inevitable

The writer introduces the poet and her poetry.

The work of American poet Jane Kenyon is influenced primarily by the circumstances and experiences of her own life. She writes carefully crafted, deceptively simple poems that connect both to her own life and to the lives of her readers. Growing out of her rural roots and her struggles with illness, Kenyon's poetry speaks in a still voice of the ordinary things in life in order to wrestle with issues of faith and mortality (Timmerman 163). One of these poems is "Let Evening Come." In this poem, the poet takes the reader on a journey into the night, but she points to hope in the face of that darkness. [1]

Narrowing her focus to the specific poem, the writer states her thesis.

She begins her analysis by explaining the stanza structure and progression.

That movement toward darkness is captured in the stanza form and in the progression of stanzas. Each three-line stanza offers a self-contained moment in the progress of transition from day to night. The first stanza positions the reader in a simple farm setting. Late afternoon fades into evening without the rumble of highways or the gleam of city lights to distract one's senses from nature, the peace emphasized by the alliteration of "l" in "Let the light of late afternoon." As the sun sinks lower on the horizon, light seeps through cracks in the barn wall, moving up the bales of hay. In the second stanza, the crickets get busy with their nighttime noises. Next, a forgotten farm hoe becomes covered with dew drops, and the silvery stars and moon appear in the sky. In the fourth stanza, complete blackness arrives as a fox returns to its empty den and the silent wind rests at close of day. The alliteration of "d" in "den" and "die down" gives a sinking, settling feeling (Timmerman 176). In the fifth stanza, a bottle and scoop keep still, untouched in their respective places, while sleep comes upon the human body. In the final stanza, Kenyon encourages readers to meet this emerging world of darkness without fear. [2]

The writer shows attention to the poem's fine details and to secondary sources on the poem.

She advances her reading of the poem by exploring images, comparisons, and symbols: the poem's "imaginative logic."

Within this stanza progression, the journey into the night is intensified by strong images, figures of speech, and symbols. The natural rhythm of work and rest on the farm is symbolized by the light that rises and falls in the first stanza (Timmerman 175). The simile comparing the crickets taking up their song to a woman picking up her knitting suggests a homespun energy and conviction. The moon revealing her "silver horn" implies that the moon does not instantly appear with brightness and beauty but rather reveals her majesty slowly as the night comes on. The den, the wind, and the shed in stanza four stress a kind of internal, hidden darkness. Then stanza five focuses on connected objects: the thoughtlessly discarded bottle resting in the ditch, oats and the scoop for feeding, human lungs and the air that fills them. Kenyon mentions the air in the lung after the bottle, ditch, scoop, and [3] oats in order to picture humanity taking its position among the established natural rhythm of the farm (Harris 31).

The refrain, "let evening come," is a powerful part of the poem's journey toward darkness, though critics interpret the line differently. Judith Harris suggests that it symbolizes an acceptance of the inevitable: Darkness will envelop the world, and night will surely come, just as mortality will certainly take its toll in time. This acceptance, in turn, acts as a release from the confinement of one's pain and trials in life. Rather than wrestle with something that cannot be beaten or worry about things that must be left undone, Kenyon advises herself and her readers to let go (31). Night intrudes upon the work and events of the day, perhaps leaving them undone just as death might cut a life short and leave it seemingly unfinished.

> The writer compares possible interpretations of a central, repeated statement in the poem.

4

By contrast, John Timmerman argues that "let" is used twelve times in a supplicatory, prayer-like manner (176). The final two lines, in turn, act as a benediction upon the supplications. The comfort of God is as inevitable as the evening, so cling to faith and hope and let evening come. Although the Comforter is mentioned only in the last two lines, that statement of faith encourages readers to find a spiritual comfort in spite of the coming of the night.

5

When asked how she came to write "Let Evening Come," Jane Kenyon replied that it was a redemptive poem given to her by the Holy Ghost. When there could be nothing—a great darkness and despair, there is a great mystery of love, kindness, and beauty (Moyers 238). In the poem's calm journey into the night, Kenyon confronts darkness and suffering with a certain enduring beauty and hope (Timmerman 161). Death will come, but there remains divine comfort. "Let Evening Come" encourages readers to release their grip on the temporary and pay attention to the Comforter who reveals Himself both day and night.

> In her conclusion, the writer offers the poet's explanation of the poem's origin and then expands on the thesis.

6

Note: The Works Cited page is not shown. For sample pages, see MLA (pages 493–534) and APA (pages 535–564).

Reading for Better Writing

Working by yourself or with a group, answer these questions:

1. Review the opening and closing paragraphs of the essay. How do they create a framework for the writer's analysis of the poem?
2. On which elements of the poem does the writer focus? Does this approach make sense for her analysis? Explain.
3. In her essay, the writer refers to the poet's life and to ideas from secondary sources. Do these references work well with her analysis? Why or why not?
4. Read the essay "Four Ways to Talk About Literature" on pages 257–258. Which approach does the student writer use to analyze Kenyon's poem? Does this approach make sense? How might another approach interpret the poem differently?

A Poem to Analyze

Now that you have read Jane Kenyon's "Let Evening Come" and Sherry Van Egdom's analysis of the poem, extend your poetry reading and interpretation skills by analyzing "My Last Duchess," the poem shown below and referenced throughout "Four Ways to Talk About Literature" on pages 257–258.

Robert Browning, a British Victorian poet, first published "My Last Duchess" in 1842. The poem is a dramatic monologue, meaning that the speaker (Duke of Ferrara) is imagined as speaking to a silent listener (an agent for a count with whom the duke is attempting to negotiate another marriage after the death of his first wife). The duke speaking in the poem is believed to be the historical Alfonso Il d'Este (1533–1598), who at the age of 25 married 14-year-old Lucrezia di Cosimo de Medici, the figure in the portrait being described by the duke. It is suspected that when Lucrezia died at the age of 17, she had been poisoned by her husband, the duke.

With this background in mind, engage "My Last Duchess" by doing the following, either on your own or with classmates:

1. **Read the poem aloud** (more than once, if helpful), paying attention to the rhythms and sounds at work.
2. **Work through the poem slowly,** line by line, to sort out what the duke is saying to the agent and why he would be saying it.
3. **Through freewriting, explore your response to the poem**—the story that it tells, the voice and personality of the duke, the ethical puzzle that it presents, or anything else that strikes you about this dramatic monologue.
4. **Use the following resources** to develop a fuller interpretation of the poem:
   - The discussion of primary and secondary research for literary analysis on pages 255-256.
   - "Four Ways to Talk About Literature" on pages 257–258.
   - The literary terms and poetry terms on pages 286–289.

My Last Duchess

That's my last Duchess painted on the wall,
Looking as if she were alive. I call
That piece a wonder, now: Frà Pandolf's hands
Worked busily a day, and there she stands.
Will't please you sit and look at her? I said
"Frà Pandolf" by design, for never read
Strangers like you that pictured countenance,
The depth and passion of its earnest glance,
But to myself they turned (since none puts by
The curtain I have drawn for you, but I)
And seemed as they would ask me, if they durst,
How such a glance came there; so, not the first
Are you to turn and ask thus. Sir, 'twas not

Her husband's presence only, called that spot
Of joy into the Duchess' cheek: perhaps
Frà Pandolf chanced to say "Her mantle laps
Over my Lady's wrist too much," or "Paint
Must never hope to reproduce the faint
Half-flush that dies along her throat": such stuff
Was courtesy, she thought, and cause enough
For calling up that spot of joy. She had
A heart—how shall I say?—too soon made glad,
Too easily impressed; she liked whate'er
She looked on, and her looks went everywhere.
Sir, 'twas all one! My favour at her breast,
The dropping of the daylight in the West,
The bough of cherries some officious fool
Broke in the orchard for her, the white mule
She rode with round the terrace—all and each
Would draw from her alike the approving speech,
Or blush, at least. She thanked men,—good! but thanked
Somehow—I know not how—as if she ranked
My gift of a nine-hundred-years-old name
With anybody's gift. Who'd stoop to blame
This sort of trifling? Even had you skill
In speech—(which I have not)—to make your will
Quite clear to such an one, and say, "Just this
Or that in you disgusts me; here you miss,
Or there exceed the mark"—and if she let
Herself be lessoned so, nor plainly set
Her wits to yours, forsooth, and made excuse,
—E'en then would be some stooping, and I choose
Never to stoop. Oh sir, she smiled, no doubt,
Whene'er I passed her; but who passed without
Much the same smile? This grew; I gave commands;
Then all smiles stopped together. There she stands
As if alive. Will't please you rise? We'll meet
The company below, then. I repeat,
The Count your master's known munificence
Is ample warrant that no just pretence
Of mine for dowry will be disallowed;
Though his fair daughter's self, as I avowed
At starting, is my object. Nay, we'll go
Together down, sir. Notice Neptune, though,
Taming a sea-horse, thought a rarity,
Which Claus of Innsbruck cast in bronze for me!

"My Last Duchess," by Robert Browning. Used under the public domain.

Analyzing a Short Story

"Good Country People" is a short story written by Flannery O'Connor. Read the piece carefully, noting how she opens the story, develops the plot, creates distinct characters, and reveals what they do and think. Then reflect on the story and what ideas or feelings it evokes. Finally, read Anya Terekhina's essay on pages 279–282 and compare her analysis with yours.

Good Country People

As you read this short story, annotate it with your thoughts and questions about its various literary qualities.

Besides the neutral expression that she wore when she was alone, Mrs. Freeman had two others, forward and reverse, that she used for all her human dealings. Her forward expression was steady and driving like the advance of a heavy truck. Her eyes never swerved to left or right but turned as the story turned as if they followed a yellow line down the center of it. She seldom used the other expression because it was not often necessary for her to retract a statement, but when she did, her face came to a complete stop, there was an almost imperceptible movement of her black eyes, during which they seemed to be receding, and then the observer would see that Mrs. Freeman, though she might stand there as real as several grain sacks thrown on top of each other, was no longer there in spirit. As for getting anything across to her when this was the case, Mrs. Hopewell had given it up. She might talk her head off. Mrs. Freeman could never be brought to admit herself wrong to any point. She would stand there and if she could be brought to say anything, it was something like, "Well, I wouldn't of said it was and I wouldn't of said it wasn't" or letting her gaze range over the top kitchen shelf where there was an assortment of dusty bottles, she might remark, "I see you ain't ate many of them figs you put up last summer." 1

They carried on their most important business in the kitchen at breakfast. Every morning Mrs. Hopewell got up at seven o'clock and lit her gas heater and Joy's. Joy was her daughter, a large blonds girl who had an artificial leg. Mrs. Hopewell thought of her as a child though she was thirty-two years old and highly educated. Joy would get up while her mother was eating and lumber into the bathroom and slam the door, and before long, Mrs. Freeman would arrive at the back door. Joy would hear her mother call, "Come on in," and then they would talk for a while in low voices that were indistinguishable in the bathroom. By the time Joy came in, they had usually finished the weather report and were on one or the other of Mrs. Freeman's daughters, Glynese or Carramae. Joy called them Glycerin and Caramel. Glynese, a redhead, was eighteen and had many admirers; Carramae, a blonde, was only fifteen but already married and pregnant. She could not keep anything on her stomach. Every morning Mrs. Freeman told Mrs. Hopewell how many times she had vomited since the last report. 2

Mrs. Hopewell liked to tell people that Glynese and Carramae were two of the finest girls she knew and that Mrs. Freeman was a lady and that she was never ashamed to take her anywhere or introduce her to anybody they might meet. Then she would tell how she had happened to hire the Freemans in the first place and 3 how they were a godsend to her and how she had had them four years. The reason for her keeping them so long was that they were not trash. They were good country people. She had telephoned the man whose name they had given as reference and he had told her that Mr. Freeman was a good farmer but that his wife was the nosiest woman ever to walk the earth. "She's got to be into everything," the man said. "If she don't get there before the dust settles, you can bet she's dead, that's all. She'll want to know all your business. I can stand him real good," he had said, "but me nor my wife neither could have stood that woman one more minute on this place." That had put Mrs. Hopewell off for a few days.

She had hired them in the end because there were no other applicants but she had made up her mind beforehand exactly how she would handle the woman. Since she was the type who had to be into everything, then, Mrs. Hopewell had decided, she would not only let her be into everything, she would see to it that she was into everything – she would give her the responsibility of everything, she would put her in charge. Mrs. Hopewell had no bad qualities of her own but she was able to use other people's in such a constructive way that she had kept them four years.

Nothing is perfect. This was one of Mrs. Hopewell's favorite sayings. Another was: that is life! And still another, the most important, was: well, other people have their opinions too. She would make these statements, usually at the table, in a tone of gentle insistence as if no one held them but her, and the large hulking Joy, whose constant outrage had obliterated every expression from her face, would stare just a little to the side of her, her eyes icy blue, with the look of someone who had achieved blindness by an act of will and means to keep it.

When Mrs. Hopewell said to Mrs. Freeman that life was like that, Mrs. Freeman would say, "I always said so myself." Nothing had been arrived at by anyone that had not first been arrived at by her. She was quicker than Mr. Freeman. When Mrs. Hopewell said to her after they had been on the place for a while, "You know, you're the wheel behind the wheel," and winked, Mrs. Freeman had said, "I know it. I've always been quick. It's some that are quicker than others."

"Everybody is different," Mrs. Hopewell said. "Yes, most people is," Mrs. Freeman said.

"It takes all kinds to make the world." "I always said it did myself."

The girl was used to this kind of dialogue for breakfast and more of it for dinner; sometimes they had it for supper too. When they had no guest they ate in the kitchen because that was easier. Mrs. Freeman always managed to arrive at some point during the meal and to watch them finish it. She would stand in the doorway if it were summer but in the winter she would stand with one elbow on top of the refrigerator and look down at them, or she would stand by the gas heater, lifting the back of her skirt slightly. Occasionally she would stand against the wall and roll her head from side to side. At no time was she in any hurry to leave. All this was very trying on Mrs. Hopewell but she was a woman of great patience. She realized that nothing is perfect and that in the Freemans she had good country people and that if, in this day and age, you get good country people, you had better hang onto them.

She had had plenty of experience with trash. Before the Freemans she had *10* averaged one tenant family a year. The wives of these farmers were not the kind you would want to be around you for very long. Mrs. Hopewell, who had divorced her husband long ago, needed someone to walk over the fields with her; and when Joy had to be impressed for these services, her remarks were usually so ugly and her face so glum that Mrs. Hopewell would say, "If you can't come pleasantly, I don't want you at all," to which the girl, standing square and rigid-shouldered with her neck thrust slightly forward, would reply, "If you want me, here I am – LIKE I AM."

Mrs. Hopewell excused this attitude because of the leg (which had been shot *11* off in a hunting accident when Joy was ten). It was hard for Mrs. Hopewell to realize that her child was thirty-two now and that for more than twenty years she had had only one leg. She thought of her still as a child because it tore her heart to think instead of the poor stout girl in her thirties who had never danced a step or had any normal good times. Her name was really Joy but as soon as she was twenty-one and away from home, she had had it legally changed. Mrs. Hopewell was certain that she had thought and thought until she had hit upon the ugliest name in any language. Then she had gone and had the beautiful name, Joy, changed without telling her mother until after she had done it. Her legal name was Hulga.

When Mrs. Hopewell thought the name, Hulga, she thought of the broad blank *12* hull of a battleship. She would not use it. She continued to call her Joy to which the girl responded but in a purely mechanical way.

Hulga had learned to tolerate Mrs. Freeman who saved her from taking walks *13* with her mother. Even Glynese and Carramae were useful when they occupied attention that might otherwise have been directed at her. At first she had thought she could not stand Mrs. Freeman for she had found it was not possible to be rude to her. Mrs. Freeman would take on strange resentments and for days together she would be sullen but the source of her displeasure was always obscure; a direct attack, a positive leer, blatant ugliness to her face – these never touched her. And without warning one day, she began calling her Hulga.

She did not call her that in front of Mrs. Hopewell who would have been *14* incensed but when she and the girl happened to be out of the house together, she would say something and add the name Hulga to the end of it, and the big spectacled Joy-Hulga would scowl and redden as if her privacy had been intruded upon. She considered the name her personal affair. She had arrived at it first purely on the basis of its ugly sound and then the full genius of its fitness had struck her. She had a vision of the name working like the ugly sweating Vulcan who stayed in the furnace and to whom, presumably, the goddess had to come when called. She saw it as the name of her highest creative act. One of her major triumphs was that her mother had not been able to turn her dust into Joy, but the greater one was that she had been able to turn it herself into Hulga. However, Mrs. Freeman's relish for using the name only irritated her. It was as if Mrs. Freeman's beady steel-pointed eyes had penetrated far enough behind her face to reach some secret fact. Something about her seemed to fascinate Mrs. Freeman and then one day Hulga realized that it was the artificial leg. Mrs. Freeman had a special fondness for the details of secret infections, hidden deformities, assaults upon children. Of diseases, she preferred the lingering or incurable. Hulga had heard Mrs. Hopewell give her the details of the hunting accident, how the leg had been literally blasted off, how she had never lost consciousness. Mrs. Freeman could listen to it any time as if it had happened an hour ago.

When Hulga stumped into the kitchen in the morning (she could walk without   *15* making the awful noise but she made it – Mrs. Hopewell was certain – because it was ugly- sounding), she glanced at them and did not speak. Mrs. Hopewell would be in her red kimono with her hair tied around her head in rags. She would be sitting at the table, finishing her breakfast and Mrs. Freeman would be hanging by her elbow outward from the refrigerator, looking down at the table. Hulga always put her eggs on the stove to boil and then stood over them with her arms folded, and Mrs. Hopewell would look at her – a kind of indirect gaze divided between her and Mrs. Freeman – and would think that if she would only keep herself up a little, she wouldn't be so bad looking. There was nothing wrong with her face that a pleasant expression wouldn't help. Mrs. Hopewell said that people who looked on the bright side of things would be beautiful even if they were not.

Whenever she looked at Joy this way, she could not help but feel that it would   *16* have been better if the child had not taken the Ph.D. It had certainly not brought her out any and now that she had it, there was no more excuse for her to go to school again. Mrs. Hopewell thought it was nice for girls to go to school to have a good time but Joy had "gone through." Anyhow, she would not have been strong enough to go again. The doctors had told Mrs. Hopewell that with the best of care, Joy might see forty-five. She had a weak heart. Joy had made it plain that if it had not been for this condition, she would be far from these red hills and good country people. She would be in a university lecturing to people who knew what she was talking about. And Mrs. Hopewell could very well picture here there, looking like a scarecrow and lecturing to more of the same. Here she went about all day in a six-year-old skirt and a yellow sweat shirt with a faded cowboy on a horse embossed on it. She thought this was funny; Mrs. Hopewell thought it was idiotic and showed simply that she was still a child. She was brilliant but she didn't have a grain of sense. It seemed to Mrs. Hopewell that every year she grew less like other people and more like herself – bloated, rude, and squint-eyed. And she said such strange things! To her own mother she had said – without warning, without excuse, standing up in the middle of a meal with her face purple and her mouth half full – "Woman! Do you ever look inside? Do you ever look inside and see what you are not? God!" she had cried sinking down again and staring at her plate, "Malebranche was right: we are not our own light. We are not our own light!" Mrs. Hopewell had no idea to this day what brought that on. She had only made the remark, hoping Joy would take it in, that a smile never hurt anyone. The girl had taken the Ph.D. in philosophy and this left Mrs. Hopewell at a complete loss. You could say, "My daughter is a nurse," or "My daughter is a school teacher," or even, "My daughter is a chemical engineer." You could not say, "My daughter is a philosopher." That was something that had ended with the Greeks and Romans. All day Joy sat on her neck in a deep chair, reading. Sometimes she went for walks but she didn't like dogs or cats or birds or flowers or nature or nice young men. She looked at nice young men as if she could smell their stupidity.

One day Mrs. Hopewell had picked up one of the books the girl had just put down and opening it at random, she read, "Science, on the other hand, has to assert its soberness and seriousness afresh and declare that it is concerned solely with what-is. Nothing – how can it be for science anything but a horror and a phantasm? If science is right, then one thing stands firm: science wishes to know nothing of nothing. Such is after all the strictly scientific approach to Nothing. We know it by wishing to know nothing of Nothing." These words had been underlined with a blue pencil and they worked on Mrs. Hopewell like some evil incantation in gibberish. She shut the book quickly and went out of the room as if she were having a chill.   17

This morning when the girl came in, Mrs. Freeman was on Carramae. "She thrown up four times after supper," she said, "and was up twict in the night after three o'clock. Yesterday she didn't do nothing but ramble in the bureau drawer. All she did. Stand up there and see what she could run up on."   18

"She's got to eat," Mrs. Hopewell muttered, sipping her coffee, while she watched Joy's back at the stove. She was wondering what the child had said to the Bible salesman. She could not imagine what kind of a conversation she could possibly have had with him.   19

He was a tall gaunt hatless youth who had called yesterday to sell them a Bible. He had appeared at the door, carrying a large black suitcase that weighted him so heavily on one side that he had to brace himself against the door facing. He seemed on the point of collapse but he said in a cheerful voice, "Good morning, Mrs. Cedars!" and set the suitcase down on the mat. He was not a bad-looking young man though he had on a bright blue suit and yellow socks that were not pulled up far enough. He had prominent face bones and a streak of sticky-looking brown hair falling across his forehead.   20

"I'm Mrs. Hopewell," she said.   21

"Oh!" he said, pretending to look puzzled but with his eyes sparkling, "I saw it said 'The Cedars' on the mailbox so I thought you was Mrs. Cedars!" and he burst out in a pleasant laugh. He picked up the satchel and under cover of a pant, he fell forward into her hall.   22

It was rather as if the suitcase had moved first, jerking him after it. "Mrs. Hopewell!" he said and grabbed her hand. "I hope you are well!" and he laughed again and then all at once his face sobered completely. He paused and gave her a straight earnest look and said, "Lady, I've come to speak of serious things."   23

"Well, come in," she muttered, none too pleased because her dinner was almost   24
ready. He came into the parlor and sat down on the edge of a straight chair and put
the suitcase between his feet and glanced around the room as if he were sizing her
up by it. Her silver gleamed on the two sideboards; she decided he had never been in
a room as elegant as this.

"Mrs. Hopewell," he began, using her name in a way that sounded almost   25
intimate, "I know you believe in Chrustian service."

"Well, yes," she murmured.   26

"I know," he said and paused, looking very wise with his head cocked on one   27
side, "that you're a good woman. Friends have told me."

Mrs. Hopewell never liked to be taken for a fool. "What are you selling?" she   28
asked. "Bibles," the young man said and his eye raced around the room before he
added, "I see you have no family Bible in your parlor, I see that is the one lack you
got!"

Mrs. Hopewell could not say, "My daughter is an atheist and won't let me keep   29
the Bible in the parlor." She said, stiffening slightly, "I keep my Bible by my bedside."
This was not the truth. It was in the attic somewhere.

"Lady," he said, "the word of God ought to be in the parlor." "Well, I think that's   30
a matter of taste," she began, "I think…"

"Lady," he said, "for a Chrustian, the word of God ought to be in every room in   31
the house besides in his heart. I know you're a Chrustian because I can see it in every
line of your face."

She stood up and said, "Well, young man, I don't want to buy a Bible and I smell   32
my dinner burning."

He didn't get up. He began to twist his hands and looking down at them, he said   33
softly, "Well lady, I'll tell you the truth – not many people want to buy one nowadays
and besides, I know I'm real simple. I don't know how to say a thing but to say it. I'm
just a country boy." He glanced up into her unfriendly face. "People like you don't
like to fool with country people like me!"

"Why!" she cried, "good country people are the salt of the earth! Besides, we all   34
have different ways of doing, it takes all kinds to make the world go 'round. That's
life!"

"You said a mouthful," he said.   35

"Why, I think there aren't enough good country people in the world!" she said,   36
stirred. "I think that's what's wrong with it!"

His face had brightened. "I didn't intraduce myself," he said. "I'm Manley   37
Pointer from out in the country around Willohobie, not even from a place, just from
near a place."

"You wait a minute," she said. "I have to see about my dinner." She went out to   38
the kitchen and found Joy standing near the door where she had been listening.

"Get rid of the salt of the earth," she said, "and let's eat."   39

Mrs. Hopewell gave her a pained look and turned the heat down under the   40 vegetables. "I can't be rude to anybody," she murmured and went back into the parlor. He had opened the suitcase and was sitting with a Bible on each knee.

"I appreciate your honesty," he said. "You don't see any more real honest people unless you go way out in the country."   41

"I know," she said, "real genuine folks!" Through the crack in the door she heard a groan.   42

"I guess a lot of boys come telling you they're working their way through college," he said, "but I'm not going to tell you that. Somehow," he said, "I don't want to go to college. I want to devote my life to Chrustian service. See," he said, lowering his voice, "I got this heart condition. I may not live long. When you know it's something wrong with you and you may not live long, well then, lady…" He paused, with his mouth open, and stared at her.   43

He and Joy had the same condition! She knew that her eyes were filling with tears but she collected herself quickly and murmured, "Won't you stay for dinner? We'd love to have you!" and was sorry the instant she heard herself say it.   44

"Yes mam," he said in an abashed voice. "I would sher love to do that!"   45

Joy had given him one look on being introduced to him and then throughout the meal had not glanced at him again. He had addressed several remarks to her, which she had pretended not to hear. Mrs. Hopewell could not understand deliberate rudeness, although she lived with it, and she felt she had always to overflow with hospitality to make up for Joy's lack of courtesy. She urged him to talk about himself and he did. He said he was the seventh child of twelve and that his father had been crushed under a tree when he himself was eight years old. He had been crushed very badly, in fact, almost cut in two and was practically not recognizable. His mother had got along the best she could by hard working and she had always seen that her children went to Sunday School and that they read the Bible every evening. He was now nineteen years old and he had been selling Bibles for four months. In that time he had sold seventy-seven Bibles and had the promise of two more sales. He wanted to become a missionary because he thought that was the way you could do most for people. "He who losest his life shall find it," he said simply and he was so sincere, so genuine and earnest that Mrs. Hopewell would not for the world have smiled. He prevented his peas from sliding onto the table by blocking them with a piece of bread which he later cleaned his plate with. She could see Joy observing sidewise how he handled his knife and fork and she saw too that every few minutes, the boy would dart a keen appraising glance at the girl as if he were trying to attract her attention.   46

After dinner Joy cleared the dishes off the table and disappeared and Mrs. Hopewell was left to talk with him. He told her again about his childhood and his father's accident and about various things that had happened to him. Every five minutes or so she would stifle a yawn. He sat for two hours until finally she told him she must go because she had an appointment in town. He packed his Bibles and thanked her and prepared to leave, but in the doorway he stopped and wring her hand and said that not on any of his trips had he met a lady as nice as her and he   47 asked if he could come again. She had said she would always be happy to see him.

Joy had been standing in the road, apparently looking at something in the distance, when he came down the steps toward her, bent to the side with his heavy valise. He stopped where she was standing and confronted her directly. Mrs. Hopewell could not hear what he said but she trembled to think what Joy would say to him. She could see that after a minute Joy said something and that then the boy began to speak again, making an excited gesture with his free hand. After a minute Joy said something else at which the boy began to speak once more. Then to her amazement, Mrs. Hopewell saw the two of them walk off together, toward the gate. Joy had walked all the way to the gate with him and Mrs. Hopewell could not imagine what they had said to each other, and she had not yet dared to ask. 48

Mrs. Freeman was insisting upon her attention. She had moved from the refrigerator to the heater so that Mrs. Hopewell had to turn and face her in order to seem to be listening. "Glynese gone out with Harvey Hill again last night," she said. "She had this sty." 49

"Hill," Mrs. Hopewell said absently, "is that the one who works in the garage?" 50

"Nome, he's the one that goes to chiropractor school," Mrs. Freeman said. "She had this sty. Been had it two days. So she says when he brought her in the other night he says, 51

'Lemme get rid of that sty for you,' and she says, 'How?' and he says, 'You just lay yourself down across the seat of that car and I'll show you.' So she done it and he popped her neck. Kept on a-popping it several times until she made him quit. This morning," Mrs. Freeman said, "she ain't got no sty. She ain't got no traces of a sty." 52

"I never heard of that before," Mrs. Hopewell said. 53

"He ast her to marry him before the Ordinary," Mrs. Freeman went on, "and she told him she wasn't going to be married in no office." 54

"Well, Glynese is a fine girl," Mrs. Hopewell said. "Glynese and Carramae are both fine girls." 55

"Carramae said when her and Lyman was married Lyman said it sure felt sacred to him. She said he said he wouldn't take five hundred dollars for being married by a preacher." 56

"How much would he take?" the girl asked from the stove. 57

"He said he wouldn't take five hundred dollars," Mrs. Freeman repeated. "Well we all have work to do," Mrs. Hopewell said. 58

"Lyman said it just felt more sacred to him," Mrs. Freeman said. "The doctor wants Carramae to eat prunes. Says instead of medicine. Says them cramps is coming from pressure. You know where I think it is?" 59

"She'll be better in a few weeks," Mrs. Hopewell said. 60

"In the tube," Mrs. Freeman said. "Else she wouldn't be as sick as she is." 61

Hulga had cracked her two eggs into a saucer and was bringing them to the table along with a cup of coffee that she had filled too full. She sat down carefully and began to eat, meaning to keep Mrs. Freeman there by questions if for any reason 62 she showed an inclination to leave. She could perceive her mother's eye on her. The first round-about question would be about the Bible salesman and she did not wish to bring it on. "How did he pop her neck?" she asked.

Mrs. Freeman went into a description of how he had popped her neck. She said he owned a '55 Mercury but that Glynese said she would rather marry a man with only a '36 Plymouth who would be married by a preacher. The girl asked what if he had a '32 Plymouth and Mrs. Freeman said what Glynese had said was a '36 Plymouth.   63

Mrs. Hopewell said there were not many girls with Glynese's common sense. She said what she admired in those girls was their common sense. She said that reminded her that they had had a nice visitor yesterday, a young man selling Bibles. "Lord," she said, "he bored me to death but he was so sincere and genuine I couldn't be rude to him. He was just good country people, you know," she said, "—just the salt of the earth."   64

"I seen him walk up," Mrs. Freeman said, "and then later – I seen him walk off," and Hulga could feel the slight shift in her voice, the slight insinuation, that he had not walked off alone, had he? Her face remained expressionless but the color rose into her neck and she seemed to swallow it down with the next spoonful of egg. Mrs. Freeman was looking at her as if they had a secret together.   65

"Well, it takes all kinds of people to make the world go 'round," Mrs. Hopewell said. "It's very good we aren't all alike."   66

"Some people are more alike than others," Mrs. Freeman said.   67

Hulga got up and stumped, with about twice the noise that was necessary, into her room and locked the door. She was to meet the Bible salesman at ten o'clock at the gate. She had thought about it half the night. She had started thinking of it as a great joke and then she had begun to see profound implications in it. She had lain in bed imagining dialogues for them that were insane on the surface but that reached below the depths that no Bible salesman would be aware of. Their conversation yesterday had been of this kind.   68

He had stopped in front of her and had simply stood there. His face was bony and sweaty and bright, with a little pointed nose in the center of it, and his look was different from what it had been at the dinner table. He was gazing at her with open curiosity, with fascination, like a child watching a new fantastic animal at the zoo, and he was breathing as if he had run a great distance to reach her. His gaze seemed somehow familiar but she could not think where she had been regarded with it before. For almost a minute he didn't say anything. Then on what seemed an insuck of breath, he whispered, "You ever ate a chicken that was two days old?"   69

The girl looked at him stonily. He might have just put this question up for consideration at the meeting of a philosophical association. "Yes," she presently replied as if she had considered it from all angles.   70

"It must have been mighty small!" he said triumphantly and shook all over with little nervous giggles, getting very red in the face, and subsiding finally into his gaze   71 of complete admiration, while the girl's expression remained exactly the same.

"How old are you?" he asked softly.   72

She waited some time before she answered. Then in a flat voice she said,   73
"Seventeen." His smiles came in succession like waves breaking on the surface of a
little lake. "I see you got a wooden leg," he said. "I think you're real brave. I think
you're real sweet." The girl stood blank and solid and silent.

"Walk to the gate with me," he said. "You're a brave sweet little thing and I liked   74
you the minute I seen you walk in the door."

Hulga began to move forward.   75

"What's your name?" he asked, smiling down on the top of her head. "Hulga,"   76
she said.

"Hulga," he murmured, "Hulga. Hulga. I never heard of anybody name Hulga   77
before. You're shy, aren't you, Hulga?" he asked.

She nodded, watching his large red hand on the handle of the giant valise.   78

"I like girls that wear glasses," he said. "I think a lot. I'm not like these people   79
that a serious thought don't ever enter their heads. It's because I may die."

"I may die too," she said suddenly and looked up at him. His eyes were very   80
small and brown, glittering feverishly.

"Listen," he said, "don't you think some people was meant to meet on account   81
of what all they got in common and all? Like they both think serious thoughts and
all?" He shifted the valise to his other hand so that the hand nearest her was free. He
caught hold of her elbow and shook it a little. "I don't work on Saturday," he said. "I
like to walk in the woods and see what Mother Nature is wearing. O'er the hills and
far away. Picnics and things. Couldn't we go on a picnic tomorrow? Say yes, Hulga,"
he said and gave her a dying look as if he felt his insides about to drop out of him. He
had even seemed to sway slightly toward her.

During the night she had imagined that she seduced him. She imagined that   82
the two of them walked on the place until they came to the storage barn beyond the
two back fields and there, she imagined, that things came to such a pass that she
very easily seduced him and that then, of course, she had to reckon with his remorse.
True genius can get an idea across even to an inferior mind. She imagined that she
took his remorse in hand and changed it into a deeper understanding of life. She
took all his shame away and turned it into something useful.   83

She set off for the gate at exactly ten o'clock, escaping without drawing Mrs.   84
Hopewell's attention. She didn't take anything to eat, forgetting that food is usually
taken on a picnic. She wore a pair of slacks and a dirty white shirt, and as an
afterthought, she had put some Vapex on the collar of it since she did not own any
perfume. When she reached the gate no one was there.

She looked up and down the empty highway and had the furious feeling that   85
she had been tricked, that he only meant to make her walk to the gate after the idea
of him. Then suddenly he stood up, very tall, from behind a bush on the opposite
embankment.

Smiling, he lifted his hat which was new and wide-brimmed. He had not worn it *86* yesterday and she wondered if he had bought it for the occasion. It was toast-colored with a red and white band around it and was slightly too large for him. He stepped from behind the bush still carrying the black valise. He had on the same suit and the same yellow socks sucked down in his shoes from walking. He crossed the highway and said, "I knew you'd come!"

The girl wondered acidly how he had known this. She pointed to the valise and *87* asked, "Why did you bring your Bibles?"

He took her elbow, smiling down on her as if he could not stop. "You can never *88* tell when you'll need the word of God, Hulga," he said. She had a moment in which she doubted that this was actually happening and then they began to climb the embankment. They went down into the pasture toward the woods. The boy walked lightly by her side, bouncing on his toes. The valise did not seem to be heavy today; he even swung it. They crossed half the pasture without saying anything and then, putting his hand easily on the small of her back, he asked softly, "Where does your wooden leg join on?"

She turned an ugly red and glared at him and for an instant the boy looked *89* abashed. "I didn't mean you no harm," he said. "I only meant you're so brave and all. I guess God takes care of you."

"No," she said, looking forward and walking fast, "I don't even believe in God." *90*

At this he stopped and whistled. "No!" he exclaimed as if he were too astonished *91* to say anything else.

She walked on and in a second he was bouncing at her side, fanning with his *92* hat. "That's very unusual for a girl," he remarked, watching her out of the corner of his eye. When they reached the edge of the wood, he put his hand on her back again and drew her against him without a word and kissed her heavily.

The kiss, which had more pressure than feeling behind it, produced that *93* extra surge of adrenalin in the girl that enables one to carry a packed trunk out of a burning house, but in her, the power went at once to the brain. Even before he released her, her mind, clear and detached and ironic anyway, was regarding him from a great distance, with amusement but with pity. She had never been kissed before and she was pleased to discover that it was an unexceptional experience and all a matter of the mind's control. Some people might enjoy drain water if they were told it was vodka. When the boy, looking expectant but uncertain, pushed her gently away, she turned and walked on, saying nothing as if such business, for her, were common enough.

He came along panting at her side, trying to help her when he saw a root that *94* she might trip over. He caught and held back the long swaying blades of thorn vine until she had passed beyond them. She led the way and he came breathing heavily behind her. Then they came out on a sunlit hillside, sloping softly into another one a little smaller. Beyond, they could see the rusted top of the old barn where the extra hay was stored.

The hill was sprinkled with small pink weeds. "Then you ain't saved?" he asked   95
suddenly, stopping.

The girl smiled. It was the first time she had smiled at him at all. "In my   96
economy," she said, "I'm saved and you are damned but I told you I didn't believe in
God."

Nothing seemed to destroy the boy's look of admiration. He gazed at her now as   97
if the fantastic animal at the zoo had put its paw through the bars and given him a
loving poke. She thought he looked as if he wanted to kiss her again and she walked
on before he had the chance.

"Ain't there somewheres we can sit down sometime?" he murmured, his voice   98
softening toward the end of the sentence.

"In that barn," she said.   99

They made for it rapidly as if it might slide away like a train. It was a large two-   100
story barn, cook and dark inside. The boy pointed up the ladder that led into the loft
and said, "It's too bad we can't go up there."

"Why can't we?" she asked. "Yer leg," he said reverently.   101

The girl gave him a contemptuous look and putting both hands on the ladder,   102
she climbed it while he stood below, apparently awestruck. She pulled herself
expertly through the opening and then looked down at him and said, "Well, come
on if your coming," and he began to climb the ladder, awkwardly bringing the
suitcase with him.

"We won't need the Bible," she observed.   103

"You never can tell," he said, panting. After he had got into the loft, he was a few   104
seconds catching his breath. She had sat down in a pile of straw. A wide sheath of
sunlight, filled with dust particles, slanted over her. She lay back against a bale, her
face turned away, looking out the front opening of the barn where hay was thrown
from a wagon into the loft. The two pink-speckled hillsides lay back against a dark
ridge of woods. The sky was cloudless and cold blue. The boy dropped down by her
side and put one arm under her and the other over her and began methodically
kissing her face, making little noises like a fish. He did not remove his hat but it was
pushed far enough back not to interfere. When her glasses got in his way, he took
them off of her and slipped them into his pocket.

The girl at first did not return any of the kisses but presently she began to and   105
after she had put several on his cheek, she reached his lips and remained there,
kissing him again and again as if she were trying to draw all the breath out of him.
His breath was clear and sweet like a child's and the kisses were sticky like a child's.
He mumbled about loving her and about knowing when he first seen her that he
loved her, but the mumbling was like the sleepy fretting of a child being put to sleep
by his mother. Her mind, throughout this, never stopped or lost itself for a second to
her feelings. "You ain't said you loved me none," he whispered finally, pulling back
from her. "You got to say that."

She looked away from him off into the hollow sky and then down at a black   106 ridge and then down farther into what appeared to be two green swelling lakes. She didn't realize he had taken her glasses but this landscape could not seem exceptional to her for she seldom paid any close attention to her surroundings.

"You got to say it," he repeated. "You got to say you love me."   *107*

She was always careful how she committed herself. "In a sense," she began, "if   *108* you use the word loosely, you might say that. But it's not a word I use. I don't have illusions. I'm one of those people who see through to nothing."

The boy was frowning. "You got to say it. I said it and you got to say it," he said.   *109*

The girl looked at him almost tenderly. "You poor baby," she murmured. "It's   *110* just as well you don't understand," and she pulled him by the neck, face-down, against her.

"We are all damned," she said, "but some of us have taken off our blindfolds   *111* and see that there's nothing to see. It's a kind of salvation."

The boy's astonished eyes looked blankly through the ends of her hair. "Okay,"   *112* he almost whined, "but do you love me or don'tcher?"

"Yes," she said and added, "in a sense. But I must tell you something. There   *113* mustn't be anything dishonest between us." She lifted his head and looked him in the eye. "I am thirty years old," she said. "I have a number of degrees."

The boy's look was irritated but dogged. "I don't care," he said. "I don't care a   *114* thing about what all you done. I just want to know if you love me or don'tcher?" and he caught her to him and wildly planted her face with kisses until she said, "Yes, yes."

"Okay then," he said, letting her go. "Prove it."   *115*

She smiled, looking dreamily out on the shifty landscape. She had seduced him   *116* without even making up her mind to try. "How?" she asked, feeling that he should be delayed a little.

He leaned over and put his lips to her ear. "Show me where your wooden leg   *117* joins on," he whispered.

The girl uttered a sharp little cry and her face instantly drained of color. The   *118* obscenity of the suggestion was not what shocked her. As a child she had sometimes been subject to feelings of shame but education had removed the last traces of that as a good surgeon scrapes for cancer; she would no more have felt it over what he was asking than she would have believed in his Bible. But she was as sensitive about the artificial leg as a peacock about his tail. No one ever touched it but her. She took care of it as someone else would his soul, in private and almost with her own eyes turned away. "No," she said.

"I known it," he muttered, sitting up. "You're just playing me for a sucker."   *119*

"On no no!" she cried. "It joins on at the knee. Only at the knee. Why do you   *120* want to see it?"

The boy gave her a long penetrating look. "Because," he said, "it's what makes   *121* you different. You ain't like anybody else."

She sat staring at him. There was nothing about her face or her round freezing-   *122* blue eyes to indicate that this had moved her; but she felt as if her heart had stopped and left her mind to pump her blood. She decided that for the first time in her life she was face to face with real innocence. This boy, with an instinct that came from beyond wisdom, had touched the truth about her. When after a minute, she said in a hoarse high voice, "All right," it was like surrendering to him completely. It was like losing her own life and finding it again, miraculously, in his.

Very gently, he began to roll the slack leg up. The artificial limb, in a white sock *123* and brown flat shoe, was bound in a heavy material like canvas and ended in an ugly jointure where it was attached to the stump. The boy's face and his voice were entirely reverent as he uncovered it and said, "Now show me how to take it off and on."

She took it off for him and put it back on again and then he took it off himself, *124* handling it as tenderly as if it were a real one. "See!" he said with a delighted child's face. "Now I can do it myself!"

"Put it back on," she said. She was thinking that she would run away with him *125* and that every night he would take the leg off and every morning put it back on again. "Put it back on," she said.

"Not yet," he murmured, setting it on its foot out of her reach. "Leave it off for *126* awhile. You got me instead."

She gave a little cry of alarm but he pushed her down and began to kiss her *127* again. Without the leg she felt entirely dependent on him. Her brain seemed to have stopped thinking altogether and to be about some other function that it was not very good at. Different expressions raced back and forth over her face. Every now and then the boy, his eyes like two steel spikes, would glance behind him where the leg stood. Finally she pushed him off and said, "Put it back on me now."

"Wait," he said. He leaned the other way and pulled the valise toward him *128* and opened it. It had a pale blue spotted lining and there were only two Bibles in it. He took one of these out and opened the cover of it. It was hollow and contained a pocket flask of whiskey, a pack of cards, and a small blue box with printing on it. He laid these out in front of her one at a time in an evenly-spaced row, like one presenting offerings at the shrine of a goddess. He put the blue box in her hand. THIS PRODUCT TO BE USED ONLY FOR THE PREVENTION OF DISEASE, she read, and dropped it. The boy was unscrewing the top of the flask. He stopped and pointed, with a smile, to the deck of cards. It was not an ordinary deck but one with an obscene picture on the back of each card. "Take a swig," he said, offering her the bottle first. He held it in front of her, but like one mesmerized, she did not move.

Her voice when she spoke had an almost pleading sound. "Aren't you," she *129* murmured, "aren't you just good country people?"

The boy cocked his head. He looked as if he were just beginning to understand *130* that she might be trying to insult him. "Yeah," he said, curling his lip slightly, "but it ain't held me back none. I'm as good as you any day in the week."

"Give me my leg," she said. *131*

He pushed it farther away with his foot. "Come on now, let's begin to have us a good time," he said coaxingly. "We ain't got to know one another good yet." *132*

"Give me my leg!" she screamed and tried to lunge for it but he pushed her down easily. "What's the matter with you all of a sudden?" he asked, frowning as he screwed the top on the flask and put it quickly back inside the Bible. "You just a while ago said you didn't believe in nothing. I thought you was some girl!" *133*

Her face was almost purple. "You're a Christian!" she hissed. "You're a fine Christian! You're just like them all – say one thing and do another. You're a perfect Christian, you're…" *134*

The boy's mouth was set angrily. "I hope you don't think," he said in a lofty indignant tone, "that I believe in that crap! I may sell Bibles but I know which end is up and I wasn't born yesterday and I know where I'm going!" *135*

"Give me my leg!" she screeched. He jumped up so quickly that she barely saw him sweep the cards and the blue box back into the Bible and throw the Bible into the valise. She saw him grab the leg and then she saw it for an instant slanted forlornly across the inside of the suitcase with a Bible at either side of its opposite ends. He slammed the lid shut and snatched up the valise and swung it down the hole and then stepped through himself. When all of him had passed but his head, he turned and regarded her with a look that no longer had any admiration in it. "I've gotten a lot of interesting things," he said. "One time I got a woman's glass eye this way. And you needn't to think you'll catch me because Pointer ain't really my name. I use a different name at every house I call at and don't stay nowhere long. And I'll tell you another thing, Hulga," he said, using the name as if he didn't think much of it, "you ain't so smart. I been believing in nothing ever since I was born!" and then the toast-colored hat disappeared down the hole and the girl was left, sitting on the straw in the dusty sunlight. When she turned her churning face toward the opening, she saw his blue figure struggling successfully over the green speckled lake. *136*

Mrs. Hopewell and Mrs. Freeman, who were in the back pasture, digging up onions, saw him emerge a little later from the woods and head across the meadow toward the highway. "Why, that looks like that nice dull young man that tried to sell me a Bible yesterday," Mrs. Hopewell said, squinting. "He must have been selling them to the Negroes back in there. He was so simple," she said, "but I guess the world would be better off if we were all that simple." *137*

Mrs. Freeman's gaze drove forward and just touched him before he disappeared under the hill. Then she returned her attention to the evil-smelling onion shoot she was lifting from the ground. "Some can't be that simple," she said. "I know I never could." *138*

Analysis of O'Connor's Short Story

In the essay below, student writer Anya Terekhina analyzes the story, "Good Country People." Note how she introduces the story, states her thesis, and then develops that idea by carefully examining the story's characters, plot, language, symbols, and theme.

"Good Country People":
Broken Body, Broken Soul

> *The writer provides background for understanding the characters in O'Connor's stories.*

Flannery O'Connor's short stories are filled with characters who are bizarre, freakish, devious, and sometimes even murderous. Every short story, according to O'Connor in *Mystery and Manners: Occasional Prose*, should be "long in depth" and meaning (94). To achieve this, O'Connor develops characters with heavily symbolic attributes and flaws, and "it is clearly evident that boldly outlined inner compulsions are reinforced dramatically by a mutilated exterior self" (Muller 22). In "Good Country People," Joy-Hulga is a typical O'Connor character—grotesque yet real. Her realness comes from her many flaws and, ironically, her flaws are a self-constructed set of illusions. Throughout the story, O'Connor carefully links Joy-Hulga's physical impairments with deeper handicaps of the soul; then, at the closing, she strips Hulga of these physical flaws while helping her realize that her corresponding beliefs are flawed as well.

O'Connor first introduces her character as Joy Hopewell, a name of optimism. However, we soon understand that her chosen name, Hulga, is more fitting. The new name distresses her mother, Mrs. Hopewell, who is "certain that she [Joy] had thought and thought until she had hit upon the ugliest name in any language" (O'Connor 1943). Hulga has connotations of "hull = hulk = huge = ugly" (Grimshaw 51), and all of these are accurate descriptions of her. Far from having a sweet temperament, Hulga stomps and sulks around the farm, "constant outrage . . . [purging] every expression from her face" (1942).

Although Hulga's demeanor could be blamed on her physical impairments, she devises her own rationalizations for behaving as she does. Ironically, each rationale is symbolized by one of her physical disabilities, yet she doesn't recognize the handicaps for what they imply.

> *The writer begins listing the protagonist's physical disabilities and explains how each one symbolizes a deeper problem in her soul.*

One of Hulga's many ailments is her weak heart, which will likely limit her life span. Hulga blames this affliction for keeping her on the Hopewell farm, making it plain that "if it had not been for this condition, she would be far from these red

1

2

3

4

hills and good country people" (1944). Having a Ph.D. in philosophy, Hulga claims to want work as a university professor, lecturing to people at her intellectual level. Hulga's weak heart functions as more than a dream-crusher; it "symbolizes her emotional detachment—and inability to love anyone or anything" (Oliver 233). She exhibits no compassion or love for anything, not even "dogs or cats or birds or flowers or nature or nice young men" (1944–45).

Hulga also suffers from poor vision. Without her eyeglasses, she is helpless.   5
Strangely though, her icy blue eyes have a "look of someone who has achieved blindness by an act of will and means to keep it" (1942). Her self-induced blindness symbolizes her blindness to reality. She is indeed intelligent, but she has packed her brain full of ideas and thoughts that only obscure common sense, let alone truth. Because of Hulga's extensive education and her focus on philosophical reasoning, she considers herself superior to everyone around her. For example, she yells at her mother, "Woman! . . . Do you ever look inside and see what you are not? God!" (1944).

> She points out the root of the protagonist's problems: her lack of belief in anything.

Hulga's last and most noticeable physical impairment is her missing leg, which   6
was "literally blasted off" (1944) in a hunting accident when she was ten years old. In *Mystery and Manners*, O'Connor stresses that the wooden leg operates interdependently at a literal and a symbolic level, which means "the wooden leg continues to accumulate meaning" throughout the story (99). Hulga's biggest physical handicap symbolizes her deepest affliction: her belief in nothing.

Hulga's philosophical studies did focus on the study of nothing, particularly on   7
the arguments of the French philosopher Nicolas Malebranche. O'Connor describes Hulga as believing "in nothing but her own belief in nothing" (*Mystery* 99). Over time, Hulga's belief in nothing develops into more than just academic study. Her nihilism becomes her religion—suitable for a woman who considers herself superior and despises platitudes. As she explains to Manley Pointer, "We are all damned . . . but some of us have taken off our blindfolds and see that there's nothing to see. It's a kind of salvation" (1952). Hulga's religious terms suggest that she uses faith in nothingness to find the meaning that she can't find elsewhere.

Hulga's nihilism is symbolized by her wooden leg, which is the only thing she   8
tends to with care: "She took care of it as someone else would his soul, in private and almost with her own eyes turned away" (1953). This limb is wooden and corresponds to Hulga's wooden soul. Whereas she believes she worships Nothing, what she

actually worships is an "artificial leg and an artificial belief" (Oliver 235).

Not realizing that her false leg and false religion cripple her both physically   *9*
and spiritually, Hulga considers seducing Manley Pointer, the Bible salesman.
She delightfully imagines that she will have to help him deal with his subsequent
remorse, and then she will instruct him into a "deeper understanding of life" (1950).
Of course, her intellectual blindness keeps her from realizing that her superiority
is only an illusion. Instead, she views Manley as "a vulnerable innocent, a naïve
Fundamentalist, and she wishes to seduce him to prove that her sophisticated
textbook nihilism is superior to his simpleminded faith" (Di Renzo 76).

The writer demonstrates how the protagonist's flaws lead her to make distorted judgments.

In classic O'Connor fashion, the characters and situation reverse dramatically   *10*
at the end of the story. Hulga and Manley are alone in a hayloft and begin
embracing. At first, Hulga is pleased with her reaction to kissing as it aligns well
with Malebranche's teachings: "it was an unexceptional experience and all a matter
of the mind's control" (1951). Soon, however, she realizes that she is enjoying the first
human connection of her life. At this point, the *innocent* Bible salesman has already
stripped Hulga of her first physical impairment: her weak heart.

Hulga hardly notices when Manley takes advantage of her next impairment: *11*
"when her glasses got in his way, he took them off of her and slipped them into his
pocket" (1952). With her heart opened and her intellectual perspective fuzzy, Hulga
swiftly descends into what she despises—platitudes. Hulga and Manley exchange
clichéd mumblings of love, and this leads Manley to ask if he can remove her
artificial leg. After brief hesitation, Hulga agrees because she feels he has touched
and understood a central truth inside her. She considers it a complete surrender,
"like losing her own life and finding it again, miraculously, in his" (1953).

She revisits the protagonist's physical disabilities, showing how the Bible salesman exploits each one.

As soon as the artificial leg is off, Manley whips out one of his Bibles, which   *12*
is hollow. Inside are whiskey, obscene playing cards, and contraceptives. In only
moments, Hulga loses control: As each of her physical handicaps is exploited, pieces
of her world view crumble, leaving her confused and weak.

In an ironic reversal, Hulga becomes the naïf and Manley becomes the cynic.   *13*
Hulga pleads in disbelief, "Aren't you . . . just good country people?" (1954). She
knows that she has reverted to her mother's platitudes: "If the language is more
sophisticated than any at Mrs. Hopewell's command, it is no less trite, and the smug
self-deception underlying it . . . is, if anything, greater" (Asals 105). Manley assumes
a startling, haughty air, exclaiming, "'I hope you don't think . . . that I believe in that

The writer reflects on the change in both characters.

crap! I may sell Bibles but I know which end is up and I wasn't born yesterday and I know where I'm going!'" (1954). Although they exchange roles, both characters use clichés to express their immature, yet authentic, worldviews.

Manley runs off with Hulga's wooden leg, leaving her vulnerable and dependent, two things she previously despised. But "Hulga's artificial self—her mental fantasy of her own perfection—has gone out the door with her artificial limb. She is stuck in the hayloft with her actual self, her body, her physical and emotional incompleteness" (Di Renzo 79). *14*

> *The closing explains how Hulga finally acknowledges the truth about herself.*

In one brief morning of delusional seduction, Hulga learns more about herself and her world than she learned in all her years of university. Forced to acknowledge her physical, emotional, and spiritual disabilities, Hulga begins to realize what she is not—neither a wise intellectual for whom there is hope, nor "good country people" who merely *hope well*. *15*

Note: The Works Cited page is not shown. For sample pages, see MLA (pages 493–534) and APA (pages 535–564).

Reading for Better Writing

Working by yourself or with a group, answer these questions:

1. In her opening paragraph, Terekhina cites Flannery O'Connor's view that every short story should be "long in depth" and meaning. Does Terekhina adequately explore that depth and meaning? Cite evidence that supports your response.

2. In her second paragraph, Terekhina analyzes Hulga Hopewell's first name; in the last paragraph, she comments on the last name. Does Terekhina's attention to names help you understand Hulga's character and the story's themes? How?

3. A writer's thesis is a type of "contract" that he or she makes with readers, spelling out what the essay will do. Review Terekhina's thesis (last sentence, first paragraph) and assess how effectively she fulfills that contract. Cite supporting details.

4. Flannery O'Connor has received strong acclaim for her clearly developed, complex characters. Does Terekhina adequately explore that complexity? Explain.

5. Many praise O'Connor for the challenging philosophical or ethical questions raised in her fiction. What questions does Terekhina identify in "Good Country People," and does she effectively discuss them?

6. What does Terekhina say about the story's plot, symbols, and diction? Then explain why she does (or does not) effectively analyze these elements?

Analyzing a Novel

Student writer Aleah Stenberg wrote the following essay to offer her interpretation of the characters and themes in Louis Erdrich's novel *Love Medicine*. As you read Stenberg's analysis, notice how she draws on specific passages in the novel.

Ah, the Power of Women: Louis Erdrich's *Love Medicine*

The introduction identifies the author, the novel, and the focus of the analysis.

While most American literature commonly portrays a negative view of women, Louise Erdrich's Native American novel, *Love Medicine*, does just the opposite. Her female characters are the catalyst around which the action of the book revolves. The two strongest women, Lulu Lamartine and Marie Kashpaw, create the dissonant nucleoli that give rise to the conflict in the novel and also trump the men in most forms of power. The matriarchal Native American culture depicted by Erdrich provides a setting in which these women can roar.

1

Aleah begins her analysis by examining the status of women in the novel and the source of their power, power that creates strong female characters.

The culture of the Chippewa highly regards mothers in particular and women in general. As a child, Lulu learns this lesson by noting the respect allotted her mother. Lulu acknowledges, "I never grew from the curve of my mother's arms" (Erdrich 68), and finds in nature manifestations of her connection to her mother's person and power. This mother/daughter bond is impenetrable for men. While Lulu mourns her mother's passing, she never mentions a father. The closest father figure she has is Uncle Nanapush, but even when conversing about his death ceremony, she does so by referencing her feelings for her mother: "I couldn't bear to think of losing him the way I had lost my mother" (71). The oldest clan matron, Rushes Bear, also alludes to the matriarchal culture of the tribe as she laments about Nector Kashpaw: "My son is marrying one of that lowlife family that insulted me. Those Lazarres breed fast and die young. I hope I'll outlive her tough breed and Nector Kashpaw will once again respect his mother" (72). Nector's actions don't insult his father or his family in a European sense; instead, he disgraces his mother. By recognizing mothers as the beating heart of the family, the Chippewa respect them accordingly.

2

In light of the reverence for women in Chippewa society, Erdrich's strongest, most prominent characters are Marie Kashpaw and Lulu Lamartine. These two are in charge of the house and rule over their husbands. Other female characters are also strong, although they play lesser roles. Rushes Bear and Sister Leopolda are strongly influential but in different times or spheres; for example, Sister Leopolda rules with a cruel hand at the Sacred Heart Convent. Erdrich's male characters have less prominent roles, and their main purpose—many times—is to be subordinated by domineering females.

3

The writer examines women's sexual power in the novel.

The women in *Love Medicine* have supremacy over the men in many aspects.   *4*
Sexual power over males guides much of the story in both Lulu and Marie's lives.
Lulu, particularly, has many affairs; she knows what she wants, gets it, and then does
away with what she doesn't like. Each of her boys and daughter is symbolic of her
conquering another man. At a young age, Lulu learned about sexual power while
listening to older women. Lulu remembers, "Rushes Bear always said that a man has
to enter and enter, repeatedly, as if in punishment for having ever left the woman's
body. She said that the woman is complete. Men must come through us to live" (82).
The idea that men are incomplete because they left the woman's body gives females
the edge in sexual relations. The man needs her; the woman is not dependant on
the man; on the contrary, she has command of the relationship. This same idea also
points to the reverence of women in Chippewa culture. The mother is the creator of
new life and the sustainer of the men she beds (whether her husband or not), and as
such, she is given great honor.

She explains how sexual power translates into political and social power.

The sexual power of women in *Love Medicine* also gives them political and   *5*
social clout. Lulu wields her political power when she denounces the proposed
tomahawk factory which would require moving her house: "Before I'd move the
Lamartine household I'd hit the tribe with a fistful of paternity suits that would
make their heads spin. Some of them had forgotten until then that I'd even had their
son. Still others must have wondered. I could see the back neck hair on the wives
all over that room prickle" (285). Lulu's sexual power gives her a platform to preside
over political decisions. Because of women's power sexually, they also are given
social influence. One of the examples in Lulu's life is deciding which Lamartine to
marry. She tells Beverly, "I am a woman of detachable parts. You should know by
now. You simply weren't playing in your league with strip poker" (115). And she
adds, "It was after I won your shorts with my pair of deuces and Henry's with my
eights, and you were naked except for your hat, that I decided which one to marry"
(115). So many men are sexually attracted to Lulu that she can pick and choose
whom she wants. In the culture the novel describes, women are venerated for their
sexuality. They can then use that given power to gain influence in tribal society and
politics.

Aleah analyzes how the power of the female characters generates the novel's central conflicts.

Matriarchal Chippewa culture; the sexual, political, and social power given to   *6*
women; and Erdrich's use of strong female characters culminate in Lulu and Marie
forming the central conflict of the piece. Both these women are strong and at odds,
the nuclei of opposing forces, two different pressure systems raging over North
Dakota. Nector Kashpaw is a main object of competition for these two. Like the

arms race of the Cold War, Marie and Lulu also engage in a race to have the most children. Lulu has many children, all by different fathers. Marie, after two of her and Nector's offspring die in childhood, rapidly adopts children and takes in young family members. These women are constantly vying for supremacy over each other. Even when they become friends, Lyman Lamartine notes, "Their statures had to be completely equal. . . . They each needed territory to control. . . . Their friendship, if that's what you'd call it, was hard to figure. Set free by Nector's death, they couldn't get enough of their own differences. They argued unceasingly about the past, and didn't agree on the present either" (311). In addition to these battles within their friendship, all other conflicts in *Love Medicine* stem from Lulu and Marie's on-going war or are in some way linked to it.

The conclusion drives home the writer's interpretation of the power of women in the novel.

Erdrich gives women center stage in *Love Medicine*. By choosing the matriarchal Chippewa tribe as her setting, she is able to create powerful female characters with dissonant relationships. Writing against the typical, American, male-dominated social order, Erdrich constructs a world in which women are in charge. Even though the female characters in the book are mothers who do laundry, cook meals, and finish long "to-do" lists, they are not held to this position. They have the power to rise above and take jurisdiction. Full of strong females, *Love Medicine* asserts a positive feminist message: women—hear them roar.

7

Note: The Works Cited page is not shown. For sample pages, see MLA (pages 493–534) and APA (pages 535–564).

Reading for Better Writing

Working by yourself or with a group, answer these questions:

1. Stenberg's essay introduces a novel (her topic) and analyzes its setting, characters, and themes. Describe how she uses the title and opening paragraphs to introduce this topic.
2. Stenberg's paper interprets one issue in the novel. What is the issue, and what is her thesis about it?
3. Review paragraphs 2-6, identify the supporting claim developed in each paragraph, and explain how Stenberg uses these points to support and clarify her main claim.
4. Describe how the writer uses her closing paragraph to refine and clarify her interpretation. Does the paragraph accomplish these goals? Explain.

"Ah, the Power of Women" by Aleah Stenberg. Used by permission of the author.

Literary Terms

Your analysis of novels, poems, plays, and films will be deeper and more sophisticated if you understand the most common literary terms.

Allusion is a reference to a person, a place, or an event in history or literature.

Analogy is a comparison of two or more similar objects, suggesting that if they are alike in certain respects, they will probably be alike in other ways, too.

Anecdote is a short summary of an interesting or humorous, often biographical event.

Antagonist is the person or thing actively working against the protagonist, or hero.

Climax is the turning point, an intense moment characterized by a key event.

Conflict is the problem or struggle in a story that triggers the action. There are five basic types of conflict:

- **Person versus person:** One character in a story is in conflict with one or more of the other characters.
- **Person versus society:** A character is in conflict with some element of society: the school, the law, the accepted way of doing things, and so on.
- **Person versus self:** A character faces conflicting inner choices.
- **Person versus nature:** A character is in conflict with some natural happening: a snowstorm, an avalanche, the bitter cold, or any other element of nature.
- **Person versus fate:** A character must battle what seems to be an uncontrollable problem. Whenever the conflict is a strange or unbelievable coincidence, the conflict can be attributed to fate.

Denouement is the outcome of a play or story. See *Resolution*.

Diction is an author's choice of words based on their correctness or effectiveness.

- **Archaic** words are old-fashioned and no longer sound natural when used, such as "I believe thee not" for "I don't believe you."
- **Colloquialism** is an expression that is usually accepted in informal situations and certain locations, as in "He really grinds my beans."
- **Heightened language** uses vocabulary and sentence constructions unlike that of standard speech or writing, as in much poetry and poetic prose.
- **Profanity** is language that shows disrespect for someone or something regarded as holy or sacred.
- **Slang** is the everyday language used by group members among themselves.
- **Trite** expressions lack depth or originality, or are overworked or not worth mentioning in the first place.
- **Vulgarity** is language that is generally considered common, crude, gross, and, at times, offensive. It is sometimes used in fiction, plays, and films to add realism.

Exposition is the introductory section of a story or play. Typically, the setting, main characters, and themes are introduced, and the action is initiated.

Falling action is the action of a play or story that follows the climax and shows the characters dealing with the climactic event or decision.

Figure of speech is a literary device used to create a special effect or to describe something in a fresh way. The most common types are *antithesis, hyperbole, metaphor, metonymy, personification, simile,* and *understatement.*

- **Antithesis** is an opposition, or contrast, of ideas.
  > "It was the best of times, it was the worst of times, it was the age of wisdom, it was the age of foolishness ..."   — Charles Dickens, *A Tale of Two Cities*
- **Hyperbole** (hi-pur´ ba-lee) is an extreme exaggeration or overstatement.
  > "I have seen this river so wide it had only one bank."
  >   —Mark Twain, *Life on the Mississippi*
- **Metaphor** is a comparison of two unlike things in which no word of comparison (*as* or *like*) is used: "Life is a banquet."
- **Metonymy** (ma-ton´a-mee) is the substituting of one term for another that is closely related to it, but not a literal restatement.
  > "Friends, Romans, countrymen, lend me your ears." (The request is for the attention of those assembled, not literally their ears.)
- **Personification** is a device in which the author speaks of or describes an animal, object, or idea as if it were a person: "The rock stubbornly refused to move."
- **Simile** is a comparison of two unlike things in which *like* or *as* is used.
  > "She stood in front of the altar, shaking like a freshly caught trout."
  >   —Maya Angelou, *I Know Why the Caged Bird Sings*
- **Understatement** is stating an idea with restraint, often for humorous effect. Mark Twain described Aunt Polly as being "prejudiced against snakes." (Because she hated snakes, this way of saying so is *understatement*.)

Genre refers to a category or type of literature based on its style, form, and content. The mystery novel is a literary genre.

Imagery refers to words or phrases that a writer uses to appeal to the reader's senses.
  > "The sky was dark and gloomy, the air was damp and raw ... "
  >   —Charles Dickens, *The Pickwick Papers*

Irony is a deliberate discrepancy in meaning. There are three kinds of irony:

- **Dramatic irony**, in which the reader or the audience sees a character's mistakes or misunderstandings, but the character does not.
- **Verbal irony**, in which the writer says one thing and means another ("The best substitute for experience is being sixteen").
- **Irony of situation**, in which there is a great difference between the purpose of a particular action and the result.

Mood is the feeling that a piece of literature arouses in the reader: *happiness, sadness, peacefulness, anxiety,* and so forth.

Paradox is a statement that seems contrary to common sense yet may, in fact, be true: "The coach considered this a good loss."

Plot is the action or sequence of events in a story. It is usually a series of related incidents that build upon one another as the story develops. There are five basic elements in a plot line: *exposition, rising action, climax, falling action,* and *resolution.*

Point of view is the vantage point from which the story unfolds.

- In the **first-person** point of view, the story is told by one of the characters: "I stepped into the darkened room and felt myself go cold."
- In the **third-person** point of view, the story is told by someone outside the story: "He stepped into the darkened room and felt himself go cold."
- **Third-person narrations** can be *omniscient*, meaning that the narrator has access to the thoughts of all the characters, or *limited*, meaning that the narrator focuses on the inner life of one central character.

Protagonist is the main character or hero of the story.

Resolution (or denouement) is the portion of the play or story in which the problem is solved. The resolution comes after the climax and falling action and is intended to bring the story to a satisfactory end.

Rising action is the series of conflicts or struggles that build a story or play toward a fulfilling climax.

Satire is a literary tone used to ridicule or make fun of human vice or weakness, often with the intent of correcting, or changing, the subject of the satiric attack.

Setting is the time and place in which the action of a literary work occurs.

Structure is the form or organization a writer uses for her or his literary work. A great number of possible forms are used regularly in literature: parable, fable, romance, satire, farce, slapstick, and so on.

Style refers to how the author uses words, phrases, and sentences to form his or her ideas. Style is also thought of as the qualities and characteristics that distinguish one writer's work from the work of others.

Symbol is a person, a place, a thing, or an event used to represent something else. For example, the dove is a symbol of peace.

Theme is the statement about life that a particular work shares with readers. In stories written for children, the theme is often spelled out clearly at the end. In more complex literature, the theme will often be more complex and will be implied, not stated.

Tone is the overall feeling, or effect, created by a writer's use of words. This feeling may be serious, mock-serious, humorous, satiric, and so on.

Poetry Terms

Alliteration is the repetition of initial consonant sounds in words.

> "Our gang paces the pier like an old myth . . ."
>
> —Anne-Marie Oomen, "Runaway Warning"

Assonance is the repetition of vowel sounds without the repetition of consonants.

> "My words like silent rain drops fell . . ."   —Paul Simon, "Sounds of Silence"

Blank verse is an unrhymed form of poetry. Each line normally consists of ten syllables in which every other syllable, beginning with the second, is stressed. As blank verse is often used in very long poems, it may depart from the strict pattern from time to time.

Consonance is the repetition of consonant sounds. Although it is very similar to alliteration, consonance is not limited to the first letters of words:

> " . . . and high school girls with clear-skin smiles . . ."   —Janis Ian, "At Seventeen"

Foot is the smallest repeated pattern of stressed and unstressed syllables in a verse (see below).

- **Iambic:** an unstressed followed by a stressed syllable (re-peat′)
- **Anapestic:** two unstressed followed by a stressed syllable (in-ter-rupt′)
- **Trochaic:** a stressed followed by an unstressed syllable (old′-er)
- **Dactylic:** a stressed followed by two unstressed syllables (o′-pen-ly)
- **Spondaic:** two stressed syllables (heart′-break′)
- **Pyrrhic:** two unstressed syllables (Pyrrhic seldom appears by itself.)

Onomatopoeia is the use of a word whose sound suggests its meaning, as in *clang or buzz.*

Refrain is the repetition of a line or phrase of a poem at regular intervals, especially at the end of each stanza. A song's refrain may be called the *chorus.*

Rhythm is the ordered or free occurrences of sound in poetry. Ordered or regular rhythm is called meter. Free occurrence of sound is called *free verse.*

Stanza is a division of poetry named for the number of lines it contains:

- **Couplet:** two-line stanza
- **Triplet:** three-line stanza
- **Quatrain:** four-line stanza
- **Quintet:** five-line stanza
- **Sestet:** six-line stanza
- **Septet:** seven-line stanza
- **Octave:** eight-line stanza

Verse is a metric line of poetry. It is named according to the kind and number of feet composing it: *iambic pentameter, anapestic tetrameter,* and so on. (See **Foot.**)

- **Monometer:** one foot
- **Dimeter:** two feet
- **Trimeter:** three feet
- **Tetrameter:** four feet
- **Pentameter:** five feet
- **Hexameter:** six feet
- **Heptameter:** seven feet
- **Octometer:** eight feet

Writing Guidelines

Planning

1. **Select a topic.** Choose a work of literature or another artwork with which you are familiar or about which you are willing to learn.

2. **Understand the work.** Read or experience it thoughtfully (two or three times, if possible), looking carefully at its content, form, and overall effect.
   - **For plays and films,** examine the plot, props, setting, characters, dialogue, lighting, costumes, sound effects, music, acting, and directing.
   - **For novels and short stories,** focus on point of view, plot, setting, characters, style, diction, symbols, and theme. (See pages 286–288.)
   - **For poems,** examine diction, tone, sound patterns, figures of speech (e.g., metaphors), symbolism, irony, structure, genre, and theme. (See page 289.)
   - **For music,** focus on harmonic and rhythmic qualities, lyrics, and interpretation.

3. **Develop a focus and approach.** Take notes on what you experience, using the list above to guide you. Seek to understand the whole work before you analyze the parts, exploring your ideas and digging deeply through freewriting and annotating. Select a dimension of the work as a focus, considering what approach to analyzing that element might work. (See "Four Ways to Talk About Literature" on pages 257–258.)

4. **Organize your thoughts.** Review the notes that you took as you analyzed the work. What key insights has your analysis led you to see? Make a key insight your thesis, and then organize supporting points logically in an outline.

Drafting

5. **Write the first draft.**

   Opening: Use ideas like the following to gain your readers' attention, identify your topic, narrow the focus, and state your thesis:
   - Summarize your subject briefly. Include the title, the author or artist, and the literary form or performance.

       Example: Michael Ondaatje's "The Time Around Scars," a poem written in quasi-free verse, deals with scars, the stories they tell, and the people who can and cannot share these stories.
   - Start with a quotation from the work and then comment on its importance.
   - Open with a general statement about the artist's style or aesthetic process.

       Example: Flannery O'Connor's stories are filled with characters who are bizarre, freakish, devious, and sometimes even murderous.
   - Begin with a general statement about the plot or performance.

       Example: In Stephen Spielberg's movie War of the Worlds, Ray Ferrier and his two children flee from their New Jersey home in a stolen minivan.

- Assert your thesis. State the key insight about the work that your analysis has revealed—the insight your essay will seek to support.

Middle: Develop or support your focus by following this pattern:

- State the main points, relating them clearly to the focus of your essay.
- Support each main point with specific details or direct quotations.
- Explain how these details prove your point.

Conclusion: Tie key points together and assert your thesis or evaluation in a fresh way, leaving readers with a sense of the larger significance of your analysis.

Revising

6. **Improve the ideas, organization, and voice.** Review your draft for its overall content and tone. Ask a classmate or writing-center tutor for help, if appropriate.

____ **Ideas:** Does the essay show clear and deep insight into specific elements of the text, artwork, or performance? Is that insight effectively developed with specific references to the work itself?

____ **Organization:** Does the opening effectively engage the reader, introduce the text or artwork, and focus attention on an element or issue? Does the middle carefully work through a "reading" of the work? Does the conclusion reaffirm the insight into the work and expand the reader's understanding?

____ **Voice:** Does the tone convey a controlled, measured interest in the text or artwork? Is the analytical attitude confident but reasonable?

Editing

7. **Edit and proofread the essay by checking issues like these:**

____ **Words:** Language, especially terminology, is precise and clear.

____ **Sentences:** Constructions flow smoothly and are varied in length and structure; quotations are effectively integrated into sentence syntax.

____ **Correctness:** The copy includes no errors in spelling, usage, punctuation, grammar, or mechanics.

____ **Design:** The page design is correctly formatted and attractive; references are properly documented according to the required system (e.g., MLA).

Publishing

8. **Publish your essay.** Submit your essay to your instructor, but consider other ways of sharing your insights about this work or artist—blogging, submitting a review to a periodical (print or online), or leading classmates in a discussion (e.g., book club, post-performance meeting, exhibition tour).

Critical-Thinking and Writing Activities

As directed by your instructor, complete the following activities.

1. Re-read "Good Country People," write your own analysis, and share the essay with your class.

2. Review "Let Evening Come" and write your own analysis of the poem. Read your essay to the class and discuss how its style and content compare with that of the essay on pages 260–261.

3. Choose a film and watch it critically, preferably twice. Then find two reviews of the film, note their theses and supporting evidence, and write an essay in which you evaluate why the reviews are (or are not) informed, insightful, and fair.

4. Attend a concert with classmates. Afterward, discuss the style of the music, the performance of the singer or group, and the content of the lyrics. Note the age of the audience and discuss how and why it responded as it did. Finally, discuss whether you found the concert worthwhile.

5. Visit an art gallery and examine an exhibit that engages you. Describe what you find appealing or intriguing and explain why. Also explain what value this exhibit might have for your community.

Learning-Objectives Checklist ✓

Have you achieved this chapter's learning objectives? Check your progress with the items below, revisiting topics in the chapter as needed. *I have* . . .

____ critically examined and assessed analyses of literature and the arts for clarity, reasoning, insight, and the writer's critical perspective (254–256).

____ assessed how each analyst's critique of an artwork might be informed by her or his purpose, readers, and topic (254–256).

____ effectively used arts-related terminology and concepts to accurately critique others' analyses and to informatively craft my own (286–289).

____ analyzed and evaluated an artwork by addressing relevant issues, including its content, form, style, special features, and impact on audiences and scholarly critics (290–291).

____ written an analysis that has an insightful thesis, clear reasoning, and relevant supporting evidence from and about the work (290–291).

____ examined (and revised where needed) my ideas, organization, and voice for weaknesses such as inadequate supporting evidence or misused literary terms 290–291).

Chapter 17

Strategies for Argumentation and Persuasion

"I wasn't convinced." "I just didn't buy it." Maybe you've said something similar while watching a political debate, viewing a TV ad, or discussing an issue in class or at work. You simply didn't find the argument logical or convincing.

College is a place where big issues get argued out—in class and out. To participate in that dialogue, you must be able to read and listen to others' arguments, analyze them, and build your own.

This chapter will help you do that. It explains what argumentation is, how to identify weak arguments, and how to construct strong ones. The three ensuing chapters then explain and model three forms of written argumentation: taking a position, persuading readers to act, and proposing a solution.

Visually Speaking   Study Figure 17.1. What does it suggest about how to build a convincing argument?

Learning **Objectives**

By working through this chapter, you will be able to

- build a convincing evidence-based argument.
- distinguish and develop three types of claims.
- assess the nature and function of nine types of evidence.
- identify and correct logical fallacies.
- draft logical claims with reliable evidence and valid warrants.
- make needed concessions, develop rebuttals, and use appropriate appeals.

© *Reuters/CORBIS*

fig. 17.1

Building Persuasive Arguments

What is an argument? Formally, an *argument* is a series of statements arranged in a logical sequence, supported with sound evidence, and expressed powerfully so as to sway your reader or listener. Arguments appear in a variety of places:

- A research paper about email surveillance by the FBI.
- An analysis of "Good Country People" (short story) or *Poisonwood Bible* (novel).
- A debate about the ethics of transferring copyrighted music over the Internet.

This chapter will outline a process commonly used to build arguments of all kinds. The process includes the following steps:

Step 1: Prepare your argument.

- **Identify your readers and purpose.** Who are your readers and what is your goal? Do you want to take a position, persuade readers to act, or offer a solution?
- **Generate ideas and gather solid evidence.** You can't base an argument on opinions. Find accurate, pertinent information about the issue and uncover all viewpoints on it.
- **Develop a line of reasoning.** To be effective, you need to link your ideas in a clear, logical sequence.

Step 2: Make and qualify your claim.

- **Draw reasonable conclusions from the evidence.** State your claim (a debatable idea) as the central point for which you will argue. For example, you might assert that something is true, has value, or should be done.
- **Add qualifiers.** Words such as "typically" and "sometimes" soften your claim, making it more reasonable and acceptable.

Step 3: Support your claim.

- **Support each point** in your claim with solid evidence.
- **Identify logical fallacies.** Test your thinking for errors in logic. (See pages 301–304.)

Step 4: Engage the opposition.

- **Make concessions,** if needed, by granting points to the opposition.
- **Develop rebuttals** that expose the weaknesses of the opposition's position, whenever possible.
- **Use appropriate appeals**—emotional "tugs" that ethically and logically help readers see your argument as convincing.

Preparing Your Argument

An argument is a reason or chain of reasons used to support a claim. To use argumentation well, you need to know how to draw logical conclusions from sound evidence. Preparing an effective argument involves a number of specific steps, starting with those discussed below.

Consider the situation.

- **Clearly identify your purpose and audience.** This step is essential for all writing, but especially true when building an argument. (See pages 28–29.)
- **Consider a range of ideas** to broaden your understanding of the issue and to help focus your thinking on a particular viewpoint. (See pages 44–45.)
- **Gather sound evidence** to support your viewpoint. (See pages 298–300.)

Develop a line of reasoning.

Argumentative writing requires a clear line of reasoning with each point logically supporting your argument. Develop the line of reasoning as you study the issue, or use either of the following outlines as a guide.

Sample Argumentative Outlines

fig. 17.2

Outline 1: **Present your supporting arguments, then address counterarguments, and conclude with the strongest argument.**

Introduction: question, concern, or claim
  1. Strong argument-supporting claim
    - Discussion and support
  2. Other argument-supporting claims
    - Discussion of and support for each argument
  3. Objections, concerns, and counterarguments
    - Discussion, concessions, answers, and rebuttals
  4. Strongest argument-supporting claim
    - Discussion and support

Conclusion: argument consolidated—claim reinforced

Outline 2: **Address the arguments and counterarguments point by point.**

Introduction: question, concern, or claim
  1. Strong argument-supporting claim
    - Discussion and support
    - Counterarguments, concessions, and rebuttals
  2. Other argument-supporting claims
    - For each argument, discussion and support
    - For each argument, counterarguments, concessions, and rebuttals
  3. Strongest argument-supporting claim
    - Discussion and support
    - Counterarguments, concessions, and rebuttals

Conclusion: argument consolidated—claim reinforced

Making and Qualifying Claims

An argument centers on a claim—a debatable statement. That claim is the thesis, or key point you wish to explain and defend so well that readers agree with it. A strong claim has the following traits:

- **It's clearly arguable**—it can be vigorously debated.
- **It's defendable**—it can be supported with sufficient arguments and evidence.
- **It's responsible**—it takes an ethically sound position.
- **It's understandable**—it uses clear terms and defines key words.
- **It's interesting**—it is challenging and worth discussing, not bland and easily accepted.

Distinguish claims from facts and opinions.

A claim is a conclusion drawn from logical thought and reliable evidence. A fact, in contrast, is a statement that can be checked for accuracy. An opinion is a personally held taste or attitude. A claim can be debated, but a fact or an opinion cannot.

> **Fact:** During the last three years, no major accident has occurred in a nuclear power plant in the U.S.
>
> **Opinion:** I think nuclear power plants are safe.
>
> **Claim:** Nuclear power and fossil fuels are two major methods of energy production, and nuclear power could be seen as the "greener" option. However, the risks of nuclear power far outweigh its benefits, making fossil fuels the safer and more environmentally friendly option.

Note: While the fact's accuracy can easily be checked, the opinion statement simply offers a personal feeling. Conversely, the claim states an idea that can be supported with reasoning and evidence.

Distinguish three types of claims.

Truth, value, and policy—these types of claims are made in an argument. The differences among them are important because each type has a distinct goal.

- **Claims of truth** state that something is or is not the case. As a writer, you want readers to accept your claim as trustworthy.

  > The Arctic ice cap will begin to disappear as early as 2050.
  >
  > The cholesterol in eggs is not as dangerous as previously feared.
  >
  > **Comment:** Avoid statements that are (1) obviously true or (2) impossible to prove. Also, truth claims must be argued carefully because accepting them (or not) can have serious consequences.
  >
  > *Sample Essay:* "Ah, the Power of Women," pages 283–285

- **Claims of value** state that something does or does not have worth. As a writer, you want readers to accept your judgment.

  > Volunteer reading tutors provide a valuable service.
  >
  > Many music videos fail to present positive images of women.
  >
  > **Comment:** Claims of value must be supported by referring to a known standard or by establishing an agreed-upon standard. To avoid a bias, base your judgments on the known standard, not on your feelings.
  >
  > *Sample Essay:* "Our Wealth: Where Is It Taking Us?" pages 331–333

- **Claims of policy** state that something ought or ought not to be done. As a writer, you want readers to approve your course of action.

  > Special taxes should be placed on gas-guzzling SUVs.
  >
  > The developer should not be allowed to fill in the pond where the endangered tiger salamander lives.
  >
  > **Comment:** Policy claims focus on action. To arrive at them, you must often first establish certain truths and values; thus an argument over policy may include both truth and value claims.
  >
  > *Sample Essay:* "Uncle Sam and Aunt Samantha," pages 351–353

Develop a supportable claim.

An effective claim balances confidence with common sense. Follow these tips:

- **Avoid all-or-nothing, extreme claims.** Propositions using words that are overly positive or negative—such as *all, best, never,* and *worst*—may be difficult to support. Statements that leave no room for exceptions are easy to attack.

  > **Extreme:** All people charged for a DUI should never be allowed to drive again.

- **Make a truly meaningful claim.** Avoid claims that are obvious, trivial, or unsupportable. None is worth the energy needed to argue the point.

  > **Obvious:** College athletes sometimes receive special treatment.
  >
  > **Trivial:** The College Rec Center is a good place to get fit.
  >
  > **Unsupportable:** Athletics are irrelevant to college life.

- **Use qualifiers to temper your claims.** Qualifiers are words or phrases that make claims more reasonable. Notice the difference between these two claims:

  > **Unqualified:** Star athletes take far too many academic shortcuts.
  >
  > **Qualified:** Some star athletes take improper academic shortcuts.

Note: The "qualified" claim is easier to defend because it narrows the focus and leaves room for exceptions. Use qualifier words or phrases like these:

almost	if done correctly	maybe	tends to
before 2012	in one case	might	typically
frequently	likely	probably some	usually

Supporting Your Claims

A claim stands or falls on its support. It's not the popular strength of your claim that matters, but rather the strength of your reasoning and evidence. To develop strong support, consider how to select and use evidence.

Gather evidence.

Several types of evidence can support claims. To make good choices, review each type, as well as its strengths and weaknesses.

- **Observations and anecdotes** share what people (including you) have seen, heard, smelled, touched, tasted, and experienced. Such evidence offers an "eyewitness" perspective shaped by the observer's viewpoint, which can be powerful but may also prove narrow and subjective.

  > A generation ago, an American child could reasonably expect to grow up with his or her father. Today, an American child can reasonably expect not to.

- **Statistics** offer concrete numbers about a topic. Numbers don't "speak for themselves," however. They need to be interpreted and compared properly—not slanted or taken out of context. They also need to be up-to-date, relevant, and accurate.

  > Pennsylvania spends $30 million annually in deer-related costs.
  > Wisconsin has an estimated annual loss of $37 million for crop damage alone.

- **Tests and experiments** provide hard data developed through the scientific method, data that must nevertheless be carefully studied and properly interpreted.

  > According to the two scientists, the rats with unlimited access to the functional running wheel ran each day and gradually increased the amount of running; in addition, they started to eat less.

- **Graphics** provide information in visual form—from simple tables to more complex charts, maps, drawings, and photographs. When poorly done, however, graphics can distort the truth. See the bar graphs in the experiment report on pages 485–490 and the sample slides used in the speech "Save Now or Pay Later" (page 392).

- **Analogies** compare two things, creating clarity by drawing parallels. However, every analogy breaks down if pushed too far.

  > It is obvious today that America has defaulted on this promissory note insofar as her citizens of color are concerned. Instead of honoring this sacred obligation, America has given the Negro people a bad check; a check which has come back marked "insufficient funds." But we refuse to believe that the bank of justice is bankrupt.
  >
  > —Martin Luther King, Jr.

- **Expert testimony** offers insights from an authority on the topic. Such testimony always has limits: Experts don't know it all, and they work from distinct perspectives, which means that they can disagree.

  > One specialist opposed to drilling is David Klein, a professor at the Institute of Arctic Biology at the University of Alaska–Fairbanks. Klein argues that if the oil industry opens up the ANWR for drilling, the number of caribou will likely decrease because the calving locations will change.

- **Illustrations, examples, and demonstrations** support general claims with specific instances, making such statements seem concrete and observable. Of course, an example may not be your best support if it isn't familiar.

  > Think about how differently one can frame Rosa Parks' historic action. In prevailing myth, Parks—a holy innocent—acts almost on whim.... The real story is more empowering: It suggests that change is the product of deliberate, incremental action.

- **Analyses** examine parts of a topic through thought patterns—cause/effect, compare/contrast, classification, process, or definition. Such analysis helps make sense of a topic's complexity, but muddles the topic when poorly done.

  > If colorism lives underground, its effects are very real. Darker-skinned African-American defendants are more than twice as likely to receive the death penalty as lighter-skinned African-American defendants for crimes of equivalent seriousness....

- **Predictions** offer insights into possible outcomes or consequences by forecasting what might happen under certain conditions. Like weather forecasting, predicting can be tricky. To be plausible, a prediction must be rooted in a logical analysis of present facts.

  > Fortunately, there is hope. Scientific research is already helping doctors do amazing things for people suffering with cancer. One treatment that has been used for some time is chemotherapy, or the use of chemicals to kill off all fast-growing cells, including cancer cells.... One of the newest and most promising treatments is gene therapy ... "

Use evidence.

Finding evidence is one thing; using it well is another. To marshal evidence in support of your claim, follow three guidelines:

1. **Go for quality and variety, not just quantity.** More evidence is not necessarily better. Instead, support your points with sound evidence in different forms. Quality evidence is ...

   - **accurate:** correct and verifiable in each detail.
   - **complete:** filled with pertinent facts.
   - **concrete:** filled with specifics.
   - **relevant:** clearly related to the claim.
   - **current:** reliably up-to-date.
   - **authoritative:** backed by expertise, training, and knowledge.
   - **appealing:** able to influence readers.

2. **Use inductive and deductive patterns of logic.** Depending on your purpose, use inductive or deductive reasoning. (See page 18.)

Induction: Inductive reasoning works from the particular toward general conclusions. In a persuasive essay using induction, look at facts first, find a pattern in them, and then lead the reader to your conclusion.

> For example, in "Nuclear Is Not the Answer," Alyssa Woudstra first examines the benefits and liabilities of nuclear energy versus fossil fuels before asserting her claim that using the latter is a better choice. (See pages 311–313.)

Deduction: Deductive reasoning—the opposite of inductive reasoning—starts from accepted truths and applies them to a new situation so as to reach a conclusion about it. For deduction to be sound, be sure the starting principles or facts are true, the new situation is accurately described, and the application is logical.

> For example, Martin Luther King opened his 1963 "I Have a Dream" speech by noting that more than one hundred years earlier, the Emancipation Proclamation promised African Americans justice and freedom. He then described the continuing unjust treatment of African Americans, deducing that the promises in the Proclamation remained unfulfilled. (See pages 334–337.)

3. **Reason using valid warrants.** To make sense, claims and their supporting reasons must have a logical connection. That connection is called the *warrant*—the often unspoken thinking used to relate the reasoning to the claim. If warrants are good, arguments hold water; if warrants are faulty, then arguments break down. In other words, beware of faulty assumptions.

Check the short argument outlined below. Which of the warrants seem reasonable and strong, and which seem weak? Where does the argument fail?

> **Reasoning:** If current trends in water usage continue, the reservoir will be empty in two years.
>
> **Claim:** Therefore, Emeryville should immediately shut down its public swimming pools.

Unstated Warrants or Assumptions:

> It is not good for the reservoir to be empty.
>
> The swimming pools draw significant amounts of water from the reservoir.
>
> Emptying the pools would help raise the level of the reservoir.
>
> No other action would better prevent the reservoir from emptying.
>
> It is worse to have an empty reservoir than an empty swimming pool.

INSIGHT Because an argument is no stronger than its warrants, you must make sure that your reasoning clearly and logically supports your claims.

Identifying Logical Fallacies

Fallacies are false arguments—that is, bits of fuzzy, dishonest, or incomplete thinking. They may crop up in your own thinking, in your opposition's thinking, or in such public "arguments" as ads, political appeals, and talk shows. Because fallacies may sway an unsuspecting audience, they are dangerously persuasive. By learning to recognize fallacies, however, you may identify them in opposing arguments and eliminate them from your own writing. In this section, logical fallacies are grouped according to how they falsify an argument.

Distorting the Issue

The following fallacies falsify an argument by twisting the logical framework.

- **Bare Assertion** The most basic way to distort an issue is to deny that it exists. This fallacy claims, "That's just how it is."

  > The private ownership of handguns is a constitutional right. (*Objection:* The claim shuts off discussion of the U.S. Constitution, the legal process of amending the Constitution, or the reasons for regulation.)

- **Begging the Question** Also known as circular reasoning, this fallacy arises from assuming in the basis of your argument the very point you need to prove.

  > We don't need a useless film series when every third student owns a DVD player or VCR. (*Objection:* There may be uses for a public film series that private video viewing can't provide. The word "useless" begs the question.)

- **Oversimplification** This fallacy reduces complexity to simplicity. Beware of phrases like "It's a simple question of." Serious issues are rarely simple.

  > Capital punishment is a simple question of protecting society.

- **Either/Or Thinking** Also known as black-and-white thinking, this fallacy reduces all options to two extremes. Frequently, it derives from a clear bias.

  > Either this community develops light-rail transportation or the community will not grow in the future. (*Objection:* The claim ignores the possibility that growth may occur through other means.)

- **Complex Question** Sometimes by phrasing a question a certain way, a person ignores or covers up a more basic question.

  > Why can't we bring down the prices that corrupt gas stations are charging? (*Objection:* This question ignores a more basic question—"Are gas stations really corrupt?")

- **Straw Man** In this fallacy, the writer argues against a claim that is easily refuted. Typically, such a claim exaggerates or misrepresents the opponents' position.

  > Those who oppose euthanasia must believe that individuals who are terminally ill deserve to suffer.

Sabotaging the Argument

These fallacies falsify the argument by twisting it. They destroy reason and replace it with something hollow or misleading.

- **Red Herring** This strange term comes from the practice of dragging a stinky fish across a trail to throw tracking dogs off the scent. When a person puts forth a volatile idea that pulls readers away from the real issue, readers become distracted. Suppose the argument addresses drilling for oil in the Arctic National Wildlife Refuge (ANWR) of Alaska, and the writer begins with this statement:

  > In 1989, the infamous oil spill of the *Exxon Valdez* led to massive animal deaths and enormous environmental degradation of the coastline. (*Objection:* Introducing this notorious oil spill distracts from the real issue—how oil drilling will affect the ANWR.)

- **Misuse of Humor** Jokes, satire, and irony can lighten the mood and highlight a truth; when humor distracts or mocks, however, it undercuts the argument. What effect would the mocking tone of this statement have in an argument about tanning beds in health clubs?

  > People who use tanning beds will just turn into wrinkled old prunes or leathery sun-dried tomatoes!

- **Appeal to Pity** This fallacy engages in a misleading tug on the heartstrings. Instead of using a measured emotional appeal, an appeal to pity seeks to manipulate the audience into agreement.

  > Affirmative action policies ruined this young man's life. Because of them, he was denied admission to Centerville College.

- **Use of Threats** A simple but unethical way of sabotaging an argument is to threaten opponents. More often than not, a threat is merely implied: "If you don't accept my argument, you'll regret it."

  > If we don't immediately start drilling for oil in the ANWR, you will soon face hour-long lines at gas stations from New York to California.

- **Bandwagon Mentality** Someone implies that a claim cannot be true because a majority of people are opposed to it, or it must be true because a majority support it. (History shows that people in the minority have often had the better argument.) At its worst, such an appeal manipulates people's desire to belong or be accepted.

  > It's obvious to intelligent people that cockroaches live only in the apartments of dirty people. (*Objection:* Based on popular opinion, the claim appeals to a kind of prejudice and ignores scientific evidence about cockroaches.)

- **Appeal to Popular Sentiment** This fallacy consists of associating your position with something popularly loved: the American flag, baseball, apple pie. Appeals to popular sentiment sidestep thought to play on feelings.

  > Anyone who has seen *Bambi* could never condone hunting deer.

Drawing Faulty Conclusions from the Evidence

This group of fallacies falsifies the argument by short-circuiting proper logic in favor of assumptions or faulty thinking.

- **Appeal to Ignorance** This fallacy suggests that because no one has proven a particular claim, it must be false; or, because no one has disproven a claim, it must be true. Appeals to ignorance unfairly shift the burden of proof onto someone else.

    > Flying saucers are real. No scientific explanation has ruled them out.

- **Hasty or Broad Generalization** Such a claim is based on too little evidence or allows no exceptions. In jumping to a conclusion, the writer may use intensifiers such as *all, every,* or *never.*

    > Today's voters spend too little time reading and too much time being taken in by 30-second sound bites. (*Objection:* Quite a few voters may, in fact, spend too little time reading about the issues, but it is unfair to suggest that this is true of everyone.)

- **False Cause** This well-known fallacy confuses sequence with causation: If *A* comes before *B, A* must have caused *B.* However, *A* may be one of several causes, or *A* and *B* may be only loosely related, or the connection between *A* and *B* may be entirely coincidental.

    > Since that new school opened, drug use among young people has skyrocketed. Better that the school had never been built.

- **Slippery Slope** This fallacy argues that a single step will start an unstoppable chain of events. While such a slide may occur, the prediction lacks evidence.

    > If we legalize marijuana, it's only a matter of time before hard drugs follow and America becomes a nation of junkies and addicts.

Misusing Evidence

These fallacies falsify the argument by abusing or distorting the evidence.

- **Impressing with Numbers** In this case, the writer drowns readers in statistics and numbers that overwhelm them into agreement. In addition, the numbers haven't been properly interpreted.

    > At 35 ppm, CO levels factory-wide are only 10 ppm above the OSHA recommendation, which is 25 ppm. Clearly, that 10 ppm is insignificant in the big picture, and the occasional readings in some areas of between 40 and 80 ppm are aberrations that can safely be ignored. (*Objection:* The 10 ppm may be significant, and higher readings may indicate real danger.)

- **Half-Truths** A half-truth contains part of but not the whole truth. Because it leaves out "the rest of the story," it is both true and false simultaneously.

    > The new welfare bill is good because it will get people off the public dole. (*Objection:* This may be true, but the bill may also cause undue suffering for some truly needy individuals.)

- **Unreliable Testimonial** An appeal to authority has force only if the authority is qualified in the proper field. If he or she is not, the testimony is irrelevant. Note that fame is not the same thing as authority.

  > On her talk show, Alberta Magnus recently claimed that most pork sold in the United States is tainted. (*Objection:* Although Magnus may be an articulate talk show host, she is not an expert on food safety.)

- **Attack Against the Person** This fallacy, also called an "*ad hominem* attack," directs attention to a person's character, lifestyle, or beliefs rather than to the issue.

  > Would you accept the opinion of a candidate who experimented with drugs in college?

- **Hypothesis Contrary to Fact** This fallacy relies on "if only" thinking. It bases the claim on an assumption of what would have happened if something else had, or had not, happened. Being pure speculation, such a claim cannot be tested.

  > If only multiculturalists hadn't pushed through affirmative action, the United States would be a united nation.

- **False Analogy** Sometimes a person will argue that X is good (or bad) because it is like Y. Such an analogy may be valid, but it weakens the argument if the grounds for the comparison are vague or unrelated.

  > Don't bother voting in this election; it's a stinking quagmire. (*Objection:* Comparing the election to a "stinking quagmire" is unclear and exaggerated.)

Misusing Language

Essentially, all logical fallacies misuse language. However, three fallacies falsify the argument, especially by the misleading use of words.

- **Obfuscation** This fallacy involves using fuzzy terms like *throughput* and *downlink* to muddy the issue. These words may make simple ideas sound more profound than they really are, or they may make false ideas sound true.

  > Through the fully functional developmental process of a streamlined target-refractory system, the U.S. military will successfully reprioritize its data throughputs. (*Objection:* What does this sentence mean?)

- **Ambiguity** Ambiguous statements can be interpreted in two or more opposite ways. Although ambiguity can result from unintentional careless thinking, writers sometimes use ambiguity to obscure a position.

  > Many women need to work to support their children through school, but they would be better off at home. (*Objection:* Does *they* refer to *children* or *women*? What does *better off* mean? These words and phrases can be interpreted in opposite ways.)

- **Slanted Language** By choosing words with strong positive or negative connotations, a writer can draw readers away from the true logic of the argument. Here is an example of three synonyms for the word stubborn that the philosopher Bertrand Russell once used to illustrate the bias in slanted language:

  > I am firm. You are obstinate. He is pigheaded.

Engaging the Opposition

Think of an argument as an intelligent, lively dialogue with readers. Anticipate their questions, concerns, objections, and counterarguments. Then follow these guidelines.

Make concessions.

By offering concessions—recognizing points made by the other side—you acknowledge your argument's limits and the truth of other positions. Paradoxically, such concessions strengthen your overall argument by making it seem more credible. Concede your points graciously, using words such as the following:

Admittedly	Granted	I agree that	I cannot argue with
It is true that	You're right	I accept	No doubt
Of course	I concede that	Perhaps	Certainly it's the case

> While foot-and-mouth disease is not dangerous to humans, other animal diseases are.

Develop rebuttals.

Even when you concede a point, you can often answer that objection by rebutting it. A good rebuttal is a small, tactful argument aimed at a weak spot in the opposing argument. Try these strategies:

1. **Point out the counterargument's limits** by putting the opposing point in a larger context. Show that the counterargument omits something important.
2. **Tell the other side of the story.** Offer an opposing interpretation of the evidence, or counter with stronger, more reliable, more convincing evidence.
3. **Address logical fallacies in the counterargument.** Check for faulty reasoning or emotional manipulation. For example, if the counterargument presents a half-truth, offer information that presents "the rest of the story."

> It is true that Chernobyl occurred more than twenty years ago, so safety measures for nuclear reactors have been greatly improved. However, that single accident is still affecting millions of people who were exposed to the radiation.

Consolidate your claim.

After making concessions and rebutting objections, you may need to regroup. Restate your claim so carefully that the weight of your whole argument can rest on it.

> Whereas bovine spongiform encephalopathy is rare, it is potentially extremely dangerous, if it is allowed to spread unchecked and untreated.

Using Appropriate Appeals

For your argument to be persuasive, it must not only be logical, but also "feel right." It must treat readers as real people by appealing to their common sense, hopes, pride, and notion of right and wrong. How do you appeal to all these concerns? Do the following: (1) build credibility, (2) make logical appeals, and (3) focus on readers' needs.

Build credibility.

A persuasive argument is credible—so trustworthy that readers can change their minds painlessly. To build credibility, observe these rules:

- **Be thoroughly honest.** Demonstrate integrity toward the topic—don't falsify data, spin evidence, or ignore facts. Document your sources and cite them wherever appropriate.
- **Make realistic claims, projections, and promises.** Avoid emotionally charged statements, pie-in-the-sky forecasts, and undeliverable deals.
- **Develop and maintain trust.** From your first word to your last, develop trust—in your attitude toward the topic, your treatment of readers, and your respect for opposing viewpoints.

Make logical appeals.

Arguments stand or fall on their logical strength, but your readers' acceptance of those arguments is often affected more by the emotional appeal of your ideas and evidence. To avoid overly emotional appeals, follow these guidelines:

- **Engage readers positively.** Appeal to their better natures—to their sense of honor, justice, social commitment, altruism, and enlightened self-interest. Avoid appeals geared toward ignorance, prejudice, selfishness, or fear.
- **Use a fitting tone.** Use a tone that is appropriate for the topic, purpose, situation, and audience.
- **Aim to motivate, not manipulate, readers.** While you do want them to accept your viewpoint, it's not a win-at-all-costs situation. Avoid bullying, guilt-tripping, name calling, and exaggerated tugs on heartstrings.
- **Don't trash-talk the opposition.** Show tact, respect, and understanding. Focus on issues, not personalities.
- **Use arguments and evidence that readers can understand and appreciate.** If readers find your thinking too complex, too simple, or too strange, you've lost them.

INSIGHT Remember the adage: The best argument is so clear and convincing that it sounds like an explanation.

Focus on readers' needs.

Instead of playing on readers' emotions, connect your argument with readers' needs and values. Follow these guidelines:

- **Know your real readers.** Who are they—peers, professors, or fellow citizens? What are their allegiances, their worries, their dreams?
- **Picture readers as resistant.** Accept that your readers, including those inclined to agree with you, need convincing. Think of them as alert, cautious, and demanding—but also interested.
- **Use appeals that match needs and values.** Your argument may support or challenge readers' needs and values. To understand those needs, study the table below, which is based loosely on the thinking of psychologist Abraham Maslow. Maslow's hierarchy ranks people's needs on a scale from the most basic to the most complex. The table begins at the bottom with *having necessities* (a basic need) and ends at the top with *helping others* (a more complex need). For example, if you're writing to argue for more affordable housing for the elderly, you'd argue differently to legislators (whose focus is on *helping others*) than to the elderly who need the housing (whose focus is on *having necessities*). Follow these guidelines:

  - Use appeals that match the foremost needs and values of your readers.
  - If appropriate, constructively challenge those needs and values.
  - Whenever possible, phrase your appeals in positive terms.
  - After analyzing your readers' needs, choose a persuasive theme for your argument—a positive benefit, advantage, or outcome that readers can expect if they accept your claim. Use this theme to help readers to care about your claims.

Reader needs . . .	Use persuasive appeals to . . .
To make the world better by helping others	values and social obligations
To achieve by being good at something getting recognition	self-fulfillment, status appreciation
To belong by being part of a group	group identity, acceptance
To survive by avoiding threats having necessities	safety, security physical needs

fig. 17.3

Critical-Thinking and Writing Activities

As directed by your instructor, complete the following critical-thinking and writing activities by yourself or with classmates.

1. Select an essay from chapters 18–20. Read the essay carefully. Then describe and evaluate the essay's argumentative strategies by answering the questions below:
    - What is the essay's main claim? Is it a claim of truth, value, or policy?
    - Is the claim arguable—that is, is it supportable, appropriately qualified, and effectively phrased?
    - What arguments does the writer develop in support of the claim? Are these arguments logical?
    - What types of evidence does the writer provide to support his or her discussion?
    - Is the evidence valid, sufficient, current, and accurate?
    - Does the writer effectively address questions, alternatives, objections, and counterarguments?

2. Review the essay that you read for the first activity, and then answer the following questions:
    - Describe the writer's tone. Does it effectively engage readers?
    - Does the argument seem credible and authoritative? Explain.
    - Identify ways that the writer connects with readers' needs and values. How does he or she develop a persuasive theme that appeals to those needs and values?

Learning-Objectives Checklist ✓

Have you achieved this chapter's learning objectives? Check your progress with the items below, revisiting topics in the chapter as needed. *I have . . .*

____ examined the process of building an argument, starting with situation analysis, researching the topic, and developing clear and logical reasoning (294–295).

____ analyzed the logical nature and persuasive effects of three types of claims: truth, value, and policy (296–297).

____ revised arguments, correcting these weaknesses: all-or-nothing claims, obvious claims, trivial assertions, and claims lacking needed qualifiers (297).

____ analyzed the strengths and weaknesses of nine types of evidence (298–299).

____ identified and corrected logical fallacies in others' arguments and in my own (301–304).

____ linked claims and their supporting reasons with valid warrants (300).

____ revised and strengthened my arguments by making needed concessions, developing rebuttals, and generating appropriate appeals (305–307).

____ drafted, revised, and edited a unified, well-reasoned argument with fitting appeals, logical claims, and current, reliable evidence (306–307).

Chapter 18

Taking a Position

Sometimes you just have to take a stand. An issue comes up that upsets you or challenges your thinking, and in response, you say, "Okay, this is what I believe, and this is why I believe it."

Learning to read and write position papers enables you to do this. The reading skills help you analyze others' positions, recognize their strengths, and identify their weaknesses. The writing skills help you probe a topic, refine your own perspective on the issues, educate others about the topic, and convince them that your position has value.

This chapter will help you refine both skills. In addition, because both skills are used across the college curriculum and at work, learning this chapter's writing skills and strategies will help you succeed in the classroom today and in the workplace throughout your career.

Visually Speaking   Study Figure 18.1. What does it suggest about how or why people take a position on an issue? What written argument might articulate the position pictured in the photograph?

Learning **Objectives**

By working through this chapter, you will be able to

- critically examine and assess the arguments in position papers.
- identify logical fallacies that are especially a danger when taking a position.
- make concessions and rebut opposing arguments.
- develop claims with reliable evidence.
- write a logical position paper in a measured, rational voice.

spirit of america / Shutterstock.com

fig. 18.1

Reading Position Writing

How should you read a position paper? The instructions below will guide you.

Consider the rhetorical situation.

Think first about how the writer uses persuasion to achieve a specific purpose, affect a particular audience, and address a given topic.

- **Purpose:** In most cases, writers produce position papers in order to educate and to persuade: they want (1) to inform readers about the nature and relevance of a topic and (2) to persuade them that the position presented in the paper is the best, most reasonable option.
- **Readers:** A writer may address a variety of readers: people opposed to the writer's position, people uncertain of what position to take, people unaware that an issue exists, or even people who agree with the writer's position but are looking for sensible reasons. Good writers shape the content, organization, and tone of position essays to effectively address such intended readers.
- **Topic:** The topics addressed in meaningful position papers are debatable issues about which informed people can reasonably disagree. Therefore, as a reader, you will learn more about a paper's topic by focusing not only on the writer's position, but also on the reasoning that she or he uses to develop that position, including her or his attention to alternative positions.

Consider qualities of strong arguments.

When reading a position paper, look for the following:

- **Informed Writing:** The writer has researched the topic thoroughly and understands it fully, including positions other than his or her own.
- **Logical Writing:** The writer presents the topic objectively, describes alternative positions fairly, and takes the position supported by the best evidence and strongest logic. The writing avoids logical fallacies such as oversimplification, either/or thinking, straw-man claims, red-herring assertions, appeals to pity, or attacks against opponents. (For information on these and other fallacies, see pages 301–304.)
- **Engaging Writing:** Rather than quarreling or pontificating, the writer converses with readers making reasonable concessions, rebutting opposing arguments, and consolidating or refocusing claims. (For details on these strategies, see page 305.)

Reading Position Papers

As you read the essays on the following pages, consider these questions:

1. What is the topic, and is it debatable, stated fairly, and addressed fully?
2. What are the writer's claims, and are they supported by reliable evidence?
3. Is the overall argument clear, unified, and free of logical fallacies?
4. Is the tone measured, reasonable, and free of manipulative language?

Sample Position Paper

Student writer Alyssa Woudstra wrote the following essay to take a position on an environmental issue—energy production.

The title partly declares the position.	**Nuclear Is Not the Answer**
Alyssa starts with common ground and narrows to her position on energy production.	In recent years, it has become popular to be "green" in all areas of life. Celebrities and corporations constantly advertise natural cleaning products, fuel-efficient cars, and energy-efficient light bulbs. Governments offer home-improvement grants to people who renovate their homes to include low-flush toilets, weather-proof windows, and additional insulation. Due to climate change and pollution, concern for the environment is rising. One major issue centers on which type of energy production is best for the environment. Nuclear power and fossil fuels are two major methods for energy production, and nuclear power could be seen as the "greener" option. However, the risks of nuclear power far outweigh its benefits, making fossil fuels the safer and more environmentally responsible option.
She examines the positives of what she actually opposes.	As a significant method of energy production, nuclear power does offer distinct advantages. The Nuclear Energy Institute's statistics show that nuclear energy accounted for fourteen percent of the world's electricity production in 2008, and that as of September 2009, thirty countries were using nuclear power ("Around the World"). This popularity speaks to nuclear power's advantages over fossil fuels. First, nuclear power plants do not release the harmful emissions that coal-burning plants do, so nuclear power does not contribute greatly to global warming (Evans 115). Second, a single nuclear power plant can produce a large amount of energy, making nuclear an efficient source ("Pros and Cons"). In fact, according to Robert Evans, "The amount of thermal energy released from just one kilogram of U235 undergoing fission is equivalent to that obtained by burning some 2.5 million kilograms, or 2500 tonnes, of coal" (116).
She turns to the disadvantages of nuclear energy: its risks and dangers.	Nevertheless, these advantages of nuclear power are outweighed by its disadvantages. Nuclear power plants produce radioactive waste, which is an enormous health and safety concern. The waste cannot simply be disposed of but must be carefully stored for hundreds of generations. The isotopes used in nuclear reactions have half-lives of thousands of years. For example, plutonium-239 has a half-life of around 24,000 years (American Assembly 24). This radioactive waste must be stored safely to prevent radiation poisoning, but it would be nearly impossible to do so for that long.
The writer reminds readers of a historical illustration.	A further danger of nuclear power is that while every safety precaution might be in place, it is possible for terrible accidents to happen. The most famous nuclear accident took place on April 26, 1986, when reactor number four at the Chernobyl Nuclear Power Plant in the Ukraine, which was then part of the Soviet Union, exploded after a power excursion. That explosion then caused the rest of the plant

_1_

_2_

_3_

_4_

to explode (Hawks et. al. 98-102). This accident released one hundred times more radiation than the bombing of Hiroshima and Nagasaki combined ("No More Chernobyls"). Chernobyl's radiation spread all over Europe, affecting people as far away as Romania and Bulgaria, exposing more than 600,000 to the effects of radiation poisoning (Medvedev 194-216). More than twenty years after Chernobyl, people are still dying from cancer that was likely caused by the disaster.

Alyssa concedes and rebuts a concern.

Whereas it is true that Chernobyl occurred more than twenty years ago, recent   5
disasters (such as the March 2011 incident at the Fukushima Nuclear Power Plant) demonstrate that additional accidents could happen at any other nuclear power plant currently in use. In addition, it is also true that if more nuclear power plants are built, the risk of similar accidents will rise.

Beyond accidents, however, is the possibility of deliberate sabotage in the form   6
of terrorism ("Pros and Cons"). If terrorists wanted to cause mass devastation, they could attack a nuclear power plant or become employees that purposely cause errors to create an explosion. On September 11, 2001, millions of people were affected at once. If a power plant were attacked, it would also affect millions, since it would cause the loss of not only many jobs but also many lives. Moreover, the risk of terrorism also surrounds the nuclear waste left behind after the reactions. Easier to obtain than pure uranium, such waste could be used to build "dirty bombs" (Evans 133).

Beyond the risks and dangers of nuclear power, still another argument against   7
it is that it is nonrenewable. Fossil fuels are also nonrenewable, but nuclear power is not an alternative in this way. In their reactors, nuclear power plants use uranium, a rare element. It is estimated that the Earth's supply of Uranium will last only thirty to sixty years, depending on how much is actually used in reactors ("Pros and Cons").

With a question, she turns to her own position, acknowledging its problems.

But is energy from fossil fuels really better than nuclear power? The burning   8
of fossil fuels (including coal, oil, and natural gas) is the most common method of energy production. Like nuclear, fossil fuels are nonrenewable. However, burning fossil fuels, for the time being, is a better option than using nuclear energy. It is true that using fossil fuels has a negative effect on the environment. In order to obtain fossil fuels, much damage is caused to the environment by drilling for oil or mining for coal. The 2010 Deepwater Horizon oil spill (also referred to as the BP oil spill) is a prime example. Also, burning fossil fuels produces gases that can aggravate respiratory conditions like asthma and emits greenhouse gases that damage the atmosphere. Moreover, particles emitted from smokestacks collect in clouds, causing acid rain (Sweet 25). With oil, spills can contaminate groundwater and surface water, creating risks to animals, plants, and humans.

Despite the fact that using fossil fuels involves many risks, it has some   9
advantages over nuclear energy. Significantly, fossil fuels are much less expensive than uranium. Although it is still expensive to access fossil fuels, it is drastically cheaper than the cost of nuclear energy. In addition, if large deposits of coal or oil

Alyssa supports her position on fossil fuels by stressing its advantages and calling for improvements.

are found, it will not be necessary to excavate in as many places to retrieve them. Although a larger area would be disturbed, fewer sites would be affected. Also, while fossil fuels are nonrenewable, they may be used wisely, conserving them until a better energy source can be established (Heron).

However, perhaps the biggest advantage of fossil fuel energy over nuclear energy lies in the possibility of progress to make current methods more environmentally friendly. At this time, burning coal for power uses only one-third of its potential energy (Heron). If scientists study more efficient uses of the coal, this waste, as well as many health and environmental concerns, could be prevented. For example, burning coal can be made cleaner through electrostatic precipitators. Also known as "smokestack scrubbers," these filters can be used in smokestacks to prevent soot particles from getting into the air. As the soot-filled air passes through the smokestack, it goes through a set of wires that negatively charge the soot particles. As the air continues through the pipe, it passes through positively charged metal plates. The negatively charged soot particles, which are made up mostly of unburned carbon, "stick" to the positively charged plates, and the particle-free air continues out the smokestack. The stuck particles are then either manually scraped or automatically shaken off by the machine itself ("Static Electricity"). If more factories used electrostatic precipitators, a large amount of air pollution would be prevented.

She restates her position and places it within a larger context of environmental changes.

Although it is not ideal, burning fossil fuels is still a better option than nuclear power until renewable energy sources such as wind, solar, and geothermal power become more available. Clearly, society must continue to work toward greater conservation and use of renewable energy. As stewards of the Earth, all humans should be concerned about the environment. If people continue to use nuclear power, the risks related to accidents, sabotage, and radioactive waste will not only be their responsibility but will also impact their descendants for many generations.

Note: The Works Cited page is not shown. For sample pages, see MLA (pages 493–534) and APA (pages 535–564).

Reading for Better Writing

Working by yourself or with a group, answer these questions:

1. Alyssa begins her essay by examining extensively an opposing position—support for nuclear energy. How effective is this strategy?

2. Review how Alyssa supports her position on energy from fossil fuels. How complete and compelling is this support?

3. Review Alyssa's reference to the BP oil spill (page 312). Then explain why this information does or does not strengthen her argument.

"Nuclear Is Not the Answer" by Alyssa Woudstra. Used by permission of the author.

Essays Taking Contrary Positions

Sometimes, a writer takes a position in response to another writer, as shown in the following essays by Gary Steiner and Natalie Angier. Steiner, a professor of philosophy at Bucknell University and author of *Animals and the Moral Community,* advocates a pure vegan lifestyle in "Animal, Vegetable, Miserable" below. Angier's essay (pages 317–319), "Sorry, Vegans: Brussel Sprouts Like to Live, Too," responds in part to Steiner. Both pieces were published in *The New York Times.*

Animal, Vegetable, Miserable

> **The writer introduces the topic.**

LATELY more people have begun to express an interest in where the meat they eat   *1* comes from and how it was raised. Were the animals humanely treated? Did they have a good quality of life before the death that turned them into someone's dinner?

Some of these questions, which reach a fever pitch in the days leading up to   *2* Thanksgiving, pertain to the ways in which animals are treated. (Did your turkey get to live outdoors?) Others focus on the question of how eating the animals in question will affect the consumer's health and well-being. (Was it given hormones and antibiotics?)

> **He states the core issue and identifies his own position.**

None of these questions, however, make any consideration of whether it is wrong   *3* to kill animals for human consumption. And even when people ask this question, they almost always find a variety of resourceful answers that purport to justify the killing and consumption of animals in the name of human welfare. Strict ethical vegans, of which I am one, are customarily excoriated for equating our society's treatment of animals with mass murder. Can anyone seriously consider animal suffering even remotely comparable to human suffering? Those who answer with a resounding no typically argue in one of two ways.

> **He summarizes opposing positions and offers an example.**

Some suggest that human beings but not animals are made in God's image and   *4* hence stand in much closer proximity to the divine than any non-human animal; according to this line of thought, animals were made expressly for the sake of humans and may be used without scruple to satisfy their needs and desires. There is ample support in the Bible and in the writings of Christian thinkers like Augustine and Thomas Aquinas for this pointedly anthropocentric way of devaluing animals.

> **He offers a second example.**

Others argue that the human capacity for abstract thought makes us capable of   *5* suffering that both qualitatively and quantitatively exceeds the suffering of any non-human animal. Philosophers like Jeremy Bentham, who is famous for having based moral status not on linguistic or rational capacities but rather on the capacity to suffer, argue that because animals are incapable of abstract thought, they are imprisoned in an eternal present, have no sense of the extended future and hence cannot be said to have an interest in continued existence.

The most penetrating and iconoclastic response to this sort of reasoning came from   *6* the writer Isaac Bashevis Singer in his story "The Letter Writer," in which he called the slaughter of animals the "eternal Treblinka."

He uses an anecdote to present a counter-argument.

The story depicts an encounter between a man and a mouse. The man, Herman Gombiner, contemplates his place in the cosmic scheme of things and concludes that there is an essential connection between his own existence as "a child of God" and the "holy creature" scuffling about on the floor in front of him.   *7*

Steiner states the story's theme and explains its relevance.

Surely, he reflects, the mouse has some capacity for thought; Gombiner even thinks that the mouse has the capacity to share love and gratitude with him. Not merely a means for the satisfaction of human desires, nor a mere nuisance to be exterminated, this tiny creature possesses the same dignity that any conscious being possesses. In the face of that inherent dignity, Gombiner concludes, the human practice of delivering animals to the table in the form of food is abhorrent and inexcusable.   *8*

He castigates "free-range" arguments.

Many of the people who denounce the ways in which we treat animals in the course of raising them for human consumption never stop to think about this profound contradiction. Instead, they make impassioned calls for more "humanely" raised meat. Many people soothe their consciences by purchasing only free-range fowl and eggs, blissfully ignorant that "free range" has very little if any practical significance. Chickens may be labeled free-range even if they've never been outside or seen a speck of daylight in their entire lives. And that Thanksgiving turkey? Even if it is raised "free range," it still lives a life of pain and confinement that ends with the butcher's knife.   *9*

He identifies his opponents' "real" reason for inaction as "not caring."

He offers one acceptable solution.

How can intelligent people who purport to be deeply concerned with animal welfare and respectful of life turn a blind eye to such practices? And how can people continue to eat meat when they become aware that nearly 53 billion land animals are slaughtered every year for human consumption? The simple answer is that most people just don't care about the lives or fortunes of animals. If they did care, they would learn as much as possible about the ways in which our society systematically abuses animals, and they would make what is at once a very simple and a very difficult choice: to forswear the consumption of animal products of all kinds.   *10*

The easy part of this consists in seeing clearly what ethics requires and then just plain doing it. The difficult part: You just haven't lived until you've tried to function as a strict vegan in a meat-crazed society. What were once the most straightforward activities become a constant ordeal. You might think that it's as simple as just removing meat, eggs and dairy products from your diet, but it goes a lot deeper than that.   *11*

He defines and advocates a pure vegan lifestyle.

To be a really strict vegan is to strive to avoid all animal products, and this includes materials like leather, silk and wool, as well as a panoply of cosmetics and medications. The more you dig, the more you learn about products you would never stop to think might contain or involve animal products in their production—like wine and beer (isinglass, a kind of gelatin derived from fish bladders, is often used to "fine," or purify, these beverages), refined sugar (bone char is sometimes used to bleach it) or Band-Aids (animal products in the adhesive). Just last week I was told that those little comfort strips on most razor blades contain animal fat.   *12*

To go down this road is to stare headlong into an abyss that, to paraphrase Nietzsche, will ultimately stare back at you.   *13*

The challenges faced by a vegan don't end with the nuts and bolts of material   *14*
existence. You face quite a few social difficulties as well, perhaps the chief one being how
one should feel about spending time with people who are not vegans.

Is it O.K. to eat dinner with people who are eating meat? What do you say when   *15*
a dining companion says, "I'm really a vegetarian—I don't eat red meat at home."
(I've heard it lots of times, always without any prompting from me.) What do you do
when someone starts to grill you (so to speak) about your vegan ethics during dinner?
(Wise vegans always defer until food isn't around.) Or when someone starts to lodge
accusations to the effect that you consider yourself morally superior to others, or that it
is ridiculous to worry so much about animals when there is so much human suffering in
the world? (Smile politely and ask them to pass the seitan.)

> **Steiner acknowledges the challenges of his position.**

Let me be candid: By and large, meat-eaters are a self-righteous bunch. The number   *16*
of vegans I know personally is . . . five. And I have been a vegan for almost 15 years,
having been a vegetarian for almost 15 before that.

Five. I have lost more friends than this over arguments about animal ethics. One   *17*
lapidary conclusion to be drawn here is that people take deadly seriously the prerogative
to use animals as sources of satisfaction. Not only for food, but as beasts of burden, as
raw materials and as sources of captive entertainment—which is the way animals are
used in zoos, circuses and the like.

These uses of animals are so institutionalized, so normalized in our society that it   *18*
is difficult to find the critical distance needed to see them as the horrors that they are:
so many forms of subjection, servitude and—in the case of killing animals for human
consumption and other purposes—outright murder.

People who are ethical vegans believe that differences in intelligence between   *19*
human and non-human animals have no moral significance whatsoever. The fact that
my cat can't appreciate Schubert's late symphonies and can't perform syllogistic logic
does not mean that I am entitled to use him as an organic toy, as if I were somehow not
only morally superior to him but virtually entitled to treat him as a commodity with
minuscule market value.

> **He concludes by stating that the core problem is humans' belief that they are fundamentally superior to animals.**

We have been trained by a history of thinking of which we are scarcely aware to   *20*
view non-human animals as resources we are entitled to employ in whatever ways we
see fit in order to satisfy our needs and desires. Yes, there are animal welfare laws. But
these laws have been formulated by, and are enforced by, people who proceed from the
proposition that animals are fundamentally inferior to human beings. At best, these laws
make living conditions for animals marginally better than they would be otherwise—
right up to the point when we send them to the slaughterhouse.

Think about that when you're picking out your free-range turkey, which has   *21*
absolutely nothing to be thankful for on Thanksgiving. All it ever had was a short and
miserable life, thanks to us intelligent, compassionate humans.

Questions on this and the following essay are on page 319.

Sorry, Vegans: Brussels Sprouts Like to Live, Too

The title introduces the topic and sets a playful tone.

I stopped eating pork about eight years ago, after a scientist happened to mention that the animal whose teeth most closely resemble our own is the pig. Unable to shake the image of a perky little pig flashing me a brilliant George Clooney smile, I decided it was easier to forgo the Christmas ham. A couple of years later, I gave up on all mammalian meat, period. I still eat fish and poultry, however, and pour eggnog in my coffee. My dietary decisions are arbitrary and inconsistent, and when friends ask why I'm willing to try the duck but not the lamb, I don't have a good answer. Food choices are often like that: difficult to articulate yet strongly held. And lately, debates over food choices have flared with particular vehemence.

Angier describes her position on meat eating as personal and arbitrary vs. strict and ideological.

In his new book, *Eating Animals,* the novelist Jonathan Safran Foer describes his gradual transformation from omnivorous, oblivious slacker who "waffled among any number of diets" to "committed vegetarian." Last month, Gary Steiner, a philosopher at Bucknell University, argued on the Op-Ed page of *The New York Times* that people should strive to be "strict ethical vegans" like himself, avoiding all products derived from animals, including wool and silk. Killing animals for human food and finery is nothing less than "outright murder," he said, Isaac Bashevis Singer's "eternal Treblinka."

She describes Steiner's position.

But before we cede the entire moral penthouse to "committed vegetarians" and "strong ethical vegans," we might consider that plants no more aspire to being stir-fried in a wok than a hog aspires to being peppercorn-studded in my Christmas clay pot. This is not meant as a trite argument or a chuckled aside. Plants are lively and seek to keep it that way. The more that scientists learn about the complexity of plants—their keen sensitivity to the environment, the speed with which they react to changes in the environment, and the extraordinary number of tricks that plants will rally to fight off attackers and solicit help from afar—the more impressed researchers become, and the less easily we can dismiss plants as so much fiberfill backdrop, passive sunlight collectors on which deer, antelope and vegans can conveniently graze. It's time for a green revolution, a reseeding of our stubborn animal minds.

She suggests Steiner's position (approves eating plants but disapproves eating meat) is logically inconsistent.

When plant biologists speak of their subjects, they use active verbs and vivid images. Plants "forage" for resources like light and soil nutrients and "anticipate" rough spots and opportunities. By analyzing the ratio of red light and far red light falling on their leaves, for example, they can sense the presence of other chlorophyllated competitors nearby and try to grow the other way. Their roots ride the underground "rhizosphere" and engage in cross-cultural and microbial trade.

Angier explains animal-plant parallels.

"Plants are not static or silly," said Monika Hilker of the Institute of Biology at the Free University of Berlin. "They respond to tactile cues, they recognize different wavelengths of light, they listen to chemical signals, they can even talk" through chemical signals. Touch, sight, hearing, speech. "These are sensory modalities and abilities we normally think of as only being in animals," Dr. Hilker said.

Plants can't run away from a threat but they can stand their ground. "They are very good at avoiding getting eaten," said Linda Walling of the University of California, Riverside. "It's an unusual situation where insects can overcome those defenses." At the smallest nip to its leaves, specialized cells on the plant's surface release chemicals to irritate the predator or sticky goo to entrap it. Genes in the plant's DNA are activated to wage systemwide chemical warfare, the plant's version of an immune response. We need terpenes, alkaloids, phenolics—let's move.   6

She supports her assertions by quoting several experts.

"I'm amazed at how fast some of these things happen," said Consuelo M. De Moraes of Pennsylvania State University. Dr. De Moraes and her colleagues did labeling experiments to clock a plant's systemic response time and found that, in less than 20 minutes from the moment the caterpillar had begun feeding on its leaves, the plant had plucked carbon from the air and forged defensive compounds from scratch.   7

She compares plants and humans.

Just because we humans can't hear them doesn't mean plants don't howl. Some of the compounds that plants generate in response to insect mastication—their feedback, you might say—are volatile chemicals that serve as cries for help. Such airborne alarm calls have been shown to attract both large predatory insects like dragon flies, which delight in caterpillar meat, and tiny parasitic insects, which can infect a caterpillar and destroy it from within.   8

Angier quotes an expert and playfully supports his opinion.

Enemies of the plant's enemies are not the only ones to tune into the emergency broadcast. "Some of these cues, some of these volatiles that are released when a focal plant is damaged," said Richard Karban of the University of California, Davis, "cause other plants of the same species, or even of another species, to likewise become more resistant to herbivores."   9

Yes, it's best to nip trouble in the bud.   10

She describes how plants communicate with insects.

Dr. Hilker and her colleagues, as well as other research teams, have found that certain plants can sense when insect eggs have been deposited on their leaves and will act immediately to rid themselves of the incubating menace. They may sprout carpets of tumorlike neoplasms to knock the eggs off, or secrete ovicides to kill them, or sound the S O S. Reporting in The Proceedings of the National Academy of Sciences, Dr. Hilker and her coworkers determined that when a female cabbage butterfly lays her eggs on a brussels sprout plant and attaches her treasures to the leaves with tiny dabs of glue, the vigilant vegetable detects the presence of a simple additive in the glue, benzyl cyanide. Cued by the additive, the plant swiftly alters the chemistry of its leaf surface to beckon female parasitic wasps. Spying the anchored bounty, the female wasps in turn inject their eggs inside, the gestating wasps feed on the gestating butterflies, and the plant's problem is solved.   11

She play-fully labels and describes the process.

Here's the lurid Edgar Allan Poetry of it: that benzyl cyanide tip-off had been donated to the female butterfly by the male during mating. "It's an anti-aphrodisiac pheromone, so that the female wouldn't mate anymore," Dr. Hilker said. "The male is trying to ensure his paternity, but he ends up endangering his own offspring." *12*

Plants eavesdrop on one another benignly and malignly. As they described in *Science* and other journals, Dr. De Moraes and her colleagues have discovered that seedlings of the dodder plant, a parasitic weed related to morning glory, can detect volatile chemicals released by potential host plants like the tomato. The young dodder then grows inexorably toward the host, until it can encircle the victim's stem and begin sucking the life phloem right out of it. The parasite can even distinguish between the scents of healthier and weaker tomato plants and then head for the hale one. *13*

In closing, Angier notes that to live, all animals must kill and eat something.

"Even if you have quite a bit of knowledge about plants," Dr. De Moraes said, "it's still surprising to see how sophisticated they can be." *14*

It's a small daily tragedy that we animals must kill to stay alive. Plants are the ethical autotrophs here, the ones that wrest their meals from the sun. Don't expect them to boast: they're too busy fighting to survive. *15*

Reading for Better Writing

Working by yourself or with a group, answer these questions:

1. On a sheet of paper, create two columns. In the left column, paraphrase Gary Steiner's core argument and list his supporting claims; and in the right column, paraphrase Natalie Angier's core argument and list her supporting claims. Explain how the positions are similar and different, and assess the strength of each writer's reasoning, taking into account the supporting claims and the evidence offered.

2. Describe each writer's voice and cite words or phrases exemplifying that voice. Then explain how each writer's voice colors his or her argument.

3. Examine each argument for logical fallacies such as either/or thinking (page 301), appeal to pity (page 302), and attack against the person (page 304). If you find examples, explain how they affect the writer's argument.

Sample Position Essay

David Blankenhorn, the founder and president of the Institute for American Values, is a Harvard graduate and the author of numerous publications, including *The Future of Marriage*. In the essay below, taken from his book, *Fatherless America*, Blankenhorn argues that America is losing its understanding of and appreciation for fatherhood.

Fatherless America

The United States is becoming an increasingly fatherless society. A generation ago, an American child could reasonably expect to grow up with his or her father. Today, an American child can reasonably expect not to. Fatherlessness is now approaching a rough parity with fatherhood as a defining feature of American childhood.

This astonishing fact is reflected in many statistics, but here are the two most important. Tonight, about 40 percent of American children will go to sleep in homes in which their fathers do not live. Before they reach the age of eighteen, more than half of our nation's children are likely to spend at least a significant portion of their childhoods living apart from their fathers. Never before in this country have so many children been voluntarily abandoned by their fathers. Never before have so many children grown up without knowing what it means to have a father.

Fatherlessness is the most harmful demographic trend of this generation. It is the leading cause of declining child well-being in our society. It is also the engine driving our most urgent social problems, from crime to adolescent pregnancy to child abuse to domestic violence against women. Yet, despite its scale and social consequences, fatherlessness is a problem that is frequently ignored or denied. Especially within our elite discourse, it remains largely a problem with no name.

> *Fatherlessness is the most harmful demographic trend of this generation. It is the leading cause of declining child well-being in our society.*

If this trend continues, fatherlessness is likely to change the shape of our society. Consider this prediction. After the year 2000, as people born after 1970 emerge as a large proportion of our working-age adult population, the United States will be a nation divided into two groups, separate and unequal. The two groups will work in the same economy, speak a common language, and remember the same national history. But they will live fundamentally divergent lives. One group will receive basic benefits—psychological, social, economic, educational, and moral—that are denied to the other group.

The primary fault line dividing the two groups will not be race, religion, class, education, or gender. It will be patrimony. One group will consist of those adults who grew up with the daily presence and provision of fathers. The other group will consist of those who did not. During the early years of this [twenty-first] century, these two groups already are roughly the same size. 5

Surely a crisis of this scale merits a response. At a minimum, it requires a serious debate. Why is fatherhood declining? What can be done about it? Can our society find ways to invigorate effective fatherhood as a norm of male behavior? Yet, to date, the public discussion on this topic has been remarkably weak and defeatist. There is a prevailing belief that not much can—or even should—be done to reverse the trend. 6

When the crime rate jumps, politicians promise to do something about it. When the unemployment rate rises, task forces assemble to address the problem. As random shootings increase, public health officials worry about the preponderance of guns. But when it comes to the mass defection of men from family life, not much happens. 7

There is debate, even alarm, about specific social problems. Divorce. Out-of-wedlock childbearing. Children growing up in poverty. Youth violence. Unsafe neighborhoods. Domestic violence. The weakening of parental authority. But in these discussions, we seldom acknowledge the underlying phenomenon that binds together these otherwise disparate issues: the flight of males from their children's lives. In fact, we seem to go out of our way to avoid the connection between our most pressing social problems and the trend of fatherlessness. 8

We avoid this connection because, as a society, we are changing our minds about the role of men in family life. As a cultural idea, our inherited understanding of fatherhood is under siege. Men in general, and fathers in particular, are increasingly viewed as superfluous to family life: either as expendable or as part of 9 the problem. Masculinity itself, understood as anything other than a rejection of what it has traditionally meant to be male, is typically treated with suspicion and even hostility in our cultural discourse. Consequently, our society is now manifestly unable to sustain, or even find reason to believe in, fatherhood as a distinctive domain of male activity.

The core question is simple: Does every child need a father? Increasingly, our society's answer is "no" or at least "not necessarily." Few idea shifts in this century are as consequential as this one. At stake is nothing less than what it means to be a man, who our children will be, and what kind of society we will become.   10

> *The core question is simple: Does every child need a father? Increasingly, our society's answer is "no" or at least "not necessarily."*

This [essay] is a criticism not simply of fatherlessness but of a culture of fatherlessness. For, in addition to losing fathers, we are losing   11
something larger: our idea of fatherhood. Unlike earlier periods of father absence in our history, we now face more than a physical loss affecting some homes. We face a cultural loss affecting every home. For this reason, the most important absence our society must confront is not the absence of fathers but the absence of our belief in fathers.

In a larger sense, this [essay] is a cultural criticism because fatherhood, much   12
more than motherhood, is a cultural invention. Its meaning for the individual man is shaped less by biology than by cultural script or story—a societal code that guides, and at times pressures, him into certain ways of acting and of understanding himself as a man.

Like motherhood, fatherhood is made up of both a biological and a social   13
dimension. Yet in societies across the world, mothers are far more successful than fathers at fusing these two dimensions into a coherent parental identity. Is the nursing mother playing a biological or social role? Is she feeding or bonding? We can hardly separate the two, so seamlessly are they woven together.

But fatherhood is a different matter. A father makes his sole biological   14
contribution at the moment of conception—nine months before the infant enters

the world. Because social paternity is only indirectly linked to biological paternity, the connection between the two cannot be assumed. The phrase "to father a child" usually refers only to the act of insemination, not to the responsibility for raising a child. What fathers contribute to their offspring after conception is largely a matter of cultural devising.

Moreover, despite their other virtues, men are not ideally suited to responsible fatherhood. Although they certainly have the capacity for fathering, men are inclined to sexual promiscuity and paternal waywardness. Anthropologically, human fatherhood constitutes what might be termed a necessary problem. It is necessary because, in all societies, child well-being and societal success hinge largely upon a high level of paternal investment: the willingness of adult males to devote energy and resources to the care of their offspring. It is a problem because adult males are frequently—indeed, increasingly—unwilling or unable to make that vital investment.   15

Because fatherhood is universally problematic in human societies, cultures must mobilize to devise and enforce the father role for men, coaxing and guiding them into fatherhood through a set of legal and extralegal pressures that require them to maintain a close alliance with their children's mother and to invest in their children. Because men do not volunteer for fatherhood as much as they are conscripted into it by the surrounding culture, only an authoritative cultural story of fatherhood can fuse biological and social paternity into a coherent male identity.   16

For exactly this reason, Margaret Mead and others have observed that the supreme test of any civilization is whether it can socialize men by teaching them to be fathers—creating a culture in which men acknowledge their paternity and willingly nurture their offspring. Indeed, if we can equate the essence of the antisocial male with violence, we can equate the essence of the socialized male with being a good father. Thus, at the center of our most important cultural imperative, we find the fatherhood script: the story that describes what it ought to mean for a man to have a child.   17

Just as the fatherhood script advances the social goal of harnessing male behavior to collective needs, it also reflects an individual purpose. That purpose, in a word, is happiness. Anthropologists have long understood that the genius of an   18 effective culture is its capacity to reconcile individual happiness with collective well-being. By situating individual lives within a social narrative, culture endows private behavior with larger meaning. By linking the self to moral purposes larger than the self, an effective culture tells us a story in which individual fulfillment transcends selfishness, and personal satisfaction transcends narcissism.

In this respect, our cultural script is not simply a set of imported moralisms, *19* exterior to the individual and designed only to compel self-sacrifice. It is also a pathway—indeed, our only pathway—to what the founders of the American experiment called the pursuit of happiness.

The stakes on this issue could hardly be higher. Our society's conspicuous *20* failure to sustain or create compelling norms of fatherhood amounts to a social and personal disaster. Today's story of fatherhood features one-dimensional characters, an unbelievable plot, and an unhappy ending. It reveals in our society both a failure of collective memory and a collapse of moral imagination. It undermines families, neglects children, causes or aggravates our worst social problems, and makes individual adult happiness—both male and female—harder to achieve.

Ultimately, this failure reflects nothing less than a culture gone awry: a culture *21* increasingly unable to establish the boundaries, erect the sign-posts, and fashion the stories that can harmonize individual happiness with collective well-being. In short, it reflects a culture that increasingly fails to "enculture" individual men and women, mothers and fathers.

In personal terms, the end result of this process, the final residue from what *22* David Gutmann calls the "deculturation" of paternity, is narcissism: a me-first egotism that is hostile not only to any societal goal or larger moral purpose but also to any save the most puerile understanding of personal happiness. In social terms, the primary results of decultured paternity are a decline in children's well-being and a rise in male violence, especially against women. In a larger sense, the most significant result is our society's steady fragmentation into atomized individuals, isolated from one another and estranged from the aspirations and realities of common membership in a family, a community, a nation, bound by mutual commitment and shared memory.

[A good father] is a cultural model, or what Max Weber calls an ideal social   23
type—an anthropomorphized composite of cultural ideas about the meaning of
paternity. I call him the Good Family Man. As described by one of the fathers [I]
interviewed . . . , a good family man "puts his family first."

A good society celebrates the ideal of the man who puts his family first. Because   24
our society is now lurching in the opposite direction, I see the Good Family Man as
the principal casualty of today's weakening fatherhood script. And because I cannot
imagine a good society without him, I offer him as the protagonist in the stronger
script that I believe is both necessary and possible.

Reading for Better Writing

Working by yourself or with a group, answer these questions:

1. What is Blankenhorn's position (thesis), and how does he introduce this idea? Which claim seems to be the most significant and when does it appear in the essay?

2. Choose five paragraphs and analyze their structure (e.g., topic sentence, supporting details, sentence structure, and transitions linking paragraphs). Then explain how these elements do or do not help present a clear message.

3. Working with a classmate, choose seven logical fallacies explained on pages 301–304. Then discuss why you believe that Blankenhorn's argument does or does not include these fallacies. Share your ideas with the class.

4. In paragraph 9, Blankenhorn makes the following claim: "Masculinity itself, understood as anything other than a rejection of what it has traditionally meant to be male, is typically treated with suspicion and even hostility in our cultural discourse." Explain what he means and why you find it a strong or weak claim.

5. Analyze three passages in which the writer uses data to support a point. Then explain why that use of data is or is not effective.

6. In paragraph 17, Blankenhorn says, "Margaret Mead and others have observed that the supreme test of any civilization is whether it can socialize men by teaching them to be fathers—creating a culture in which men acknowledge their paternity and willingly nurture their offspring." Explain what the quotation means and why it does or does not support the writer's thesis.

7. In paragraph 22, the writer says, "In personal terms, the end result of this process, the final residue from what David Gutmann calls the 'deculturation' of paternity, is narcissism." Define narcissism and explain how Blankenhorn's use of the term does or does not develop his argument.

David Blankenhorn, "Fatherless America," from FATHERLESS AMERICA: Confronting Our Most Urgent Social Problem, 1995, pp. 1-5. Copyright (c) 1996 David Blankenhorn. Reprinted by permission of Basic Books, a member of Perseus BooksGroup.

Writing Guidelines

Note: For in-depth help on developing persuasive arguments, see pages 293–308.

Planning

1. **Select a debatable topic.** Review the list below and add topics as needed.

   - **Current Affairs:** Explore recent trends, new laws, and emerging controversies discussed in the news media, blogs, or online discussion groups.
   - **Burning Issues:** What issues related to family, work, education, recreation, technology, the environment, or popular culture do you care about?
   - **Dividing Lines:** What issues divide your communities? Religion, gender, politics, regionalism, nationalism? Choose a topic and freewrite to clarify your position.
   - **Fresh Fare:** Avoid tired issues unless you take a fresh perspective.

2. **Take stock.** Before you dig into your topic, assess your starting point. What is your current position on the topic? Why? What evidence do you have?

3. **Get inside the issue.** To take a defensible position, study the issue carefully:

   - **Investigate all possible positions** on the issue and research as needed.
   - **Do firsthand research** that produces current, relevant information.
   - **Write your position** at the top of a page. Below it, set up "Pro" and "Con" columns. List arguments in each column.
   - **Develop reasoning** that supports your position and test it for the following: (a) no logical fallacies, such as slanted language, oversimplification, either/or thinking, straw-man and red-herring claims, appeals to pity, and personal attacks (see pages 301–304); and (b) an effective range of support: statistics, observations, expert testimony, comparisons, experiences, and analysis (see pages 298–299).

4. **Refine your position.** By now, you may have sharpened or radically changed your initial position on the topic. Before you organize and draft your essay, reflect on those changes. If it helps, use this formula:

   I believe this to be true about _____.

5. **Organize your argument and support.** Now you've committed yourself to a position. Before drafting, review these organizational options:

   - **Traditional Pattern:** Introduce the issue, state your position, support it, address and refute opposition, and restate your position.
   - **Blatant Confession:** Place your position statement in the first sentence.
   - **Delayed Gratification:** Describe various positions on the topic, compare and contrast them, and then take and defend your position.
   - **Changed Mind:** If your research changed your mind, explain how and why.
   - **Winning Over:** If readers oppose your position, address their concerns by anticipating and answering each objection or question.

Drafting

6. **Write your first draft.** Using freewriting and/or your notes, draft the paper.
   - **Opening:** Seize the reader's attention, possibly with a bold title—or raise concern for the issue with a dramatic story, a pointed example, a vivid picture, a thought-provoking question, or a personal confession. Supply background information that readers need to understand the issue.
   - **Development:** Deepen, clarify, and support your position statement, using solid logic and reliable support. Address opposing views fairly as part of a clear, well-reasoned argument that helps readers understand and accept your position.
   - **Closing:** End on a lively, thoughtful note that stresses your commitment. If appropriate, make a direct or indirect plea to readers to adopt your position.

Revising

7. **Improve the ideas, organization, and voice.** Ask a classmate or someone from the college's writing center to read your position paper for the following:
   - ____ **Ideas:** Does the writing effectively establish and defend a stand on a debatable issue? Is the position clearly stated and effectively qualified and refined? Do the reasoning and support help the reader understand and appreciate the position?
   - ____ **Organization:** Does the opening effectively raise the issue? Does the middle offer a carefully sequenced development and defense of the position? Does the closing successfully drive home the position?
   - ____ **Voice:** Is the voice thoughtful, measured, committed, and convincing?

Editing

8. **Edit and proofread the essay by addressing these issues:**
   - ____ **Words:** Language is precise, concrete, and lively—no jargon, clichés, or insults.
   - ____ **Sentences:** Constructions vary in length and flow smoothly.
   - ____ Correctness: The copy includes no errors in spelling, usage, punctuation, grammar, or mechanics.
   - ____ **Design:** The page design is correctly formatted and attractive; information is properly documented according to the required system (e.g., MLA, APA).

Publishing

9. **Publish your essay.** Submit your position paper according to your instructor's requirements. In addition, seek a forum for your position—with peers in a discussion group, with relatives, or online.

Critical-Thinking and Writing Activities

As directed by your instructor, complete the following critical-thinking and writing activities by yourself or with classmates.

1. Review Alyssa Woudstra's essay, "Nuclear Is Not the Answer." Then research this or another energy-related topic and write an essay in which you take a clear, well-reasoned position on one or more key issues.

2. Review Gary Steiner's and Natalie Angier's essays on what we should or should not eat. Then research the topic and develop your own argument in which you address relevant issues that they raise, as well as other issues that you think are relevant. Seek to state your position clearly and support your claims with reliable evidence.

3. Review David Blankenhorn's essay, "Fatherless America," paying special attention to the way he builds his argument with clear, well-documented claims. Then write your own position paper in which you oppose or support a claim about family in society.

4. Draft or revise a position paper that addresses a controversial issue that exists within a community to which you belong (e.g., city, neighborhood, generation, race or ethnic group, gender, consumer group, online network) by respectfully describing opposing ideas and showing how each view is or is not reasonable and acceptable.

Learning-Objectives Checklist ✓

Have you achieved this chapter's learning objectives? Check your progress with the items below, revisiting topics in the chapter as needed. *I have . . .*

____ critically examined position papers for a convincing argument with well-crafted claims, reliable evidence, and valid warrants (310).

____ identified these logical fallacies in others' writing and corrected them in my own writing: oversimplification, either/or thinking, straw-man and red-herring claims, appeals to pity, and personal attacks (301–304).

____ chosen and researched a debatable topic, compared and contrasted arguments both for and against, discerned the most convincing position, and outlined the argument in a clear, logical pattern (326–327).

____ drafted, revised, and edited a well-reasoned position paper in a measured but compelling voice (326–327).

____ analyzed and strengthened my writing by answering opponents' questions, making reasonable concessions, and rebutting opposing positions (326–327).

____ scrutinized and revised my writing to clarify my claims, insert needed transitions, and achieve a smooth and correct presentation of my position (326–327).

____ corrected errors in mechanics, usage, and grammar and developed an attractive page design (327).

Chapter 19

Persuading Readers to Act

Persuading people to do something is challenging, requiring that you convince them to believe you, to rethink their own perspectives, and to take a concrete step. In the end, you need to change people's minds in order to change their actions.

Writers achieve this goal with sound logic, reliable support, and fitting appeals. Every day, persuasive writing like this appears in newsletters, editorials, marketing documents, business proposals, academic journals, white papers, and traditional essays.

Because persuasive writing is so common, you can expect to read and write versions of it in college and in the workplace. As you read the essays in this chapter, carefully analyze how writers develop convincing appeals for action. Then when you write your own essay, try these same strategies.

Visually Speaking Review Figure 19.1. What does it suggest about how or why people persuade others to act on an issue?

Learning **Objectives**

By working through this chapter, you will be able to

- critically examine and assess the arguments in call-to-action papers.
- identify logical fallacies that are especially a danger in call-to-action writing.
- support claims with appropriate and convincing evidence.
- develop reasonable claims, especially a thesis that calls for action.
- write a compelling call-to-action paper in a mature, informed voice.

Scott Rothstein / Shutterstock.com

fig. 19.1

Reading Persuasive Writing

How should you read writing that urges you to act on an issue? The instructions below offer helpful instructions.

Consider the rhetorical situation.

When reading an appeal to act, anticipate what the writer wants people to do, what readers he or she has in mind, and how the topic is treated.

- **Purpose:** Whether in academics, the workplace, or public life, writers call for action because they believe change is needed. Something is not right. Something needs to be improved or fixed. The writer's goal is to convince readers to care about the issue strongly enough to take a concrete step.
- **Readers:** The intended readers are people whom the writer believes need to be pressed to act. Readers may be unaware of the issue, may feel overwhelmed by it, may have an interest in not acting, or may not care enough about the issue to actually act. The writer thus educates and urges such readers.
- **Topic:** In academics, the topics addressed might be related to a specific discipline (e.g., educational mentoring campaign, expanding an arts program), a political or social issue (e.g., shelter for abused women, Special Olympics program), or a general humanitarian concern (e.g., help for victims of an epidemic, a flood, or a war).

Look for convincing qualities.

When reading an appeal to act, look for the following:

- **Compelling Argument:** The writer accurately describes the issue, convinces readers of its importance, and calls for a doable and effective action. The writer's claims are fact based and reasonable, not extreme, trivial, or unqualified (see pages 296–297).
- **Logical Argument:** The argument is based on reliable evidence such as appropriate anecdotes, tests, experiments, analogies, and expert testimony (see pages 298–299); and the argument avoids logical fallacies such as half-truths, unreliable testimonials, attacks against a person, and false analogies (see pages 301–304).
- **Mature Voice:** The writing sounds informed and genuine; it includes no manipulative appeals, quarrelsome language, or demeaning accusations.

Reading Call-to-Action Writing

As you read the essays on the following pages, consider these questions:

1. What is the issue, and what action is requested to address it?
2. Who are the intended readers, and what capacity to act do they have?
3. Are the writer's claims accurate, compelling, and logical?
4. Is the argument's tone informed, genuine, and respectful?
5. Is the writing convincing—does it move readers to do what the writer requests?

Sample Persuasive Essay

Henry Veldboom, a student with children of his own, wrote this essay to call North American readers to reconsider what they value.

Outline

Introduction: the issue of North American wealth and its real cost
1. Modern capitalism is based on harmful consumerism.
2. Consumers must consider the results of their consumption.
3. People must examine especially how consumerism impacts children.

Conclusion: individual consumer change necessary for social change

Title: issue and central question

Introduction: North American wealth and its real cost

1 Modern capitalism is based on harmful consumerism.

2 Consumers must consider the results of their consumption.

Our Wealth: Where Is It Taking Us?

North America's wealth and the lifestyle it affords are known throughout the world. This knowledge has created a belief that wealth and happiness are synonymous, which in turn has perpetuated the dreams of people around the globe who hope to achieve the same successes witnessed here in the West. Is there truth to the idea that wealth and happiness coexist? Ask North Americans if they would willingly trade life here for that in a struggling country and they would likely say "No." Their wealth has made their lives quite comfortable. Most would admit to enjoying the lifestyle such wealth allows; few would want to give it up. But what is this wealth really costing North Americans—especially children?

While North American wealth grew out of the capitalism that culminated in the nineteenth-century Industrial Revolution, today's capitalism is a system largely based on consumerism—an attitude that values the incessant acquisition of goods in the belief that they are necessary and beneficial. The goal, then, of a modern capitalist economy is to produce many goods as cheaply as possible and have these goods purchased on a continual basis. The forces behind capitalism— business owners at the demand of stockholders—employ an ever-expanding array of marketing techniques to accomplish the goal of selling products. Expert on marketing George Barna defines marketing as the process of directing "goods and services from the producer to the consumer, to satisfy the needs and desires of the consumer and the goals of the producer" (41). On the receiving end of today's capitalism are consumers whose needs are in general self-serving and based on self-actualization. Corporations promote this way of thinking and capitalize on it through marketing techniques. Social commentator Benjamin Barber describes this modern interaction in the following way: "[This thinking] serves capitalist consumerism directly by nurturing a culture of impetuous consumption necessary to selling puerile goods in a developed world that has few genuine needs" (81).

Admittedly, deciphering genuine needs from superfluous wants is not an easy task. However, putting debates about materialism aside, people must consider the results of their consumption. The 2008-2009 economic upheaval still lingers in

1

2

3

people's minds despite the recent upward trend in the North American economy. When such financial turmoil happens, the typical response is to lay blame. Some people are quick to accuse corporations of causing the turmoil and governments of allowing corporations to operate as they do. Noted journalist and anti-establishment advocate Linda McQuaig comments on the shift in the 1970s that gave individuals more freedoms; in turn, corporations accommodated the lax attitudes of government to themselves and were "ensured freedom from their restraints on their profit-making" (22). Do North American corporations and governments share the responsibility to properly use wealth and direct the economy? Yes, they most certainly do. However, individuals must also examine their own fiscal responsibility. McQuaig addresses this issue as well, highlighting "the power and centrality of greed in our culture" (23). She raises a word that no one wants to be labeled with— greed. When people begin discussing their financial woes in relation to individual greed, the blame rests squarely on each member of society.

3 People must examine how consumerism harms children.

The behavior that has led to the current financial crisis is not only impacting adults but also putting children at risk. Deceptive marketing tactics make use of psychological knowledge and social patterning research to convince consumers to purchase particular products. Adults who possess the mental capacity to discern motives and detect subversion are being effectively manipulated by cunning advertising techniques, resulting in massive debt loads, addiction, and bankruptcy. However, the greater concern with these marketing practices is that they are being aimed at children who have less ability to defend themselves. Psychiatrist Susan Linn describes the marketing aimed at children as "precisely targeted, refined by scientific method, and honed by child psychologists . . ." (5). It isn't the case that children are getting caught in marketing traps set for adults; rather, kids are being targeted. Linn remarks that developmental psychology which was once used solely for treating children's mental health is now used to determine "weaknesses" in children's thinking in order to exploit these weaknesses (24). The weaknesses are due to children's brains not having reached full cognitive development, resulting in unstable patterns of thinking in areas such as reasoning, memory, and problem solving (Weiten 47). At such a disadvantage, children are unable to withstand the marketing ploys aimed at them.

(a) marketing manipulation

(b) influence on parental spending

Knowing that children are the targets of aggressive mass marketing is all the more serious when the scope of the situation is considered. Much research has been done on purchasing patterns, and while the fact that North Americans spend large amounts of money on goods may not be surprising, when children are added to the equation the picture changes. Expert on consumerism, economics, and family studies Juliet Schor has done a considerable amount of convincing research in this area. She comments on the purchasing influence of children and notes that children aged four to twelve influenced an estimated $670 billion of adult purchasing in 2004 (23). Children having influence on such large amounts of money being spent catches the attention of producers who consequently aim their marketing at kids in order to sell adult products. Schor also notes the results of a Nickelodeon (an entertainment

4

5

company) study that states when it comes to recognizing brands, "the average ten year old has memorized 300 to 400 brands" (25). Kids know the products and they know what they want; the dollar amount parents are spending in response to their children reflects this.

(c) physical and mental health problems

The effects of aggressive marketing and consumerism on North American children are exhibited in a wide range of health problems. At first glance, the relationship between consumerism and children's health may appear to be coincidental. However, much research shows a direct link between marketing to children and their health. Having done her own research and examined other studies, Juliet Schor concludes that "the more [children] buy into the commercial and materialist messages, the worse they feel about themselves, the more depressed they are, and the more they are beset by anxiety, headaches, stomachaches, and boredom" (173). (On a related note, the time spent by children sitting in front of televisions and computers is an important factor in this outcome. These media are the prime vehicles for advertising and are contributing to sedentary lifestyles, which in turn cause health problems.) Materialism is having an effect not only on adults but also on youth. When children are asked what they aspire to be, the top answer is "to be rich" (37). The health of the minds and bodies of North American children is deteriorating as a result of consumerism and the new capitalism.

5

Conclusion: Individual consumers must change if society is to change.

Having examined the current state of North American society in terms of the economic and personal health related to the new capitalism, one begins to see that society is in a situation that is neither beneficial nor sustainable. Changes must be made. If the response is to look for someone or something to blame, everyone must stop and take a look in the mirror. Changing habits and attitudes must start with the individual. While adopting a particular economic ideology is not the point, North Americans must take a hard look at their society and decide if this is how they want to live. If this society carries on unchanged, what future will its children have? North America has an abundance of wealth; the decision of where to go with it must be made: time is running out.

6

Note: The Works Cited page is not shown. For sample pages, see MLA (pages 493–534 and APA (pages 535–564).

Reading for Better Writing

Working by yourself or with a group, answer these questions:

1. In his title, Veldboom identifies the issue as wealth. How does he clarify and deepen the issue in the essay's opening paragraphs?

2. While acknowledging economic and social systems, Veldboom stresses individual values and responsibilities. How effective is this emphasis?

3. What action does the essay call for? Do you find the action practical and compelling? Why or why not?

"Our Wealth: Where Is It Taking Us?" by Henry Veldboom. Used by permission of the author.

Sample Persuasive Speech

Dr. Martin Luther King, Jr., was a leader in the Civil Rights Movement during the 1950s and 1960s. On August 28, 1963, he delivered this persuasive speech to a crowd of 250,000 people gathered at the Lincoln Memorial in Washington, D.C.

I Have a Dream

King starts with a tragic contrast.

Five score years ago, a great American, in whose symbolic shadow we stand, signed the Emancipation Proclamation. This momentous decree came as a great beacon light of hope to millions of Negro slaves who had been seared in the flames of withering injustice. It came as a joyous daybreak to end the long night of captivity.   *1*

He uses figurative language to describe the present situation.

But one hundred years later, we must face the tragic fact that the Negro is still not free. One hundred years later, the life of the Negro is still sadly crippled by the manacles of segregation and the chains of discrimination. One hundred years later, the Negro lives on a lonely island of poverty in the midst of a vast ocean of material prosperity. One hundred years later, the Negro is still languishing in the corners of American society and finds himself an exile in his own land. So we have come here today to dramatize an appalling condition.   *2*

An analogy clarifies the problem.

In a sense we have come to our nation's Capitol to cash a check. When the architects of our republic wrote the magnificent words of the Constitution and the Declaration of Independence, they were signing a promissory note to which every American was to fall heir. This note was a promise that all men would be guaranteed the unalienable rights of life, liberty, and the pursuit of happiness.   *3*

It is obvious today that America has defaulted on this promissory note insofar as her citizens of color are concerned. Instead of honoring this sacred obligation, America has given the Negro people a bad check; a check which has come back marked "insufficient funds." But we refuse to believe that the bank of justice is bankrupt. We refuse to believe that there are insufficient funds in the great vaults of opportunity of this nation. So we have come to cash this check—a check that will give us upon demand the riches of freedom and the security of justice. We have also come to this hallowed spot to remind America of the fierce urgency of now. This is no time to engage in the luxury of cooling off or to take the tranquilizing drug of gradualism. Now is the time to make real the promises of Democracy. Now is the time to rise from the dark and desolate valley of segregation to the sunlit path of racial justice. Now is the time to open the doors of opportunity to all of God's children. Now is the time to lift our nation from the quicksands of racial injustice to the solid rock of brotherhood.   *4*

Repeated words and phrases create urgency.

It would be fatal for the nation to overlook the urgency of the moment and   5
to underestimate the determination of the Negro. This sweltering summer of the
Negro's legitimate discontent will not pass until there is an invigorating autumn of
freedom and equality. 1963 is not an end, but a beginning. Those who hope that the
Negro needed to blow off steam and will now be content will have a rude awakening
if the nation returns to business as usual. There will be neither rest nor tranquility in
America until the Negro is granted his citizenship rights. The whirlwinds of revolt
will continue to shake the foundations of our nation until the bright day of justice
emerges.

> King addresses specific audiences in turn.

But there is something I must say to my people who stand on the warm   6
threshold which leads into the palace of justice. In the process of gaining our
rightful place we must not be guilty of wrongful deeds. Let us not seek to satisfy
our thirst for freedom by drinking from the cup of bitterness and hatred. We must
forever conduct our struggle on the high plane of dignity and discipline. We must
not allow our creative protest to degenerate into physical violence. Again and again
we must rise to the majestic heights of meeting physical force with soul force. The
marvelous new militancy which has engulfed the Negro community must not lead
us to a distrust of all white people, for many of our white brothers, as evidenced by
their presence here today, have come to realize that their destiny is tied up with our
destiny and their freedom is inextricably bound to our freedom. We cannot walk
alone.

> He responds to the arguments of opponents.

And as we talk, we must make the pledge that we shall march ahead. We cannot   7
turn back. There are those who are asking the devotees of civil rights, "When will
you be satisfied?" We can never be satisfied as long as the Negro is the victim of the
unspeakable horrors of police brutality. We can never be satisfied as long as our
bodies, heaving with the fatigue of travel, cannot gain lodging in the motels of the
highways and the hotels of the cities. We cannot be satisfied as long as the Negro's
basic mobility is from a smaller ghetto to a larger one. We can never be satisfied as
long as a Negro in Mississippi cannot vote and a Negro in New York believes he has
nothing for which to vote. No, no, we are not satisfied, and we will not be satisfied
until justice rolls down like waters and righteousness like a mighty stream.

> Appropriate emotional appeals are used in the context of suffering.

I am not unmindful that some of you have come here out of great trials and   8
tribulations. Some of you have come fresh from narrow jail cells. Some of you have
come from areas where your quest for freedom left you battered by the storms
of persecution and staggered by the winds of police brutality. You have been the
veterans of creative suffering. Continue to work with the faith that unearned
suffering is redemptive.

Go back to Mississippi, go back to Alabama, go back to South Carolina, go back   *9*
to Georgia, go back to Louisiana, go back to the slums and ghettos of our northern
cities, knowing that somehow this situation can and will be changed. Let us not
wallow in the valley of despair.

I say to you today, my friends, that in spite of the difficulties and frustrations of   *10*
the moment I still have a dream. It is a dream deeply rooted in the American dream.

I have a dream that one day this nation will rise up and live out the true   *11*
meaning of its creed: "We hold these truths to be self-evident; that all men are
created equal."

I have a dream that one day on the red hills of Georgia the sons of former slaves   *12*
and the sons of former slaveowners will be able to sit down together at the table of
brotherhood.

I have a dream that the state of Mississippi, a desert state sweltering with the   *13*
heat of injustice and oppression, will be transformed into an oasis of freedom and
justice.

I have a dream that my four little children will one day live in a nation   *14*
where they will not be judged by the color of their skin but by the content of their
character.

I have a dream today.   *15*

I have a dream that the state of Alabama, whose governor's lips are presently   *16*
dripping with the words of interposition and nullification, will be transformed into
a situation where little black boys and black girls will be able to join hands with little
white boys and girls and walk together as sisters and brothers.

I have a dream today.   *17*

I have a dream that one day every valley shall be exalted, every hill and   *18*
mountain shall be made low, the rough places will be made plain, and the crooked
places will be made straight, and the glory of the Lord shall be revealed, and all flesh
shall see it together.

This is our hope. This is the faith with which I return to the South. With this   *19*
faith we will be able to hew out of the mountain of despair a stone of hope. With this
faith we will be able to transform the jangling discords of our nation into a beautiful
symphony of brotherhood. With this faith we will be able to work together, to pray
together, to struggle together, to go to jail together, to stand up for freedom together,
knowing that we will be free one day.

This will be the day when all God's children will be able to sing with new   *20*
meaning.

> The repetition of key phrases becomes a persuasive refrain.

> King's vision offers hope and motivates readers to change society.

He appeals to ideals and to humanity's better nature, ending with a vision of a just society.

My country 'tis of thee 21

Sweet land of liberty,

Of thee I sing,

Land where my fathers died,

Land of the pilgrims' pride,

From every mountainside

Let freedom ring.

And if America is to be a great nation this must become true. So let freedom 22
ring from the prodigious hilltops of New Hampshire. Let freedom ring from the
mighty mountains of New York. Let freedom ring from the heightening Alleghenies
of Pennsylvania!

Let freedom ring from the snow-capped Rockies of Colorado! 23

Let freedom ring from the curvaceous peaks of California! 24

But not only that; let freedom ring from Stone Mountain of Georgia! 25

Let freedom ring from Lookout Mountain of Tennessee! 26

Let freedom ring from every hill and molehill of Mississippi! From every 27
mountainside, let freedom ring.

The closing urges readers to work for a better future.

When we let freedom ring, when we let it ring from every village and every 28
hamlet, from every state and every city, we will be able to speed up that day when
all of God's children, black men and white men, Jews and Gentiles, Protestants and
Catholics, will be able to join hands and sing in the words of the old Negro spiritual,
"Free at last! Free at last! Thank God almighty, we are free at last!"

Reading for Better Writing

Working by yourself or with a group, answer these questions:

1. King is actually speaking to several audiences at the same time. Who are these different audiences? How does King address each?
2. For what specific changes does King call? What does he want his listeners to do?
3. Explore the writer's style. How does he use religious imagery, comparisons, and analogies? How does repetition function as a persuasive technique?
4. In a sense, King's speech addresses a gap between reality and an ideal. How does he present this gap?

Sample Persuasive Essay

Kofi Annan, the former Secretary General of the United Nations, wrote the essay below in order to urge readers worldwide to help address AIDS and famine in Africa.

In Africa, AIDS Has a Woman's Face

The title and introduction aim to create urgency about the issue.

A combination of famine and AIDS is threatening the backbone of Africa—the women who keep African societies going and whose work makes up the economic foundation of rural communities. For decades, we have known that the best way for Africa to thrive is to ensure that its women have the freedom, power, and knowledge to make decisions affecting their own lives and those of their families and communities. At the United Nations, we have always understood that our work for development depends on building a successful partnership with the African farmer and her husband.   *1*

Stressing the importance of women in African societies, Annan outlines the double catastrophe happening.

Study after study has shown that there is no effective development strategy in which women do not play a central role. When women are fully involved, the benefits can be seen immediately: families are healthier; they are better fed; their income, savings and reinvestment go up. And, what is true of families is true of communities and, eventually, of whole countries.   *2*

But today, millions of African women are threatened by two simultaneous catastrophes: famine and AIDS. More than 30 million people are now at risk of starvation in southern Africa and the Horn of Africa. All of these predominantly agricultural societies are also battling serious AIDS epidemics. This is no coincidence: AIDS and famine are directly linked.   *3*

Because of AIDS, farming skills are being lost, agricultural development efforts are declining, rural livelihoods are disintegrating, productive capacity to work the land is dropping, and household earnings are shrinking—all while the cost of caring for the ill is rising exponentially. At the same time, H.I.V. infection and AIDS are spreading dramatically and disproportionately among women. A United Nations report released last month shows that women now make up 50 percent of those infected with H.I.V. worldwide—and in Africa that figure is now 59 percent. Today, AIDS has a woman's face.   *4*

AIDS has already caused immense suffering by killing almost 2.5 million Africans this year alone. It has left 11 million African children orphaned since the epidemic began. Now it is attacking the capacity of these countries to resist famine by eroding those mechanisms that enable populations to fight back—the coping abilities provided by women.   *5*

In famines before the AIDS crisis, women proved more resilient than men. Their survival rate was higher, and their coping skills were stronger. Women were the ones who found alternative foods that could sustain their children in time of drought. Because droughts happened once a decade or so, women who had experienced previous droughts were able to pass on survival techniques to younger   *6*

Pixel Embargo / Shutterstock.com

women. Women are the ones who nurture social networks that can help spread the burden in times of famine.

Annan contrasts women's situation before and after the arrival of AIDS.

But today, as AIDS is eroding the health of Africa's women, it is eroding the skills, experience and networks that keep their families and communities going. Even before falling ill, a woman will often have to care for a sick husband, thereby reducing the time she can devote to planting, harvesting and marketing crops. When her husband dies, she is often deprived of credit, distribution networks or land rights. When she dies, the household will risk collapsing completely, leaving children to fend for themselves. The older ones, especially girls, will be taken out of school to work in the home or the farm. These girls, deprived of education and opportunities, will be even less able to protect themselves against AIDS.   7

He presses for a new combination of necessary, related actions.

Because this crisis is different from past famines, we must look beyond relief measures of the past. Merely shipping in food is not enough. Our effort will have to combine food assistance and new approaches to farming with treatment and prevention of H.I.V. and AIDS. It will require creating early-warning and analysis systems that monitor both H.I.V. infection rates and famine indicators. It will require new agricultural techniques, appropriate to a depleted work force. It will require a renewed effort to wipe out H.I.V.-related stigma and silence.   8

It will require innovative, large-scale ways to care for orphans, with specific measures that enable children in AIDS-affected communities to stay in school. Education and prevention are still the most powerful weapons against the spread of H.I.V. Above all, this new international effort must put women at the center of our strategy to fight AIDS.   9

He points to hopeful signs and cases as a way of convincing readers that change can happen.

Experience suggests that there is reason to hope. The recent United Nations report shows that H.I.V. infection rates in Uganda continue to decline. In South Africa, infection rates for women under 20 have started to decrease. In Zambia, H.I.V. rates show signs of dropping among women in urban areas and younger women in rural areas. In Ethiopia, infection levels have fallen among young women in the center of Addis Ababa.   10

We can and must build on those successes and replicate them elsewhere. For that, we need leadership, partnership, and imagination from the international community and African governments. If we want to save Africa from two catastrophes, we would do well to focus on saving Africa's women.   11

Reading for Better Writing

Working by yourself or with a group, answer these questions:

1. How does the writer introduce the topic and focus the essay? Explain.
2. What does Annan ask readers to do? Is his request clear and convincing? Why?
3. Choose a paragraph that you find particularly convincing and explain why.

Sample Persuasive Essay

In the following essay, Barbara Ehrenreich argues that whereas America's poor citizens sometimes loiter, trespass, or panhandle, most do these things because they're poor—not because they're criminals. In response to such behavior, she urges readers to show compassion and to act on behalf of the poor.

Is It Now a Crime to Be Poor?

As you read, highlight strategies and take marginal notes exploring how Ehrenreich raises the issue and calls for action.

It's too bad so many people are falling into poverty at a time when it's almost illegal to be poor. You won't be arrested for shopping in a Dollar Store, but if you are truly, deeply, in-the-streets poor, you're well advised not to engage in any of the biological necessities of life—like sitting, sleeping, lying down, or loitering. City officials boast that there is nothing discriminatory about the ordinances that afflict the destitute, most of which go back to the dawn of gentrification in the '80s and '90s. "If you're lying on a sidewalk, whether you're homeless or a millionaire, you're in violation of the ordinance," a city attorney in St. Petersburg, Fla., said in June, echoing Anatole France's immortal observation that "the law, in its majestic equality, forbids the rich as well as the poor to sleep under bridges."   *1*

In defiance of all reason and compassion, the criminalization of poverty has actually been intensifying as the recession generates ever more poverty. So concludes a new study from the National Law Center on Homelessness and Poverty, which found that the number of ordinances against the publicly poor has been rising since 2006, along with ticketing and arrests for more "neutral" infractions like jaywalking, littering or carrying an open container of alcohol. *[See Homes Not Handcuffs: The Criminalization of Homelessness in U.S. Cities.]*   *2*

The report lists America's 10 "meanest" cities—the largest of which are Honolulu, Los Angeles and San Francisco—but new contestants are springing up every day. The City Council in Grand Junction, Colo., has been considering a ban on begging, and at the end of June, Tempe, Ariz. carried out a four-day crackdown on the indigent. How do you know when someone is indigent? As a Las Vegas statute puts it, "An indigent person is a person whom a reasonable ordinary person would believe to be entitled to apply for or receive" public assistance.   *3*

That could be me before the blow-drying and eyeliner, and it's definitely Al Szekely at any time of day. A grizzled 62-year-old, he inhabits a wheelchair and is often found on G Street in Washington—the city that is ultimately responsible for the bullet he took in the spine in Fu Bai, Vietnam, in 1972. He had been enjoying the luxury of an indoor bed until last December, when the police swept through the shelter in the middle of the night looking for men with outstanding warrants.   *4*

It turned out that Mr. Szekely, who is an ordained minister and does not drink, do drugs or curse in front of ladies, did indeed have a warrant—for not appearing in court to face a charge of "criminal trespassing" (for sleeping on a sidewalk in a   *5*

Washington suburb). So he was dragged out of the shelter and put in jail. "Can you imagine?" asked Eric Sheptock, the homeless advocate (himself a shelter resident) who introduced me to Mr. Szekely. "They arrested a homeless man in a shelter for being homeless."

The viciousness of the official animus toward the indigent can be breathtaking. 6 A few years ago, a group called Food Not Bombs started handing out free vegan food to hungry people in public parks around the nation. A number of cities, led by Las Vegas, passed ordinances forbidding the sharing of food with the indigent in public places, and several members of the group were arrested. A federal judge just overturned the anti-sharing law in Orlando, Fla., but the city is appealing. And now Middletown, Conn., is cracking down on food sharing.

If poverty tends to criminalize people, it is also true that criminalization 7 inexorably impoverishes them. Scott Lovell, another homeless man I interviewed in Washington, earned his record by committing a significant crime—by participating in the armed robbery of a steakhouse when he was 15. Although Mr. Lovell dresses and speaks more like a summer tourist from Ohio than a felon, his criminal record has made it extremely difficult for him to find a job.

For Al Szekely, the arrest for trespassing meant a further descent down the 8 circles of hell. While in jail, he lost his slot in the shelter and now sleeps outside the Verizon Center sports arena, where the big problem, in addition to the security guards, is mosquitoes. His stick-thin arms are covered with pink crusty sores, which he treats with a regimen of frantic scratching.

For the not-yet homeless, there are two main paths to criminalization—one 9 involving debt, and the other skin color. Anyone of any color or pre-recession financial status can fall into debt, and although we pride ourselves on the abolition of debtors' prison, in at least one state, Texas, people who can't afford to pay their traffic fines may be made to "sit out their tickets" in jail.

Often the path to legal trouble begins when one of your creditors has a court 10 issue a summons for you, which you fail to honor for one reason or another. (Maybe your address has changed or you never received it.) Now you're in contempt of court. Or suppose you miss a payment and, before you realize it, your car insurance lapses; then you're stopped for something like a broken headlight. Depending on the state, you may have your car impounded or face a steep fine—again, exposing you to a possible summons. "There's just no end to it once the cycle starts," said Robert Solomon of Yale Law School. "It just keeps accelerating."

By far the most reliable way to be criminalized by poverty is to have the wrong- 11 color skin. Indignation runs high when a celebrity professor encounters racial profiling, but for decades whole communities have been effectively "profiled" for the suspicious combination of being both dark-skinned and poor, thanks to the "broken windows" or "zero tolerance" theory of policing popularized by Rudy Giuliani, when he was mayor of New York City, and his police chief William Bratton.

Flick a cigarette in a heavily patrolled community of color and you're littering;   *12*
wear the wrong color T-shirt and you're displaying gang allegiance. Just strolling
around in a dodgy neighborhood can mark you as a potential suspect, according
to *Let's Get Free: A Hip-Hop Theory of Justice,* an eye-opening new book by Paul
Butler, a former federal prosecutor in Washington. If you seem at all evasive, which
I suppose is like looking "overly anxious" in an airport, Mr. Butler writes, the police
"can force you to stop just to investigate why you don't want to talk to them." And
don't get grumpy about it or you could be "resisting arrest."

There's no minimum age for being sucked into what the Children's Defense   *13*
Fund calls "the cradle-to-prison pipeline." In New York City, a teenager caught
in public housing without an ID—say, while visiting a friend or relative—can
be charged with criminal trespassing and wind up in juvenile detention, Mishi
Faruqee, the director of youth justice programs for the Children's Defense Fund of
New York, told me. In just the past few months, a growing number of cities have
taken to ticketing and sometimes handcuffing teenagers found on the streets during
school hours.

In Los Angeles, the fine for truancy is $250; in Dallas, it can be as much as   *14*
$500—crushing amounts for people living near the poverty level. According to the
Los Angeles Bus Riders Union, an advocacy group, 12,000 students were ticketed for
truancy in 2008.

Why does the Bus Riders Union care? Because it estimates that 80 percent of the   *15*
"truants," especially those who are black or Latino, are merely late for school, thanks
to the way that over-filled buses whiz by them without stopping. I met people in Los
Angeles who told me they keep their children home if there's the slightest chance of
their being late. It's an ingenious anti-truancy policy that discourages parents from
sending their youngsters to school.

The pattern is to curtail financing for services that might help the poor while   *16*
ramping up law enforcement: starve school and public transportation budgets,
then make truancy illegal. Shut down public housing, then make it a crime to be
homeless. Be sure to harass street vendors when there are few other opportunities
for employment. The experience of the poor, and especially poor minorities, comes
to resemble that of a rat in a cage scrambling to avoid erratically administered
electric shocks.

And if you should make the mistake of trying to escape via a brief marijuana-   *17*
induced high, it's "gotcha" all over again, because that of course is illegal too. One
result is our staggering level of incarceration, the highest in the world. Today the
same number of Americans—2.3 million—reside in prison as in public housing.

Meanwhile, the public housing that remains has become ever more prisonlike,   *18*
with residents subjected to drug testing and random police sweeps. The safety net, or
what's left of it, has been transformed into a dragnet.

Some of the community organizers I've talked to around the country think   *19*
they know why "zero tolerance" policing has ratcheted up since the recession
began. Leonardo Vilchis of the Union de Vecinos, a community organization in Los
Angeles, suspects that "poor people have become a source of revenue" for recession-
starved cities, and that the police can always find a violation leading to a fine. If
so, this is a singularly demented fund-raising strategy. At a Congressional hearing
in June, the president of the National Association of Criminal Defense Lawyers
testified about the pervasive "overcriminalization of crimes that are not a risk to
public safety," like sleeping in a cardboard box or jumping turnstiles, which leads to
expensively clogged courts and prisons.

A Pew Center study released in March found states spending a record $51.7   *20*
billion on corrections, an amount that the center judged, with an excess of
moderation, to be "too much."

But will it be enough—the collision of rising prison populations that we can't   *21*
afford and the criminalization of poverty—to force us to break the mad cycle of
poverty and punishment? With the number of people in poverty increasing (some
estimates suggest it's up to 45 million to 50 million, from 37 million in 2007) several
states are beginning to ease up on the criminalization of poverty—for example,
by sending drug offenders to treatment rather than jail, shortening probation and
reducing the number of people locked up for technical violations like missed court
appointments. But others are tightening the screws: not only increasing the number
of "crimes" but also charging prisoners for their room and board—assuring that
they'll be released with potentially criminalizing levels of debt.

Maybe we can't afford the measures that would begin to alleviate America's   *22*
growing poverty—affordable housing, good schools, reliable public transportation
and so forth. I would argue otherwise, but for now I'd be content with a consensus
that, if we can't afford to truly help the poor, neither can we afford to go on
tormenting them.

Reading for Better Writing

Working by yourself or with a group, answer these questions:

1. Note how Ehrenreich uses the title, opening sentence, and opening paragraph
   to introduce her topic and focus her argument. Are these strategies effective?
2. Identity two passages in which the writer makes a claim and then supports it
   by citing a study or an academic authority. Is this strategy convincing?
3. Cite two passages in which the writer uses an anecdote or illustration to
   support a claim. Do these strategies strengthen her argument?
4. Precisely what does the writer want her readers to do? Why might she have
   published this appeal in *The New York Times*?

*Barbara Ehrenreich, "Is It Now a Crime to Be Poor" from The New York Times, August 8, 2009. Reprinted by permission of
International Creative Mangangement, Inc. Copyright (c) 2009 by Barbara Ehrenreich.*

Writing Guidelines

Note: For in-depth help on developing persuasive arguments, see pages 293–308.

Planning

1. **Select a topic.** List issues about which you feel passionately such as community problems, international issues, disaster-relief efforts, educational outreach programs, environmental clean-up efforts, or social or political campaigns. Then choose a related topic that is debatable, significant, current, and manageable.

Not Debatable	Debatable
Statistics on spending practices	The injustice of consumerism
The existence of racism	Solutions to racism
Recyclables are dumped in landfills	Tax on paper/plastic grocery bags

2. **Choose and analyze your readers.** Think about who your readers are and why they might resist the change that you advocate.

3. **Narrow your focus and determine your purpose.** Should you focus on one aspect of the issue or all of it? What should you and can you try to change? How might you best organize your argument?.

4. **Generate ideas and support.** Use prewriting strategies like those below to develop your thinking and gather support:
   - Set up "opposing viewpoints" columns in which you list arguments accepted by advocates of each position.
   - Research the issue to find current, reliable sources from many perspectives.
   - Research other calls to action on this issue, noting their appeals, supporting evidence, and success.
   - Brainstorm the range of actions that might be taken in response to the issue. For each action, explore how attractive and doable it might be for your readers.
   - Consider what outcomes or results you want.

5. **Organize your thinking.** Consider using the following strategies:
   - Make a sharp claim (like those below) that points toward action:
     On the issue of _____, I believe _____.
     Therefore, we must change _____.
   - Review the evidence, and develop your line of reasoning by generating an outline or using a graphic organizer. (See pages 48–53.)
     Simple Outline: Introduction: the issue and initial claim
     Describing the issue and its importance: point 1, 2, etc.
     Explaining possible actions and benefits: point 1, 2, etc.
     Conclusion: call to specific action

Drafting

6. Write your first draft. As you write, remember your goal and specific readers:

- **Opening:** Gain the readers' attention, raise the issue, help the readers care about it, and state your claim.
- **Development:** Decide where to place your most persuasive supporting argument: first or last. Anticipate readers' questions and objections, and use appropriate logical and emotional appeals to overcome their resistance to change.
- **Closing:** Restate your claim, summarize your support, and call your readers to act.
- **Title:** Develop a thoughtful, energetic working title that stresses a vision or change. (For ideas, scan the titles of the sample essays in this chapter.)

Revising

7. Improve the ideas, organization, and voice. Ask a classmate or someone from the college's writing center to read your call-to-action paper for the following:

____ **Ideas:** Does the writing prompt readers to change their thinking and behavior? Does the essay show effective reasoning, good support, and a clear call to action—without logical fallacies such as half-truths, unreliable testimonials, attacks against a person, and false analogies (see pages 301–304)?

____ **Organization:** Does the opening engagingly raise the issue? Does the middle carefully press the issue and the need for action? Does the closing successfully call for specific changes and actions?

____ **Voice:** Is the tone energetic but controlled, confident but reasonable? Does the writing inspire readers to join your cause and act?

Editing

8. Edit and proofread the essay by checking issues like these:

____ **Words:** Language is precise, concrete, and easily understood—no jargon, clichés, doublespeak, or loaded terms.

____ **Sentences:** Constructions flow smoothly and are varied in structure.

____ **Correctness:** The copy includes no errors in grammar, punctuation, usage, or spelling.

____ **Design:** The page design is correctly formatted and attractive; information is properly documented according to the required system (e.g., MLA, APA).

Publishing

9. Prepare and publish your final essay. Submit the essay to your instructor. If appropriate, solicit feedback from others—perhaps on a Web site or in a newspaper.

Critical-Thinking and Writing Activities

As directed by your instructor, complete the following critical-thinking and writing activities by yourself or with classmates.

1. The four essays in this chapter address significant social and ethical issues: wealth and poverty, health and famine, racial equality. List topics like these, choose one, narrow the focus to a specific issue, and then write an essay that persuades readers to do something related to the issue.

2. If you are a natural sciences major, consider debatable issues that are central to studying and applying the sciences—environmental, medical, biotechnical, and agricultural issues, for example. If you are a social science or humanities major, do the same brainstorming in your area. Then chose an issue where you see a need for change and write an essay in which you describe the issue and persuade readers to take the action that you recommend.

3. As a service project, visit an administrator at a local nonprofit agency (e.g., school, hospital, church, employment office, YMCA) and offer to write an editorial, news article, or letter in which you describe one of the agency's needs and persuade readers to offer their help.

4. What issues have come up in your job? Contemplate issues such as pay equity, equal opportunity, management policies, and unsafe work conditions. Then write a persuasive report to a decision maker or to fellow employees.

Learning-Objectives Checklist ✓

Have you achieved this chapter's learning objectives? Check your progress with the items below, revisiting topics in the chapter as needed. *I have . . .*

____ critically examined and evaluated call-to-action papers for logical, evidence-based, arguments that effectively address the writers' situations (330).

____ identified these logical fallacies in others' writing and corrected them in my own writing: half-truths, unreliable testimonials, personal attacks, and false analogies (301–304).

____ strengthened my appeals with appropriate supporting evidence such as anecdotes, tests, experiments, analogies, and expert testimony (298–299).

____ developed reasonable claims, especially my call to action, rather than claims that are extreme, trivial, unqualified, or unwarranted (296–297).

____ integrated clarifying definitions and analyzed key cause-effect relationships.

____ researched and written a convincing call-to-action essay that develops its argument in a mature, informed voice (344–345).

____ edited my essay for all errors in mechanics, usage, grammar, and page design (345).

Chapter 20

Proposing a Solution

Proposals are prescriptions for change. As such, they challenge readers to care about a problem, accept a solution, and act on it. A strong proposal offers a logical, practical, and creative argument that leads toward positive change, whether it's helping immigrants acquire citizenship, giving youthful law breakers lenient sentences, or requiring both men and women to register for the military draft.

Proposal writers argue for such remedies in all areas of life. In your college courses, you'll be challenged to generate solutions to many difficult problems. In your community, you may participate in policy making and civic development. In the workplace, you may write proposals that justify expenditures, sell products, or troubleshoot problems. In each situation, you'll have to clearly explain the problem, offer a solution, argue for adopting it, and possibly also explain how to implement it.

Visually Speaking   Review Figure 20.1. What does it suggest about problems and solutions? What problem-solution writing might relate to this image?

Learning **Objectives**

By working through this chapter, you will be able to

- critically examine and assess the arguments in problem-solution essays.

- analyze a problem's history, causes, and effects.

- analyze a solution's benefits and drawbacks.

- identify logical fallacies that are especially a danger in problem-solution writing.

- write a convincing essay that logically analyzes a problem and proposes a reasonable, reliable solution.

China Photos / Getty Images News / Getty Images

fig. 20.1

Reading Problem-Solution Writing

The instructions below will help you understand and use problem-solution logic.

Consider the rhetorical situation.

When reading problem-solution writing, think about its purpose, audience, and topic.

- **Purpose:** Problem-solution writing aims to inform: to describe a problem accurately, to present workable solutions, and to explain the strengths and weaknesses of each. However, such writing also aims to persuade: to convince readers that a problem is urgent, that one solution is better than others, or that readers should implement it.
- **Readers:** Potentially, writers could have four groups of readers: people responsible for the problem, decision makers with the power to adopt a solution, people affected by the problem, and a public who just want information about the problem. When reading the document, note whether it (1) offers all of its readers the information that they need and (2) communicates in language that they can understand and trust.
- **Topic:** Clearly, problem-solution writing focuses on a problem, but it can be a problem broadly conceived—perhaps as a challenge or an opportunity. Across the college curriculum, such problems are typically discipline-related (e.g., dyslexia in Education, oil spills in Environmental Studies, agoraphobia in Psychology). In the workplace, problem-solution reasoning is used in documents such as proposals.

Consider the reasoning.

When reading problem-solution writing, look for the following:

- **Accurate Description:** The writer correctly describes the problem, including relevant details regarding its history, causes, effects, dangers, costs, and direct or indirect impact on readers. The writing also describes all reasonable solutions, including details about their history, side effects, costs, successes, and failures.
- **Thorough Analysis:** The writer carefully analyzes the problem, each solution, and why the recommended solution is the best choice. The writer supports all claims with reliable data and logical reasoning.
- **Rational Argument:** The writer's claims and appeals for action are thoughtful, stated in objective terms, and presented in a measured, informed voice.

Reading Problem-Solution Writing

As you read the essays in this chapter, consider these questions:

1. What is the problem, what is its history, and why should the problem be resolved?
2. What is the solution, how does it resolve the problem, and with what side effects?
3. What action does the writer call for, and is it beneficial, realistic, and cost effective?
4. Are persuasive statements reasonable, well-documented, and free of fallacies?

Sample Problem-Solution Essay

Journalism major Renee Wielenga wrote and published "Dream Act . . ." as a newspaper article. She then revised the piece as an essay, but retained the problem-solution reasoning used in her original article.

Outline

Introduction: (Problem) Students' dreams foiled by immigration laws; (Solution) Dream Act offers route to legal residency.

1. Bill's requirements for residency and citizenship
2. Bill's origin and increasing support
3. Bill's remaining impediments

Conclusion: The Dream Act warrants readers' support.

Title: the problem and solution	**Dream Act May Help Local Student Fight for Residency**

Introduction: (Problem) Students' dreams foiled by immigration laws

Attending college, joining the military, creating a career path: these are dreams *1* for most U.S. high school graduates. But for Maria Lopez, a senior at San Marshall High School who has lived in the U.S for seven years, there is only one legal option: return to Mexico. She is one of nearly 65,000 high school students each year who do not have the opportunity to pursue their dreams because they arrived in the U.S. illegally. Like many of these students, Maria is highly motivated, hard working, and excited to be involved in her high school. However, Maria's parents brought her to this country without going through the legal immigration process. As a result, by law she is an undocumented alien who has no method to achieve legal residency while living in the U.S.

(Solution) Dream Act offers route to legal residency.

Currently, children like Maria have only one route to legal residency: go back *2* to their country of birth, file the proper paperwork, and then return to the U.S. Unfortunately, attempts to return legally are often difficult, with roadblocks such as a ten-year restriction on re-entering the U.S. However, one piece of proposed federal legislation could help these young people pursue their dreams: The Development, Relief, and Education for Alien Minors Act (S. 729), better known as the Dream Act, is an amendment to the Illegal Immigration Reform and Immigrant Responsibility Act of 1996.

1 Bill's requirements for residency and citizenship

The current version of this bill would grant eligible immigrant students six *3* years of conditional residency during which they could earn full citizenship. To be eligible for conditional residency, a student must: (1) graduate from a U.S. high school or obtain a GED, (2) be of good moral character, (3) have arrived in the U.S. under the age of 16, (4) have proof of residence in the U.S. for at least five consecutive years since the arrival date, and (5) be between the ages of 12 and 35 at the time of the bill's enactment. To gain full citizenship, the student must do one of the following during his or her residency: (1) complete at least two years of work toward a four-year college degree, (2) earn a two-year college degree, or (3) serve in the military for two years. If, within the six-year period, a student does not complete either the college requirement or the military-service requirement, the person would lose his or her temporary residency and be subject to deportation.

2 Bill's origin and increasing support

While the Dream Act was first introduced in 2001, and its progress toward approval has been slow, the bill's popularity has grown each year since then. For example, in March 2009, the bill was re-introduced in the U.S. Senate by Richard Durbin (D-IL) and Richard Lugar (R-IN). Also at that time, Howard Berman (D-CA), Lincoln Diaz-Balart (R-FL), Lucille Roybal-Allard (D-CA), and a number of other legislators introduced the bill in the House of Representatives where the document is called the American Dream Act (H.R. 1751). In addition to these officials, many citizens such as Maria's guidance counselor, Ben Barry, favor the bill, believing that it would give immigrant students a chance to give back to the country that has given so much to them, and the bill would offer those students an opportunity to utilize their hard-earned education and talents.

3 Bill's remaining impediments

However, as of January 2013, the bill remains in the first step in the legislative process—a process in which bills go to committees or "mini congresses" that deliberate, investigate, and revise the bill before it is brought up for general debate in either the Senate or the House of Representatives. The disheartening fact, though, is that the majority of bills never make it out of these committees. Furthermore, supporters of Comprehensive Immigration Reform (CIR) are in favor of including the Dream Act as part of CIR, which could make the Dream Act subject to change yet again.

Conclusion: The Dream Act warrants our support.

Given such debates, it might be a long time before the bill becomes law, thereby dashing the dreams of nearly 65,000 high school students like Maria who can't wait another year because they may already be in deportation proceedings. We need to step up and educate our Representatives and Senators about the importance of passing the Dream Act on its own instead of including the bill along with CIR. We need to urge them to debate and approve the Dream Act now, thereby making Maria's dreams—and the dreams of thousands of students like her—a reality!

Reading for Better Writing

Working by yourself or with a group, answer these questions:

1. What problem does Wielenga address, and how does she get readers to care about it?
2. What solution does she propose, and how does she explain or assert its value?
3. In paragraph 6, Wielenga urges readers to promote her solution. Explain why you do or do not find her rationale for action convincing.
4. As noted in the introduction, Wielenga published an earlier form of this essay in a newspaper. Given its content and tone, explain why you think this version of the piece might be appropriate for a news article, an editorial, or both.

"Dream Act May Help Local Student Fight for Residence" by Renee Wielenga. Used by permission of the author.

Sample Problem-Solution Essay

Anna Quindlen has written more than a dozen books, including best-selling novels such as *Rise and Shine* and *Black and Blue*, and nonfiction books such as *Being Perfect* and *Living Out Loud*. In addition, she has written a Pulitzer Prize winning column for *The New York Times*, as well as many essays such as "Uncle Sam and Aunt Samantha."

Uncle Sam and Aunt Samantha

> **Each of the first five paragraphs is one sentence long.**

One out of every five new recruits in the United States military is female. 1

The Marines gave the Combat Action Ribbon for service in the Persian Gulf to 23 women. 2

Two female soldiers were killed in the bombing of the *USS Cole*. 3

The Selective Service registers for the draft all male citizens between the ages of 18 and 25. 4

What's wrong with this picture? 5

> **The writer identifies the problem that she wants solved.**

As Americans read and realize that the lives of most women in this country are as different from those of Afghan women as a Cunard cruise is from maximum-security lockdown, there has nonetheless been little attention paid to one persistent gender inequity in U.S. public policy. An astonishing anachronism, really: While women are represented today in virtually all fields, including the armed forces, only men are required to register for the military draft that would be used in the event of a national-security crisis. 6

> **She provides background about the source and history of the problem.**

Since the nation is as close to such a crisis as it has been in more than sixty years, it's a good moment to consider how the draft wound up in this particular time warp. It's not the time warp of the Taliban, certainly, stuck in the worst part of the 13th century, forbidding women to attend school or hold jobs or even reveal their arms, forcing them into sex and marriage. Our own time warp is several decades old. The last time the draft was considered seriously was twenty years ago, when registration with the Selective Service was restored by Jimmy Carter after the Soviet invasion of, yep, Afghanistan. The president, as well as the Army chief of staff, asked at the time for the registration of women as well as men. 7

The president, as well as the Army chief of staff, asked at the time for the registration of women as well as men.

Amid a welter of arguments—women interfere with esprit de corps, women   8
don't have the physical strength, women prisoners could be sexually assaulted,
women soldiers would distract male soldiers from their mission—Congress shot
down the notion of gender-blind registration. So did the Supreme Court, ruling that
since women were forbidden to serve in combat positions and the purpose of the
draft was to create a combat-ready force, it made sense not to register them.

But that was then, and this is now. Women have indeed served in combat   9
positions, in the Balkans and the Middle East. More than 40,000 managed to serve
in the Persian Gulf without destroying unit cohesion or failing because of upper-
body strength. Some are even now taking out targets in Afghanistan from fighter
jets, and apparently without any male soldier's falling prey to some predicted excess
of chivalry or lust.

Talk about cognitive dissonance. All these   10
military personnel, male and female alike, have
come of age at a time when a significant level of
parity was taken for granted. Yet they are supposed
to accept that only males will be required to defend
their country in a time of national emergency. This
is insulting to men. And it is insulting to women.
Caroline Forell, an expert on women's legal rights
and a professor at the University of Oregon School

> *Yet they are supposed to accept that only males will be required to defend their country . . .*

A quotation helps to explain why the writer understands the situation to be a problem.

of Law, puts it bluntly: "Failing to require this of women makes us lesser citizens."

Neither the left nor the right has been particularly inclined to consider this   11
issue judiciously. Many feminists came from the antiwar movement and have let
their distaste for the military in general and the draft in particular mute their
response. In 1980 NOW [National Organization for Women] released a resolution
that buried support for the registration of women beneath opposition to the draft,
despite the fact that the draft had been redesigned to eliminate the vexing inequities
of Vietnam, when the sons of the working class served and the sons of the Ivy
League did not. Conservatives, meanwhile, used an equal-opportunity draft as the
linchpin of opposition to the Equal Rights Amendment, along with the terrifying
specter of unisex bathrooms. (I have seen the urinal, and it is benign.) The legislative
director of the right-wing group Concerned Women for America once defended the

The writer anticipates and addresses counter-arguments to her position.

existing regulations by saying that most women "don't want to be included in the draft." All those young men who went to Canada during Vietnam and those who today register with fear and trembling in the face of the Trade Center devastation might be amazed to discover that lack of desire is an affirmative defense.

She supports her position with statistics as well as personal anecdotes and comparisons to other situations.

Parents face a series of unique new challenges in this more egalitarian world, *12* not the least of which would be sending a daughter off to war. But parents all over this country are doing that right now, with daughters who enlisted; some have even expressed surprise that young women, in this day and age, are not required to register alongside their brothers and friends. While all involved in this debate over the years have invoked the assumed opposition of the people, even ten years ago more than half of all Americans polled believed women should be made eligible for the draft. Besides, this is not about comfort but about fairness. My son has to register with the Selective Service this year, and if his sister does not when she turns 18, it makes a mockery not only of the standards of this household but of the standards of this nation.

The writer appeals to the reader's logic and ethics.

It is possible in Afghanistan for women to be treated like little more than fecund pack animals precisely because gender fear and ignorance and hatred have been codified and permitted to hold sway. In this country, largely because of the concerted efforts of those allied with the women's movement over a century of struggle, much of that bigotry has been beaten back, even buried. Yet in improbable places the creaky old ways surface, the ways suggesting that we women

13

> *This is a responsibility that should fall equally upon all, male and female alike.*

were made of finer stuff. The finer stuff was usually porcelain, decorative and on the shelf, suitable for meals and show. Happily, the finer stuff has been transmuted into the right stuff. But with rights come responsibilities, as teachers like to tell their students. This is a responsibility that should fall equally upon all, male and female alike. If the empirical evidence is considered rationally, if the decision is divested of outmoded stereotypes, that's the only possible conclusion to be reached.

Reading for Better Writing

Working by yourself or with a group, answer these questions:

1. Which problem(s) does Quindlen identify? Which solution(s) does she propose? To what extent would the proposed solution(s) solve the problem(s) Quindlen discusses?

2. Review the section in chapter 17 about "Identifying Logical Fallacies" (see pages 301–304). Quindlen's opponents might accuse her of "either/or thinking," pointing out that instead of addressing only two options, she could also have argued to end the draft for everyone. Which other logical fallacies might Quindlen's opponents accuse her of making? Would you agree with them? Why or why not?

3. Which strategies does Quindlen use to try to convince readers that the situation she describes is problematic?

4. Why does the writer acknowledge that there may be opposition to her description of the problem and to her proposed solution?

5. Why does the essay open with a series of one-sentence paragraphs? How might the effect of the essay differ if these sentences had been combined into one paragraph?

6. Carefully re-read paragraph 8 in which Quindlen cites "a welter of arguments" that were lodged by those who oppose requiring women to register for the draft. Describe how she states their arguments and explain why her tone and phrasing are or are not fair.

7. Review Quindlen's statement in paragraph 8 that both Congress and the Supreme Court had ruled that "since women were forbidden to serve in combat positions, and the purpose of the draft was to create a combat-ready force, it made sense not to register them." Then summarize her counter-argument and explain why it is or is not convincing.

8. In January 2013, U.S. military administrators, led by Secretary of Defense Leon Panetta, changed the policy cited above by opening all combat roles to any qualified service personnel, regardless of gender. However, they did not change the policy requiring that only males must register for the draft. If Quindlen were to revise this essay (first published in 2001), how might she use the 2013 ruling to strengthen her analysis of both the problem and her solution?

Sample Problem-Solution Essay

Malcolm Gladwell, author of *The Tipping Point, Blink, Outliers,* and *What the Dog Saw,* writes regularly for *The New Yorker* magazine. Gladwell was born in England, grew up in Ontario, and graduated from the University of Toronto. In the commentary below, he takes a stand on the punishment of students. As you read his argument, take note of his appeals to logic, credibility, and/or emotion.

No Mercy

> As you read, take notes about how the writer presents the problem, and proposes and supports his solution.

In 1925, a young American physicist was doing graduate work at Cambridge University, in England. He was depressed. He was fighting with his mother and had just broken up with his girlfriend. His strength was in theoretical physics, but he was being forced to sit in a laboratory making thin films of beryllium. In the fall of that year, he dosed an apple with noxious chemicals from the lab and put it on the desk of his tutor, Patrick Blackett. Blackett, luckily, didn't eat the apple. But school officials found out what happened, and arrived at a punishment: the student was to be put on probation and ordered to go to London for regular sessions with a psychiatrist. *1*

Probation? These days, we routinely suspend or expel high-school students for doing infinitely less harmful things, like fighting or drinking or taking drugs—that is, for doing the kinds of things that teenagers do. This past summer, Rhett Bomar, the starting quarterback for the University of Oklahoma Sooners, was cut from the team when he was found to have been "overpaid" (receiving wages for more hours than he worked, with the apparent complicity of his boss) at his job at a car dealership. Even in Oklahoma, people seemed to think that kicking someone off a football team for having cut a few corners on his job made perfect sense. This is the age of zero tolerance. Rules are rules. Students have to be held accountable for their actions. Institutions must signal their expectations firmly and unambiguously: every school principal and every college president, these days, reads from exactly the same script. What, then, of a student who gives his teacher a poisoned apple? Surely he ought to be *2*

> *Even in Oklahoma, people seemed to think that kicking someone off a football team for having cut a few corners on his job made perfect sense.*

expelled from school and sent before a judge.

Suppose you cared about the student, though, and had some idea of his   3
situation and his potential. Would you feel the same way? You might. Trying to
poison your tutor is no small infraction. Then again, you might decide, as the dons
at Cambridge clearly did, that what had happened called for a measure of leniency.
They knew that the student had never done anything like this before, and that he
wasn't well. And they knew that to file charges would almost certainly ruin his
career. Cambridge wasn't sure that the benefits of enforcing the law, in this case,
were greater than the benefits of allowing the offender an unimpeded future.

Schools, historically, have been home to this kind of discretionary justice. You   4
let the principal or the teacher decide what to do about cheating because you know
that every case of cheating is different—and, more to the point, that every cheater
is different. Jimmy is incorrigible, and needs the shock of expulsion. But Bobby just
needs a talking to, because he's a decent kid, and Mary and Jane cheated because
the teacher foolishly stepped out of the classroom in the middle of the test, and the
temptation was simply too much. A Tennessee study found that after zero-tolerance
programs were adopted by the state's public schools the frequency of targeted
offenses soared: the firm and unambiguous punishments weren't deterring bad
behavior at all. Is that really a surprise? If you're a teenager, the announcement that
an act will be sternly punished doesn't always sink in, and it isn't always obvious
when you're doing the thing you aren't supposed to be doing. Why? Because you're a
teenager.

Somewhere along the way—perhaps in response   5
to Columbine—we forgot the value of discretion in
disciplining the young. "Ultimately, they have to
make right decisions," the Oklahoma football coach,
Bob Stoops, said of his players, after jettisoning his
quarterback. "When they do not, the consequences
are serious." Open and shut: he sounded as if he were
talking about a senior executive of Enron, rather
than a college sophomore whose primary obligation
at Oklahoma was to throw a football in the direction

> *Somewhere along the way—perhaps in response to Columbine—we forgot the value of discretion in disciplining the young.*

of young men in helmets. You might think that if the University of Oklahoma was so touchy about its quarterback being "overpaid" it ought to have kept closer track of his work habits with an on-campus job. But making a fetish of personal accountability conveniently removes the need for institutional accountability. (We court-martial the grunts who abuse prisoners, not the commanding officers who let the abuse happen.) To acknowledge that the causes of our actions are complex and muddy seems permissive, and permissiveness is the hallmark of an ideology now firmly in disgrace. That conservative patron saint Whittaker Chambers once defined liberalism as Christ without the Crucifixion. But punishment without the possibility of redemption is worse: it is the Crucifixion without Christ.

As for the student whose career Cambridge saved? He left at the end of the   6
academic year and went to study at the University of Göttingen, where he made important contributions to quantum theory. Later, after a brilliant academic career, he was entrusted with leading one of the most critical and morally charged projects in the history of science. His name was Robert Oppenheimer.

Reading for Better Writing

Working by yourself or with a group, answer these questions:

1. Malcolm Gladwell frames his commentary by beginning and ending with the story of Robert Oppenheimer. How does Gladwell present this story? What is its role in communicating his position?

2. Describe the phenomenon that Gladwell claims is a problem and explain how he supports that claim.

3. In paragraphs 2 and 5, Gladwell contrasts Oppenheimer's experience with that of Rhett Bomar. What differences does Gladwell emphasize?

4. At the beginning of paragraph 3, Gladwell uses the pronoun "you" as part of a "what if" appeal to his readers. Here and elsewhere in the essay, what is the impact of Gladwell speaking directly to readers?

5. Describe the solution that Gladwell argues will address the problem. Then explain why you do or do not agree, citing examples to support your position.

6. At the end of paragraph 5, Gladwell refers to Christ and the Crucifixion. How does this reference contribute to his argument?

Writing Guidelines

Planning

1. **Select and narrow a topic.** Brainstorm possibilities from this list:

   - **People Problems:** Consider generations—your own or a relative's. What problems face this generation? How can they be solved?
   - **College Problems:** List problems faced by college students. In your major, what problems are experts trying to solve?
   - **Social Problems:** What problems do our communities and country face? Where do you see suffering, injustice, inequity, waste, or harm?
   - **Workplace Problems:** What job-related problems have you experienced or might you experience?

   Then test your topic:

   - Is the problem real, serious, and currently—or potentially—harmful?
   - Do you care about this problem and believe that it must be solved? Why?
   - Can you offer a workable solution—or should you focus on part of the problem?

2. **Identify and analyze your audience.** You could have four audiences: people responsible for the problem, decision makers with the power to deliver change, people affected by the problem, and a public that wants to learn about it.

   - What do readers know about the problem? What are their questions or concerns?
   - Why might they accept or resist change? What solution might they prefer?
   - What arguments and evidence would convince them to acknowledge the problem, to care about it, and to take action?

3. **Probe the problem.** If helpful, use the graphic organizer on page 53.

   - **Define the problem.** What is it, exactly? What are its parts or dimensions?
   - **Determine the problem's seriousness.** Why should it be fixed? Who is affected and how? What are its immediate, long-term, and potential effects?
   - **Analyze causes.** What are its root causes and contributing factors?
   - **Explore context.** What is the problem's background, history, and connection to other problems? What solutions have been tried in the past? Who, if anyone, benefits from the problem's existence?
   - **Think creatively.** Look at the problem from other perspectives—other states and countries, both genders, different races and ethnic groups, and so on.

4. **Choose the best solution.** List all imaginable solutions—both modest and radical fixes. Then evaluate the alternatives:

   - List criteria that any solution should meet.
   - List solutions and analyze their strengths, weaknesses, costs, and so on.
   - Choose the best solution and gather evidence supporting your choice.

Drafting

5. **Outline your proposal and complete a first draft.** Describe the problem, offer a solution, and defend it using strategies that fit your purpose and audience.

   - **The problem:** Inform and/or persuade readers about the problem by using appropriate background information, cause-effect analysis, examples, analogies, parallel cases, visuals, and expert testimony.
   - **The solution:** If necessary, first argue against alternative solutions. Then present your solution, stating what should happen, who should be involved, and why.
   - **The support:** Show how the solution solves the problem. Use facts and analysis to argue that your solution is feasible and to address objections. If appropriate, use visuals such as photographs, drawings, or graphics to help readers grasp the nature and impact of the problem.

Revising

6. **Improve the ideas, organization, and voice.** Ask a classmate or someone from your college's writing center to read your problem-solution paper for the following:

   ___ **Ideas:** Does the solution fit the problem? Is the proposal precise, well researched, and well reasoned—free from oversimplification and obfuscation?

   ___ **Organization:** Does the writing move convincingly from problem to solution, using fitting compare-contrast, cause-effect, and process structures?

   ___ **Voice:** Is the tone positive, confident, objective, and sensitive to opposing viewpoints—and appropriate to the problem's seriousness?

Editing

7. **Edit and proofread the essay.** Look for these issues:

   ___ **Words:** Words are precise, effectively defined, and clear.

   ___ **Sentences:** Sentences are smooth, energetic, and varied in structure.

   ___ **Correctness:** The copy has correct grammar, spelling, usage, and mechanics.

   ___ **Design:** The design includes proper formatting and documentation.

Publishing

8. **Prepare and share your final essay.** Submit your essay to your instructor, but also consider sharing it with readers who have a stake in solving the problem.

Critical-Thinking and Writing Activities

As directed by your instructor, complete the following critical-thinking and writing activities by yourself or with classmates.

1. Note that Renee Wielenga initially wrote "Dream Act May Help Local Student Fight for Residency" in journalistic style and published the piece in a regional newspaper. Select a problem in your community, research the problem, and then write a news article or an editorial on the topic. Use problem-solution reasoning and submit the piece to your college or community newspaper.

2. Review the section in chapter 17 about "Engaging the Opposition" (page 305). Also review how Anna Quindlen engages her opposition in "Uncle Sam and Aunt Samantha." Then consider a persuasive piece that you are drafting or revising. How might you engage the opposition in a dialogue about your arguments? Revise your writing as needed.

3. Review chapter 17 for "Identifying Logical Fallacies" (pages 301–304). Write a humorous problem-solution essay in which you make an argument that includes a number of obvious logical fallacies. Share your writing with the class.

4. What are some challenges facing the planet Earth and the human race in the foreseeable future? Find a focused challenge and write a proposal that addresses it.

Learning-Objectives Checklist ✓

Have you achieved this chapter's learning objectives? Check your progress with the items below, revisiting topics in the chapter as needed. *I have . . .*

____ critically examined and evaluated problem-solution essays for clear information, logical claims, reliable evidence, and arguments that effectively address the writers' situations (348).

____ analyzed a problem's history, causes, effects, and impact on my intended readers (358–359).

____ researched potential solutions, evaluated their strengths and weaknesses, selected the best solution, and rationally explained my choice (358–359).

____ identified and corrected logical fallacies such as obfuscation, oversimplification, false cause, and slanted language (301–304).

____ integrated needed definitions and pointed out clarifying comparisons, contrasts, and classifications.

____ produced accurate descriptions, thorough analyses, and well-organized, rational arguments (358–359).

____ written, revised, and edited a convincing essay that logically analyzes a problem, proposes a reasonable solution, and advocates its implementation (358–359).

Chapter 21

Taking Essay Tests

There is nothing more disheartening than sitting down to take a test for which you're not prepared. The results are predictable—and they're not pretty. Conversely, there is nothing more exhilarating than walking out of a classroom after nailing a test. This is especially true in a college setting, where tests count for so much and second chances and extra credit are rare.

Many of the writing skills that you've already developed should serve you well in taking essay tests. For example, the instructions for essay tests commonly direct students to describe, analyze, classify, persuade, and more.

This chapter will help you perform these writing tasks within your specific rhetorical situation—a written exam. As a bonus, the chapter suggests a variety of other helpful ways to improve your test-taking skills.

Visually Speaking   Study Figure 21.1. Then list the many ways that focus is crucial to success when running races or taking essay tests.

Learning **Objectives**

By working through this chapter, you will be able to

- create study groups and memory guides.
- differentiate and interpret key words in essay questions.
- transform questions into topic sentences and thesis statements.
- generate answers that are clear, thoughtful, unified, and correct.
- implement tips for taking essay and objective tests.

fig. 21.1

Reviewing for Tests

Do you consider yourself a "bad" test taker? Do you know the material, yet somehow perform poorly on tests? Do you feel overwhelmed by all the information you have to cover when studying for a test? Does even the thought of studying so much material make you nervous? What you need is a positive mental attitude—and good study habits. Together they can make the difference between "spacing" during a test and "acing" an exam.

Perform daily reviews.

Why daily? Begin your reviews on the first day of class; if you miss a day, dust yourself off and keep going. Daily reviews are especially good because you tend to forget new information rapidly. Reviewing while the material is fresh in your mind helps to move it from your short-term memory into your long-term memory.

How much time? Even spending five or ten minutes on your review before or after each class will pay big dividends. Depending on the day's class, you may read through (or talk through) your notes, look over the headings in a reading assignment, skim any summaries you have, or put information into graphic organizers.

What to Do

- Put "Daily review of . . ." on your "To Do" list, calendar, or date book.
- Use the buddy system. Make a pact with a classmate and review together.
- Put your subconscious to work by reviewing material before you go to sleep.

Perform longer weekly reviews.

Why weekly? More than anything else, repetition helps anchor memory. You can cram a lot of data into your brain the night before an exam, but a day or two later you won't remember much of anything. And when final exam time comes, you'll have to learn the material all over again.

How much time? Plan to spend about one hour per week for each class. (This review can take place either by yourself or with a study group.) Remember that repetition is the single most important factor in retaining what you learn.

What to Do

- Make mind maps and flash cards of important information.
- Practice answering review questions by saying them aloud and by writing out short answers.
- Test your understanding of a subject by teaching or explaining it to someone else.
- Organize a study group. (See page 363.)

Forming a Study Group

A study group can keep you interested in a subject, force you to keep up with classwork, and increase your retention of study material. Group energy can be more powerful than individual energy. You will hear other points of view and other ways to approach a subject that you may never have thought of on your own. To get started, follow these guidelines.

1. **Find five to six people.**
   - Consider people who seem highly motivated and collaborative.
   - Ask your instructor to inform the class about the opportunity.

2. **Consider working online.**
   - Check first with your instructor and student services about the availability of chat rooms on your campus network.
   - Go to any search engine (Yahoo!, Google, Bing, and so on) and enter the term "chat room." For example, Yahoo! provides both private and public chat rooms ("clubs") free.
   - Use other options such as Skype or Facebook Chat.

3. **Arrange a time and place.**
   - Select a site where you can converse freely without distractions.
   - Agree on a time limit for the initial session.
   - Choose somebody in the group to keep everyone on task (or rotate this duty) and agree to accept any prodding and nudging with good humor.

4. **Set realistic goals and decide on a plan of action.**
   - Discuss what the group needs to accomplish and what your goals are.
   - Agree to practice "people skills" (listening, observing, cooperating, responding, and clarifying).
   - Decide which parts of the coursework you will review (lectures? labs? texts? exam questions?).

5. **Evaluate at the end of the first session.**
   - Honestly and tactfully discuss any problems that arose.
   - Ask who wants to continue. (It may be obvious at the first meeting that the group won't work well for all members.)
   - Choose a time (and place) for your next session.
   - Determine an agenda for the next session.
   - Exchange necessary information such as phone numbers, email addresses, user names for online networks, and so forth.

jocic / Shutterstock.com

Consider the Testing Situation

As you prepare to take an essay test, think about the test's purpose, readers, and topic.

- **Purpose:** Consider, first of all, how the essay test fits within the course. For example, how does this test match up with certain course goals? Then consider the purpose of a specific essay question, remembering that your goal is not simply to recall information and record it on the page. Rather, your goal is to come up with a solid, thoughtful idea (a thesis) in response to the question, and then effectively elaborate and support that idea. To that end, read the question carefully, noting the assigned topic, as well as the key terms (such as *evaluate, explain,* or *classify*) that clarify your task and suggest how you might organize your answer. (Pages 365–366 include definitions of eighteen terms that are commonly used in essay-test questions.)

- **Readers:** When you write an essay test, your primary reader is probably your instructor. Start, then, by considering your instructor's expectations and assessment criteria. What does he or she value? What thinking moves has your instructor modeled and emphasized in class? Thinking about your reader will help you make choices such as what issues to address, what supporting evidence to cite, what terms need defining, or how to focus your writing. For example, if your instructor asks you to take a position on a debatable topic, he or she is likely interested in what position you take, but possibly more interested in whether you state your claims clearly, support them logically, address opposing points of view, and shape your essay into a rational, informed, and convincing argument.

- **Topic:** The topics that you're asked to address in essay tests will obviously vary, depending on the subject matter that you're studying. When preparing for an essay test, study topics and related issues stressed in class and/or in your assigned readings. Then think about—and be ready to explain—how and why these topics and issues are relevant to your coursework and discipline. To help you remember information that you might include in your writing, use these memory strategies:

Tips to improve your memory

- **Intend to remember.** Scientists say that our brains never forget anything: It's our recall that is at fault. We remember the things that are important to us.
- **Link new information** to things you already know.
- **Organize your material.** Understand the big picture and then divide the information you need to know into smaller, more manageable categories.
- **Review new material as soon as possible.** The sooner you review (and the more regularly), the more likely you will remember.

Taking the Essay Test

Your instructors expect you to include all the right information, and they expect you to organize it in a clear, thoughtful way. In addition, they expect you to evaluate, synthesize, predict, analyze, and write a worthwhile answer.

Look for key words.

Key words, like those listed and defined below, will help you understand your writing tasks and compose focused, well-organized answers. Study the terms now and pay special attention to them when you read test questions.

Also note that many of the terms have been discussed at length in chapters 10–20, and review this information as needed.

Analyze To analyze is to break down a larger problem or situation into separate parts or relationships.

  ▊ Analyze the major difficulties found at urban housing projects.

Classify To classify is to place persons or things (especially animals and plants) together in a group because they share similar characteristics. Science uses a special classification or group order: phylum, class, order, family, genus, species, and variety.

  ▊ Classify three kinds of trees found in the rainforests of Costa Rica.

Compare To compare is to use examples to show how things are similar and different, placing the greater emphasis on similarities.

  ▊ Compare the vegetation in the rainforests of Puerto Rico with the vegetation in the rainforests of Costa Rica.

Contrast To contrast is to use examples to show how things are different in one or more important ways.

  ▊ Contrast the views of George Washington and Harry S. Truman regarding the involvement of the United States in world affairs.

Compare and contrast To compare and contrast is to use examples that show the major similarities and differences between two things (or people, events, ideas, and so forth). In other words, two things are used to clarify each other.

  ▊ Compare and contrast people-centered leadership with task-centered leadership.

Define To define is to give the meaning for a term. Generally, defining involves identifying the class to which a term belongs and explaining how it differs from other things in that class.

  ▊ Define the term "emotional intelligence" as it pertains to humans.

Describe To describe is to give a detailed sketch or impression of a topic.

▌ Describe how the Euro tunnel (the Chunnel) was built.

Diagram To diagram is to explain with lines or pictures—a flowchart, map, or other graphic device. Generally, a diagram will label the important points or parts.

▌ Diagram the parts of a DNA molecule.

Discuss To discuss is to review an issue from all sides. A discussion answer must be carefully organized to stay on track.

▌ Discuss how Rosa Parks's refusal to move to the back of the bus affected the civil rights movement.

Evaluate To evaluate is to make a value judgment by giving the pluses and minuses along with supporting evidence.

▌ Evaluate the efforts of midsized cities to improve public transportation services.

Explain To explain is to bring out into the open, to make clear, and to analyze. This term is similar to *discuss* but places more emphasis on cause/effect relationships or step-by-step sequences.

▌ Explain the effects of global warming on a coastal city like New Orleans.

Justify To justify is to tell why a position or point of view is good or right. A justification should be mostly positive—that is, the advantages are stressed over the disadvantages.

▌ Justify the use of antilock brakes in automobiles.

Outline To outline is to organize a set of facts or ideas by listing main points and subpoints. A good outline shows at a glance how topics or ideas fit together or relate to one another.

▌ Outline the events that caused the United States to enter World War II.

Prove To prove is to bring out the truth by giving evidence to back up a point.

▌ Prove that Atticus Finch in *To Kill a Mockingbird* provided an adequate defense for his client.

Review To review is to reexamine or to summarize the key characteristics or major points of the topic. Generally speaking, a review presents material in the order in which it happened or in decreasing order of importance.

▌ Review the events since 1976 that have led to the current hip-hop culture.

State To state is to present a concise statement of a position, fact, or point of view.

▌ State your reasons for voting in the last national election.

Summarize To summarize is to present the main points of an issue in a shortened form. Details, illustrations, and examples are usually omitted.

▌ Summarize the primary responsibilities of a school in a democracy.

Trace To trace is to present—in a step-by-step sequence—a series of facts that are somehow related. Usually the facts are presented in chronological order.

▌ Trace the events that led to the fall of the Union of Soviet Socialist Republics.

Plan and write the essay-test answer.

To help you write fluently and use your time efficiently, use an effective writing process, like the one described below.

1. **Reread the question several times.** (Pay special attention to any key words used in the question.)
2. **Rephrase the question into a topic sentence/thesis statement** with a clear point.

> **Question:** Explain why public housing was built in Chicago in the 1960s.
>
> **Thesis statement:** Public housing was built in Chicago because of the Great Migration, the name given to the movement of African Americans from the South to the North.

3. **Outline the main points you plan to cover in your answer.** Time will probably not allow you to include all supporting details in your outline.
4. **Write your essay (or paragraph).** Begin with your thesis statement (or topic sentence). Add whatever background information may be needed, and then follow your outline, writing as clearly as possible.

One-Paragraph Answer

If you feel that only one paragraph is needed to answer the question, use the main points of your outline as supporting details for your thesis statement.

Question: Explain why public housing was built in Chicago in the 1960s.

Topic Sentence

Public housing was built in Chicago because of the Great Migration, the name given to the movement of African Americans from the South to the North. The mechanical cotton picker, introduced in the 1920s, replaced field hands in the cotton fields of the South. At that time, Chicago's factories and stockyards were hiring workers. In addition, Jim Crow laws caused hardships and provided reasons for African Americans to move north. Finally, some African Americans had family

Supporting Details

and relatives in Chicago who had migrated earlier and who, it was thought, could provide a home base for the new migrants until they could get work and housing. According to the U.S. Census Reports, there were 109,000 African Americans in Chicago in 1920. By 1960, there were more than 800,000. However, this increase in population could have been handled except that the public wanted to keep the African Americans in the Black Belt, an area in South Chicago. Reluctant lending agencies and realtors made it possible for speculators to operate. Speculators

Conclusion

increased the cost of houses by 75 percent. All of these factors led to a housing shortage for African Americans, which public housing filled.

Multi-paragraph Answer

If the question is too complex to be handled in one paragraph, your opening paragraph should include your thesis statement and any essential background information. Begin your second paragraph by rephrasing one of the main points from your outline (Figure 21.2) into a suitable topic sentence. Support this topic sentence with examples, reasons, or other appropriate details. Handle additional paragraphs in the same manner. If time permits, add a summary or concluding paragraph to bring all of your thoughts to a logical close.

Question: Explain the advantages and disadvantages of wind energy.

Thesis: Wind energy has an equal number of advantages and disadvantages.

fig. 21.2

Outline

I. Advantages of wind energy
   A. Renewable
   B. Economical
   C. Nonpolluting
II. Disadvantages of wind energy
   A. Intermittent
   B. Unsightly
   C. A danger to some wildlife

The introductory paragraph sets up the essay's organization.

Wind energy has an equal number of advantages and disadvantages. It is renewable, economical, and nonpolluting; but it is also intermittent, unsightly, and a danger to the bird population.

Wind energy is renewable. No matter how much wind energy is used today, there will still be a supply tomorrow. As evidence indicates that wind energy was used to propel boats along the Nile River about 5000 B.C.E., it can be said that wind is an eternal, renewable resource.

Wind energy is economical. The fuel (wind) is free, but the initial cost for wind turbines is higher than for fossil-fueled generators. However, wind energy costs do not include fuel purchases and only minimal operating expenses. Wind power reduces the amount of foreign oil the United States imports and reduces health and environmental costs caused by pollution. Is it possible to sell excess power? The Public Utilities Regulatory Policy Act of 1978 (PURPA) states that a local electric company must buy any excess power produced by a qualifying individual. This act encourages the use of wind power.

Each paragraph follows a point in the outline.

Wind energy does not pollute. Whether one wind turbine is used by an individual or a wind farm supplies energy to many people, no air pollutants or greenhouse gases are emitted. California reports that 2.5 billion pounds of carbon dioxide and 15 million pounds of other pollutants have not entered the air thanks to wind energy.

How unfortunate is it that wind energy is intermittent? If a wind does not blow, 5 there is little or no electrical power. One way to resolve this dilemma is to store the energy that wind produces in batteries. The word intermittent also refers to the fact that wind power **is not** always available at the places where it is most needed. Often the sites that offer the greatest winds are located in remote locations far from the cities that demand great electrical power.

Specific details explain the main point.

Are wind turbines unsightly? A home-sized wind machine rises about 30 feet 6 with rotors between 8 and 25 feet in diameter. The largest machine in Hawaii stands about 20 stories high with rotors a little longer than the length of a football field. This machine supplies electricity to 1,400 homes. Does a single wind turbine upset the aesthetics of a community as much as a wind farm? The old adage "Beauty is in the eye of the beholder" holds up wherever wind turbines rotate. If ongoing electrical costs are almost nil, that wind turbine may look beautiful.

Questions help the reader understand the issue.

How serious is the issue of bird safety? The main questions are these: (1) 7 Why do birds come near wind turbines? (2) What, if any, are the effects of wind development on bird populations? (3) What can be done to lessen the problem? If even one bird of a protected species is killed, the Endangered Species Act has been violated. If wind turbines kill migratory birds, the Migratory Bird Treaty Act has been violated. As a result, many countries and agencies are studying the problem carefully.

The ending makes a final conclusion.

The advantages of wind energy seem to outweigh the disadvantages. The wind- 8 energy industry has been growing steadily in the United States and around the world. The new wind turbines are reliable and efficient. People's attitudes toward wind energy are mostly positive. Many manufacturers and government agencies are now cooperating to expand wind energy, making it the fastest-growing source of electricity in the world.

Reading for Better Writing

Working by yourself or with a group, answer these questions:

1. How does the writer provide a clear focus and logical organization in the essay answer? How soon are the focus and organization provided? What advantages does this approach offer the writer? The reader?

2. How do the sentences used to introduce the advantages differ from the sentences used to introduce the disadvantages? How does this technique aid the reader?

3. Why must the paragraphs in the body contain specific facts and examples? Which facts and examples does this writer use?

Quick Guide

Writing Under Pressure: The Essay Test

Make sure you are ready for the test both mentally and physically.

- **Before the test is distributed, mentally review your writing situation:** purpose, readers, and possible topics.

- **Receive the test and carefully listen to or read the instructions.**
    1. How much time do you have to complete the test?
    2. Do all the essay questions count equally?
    3. Can you use any aids, such as a dictionary or handbook?
    4. Are there any corrections, changes, or additions to the test?

- **Begin the test immediately and watch the time.** Don't spend so much time answering one question that you run out of time before answering the others.

- **Read all the essay questions carefully,** paying special attention to the key words. (See pages 365–366.)

- **Ask the instructor for clarification** if you don't understand something.

- **Rephrase each question into a controlling idea for your essay answer.** (This idea becomes your thesis statement.)

- **Think before you write.** Jot down all the important information and work it into a brief outline. Do this on the back of the test sheet or on a piece of scrap paper.

- **Use a logical pattern of organization and a strong topic sentence for each paragraph.** Tie points together with clear, logical transitions.

- **Write concisely,** but don't use abbreviations or nonstandard language.

- **Be efficient.** Write about those areas of the subject of which you are most certain first; then work on other areas as time permits.

- **Keep your test paper neat and use reasonable margins.** Neatness is always important, and readability is a must, especially on an essay exam.

- **Revise and proofread.** Read through your essay as carefully and completely as time permits.

Note: Also see "Tips for Coping with Test Anxiety," page 372.

Taking an Objective Test

Even though objective tests are generally straightforward and clear, following some tips can help you avoid making foolish mistakes.

True/False Test

- Read the entire question before answering. Often the first half of a statement will be true or false, while the second half is just the opposite. For an answer to be true, the entire statement must be true.
- Read each word and number. Pay special attention to names, dates, and numbers that are similar and could be easily confused.
- Beware of true/false statements that contain words such as *all, every, always,* and *never.* Very often these statements will be false.
- Watch for statements that contain more than one negative word. Remember: Two negatives make a positive. (***Example:*** It is unlikely ice will not melt when the temperature rises above 32 degrees F.)

Matching Test

- Read through both lists quickly before you begin answering. Note any descriptions that are similar and pay special attention to the differences.
- When matching a word to a word, determine the part of speech of each word. If the word is a verb, for example, match it with another verb.
- When matching a word to a phrase, read the phrase first and look for the word it describes.
- Cross out each answer as you find it—unless you are told that the answer can be used more than once.
- Use capital letters rather than lowercase letters because they are less likely to be misread by the person correcting the test.

Multiple-Choice Test

- Read the directions to determine whether you are looking for the correct answer or the best answer. Also, check whether some questions can have two (or more) correct answers.
- Read the first part of the question, checking for negative words such as *not, never, except,* and *unless.*
- Try to answer the question in your mind before looking at the choices.
- Read all the choices before selecting your answer. This step is especially important on tests in which you must select the best answer, or on tests where one of your choices is a combination of two or more answers. (***Example:*** d. Both a and b / e. All of the above / f. None of the above)

Tips for Coping with Test Anxiety

Consider the following advice:

- **Study smart.** Use a variety of study and memory techniques to help you see your coursework from several different angles.

- **Review with others.** Join a study group and prepare with the members. Also, ask a classmate or family member to put you to the test.

- **Prepare yourself both physically and mentally.** Get a good night's sleep and eat a healthful, light meal before the test (doughnuts and coffee are not a healthful, light meal).

- **Get some exercise.** Aerobic exercise (running, swimming, walking, aerobics) is a great way to relieve stress, and exercise has been proven to help you think more quickly and more clearly.

- **Hit the shower.** Hot water is relaxing, cold water is stimulating, and warm water is soothing. Take your pick.

- **Get to class early ... but not too early!** Hurrying increases anxiety, but so does waiting.

- **Relax.** Take a few deep breaths, close your eyes, and think positive thoughts. The more relaxed you are, the better your memory will serve you.

- **Glance through the entire test.** Then plan your time, and pace yourself accordingly. You don't want to discover with only 5 minutes of class time left that the last question is an essay that counts for 50 percent of your grade.

- **Begin by filling in all the answers you know.** This process relieves anxiety and helps to trigger answers for other questions that you may not know immediately. Also, jot down important facts and formulas that you know you will need later on.

- **Don't panic.** If other people start handing in their papers long before you are finished, don't worry. They may have given up or rushed through the exam. The best students often finish last.

Bottom Line

The better you prepare for a test—mentally and physically—the less likely you'll be to suffer serious test anxiety.

Chapter 22

Writing for the Workplace

One thing you already know about college life is that you have to do a lot of writing in your courses—and it has to be good. By writing well, you make a positive impression in the classroom. But did you know that life outside the classroom also requires lots of writing?

This chapter will help you write work-related documents. Sample letters and memos will help you communicate effectively with people ranging from the registrar to scholarship committees. The sample application essay and résumés will help you apply for a job, a program, or an internship. In addition, the email writing instructions will help you take care of business with other readers, no matter where in the world they might be.

Visually Speaking   What does Figure 22.1 suggest about how and why people write in the workplace?

Learning **Objectives**

By working through this chapter, you will be able to

- accurately analyze your workplace-writing situation.
- produce clear, properly formatted letters, memos, and emails.
- write persuasive job-search correspondence.
- write organized, detailed, and effectively formatted résumés.

bikeriderlondon / Shutterstock.com

fig. 22.1

Writing the Business Letter

Business letters do many things—for example, share ideas, promote products, or ask for help. Putting a message in writing gives you time to think about, organize, and edit what you want to say. In addition, a written message serves as a record of important details for both the sender and the recipient.

Parts of the Business Letter

1. **Heading** The heading gives the writer's complete address, either in the letterhead (company stationery) or typed out, followed by the date.

2. **Inside Address** The inside address gives the reader's name and address.
   - If you're not sure which person to address or how to spell someone's name, you could call the company or check their Web site for the information.
   - If the person's title is a single word, place it after the name and a comma (Mary Johnson, President). A longer title goes on a separate line.

3. **Salutation** The salutation begins with *Dear* and ends with a colon, not a comma.
   - Use *Mr.* or *Ms.* plus the person's last name, unless you are well acquainted. Do not guess at *Miss.* or *Mrs.*
   - If you can't get the person's name, replace the salutation with *Dear* or *Attention* followed by the title of an appropriate reader. (*Examples:* Dear Dean of Students: or Attention: Personnel Manager)

   Note: See pages 102–104 for a complete list of "unbiased" ways to refer to an individual or a particular group.

4. **Body** The body should consist of single-spaced paragraphs with double-spacing between paragraphs. (Do not indent the paragraphs.)
   - If the body goes to a second page, put the reader's name at the top left, the number 2 in the center, and the date at the right margin.

5. **Complimentary Closing** For the complimentary closing, use *Sincerely, Yours sincerely,* or *Yours truly* followed by a comma; use *Best wishes* if you know the person well.

6. **Signature** The signature includes the writer's name both handwritten and typed.

7. **Initials** When someone types the letter for the writer, that person's initials appear (in lowercase) after the writer's initials (in capitals) and a colon.

8. **Enclosure** If a document (brochure, form, copy, or other form) is enclosed with the letter, the word *Enclosure* or *Encl.* appears below the initials.

9. **Copies** If a copy of the letter is sent elsewhere, type *cc:* beneath the enclosure line, followed by the person's or department's name.

Formatting a Letter

fig. 22.2

Heading

Box 143
Balliole College
Eugene, OR 97440-5125
August 29, 2013

Four to Seven Spaces

Inside Address

Ms. Ada Overlie
Ogg Hall, Room 222
Balliole College
Eugene, OR 97440-0222

Double Space

Salutation

Dear Ms. Overlie:

Double Space

Body

As the president of the Earth Care Club, I welcome you to Balliole Community College. I hope the year will be a great learning experience both inside and outside the classroom.

Double Space

That learning experience is the reason I'm writing—to encourage you to join the Earth Care Club. As a member, you could participate in the educational and action-oriented mission of the club. The club has most recently been involved in the following:

- Organizing a reduce, reuse, recycle program on campus
- Promoting cloth rather than plastic bag use among students
- Giving input to the college administration on landscaping, renovating, and building for energy efficiency
- Putting together the annual Earth Day celebration

Double Space

Which environmental concerns and activities would you like to focus on? Bring them with you to the Earth Care Club. Simply complete the enclosed form and return it by September 9. Then watch the campus news for details on our first meeting.

Double Space

Yours sincerely,

Complimentary Closing and Signature

Dave Wetland   **Four Spaces**

Dave Wetland
President

Double Space

**Initials
Enclosure
Copies**

DW:kr
Encl. membership form
cc: Zachary Clark, membership committee

Writing Memos and Email

A memorandum is a written message sent from one person to one or more other people within the same organization. As such, a memo is less formal than a letter. A memo can vary in length from a sentence or two to a four- or five-page report, and a memo can be delivered in person, dropped in a mailbox, or sent via email.

Memos are written to create a flow of information within an organization—asking and answering questions, describing procedures and policies, or reminding people about appointments and meetings. Here are some guidelines:

- **Write memos only when necessary,** and only to those people who need them.
- **Distribute them through the appropriate media**—mail, fax, bulletin boards, kiosk, or email.
- **Make your subject line precise** (a brief summary) so that the topic is clear and the memo is easy to file.
- **Get to the point:** (1) state the subject, (2) give necessary details, and (3) state the response you want.

Date: September 24, 2013

To: All Users of the Bascom Hill Writing Lab

From: Kerri Kelley, Coordinator

Subject: New Hours/New Equipment for Writing Lab

The subject line clarifies the memo's purpose.

Beginning October 1, the Bascom Hill Writing Lab will expand its weekend hours as follows: Fridays, 7:00 a.m.–11:00 p.m.; Saturdays, 8:00 A.M.–11:00 p.m.

The main point is stated immediately.

Also, six additional computers will be installed next week, making it easier to get computer time. We hope these changes will help meet the increased demand for time and assistance we've experienced this fall. Remember, it's still a good idea to sign up in advance. To reserve time, call the lab at 462.7722 or leave your request at bhill@madwis.edu.

Readers are asked to take note of a few final facts.

Finally, long-range planners, mark your calendars. The lab will be closed on Thanksgiving Day morning and open from 1:00 p.m. to 11:00 p.m. We will also be closed on Christmas and New Year's Day. We will post our semester-break hours sometime next month.

Sending Email

Email enables people to correspond through computer networks around the globe. Although some prefer to send quick notes via text messaging or social networks, email is still widely used in professional contexts because it allows you to do the following:

- Send, forward, and receive many messages quickly and efficiently, making it ideal for group projects and other forms of collaboration
- Set up mailing lists (specific groups of email addresses) so that you can easily send the same message to several people at the same time
- Organize messages in "folders" for later reference, and reply to messages

Tips for email

- **Revise and edit messages for clarity and correctness before sending them.** Confusing sentences, grammatical errors, and typos limit your ability to communicate on a computer screen just as they do on paper.

- **Use email responsibly.** Sooner or later you will send email to the wrong person, or a reader will forward your message to another person without your permission. Also understand that your email messages and attachments could remain on your organization's server for years! Keep these possibilities in mind at all times, and never write anything that would embarrass you if the wrong party gained access to it.

- **Make messages easy to read and understand.** (1) Provide a clear, complete subject line so readers can scan it and decide whether to read or delete the message. (2) Type short paragraphs. Figure 22.3 provides an example.

Send　Chat　Attach　Address　Fonts　Colors　Save As Draft	
To:	"Sherry West" SWEST@stgeorge.edu
From:	outreach@stgeorge.edu
Subject:	Agenda for Student Outreach Committee Meeting

fig. 22.3

Please remember that our next meeting is this Wednesday, September 25, at 8:00 p.m. in SUB Room 201. We'll discuss the following agenda items:

1. The minutes of our September 11 meeting
2. A proposal from SADD about Alcohol Awareness Week
3. A progress report on the Habitat for Humanity project

Before the meeting, please review the minutes and the SADD proposal attached to this message.

Applying for a Job

When you apply for some jobs, you have to do nothing more than fill out an application form. With other jobs, it's a different story. You may be required to write a letter of application, gather letters of recommendation, write an application essay, and put together a résumé. The following pages provide models to fit nearly every occasion.

Sample Letter of Application

Your letter of application (or cover letter) introduces you to an employer and often highlights information on an accompanying résumé. Your goal in writing this letter is to convince the employer to invite you for an interview.

Ogg Hall, Room 222
Balliole College
Eugene, OR 97440-0222
September 2, 2013

Address a specific person, if possible.

Professor Edward Mahaffy
Greenhouse Coordinator
Balliole College
Eugene, OR 97440-0316

Dear Professor Mahaffy:

State the desired position and your chief qualification.

I recently talked with Ms. Sierra Arbor in the Financial Aid Office about work-study jobs for 2013-2014. She told me about the Greenhouse Assistant position and gave me a job description. As a full-time Balliole student, I'm writing to apply for this position. I believe that my experience qualifies me for the job.

Focus on how your skills meet the reader's needs.

As you can see from my résumé, I spent two summers working in a raspberry operation, doing basic plant care and carrying out quality-control lab tests on the fruit. Also, as I was growing up, I learned a great deal by helping with a large farm garden. In high school and college, I studied botany. Because of my interest in this field, I'm enrolled in the Environmental Studies program at Balliole.

Request an interview and thank the reader.

I am available for an interview. You may phone me any time at 341.3611 (and leave a message on my machine) or email me at dvrl@balliole.edu. Thank you for considering my application.

Yours sincerely,

Ada Overlie

Ada Overlie

Encl. résumé

Sample Recommendation-Request Letter

When you apply for a job or program, it helps to present references or recommendations to show your fitness for the position. To get the support you need from people familiar with your work (instructors and employers), you need to ask for that support. You can do so in person or by phone, but a courteous and clear letter or email message makes your request official and helps the person complete the recommendation effectively. Here is a suggested outline:

- **Situation:** Remind the reader of your relationship to him or her; then ask the person to write a recommendation or to serve as a reference for you.
- **Explanation:** Describe the work you did for the reader and the type of job, position, or program for which you are applying.
- **Action:** Explain what form the recommendation should take, to whom it should be addressed, and where and when it needs to be sent.

2456 Charles Street
Lexington, KY 40588-8321
March 19, 2013

Dr. Rosa Perez
271 University Boulevard
University of Kentucky
Lexington, KY 40506-1440

Dear Dr. Perez:

The Situation

As we discussed on the phone, I would appreciate your writing a recommendation letter for me. You know the quality of my academic work, my qualities as a person, and my potential for working in the medical field.

The Explanation

As my professor for Biology 201 and 202, you are familiar with my grades and work habits. As my adviser, you know my career plans and understand whether I have the qualities needed to succeed in the medical profession. I am asking you for your recommendation because I am applying for summer employment with the Lexington Ambulance Service. I recently received my Emergency Medical Technician (Basic) license to prepare for such work.

The Action

Please send your letter to Rick Falk, EMT Coordinator, at the University Placement Office by April 8. Thank you for your help. Let me know if you need any other information (phone 231.6700; email jnwllms@ukentucky.edu).

Yours sincerely,

Jon Williams

Jon Williams

The Application Essay

For some applications, you may be asked to submit an essay, a personal statement, or a response paper. For example, you might be applying for admission to an academic program (social work, engineering, optometry school) or for an internship, a scholarship, or a research grant. Whatever the situation, what you write and how well you write it will be important factors in the success of your application.

On the facing page is a model application essay. Jessy Jezowski wrote this essay as part of her application to a college social work program.

Tips for an application essay

- **Understand what you are being asked to write and why.** How does the essay fit into the entire application? Who will read your essay? What will they look for?

- **Focus on the instructions for writing the essay.** What type of question is it? What topics are you asked to write about? What hints do the directions give about possible organization, emphasis, style, length, and method of submitting the essay?

- **Be honest with yourself and your readers.** Don't try to write only what you think readers want to hear.

- **Think about your purpose and readers:**
  - What do you want to gain (internship, scholarship, job interview), and how could your writing help you gain it?
  - Who are your readers? What do they know about you? What should they know?

- **Develop your essay using the following organization** (if the instructions allow for it):
  - An introduction with a fresh, interesting opening statement and a clear focus or theme
  - A body that develops the focus or theme clearly and concisely—with some details and examples—in a way appropriate to the instructions
  - A conclusion that stresses a positive point and looks forward to participating in the program, internship, organization, or position
  - Write in a style that is personal but professional. Use words that fit the subject and the readers. Avoid clichés, and balance generalizations with concrete examples and details.

- **Refine your first draft into a polished piece.** First, get feedback from another student or, if appropriate, a professor, and revise the essay. Second, edit the final version thoroughly: You don't want typos, incorrect names, and grammar errors to derail your application.

February 28, 2013

Jessy Jezowski

Personal Statement

The opening provides a clear focus for the essay.

While growing up in Chicago, I would see people hanging out on street corners, by grocery stores, and in parks—with no home and barely any belongings. Poverty and its related problems are all around us, and yet most people walk by them with blinders on. I have found myself quick to assume that someone else will help the poor man on the corner, the woman trapped in an abusive relationship, or the teenager struggling with an eating disorder. But I know in my heart that all members of society are responsible to and for each other. Social welfare issues affect every member of society— including me.

The writer demonstrates knowledge of the field and explains what she hopes to learn.

Because these issues are serious and difficult to solve, I wish to major in social work and eventually become a social worker. In the major, I want to gain the knowledge, skills, and attitudes that will make me part of the solution, not part of the problem. By studying social work institutions, the practices of social work, and the theory and history behind social work, I hope to learn how to help people help themselves. When that pregnant teenager comes to me, I want to have strong, practical advice—and be part of an effective social work agency that can help implement that advice.

Two concrete examples help back up her general statements.

I am especially interested at this point in working with families and teenagers, in either a community counseling or school setting. Two experiences have created this interest. First, a woman in my church who works for an adoption agency, Ms. Lesage, has modeled for me what it means to care for individuals and families within a community and around the world. Second, I was involved in a peer counseling program in high school. As counselors, we received training in interpersonal relationships and the nature of helping. In a concrete way, I experienced the complex challenges of helping others.

The conclusion summarizes her goals for the future.

I believe strongly in the value of all people and am interested in the well-being of others. As a social worker, I would strive to make society better (for individuals, families, and communities) by serving those in need, whatever their problems.

Preparing a Résumé

A strong résumé isn't generic—a ho-hum fill-in-the-blanker. Rather, it's a vivid word picture of your skills, knowledge, and past responsibilities. It says exactly who you are by providing the kind of information listed below.

- **Personal Data:** name, address, phone number, email address (enough for the reader to identify you and reach you easily).

- **Job Objective:** the type of position you want and the type of organization for which you want to work.

- **Skills Summary:** the key qualities and skills you bring to a position, listed with supporting details. Here are some skill areas that you might consider for your own résumé:

  - Communication
  - Organization
  - Problem solving
  - Computer
  - Sales, marketing, public relations
  - Working with people, counseling, training
  - Management (people, money, other resources)
  - Languages

- **Experience:** positions you've held (where and when), and your specific duties and your accomplishments.

- **Education:** degrees, courses, and special projects.

- **Other Experiences:** volunteer work, awards, achievements, tutoring jobs, extra-curricular activities (related to your job objective), licenses, and certifications.

Tips for résumé writing

- **Design each résumé to fit the particular job.**

- **Be specific**—use numbers, dates, and names.

- **Present information first that is the most impressive** and/or most important to the job for which you are applying. This guideline will help you determine whether to put your experience or your education first.

- **Use everyday language** and short, concise phrases.

- **Be parallel**—list similar items using similar structures.

- **Use boldface type, underlining, white space, and indentations** to make your résumé more readable.

- **Get someone else's reaction**; then revise and proofread.

Sample Résumé

Ada Overlie

Present contact information and employment objectives.

Home
451 Wiser Lake Road
Ferndale, WA 98248-8941
360.354.5916

School
Ogg Hall, Room 222
Balliole College
Eugene, OR 97440-0222
Phone: 503.341.3611
Email: dvrl@balliole.edu

Job Objective: Part-time assistant in a nursery or greenhouse.

Skills Summary:

Feature skills with appropriate headings and lists.

Horticultural Skills: Familiar with garden planting, care, and harvesting practices—
        planning, timing, companion planting, fertilizing.

Lab Skills: Familiar with procedures for taking fruit samples, pureeing
        them, checking for foreign objects, and testing sugar content.

Experience:

List work and education chronologically, from most to least current.

Summers 2011 and 2012: Lab Technician.
        Mayberry Farms and Processing Plant, Ferndale, WA.
        Worked in Quality Control testing raspberries to make sure they met company
        standards.

Summers 2009 and 2010: Camp Counselor.
        Emerald Lake Summer Camp, Hillsboro, WA.
        Supervised 12-year-olds in many camp activities, including nature
        hikes in which we identified plants and trees.

Education:

Format for paper only; boldface, underlining, bulleted or indented lists, two columns.

August 2012 to present: Balliole College, Eugene, OR.
        Environmental Studies and Communication major.
        Courses completed and in progress include Environmental Studies
        and General Botany. First semester GPA 3.7.

August 2008 to June 2012: Ferndale High School, Ferndale, WA.
        Courses included Biology, Agriculture, U.S. Government, and Economics.
        Special Projects: Completed research papers on clean-water legislation
        and organic farming practices.

Offer references.

References available upon request.

Sample Electronic Résumé

To find employees, companies often use computer programs to search electronic résumés for keywords (especially nouns) found in job descriptions or ads. Anticipating such a search, Jonathan Greenlind identified keywords and inserted them into his job description and résumé.

Present contact information and employment objective.

Jonathan L. Greenlind
806 5th Avenue
Waterloo, Iowa 50701
Telephone: 319.268.6955
Email: grnlnd@aol.com

OBJECTIVE

Position as hydraulics supervisor that calls for hydraulics expertise, technical skills, mechanical knowledge, reliability, and enthusiasm

List skills, experiences, and education using many keywords.

SKILLS

Operation and repair specialist in main and auxiliary power systems, subsystems, landing gears, brakes and pneumatic systems, hydraulic motors, reservoirs, actuators, pumps and cylinders from six types of hydraulic systems

Dependable, resourceful, strong leader, team worker

Format for email:
• one column
• bullets
• simple sans serif typeface
• flush-left margin
• ASCII or RTF text (readable by all computers)

EXPERIENCE

Aviation Hydraulics Technician
United States Navy (2007–present)

• Repair, test, and maintain basic hydraulics, distribution systems, and aircraft structural hydraulics systems
• Manufacture low-, medium-, and high-pressure rubber and Teflon hydraulic hoses, and aluminum stainless-steel tubing
• Perform preflight, postflight, and other periodic aircraft inspections
• Operate ground-support equipment
• Supervise personnel

Aircraft Mechanic
Sioux Falls International Airport (2005–2007)
Sioux Falls, South Dakota

• Performed fueling, engine overhauls, minor repairs, and tire and oil changes of various aircraft

EDUCATION

• United States Navy (2007–2011)
• Certificate in Hydraulic Technical School "A", GPA 3.8/4.0
• Certificate in Hydraulic, Pneumatic Test Stand School, GPA 3.9/4.0
• Courses in Corrosion Control, Hydraulic Tube Bender, Aviation Structural Mechanics
• Equivalent of 10 semester hours in Hydraulic Systems Maintenance and Structural Repair

Offer references.

References available upon request.

Chapter 23

Preparing Oral Presentations

Throughout your academic and professional career, you will give many oral presentations. In each situation, start by identifying the following:

- **Your purpose:** Am I trying to persuade, inspire, inform, or teach?
- **Your audience:** What are their ages, interests, knowledge of the topic, and attitude toward me?
- **Your topic:** What should I speak about, and where can I find the best information?

This chapter will help you answer these questions and develop a strong speech.

Visually Speaking   What does Figure 23.1 suggest about the nature and impact of public speaking?

Learning **Objectives**

By working through this chapter, you will be able to

- accurately analyze your presentation situation.
- create an opening, middle, and closing that fit the situation.
- develop list, outline, and/or manuscript forms of a speech, complete with cues for audiovisual effects.
- effectively use presentation software.
- plan, write, rehearse, and deliver an effective presentation.

hxdbzxy / Shutterstock.com

fig. 23.1

Organizing Your Presentation

After you've gathered your information, you must organize and develop the message. How? Start by thinking about your presentation as having three distinct parts: (1) an introduction, (2) a body, and (3) a conclusion. The guidelines on this page and the following two pages will help you integrate, organize, and refine all the parts so they communicate the message and achieve your purpose.

Prepare an introduction.

For any speaking situation, you should develop an introduction that does the following things:

- Greets the audience and grabs their attention
- Communicates your interest in them
- Introduces your topic and main idea
- Shows that you have something worthwhile to say
- Establishes an appropriate tone

You may greet the audience in many ways, including introducing yourself or making appropriate comments about the occasion, the individuals present, or the setting. Following these comments, introduce your topic and main idea as quickly and as clearly as you can. For example, you could open with one of these attention-grabbing strategies:

- A little-known fact or statistic
- A series of questions
- A humorous story or anecdote
- An appropriate quotation
- A description of a serious problem
- A cartoon, picture, or drawing
- A short demonstration
- A statement about the topic's importance
- An eye-catching prop or display
- A video or an audio clip

fyi As a matter of courtesy, audiences will generally give you their attention—but only for about thirty seconds. After that, you must *earn* it by presenting information that they believe is worth hearing.

razihusin / Shutterstock.com

Develop the body.

The body of your presentation should deliver the message—and supporting points—so clearly that the audience understands the presentation after hearing it only once. The key to developing such a clear message is choosing an organizational pattern that fits your purpose.

Before you outline the body, take a moment to review what you want your presentation to do: Explain a problem? Promote an idea? Teach a process? Be sure the organizational pattern will help you do that. For example, if you want to teach a process, the outline should list the process steps in chronological order. If your outline is clear, you may begin to write.

Organizational Patterns

Organizational patterns for explaining a process and other purposes are listed below.

- **Chronological order:** Arrange information according to the time order in which events (or steps in a process) take place.
- **Order of importance:** Arrange information according to its importance—greatest to least or least to greatest.
- **Comparison/contrast:** Give information about subjects by comparing and contrasting them.
- **Cause/effect:** Give information about a situation or problem by showing the causes and the effects.
- **Order of location:** Arrange information about subjects according to where things are located in relation to each other.
- **Problem/solution:** Describe a problem and then present a solution for it.

Writing an Outline or a Manuscript

After deciding how to organize your message, write it out in either outline or manuscript form. For help, see the tips below and the model on pages 389–391.

Body-Building Tips

- Build your presentation around several key ideas. (Don't try to cover too much ground.)
- Write with a personal, natural voice.
- Support your main points with reliable facts and clear examples.
- Present your information in short, easy-to-follow segments.
- Use positive, respectful language. (Avoid jargon.)
- Use graphic aids and handouts.

Come to a conclusion.

A strong introduction and conclusion work like bookends supporting the body of the presentation. The introduction gets the audience's attention, sets the tone, states the main idea, and identifies the key points of the message. Almost in reverse, the conclusion reviews those points, restates the main idea, reinforces the tone, and refocuses the audience on what it should think about or do. Together, those bookends emphasize and clarify the message so that listeners will understand and remember it.

Concluding Strategies

Here are some strategies—which you can use alone or in combination—for concluding a presentation:

- Review your main idea and key points.
- Issue a personal challenge.
- Come "full circle." (State those arguments or details that back up your original point.)
- Recommend a plan of action.
- Suggest additional sources of information.
- Thank the audience and ask for questions.

Hold a Q & A session.

After your presentation, you may want to invite your audience to ask questions. Very often, a Q & A session is the real payoff for participants. They can ask for clarification of points or inquire about how your message applies to their personal situations. Audience members may even offer their own insights or solutions to problems mentioned in the presentation.

Q & A Tips

The following suggestions will help you lead a good Q & A session:

- Listen carefully and think about each part of the question.
- Repeat or paraphrase questions for the benefit of the entire group.
- Answer the questions concisely and clearly.
- Respond honestly when you don't know the answer, and offer to find one.
- Ask for a follow-up question if someone seems confused after your answer.
- Look directly at the group when you answer.
- Be prepared to pose an important question or two if no one asks a question.
- Conclude by thanking the audience for their participation.

Writing Your Presentation

How much of your presentation you actually write out depends on your topic, audience, purpose, and—of course—personal style. The three most common forms to use when making a presentation are a list, an outline, and a manuscript (Figure 23.2).

List: Use a list for a short, informal speech such as an after-dinner introduction. Think about your purpose and then list the following:

- Your opening sentence (or two)
- A summary phrase for each of your main points
- Your closing sentence

Outline: Use an outline for a more complex or formal topic. You can organize your material in greater detail without tying yourself to a word-for-word presentation. Here's one way you can do it:

- Opening (complete sentences)
- All main points (sentences)
- Supporting points (phrases) quotations (written out) all supporting technical details, statistics, and sources (listed)
- Closing (complete sentences)

Wherever appropriate, include notes on visual aids (in caps or boldface).

Manuscript: Use the guidelines below if you plan to write out your presentation word for word:

- Double-space and number pages (or cards).
- Use complete sentences on a page (do not run sentences from one page to another).
- Mark difficult words for pronunciation.
- Mark the script for interpretation using symbols such as boldface or italics to signal emphasis or vocal color.

List

1. Opening sentence or two
2. Phrase 1
   Phrase 2
   Phrase 3
3. Closing sentence

Outline

I. Opening statement
   A. Point with support
   B. Point (purpose or goal)
      [VISUAL 1]
II. Body (with 3-5 main points)
   A. Main point
      1. Supporting details
      2. Supporting details
   B. Main point
      1. Supporting details
      2. Supporting details
   C. Main point
      1. Supporting details
      2. Supporting details
III. Closing statement
   A. Point, including restatement of purpose
   B. Point, possibly a call to action
      [VISUAL 2]

fig. 23.2

Sample Speech

In her formal presentation below, student Burnette Sawyer argues that college students must begin a retirement savings plan today. Notice that she uses italics to mark words needing vocal color and boldface to mark words needing emphasis. She places all visual aid cues in color.

Save Now or Pay Later

Imagine that you've finished school, gotten a job, worked hard all week, and this dollar bill represents your whole paycheck. [hold up dollar bill] As your employer, I'm about to hand you the check when I stop, tear off about 20 percent like this, give it to Uncle Sam, and say, "Here's my employee's income tax." Then I tear off another 30 percent like this, give that to Uncle Sam too, and say, "And here's her Medicare and Social Security tax." *1*

> The speaker begins with an anecdote.

Finally, I give you this half and say, "Here, hard worker, this is what's left of your *whole paycheck.*" *2*

> She tears the dollar for emphasis.

Does that sound like science fiction? *3*

Senator Alan Simpson doesn't think so. In the magazine *Modern Maturity,* he says that unless legislation changes the Social Security system, our generation will have to pay 20 percent [SLIDE 1] of our paychecks as income tax, and 30 percent [SLIDE 2] as Social Security tax. That means we can keep just **50 percent** [SLIDE 3] of what we earn. *4*

But the news gets **worse**. Remember this 30 percent that we paid to Social Security? [hold up piece of dollar bill] Well, that won't be enough money for retired people to live on in the year 2043. Remember that year, 2043—we'll come back to that soon. *5*

> The speaker asks questions to involve the audience.

What's the problem? The Social Security system can't ensure our savings for retirement. *6*

What's the solution? We have to start our own savings plans, and the earlier, the better. *7*

Ever since the Social Security system started back in 1935 [SLIDE 4], it has never been secure. While the system has been "fixed" a number of times, these fix-it jobs haven't solved the problem. For example, writer Keith Carlson points out that in 1983 [SLIDE 5] Congress raised payroll taxes, extended the retirement age, and said that the system would be in good financial shape until 2056. *8*

> Throughout the speech, she uses 11 slides to give her listeners a clear understanding of the main points.

But then, says Carlson, *just nine years later,* a report came out saying that Congress had been **wrong**. The report [SLIDE 6] said in 1992 that Social Security money wouldn't even last that long—it would run out by 2043. *Remember that year, 2043?* That's before most of us are supposed *to retire at age 67*! *9*

Do you think this news is bad? The AARP Bulletin reported on the Bipartisan *10* Commission on Entitlement and Tax Reform. This commission warned that entitlement programs like Social Security [SLIDE 7] are growing so fast they could "bankrupt the country" by the year 2029—long before we retire!

So what should we do? In three years, many of us will vote in a presidential *11* election for the first time. Both Democrats and Republicans say they have a plan to fix Social Security. What if we all vote for the presidential candidate with the best plan? Will that save our retirement funds? **Don't count on it!** As the track record for Social Security shows, one more fix-it job won't fix the system. We have to start our own retirement plans—and do it early in our careers.

In fact, in his book *Retirement 101,* Willard Enteman says that we should start a *12* personal savings plan the day we get our first paychecks. In sociology class last week, Mr. Christians made the same point. He gave us this bar graph [SLIDE 8] showing that if our goal is to save $500,000 by age 67, we had better *start early* before saving gets too expensive.

As you can see from the graph, if we start saving when we're 25, we can reach *13* $500,000 by saving just $121 a month. [SLIDE 9] If we wait until we're 35, we'll have to save $282 a month. [SLIDE 10] If we wait until we're 45, we'll have to put away $698 a month. [SLIDE 11] And if we wait until we're 55, we'll need $2,079 a month.

Look at the difference. To reach $500,000 by age 67 would cost $121 a month if *14* we start at 25, and $2,079 a month if we start at 55.

What's my point? The Social Security system *can't promise* us financial security *15* when we retire.

What's the solution? We have to start our own savings plans; and the *earlier* we *16* start, the *easier* it will be to reach our goals.

Note: Sample slides for this presentation are shown on page 392.

> The closing paragraphs help listeners reflect on the subject.

Marking Your Presentation

As you rehearse your presentation, decide which words or phrases to emphasize, where to pause, and where to add visual aids. Then use the symbols and text enhancements below to mark the copy of your presentation.

Italic or **boldface**	for additional feeling or emotion
Underlining	for greater volume or emphasis
Dash, diagonal, ellipsis	for a pause—or / a break in the flow
Brackets	for actions or [visual aids]

Use visual aids.

While constructing your presentation, think about visual aids that would grab the audience's attention and help them understand the message. For example, in her speech, Burnette Sawyer used the computer-generated graphics in Figures 23.3–23.5. (See pages 390–391.)

Sample Graphics

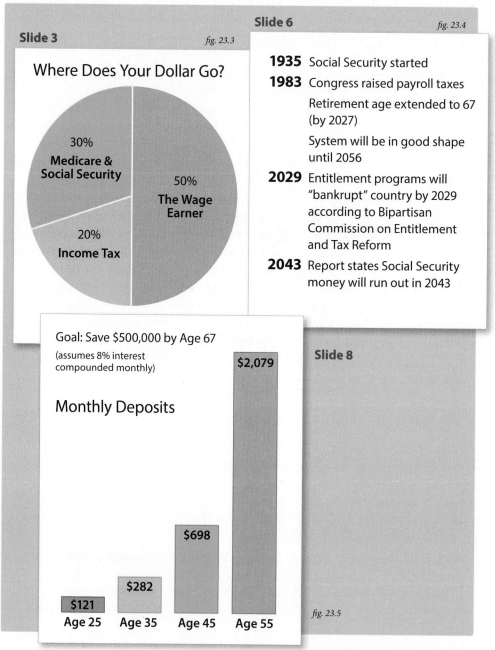

Slide 3 *fig. 23.3*

Where Does Your Dollar Go?

- 30% Medicare & Social Security
- 50% The Wage Earner
- 20% Income Tax

Slide 6 *fig. 23.4*

1935 Social Security started

1983 Congress raised payroll taxes

Retirement age extended to 67 (by 2027)

System will be in good shape until 2056

2029 Entitlement programs will "bankrupt" country by 2029 according to Bipartisan Commission on Entitlement and Tax Reform

2043 Report states Social Security money will run out in 2043

Goal: Save $500,000 by Age 67
(assumes 8% interest compounded monthly)

Monthly Deposits

- $121 Age 25
- $282 Age 35
- $698 Age 45
- $2,079 Age 55

Slide 8

fig. 23.5

Developing Computer Presentations

To help you use presentation software effectively, follow the guidelines below.

1. **Develop a design.** Be sure your graphic design fits your topic and your audience—polished for a serious topic, casual for an informal topic.

2. **Create pages.** If a main idea has several parts, present each one on its own page. Each click of the mouse button (or computer key) should reveal a new detail.

3. **Use transitions.** Dissolves, fades, wipes, and other transitional effects refine a computer presentation and keep the audience's attention (as long as the devices don't detract from the message).

4. **Add sound.** Just as graphics and animation can enhance a presentation, so, too, can sound. Music can serve as an introduction or backdrop, and sound effects can add emphasis. Voice recording can add authority and help drive home key points.

   > **Tip for speakers:** Text can be animated to appear from off-screen at just the right moment. Graphics can be made to appear one element at a time, and illustrations can change before the viewer's eyes. Remember to use special effects—especially animation—wisely.

5. **Fine-tune your presentation.** Practice delivering your presentation while clicking through your pages. Try it with an audience of fellow students, if possible, and ask for their input.

6. **Check for word choice and style.** Make sure that the words on the screen are key words. Use these words as talking points—don't try to cover any point word for word. Also, check that transitions, animations, and sounds are smooth and not disruptive.

7. **Edit the final version.** Check spelling, punctuation, usage, and other mechanics. Remember: On-screen errors are glaringly obvious to everyone.

8. **Rehearse.** Perform your presentation for a friend or family member. Practice running the equipment until you can use it with confidence.

9. **Make a backup copy.** Protect all the effort you invested in your presentation.

 Choose an easy-to-read font and type-size. In most situations, 36-point headings and 24-point text work well. However, the type-size needed depends on a number of variables, including the screen size, lens type, and audience's distance from the screen.

Overcoming Stage Fright Checklist

While it's okay to feel a little nervous before a presentation (the emotion keeps you alert), stage fright can limit your ability to communicate. The remedy for stage fright is confidence—confidence in what to say and how to say it. To develop that confidence, do the following:

Personal Preparation

____ Know your subject well.

____ Rehearse the presentation thoroughly, including the use of visuals.

____ Schedule your time carefully, making sure to arrive early.

____ Try to relax before the presentation by stretching or doing a deep-breathing exercise, remembering that your presentation can be successful without being perfect.

The Room and Equipment

____ See that the room is clean, comfortable, and well lit.

____ Make sure tables and chairs are set up and arranged correctly.

____ Check that AV equipment is in place and working.

____ Test the microphone volume.

____ Position the screen and displays for good visibility.

Personal Details

____ Check your clothing and hair.

____ Arrange for drinking water to be available.

____ Put your script and handouts in place.

Speaking Strategies

____ Be confident, positive, and energetic.

____ Maintain eye contact when speaking or listening.

____ Use gestures naturally—don't force them.

____ Provide for audience participation; survey the audience: "How many of you . . . ?"

____ Maintain a comfortable, erect posture.

____ Speak up and speak clearly—don't rush.

____ Reword and clarify when necessary.

____ After the presentation, ask for questions and answer them clearly.

____ Thank the audience.

III. Research and Writing

Chapter 24

Getting Started: From Planning Research to Evaluating Sources

At first glance, research looks like a dry-as-dust business carried out by obsessed scholars in dim libraries and mad scientists in cluttered laboratories. Research couldn't be further from the reality of your life.

But is it? Consider car tires. Before these were mounted, scientists researched which materials would resist wear and which adhesives would keep treads on steel belts. Sloppy research could cause blowouts; good research builds safe tires.

For you, the rewards of research projects can be great— new insights into a subject that really interests you, a deepened understanding of your major or profession, reliable knowledge to share with others, and sharpened thinking skills. This chapter will help you get started on such a project.

Visually Speaking   Figure 24.1 shows one form of research in action. Study the details. What does this image suggest about research? What other images would capture other dimensions of research today?

Learning **Objectives**

By working through this chapter, you will be able to

- interpret the rhetorical situation for research.
- identify the phases of the research process.
- focus a research assignment into a manageable project.
- identify primary, secondary, and tertiary sources.
- generate a research plan.
- choose different information resources and sites.
- perform keyword searches.
- examine and evaluate print and digital resources.
- produce a working bibliography.
- choose a note-taking system.
- summarize, paraphrase, and quote source material.

kurhan / Shutterstock.com

fig. 24.1

Quick Guide

Papers with Documented Research

When you work on a research project, you ask important questions, look systematically for answers, and share your conclusions with readers. The rhetorical situation for such a project centers on the writer's purpose of inquiring into a topic so as to advance understanding for him- or herself and the reader. In other words, it's all about curiosity, discovery, and dialogue.

- **Starting Point:** The assignment usually relates to a course concept, so consider what your instructor wants you to learn and how your project will be evaluated. Then take ownership of the project by looking for an angle that makes the writing relevant for you.

- **Purpose:** The project requires you to conduct research and share results. Your main goal is to discover the complex truth about a topic and clarify that discovery for others.

- **Form:** The traditional research paper is a fairly long essay (5 to 15 pages) complete with thesis, supporting paragraphs, integrated sources, and careful documentation. However, you may be asked to shape your research into a field report, a Web site, or a multimedia presentation.

- **Audience:** Traditionally, research writing addresses "the academic community," a group made up mainly of instructors and students. However, your actual audience may be more specific: addicted smokers, all Floridians, fellow immigrants, and so on.

- **Voice:** The tone is usually formal or semiformal, but check your instructor's expectations. In any research writing, maintain a thoughtful, confidently measured tone. After all, your research has made you somewhat of an authority on the topic.

- **Point of View:** Generally, research writers avoid the pronouns "I" and "you" in an effort to remain properly objective and academic sounding. Unfortunately, this practice can result in an overuse of both the pronoun "one" and the passive voice. Some instructors encourage students to connect research with experience, meaning that you may use the pronouns "I" and "you" occasionally. Be careful, however, to keep the focus where it belongs—on the topic. Bottom line: Follow your instructor's requirements concerning pronoun use. For more on developing a strong academic style for your research writing, see pages 77–78.

INSIGHT The best research writing centers on your ideas—ideas you develop through thoughtful engagement with sources. In poor research papers, the sources dominate, and the writer's perspective disappears.

The Research Process: A Flowchart

The research process involves getting started, planning, conducting the research, and organizing the results. This process is flexible enough to be adapted to diverse research projects. In fact, real research is typically dynamic: You might think during the planning phase that you've nailed down your topic, only to discover a surprising topical detour while conducting research. Generally, however, the research process maps out as shown in Figure 24.2. When you get your assignment—whether to write a five-page paper on pasteurization or to develop a Web site on Middle Eastern political conflicts—review the process and tailor it to the task.

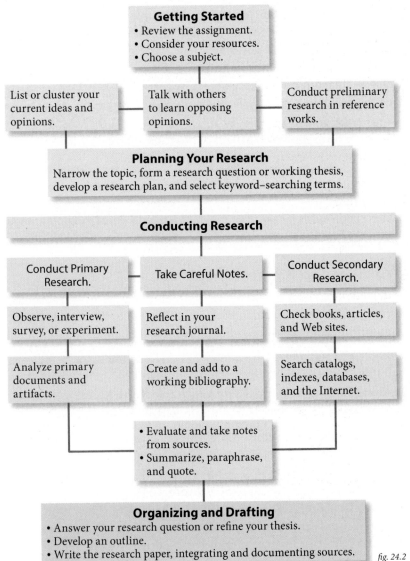

Getting Started
- Review the assignment.
- Consider your resources.
- Choose a subject.

List or cluster your current ideas and opinions.

Talk with others to learn opposing opinions.

Conduct preliminary research in reference works.

Planning Your Research
Narrow the topic, form a research question or working thesis, develop a research plan, and select keyword–searching terms.

Conducting Research

Conduct Primary Research.

Take Careful Notes.

Conduct Secondary Research.

Observe, interview, survey, or experiment.

Reflect in your research journal.

Check books, articles, and Web sites.

Analyze primary documents and artifacts.

Create and add to a working bibliography.

Search catalogs, indexes, databases, and the Internet.

- Evaluate and take notes from sources.
- Summarize, paraphrase, and quote.

Organizing and Drafting
- Answer your research question or refine your thesis.
- Develop an outline.
- Write the research paper, integrating and documenting sources.

fig. 24.2

Getting Focused

Early in your project, get focused by narrowing your topic, brainstorming research questions, and developing a working thesis. For help understanding assignments and selecting topics, as well as other prewriting strategies, see pages 32–37.

Establish a narrow, manageable topic.

To do good research, you need an engaging, manageable topic. Once you have a broad topic, narrow your focus to a specific feature or angle that allows for in-depth research. Try these strategies:

- **Check your topic in the Library of Congress subject headings, available in your library in print.** An online version is available at classificationweb.net (a subscription service) or at authorities.loc.gov (free). Note "narrower terms" listed (see page 410).
- **Read about your topic.** By consulting specialized reference works, explore background that directs you to subtopics (see page 441).
- **Check the Internet.** For example, follow a subject directory to see where your topic leads (see pages 448–451).
- **Freewrite to discover which aspect of the topic interests you most:** a local angle, a connection with a group of people, or a personal concern.

Broad Topic	Manageable Focus
Homelessness	Homeless Families in Los Angeles
Bacteria and Viruses	Bacterial Resistance to Antibiotics
Alternative Energy Sources	Hydrogen Fuel-Cell Vehicles

Brainstorm research questions.

Good research questions help you find meaningful information and ideas about your topic. These questions sharpen your research goal, and the answers will become the focus of your writing. Brainstorm questions by following these guidelines:

List both simple and substantial questions. Basic questions aim for factual answers. More complex questions get at analysis, synthesis, and evaluation.

- **Question of fact:** How long did Kim Jong Il rule North Korea?
- **Question of interpretation:** How did Kim Jong Il maintain power?

List main and secondary questions. Ask a primary question about your topic—the main issue that you want to get at. Then brainstorm secondary questions that you need to research to answer your primary question.

- **Main Question:** Should consumers buy hydrogen fuel-cell cars?
- **Secondary Questions (Who, What, When, Where, Why, How):** Who has developed hydrogen fuel-cell cars? What is a hydrogen fuel-cell car? When were these cars developed? Where are hydrogen fuel-cell cars currently used? Why are they being developed? How does one work?

Testing Your Main Research Question

_____ Is the question so broad that I can't answer it in the project's time and page limits?

_____ Is the question so narrow that I won't be able to find sources?

_____ Is the question so simple that it will be too easy to answer?

_____ Will the question lead to significant sources and intellectual challenge?

_____ Am I committed to answering this question? Does it interest me?

_____ Will the question and answers interest my readers?

Develop a working thesis.

A working thesis offers a preliminary answer to your main research question. As your initial perspective on the topic, a good working thesis keeps you focused during research, helping you decide whether to carefully read a particular book or just skim it, fully explore a Web site or quickly browse through it. Make your working thesis a statement that demands "Prove it!" Don't settle for a simple statement of fact about your topic; instead, choose a working thesis that seems debatable or that requires some explanation. Try this formula:

Formula:

Working Thesis = limited topic + tentative claim, statement, or hypothesis

Examples:

E-communication technologies are rewiring our brains.

Downtown revitalization will have distinct economic, environmental, and social benefits.

Internet dating is weakening long-term relationships.

Working Thesis Checklist

_____ Does my working thesis focus on a single, limited topic?

_____ Is my working thesis stated in a clear, direct sentence?

_____ Does my working thesis convey my initial perspective about the topic?

_____ Do I have access to enough good information to support this working thesis?

_____ Does my working thesis direct me to write a paper that meets all assignment requirements?

INSIGHT Your working thesis is written in sand, not stone. It may change as you research the topic because sources may push you in new directions. In fact, such change shows that you are engaging your sources and growing in your thinking.

Understanding Primary, Secondary, and Tertiary Sources

Information sources for your project can be primary, secondary, or tertiary, depending on their nearness to your topic. With your college assignments, you will likely be expected to rely upon primary and secondary sources, not tertiary sources. As part of project planning, then, you need to understand the distinction between primary, secondary, and tertiary sources.

Primary Sources

A primary source is an original source, one that gives firsthand information on a topic: the source is close to the issue or question. This source (such as a log, a person, a document, or an event) informs you directly about the topic, not through another person's explanation or interpretation. Common primary sources are observations, interviews, surveys, experiments, documents, and artifacts. Frequently, you generate the primary source yourself; sometimes, that primary information is available in published form.

> ***Example:*** For a project on Jane Austen's *Pride and Prejudice* in fiction and film, these sources would be primary: the text of the novel itself, the 2005 film adaptation of the novel, Jane Austen's letters, and an interview with a screen writer who adapts novels into films.

> **Strengths of Primary Research:** Primary sources produce information precisely tailored to your research needs, giving you direct, hands-on access to your topic. If, for example, you were researching the impact of tornados on communities, interviews with survivors would provide information directly tailored to your project.

> **Downsides of Primary Research:** Primary research can take a lot of time and many resources, as well as specialized skills (e.g., designing surveys and analyzing statistics).

Secondary Sources

Secondary sources present information one step removed from the origin: information has been collected, compiled, summarized, analyzed, synthesized, interpreted, and evaluated by someone studying primary sources and other secondary sources. Scholarly studies, journal articles, and documentaries are typical examples of such resources. Typically, you track down secondary resources in your library, through library databases, and on the free Web (see pages 437–457).

> ***Example:*** For a project on Jane Austen's *Pride and Prejudice* in fiction and film, these sources would be secondary: books and articles by scholars on Austen and on film, literary biographies about Austen's life, and film reviews.

▲ **Strengths of Secondary Research:** Good secondary sources—especially scholarly ones that have gone through a peer review process—offer quality information in the form of expert perspectives on and analysis of your topic. As such, secondary sources can save you plenty of research labor while providing you with extensive data. In addition, secondary sources can help you see your topic from multiple angles through multiple perspectives; they can tell you the story of research done on your topic.

▼ **Downside of Secondary Research:** Because secondary research isn't written solely with you and your project in mind, you may need to do some digging to find relevant data. Moreover, the information that you do find may be filtered through the researcher's bias. In fact, the original research related through the secondary source may be faulty, a point suggesting that the quality of secondary sources can vary greatly (especially on the free Web). Finally, because knowledge about your topic can grow or radically change over time, secondary sources can become dated.

Tertiary Sources

Some resources are tertiary—essentially reports of reports of research. That is, writers of tertiary sources are not reporting on the primary research they themselves have done but are compiling information based on their reading of secondary sources. Examples of tertiary sources would include some articles in popular magazines and entries in Wikipedia (see page 452).

Example: For a project on Jane Austen's *Pride and Prejudice* in fiction and film, these sources would be tertiary: an online discussion group exchanging thoughts on a recent Austen biography, and a Wikipedia entry on Austen.

▲ **Upside of Tertiary Research:** Tertiary sources are typically easy to find, easy to access, and easy to read. Note, for example, that a free-Web search of a specific topic frequently lists a Wikipedia entry in the first ten items. Used cautiously, such tertiary sources can serve as one starting point for your research—to find basic facts that you'll likely have to verify elsewhere, some ideas for narrowing your topic, or some leads and links for further research.

▼ **Downside of Tertiary Research:** The main weakness of tertiary sources is their distance from the original research and information. Because the information and ideas have been passed along in this way, the possibility of error, distortion, gaps, and over-simplification of complex issues is greater than with primary and secondary sources. Generally, tertiary sources lack the reliability and depth necessary for college-level research projects.

fyi Whether a source is primary, secondary, or tertiary often depends on what your focused topic is. For example, if you were studying why power brown-outs happen during heat waves, a newspaper editorial on the topic would be secondary. But if you were focusing on public attitudes towards and responses to brown-outs, the editorial might prove primary. In other words, a given source is not always primary or always secondary: proximity depends on the research context.

Developing a Research Plan

It pays to plan your research, including decisions about primary, secondary, and tertiary sources. In fact, minutes spent planning research can save hours doing research. With your limited topic, main research question, and working thesis in front of you, plan your project more fully using the research tips on the next two pages.

Choose research methods.

Consider these questions: What do you already know about the topic? What do you need to know? Which resources will help you answer your research question? Which resources does the assignment require? Based on your answers, map out a research plan that draws resources from fitting categories.

Background research: To find information about your topic's context, central concepts, and key terms, take these steps:

- Use the Library of Congress subject headings to find keywords for searching the library catalog, periodical databases, and the Internet (see page 410).
- Conduct a preliminary search of the library catalog, journal databases, and the Internet to confirm that good resources on your topic exist.
- Use specialized reference works to find background information, definitions, facts, and statistics (see page 441).

Field or primary research: If appropriate for your project, conduct field research:

- Use interviews (pages 434–435) or surveys (page 430–431) to get key information from experts or others.
- Conduct observations or experiments (page 436) to obtain hard data.
- Analyze key documents or artifacts (pages 432–433).

Library research: Select important library resources:

- Use scholarly books to get in-depth, reliable material (pages 437–441).
- Use periodical articles (print or electronic) to get current, reliable information (pages 408–413). Select from news sources, popular magazines, scholarly journals, and trade journals.
- Consider other library resources, such as a documentary, recorded interview, pamphlet, marketing study, or government publication.

Free-Web research: Plan effective free-Web searches using the following:

- Search engines and subject guides: Choose tools that will lead you to quality resources (pages 448–451).
- Expert guidance: Select reputable Web sites that librarians or other experts recommend (page 454).
- Evaluation: Test all Web resources for reliability (pages 454–457).
- Limitations: How many Web resources are you allowed to use, if any?

Get organized to do research.

An organized approach to doing your research will save you time, help you work efficiently, and prevent frustration. Get organized by addressing these issues:

Establishing Priorities for Resources, Time, and Effort

- How much research material do you need?
- What range of resources will give you quality, reliable information?
- Which types of research does the assignment specify? Are you limited, for example, in the number of Internet sources you can use?
- What are the project's priorities: What must you do? Which tasks are secondary in nature?
- What weight does the project carry in the course? How should you match your time and effort with that weight?

INSIGHT Gather more information than you could ever use in your paper. That richness gives you choices and allows you to sift for crucial information.

Selecting Research Methods and Systems

- **Given the resources and technologies available, select methods that help you do research efficiently:** signing out hard-copy library holdings or using interlibrary loan; photocopying book sections and journal articles; printing, saving, downloading, bookmarking, or emailing digital materials.
- **Develop a note-taking system.** Choose from the note-card, double-entry notebook, copy-and-annotate, and research-log methods (pages 418–421). In addition, set up a working bibliography (pages 416–417).
- **Choose and review a documentation system.** It's likely that your instructor will designate a system such as MLA (pages 493–534) or APA (pages 535–564). If he or she doesn't do so, then use a method that suits the subject matter and discipline. Review the system's basic rules and strategies.

Establishing a Schedule

The time frame for completing a research project obviously varies from one assignment to the next. What you have to work with is the time frame between getting the assignment and turning in the project at the deadline, whether that time frame is two weeks or two months, along with any intermediate deadlines set by your instructor for specific phases of the project (e.g., topic selection, project proposal, working bibliography, first draft). Generally, however, you should spend about half your time on research and half on writing. To stay on track, sketch out a preliminary schedule with tentative deadlines for completing each phase of your work.

Writing a Research Proposal

For some research projects, you may need to submit a proposal early in the process. The proposal seeks to explain what you plan to research, why, and how. Such a proposal has several aims: (1) to show that the research is valid (makes good scholarly sense), (2) to argue that the research is valuable (will lead to significant knowledge), (3) to communicate your enthusiasm for the project, and (4) to demonstrate that your plan is workable within the constraints of the assignment—all in order to gain your instructor's feedback and approval. Note the parts modeled in the sample proposal.

Understand the parts of a research proposal.

1. **Introduction:** In a brief paragraph, state your research idea, explaining why the topic is important and worth researching. Provide any background information that the instructor may need.

2. **Description:** Discuss your proposed research topic by identifying the central issue or concern about the topic, indicating the main question that you want to answer through research, listing secondary questions that relate to the main question, stating a working thesis or hypothesis in response to the main question, and explaining the research outcomes that you expect from the study.

3. **Plan (methods and procedures):** Explain how you plan to answer your questions, how you plan to research your topic. Include an explanation of your primary research (the "firsthand" investigation), a description of research tools you plan to use (e.g., catalogs, reference works, lab equipment, survey software), and a working bibliography indicating your initial survey of resources.

4. **Schedule:** List deadlines that are part of the assignment and deadlines that you've set for yourself.

5. **Approval Request:** Ask for feedback and approval from your instructor.

Sample Research Proposal

The research proposal below offers a student's plan for analyzing Jane Austen's *Pride and Prejudice,* both the novel and the film adaptation.

Film Studies 201 Proposal:
Jane Austen's *Pride and Prejudice* as Fiction and Film

Gwendolyn Mackenzie

Nearly 200 years after her death, Jane Austen's novels still captivate readers, filmmakers, and filmgoers—including me. For my research paper, I will explore one aspect of this phenomenon within *Pride and Prejudice* and the 2005 film adaptation directed by Joe Wright.

Description: Specifically, I want to see how the novel and film explore gender prejudice. My main research question is, What sense do these texts make of prejudice as it relates to relationships between men and women? My working thesis is that the 2005 film portrayal of gender inequality in *Pride and Prejudice* highlights and intensifies the issue of gender inequality introduced in the novel.

This study of gender prejudice will allow me (1) to appreciate the treatment of this theme in fiction and in film, (2) to understand film adaptations more fully, and (3) to explain in a small way the Jane Austen phenomenon. As part of the project, I will write a 6-8 page paper.

Plan: My primary research will involve rereading the novel and reviewing the 2005 film adaptation. In terms of secondary research, I have done an initial search of our library's catalog and of EBSCOhost for books and articles. This is my working bibliography:

Primary Sources

Austen, Jane. *Pride and Prejudice: An Authoritative Text, Background and Sources, Criticism.* Ed. Donald J. Gray. New York: Norton, 2001. Print.

Wright, Joe, dir. *Pride and Prejudice.* Universal Pictures, 2005. Film.

Secondary Sources

Cartmell, Deborah, and Imelda Whelehan. *Adaptations: From Text to Screen, Screen to Text.* London: Routledge, 2004. Print.

Crusie, Jennifer. *Flirting with Pride and Prejudice: Fresh Perspectives on the Original Chick-Lit Masterpiece.* Dallas: BenBella, 2005. Print.

Grandi, Roberta. "The Passion Translated: Literary and Cinematic Rhetoric in *Pride and Prejudice* (2005)." *Literature Film Quarterly* 36.1 (2008): 45-51. Print.

McFarlane, Brian. "Something Old, Something New: 'Pride and Prejudice' on Screen." *Screen Education* (2005): 6-14. Print.

Stovel, Nora Foster. "From Page to Screen: Dancing to the Altar in Recent Film Adaptations of Jane Austen's Novels." *Persuasions: The Jane Austen Journal* (2006): 185-198. EBSCOhost. Web. 6 Nov. 2013.

Sutherland, Kathryn. *Jane Austen's Textual Lives: From Aeschylus to Bollywood.* Oxford: Oxford UP, 2007. Print.

Todd, Janet M. *The Cambridge Introduction to Jane Austen.* Cambridge; Cambridge UP, 2006. NetLibrary. Web. 6 Nov. 2013.

Schedule: Here is my schedule for completing this project:
1. Finish rereading the novel and reviewing the film: November 14.
2. Complete secondary research: November 20.
3. Develop outline for paper: November 23.
4. Finish first draft of paper: November 30.
5. Revise, edit, and proofread paper: December 4.
6. Submit paper: December 6.

Approval Request: Dr. Rajan, I would appreciate your feedback on my proposed project, as well as your approval of my plan.

Exploring Information Resources and Sites

To conduct thorough, creative, but efficient research, you need a sense of which types of resources are available for your project and where to find them. Check the tables that follow.

Consider different information resources.

Examine the range of resources available: Which will give you the best information for your project? While one project (for example, a sociological report on airport behaviors) might require personal, direct sources, another project (for example, the effects of the September 11, 2001, terrorist attacks on the air transportation industry) might depend on government reports, business publications, and journal articles. Generally, a well-rounded research paper relies on a range of quality resources; in particular, it avoids relying on insubstantial Web information.

fig. 24.3

Type of Resource	Examples
Personal, direct resources	Memories, diaries, journals, logs, experiments, tests, observations, interviews, surveys
Reference works (print and electronic)	Dictionaries, thesauruses, encyclopedias, almanacs, yearbooks, atlases, directories, guides, handbooks, indexes, abstracts, catalogs, bibliographies
Books (print and electronic)	Nonfiction, how-to, biographies, fiction, trade books, scholarly and scientific studies
Periodicals and news sources	Print newspapers, magazines, and journals; broadcast news and news magazines; online magazines, news sources, and discussion groups
Audiovisual, digital, and multimedia resources	Graphics (tables, graphs, charts, maps, drawings, photos), audiotapes, CDs, videos, DVDs, Web pages, online databases
Government publications	Guides, programs, forms, legislation, regulations, reports, records, statistics
Business and nonprofit publications	Correspondence, reports, newsletters, pamphlets, brochures, ads, catalogs, instructions, handbooks, manuals, policies and procedures, seminar and training materials

Consider different information sites.

Where do you go to find the resources that you need? Consider the information "sites" listed below, remembering that many resources may be available in different forms in different locations. For example, a journal article may be available in library holdings or in an electronic database.

fig. 24.4

Information Location	Specific "Sites"
People	Experts (knowledge area, skill, occupation) Population segments or individuals (with representative or unusual experiences)
Libraries	General: public, college, online Specialized: legal, medical, government, business
Computer resources	Computers: software, disks Networks: Internet and other online services (email, limited-access databases, discussion, groups, MUDs, chat rooms, Web sites, blogs, YouTube, image banks, wikis); intranets
Mass media	Radio (AM and FM) Television (network, public, cable, satellite) Print (newspapers, magazines, journals)
Testing, training, meeting, and observation sites	Plants, facilities, field sites, laboratories Research centers, universities, think tanks Conventions, conferences, seminars Museums, galleries, historical sites
Municipal, state, and federal government offices	Elected officials, representatives Offices and agencies, Government Printing Office Web sites (GPO, www.gpoaccess.gov)
Business and nonprofit publications	Computer databases, company files Desktop reference materials Bulletin boards (physical and electronic) Company and department Web sites Departments and offices Associations, professional organizations Consulting, training, and business information services

Conducting Effective Keyword Searches

Keyword searching can help you find information in electronic library catalogs, online databases that index periodical articles (for example, EBSCOhost), print indexes to periodical publications (for example, *Business Periodicals Index*), Internet resources, print books, and e-books. Learn to choose keywords and use specific search strategies.

Choose keywords carefully.

Keywords give you "compass points" for navigating through a sea of information. That's why choosing the best keywords is crucial. Consider these tips:

1. **Brainstorm a list of possible keywords**—topics, titles, and names—based on your current knowledge and/or background reading.

2. **Consult the Library of Congress subject headings.** These headings, available in print or online at classificationweb.net (subscription) or at authorities.loc.gov (free), contain the keywords librarians use when classifying materials. For example, if you looked up *immigrants*, you would find the entry below, indicating keywords to use and tips to follow (including that the topic may subdivide geographically), along with narrower, related, and broader terms. When you are conducting subject searches of catalogs and databases, these are the terms that will get you the best results.

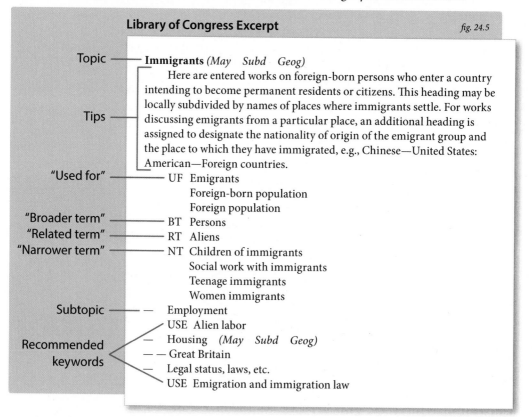

Library of Congress Excerpt   *fig. 24.5*

Topic —— **Immigrants** *(May   Subd   Geog)*

Tips ——   Here are entered works on foreign-born persons who enter a country intending to become permanent residents or citizens. This heading may be locally subdivided by names of places where immigrants settle. For works discussing emigrants from a particular place, an additional heading is assigned to designate the nationality of origin of the emigrant group and the place to which they have immigrated, e.g., Chinese—United States: American—Foreign countries.

"Used for" —— UF Emigrants
            Foreign-born population
            Foreign population

"Broader term" —— BT Persons

"Related term" —— RT Aliens

"Narrower term" —— NT Children of immigrants
            Social work with immigrants
            Teenage immigrants
            Women immigrants

Subtopic —— — Employment
            USE Alien labor

Recommended keywords — Housing *(May   Subd   Geog)*
            — — Great Britain
            — Legal status, laws, etc.
            USE Emigration and immigration law

Use keyword strategies.

The goal of a keyword search is to find quality research sources. To ensure that you identify the best resources available, follow these strategies:

1. **Get to know the database.** Look for answers to these questions:
   - What material does the database contain? What time frames?
   - What are you searching—authors, titles, subjects, full text?
   - What are the search rules? How can you narrow the search?

2. **Use a shotgun approach.** Start with the most likely keyword. If you have no "hits," choose a related term. Once you get some hits, check the citations for clues regarding which words to use as you continue searching.

3. **Use Boolean operators to refine your search.** When you combine keywords with Boolean operators—such as those below—you will obtain better results.

Boolean Operators

fig. 24.6

Narrowing a Search **And, +, not, -** Use when one term gives you too many hits, especially irrelevant ones.	buffalo and bison *or* buffalo + bison buffalo not water +buffalo –water	Searches for citations containing both keywords Searches for "buffalo" but not "water," so that you eliminate material on water buffalo
Expanding a Search **Or** Combine a term providing few hits with a related word	buffalo or bison	Searches for citations containing either term
Specifying a Phrase **Quotation marks** Indicate that you wish to search for the exact phrase enclosed	"reclamation project"	Searches for the exact phrase "reclamation project"
Sequencing Operations **Parentheses** Indicate that the operation should be performed before other operations in the search string	(buffalo or bison) and ranching	Searches first for citations containing either "buffalo" or "bison" before checking the resulting citations for "ranching"
Finding Variations **Wild card symbols** Depending on the database, symbols such as $, ?, or # can find variations of a word.	ethic# ethic$	Searches for terms like *ethics* and *ethical*

Engaging and Evaluating Sources

Using reliable benchmarks, you should test all sources before you rely on them in your writing. After all, credible sources help your own credibility; sources that aren't credible destroy it. The benchmarks on the next four pages will help you test your sources' usefulness and reliability.

Engage your sources.

Engaged reading is the opposite of passive reading—treating all sources equally, swallowing whole what's in the material, or looking only for information that supports your opinion. Full engagement involves these practices:

Test each source to see if it's worth reading. When reviewing source citations and generating a working bibliography, study titles, descriptions, lengths, and publication dates, asking these questions:

- How closely related to my topic is this source?
- Is this source too basic, overly complex, or just right?
- What could this source add to my overall balance of sources?

If you were writing about the International Space Station, for example, you might find a ten-page article in *Scientific American* more valuable and insightful than a brief news article on a specific event onboard or a *Star Trek* fan's blog on the topic.

INSIGHT Don't reject a source simply because it disagrees with your perspective. Good research engages rather than ignores opposing points of view.

Skim sources before reading in-depth. Consider marking key pages or passages with sticky notes, tabs, or a digital bookmark.

- Review the author biography, preface, and/or introduction to discover the perspective, approach, scope, and research methods.
- Using your keywords, review any outline, abstract, table of contents, index, or home page to get a sense of coverage.

Read with an open but not an empty mind. Carry on a dialogue with the source, asking questions like "Why?" and "So what?"

- Note the purpose and audience. Was the piece written to inform or persuade? Is it aimed at the public, specialists, supporters, or opponents?
- Read to understand the source: What's clear and what's confusing?
- Relate the source to your research question: How does the source affirm or challenge your ideas? Synthesize what you read with what you know.
- Record your reactions to it—what it makes you think, feel, believe.
- Consider how you might use this source in your writing—key facts, important ideas, opposing perspectives, or examples.
- Check footnotes, references, appendices, and links for leads on other sources.

Rate source reliability and depth.

You should judge each source on its own merit. Generally, however, types of sources can be rated for depth and reliability, as shown in the table below, based on their authorship, length, topic treatment, documentation, publication method, review process, distance from primary sources, allegiances, stability, and so on. Use the table to

1. target sources that fit your project's goals,
2. assess the approximate quality of the sources you're gathering, and
3. build a strong bibliography that readers will respect.

fig. 24.7

Deep, Reliable, Credible Sources

Scholarly Books and Scholarly Articles: largely based on careful research; written by experts for experts; address topics in depth; involve peer review and careful editing; offer stable discussion of topic

Trade Books and Articles in Quality, Specialized Magazines: largely based on careful research; written by experts for educated general audience. *Sample periodicals: The Atlantic, Scientific American, Nature, Orion*

Government Resources: books, reports, Web pages, guides, statistics developed by experts at government agencies; provided as service to citizens; relatively objective. *Sample source: Statistical Abstract of the United States*

Reviewed Official Online Documents: Internet resources posted by legitimate institutions—colleges and universities, research institutes, service organizations; although offering a particular perspective, sources tend to be balanced.

Reference Works and Textbooks: provide general and specialized information; carefully researched, reviewed, and edited; lack depth for focused research (e.g., general encyclopedia entry).

News and Topical Stories from Quality Sources: provide current affairs coverage (print and online), introduction-level articles of interest to general public; may lack depth and length. *Sample sources: the Washington Post, the New York Times; Time, Psychology Today; NPR's All Things Considered*

Popular Magazine Stories: short, introductory articles often distant from primary sources and without documentation; heavy advertising. *Sample sources: Glamour, Seventeen, Reader's Digest*

Business and Nonprofit Publications: pamphlets, reports, news releases, brochures, manuals; range from informative to sales-focused.

List Server Discussions, Usenet Postings, Blog Articles, Talk Radio Discussions: highly open, fluid, undocumented, untested exchanges and publications; unstable resource.

Unregulated Web Material: personal sites, joke sites, chat rooms, special-interest sites, advertising and junk email (spam); no review process, little accountability, biased presentation.

Shallow, Unreliable, Not Credible Sources

Tabloid Articles (print and Web): contain exaggerated and untrue stories written to titillate and exploit. *Sample source: National Enquirer*

Evaluate print and online sources.

As you work with a source, you need to test its reliability. The benchmarks that follow apply to both print and online sources; note, however, the additional tests offered for Web sources. For more on evaluating material on the Web, see pages 454–455.

Credible author An expert is an authority—someone who has mastered a subject area. Is the author an expert on this topic? What are her or his credentials, and can you confirm them? For example, an automotive engineer could be an expert on hydrogen fuel-cell technology, whereas a celebrity in a commercial would not.

> **Web test:** Is an author indicated? If so, are the author's credentials noted and contact information offered (for example, an email address)?

Reliable publication Has the source been published by a scholarly press, a peer-reviewed professional journal, a quality trade-book publisher, or a trusted news source? Did you find this resource through a reliable search tool (for example, a library catalog or database)?

> **Web test:** Which individual or group posted this page? Is the site rated by a subject directory or library organization? How stable is the site—has it been around for a while and does material remain available, or is the site "fly-by-night"? Check the site's home page, and read "About Us" pages and mission statements, looking for evidence of the organization's perspective, history, and trustworthiness.

Unbiased discussion While all sources come from a specific perspective and represent specific commitments, a biased source may be pushing an agenda in an unfair, unbalanced, incomplete manner. Watch for bias toward a certain region, country, political party, industry, gender, race, ethnic group, or religion. Be alert to connections among authors, financial backers, and the points of view shared. For example, if an author has functioned as a consultant to or a lobbyist for a particular industry or group (oil, animal rights), his or her allegiances may lead to a biased presentation of an issue.

> **Web test:** Is the online document one-sided? Is the site nonprofit (.org), government (.gov), commercial (.com), educational (.edu), business (.biz), informational (.info), network-related (.net), or military (.mil)? Is the site U.S. or international? Is this organization pushing a cause, product, service, or belief? How do advertising or special interests affect the site? You might suspect, for example, the scientific claims of a site sponsored by a pro-smoking organization.

Web Link: Beware especially of masquerade sites— those that appear to be legitimate but are joke sites or, worse, propaganda lures. Check, for example, www.dhmo.org.

Current information A five-year-old book on computers may be outdated, but a forty-year-old book on Abraham Lincoln could still be the best source. Given what you need, is this source's discussion up-to-date?

> ▌ *Web test:* When was the material originally posted and last updated? Are links live or dead?

Accurate information Bad research design, poor reporting, and sloppy documentation can lead to inaccurate information. Check the source for factual errors, statistical flaws, and conclusions that don't add up.

> ▌ *Web test:* Is the site information-rich or -poor? More specifically, is it filled with helpful, factual materials or fluffy with thin, unsubstantiated opinions? Can you trace and confirm sources by following links or conducting your own search?

Full, logical support Is the discussion of the topic reasonable, balanced, and complete? Are claims backed up with quality evidence? Does the source avoid faulty assumptions, twisted statistical analysis, logical fallacies, and unfair persuasion tactics? (See pages 301–304, for help.)

> ▌ *Web test:* Does the Web page offer well-supported claims and helpful links to additional information?

Quality writing and design Is the source well written? Is it free of sarcasm, derogatory terms, clichés, catch phrases, mindless slogans, grammar slips, and spelling errors? Generally, poor writing correlates with sloppy thinking.

> ▌ *Web test:* Are words neutral ("conservative perspective") or emotionally charged ("fascist agenda")? Are pages well designed—with clear rather than flashy, distracting multimedia elements? Is the site easy to navigate?

Positive relationship with other sources Does the source disagree with other sources? If yes, is the disagreement about the facts themselves or about how to interpret the facts? Which source seems more credible?

> ▌ *Web test:* Is the site's information logically consistent with print sources? Do other reputable sites offer links to this site?

INSIGHT Engage and evaluate visual resources as thoroughly as verbal materials. For example, ask yourself what tables, graphs, and photos really "say":

- Is the graphic informative or merely decorative?
- Does the graphic create a valid or manipulative central idea? For example, does the image seek to bypass logic by appealing to sexual impulses or to crude stereotypes?
- What does the graphic include and exclude in terms of information?
- Is the graphic well designed and easy to understand, or is it cluttered and distorted?
- Is a reliable source provided?

Creating a Working Bibliography

A working bibliography lists sources you have used and intend to use. It helps you track your research, develop your final bibliography, and avoid plagiarism. Here's what to do: Choose an orderly method.

Select an efficient approach for your project:

- **Paper note cards:** Use 3 x 5-inch cards, and record one source per card.
- **Paper notebook:** Use a small, spiral-bound book to record sources.
- **Computer program:** Record source information electronically, either by capturing citation details from online searches or by recording bibliographic information using word-processing software or research software such as TakeNote, EndNote Plus, or Bookends Pro.

Including Identifying Information for Sources

Start by giving each source its own code number or letter: Doing so will help you when drafting and documenting your paper. Then include specific details for each kind of source listed below, shown on the facing page.

  A. Books: author, title and subtitle, publication details (place, publisher, date)
  B. Periodicals: author, article title, journal name, publication information (volume, number, date), page numbers
  C. Online sources: author (if available), document title, site sponsor, database name, publication or posting date, access date, other publication information, URL
  D. Primary or field research: date conducted, name and/or descriptive title of person interviewed, place observed, survey conducted, document analyzed

Adding Locating Information

Because you may need to retrace your research footsteps, include details about your research path:

  A. Books: Include the Library of Congress or Dewey call number.
  B. Articles: Note where and how you accessed them (stacks, current periodicals, microfilm, database).
  C. Web pages: Record the complete URL, not just the broader site address.
  D. Field research: Include a telephone number or an email address.

INSIGHT Consider recording bibliographic details in the format of the documentation system you are using—MLA (pages 493–534) or APA (pages 535–564), for example. Doing so now will save time later. In addition, some research software allows you to record bibliographic information and then format it according to a specific system.

Annotate the source.

Add a note about the source's content, focus, reliability, and usefulness, as shown in Figure 24.8.

Sample Working Bibliography Entries   *fig. 24.8*

A. Book Source Note:

> #2
>
> Howells, Coral Ann. *Alice Munro.*
>
> Contemporary World Writers. Manchester and New York: Manchester UP, 1998. Print.
>
> PS 8576.U57 Z7 1998
>
> Book provides good introduction to Alice Munro's fiction, chapters arranged by Munro's works; contains intro, conclusion, and bibliography; 1998 date means author doesn't cover Munro's recent fiction.

B. Periodical Source Note

> #5
>
> Valdes, Marcela. "Some Stories Have to Be Told by Me: A Literary History of Alice Munro." *Virginia Quarterly Review* 82.3 (Summer 2006): 82-90.
>
> EBSCOhost Academic Search Premier http://web.ebscohost.com accessed 17 April 2013.
>
> Article offers good introduction to Munro's life, her roots in Ontario, her writing career, and the key features of her stories.

C. Internet Source Note:

> #3
>
> "Alice Munro." Athabasca University Centre for Language and Literature: Canadian Writers. Updated 11 Oct. 2012. Accessed 17 April 2013.
>
> http://www.athabascau.ca/writers/munro.html site offers good introduction to Munro's writing, along with links to bibliography and other resources.

D. Interview Source Note:

> #4
>
> Thacker, Robert. Email interview. 7 March 2013.
>
> rthacker@mdu.edu
>
> Author of critical biography on Munro, *Alice Munro: Writing Her Lives,* offered really helpful insights into her creative process, especially useful for story "Carried Away."

Developing a Note-Taking System

Accurate, thoughtful notes create a foundation for your research writing. The trick is to practice some sensible strategies and choose an efficient method.

Develop note-taking strategies.

What are you trying to do when you take notes on sources? What you are not doing is (a) collecting quotations to plunk in your project, (b) piling isolated grains of data into a large stack of disconnected facts, or (c) intensively reading and taking notes on every source you find. Instead, use these strategies:

Be selective. Guided by your research questions and working thesis, focus on sources that are central to your project. From these sources, record information clearly related to your limited topic, but also take notes on what surprises or puzzles you. Be selective, avoiding notes that are either too meager or too extensive. Suppose, for example, that you were writing a paper on the engineering problems facing the International Space Station. If you were reading an article on the history and the future of this facility, you might take careful notes on material describing the station's technical details, but not on astronauts' biographies.

Develop accurate, complete records. Your notes should . . .
- Accurately summarize, paraphrase, and quote sources (pages 422–424).
- Clearly show where you got your information.
- Cover all the research you've done—primary research (e.g., interviews, observations), books and periodical articles, and online sources.

Engage your sources. Evaluate what you are reading and develop your own responses. (See pages 4–9.) For example, with an article about the International Space Station, you might test the author's biases, credentials, and logic; and you might respond with knowledge you have gained about other space endeavors.

Take good notes on graphics in sources—tables, line graphs, photographs, maps, and so on. Such graphics are typically packed with information and powerfully convey ideas. (See "Critical Thinking Through Viewing," pages 10–15.)

INSIGHT   Different disciplines use different note-taking practices. In your major, learn these practices through courses that introduce you to the subject matter. Here are two examples:
- In literature studies, students conduct literary analyses by annotating print texts. Students may also take notes through keyword searches of e-books (for example, a Shakespeare play) and reviews of literary criticism.
- In environmental studies, students conduct research by (a) taking notes on published research to develop literature reviews, and (b) using a standard field notebook to collect data, make drawings, and reflect on results.

Employ note-taking systems.

A good note-taking system should help you do the following:

- Avoid unintentional plagiarism by developing accurate records, distinguishing among sources, and separating source material from your own ideas.
- Work efficiently at gathering what you need for the project.
- Work flexibly with a wide range of resources—primary and secondary, print and electronic, verbal and visual.
- Engage sources through creative and critical reflection.
- Record summaries, paraphrases, and quotations correctly.
- Be accurate and complete so that you need not reread sources.
- Efficiently develop your paper's outline and first draft.

Four note-taking systems are outlined on the pages that follow. Choose the system that works best for your project, or combine elements to develop your own.

System 1: Paper or electronic note cards. Using paper note cards is the traditional method of note taking; however, note-taking software is now available with most word-processing programs and special programs like TakeNote, EndNote Plus, and Bookends Pro. Here's how a note-card system works:

1. Establish one set of cards (3 × 5 inches, if paper) for your bibliography.
2. On a second set of cards (4 × 6 inches, if paper), take notes on sources:
   - Record one point from one source per card.
   - Clarify the source: List the author's last name, a shortened title, or a code from the matching bibliography card. Include a page number.
   - Provide a topic or heading: Called a slug, the topic helps you categorize and order information.
   - Label the note as a summary, paraphrase, or quotation of the original.
   - Distinguish between the source's information and your own thoughts.

fig. 24.9

	1
Slug	PROBLEMS WITH INTERNAL-COMBUSTION CARS
Quotation	"In one year, the average gas-powered car produces five tons of carbon dioxide, which as it slowly builds up in the atmosphere causes global warming." (p. 43)
Page Number	
Comments	– helpful fact about the extent of pollution caused by the traditional i-c engine
	– how does this number compare with what a hybrid produces?
Source	#7

Upside: Note cards are highly systematic, helping you categorize material and organize it for an outline and a first draft.

Downside: The method can be initially tedious and time-consuming.

System 2: Copy (or save) and annotate. The copy-and-annotate method involves working with photocopies, print versions, or digital texts of sources:

1. Selectively photocopy, print, and/or save important sources. Copy carefully, making sure you have full pages, including the page numbers.
2. As needed, add identifying information on the copy—author, publication details, and date. Each page should be easy to identify and trace. When working with books, simply copy the title and copyright pages and keep them with the rest of your notes.
3. As you read, mark up the copy and highlight key statements. In the margins or digital file, record your ideas:
   - Ask questions. Insert a "?" in the margin, or write out the question.
   - Make connections. Draw arrows to link ideas, or make notes like "see page 36."
   - Add asides. Record what you think and feel while reading.
   - Define terms. Note important words that you need to understand.
   - Create a marginal index. Write keywords to identify themes and main parts.

Upside: Copying, printing, and/or saving helps you record sources accurately; annotating encourages careful reading and thinking.

Downside: Organizing material for drafting is inconvenient; when done poorly, annotating and highlighting involve skimming, not critical thinking.

System 3: The computer notebook or research log. The computer notebook or research log method involves taking notes on a computer or on sheets of paper. Here's how it works:

1. Establish a central location for your notes—a notebook, a file folder, a binder, or an electronic folder.
2. Take notes one source at a time, making sure to identify the source fully. Number your note pages.
3. Using your initials or some other symbol, distinguish your own thoughts from source material.
4. Use codes in your notes to identify which information in the notes relates to which topic in your outline. Then, under each topic in the outline, write the page number in your notes where that information is recorded. With a notebook or log, you may be able to rearrange your notes into an outline by using copy and paste—but don't lose source information in the process!

Upside: Taking notes feels natural without being overly systematic.

Downside: Outlining and drafting may require time-consuming paper shuffling.

System 4: The double-entry notebook. The double-entry notebook involves parallel note taking—notes from sources beside your own brainstorming, reaction, and reflection. Using a notebook or the columns feature of your word-processing program, do the following:

1. Divide pages in half vertically.
2. In the left column, record bibliographic information and take notes on sources.
3. In the right column, write your responses. Think about what the source is saying, why the point is important, whether you agree with it, and how the point relates to other ideas and other sources.

Upside: This method creates accurate source records while encouraging thoughtful responses; also, it can be done on a computer.

Downside: Organizing material for drafting may be a challenge.

fig. 24.10

Cudworth, Erika. *Environment and Society.* Routledge Introductions to Environment Series. London and New York: Routledge, 2003. Print.	
Ch. 6 "Society, 'Culture' and 'Nature'— Human Relations with Animals"	I've actually had a fair bit of personal experience with animals—the horses, ducks, dogs, and cats on our hobby farm. Will this chapter make trouble for my thinking?
chapter looks at how social scientists have understood historically the relationship between people and animals (158)	
the word <u>animal</u> is itself a problem when we remember that people too are animals but the distinction is often sharply made by people themselves (159)	Yes, what really are the connections and differences between people and animals? Is it a different level of intelligence? Is there something more basic or fundamental? Are we afraid to see ourselves as animals, as creatures?
"In everyday life, people interact with animals continually." (159)–author gives many common examples	Many examples—pets, food, TV programs, zoos—apply to me. Hadn't thought about how much my life is integrated with animal life! What does that integration look like? What does it mean for me, for the animals?

Summarizing, Paraphrasing, and Quoting Source Material

As you work with sources, you must decide what to put in your notes and how to record it—as a summary, a paraphrase, or a quotation. Use these guidelines:

- How relevant is the passage to your research question or working thesis?
- How strong and important is the information offered?
- How unique or memorable is the thinking or phrasing?

The more relevant, the stronger, and the more memorable the material is, the more likely you should note it. The passage below comes from an article on GM's development of fuel-cell technology. Review the passage; study how the researcher summarizes, paraphrases, and quotes from the source; and then practice these same strategies as you take notes on sources.

From Burns, L. D., McCormick, J. B., and Borroni-Bird, C. E. "Vehicle of Change." *Scientific American 287*(4), 64-73.

When Karl Benz rolled his Patent Motorcar out of the barn in 1886, he literally set the wheels of change in motion. The advent of the automobile led to dramatic alterations in people's way of life as well as the global economy—transformations that no one expected at the time. The ever-increasing availability of economical personal transportation remade the world into a more accessible place while spawning a complex industrial infrastructure that shaped modern society.

Now another revolution could be sparked by automotive technology: one fueled by hydrogen rather than petroleum. Fuel cells—which cleave hydrogen atoms into protons and electrons that drive electric motors while emitting nothing worse than water vapor—could make the automobile much more environmentally friendly. Not only could cars become cleaner, they could also become safer, more comfortable, more personalized—and even perhaps less expensive. Further, these fuel-cell vehicles could be instrumental in motivating a shift toward a "greener" energy economy based on hydrogen. As that occurs, energy use and production could change significantly. Thus, hydrogen fuel-cell cars and trucks could help ensure a future in which personal mobility—the freedom to travel independently—could be sustained indefinitely, without compromising the environment or depleting the earth's natural resources.

A confluence of factors makes the big change seem increasingly likely. For one, the petroleum-fueled internal-combustion engine (ICE), as highly refined, reliable and economical as it is, is finally reaching its limits. Despite steady improvements, today's ICE vehicles are only 20 to 25 percent efficient in converting the energy content of fuels into drive-wheel power. And although the U.S. auto industry has cut exhaust emissions substantially since the unregulated 1960s—hydrocarbons dropped by 99 percent, carbon monoxide by 96 percent and nitrogen oxides by 95 percent—the continued production of carbon dioxide causes concern because of its potential to change the planet's climate.

Summarize useful passages.

Summarizing condenses in your own words the main points in a passage. Summarize when the source provides relevant ideas and information on your topic.

1. **Reread the passage,** jotting down a few key words.
2. **State the main point in your own words.** Add key supporting points, leaving out examples, details, and long explanations. Be objective: Don't include your reactions.
3. **Check your summary against the original,** making sure that you use quotation marks around any exact phrases you borrow.

Sample Summary:

> While the introduction of the car in the late nineteenth century has led to dramatic changes in society and world economics, another dramatic change is now taking place in the shift from gas engines to hydrogen technologies. Fuel cells may make the car "greener," and perhaps even safer, cheaper, and more comfortable. These automotive changes will affect the energy industry by making it more environmentally friendly; as a result, people will continue to enjoy mobility while transportation moves to renewable energy. One factor leading to this technological shift is that the internal-combustion engine has reached the limits of its efficiency, potential, and development—while remaining problematic with respect to emissions, climate change, and health.

Paraphrase key passages.

Paraphrasing involves putting a passage from the source into your own words—keeping the content but phrasing it in your own voice and style, so to speak. Typically, you would paraphrase a passage that contains important points, explanations, or arguments but that is not phrased memorably or clearly. The passage might be primarily factual, making direct quotation unnecessary, or the passage might be technical, dense, and complex, requiring that you put it in plainer terms. To paraphrase effectively, follow these steps:

1. **Review the passage** to make sure that you have the gist of the whole.
2. **Go through the passage carefully,** sentence by sentence, doing the following:
   - State the ideas in your own words, substituting terms and defining words as needed.
   - Rework the sentence patterns, as needed—changing syntax, combining clauses, and so on—so that the passage takes on your voice.
   - If you do borrow phrases directly, put them in quotation marks.
3. **Check your paraphrase against the original:** Is the meaning accurate and complete? Have you fairly "translated" the source into your own wording and voice?

Sample Paraphrase of the Second Paragraph in the Passage:

> Automobile technology may lead to another radical economic and social change through the shift from gasoline to hydrogen fuel. By breaking hydrogen into protons and electrons so that the electrons run an electric motor with only the by-product of water vapor, fuel cells could make the car a "green" machine. But this technology could also increase the automobile's safety, comfort, personal tailoring, and affordability. Moreover, this shift to fuel-cell engines in automobiles could lead to drastic, environmentally friendly changes in the broader energy industry, one that will be now tied to hydrogen rather than fossil fuels. The result from this shift will be radical changes in the way we use and produce energy. In other words, the shift to hydrogen-powered vehicles could promise to maintain society's valued mobility, while the clean technology would preserve the environment and its natural resources.

Quote crucial phrases, sentences, and passages.

Quoting records statements or phrases in the original source word for word. Quote nuggets only—statements that are well phrased or authoritative:

1. **Note the quotation's context**—how it fits in the author's discussion.
2. **Copy the passage word for word,** enclosing it in quotation marks and checking its accuracy.
3. **If you omit words, note that omission with an ellipsis.** If you change any word for grammatical reasons, put changes in brackets. (See page 479).

Sample Quotation:

> "[H]ydrogen fuel-cell cars and trucks could help ensure a future in which personal mobility . . . could be sustained indefinitely, without compromising the environment or depleting the earth's natural resources."

Note: This sentence captures the authors' main claim about the benefits and future of fuel-cell technology.

INSIGHT Whether you are summarizing, paraphrasing, or quoting, aim to be true to the source by respecting the context and spirit of the original. Avoid shifting the focus or ripping material out of its context and forcing it into your own. For example, in the sample passage the authors discuss the limits of the internal-combustion engine. If you were to claim that these authors are arguing that the internal-combustion engine was an enormous engineering and environmental mistake, you would be twisting their comments to serve your own writing agenda.

 For instruction on effectively integrating quotations, paraphrases, and summaries into your writing, see pages 476–479.

Avoiding Unintentional Plagiarism

Careful note taking helps prevent unintentional plagiarism. Plagiarism—using source material without giving credit—is treated more fully in chapter 26; essentially, however, unintentional plagiarism happens when you accidentally use a source's ideas, phrases, or information without documenting that material. At the planning stage of your project, you can prevent this problem from happening by adhering to principles of ethical research and following some practical guidelines.

Practice the principles of ethical research.

Because of the nature of information and the many challenges of working with it, conducting ethical research can be very complex and involved. To start with, however, commit to these principles of ethical research:

- Do the research and write the paper yourself.
- Adhere to the research practices approved in your discipline.
- Follow school- and discipline-related guidelines for working with people, resources, and technology.
- Avoid one-sided research that ignores or conceals opposition.
- Present real, accurate data and results—not "fudged" or twisted facts.
- Treat source material fairly in your writing.

Practices That Prevent Unintentional Plagiarism

The principles of ethical research above find expression when you prevent unintentional plagiarism. Do so by following these practices:

- Maintain an accurate working bibliography (pages 416–417).
- When taking notes, distinguish source material from your own reflection by using quotation marks, codes, and/or separate columns or note cards.
- When you draft your paper, transfer source material carefully by coding material that you integrate into your discussion, using quotation marks, double-checking your typing, or using copy and paste to ensure accuracy.
- Take time to do the project right—both research and writing. Avoid pulling an all-nighter during which you can't properly work with sources.

Practices That Prevent Internet Plagiarism

An especially thorny area related to unintentional plagiarism centers on the Internet. As with traditional print sources, Internet sources must be properly credited; in other words, Web material cannot simply be transferred to your paper without acknowledgement. So treat Web sources like print sources. And if you copy and paste digital material while taking notes and drafting, always track its origins with codes, abbreviations, or separate columns.

Critical-Thinking and Writing Activities

As directed by your instructor, complete the following activities.

1. Using all that you have learned in this chapter, develop a research proposal that identifies a topic of interest to you, clarifies the value of the research, maps out research methods (including a working bibliography of five to ten sources), and establishes a workable schedule.

2. If you have not already done so, get the resources that you listed in your research proposal's working bibliography (activity 1 above). Then do the following:

   - Identify each source as primary, secondary, or tertiary. Consider the relative value of these sources for your project.
   - Test the reliability of your sources, both print and digital. Refer to the scale on page 413 and the questions on pages 414-415. Are the sources credible enough for your project?
   - From your bibliography, choose a short article or a passage from a longer source. Read that material carefully and do the following: (a) write a summary of the material, (b) choose a paragraph and paraphrase it, and (c) choose a key statement to quote directly, indicating why it is worthy of quotation.

Learning-Objectives Checklist ✓

Have you achieved this chapter's learning objectives? Check your progress with the items below, revisiting topics in the chapter as needed. *I have . . .*

_____ analyzed the rhetorical situation of my research project (398).

_____ identified the phases of the research process (399).

_____ focused my research project by establishing a manageable topic, brainstorming questions, and developing a working thesis (400–401).

_____ differentiated the nature and uses of primary, secondary, and tertiary sources (402–403).

_____ generated a research plan by choosing research methods and getting organized to do research, as well as composing a research proposal, if required (404–407).

_____ chosen fitting information sources from promising information sites (408–409).

_____ performed effective keyword searches by choosing productive keywords and implementing search strategies (410–411).

_____ critically engaged print and digital sources, evaluating them for depth, reliability, credibility, lack of bias, currency, and accuracy (412–415).

_____ produced and maintained an orderly, accurate working bibliography (416–417).

_____ chosen a note-taking system that allows me to keep accurate, complete records and engage my sources (418–421).

_____ accurately summarized, paraphrased, and quoted material from sources in my notes (422–424).

_____ identified principles of ethical research and implemented them in my own project (425).

Chapter 25

Conducting Research: Primary, Library, Web

Today, conducting research is both easy and difficult. It's easy because research technology is powerful and many research methods are available. It's difficult because that technology and those methods provide access to so much information—the good, the bad, and the ugly.

How do you meet this challenge and conduct quality research? First, consider whether your project would benefit from primary research—gathering information firsthand by observing sites, interviewing people, and analyzing documents, for example. Second, learn how to use an expert resource—your college library. The library is your gateway to quality print and electronic materials. Third, learn to access reliable resources on the free Web.

Visually Speaking "Libraries are research centers." Think about this statement in light of Figure 25.1, and relate this idea to your own experience of research, inside and outside of libraries.

Learning **Objectives**

By working through this chapter, you will be able to

- choose, design, and conduct primary research for your project.
- identify, locate, retrieve, and work with library resources.
- implement free-Web research tools to locate and evaluate free-Web resources.

Jens Goepfert / Shutterstock.com

fig. 25.1

Planning Primary Research

As discussed on pages 402–403, resources can be primary, secondary, or tertiary. Doing primary research is particularly hands-on and requires careful planning. To do truly useful primary research, you need to choose methods that will gather information directly related to your main research question and learn the proper methods of doing such research. To start your planning, consider these factors:

- **The assignment:** Does the assignment dictate a particular form of primary research?
- **The field of study:** Does the course's subject matter point you towards particularly valued methods of primary research?
- **The topic:** How might your understanding of the topic deepen with information gathered through a particular method?
- **The timing:** How much time do you have for doing primary research?
- **The audience:** What forms of primary research will your readers expect, respect, or value?

Methods of Primary Research

After considering the factors above, review the methods below and choose those that make sense for your project. You can find instruction for each method at the page numbers indicated.

- **Surveys and Questionnaires** (pages 430–431) gather information from representative groups of people as responses you can review, tabulate, and analyze, most often statistically. Whether gathering simple facts or personal opinions, such research can give you strong insights into how the group thinks about your issue; however, it may be difficult to gather complex responses.

- **Analyses of Texts, Documents, Records, and Artifacts** (pages 432–433) involve studying original correspondence, reports, legislation, images, literary works, historical records, and so on. Such research provides a direct experience of your topic and insights into its immediate nature, products, or remnants, but the quality of research depends on how fully and effectively you analyze the "text" in question.

- **Interviews** (pages 434–435) involve consulting people through a question-and-answer dialogue. Interviewees can be either experts on your topic or people who have had a particular experience with the topic, either witnessing it or involved in some way. Interviewing experts can add authoritative input, though experts sometimes disagree. Interviewing someone with experience of your topic can give an inside perspective into its causes and effects, as well as its personal dimensions.

- **Observations** (page 436) involve systematically examining and analyzing places, spaces, scenes, equipment, work, events, and other sites or phenomena. Whether you rely simply on your five senses or use scientific techniques, observation provides a range of information—from personal impressions to precise data (e.g., measurements).

- **Experiments** (see IMRAD report, pages 485–491) test hypotheses—predictions about why things are as they are or happen as they do—so as to arrive at conclusions that can be tentatively accepted, related to other knowledge, and acted upon. Such testing often explains cause-effect relationships for varied natural, social, or psychological phenomena, offering a degree of scientific certainty about the forces at work in your topic.

Principles for Doing Primary Research

Whatever primary research you choose to do, you should conduct that research in a systematic, careful manner in order to generate valid, reliable primary information and ideas. Here are some principles common to doing any method of primary research:

1. **Locate a reliable source.** Make sure, in other words, that the person, place, group, document, or image is the real thing—an authoritative, representative, respected source of information. Whether you find your source in a print publication (e.g., a version of a Shakespeare play published by a scholarly press), on the Internet (e.g., a piece of legislation), in an archive or museum (e.g., a sculpture), through personal contact (e.g., a home visit), or through exploration (e.g., a ravine in your city)—make sure that the source matches your research need and has the right "weight" for your project.

2. **Aim for objectivity.** You should approach most primary research with an objective frame of mind: remain open to the evidence that arises by keeping your wishes in check; otherwise, your research will be slanted and your readers will recognize the biases in your thinking.

3. **Get ready through background research.** That is, don't go cold into your primary research. Do your homework first—learning the key concepts and perspectives on your topic, the theories debated, and the knowledge that has already been built by others. That way, your primary research will grow out of some foundational thinking and be driven by a specific purpose and specific questions.

4. **Use the right tools.** Each method of primary research requires tools—physical tools (e.g., field notebook, instruments), software (e.g., survey software, spreadsheet software), or analytical tools (e.g., the ability to sort out causes and effects). Make sure that you have reliable tools and are using them effectively.

5. **Gather and work with data carefully.** Primary information is only as good as the care with which it is gathered, interpreted, and presented. Keep accurate, complete records of your research; in some projects, you may even have to include such records and "raw data" in an appendix. Above all, work ethically with your data by avoiding errors, gaps and omissions, and by not fudging your data or doctoring graphics.

fyi If your research involves working with people, typically called "human subjects," strive to (1) do no harm, whether psychological, social, or financial, and (2) respect individual autonomy—participants' rights, dignity, and privacy, for example. Check if your school has a research-ethics committee that reviews, approves, and oversees such research by students.

Conducting Surveys

One source of primary information that you can use for research projects is a survey or questionnaire. Surveys can collect facts and opinions from a wide range of people about virtually any topic. To get valid information, follow these guidelines:

1. **Find a focus.**
   - Limit the purpose of your survey.
   - Target a specific audience.

2. **Ask clear questions.**
   - Phrase questions so they can be easily understood.
   - Use words that are objective (not biased or slanted).

3. **Match your questions to your purpose.**
   - Closed questions give respondents easy-answer options, and the answers are easy to tabulate. Closed questions can provide two choices (*yes* or *no, true* or *false*), multiple choices, a rating scale (*poor 1 2 3 excellent*), or a blank to fill.
   - Open-ended questions bring in a wide variety of responses and more complex information, but they take time to complete, and the answers can be difficult to summarize.

4. **Organize your survey so that it's easy to complete.**
   - In the introduction, state who you are and why you need the information. Explain how to complete the survey and when and where to return it.
   - Guide readers by providing numbers, instructions, and headings.
   - Begin with basic questions and end with any complex, open-ended questions that are necessary. Move in a logical order from one topic to the next.

5. **Test your survey before using it.**
   - Ask a friend or classmate to read your survey and help you revise it, if necessary, before printing it.
   - Try out your survey with a small test group. If the test group seems to misunderstand or misinterpret a question, then revise it.

6. **Conduct your survey.**
   - Distribute the survey to a clearly defined group that won't prejudice the sampling (random or cross section).
   - Get responses from a sample of your target group (10 percent at minimum).
   - Tabulate responses carefully and objectively.

Note: To develop statistically valid results, you may need expert help. Check with your instructor. In addition, consider online survey tools such as SurveyMonkey.com and LimeSurvey.org.

Sample Survey

Confidential Survey

The introduction includes the essential information about the survey.

My name is Cho Lang, and I'm conducting research about the use of training supplements. I'd like to hear from you, Alfred University's athletes. Please answer the questions below by circling or writing out your responses. Return your survey to me, care of the Dept. of Psychology, through campus mail by Friday, April 5. Your responses will remain confidential.

The survey begins with clear, basic questions.

1. Circle your gender.   **Male**   **Female**

2. Circle your year.
   Freshman   **Sophomore**   **Junior**   **Senior**

3. List the sports that you play.

4. Are you presently using a training supplement?
   Yes   **No**

   Note: If you circled "no," you may turn in your survey at this point.

The survey asks an open-ended question.

5. Describe your supplement use (type, amount, and frequency).

6. Who supervises your use of this training supplement?
   Coach   **Trainer**   **Self**   **Others**

7. How long have you used it?
   Less than 1 month   **1–12 months**   **12+ months**

The survey covers the topic thoroughly.

8. How many pounds have you gained while using this supplement?

9. How much has your athletic performance improved?
   None   1   2   3   4   5   **Greatly**

10. Circle any side effects you've experienced.
    Dehydration   **Nausea**   **Diarrhea**

Analyzing Texts, Documents, Records, and Artifacts

An original document or record is one that relates directly to the event, issue, object, or phenomenon you are researching. Examining original documents and artifacts can involve studying letters, email exchanges, case notes, literary texts, sales records, legislation, and material objects such as tools, sculptures, buildings, and tombs. As you analyze such documents and records, you examine evidence in an effort to understand a topic, arrive at a coherent conclusion about it, and support that judgment. How do you work with such diverse documents, records, and artifacts? Here are some guidelines:

Choose evidence close to your topic.

Which texts, documents, records, and artifacts originated from or grew out of the topic you are researching? The closer to the topic, the more primary the source. Select materials that are directly related to your research questions and/or working thesis.

> **Example:** If you were studying English labor riots of the 1830s, you could investigate these primary sources:
> - To identify the rioters, names from police reports or union membership lists
> - To understand what rioters were demanding, copies of speeches given at demonstrations
> - To learn the political response to the riots, political speeches or legislation
> - To get at the attitudes of people from that time, newspaper reports, works of art, or novels from the period
> - To find people's personal stories and private opinions related to the riots, personal letters, diaries, family albums, gravestones, and funeral eulogies

Put the document or artifact in context.

So that the material takes on meaning, clarify its external and internal natures. First, consider its external context—the five W's and H: What exactly is it? Who made it, when, where, why, and how? Second, consider its internal nature—what the document means, based on what it can and cannot show you: What does the language mean or refer to? What is the document's structure? What are the artifact's composition and style?

> **Example:** If you were examining Mary Wollstonecraft's *A Vindication of the Rights of Woman* in a history or women's studies course, you would consider the following:
> - **External Context:** who Mary Wollstonecraft was; when and why she wrote *A Vindication* and under what conditions; for whom she wrote it and their response; the type of document it is
> - **Internal Context:** Wollstonecraft's essential argument and evidence; the nature of her views, their relationship to her times, and their relevance today

Frame your examination with questions.

To make sense of the text, document, record, or artifact, understand what you are looking for and why. List the secondary questions that you want to answer in relation to the main question behind your research project.

> *Example:* To study the legislative background behind the development of cleaner cars, such as the hybrid-fuel vehicle, you could access various documents on the Clean Air Act of 1990 (for example, *The Plain English Guide to the Clean Air Act*, an EPA publication). As you study this legislation, you could frame your reading with these additional questions:
> - What are the requirements of the Clean Air Act?
> - Specifically, how do those requirements affect automotive technology?
> - Which research projects will likely influence these requirements?
> - Are schedules for change or deadlines written into the Clean Air Act?

Draw coherent conclusions about meaning.

Make sense of the source in relation to your research questions. What connections does it reveal? What important developments? What cause/effect relationships? What themes?

> *Example:* A study of the Clean Air Act might lead you to conclusions regarding how environmental legislation relates to the development of hybrid technology—for example, that the United States must produce cleaner cars if it hopes to gain improved air quality.

INSIGHT Studying primary documents and artifacts is central to many disciplines—history, literature, theology, philosophy, political studies, and archaeology, for example. Good analysis depends on asking research questions appropriate for the discipline. With the English labor riots of the 1830s again as an example, here's what three disciplines might ask:

- **Political science:** What role did political theories, structures, and processes play in the riots—both in causing and in responding to them?
- **Art:** How were the concerns of the rioters embodied in the new "realist" style of the mid-1800s? Did artists sympathize with and address an alienated working-class audience? How did art comment on the social structures of the time?
- **Sociology:** What type and quality of education did most workers have in the 1830s? How did that education affect their economic status and employment opportunities? Did issues related to the riots prompt changes in the English educational system? What changes and why?

With these examples in mind, consider your own major: What questions would this discipline ask of the English labor riots, of Mary Wollstonecraft's *A Vindication of the Rights of Woman*, or of the Clean Air Act of 1990?

Conducting Interviews

The purpose of an interview is simple: To get information, you talk with someone who has significant experience or someone who is an expert on your topic. Use the guidelines below whenever you conduct an interview.

1. **Before the interview,** research the topic and the person you are planning to interview.
   - Arrange the interview in a thoughtful way. Explain to the interviewee your purpose and the topics to be covered.
   - Think about the specific ideas you want to cover in the interview and write questions for each. Addressing the 5 W's and H (*Who? What? Where? When? Why?* and *How?*) is important for good coverage.
   - Organize your questions in a logical order so the interview moves smoothly from one subject to the next.
   - Write the questions on the left side of a page. Leave room for quotations, information, and impressions on the right side.

2. **During the interview,** try to relax so that your conversation is natural and sincere.
   - Provide some background information about yourself, your project, and your plans for using the interview information.
   - Use recording equipment only with the interviewee's permission.
   - Jot down key facts and quotations.
   - Listen actively. Show that you're listening through your body language—eye contact, nods, smiles. Pay attention not only to what the person says, but also to how he or she says it.
   - Be flexible. If the person looks puzzled by a question, rephrase it. If the discussion gets off track, redirect it. Based on the interviewee's responses, ask follow-up questions, and don't limit yourself to your planned questions only.
   - End positively. Conclude by asking if the person wants to add, clarify, or emphasize anything. (Note: important points may come up late in the interview.) Thank the person, gather your notes and equipment, and part with a handshake.

3. **After the interview,** do the appropriate follow-up work.
   - As soon as possible, review your notes. Fill in responses you remember but couldn't record at the time.
   - Analyze the results. Study the information, insights, and quotations you gathered. What do they reveal about the topic? How does the interview confirm, complement, or contradict other sources on the topic? What has the interview added to your understanding?
   - Thank the interviewee with a note, an email, or a phone call.
   - If necessary, ask the interviewee to check whether your information and quotations are accurate.
   - Offer to send the interviewee a copy of your writing.

Sample Interview Note-Taking Sheet

Below, note how the researcher sets up questions for an interview with an automotive engineer regarding hybrid technology. The interviewer begins with identifying information for future reference, and then moves from a basic "connecting" question into the technology's principles, strengths, challenges, and future. On the right, he would leave room (approximately half the sheet) for taking notes.

Interview with Jessica Madison,
automotive engineer for Future Fuel Corporation
(email jmadison@futurefuel.com; phone 555-555-5555)
January 22, 2014: 2:30 p.m.

Notes, quotations,
observations:

Preliminaries: thanks/appreciation; introduction of myself; background, purpose, hoped-for outcome of research (report on hybrids' environmental potential)

Initial Question

1. Please tell me about your research into hybrid technology. When and how did you become interested? What discoveries have you made?

Hybrid Technology: Principles

2. How does hybrid technology actually work? What's the principle behind the hybrid vehicle?

3. How is the hybrid engine different from the traditional internal-combustion engine?

Strengths and Challenges

4. What are the strengths of hybrid vehicles?

5. What are some of the challenges of hybrids? Some of the weaknesses?

The Future/Viability

6. Where is hybrid technology going? What's the next generation of clean-car technology?

7. What are the benefits or drawbacks of society investing in hybrids? Why should the average person care about hybrid technologies?

8. Would you like to add or clarify anything about hybrid technologies?

Closing: thank for taking time, offering insights

Making Observations

Observation places you at a site directly related to your topic. Whether you are examining people's behavior, natural phenomena, or a location's features, observation can gather subjective impressions, sensory data, various recordings, or concrete measurements.

Prepare to observe.

1. **Know your goal.** Do you need to understand a place or a process? Solve a problem? Answer a question? What kind of information do you want to gather?

2. **Consider possible perspectives and vantage points.** Should you observe the site passively or interact with it? Should you simply record data or also include impressions? Should you observe from one position or several?

3. **Plan your observation.** Preparation involves both academic and practical issues: doing sufficient background research; listing questions to answers; seeking permission to observe, if needed; taking safety precautions; considering timing issues; and gathering observation tools.

Conduct your observations.

1. **Be flexible but focused.** Follow your plan, but be open to surprises. Pay attention to the big picture (the context, time frame, and surroundings), but focus on your observational goal by filtering out unnecessary details.

2. **Identify your position.** Where are you in the site? What is your angle? More broadly, what is your personal and/or cultural stance here?

3. **Take notes on specific details and impressions.** While being careful not to miss too much, jot down data for later review—conditions, appearances, actions, events, and so on. If appropriate, focus on your five senses: sight, sound, smell, touch, and taste.

4. **Gather other forms of evidence.** Take measurements, record images and sound, gather samples, interview people, study event programs, get brochures.

Make sense of your observations.

1. **Complete and review your notes and evidence.** As soon as possible, flesh out your notes a bit more fully—while your memory is still good. Then examine closely everything that you have written, recorded, and collected, looking for patterns and themes.

2. **List your conclusions.** Describe what has been clarified about your topic through the observation.

3. **Relate your observations to your other research.** Explore how your observations confirm, contradict, complement, or build on other sources of information.

Becoming Familiar with the Library

The library door is your gateway to information. Inside, the college library holds a wide range of research resources, from books to periodicals, from reference librarians to electronic databases.

To improve your ability to succeed at all your research assignments, become familiar with your college library system. Take advantage of tours and orientation sessions to learn its physical layout, resources, and services. Check your library's Web site for policies, tutorials, and research tools. The college library offers a variety of resources for your research projects.

Librarians: Librarians are information experts:
- Librarians manage the library's materials and guide you to resources.
- They help you perform online searches.

Collections: The library collects and houses a variety of materials:
- **Books and electronic materials**—CD-ROMs, CDs, and DVDs
- **Periodicals**—journals, magazines, and newspapers (print or microform)
- **Reference materials**—directories, indexes, handbooks, encyclopedias, and almanacs
- **Special collections**—government publications, historical documents, and original artifacts

Research tools: The library contains many tools that direct you to materials:
- The online catalog allows you to search everything in the library.
- Print indexes and subscription databases (Lexis-Nexis, EBSCOhost, ProQuest Direct) point you to abstracts and full-text articles.
- Internet access connects you with other library catalogs and online references.

Special services: Special services may also help you to complete research:
- Interlibrary loan allows you to obtain books and articles not available in your library.
- "Hold" allows you to request a book that is currently signed out.
- "Reserve" materials give you access to materials recommended by your instructors or heavily in demand.
- The reference desk can help you find information quickly, point you to the right resources, and help you with a search.
- Photocopiers, scanners, and presentation software help you perform and share your research.

Cross-Curricular Connection: As you advance in your field of study, become especially familiar with the reference holdings, journals, book stacks, and Web resources related to your major.

Searching the Catalog

Library materials are catalogued so they are easy to find. In most college libraries, books, videos, and other holdings are catalogued in an electronic database. To find material, use book titles, author names, and related keyword searching. (See also pages 410–411.)

Sample Electronic Catalog

fig. 25.2

◉ Keyword   ◯ Browse   ◯ Exact

[   ]

| Search Everything | Author | Title | Subject | Series | Periodical Title |

1. Enter the word(s) you want to find.
   Keyword returns records containing the word(s) entered.
   Browse returns catalog headings *beginning* with the first word entered.
   Exact returns records that *exactly* match the word(s) entered.
2. Choose a target search field.
   Search everything targets all indexed fields within a record.
   All other choices target specified fields within a record.

When you find a citation for a book or other resource, the result will provide some or all of the following information. Use that information to determine whether the resource is worth exploring further and to figure out other avenues of research. Note that a number of items appearing in blue, underlined type provide links to related books and other resources in the catalog.

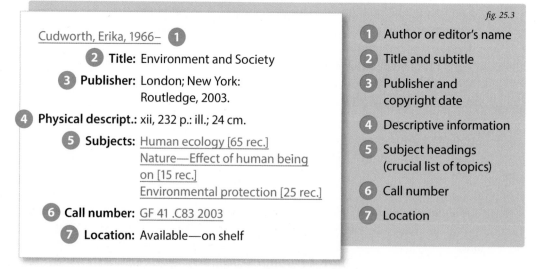

fig. 25.3

Cudworth, Erika, 1966– **1**

2 **Title:** Environment and Society

3 **Publisher:** London; New York: Routledge, 2003.

4 **Physical descript.:** xii, 232 p.: ill.; 24 cm.

5 **Subjects:** Human ecology [65 rec.]
Nature—Effect of human being on [15 rec.]
Environmental protection [25 rec.]

6 **Call number:** GF 41 .C83 2003

7 **Location:** Available—on shelf

1 Author or editor's name

2 Title and subtitle

3 Publisher and copyright date

4 Descriptive information

5 Subject headings (crucial list of topics)

6 Call number

7 Location

Locating Resources by Call Numbers

Library of Congress (LC) call numbers combine letters and numbers to specify a resource's broad subject area, topic, and authorship or title. Finding a book, DVD, or other item involves combining both the alphabetical and the numerical order. Here is a sample call number for *Arctic Refuge: A Vanishing Wilderness?*:

VIDEO QH84.1.A72 1990

subject area (QH) topic number (84) subtopic number (1) cutter number (A72)

To find this resource in the library, first note the tab VIDEO. Although not part of the call number, this locator may send you to a specific area of the library. Once there, follow the parts of the call number one at a time:

1. Find the library section on natural history containing videos with the "QH" designation.
2. Follow the numbers until you reach "84."
3. Within the "84" items, find those with the subtopic "1."
4. Use the cutter "A72" to locate the resource alphabetically with "A," and numerically with "72."

Note: In the LC system, pay careful attention to the arrangement of subject area letters, topic numbers, and subtopic numbers: Q98 comes before QH84; QH84 before QH8245; QH84. A72 before QH84.1.A72.

Classification Systems

The LC classification system combines letters and numbers. The Dewey decimal system, which is used in some libraries, uses numbers only. Here is a list of the subject classes for both the LC and Dewey systems.

The Library of Congress and Dewey Decimal Systems   *fig. 25.4*

LC Category		Dewey Decimal	LC Category		Dewey Decimal
A	General Works	000–999	K	Law	340–349
B	Philosophy	100–199	L	Education	370–379
	Psychology	150–159	M	Music	780–789
	Religion	200–299	N	Fine Arts	700–799
C	History: Auxiliary		P	Language	800–899
	Sciences	910–929		Literature	400–499
D	History: General and		Q	Science	500–599
	Old World	930–999	R	Medicine	610–619
E–F	History of the Americas	970–979	S	Agriculture	630–639
G	Geography	910–919	T	Technology	600–699
	Anthropology	571–573	U	Military Science	355–359, 623
	Recreation	700–799	V	Naval Science	359, 623
H	Social Sciences	300–399	Z	Bibliography and	010–019
J	Political Science	320–329		Library Science	020–029

Using Books in Research

Your college library contains a whole range of books for you to use. Unfortunately, for most research projects you simply don't have time to read an entire book, and rarely do the entire contents relate to your topic. Instead, use the strategies outlined below.

Approach the book systematically.

1. **Identify the book type.** Trade books are typically written for a broad public and published by for-profit presses. Often written by experts, such books can be filled with reliable, useful information for a lay audience, though quality, depth, and reliability can vary. Example: *Flirting with* Pride & Prejudice: *Fresh Perspectives on the Original Chick-Lit Masterpiece.* By comparison, scholarly books are typically written for a specialized audience and college-level students. Published by university presses and other respected scholarly presses, such studies typically provide advanced research findings. Example: *Jane Austen on Screen* (Cambridge University Press).

2. **Check out front and back information.** The title and copyright pages give the book's full title and subtitle; the author's name; and publication information, including publication date and Library of Congress subject headings. The back may contain a note on the author's credentials and other publications.

3. **Scan the table of contents.** Examine the contents page to see what the book covers and how it is organized. Ask yourself which chapters are relevant to your project.

4. **Using key words, search the index.** Check the index for coverage and page locations of the topics most closely related to your project. Are there plenty of pages, or just a few? A scattered mention of key words likely represents more superficial coverage than concentrated, in-depth coverage.

5. **Skim the preface, foreword, or introduction.** The opening materials will often indicate the book's perspective, explain its origin, and preview its contents.

6. **Check appendices, glossaries, or bibliographies.** These special sections may be a good source of tables, graphics, definitions, statistics, and clues for further research.

7. **Carefully read appropriate chapters and sections.** Think through the material you've read and take good notes. (See pages 418–421.) Follow references to authors and other works to do further research on the topic. Study footnotes and endnotes for insights and leads.

fyi Consider these options for working productively with books:
- When you find a helpful book, browse nearby shelves for more books.
- To confirm a book's quality, check the Internet or a periodical database for for a review.
- If your library subscribes to an e-book service such as NetLibrary, you have access to thousands of books in electronic form. You can conduct electronic searches, browse or check out promising books, and read them online.

Using Reference Resources

Reference works, whether print or digital, are information-rich resources that can give you an overview of your topic, supply basic facts, share common knowledge about your topic, and offer ideas for focusing and furthering your research. While some reference resources are available on the free Web (see, for example, the discussion of Wikipedia on pages 452–453), your library offers you excellent access to reference resources in both print and digital formats. Consider options like those below.

Check reference works that supply information.

- **Encyclopedias** supply facts and overviews for topics arranged alphabetically. General encyclopedias cover many fields of knowledge: *Encyclopedia Britannica* (online version). Specialized encyclopedias focus on a single topic: *Encyclopedia of American Film Comedy.*
- **Almanacs, yearbooks, and statistical resources,** normally published annually, contain diverse facts. For example, the *Statistical Abstract of the United States* provides data on population, geography, politics, employment, business, science, and industry.
- **Vocabulary resources** supply information on languages. General dictionaries, such as *The American Heritage College Dictionary,* supply definitions and histories for a whole range of words. Specialized dictionaries define words common to a field, topic, or group: *The New Harvard Dictionary of Music.* Bilingual dictionaries translate words from one language to another.
- **Biographical resources** supply information about people. General biographies cover a broad range of people. Other biographies focus on people from a specific group. *Examples: Who's Who in America, World Artists 1980–1990.*
- **Directories** supply contact information for people, groups, and organizations. *Examples: USPS ZIP Code Lookup and Address Information* (online).

Check reference works that are research tools.

- **Guides and handbooks** help readers explore specific topics: *The Handbook of North American Indians, A Guide to Prairie Fauna.*
- **Indexes** point you to useful resources. Whether general or specialized, such as indexes are available online in databases your library subscribes to. (See pages 442–445.)
- **Bibliographies** list resources on a specific topic. A good, current bibliography can be used as an example when you compile your own bibliography on a topic.
- **Abstracts,** like indexes, direct you to articles on a particular topic. But abstracts also summarize those materials so you learn whether a resource is relevant before you invest time in locating and reading it. Such abstracts are typically incorporated into many online subscription databases.

Finding Articles Via Databases

Periodicals are publications or broadcasts produced at regular intervals (daily, weekly, monthly, quarterly). Although some periodicals are broad in their subject matter and audience, as a rule they focus on a narrow range of topics geared toward a particular audience.

- **Daily newspapers and newscasts** provide up-to-date information on current events, opinions, and trends—from politics to natural disasters *(Wall Street Journal, USA Today, The NewsHour)*.
- **Weekly and monthly magazines** generally provide more in-depth information on a wide range of topics *(Time, Newsweek, 60 Minutes)*.
- **Journals**, generally published quarterly, provide specialized scholarly information for a narrowly focused audience *(English Journal)*.

With thousands of periodicals available, how do you find helpful articles? Learn (a) which search tools your library offers, (b) which periodicals it has available in which forms, and (c) how to gain access to those periodicals.

Search online databases.

If your library subscribes to EBSCOhost, Lexis-Nexis, or another database service, use keyword searching (see pages 410–411) to find citations on your topic. You might start with the general version of such databases, such as EBSCOhost's Academic Search Premier, which provides access to more than 4,100 scholarly publications covering all disciplines.

- **Basic Search:** Figure 25.5 shows an EBSCOhost search screen for a search on hybrid electric cars. Notice how limiters, expanders, and other advanced features help you find the highest-quality materials.

fig. 25.5

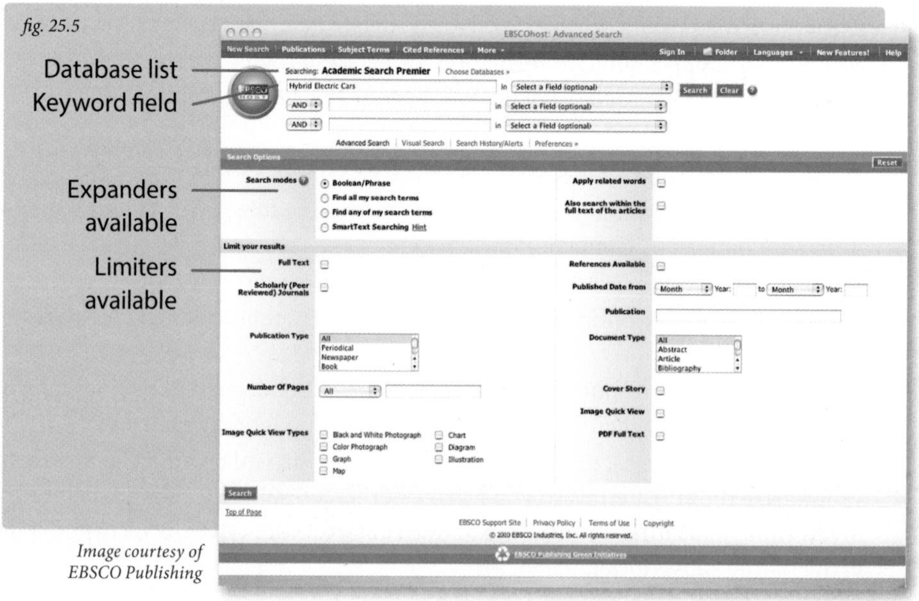

Database list
Keyword field
Expanders available
Limiters available

Image courtesy of EBSCO Publishing

- **Advanced Search:** A more focused research strategy would involve turning to specialized databases, which are available for virtually every discipline and are often an option within search services such as EBSCOhost (for example, Business Source Elite, PsycINFO, ERIC) and Lexis-Nexis (for example, Legal, Medical, and Business databases). If a basic search turns up little, turn to specialized databases, seeking help from a librarian if necessary. For a list of specialized databases, see page 445.

fyi Particularly if you need articles published before 1985, you may need to go to the *Readers' Guide to Periodical Literature* or another print index. While databases are converting pre-1985 articles to digital form (for example, the JSTOR database), many excellent periodical articles are available only in print. To use the *Reader's Guide*, consult a librarian.

Generate citation lists of promising articles.

Your database search should generate lists of citations, brief descriptions of articles that were flagged through keywords in titles, subject terms, abstracts, and so on. For example, a search focused on hybrid electric cars leads to the results shown in Figure 25.6. At this point, study the results and do the following:

- Refine the search by narrowing or expanding it.
- Mark specific citations for "capture" or further study.
- Re-sort the results.
- Follow links in a specific citation to further information.

fig. 25.6

Folder feature for "capturing" citations

"Sort" options

Numbered citations including titles, authors, journal information, length, location notes

Article links indicating article availability and format

Image courtesy of EBSCO Publishing

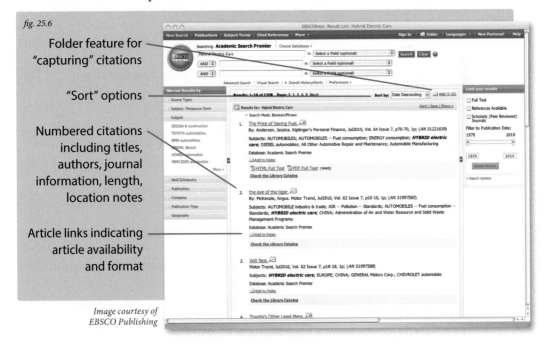

Study citations and capture identifying information.

By studying citations (especially abstracts), you can determine three things:

- Is this article relevant to your research?
- Is an electronic, full-text version available?
- If not, does the library have this periodical?

To develop your working bibliography (see pages 416–417), you should also "capture" the article's identifying details by using the save, print, or email function, or by recording the periodical's title, the issue and date, and the article's title and page numbers. These functions are shown in the EBSCOhost citation in Figure 25.7.

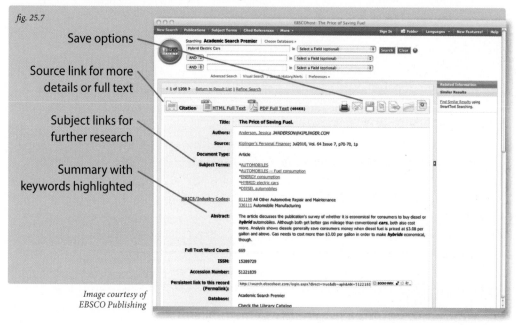

fig. 25.7

Save options

Source link for more details or full text

Subject links for further research

Summary with keywords highlighted

Image courtesy of
EBSCO Publishing

Find and retrieve the full text of the article.

When citations indicate that you have promising articles, access those articles efficiently, preferably through a direct link in the citation to an electronic copy. From there you can print, save, or email the article. If the article is not available electronically, track down a print version:

- Check the online citation to see if your library has the article. If necessary, check your library's inventory of periodicals held; this list should be available online and/or in print. Examine especially closely the issues and dates available, the form (print or microfilm), and the location (bound or current shelves).
- To get the article, follow your library's procedure. You may have to submit a request slip so that a librarian can get the periodical, or you may be able to get it yourself in the current, bound, or microfilm collection. If the article is not available online or in your library, use interlibrary loan.

Databases for Disciplines

Most libraries offer access to databases from a wide range of disciplines. Check your library's Web site for access to databases like these:

- **Agricola** offers citations from the National Agricultural Library group—with materials focused on issues from animal science to food and nutrition.
- **ARTbibliographies Modern** abstracts articles, books, catalogs, and other resources on modern and contemporary art.
- **CAIRSS for Music** offers bibliographic citations for articles on music-related topics, from music education to music therapy.
- **Communication & Mass Media Complete** offers access to resources on topics like public speaking and TV broadcasting.
- **Engineering E-journal Search Engine** offers free, full-text access to more than 150 online engineering journals.
- **ERIC** offers citations, abstracts, and digests for more than 980 journals in the education field.
- **First Search**, a fee-based information service, offers access to more than 30 scholarly databases in a range of disciplines.
- **GPO**, the Government Printing Office, offers access to records for U.S. government documents (e.g., reports, hearings, judicial rules, addresses, and so on).
- **Health Source** offers access to abstracts, indexing, and full-text material on health-related topics, from nutrition to sports medicine.
- **Ingenta** offers citations for more than 25,000 journals, most in the sciences.
- **JSTOR** offers full-text access to scholarly articles in a full range of disciplines, articles once available only in print.
- **Math Database** offers article citations for international mathematics research.
- **Medline** offers access to journals in medicine and medicine-related disciplines through references, citations, and abstracts.
- **MLA Bibliography** provides bibliographic citations for articles addressing a range of modern-language and literature-related topics.
- **National Environmental Publications Internet Site (NEPIS)** offers access to more than 6,000 EPA documents (full text, online).
- **PsycINFO** offers access to materials in psychology and psychology-related fields (for example, social work, criminology, organizational behavior).
- **Scirus** indexes science resources, citing article titles and authors, source publication information, and lines of text indicating the article's content.
- **Vocation and Career Collection** offers full-text access to more than 400 trade- and industry-related periodicals.
- **Worldwide Political Science Abstracts** offers bibliographic citations in politics-related fields, from public policy to international law.

Understanding Internet Basics

Did you know that the World Wide Web and the Internet are not the same? Do you know what the *deep Web* is? Can you identify the parts of a Web page? These two pages provide basic definitions and explanations of the digital world.

- The **Internet** is a vast array of interconnected computers and computer networks. It began in 1969 with the ARPANET, a connection of U.S. government computers. Since then, the Internet has expanded into a worldwide system. Email, cell phones, and satellites all access and use the Internet, as do people on the World Wide Web.

- The **World Wide Web** is a huge collection of Web sites and pages on the Internet, accessible through the hypertext transfer protocol (HTTP). Put simply, this protocol is a set of rules that allow computers to trade information. The World Wide Web was begun in 1989 by a British engineer named Tim Berners-Lee.

- A **uniform resource locator (URL)** is the Web address for each page available on the World Wide Web. Just as every home and business has a specific street address, every Web site has a specific Web address that allows other computers to find and access it.

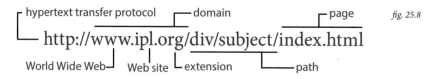

fig. 25.8

- A **domain name** is the Web site address, often beginning with www and ending with an extension that indicates what type of site it is. Here is a list of common domain types:

.com	a commercial or business site
.gov	a government site, for federal, state, or local government
.edu	an educational site
.org	a site for a nonprofit organization
.net	a site for an organization that belongs to the Internet's infrastructure
.mil	a military site
.biz	a business site
.info	an information site

Such domain names apply particularly to U.S. Web sites. If a Web site originates in another country, the domain typically is a two-letter nation abbreviation. Examples: .ca for Canada; .uk for United Kingdom. Keep this in mind as you access Web sites for your research.

- A **Web browser** is a program on your computer that provides access to the Web. Common browsers include Chrome, Internet Explorer, and Safari.

- A **Web page** is a specific grouping of information on the Web (Figure 25.9). Web pages often include text, graphics, photographs, videos, and hyperlinks—which are words or graphics that can be clicked to take the user to different Web pages.

- A **search engine** is a specialized Web page that allows you to find specific terms on sites throughout the Web. Here are some popular search engines:

Google	http://www.google.com
Bing	http://www.bing.com
Yahoo	http://www.yahoo.com

- A **metasearch engine** is a Web page that searches several other search engines at once, compiling the information. Here are some popular metasearch engines:

Ask	http://www.ask.com
Dog Pile	http://www.dogpile.com
Ixquick	http://www.ixquick.com

- A **deep-Web** tool is an Internet search engine or database that can access materials not available to basic search engines, materials found on what is called the *deep Web*.

Complete Planet	http://www.completeplanet.com

Common Web page Elements

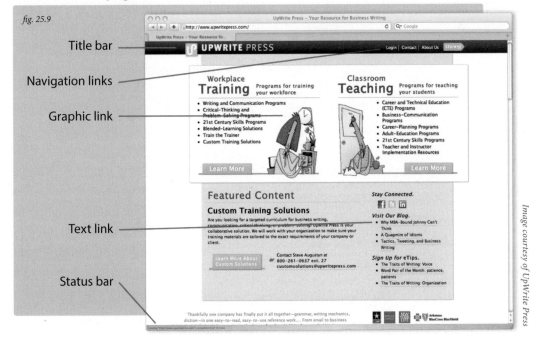

fig. 25.9

Title bar

Navigation links

Graphic link

Text link

Status bar

Image courtesy of UpWrite Press

Using a Subject Guide/Directory

A subject tree, sometimes called a *subject guide* or *directory*, lists Web sites that have been organized into categories by experts who have reviewed those sites. As such, a subject tree includes sites selected for reliability and quality.

1. **Search out the subject trees available to you.** Check whether your library subscribes to a service such as NetFirst, a database in which subject experts have cataloged Internet resources by topic. Here are some other common subject directories:

   WWW Virtual Library http://vlib.org/Overview.html
   Ipl2 http://www.ipl.org/
   Google Directory http://www.google.com/dirhp
   LookSmart http://looksmart.com

2. **Follow categories from broad to specific.** A subject tree is arranged from general to specific, so you will need to begin by clicking on a broad category to see a more selective list. Clicking on subcategories will take you to progressively more focused lists. Read the name of a site, review the information beneath the name, check out the domain and extension, and decide if the site is worth exploring. If so, click on it. If not, go back and continue your search. Figure 25.10 illustrates common subject guide elements.

Common Subject Guide Elements

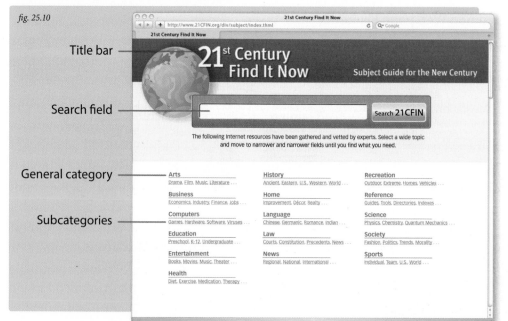

fig. 25.10

Using Search and Metasearch

Search and metasearch engines provide quick and powerful access to much of the content of the Web. They are invaluable tools for researchers. This page gives tips for getting the most out of your searches, and the next two pages look at search in depth.

1. **Select effective keywords:** Keywords are words or phrases that the search engine looks for across the Web. The more specific a keyword or phrase is, the more tightly a search will be focused. Here are a set of keywords for the research topic of "games used to simulate real-world scenarios":

General **game**	This general term will produce a very unfocused list of millions of Web sites, ranging from stores selling games to recipes for cooking game.
simulation	This more-specific term will narrow the search considerably, but will show off-topic sites such as suppliers of simulated wood products.
simulation game	This set of keywords is much more specific, but the engine will also find sites using both words but not in combination.
"simulation game" Specific	The quotation marks around this search will turn up only sites that use the exact phrase "simulation game."

2. **Use Boolean operators:** In addition to using quotation marks, you can use words and symbols to make your search specific. (See also page 411.)

game and **war**	*and* indicates sites with both terms
game + **war**	+ indicates sites with both terms
game not **war**	*not* indicates sites with the first term but not the second
game – **war**	– indicates sites with the first term but not the second
game or **simulation**	*or* indicates sites with either term

3. **Act on search results:** Once a search engine has generated a list of possible sites, you need to survey the results and act on them.
   - Read the name of the site and determine how the term is used.
   - Review the domain and extension to decide if you will click it.
   - Look for information and links.

Using Search Engines as Research Tools

Like millions of people, you probably "Google it" when you have a question. But how should you use search engines for college research projects? A search engine is a program that automatically scours a large amount of Web material using keywords and commands that you submit. In that respect, the search is only as productive as the terms you use, the quality of the search program, and the amount and areas of the Web that the engine searches. When you use search engines, be aware of the issues below, and use the tips on the following page to work around the limitations discussed.

- **Web Coverage:** Even though the largest search engines search billions of Web resources, those pages represent just a portion of the Web—as little as 20 percent. The point to keep in mind is that any given search engine is not searching the entire Web for you and may be focusing on particular kinds of pages and documents. Moreover, a given engine may not be searching each resource in its entirety but only certain portions (e.g., citations) or up to a certain size of the document.

- **Resource Ranking:** A search engine returns results in a ranking of resources based on complex mathematical algorithms—a weighing of a variety of criteria that differ from one engine to the next. One criterion used is the number of times your keywords appear in a given resource. A second criterion might be the number and type of links to a given page—a measure, in other words, of the site's importance or popularity on the Web. A third criterion relates to your search history: given sites that you have looked at in the past, what types of sites do you prefer? Algorithms answer this question by *personalizing* your search, potentially creating what Eli Pariser calls a "filter bubble"—results restricted to your interests and biases. One more point: organizations on the Web work very hard to make sure that their pages get ranked near the top of searches; some companies hire consultants to help achieve this result or even try to fool the programs. In other words, what you are getting in your search is not necessarily an objective listing of the most relevant and reliable resources for an academic research project.

- **Search Habits:** Using search engines is complicated not just by algorithms but by the habits of users themselves. Studies suggest, for example, that very few users look past the first three hits returned by a search, in fact, that only one percent of searchers go past the first ten hits. (You can understand, then, why some organizations work so hard to get into that top-ten list for specific keyword searches.) Moreover, very few users go on to refine their search after the initial results, supposedly satisfied with what they have found, although studies also suggest that few users can effectively evaluate the returned resources in terms of their quality, authority, objectivity, and timeliness (currency of information). The implications for your college research projects are clear: such search habits rarely lead to quality resources that you can use in an academic project.

Use search engines well.

Given how search engines work, what practices should you follow in using them for an academic research project? Obviously, start by following the assignment's restrictions about using free-Web resources. But here are four additional guidelines:

1. **Restrict search-engine use to specific purposes.** Generally, a search engine is useful for college research projects in these circumstances:

   - You have a very narrow topic in mind or an exact question you need answered.
   - You have a highly specific word or phrase to use in your search.
   - You want a large number of results.
   - You are looking for a specific type of Internet file.
   - You have the time to sort the material for reliability.

2. **Learn to do advanced searches.** Basic searches tend to lead to basic results. Most search engines actually allow you to do quite complex searches through advanced-search screens. With these, you can employ Boolean logic to a degree, use limiters and expanders, and refine your results in other ways. Study the search engine's help pages for instructions on how to benefit from these advanced-searching techniques.

3. **Approach results with suspicion.** Given the wide-ranging quality and reliability of material on the free Web, it is imperative that you evaluate resources that you find through search engines. See "Evaluating Online Sources" on pages 454–457.

4. **Use search engines that seem to give you more quality results.** Try out a variety of search engines using the same search, and compare the results. While you generally want to choose search engines that cover a large portion of the Web, offer quality indexing, and give you high-powered search capabilities, you also want to consider a search-engine's information focus: try out search engines whose goals seem more obviously focused on academics.

   - **Internet Public Library:** http://www.ipl.org Offering access to electronic reference resources, to e-books and electronic articles, and to special collections, this site's chief resource is its subject collections of Web resources.
   - **Infomine:** http://infomine.ucr.edu Subtitled Scholarly Internet Resource Collections, this librarian-built site is designed for college and university faculty and students; the site offers researchers access to databases, electronic journals and books, and more, including government information.
   - **LookSmart Find Articles.com:** http://findarticles.com This commercial site can give you citations for articles on your topic, although getting full-text access may involve fees.
   - **Google Scholar:** http://scholar.google.com While it indexes just a small portion of all published articles, Google Scholar can help you build citations from a variety of sources, citations you can then find in your library's subscription databases. Moreover, it ranks articles by weighing the full text, the author, the publication, and frequency of citation in other sources.

Understanding the Uses and Limits of Wikipedia

You likely recognize Figure 25.11—an article from Wikipedia. From Wikipedia's beginning in 2001 to today, a large population of volunteer writers and editors has made it a top-ten Internet-traffic site. But is Wikipedia acceptable for college-level research? Put simply, Wikipedia is a controversial resource for academic research.

fig. 25.11

1. Semi-protected article icon
2. History tab
3. Discussion page
4. Title
5. Introduction
6. Links
7. Search field
8. Wikipedia's menus
9. Contents menu
10. Essential facts

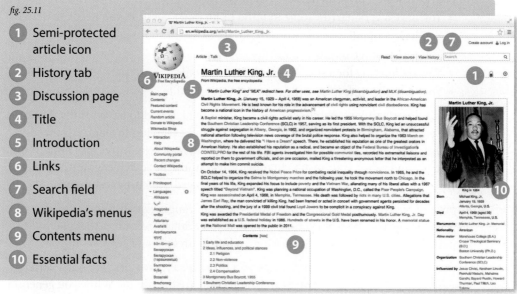

Image courtesy of Wikipedia

Know Wikipedia's strengths.

Because of its wiki nature, Wikipedia offers researchers a number of advantages.

- **Consensus Model of Knowledge:** Articles represent a collaborative agreement about a topic—a topical knowledge base that is fair and fairly comprehensive. Generally, articles improve over time, offering "open-source" knowledge.
- **Currency of Information:** Because they are Web-based, articles are regularly monitored and updated—a distinct advantage over print encyclopedias.
- **Breadth of Information:** With its size and global community, Wikipedia offers articles on a wide range of topics—especially strong in pop culture, current events, computer, and science topics.
- **Links:** Articles are linked throughout so that readers can pursue associated topics, sources, recommended reading, and related categories.

Understand Wikipedia's standards for truth.

Wikipedia applies a different standard of truth than more traditional sources of information. In his revealing article, "Wikipedia and the Meaning of *Truth*" (see pages 244–249), Simson L. Garfinkle explains this standard of truth.

Know Wikipedia's weaknesses.

In some ways, Wikipedia's strengths are closely related to its weaknesses for college-level research. Consider these issues:

- **Popularity Model of Knowledge:** The dynamics of popularity can lead to bias, imbalance, and errors. In some ways, this approach minimizes the value of training, education, and expertise while promoting a kind of democracy of knowledge.
- **Anonymity of Authorship:** Wikipedia allows contributors to remain anonymous. Researchers thus have little way of checking credentials and credibility.
- **Variable Quality of Content:** While many well-established articles are quite stable, balanced, and comprehensive, other articles can be partial, driven by a biased perspective, erroneous, and poorly sourced.
- **Variable Coverage:** Wikipedia's strength in some content areas is matched by gaps and incompleteness in other content areas.
- **Vulnerability to Vandalism:** Wikipedia has a number of processes in place to limit people from harming articles with misinformation, with the result that most vandalism is corrected within hours, but some errors have persisted for months.
- **Tertiary Nature of Information:** For most research projects, Wikipedia articles function as tertiary sources—reports of reports of research. As such, Wikipedia articles are not substantial enough for academic projects.

Use Wikipedia cautiously.

Based on Wikipedia's strengths and weaknesses, follow these guidelines:

1. **Respect your assignment.** Instructors may give you varied instruction about using Wikipedia. Respect their guidelines.
2. **Verify Wikipedia information.** If you use information from Wikipedia, also use other more traditional sources to verify that information.
3. **Use Wikipedia as a semi-authoritative reference source.** Generally, the more academic your research assignment, the less you should rely on Wikipedia articles, which are essentially sources of basic and background information.
4. **Use Wikipedia as one starting point.** From a Wikipedia article, you can learn what is considered "open-source" knowledge on your topic, gather ideas for developing a topic, find links to related topics and other resources, and begin to build a bibliography.
5. **Study individual articles to get a sense of their reliability.** When you find a Wikipedia article relevant to your research project, check the article for quality and stability. Use the evaluation criteria on the following pages, but also check the article's history, its discussion page, any tags or icons indicating the article's state, and the "what links here" link in the toolbox at the left of the screen.

Evaluating Online Sources

The Internet contains a wealth of information, but much of it is not suitable for college-level research writing. The information may be incorrect, biased, outdated, plagiarized, or otherwise unreliable. These pages discuss issues to watch for.

Assignment Restrictions

Before engaging any Web resources, carefully review your assignment and note any restrictions on what type of sources may be used. If Web resources are allowed, abide by the number or percentage indicated in the assignment.

Author/Organization

When using Web resources, make sure the sites are sponsored by legitimate, recognizable organizations: government agencies, nonprofit groups, and educational institutions. For most projects, avoid relying on personal or special-interest sites, as well as chat rooms, blogs, news groups, or wikis. (These sources may help you explore a topic, but they do not provide scholarly material suitable for most research writing.)

Balance or Bias

Be aware of the purpose of a site or an article. Editorials and reviews, for example, express the point of view of a given author but are not sources for unbiased information. Unless your purpose is to show the author's point of view or point out two sides of an argument, avoid sources that show a bias toward or against a specific region, country, political party, industry, gender, race, ethnic group, or religion. Also, avoid sites that promote a specific cause, product, service, or belief.

Quality of Information

Test the quality of information on a site. Note whether the information is current (when was it posted/updated last) and check it against other sources for corroboration. Also, favor sites with a depth of information and those that show they truly engage their topic rather than treating it superficially.

Quality of Writing and Design

Avoid sites that show sloppy editing and poor design. These surface flaws can reveal a lack of scholarly rigor or serious commitment on the part of the site's creators. At the same time, don't be fooled by flashy sites where the design masks problems with the content.

Evaluation Checklist

Use this checklist to assess the reliability of Web sources. The more items you check off, the more reliable the source is.

Assignment Restrictions

____ 1. Does the source fit with the type and number allowed in the assignment?

Author/Organization

____ 2. Is the person or organization behind the site reliable?

____ 3. Is contact information for the person or organization provided?

____ 4. Is the site well known and well connected in the field?

____ 5. Does the site have a clear "About Us" page and mission statement?

Balance or Bias

____ 6. Is the material on the site balanced and unbiased?

____ 7. Does the site avoid unfair and inflammatory language?

____ 8. Does the site avoid pushing a particular product, cause, service, or belief?

____ 9. Does the site provide ample support for its claims?

____ 10. Does the site avoid logical fallacies and twisted statistics? (See pages 301–304.)

Quality of Information

____ 11. Is the material current?

____ 12. Is the Web site often updated?

____ 13. Is the Web site information-rich?

____ 14. Is the information backed up by other reputable print and online sources?

Quality of Writing and Design

____ 15. Is the text free of errors in punctuation, spelling, and grammar?

____ 16. Is the site effectively and clearly designed?

Gts / Shutterstock.com

Sample Evaluations

Assignment Restrictions

- The site shown in Figure 25.12 would be appropriate for most assignments about the life and work of William Faulkner, as long as free-Web sources are allowed.

Author/ Organization

- This site is sponsored by the University of Mississippi, a scholarly source for information, and the article's author, Dr. John B. Padgett, is an authority on Faulkner.

Balance or Bias

- The site clearly extols Faulkner as a great writer but does not shy from showing his shortcomings. The claims are fair and amply supported, without logical fallacies.

Quality of Information

- The Web site is current, often updated, and information-rich. It is also connected to many other Faulkner resources available on the Web.

Quality of Writing and Design

- The site is well designed, with easy navigation, readable text, informative headings, helpful photos, and strong links. The text is well written and well edited.

fig. 25.12

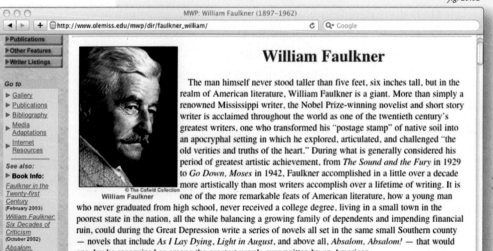

MWP: William Faulkner (1897–1962)

http://www.olemiss.edu/mwp/dir/faulkner_william/

▶Publications
▶Other Features
▶Writer Listings

Go to
▶ Gallery
▶ Publications
▶ Bibliography
▶ Media Adaptations
▶ Internet Resources

See also:
▶ Book Info:

Faulkner in the Twenty-first Century (February 2003)

William Faulkner: Six Decades of Criticism (October 2002)

Absalom, Absalom! (September 2002)

Faulkner and the Politics of Reading, by Karl Zender (August 2002)

Faulkner and Postmodernism, edited by John Duvall and Ann Abadie (July 2002)

New Orleans Sketches (June 2002)

The Unvanquished (Large Print

William Faulkner

The man himself never stood taller than five feet, six inches tall, but in the realm of American literature, William Faulkner is a giant. More than simply a renowned Mississippi writer, the Nobel Prize-winning novelist and short story writer is acclaimed throughout the world as one of the twentieth century's greatest writers, one who transformed his "postage stamp" of native soil into an apocryphal setting in which he explored, articulated, and challenged "the old verities and truths of the heart." During what is generally considered his period of greatest artistic achievement, from *The Sound and the Fury* in 1929 to *Go Down, Moses* in 1942, Faulkner accomplished in a little over a decade more artistically than most writers accomplish over a lifetime of writing. It is one of the more remarkable feats of American literature, how a young man who never graduated from high school, never received a college degree, living in a small town in the poorest state in the nation, all the while balancing a growing family of dependents and impending financial ruin, could during the Great Depression write a series of novels all set in the same small Southern county — novels that include *As I Lay Dying*, *Light in August*, and above all, *Absalom, Absalom!* — that would one day be recognized as among the greatest novels ever written by an American.

© The Cofield Collection
William Faulkner

The Early Years

William Cuthbert Falkner (as his name was then spelled) was born on September 25, 1897, in New Albany, Mississippi, the first of four sons born to Murry and Maud Butler Falkner. He was named after his great-grandfather, William Clark Falkner, the "Old Colonel," who had been killed eight years earlier in a duel with his former business partner in the streets of Ripley, Mississippi. A lawyer, politician, planter, businessman, Civil War colonel, railroad financier, and finally a best-selling writer (of the novel *The White Rose of Memphis*), the Old Colonel, even in death, loomed as a larger-than-life model of personal and professional success for his male descendants.

A few days before William's fifth birthday, the Falkners moved to Oxford, Mississippi, at the urging of Murry's father, John Wesley Thompson Falkner. Called the "Young Colonel" out of homage to his father rather than to actual military service, the younger Falkner had abruptly decided to sell the railroad begun by his father. Disappointed that he

Related Links & Info

© The Cofield Collection
William Clark Falkner

Courtesy of Dr. John B. Padgett/Brevard College

- As a blog, the site shown in Figure 25.13 would not be appropriate for an assignment about the life and work of William Faulkner. A site such as this should be recognized as reflective only of the writer's opinion, not of reliable information or fact.

- There is no author or organization listed for this Web site. The domain name—myviewsonliterature.wordpress.com—shows that this is a personal opinion blog. Its lack of connection to other Web sites shows it represents an isolated opinion.

- This blog post shows a strong bias against William Faulkner. The few facts cited inadequately support the writer's main point, and logical fallacies are apparent. The tone of the post is unscholarly, with inflammatory language.

- Though this Web site is frequently updated, the blog post does not represent current scholarship about William Faulkner. The Web site is information-poor and is not backed up by any reputable print or online sources.

- The site has an amateurish design and numerous errors, including the persistent misspelling of William Faulkner's name. The writing is slipshod, and the editing is poor.

fig. 25.13

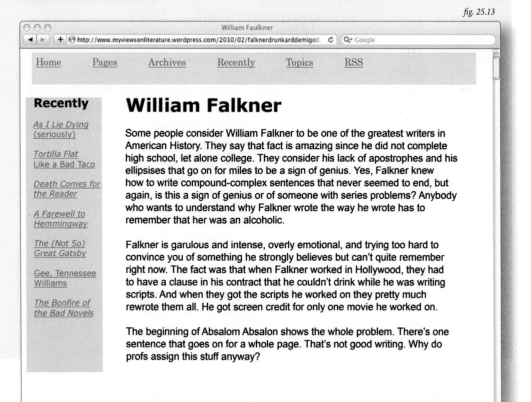

Critical-Thinking and Writing Activities

As directed by your instructor, complete the following activities.

1. Think about a research project that you have done or are doing now. How might primary research and library research (scholarly books and journals) strengthen your writing? Why not do all your research on the free Web?

2. Working with your library's Web site and its orientation tools, identify where you can physically and/or electronically locate books, reference resources, and journals.

3. Explore your library's handouts and Web site for information about Internet research. What services, support, and access does the library provide?

4. Brainstorm issues related to food production, consumption, or culture. Choosing one issue, use your library's catalog and database tools to track down and evaluate print books and periodical articles. Then do a free-Web search of the topic, comparing the results.

5. Using the variety of methods outlined in this chapter, work with some classmates to search the Internet for information on a controversial topic, event, person, or place. Carefully analyze and evaluate the range of Web information you find.

Learning-Objectives Checklist ✓

Have you achieved this chapter's learning objectives? Check your progress with the items below, revisiting topics in the chapter as needed. *I have . . .*

___ effectively planned primary research, if needed for my project, following sound principles and practices (428–429).

___ performed primary research successfully, whether conducting a survey, analyzing documents or artifacts, doing an interview, or making observations (430–436).

___ familiarized myself with the library and its research tools (437).

___ performed keyword searches of the catalog, locating through call numbers relevant books and other resources for my project (438–439).

___ approached books systematically in order to work with them productively (440).

___ located and mined reference works relevant to my topic (441).

___ searched library databases to generate citations of periodical articles, studied those citations, and retrieved promising articles (442–445).

___ differentiated elements of the Internet related to research, including the distinction between the free Web and the deep Web (446–451).

___ effectively searched the Web using subject directories and search engines, aware of the strengths and limits of such tools and such resources as Wikipedia (452–453).

___ carefully evaluated free-Web resources in terms of authorship or sponsorship, balance, quality of information, and quality of writing and design (454–455).

Chapter 26

Building Credibility: Avoiding Plagiarism

"That's incredible!" is normally a positive exclamation of amazement. But maybe it's an exclamation that you do not want to hear about your research writing, if "incredible" means "unbelievable." If your paper is unbelievable, your credibility as a researcher and a writer is seriously damaged.

Obviously, you want to draft a strong, well-documented paper—a credible discussion of your carefully researched topic. While the next chapter focuses on drafting such a paper, this chapter prepares you for drafting by explaining how to build and maintain credibility. It starts with these principles:

1. Write the paper yourself. Take ownership of your thinking, research, and writing.
2. Be honest, accurate, and measured.
3. Show respect to your reader, the topic, and opposing viewpoints.
4. Establish your credentials by showing that you have done careful research.

Visually Speaking   Copying—what's wrong with it? Using Figure 26.1 as a starting point, reflect on the nature of copying as an issue in life and in research.

Learning **Objectives**

By working through this chapter, you will be able to

- differentiate between poor and effective uses of sources in your writing.
- define and recognize plagiarism.
- explain why plagiarism is a serious academic offense.
- prevent plagiarism within your own writing.
- distinguish other source abuses and avoid them in your writing.

Jason Benz Bennee / Shutterstock.com

fig. 26.1

Developing Credibility through Source Use

Your credibility—how fully readers trust and believe you—is partly rooted in how well you treat your sources. While abuses such as distorting a source's ideas damage your credibility, good practices enhance it. Contrast the passages below and on the next page.

Writing with Poor Use of Sources

A poor paper might read like a recitation of unconnected facts, unsupported opinions, or undigested quotations. It may contain contradictory information or illogical conclusions. A source's ideas may be distorted or taken out of context. At its worst, poor source use involves plagiarism.

> The writing offers weak generalizations in several spots.

It goes without saying that cell phone usage has really increased a lot, from the beginning of the cell phone's history until now. How many people still don't have a cell—basically, no one! The advantages of cell phones are obvious, but has anyone really thought about the downside of this technological innovation? For example, there's "rinxiety," where people believe that their cell phones are ringing but they're not. Two-thirds of cell users have reported this feeling, which some experts believe to be a rewiring of the nervous system similar to phantom limb pain, while other experts thinks it's about the pitch of cell rings. It's not good.   *1*

> Material from sources is clearly borrowed but not referenced through in-text citation.

But the most serious problem with cell phones is without a doubt driving while talking or texting. Due to the increasing complexity of mobile phones –often more like mobile computers in their available uses– it has introduced additional difficulties for law enforcement officials in being able to tell one usage from another as drivers use their devices. This is more apparent in those countries who ban both hand-held and hands-free usage, rather than those who have banned hand-held use only, as officials cannot easily tell which function of the mobile phone is being used simply by visually looking at the driver. This can mean that drivers may be stopped for using their device illegally on a phone call, when in fact they were not; instead using the device for a legal purpose such as the phones' incorporated controls for car stereo or satnav usage – either as part of the cars' own device or directly on the mobile phone itself.   *2*

> A passage from an online source is copy-and-pasted into the paper without credit.

> The writer uses a visual without indicating the source or effectively discussing its meaning.

The question arises, is the cell phone even being used as a phone? And are these other uses legitimate or just gimmicks? This chart makes the point.   *3*

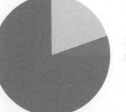

Cell Phone Usage

- Text Messaging
- Making Phone Calls
- Checking the Time

Writing with Strong Use of Sources

A strong paper centers on the writer's ideas—ideas advanced through thoughtful engagement with and crediting of sources. It offers logical analysis or a persuasive argument built on reliable information from quality sources that have been treated with intellectual respect. Note these features at work in the excerpt below from student writer Brandon Jorritsma's essay on cell-phone dependency.

Facts and ideas are credited through in-text citations, which are linked to full source information on a works-cited page.

The writer builds on and reasons with source material.

This dependency on cells is reflected in the phenomenon that has come to be termed "rinxiety." Frequent cell phone users are reporting numerous instances of either hearing their phones ring or feeling them vibrate, even if their phones are not around. Two thirds of cell phone users in a recent survey report having experienced this ("Phantom Ringing"), which is thought by some to be a rewiring of the nervous system similar to phantom limb pain (Lynch). Others theorize that it is a result of the pitch of typical cell rings being similar to elements of commonplace sounds, such as running water, music, traffic, and television (Lynch, Goodman). Regardless of the particular explanation, the experience of rinxiety is more common among young, frequent users of cell phones, which seems to indicate a constant expectation of calls ("Phantom Ringing"). This expectation is damaging to relationships because someone expecting a phone call or email to arrive at any moment is not mentally present in other interactions he or she may be involved in. We've all experienced being around someone who was waiting on a phone call. How much more distracted would that person be if he or she were subconsciously expecting a phone call every hour of the day?

Direct quotations from sources are indicated with quotation marks.

A case study from a source makes a concept concrete through cause-effect reasoning.

The corollary of constantly expecting incoming cell communication is the constant impulse to send out messages. Fifty-two percent of respondents to an informal survey at CSU, Fresno, admitted to being "preoccupied with the next time they could text message," and forty-six percent of students "reported irritability when unable to use their cell phones" (Lui). In a study of an international sample of cell phone users, some respondents recounted how they felt anxiety if they forgot to take their phone out of the house with them (Jarvenpaa 12). Even when the phone was not anywhere near them, they couldn't escape its demands on their attention. The phone has moved from being an object of utility to being one of psychological necessity, which constantly demands attention from its user regardless of its proximity or restrictions on its use. Lauren Hawn, a student at Pennsylvania State University, reports that when she is near her cell, she does the following: "I seem to look at it a lot and check the time [on the phone's digital display] even when I don't need to" (qtd. in Lynch). Hawn does not consciously think that there is a phone call or text message . . . .

"Weak Signals: How Cellular Phones Inhibit Communication" by Brandon Jorritsma. Reprinted by permission of the author.

Recognizing Plagiarism

The road to plagiarism may be paved with the best intentions—or the worst. Either way, the result is still a serious academic offense. As you write your research paper, do everything you can to stay off that road! Start by studying your school's and your instructor's guidelines on plagiarism and other academic offenses. Then study the following pages.

What is plagiarism?

Plagiarism is using someone else's words, ideas, or images (what's called intellectual property) so they appear to be your own. When you plagiarize, you use source material—whether published in print or online—without acknowledging the source. In this sense, plagiarism refers to a range of thefts:

- Submitting a paper you didn't write yourself
- Pasting large chunks of a source into your paper and passing it off as your own work
- Using summaries, paraphrases, or quotations without documentation
- Using the exact phrasing of a source without quotation marks
- Mixing up source material and your own ideas—failing to distinguish between the two

 Plagiarism refers to more than "word theft." Because plagiarism is really about failing to credit ideas and information, the rules also apply to visual images, tables, graphs, charts, maps, music, videos, and so on.

What does plagiarism look like?

Plagiarism refers to a range of source abuses. What exactly do these violations look like? Read the passage below, and then review the five types of plagiarism that follow, noting how each example misuses the source.

> **The passage below is from page 87 of "Some Stories Have to Be Told by Me: A Literary History of Alice Munro," by Marcela Valdes, published in the *Virginia Quarterly Review* 82.3 (2006).**
>
> What makes Munro's characters so enthralling is their inconsistency; like real people, at one moment they declare they will cover the house in new siding, at the next, they vomit on their way to the hospital. They fight against and seek refuge in the people they love. The technique that Munro has forged to get at such contradictions is a sort of pointillism, the setting of one bright scene against another, with little regard for chronology.

Using Copy and Paste

It is unethical to take chunks of material from another source and splice them into your paper without acknowledgment. In the example below, the writer pastes in a sentence from the original article (boldfaced) without using quotation marks or a citation. Even if the writer changed some words, it would still be plagiarism.

> Life typically unfolds mysteriously for Munro's characters, with unexplained events and choices. **Like real people, at one moment they declare they will cover the house in new siding, at the next, they vomit on their way to the hospital.**

Failing to Cite a Source

Borrowed material must be documented. Even if you use information accurately and fairly, don't neglect to cite the source. Below, the writer correctly summarizes the passage's idea but offers no citation.

> For the reader, the characters in Munro's stories are interesting because they are so changeable. Munro shows these changes by using a method of placing scenes side by side for contrast, without worrying about the chronological connections.

Neglecting Necessary Quotation Marks

Whether it's a paragraph or a phrase, if you use the exact wording of a source, that material must be enclosed in quotation marks. In the example below, the writer cites the source but doesn't use quotation marks around a phrase taken from the original (boldfaced).

> What makes Munro's characters so typically human is that they **fight against and seek refuge in the people they love (Valdes 87).**

Confusing Borrowed Material with Your Own Ideas

Through carelessness (often in note taking), you may confuse source material with your own thinking. Below, the writer indicates that he borrowed material in the first sentence, but fails to indicate that he also borrowed the next sentence.

> As Marcela Valdes explains, "[w]hat makes Munro's characters so enthralling is their inconsistency" (87). **To achieve this sense of inconsistency, Munro places brightly lit scenes beside each other in a kind of pointillist technique.**

Submitting Another Writer's Paper

The most blatant plagiarism is taking an entire piece of writing and claiming it as your own work. Examples:

- Downloading, reformatting, and submitting an article as your own work
- Buying a paper from a "paper mill" or taking a "free" paper off the Internet
- Turning in another student's work as your own (see "Falstaffing" on page 467)

fyi Just as it's easy to plagiarize using the Internet, it's easy for your professors to recognize and track down plagiarism using Internet tools.

Understanding Why Plagiarism Is Serious

Perhaps the answer is obvious. But some people operate with the notion that material on the Internet is "free" and, therefore, fair game for research writing. After all, a lot of stuff on the Web doesn't even list an author, so what's the harm? Here's some food for thought:

Academic Dishonesty

At its heart, plagiarism is cheating—stealing intellectual property and passing it off as one's own work. Colleges take such dishonesty seriously. Plagiarism, whether intentional or unintentional, will likely be punished in one or more ways:

- A failing grade for the assignment
- A failing grade for the course
- A note on your academic transcript (often seen by potential employers) that failure resulted from academic dishonesty
- Expulsion from college

Theft from the Academic Community

The research paper represents your dialogue with other members of the academic community—classmates, the instructor, others in your major, others who have researched the topics, and so on. When you plagiarize, you short-circuit the dialogue:

- You gain an unfair advantage over your classmates who follow the rules and earn their grades.
- You disrespect other writers, researchers, and scholars.
- You disrespect your readers by passing off others' ideas as your own.
- You insult your instructor, a person whose respect you need.
- You harm your college by risking its reputation and its academic integrity.

Now and in the Future

Because research projects help you master course-related concepts and writing skills, plagiarism robs you of an opportunity to learn. Moreover, you rob yourself of your integrity and reputation. After all, as a student you are seeking to build your credibility within the broader academic community, your major, and your future profession.

In addition, research projects often train you for your future work in terms of research, thinking, and writing skills—skills that you will need to succeed in the workplace. If you do not learn the skills now, you will enter the workplace without them—a situation that your employer will, at some point, find out.

 One tool to deter plagiarism is Turnitin.com. Students submit their papers for comparison against millions of Web pages and other student papers. Students and instructors get reports about originality and matching text.

Avoiding Plagiarism

Preventing plagiarism begins the moment you get an assignment. Essentially, prevention requires your commitment and diligence throughout the project. Follow these tips:

1. **Resist temptation.** With the Internet, plagiarism is a mouse click away. Avoid last-minute all-nighters that make you desperate; start research projects early. Note: It's better to ask for an extension or accept a penalty for lateness than to plagiarize.

2. **Play by the rules.** Become familiar with your college's definition, guidelines, and policies regarding plagiarism so that you don't unknowingly violate them. When in doubt, ask your instructor for clarification.

3. **Take orderly, accurate notes.** From the start, carefully keep track of source material and distinguish it from your own thinking. Specifically, do the following:
   - Maintain an accurate working bibliography (pages 416–417).
   - Adopt a decent note-taking system (pages 418–421).
   - Accurately summarize, paraphrase, and quote sources (pages 422–424).

4. **Document borrowed material.** Credit information that you have summarized, paraphrased, or quoted from any source, whether that information is statistics, facts, graphics, phrases, or ideas. Readers can then see what's borrowed and what's yours, understand your support, and do their own follow-up research.

> **Common Knowledge Exception:** Common knowledge is information—a basic fact, for instance—that is generally known to readers or easily found in several sources, particularly reference works. Such knowledge need not be cited. However, when you go beyond common knowledge into research findings, interpretations of the facts, theories, explanations, claims, arguments, and graphics, you must document the source. Study the examples below, but whenever you are in doubt, document.
>
> *Examples:*
> - The fact that automakers are developing hybrid-electric cars is common knowledge, whereas the details of GM's AUTOnomy project are not.
> - The fact that Shakespeare wrote *Hamlet* is common knowledge, whereas the details of his sources are not.

5. **Work carefully with source material in your paper.** See pages 476–479 for more on integrating and documenting sources, but here, briefly, are your responsibilities:
   - Distinguish borrowed material from your own thinking by signaling where source material begins and ends.
   - Indicate the source's origin with an attributive phrase and a citation (parenthetical reference or footnote).
   - Provide full source information in a works-cited or references page.

Avoiding Other Source Abuses

Plagiarism, though the most serious offense, is not the only source abuse to avoid when writing a paper with documented research. Consider these pitfalls, which refer again to the sample passage on page 462.

Using Sources Inaccurately

When you get a quotation wrong, botch a summary, paraphrase poorly, or misstate a statistic, you misrepresent the original. In this quotation, the writer carelessly uses several wrong words that change the meaning, as well as adding two words that are not in the original.

> As Marcela Valdes explains, "[w]hat makes Munro's characters so appalling is their consistency. . . . They fight against and seek refuse in the people they say they love" (87).

Using Source Material Out of Context

By ripping a statement out of its context and forcing it into yours, you can make a source seem to say something that it didn't really say. This writer uses part of a statement to say the opposite of the original.

> According to Marcela Valdes, while Munro's characters are interesting, Munro's weakness as a fiction writer is that she shows "little regard for chronology" (87).

Overusing Source Material

When your paper reads like a string of references, especially quotations, your own thinking disappears. The writer below takes the source passage, chops it up, and splices it together.

> Anyone who has read her stories knows that "[w]hat makes Munro's characters so enthralling is their inconsistency." That is to say, "like real people, at one moment they declare they will cover the house in new siding, at the next, they vomit on their way to the hospital." Moreover, "[t]hey fight against and seek refuge in the people they love." This method "that Munro has forged to get at such contradictions is a sort of pointillism," meaning "the setting of one bright scene against another, with little regard for chronology" (Valdes 87)

"Plunking" Quotations

When you "plunk" quotations into your paper by failing to prepare the reader for them and follow them up, the discussion becomes choppy and disconnected. The writer below interrupts the flow of ideas with a quotation "out of the blue." In addition, the quotation hangs at the end of a paragraph with no follow-up.

> Typically, characters such as Del Jordan, Louisa Doud, and Almeda Roth experience a crisis through contact with particular men. "They fight against and seek refuge in the people they love" (Valdes 87).

Using "Blanket" Citations

Your reader shouldn't have to guess where borrowed material begins and ends. For example, if you place a parenthetical citation at the end of a paragraph, does that citation cover the whole paragraph or just the final sentence?

Relying Heavily on One Source

If your writing is dominated by one source, readers may doubt the depth and integrity of your research. Instead, your writing should show your reliance on a balanced diversity of sources.

Failing to Match In-Text Citations to Bibliographic Entries

All in-text citations must clearly refer to accurate entries in the works-cited, references, or endnotes page. Mismatching occurs in the following circumstances:

- An in-text citation refers to a source that is not listed in the bibliography.
- A bibliographic resource is never actually referenced anywhere in the paper.

Related Academic Offenses

Beyond plagiarism and related source abuses, steer clear of these academic offenses:

Double-dipping: When you submit one paper in two different classes or otherwise turn in a paper you have turned in before without permission from both instructors, you take double credit for one project.

Falstaffing: This practice refers to a particular type of plagiarism in which one student submits another student's work. Know that you are guilty of Falstaffing if you let another student submit your paper.

Copyright violations: When you copy, distribute, and/or post in whole or in part any intellectual property without permission from or payment to the copyright holder, you commit a copyright infringement, especially when you profit from this use. To avoid copyright violations in your research projects, do the following:

- **Observe fair use guidelines:** Quote small portions of a document for limited purposes, such as education or research. Avoid copying large portions for your own gain.
- **Understand what's in the public domain:** You need not obtain permission to copy and use public domain materials—primarily documents created by the government, but also some material posted on the Internet as part of the "copy left" movement.
- **Observe intellectual property and copyright laws:** First, know your college's policies on copying documents. Second, realize that copyright protects the expression of ideas in a range of materials—writings, videos, songs, photographs, drawings, computer software, and so on. Always obtain permission to copy and distribute copyrighted materials.
- **Avoid changing a source** (e.g., a photo) without permission of the creator or copyright holder.

Critical-Thinking and Writing Activities

As directed by your instructor, complete the following critical-thinking and writing activities by yourself or with classmates.

1. Find three articles on the same topic, articles from different media (e.g., newspaper, magazine, Web site). Explore how each writer attempts to establish and build credibility. How well does each succeed?

2. With some classmates, debate the seriousness of plagiarism and the use of tools such as Turnitin.com.

3. Research your school's academic-integrity policies. How does your school define plagiarism, and how does it address it in its policies and procedures?

4. Compare and contrast the writing samples on pages 460–461 showing poor and strong use of sources. Then examine a research paper that you wrote recently. Is your writing closer to the poor or strong model? What improvements do you need to make in your working with sources?

5. Review the list of source abuses on pages 466–467. Which of these abuses is most common in research writing? Which abuse is most serious? Write a paragraph focusing on one type of source abuse and explaining its effect on scholarship.

Learning-Objectives Checklist ✓

Have you achieved this chapter's learning objectives? Check your progress with the items below, revisiting topics in the chapter as needed. *I have...*

_____ differentiated between writing that uses sources poorly and writing that uses sources effectively (460–461).

_____ defined plagiarism and distinguished the various forms that it might take (462–463).

_____ explained the seriousness of plagiarism as a form of academic dishonesty that harms the academic community, as well as my own integrity now and in the future (464).

_____ prevented plagiarism in my own writing, following strategies that include knowing the difference between material that must be credited and material that is common knowledge (465).

_____ distinguished other source abuses, from inaccurate use of a source to mismatched in-text citations and bibliographic entries, and avoided these abuses in my writing (466–467).

_____ identified and avoided academic offenses such as double dipping, falstaffing, and copyright violations (467).

Chapter 27

Drafting Papers with Documented Research

When you write a research paper, you enter a larger conversation about your topic. Because you are seeking to add your voice to the conversation, the paper should center on your own ideas while thoughtfully engaging with the ideas of others. Crediting sources ensures that each voice in the conversation is fairly represented.

This chapter explains how to make the shift from researching your topic to writing about it, focuses on effective and conscientious use of sources in your writing, and helps you write a first draft of your paper. The chapter then shows you good research-writing practices at work in a humanities essay and a science report.

Visually Speaking   Scales like the one shown in Figure 27.1 are all about weighing and balancing. In what ways does drafting research-based writing involve mental versions of these activities?

Learning **Objectives**

By working through this chapter, you will be able to

- examine your research findings so as to deepen your thinking on a topic.

- assess and strengthen your working thesis.

- organize your writing with your research findings in mind.

- draft your essay so as to respect, smoothly integrate, and effectively document source material.

- compare and contrast research-writing practices in the humanities and the sciences.

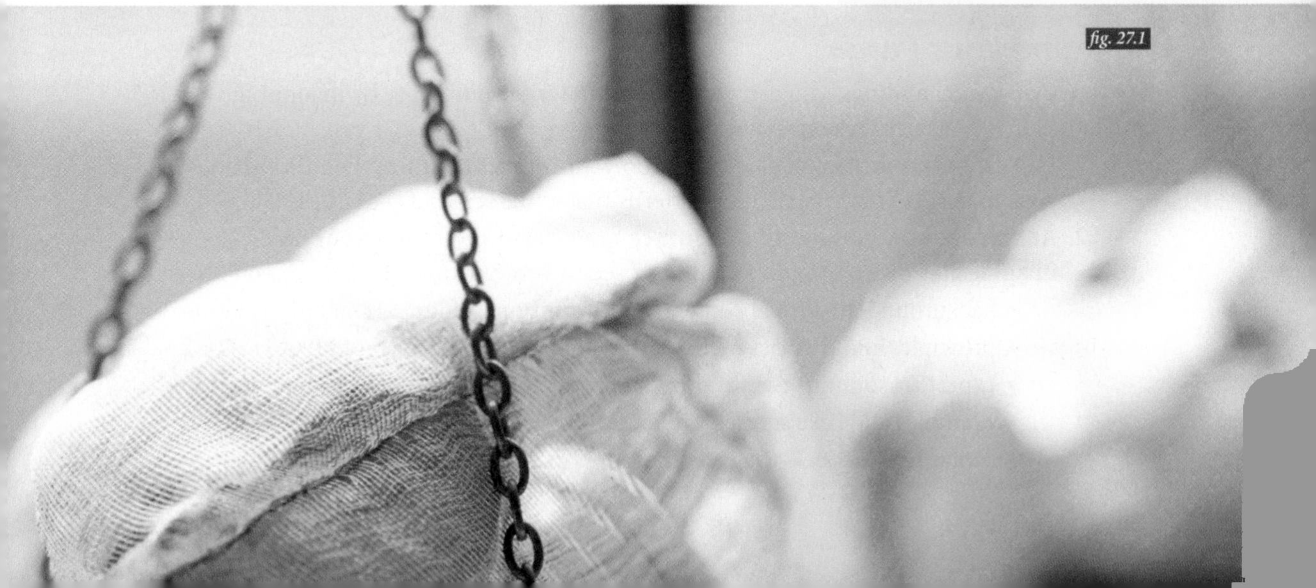

image100/Corbis

fig. 27.1

Reviewing Your Findings

With every research project, the time comes when you must transition from exploring your topic to sharing discoveries, from research to writing. To start this transition, take time to review your findings—to go over your notes as many times as necessary, using them to stimulate your thinking and planning. Try these strategies, in particular:

Conduct Q & A

Early in your project, you may have generated a set of research questions (see page 400). Now that you have completed the bulk of your research, you might do the following Q & A activity to clarify how your research has impacted your thinking:

- **Review your primary research question:** What answers has your research produced? Are the answers affirming, engaging, or unsettling?
- **Review your secondary research questions:** What information have you found to answer these questions? How do the answers enhance your thinking?

Deepen Your Thinking on the Topic

During note-taking, you focused on making sense of what individual sources said about your topic. Now, take these steps to deepen and expand your thinking:

- **Identify key discoveries.** What central ideas and new facts have you learned through research? What conclusions have you reached, and why?
- **Identify connections between sources.** How are your sources related to each other? Do they share similar points of view and similar conclusions? Do some sources build on other sources? Which one was published first, second, third, etc.?
- **Identify differences between sources.** In what ways and on what issues do sources disagree? Why? What sense do you make of the differences?
- **Identify limits and gaps.** What issues do your sources not cover? For what questions have you not found answers? How are these gaps important for your project?

Imagine Your Paper

As you review your findings, you can also prepare to write your paper by imagining what it might include. Consider these strategies:

1. **Look for organizational clues.** How do your sources organize their discussions of your topic? Are there particular patterns that make sense of the issues?
2. **Anticipate how you might use source material.** As you study your notes, imagine how different points could be used in your writing. Here are possibilities:
   - background, historical context, and definitions—foundational information
   - principles and theories—idea "tools" for exploring your topic
   - expert reasoning—the thinking of those most knowledgeable about the topic
   - examples and case studies—illustrations that vivify an idea
   - concrete evidence—the facts that support your claims

Sharpening Your Working Thesis

As you prepare to draft your research paper, you might refine your focus by revisiting and revising your working thesis (page 45).

Deepen Your Thesis

Review your working thesis. Given the research that you have completed, does this thesis stand up? It is possible, of course, that your research has led you to a conclusion quite different from your original working thesis. If so, rewrite your thesis accordingly. However, you might also retain your original thesis but strengthen it by using these strategies:

1. **Use richer, clearer terms.** Test your working thesis for vague, broad, or inappropriate terms or concepts. Replace them with terms that have rich meanings, are respected in discussions of your topic, and refine your original thinking.

2. **Introduce qualifying terms where needed.** With qualifying terms such as "normally," "often," and "usually," as well as with phrases that limit the reach of your thesis, you are paradoxically strengthening your thesis by making it more reasonable.

3. **Stress your idea through opposition.** You can deepen your working thesis by adding an opposing thought (usually phrased in a dependent clause).

> **Original Working Thesis:** In Alice Munro's "An Ounce of Cure," infatuation messes with the narrator's head so her life gets turned upside down.
>
> **Revised Working Thesis:** While Alice Munro's "An Ounce of Cure" tells a simple story of infatuation leading to confusion and trouble, the story is more importantly about the "plots of life"—the ways in which the narrator experiences life as a competing set of stories (romance, fairy tale, farce), none of which does justice to the complexity of real life.

Question Your Thesis

You can also sharpen your working thesis by questioning it—viewing it from your readers' point of view. What questions might readers have, given the phrasing of your thesis? Here, for example, are questions about the revised working thesis above:

- In what ways is the story primarily about infatuation? What kinds of trouble flow from the infatuation? What confusions?
- What do you mean by the phrase "plots of life" and where does it come from?
- What is the nature of the types of stories listed? In what ways are they "competing"?
- How is real life more complex than these fictional stories? Does the narrator experience real life? If so, where and how?

Probing your thesis in this way can help you (1) decide which questions you want to answer in your paper, and (2) imagine a question-answer structure for your paper.

Considering Methods of Organization

Before drafting, explore which methods of organization would work well for your paper. For help, see chapter 3, "Planning." The discussion on this page and the next will help you make choices, but start by avoiding these simplistic patterns:

- The five-paragraph essay: Popularly known as the high school hamburger, this structure is too basic and limiting for most college research projects.
- Information regurgitation: Generally, college-level research requires analytical thinking about information, not just the presentation of data.
- A series of source summaries: Your paper should not be structured simply as a summary of one source after another.

Organizational Practices That Consider Sources

Because the writing you are doing is research based, you want to factor your sources into your thinking about organization. Here are some ideas that may work with your project.

Consider where to position primary and secondary sources. Different writing projects require different approaches to using, balancing, and integrating primary and secondary sources (pages 402–403). Where and how should you work in primary sources—interview material, survey data, textual and artifact analysis, observation results? Where and how should you bring in secondary sources—scholarly books, journal articles, and the like? *Example:* In a literary analysis, you might rely on primary textual analysis of a novel throughout your paper but support—or establish the context for—that analysis with secondary-source information from biographical research placed early in your paper.

Order your writing around key sources. While you shouldn't organize your whole paper as a series of source summaries, sometimes your writing can take direction specifically from the sources that you have researched. Consider these options:

- **Make one of your key points a response to a specific source.** Did a particular source stand out as especially supportive of or especially contrary to your own thinking? Shape part of your paper as an affirmation or rebuttal of the source.
- **Structure your paper around a dialogue with sources.** Do your sources offer multiple, divergent, even contradictory perspectives on your topic? If they do, consider organizing your paper around a dialogue with these sources.

Map out relationships between sources and ideas. Having reviewed your findings and sharpened your working thesis, consider how your sources support that thesis. To visualize your options, create a diagram, map, or flowchart that shows where particular sources speak to particular points.

Put your discussion in context. Often, the early part of your paper will involve establishing a context for exploring your topic. Consider, then, tapping your sources to present necessary background, explain key terms, describe the big picture, set out key principles, or establish a theoretical framework for your discussion.

Traditional Organizational Patterns

As shown in the "writing moves" chart on page 57, organizing your paper into an opening, middle, and closing can involve a variety of strategies. The traditional patterns below offer sound methods for developing your thinking. Each choice offers a basic structure for your paper, but several patterns may be useful within your paper's body. As indicated, full instruction for many of these patterns can be found elsewhere in this book.

- **Analysis** clarifies how something works by breaking the object or phenomenon into parts or phases and then showing how they work together. See page 161–292.

- **Argumentation** asserts and supports a main claim with supporting claims, logical reasoning about each claim, and concrete evidence to back up the reasoning. This pattern also includes acknowledging and countering any opposition, as well as reasserting the main claim (perhaps in a modified form). See pages 293–308.

- **Cause-effect** can (1) explore the factors that led to an event or phenomenon, (2) explore the consequences of an event or phenomenon, or (3) do both. See pages 161–180.

- **Chronological order** arranges items in a temporal sequence (order of events, steps in a process). See pages 138–139.

- **Classification** places items within categories. Each category is characterized by what the items share with each other and by what makes them different from items in the other categories. See pages 203–216.

- **Comparison-contrast** examines two or more items for similarities, differences, or both. Such a study typically holds the items side by side, comparing or contrasting traits point by point. See pages 181–202.

- **Definition** clarifies a term's meaning through appropriate strategies: explaining the term's origin and history, offering examples and illustrations, elaborating key concepts at the heart of the term, and so on. See pages 235–252.

- **Description** orders details in terms of spatial relationships, sounds, components, color, form, texture, and so on. See pages 138–139.

- **Evaluation** measures the strength or quality of something against particular standards, standards that are already accepted or that are established prior to the evaluation.

- **Order of importance** arranges items from most to least important, or least to most.

- **Partitioning** breaks down an object, a space, or a location into ordered parts, or a process into steps or phases.

- **Problem-solution** describes a problem, explores its causes and effects, surveys possible solutions, proposes the best one, and defends it as desirable and doable. This pattern may also involve explaining how to implement the solution. See pages 347–360.

- **Question-answer** moves back and forth from questions to answers in a sequence that logically clarifies a topic.

Considering Drafting Strategies

With research writing, developing the first draft involves exploring your own thinking in relation to the ideas and information that you have discovered through research. Your goal is to develop and support your ideas—referring to and properly crediting sources, but not being dominated by them. Such drafting requires both creativity and care: the creativity to see connections and to trace lines of thinking, and the care to respect ideas and information that you are borrowing from sources. Consider the tips below.

Choose a Drafting Method

Before starting your draft, choose a drafting method that makes sense for your project (its complexity, formality, etc.) and your writing style. Here are two options:

Writing Systematically

1. Develop a detailed outline, including supporting evidence, such as the formal sentence outline on page 50.
2. Arrange all your research notes in the precise order of your outline.
3. Write methodically, following your thesis, outline, and notes. However, be open to taking your writing in an interesting direction and modifying your outline as you write.
4. Cite sources as you draft.

Writing Freely

1. Review your working thesis and notes. Then set them aside.
2. If you need to, jot down a brief outline (see the basic list on page 48).
3. Write away—get all your research-based thinking down without stressing about details and flow.
4. Going back to your notes, develop your draft further and carefully integrate and cite research material.

Respect Your Sources While Drafting

Research writing involves handling your sources with care, including during the first draft. While drafting, try to have source material at your fingertips so that you can integrate summaries, paraphrases, and quotations without disrupting the flow and energy of your drafting. Moreover, take care not to overwhelm your draft with source material. As you draft, keep the focus on your own ideas:

- **Avoid strings of references and chunks of source material** without your discussion, explanation, or interpretation in between.
- **Don't offer entire paragraphs of material from a source** (whether paraphrased or quoted) with a single in-text citation at the end: when you do so, your thinking disappears.
- **Be careful not to overload your draft with complex information** and dense data lacking explanation.
- **Resist the urge to copy-and-paste big chunks from sources.** Even if you document the sources, your paper will quickly become a patchwork of source material with a few stitches (your slim contribution) holding the paper together.

Reason with the Evidence

Your paper presents the weight of your research findings in the light of your best thinking. Here you support your thesis with a line of reasoning that is carefully thought out and backed up by evidence. That line of reasoning is typically carried by well-developed paragraphs. A typical body paragraph starts with a topic sentence that makes a point in support of your thesis, then elaborates that point with careful reasoning and detailed evidence, and finishes with a concluding sentence that reiterates and advances the idea.

Sample Body Paragraph Showing Reasoning with Evidence:

Topic Sentence: idea elaborating and supporting thesis

Development of idea through reasoning

Support of idea through reference to evidence from source material

Concluding statement of idea

Finally, Fairtrade consumers can misjudge producers. Whereas Fairtrade has been rightly criticized for inadvertently spreading a sort of neo-colonial attitude, consider, for instance, the problem of quality control that was explored earlier: that Fairtrade does not press producers to develop high-quality products. "Companies such as Green & Black's," on the other hand, "say they aid farmers more by helping them to improve quality and go organic rather than just guaranteeing a price" (Beattie 34). The Fairtrade model ensures that producers will never be able to grow beyond the need for a fixed minimum, while alternate models seek to empower producers. It is not hard to see which paradigm is rife with paternalistic, colonialist implications. Getting consumers in the right frame of mind is not an irrelevant need. As Ian Hussey puts it, "decolonization is not just a material process, but also a mental one" (17). Fair trade, he says, "serves to reinforce racist and colonial distinctions between the poor Global South farmer and the benevolent Global North consumer" (15). In the long run, this mindset is destructive in that it denigrates Fairtrade producers as charity cases rather than potential partners.

As your writing unfolds, make sure that your thinking is sound. To that end, consider these points:

- **Supporting Ideas:** Your topic sentence is essentially a claim—an idea that explains or argues a point. Clearly and logically tie your claim to your thesis.
- **Reasons:** These sentences develop and deepen the claim in the topic sentence. However, reasoning also functions to explain the evidence when you present it. Just remember that the evidence does not generally speak for itself: you will likely have to introduce it to your reader, who is seeing it for the first time.
- **Evidence:** This material is foundational to your thinking—the facts, statistics, quotations, artifacts, illustrations, case studies, and more that you have gathered through research. Always choose evidence that clarifies and convinces, and aim for providing a level of detail that makes your discussion concrete, clear, and convincing.

Using Source Material in Your Writing

After you've found good sources and taken good notes on them, you want to use that research effectively in your writing. Specifically, you want to show (1) what information you are borrowing and (2) where you got it. By doing so, you create credibility. This section shows you how to develop credibility by integrating and documenting sources so as to avoid plagiarism and other abuses (see chapter 26). ***Note:*** For a full treatment of documentation, see chapter 28 (MLA) and chapter 29 (APA).

Integrate source material carefully

Source material—whether a summary, a paraphrase, or a quotation—should be integrated smoothly into your discussion. Follow these strategies:

The Right Reasons

Focus on what you want to say, not on all the source material you've collected. Use sources to do the following:

- **Deepen and develop your point** with the reasoning offered by a source.
- **Support your point and your thinking** about it with evidence—with facts, statistics, details, and so on.
- **Give credibility to your point** with an expert's supporting statement.
- **Bring your point to life** with an example, an observation, a case study, an anecdote, or an illustration.
- **Address a counterargument** or an alternative.

Quotation Restraint

In most research documents, restrict your quoting to nuggets:

- **Key statements by authorities** (e.g., the main point that a respected Shakespeare scholar makes about the role of Ophelia in Hamlet)
- **Well-phrased claims and conclusions** (e.g., a powerful conclusion by an ethicist about the problem with the media's coverage of cloning debates and technological developments)
- **Passages where careful word-by-word analysis and interpretation** are important to your argument (e.g., an excerpt from a speech made by a politician about the International Space Station—a passage that requires a careful analysis for the between-the-lines message)

Quotations, especially long ones, must pull their weight, so generally paraphrase or summarize source material instead.

Primary Document Exception: When a primary text (a novel, a piece of legislation, a speech) is a key piece of evidence or the actual focus of your project, careful analysis of quoted excerpts is required. See pages 432–433 for more.

Smooth Integration

When you use quotations, work them into your writing as smoothly as possible. To do so, you need to pay attention to style, punctuation, and syntax. (See pages 478–479.)

Use enough of the quotation to make your point without changing the meaning of the original. Use quotation marks around key phrases taken from the source.

> Ogden, Williams, and Larson also conclude that the hydrogen fuel-cell vehicle is "a strong candidate for becoming the Car of the Future," given the trend toward "tighter environmental constraints" and the "intense efforts underway" by automakers to develop commercially viable versions of such vehicles (25).

Integrate all sources thoughtfully. Fold source material into your discussion by relating it to your own thinking. Let your ideas guide the way, not your sources, by using this pattern:

1. **State and explain your idea,** creating a context for the source.
2. **Identify and introduce the source,** linking it to your discussion.
3. **Summarize, paraphrase, or quote the source,** providing a citation in an appropriate spot.
4. **Use the source by explaining, expanding, or refuting it.**
5. **When appropriate, refer back to a source** to further develop the ideas it contains.

Sample Passage: Note the integration of sources in the paragraph below.

Writer's ideas	The motivation and urgency to create and improve hybrid-electric technology comes from a range of complex forces. Some of these forces are economic, others
Attributive phrase	environmental, and still others social. In "Societal Lifestyle Costs of Cars with Alternative Fuels/Engines," Joan Ogden, Robert Williams, and Eric Larson argue
Paraphrase, quotation, or summary	that "[c]ontinued reliance on current transportation fuels and technologies poses serious oil supply insecurity, climate change, and urban air pollution risks" (7).
Citation	Because of the nonrenewable nature of fossil fuels as well as their negative side
Commentary	effects, the transportation industry is confronted with making the most radical changes since the introduction of the internal-combustion automobile more than
Conclusion	100 years ago. Hybrid-electric vehicles are one response to this pressure.

Fabio Berti / Shutterstock.com

Effectively document your sources

Just as you need to integrate source material carefully into your writing, so you must also carefully document where that source material comes from. Readers should recognize which material is yours and which material is not.

Identify clearly where source material begins. Your discussion must offer a smooth transition to source material. Follow the guidelines below:

- For first reference to a source, use an attributive statement that indicates some of the following: author's name and credentials, title of the source, nature of the study or research, and helpful background.

  > **Joan Ogden, Robert Williams, and Eric Larson, members of the Princeton Environmental Institute, explain** that modest improvements in energy efficiency and emissions reductions will not be enough over the next century because of anticipated transportation increases (7).

- For subsequent references to a source, use a simplified attributive phrase, such as the author's last name or a shortened version of the title.

  > **Ogden, Williams, and Larson go on to argue** that "[e]ffectively addressing environmental and oil supply concerns will probably require radical changes in automotive engine/fuel technologies" (7).

- In some situations, such as providing straightforward facts, simply skip the attributive phrase. The parenthetical citation supplies sufficient attribution.

  > Various types of transportation are by far the main consumers of oil (three fourths of world oil imports); moreover, these same technologies are responsible for one fourth of all greenhouse gas sources (Ogden, Williams, and Larson 7).

- The verb you use to introduce source material is key. Use fitting verbs, such as those in the table below—verbs indicating that the source informs, analyzes, or argues. Normally, use the present tense. Use the past tense only to stress the "pastness" of a source.

  > In their 2004 study, "Societal Lifecycle Costs of Cars with Alternative Fuels/ Engines," Ogden, Williams, and Larson **present** a method for comparing and contrasting alternatives to internal-combustion engines. Earlier, these authors **made** preliminary steps . . .

Verbs for Signal Phrases

accepts	considers	explains	rejects	contrasts
contradicts	highlights	reminds	adds	insists
identifies	responds	affirms	criticizes	shows
shares	argues	declares	interprets	believes
asserts	defends	lists	states	describes
denies	maintains	stresses	cautions	points out
outlines	suggests	claims	disagrees	urges
supports	compares	discusses	praises	confirms
concludes	emphasizes	proposes	verifies	
enumerates	refutes	warns	acknowledges	

Indicate where source material ends. Closing quotation marks and a citation, as shown below, indicate the end of a source quotation. Generally, place the citation immediately after any quotation, paraphrase, or summary. However, you may also place the citation early in the sentence or at the end if the parenthetical note is obviously obtrusive. When you discuss several details from a page in a source, use an attributive phrase at the beginning of your discussion and a single citation at the end.

> As the "Lifestyle Costs" study concludes, when greenhouse gases, air pollution, and oil insecurity are factored into the analysis, alternative-fuel vehicles "offer lower LCCs than typical new cars" (Ogden, Williams, and Larson 25).

Set off longer quotations. If a quotation is longer than four typed lines, set it off from the main text. Generally, introduce the quotation with a complete sentence and a colon. Indent the quotation one inch (10 spaces) and double-space it, but don't put quotation marks around it. Put the citation outside the final punctuation mark.

> Toward the end of the study, Ogden, Williams, and Larson argue that changes to the fuel-delivery system must be factored into planning:
>
>> In charting a course to the Car of the Future, societal LCC comparisons should be complemented by considerations of fuel infrastructure requirements. Because fuel infrastructure changes are costly, the number of major changes made over time should be minimized. The bifurcated strategy advanced here—of focusing on the H2 FCV for the long term and advanced liquid hydrocarbon-fueled ICEVs and ICE/HEVs for the near term—would reduce the number of such infrastructure changes to one (an eventual shift to H2). (25)

Mark changes to quotations

You may shorten or change a quotation so that it fits smoothly into your sentence—but don't alter the original meaning. Use an ellipsis to indicate that you have omitted words from the original. An ellipsis is three periods with spaces between them.

> In their projections of where fuel-cell vehicles are heading, Ogden, Williams, and Larson discuss GM's AUTOnomy vehicle, with its "radical redesign of the entire car. . . . In these cars, steering, braking, and other vehicle systems are controlled electronically rather than mechanically" (24).

Use square brackets to indicate a clarification or to change a pronoun or verb tense or to switch around uppercase and lowercase.

> As Ogden, Williams, and Larson explain, "[e]ven if such barriers [the high cost of fuel cells and the lack of an H2 fuel infrastructure] can be overcome, decades would be required before this embryonic technology could make major contributions in reducing the major externalities that characterize today's cars" (25).

To indicate a spelling error or typographical error in the original source, add [sic] immediately after the error.

fyi Part I of this text, especially chapters 2–7, contains additional help on working through the writing process, including attention to working with sources.

Sample Research Paper: A Humanities Essay

As discussed on page 133, the humanities study aspects of human experience, as well as the ideas that grow out of that experience. Student writer Paige Greco does that in the humanities essay below: she explores the relationship between actors and audiences in the reconstructed Shakespeare Globe Theatre. As you read Paige's essay, explore how it is rooted in research and how she reasons with that research. Note: the sample essay shows source documentation according to the MLA style. However, the paper does not show MLA format rules (heading, margins, spacing, etc.). Those details are addressed in chapter 28.

The title indicates the essay's focus.	## The Audience-Actor Relationship at Shakespeare's Globe
The introduction identifies the problem to be explored: the value of the Globe reconstruction.	In spite of the populist impulses that drove Sam Wanamaker's efforts to rebuild the Globe Theatre in London, there were doubts as to whether the public, or anyone without a scholarly interest in Shakespeare, would even be interested in seeing Shakespeare performed in a drafty, thatch-covered theatre. Former Artistic Director Mark Rylance reflected that "although it's hard to believe now, we were not even sure that anyone would come and stand for a show in this 'old' building. No former reconstruction had dared to have standing room even in warmer, drier climates. What would people do when it rained?" (Rylance 104). Throughout
The voices of those involved in the reconstruction focus the essay on the theatre experience.	its various phases, the reconstruction was treated as a learning experience—a grand experiment in applying historical and archaeological research, re-learning Elizabethan construction techniques and numerous other skills. When asked in an interview whether he viewed this "'old' building" as an experimental theatre, Rylance replied, "It has always appeared to me as the most experimental theatre space in England. The space itself is an experiment" (Rylance 103).
At the end of her introduction, Greco identifies her particular focus: the actor-audience relationship in the Globe.	In order to build the most authentic reconstruction of an Elizabethan playhouse that their combined expertise could produce, Wanamaker and his architect, Theo Crosby, took pains to involve Shakespeare scholars in the planning phases of the Globe project. Wanamaker traveled to universities and conferences to drum up academic and financial interest in the project, while Crosby organized seminars with theatre scholars at his architectural firm to debate, and eventually decide, the final shape the theatre would take. Through the reconstruction of the Globe and the staging of Shakespeare's plays in the resulting authentic replica of the space for which the playwright created his plays, the scholars interviewed by Crosby hoped to test a multitude of theories about Elizabethan stagecraft and Shakespeare's stagecraft in particular. In the midst of the company's experimentation with acting

1

2

and stagecraft in the finished theatre, one of the most striking discoveries has been in regards to something fundamental: the audience.

Even in the early days of the reconstruction effort, investigating the relationship of the Elizabethan actor to his audience was considered among the paramount reasons to build a theatre. In a paper given at a conference at Wayne State University in 1979, Bernard Beckerman wondered, "What will it be like to stand where the groundlings stood and see the actors loom above us? Or how will it affect our response to sit in one of the better places of the gallery watching them strut past the heads of the groundlings? Until we live these moments, we cannot know how they might alter our feeling for Shakespearean performance" (158). Only by recreating the theatre can we possibly see through the eyes of a playgoer of Shakespeare's time. In modern theatres, audiences no longer stand at the edge of the stage, the actors' feet at eye level. We cannot "live these moments" of interaction without a space that mirrors the conditions of the original.

Even scholars who were otherwise enthusiastic about the possibility of recreating the theatrical space of the Globe pointed out that complete authenticity was impossible to achieve. Franklin J. Hildy quotes Edward Everett Hale Jr.'s observation that the audience itself can detract from perfect authenticity: "It is impossible by any act of imagination or anything else to put ourselves psychologically into the time of Shakespeare; and as an audience can never be an Elizabethan audience, so it would be futile to have the play an Elizabethan play, for even if the conditions were correct, we should be incorrect (qtd. in Hildy 31). Even if we get the costumes right, even if we get the theatre right, we cannot transform ourselves into Elizabethan people with Elizabethan mindsets and Elizabethan tastes. No matter what, we are products of our modern culture. Hildy, having engaged this commonly voiced reservation, comes to the conclusion that Hale's point does not invalidate the scholastic potential of the Globe reconstruction: "But whatever the parameters on uncertainty, the International Shakespeare Globe Centre will be the first working reconstruction to have organized its audience in the same relationship to performers and to each other that prevailed in Shakespeare's time" (31). Hildy points out that the modernity of the audience need not prevent us from gleaning new, practical information about the impact of the space on the way the audience and the actors interact.

When the construction of the theatre, now called Shakespeare's Globe, was completed in 1995, the actors could begin to test the scholars' theories. First,

---

The writer discusses scholarly debates about the actor-audience experience.

Contrasting perspectives are given voice and discussed.

With a clear transition, Greco turns from theory to actual theatre experience once the Globe was completed.

though, they would have to learn how to use the building. Since no one had acted in an Elizabethan playhouse in four hundred years, the artistic directorate decided that there would be a short "workshop season" which Barry Day describes as "an opportunity for a handful of actors and directors to try out some of the theories on Shakespearean theatre that had been so far confined to learned dissertations or crude physical approximations" (290). Among this select group was Sir Peter Hall, an eminent director of Shakespeare for the modern stage. During the workshop season, he realized that the way soliloquies were performed on the modern stage would have to change at Shakespeare's Globe: "Given the design of the stage and the proximity of the audience, he [Hall] was now convinced, the actor would have had to take that audience into his confidence, which would mean moving around the stage, so as to face them all in turn" (Day 296). Given that the daylight flooding into the roofless yard illuminated the audience and the actors equally, it was no longer practical for an actor to ignore the presence of the audience. Hill concluded that Shakespeare had not intended his characters to speak to an empty room, but to the throngs that faced him. As the company of actors produced Shakespeare's plays in the space, many of them, including Art Director Mark Rylance, came to similar conclusions:

> Eventually, in my last years, I really came to feel that it was not just about speaking, it was about thinking of the audience as other actors, and not just when you were projecting on them the role of the helpful crowd, like Henry's army or the citizens of Venice at the trial in *The Merchant of Venice*. It was more about the fact that anything they did was like another player on the stage doing something, so they were always there and when you were alone, they were your conscience or your soul. (Rylance 107)

For both Hill and Rylance, the interaction with the audience afforded by the unique theatrical space of Shakespeare's Globe changed the way they interpreted the role of the audience in the play. No longer were the audience members invisible beyond the illumination of the footlights; they were engaged in the creation of the performance. Since the audience is clearly visible to the performers from the Globe's stage, the interaction between the audience and the actors influences the actors' performance.

Paul Chahidi, an actor in the Globe's company, points out, "The fundamental area in which this theatre reveals so much is in the symbiotic relationship between the words of the playwright, the actor, the audience and the architecture of the

She focuses on the directorial experience.

A long quotation articulates a key point in concrete terms.

Greco turns to the actor's experience of the Globe.

6

7

8

building, which are all intrinsically linked; you cannot separate one from the other" (Rylance, Vazquez, and Chahidi 204). No theatre works without an audience, but in no other theatre does the audience play such a vital role in the performance. In Shakespeare's time, it was not uncommon for the audience to comment on the performance. Given that the actors at the Globe address the audience so directly, as Tim Carroll points out,

> the possibility has to be there that the audience will answer him back. The audience does not do it very often, but just occasionally, something interesting happens, such as in Barry Kyle's 2001 production of King Lear when Edmund was wondering aloud which of Goneril or Regan he should take as his mistress (and of course wondering aloud means asking the audience). Someone shouted out "Have them both." Michael Gould's response to this was a facial gesture that was unmistakable: "That's not a bad idea." (40)

9

The writer pulls together her thinking about the audience experience.

The audience at the Globe is not passive—the space makes them complicit in the performance. They become, for the actor, a helpful crowd, the sea, or the landscape. From the stage, the varying heights of the groundlings can suggest the gently rolling waves of the ocean or the undulating hills of the countryside. The groundlings also suffer the effects of ill weather along with the actors. For the audience in the galleries, the groundlings become part of the sweep of the stage. Not only can the actors see the audience—the members of the audience can see each other and recognize the communal nature of the performance.

10

The conclusion stresses the value and meaning of the Globe reconstruction.

Now that there are actors strutting and fretting about the stage, looming over groundlings, we can live the moments in an actual Elizabethan theatre that Bernard Beckerman imagined so many decades ago. In an interview about her experiences with Shakespeare's Globe, actor and educator Yolanda Vasquez claims, "That is what this space should be about—discovery, about seeing how these plays may have worked in the past, how we can learn from that, what we can do with them now and how we can go forward. Then it does not become a museum or archaic; it is something fruitful and in the moment" (Rylance, Vazquez, and Chahidi 202). Even though the yard and the galleries are now filled with modern theatregoers instead of Elizabethans, the beams and thatch of Shakespeare's Globe have allowed us to discover new and different theatrical experiences.

11

Works Cited

Beckerman, Bernard. "The Uses and Management of the Elizabethan Stage." *The Third Globe: Symposium for the Reconstruction of the Globe Playhouse, Wayne State University, 1979.* Ed. C. Walter Hodges, S. Schoenbaum, and Leonard Leone. Detroit: Wayne State UP, 1981. 151-63. Print.

Carroll, Tim. "'Practising Behaviour to His Own Shadow.'" Carson and Karim-Cooper 37-44.

Carson, Christie, and Farah Karim-Cooper, eds. *Shakespeare's Globe: A Theatrical Experiment.* New York: Cambridge UP, 2008. Print.

Day, Barry. *This Wooden "O": Shakespeare's Globe Reborn.* London: Oberon, 1996. Print.

Hildy, Franklin J. "Reconstructing Shakespeare's Theatre." *New Issues in the Reconstruction of Shakespeare's Theatre: Proceedings of the Conference Held at the University of Georgia, February 16-18, 1990.* Ed. Hildy. New York: Peter Lang, 1990. 1-37. Print.

Rylance, Mark. "Research, Materials, Craft: Principles of Performance." Carson and Karim-Cooper 103-14.

Rylance, Mark, Yolanda Vazquez, and Paul Chahidi. "Discoveries from the Globe Stage." Carson and Karim-Cooper 194-210.

All works referenced through in-text citation in the paper are correctly listed in the Works-Cited page

Reading for Better Writing

Working by yourself or with a group, do the following:

1. In a discussion of her paper, Paige Greco indicated that her interest in writing about the reconstructed Globe Theatre grew out of her experience of visiting the theatre several years earlier. In what ways does that experience shine through in the essay, even though Greco doesn't mention it?

2. Humanities essays tend to be about ideas, whether creative, historical, or theoretical. Writers of such essays aim to understand more deeply human experience and humanity's place in the world. In what ways does this essay demonstrate this humanities approach to knowledge?

3. Review the essay's sources as listed in the Works Cited, but also as they are referred to and used in the paper itself. What does this review suggest to you about the nature of research in the humanities?

"The Audience-Actor Relationship at Shakespeare's Globe" by Paige Greco. Reprinted by permission of the author.

Sample Research Paper: Science IMRAD Report

As discussed on pages 134–135, a common form of research writing in the natural and social sciences is the experiment report, often called the IMRAD report because of its structure: an *introduction* establishing the problem, a *methods* section detailing experimental procedures, a *results* section providing the data, and a *discussion* that interprets the data. This structure is rooted in the scientific method, a procedure by which experiments are set up to test hypotheses about why things happen.

In the report below, student writers Dana Kleckner, Brittany Korver, Nicolette Storm, and Adam Verhoef share the results of an experiment in which they tested a hypothesis about the impact of an invasive plant species, Eastern Red Cedar, on Midwestern native species. Note: the sample essay shows source documentation according to the APA style. However, the paper does not show in detail APA format rules (running head, margins, spacing, etc.). Those details are addressed in chapter 29. Note, as well, that documentation in the natural sciences often follows CSE format: for more information, check councilscienceeditors.org.

> The title contains key terms identifying the experiment's cause-effect focus.

The Effects of the Eastern Red Cedar on Seedlings and Implications for Allelopathy

Abstract

The Eastern Red Cedar *(Juniperus virginiana)* is an invasive species that threatens native tall-grass prairies in much of the Midwest (Norris, Blair, Johnson, & McKane, 2001). In an effort to learn more about its invasive characteristics, we decided to test for possible allelopathic properties. Allelopathy refers to the growth inhibition of one species by another species releasing toxins from its tissues (Simberloff, 1995). In this study, the germination and survival of black-eyed Susans *(Rudbeckia hirta)* and poppies *(Papaver orientale)* were examined. Seeds were planted in soil gathered from under three eastern red cedar trees at Oak Grove State Park (Northwestern Iowa) and in soil from three non-cedar locations at this park. Germination and survival of the seedlings in controlled conditions were documented over thirty-two days. We found no significant difference between germination and survival proportions of the two seed types between the cedar and non-cedar soil. This led us to conclude that the eastern red cedar does not negatively affect the germination and survival of the selected seed types.

> The abstract summarizes the experiment and its findings

1

Introduction

> The introduction offers background and surveys past research.

Several factors can give a plant dominance in an area. One of these factors is the production of allelopathic chemicals. Allelopathy is the secretion of chemicals by one plant that suppresses the growth of other nearby plants (Simberloff, 1995).

2

This phenomenon reduces competition for limited resources. One possible method of allelopathy is the secreting of chemicals through the roots, directly into the soil. The chemicals can also be stored in the leaves, flowers, fruits, and seeds, releasing chemicals into the soil as they decompose (Norris, Blair, & Johnson., 2007). These allelopathic properties are present in several invasive species, such as the Japanese Red Pine (Node et al., 2003).

The object in this experiment was to test for allelopathic capabilities of the eastern red cedar *(Juniperus virginiana)*. The eastern red cedar is a pioneer invader in the Midwest, quickly populating disturbed land (Norris et al., 2001). This invasion is problematic in certain areas of the Midwest, as it often changes the native ecology of the area it invades, namely tall-grass prairies (Norris et al., 2001). In the effort to preserve native ecosystems, a correct understanding of the characteristics of invaders is useful. The knowledge of the allelopathic properties of this species could assist in preservation efforts.

The writers identify the specific problem, explain the value of their research, and state their hypothesis.

We predicted that eastern red cedars are allelopathic and that the soil around cedar trees would have a negative effect on the germination and lifespan of other plants. We hypothesized that seeds planted in cedar soil would germinate at a lower frequency and have shorter life spans than those planted in non-cedar soil under the same conditions.

Methods

The experiment took place from March 19 to April 20, 2009, in the Northwestern College biology lab. Our professors collected soil from Oak Grove State Park near Hawarden, Iowa, several months in advance. They gathered soil from three different locations under three different cedars trees and from three nearby non-cedar locations. They placed the soils under sun lamps to dry, and then stored the soil in plastic ziplock bags.

The writers detail the experimental procedure using precise terms and steps.

To prepare for this experiment, two rows of evenly spaced holes were drilled into 18 potting trays for drainage. Each tray was labeled with the soil's location number and the soil type (cedar or non-cedar). From each specified location, soil was measured out equally and placed into the trays. In an effort to make the growing conditions realistic, any foreign plant roots, stems, etc. were left in the soil.

They explain choices made during the experiment.

Black-eyed Susans *(Rudbeckia hirta)* and poppies *(Papaver orientale)* were chosen because of their equal planting depth and equal time for seed germination. Two rows were planted in each tray with 10 evenly spaced black-eyed Susan seeds on one side and ten evenly spaced poppy seeds on the other side (both were planted according to the directions on the packages).

3

4

5

6

7

On March 19, each tray was placed approximately 35cm. under sun lamps that ran on a 12hrs. on/12hrs. off cycle. Each day, the trays were watered and rotated so that they received an equal amount of light and warmth. When a seed germinated, the date and the plant location in the tray were documented. If the plant died, the date of the death was recorded. Any foreign species that grew were left so as not to disturb the soil. On April 20, thirty-two days later, the data were compiled. The number of each species that germinated at each location and the number of days each plant survived were recorded.   *8*

Using Microsoft Excel, we first ran ANOVAs to see if there were any significant differences in germination rates among the three cedar soil sites or any significant difference in germination rates among the non-cedar sites. Then we ran paired t-tests on germination for each seed type between the cedar and non-cedar soils. To compare the percentage of surviving seedlings between cedar and non-cedar soils, we ran an ANOVA for each seed type.   *9*

Results

We found no significant differences related to location in germination of black-eyed Susan seeds (ANOVA: F=2.71, F-crit=5.14, df=8, p-value=0.14) (Fig.1) or poppy seeds (ANOVA: F=0.37, F-crit=5.14, df=8, p-value=0.7) (Fig. 1) among the three cedar sites. We also found that there were no significant differences related to location in the germination of black-eyed Susans (ANOVA: F=1.63, F-crit=5.14, df=8, p-value=0.27) (Fig. 2) or poppies (ANOVA: F=0.31, F-crit=5.14, df=8, p-value=0.74) (Fig. 2) among the three non-cedar sites. Knowing that there were no significant differences in germination among the sites, we condensed the data into four different groups: black-eyed Susan cedar, black-eyed Susan non-cedar, poppy cedar, and poppy non-cedar.   *10*

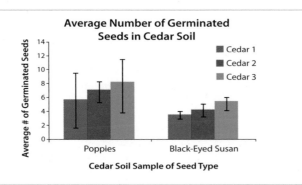

Figure 1. There is no significant difference in seed germination among the three cedar soils for poppies (p=.7) or black-eyed Susans (p=.14). Bars represent standard deviation.

To keep the focus on actions rather than themselves as actors, the writers use passive voice (but mainly in the Methods section).

The results are stated in neutral, precise terms and portrayed in figures.

Figures effectively visualize the experimental data, and are properly titled, numbered, and captioned.

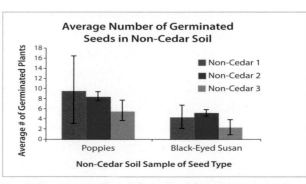

Figure 2. There is no significant difference in seed germination among the three non-cedar soils for poppies (p=.74) or black-eyed Susans (p=.27). Bars represent standard deviation.

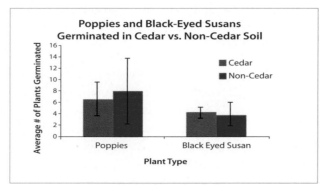

Figure 3. There is no significant difference in germination between cedar and non-cedar soil for poppies (p=.48) or black-eyed Susans (p=.77). Bars represent standard deviation.

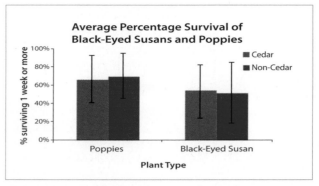

Figure 4. There is no significant difference in seedling survival between cedar and non-cedar soil for poppies (p=.82) or black-eyed Susans (p=.92). Bars represent standard deviation.

The two paired t-tests comparing seed germination in cedar soil versus non-cedar soil showed no significant differences in black-eyed Susan germination between the two soil types (t=0.31, p=0.77) (Fig.3) or in poppy germination between the two soil types (t=-0.78, p=0.46) (Fig.3).

When comparing survivorship of the two seedling types in each soil, we defined surviving plants as those that lived for seven days or more. We ran ANOVAs and found that there was no significant difference between the proportion of seedlings that survived in cedar versus non-cedar soil for black-eyed Susans (ANOVA: F=0.01, F-crit=4.49, df=1, p=0.92) (Fig. 4) or for poppies (ANOVA: F=0.06, F-crit=4.49, df=1, p=0.82) (Fig. 4).

Discussion

In this experiment, we sought to discover whether eastern red cedar soil is allelopathic. We predicted that cedar soil was allelopathic and hypothesized that if our prediction were correct, seeds planted in non-cedar soil would show higher germination and higher survival. We tested for significant differences in soil sites, germination of the two seeds types between soil types, and survival percentages of the seed types between soil types. None of these tests yielded a significant difference.

If the black-eyed Susans and poppies are good representatives of typically affected plants, then eastern red cedar soil appears not to reduce germination or survival. For those concerned with protecting native ecosystems from these invaders, the implications seem positive. An allelopathic invader would produce more damage than a non-allelopathic invader not only in the secretion of chemicals, but also in those chemicals remaining to harm desirable native species even if that invader is removed (Medley & Krisko, 2007).

However, even if cedars do not release allelopathic chemicals, a study conducted in the tall grass prairies of Kansas found that the eastern red cedar increased the amount of above-ground biomass and surface-litter nitrogen pools that are linked to the conversion of grassland to forest (Norris et al., 2007). Though this is not allelopathy, the invasive eastern red cedar still changes the composition of the soil in a manner that could affect the growth of other plants (Norris et al., 2007).

Also, though the cedar soil appeared not to be allelopathic in our study, we are hesitant to make an assessment of the eastern red cedar's affect on other plant types. Several factors may have confounded our non-allelopathic conclusion. The cedar's chemical may simply not be allelopathic to the types of plants we chose (Medley & Krisko, 2007). We purchased the seeds at a local Bomgaars store, and these seeds

The writers restate their purpose and hypothesis, and then interpret the results of their experiment.

They consider the broader implications of their study.

11

12

13

14

15

are domesticated strains. Domesticated strains may be more resistant to allelopathic chemicals and selected for high germination (Node et al., 2003). If allelopathic chemicals are present, the chemicals may have been affected by the storage period and drying process and consequently have a different effect on seedlings (Norris et al., 2001).   *16*

Though we doubt that chemicals affected the outcome of our study, we had several slight complications. In one of our planting boxes, more than ten poppies germinated. This was likely due to accidentally planting more than ten of the tiny seeds. In our statistics, we chose to count them all because excessive seeds were likely accidentally planted in other boxes as well. A recording complication occurred when some poppies germinated outside of their row in their container. The species type of some of the small seedlings was hard to distinguish as they were mixed together.

The writers identify complicating factors and reflect on the experiment's method.

If we repeated this experiment, we would change both materials and methods.   *17*
We would grow separate seed types in separate containers so there would be no confusion as to the species. We would also be more attentive to the seeds during the planting process, so none would stick together and distort our data. To see if the drying process was a factor, in addition to planting in dried soil, we would plant in freshly gathered soil. Finally, we would use plant species that are actually threatened by possible cedar allelopathy instead of species to which this possibility is irrelevant in real life. A native tall grass may react much differently to cedar soil and would provide more interesting and relevant application.

Smit / Shutterstock.com

References

Medley, K., & Krisko, B. (2007). Physical site conditions and land use history as factors influencing the conservation of regrowth forests in a southwest Ohio nature reserve. *Natural Areas Journal, 27*(1), 31-40. doi:10.3375/0885-8608

Node, M., Tomita-Yokotani, K., Suzuki, T., Kosemura, S., Hirata, H., Hirata, K., . . . Hasegawa, K. (2003). Allelopathy of pinecone in Japanese red pine tree (*Pinus densiflora Sieb. et Zucc.*). *Weed Biology & Management, 3*(2), 111-116. doi:10.1046/j.1445-6664.2003.00092.x

Norris, M. D., Blair, J.M., Johnson, L. C., & McKane, R. B. (2001). Assessing changes in biomass, productivity, and C and N stores following *Juniperus virginiana* forest expansion into tallgrass prairie. *Canadian Journal of Forest Research, 31*(11), 1940. doi:10.1139/x01-132

Norris, M. D., Blair, J. M., & Johnson, L. C. (2007). Altered ecosystem nitrogen dynamics as a consequence of land cover change in tallgrass prairie. *American Midland Naturalist, 158*(2), 432-445. doi:10.1674/0003-0031

Simberloff, D. (1995). Introduced species. In *Encyclopedia of environmental biology* (pp. 323-336). San Diego, CA: Academic Press.

Reading for Better Writing

Working by yourself or with a group, do the following:

1. Where do the writers discuss the experiment's purpose and value? Are their efforts convincing?
2. What role does secondary research play in this report? Where and how is it referred to, and for what purpose?
3. In the "Methods" section, what strategies do the writers use to ensure that the experiment can be repeated?
4. In the "Results" section, what is the relationship between the writers' statements and the four figures?
5. In the "Discussion" section, how do the writers interpret the experiment results? Are their interpretations and conclusions sound? Why or why not?

"The Effects of the Eastern Red Cedar on Seedlings and Implications for Allelopathy" by Dana Kleckner, Brittany Korver, Nicolette Storm, and Adam Verhoef

Critical-Thinking and Writing Activities

As directed by your instructor, complete the following critical-thinking and writing activities by yourself or with classmates.

1. The first pages of this chapter focus on making the transition from research to writing, as well as on strategies for engaging your research findings, developing your research-based thinking, and drafting your research paper. What does this instruction suggest about the nature and purpose of research writing? How does it differ from other forms of writing?

2. Review a research paper that you wrote in the past. Does that paper follow the principles for using, integrating, and documenting source material, as outlined in this chapter? How might you improve the treatment of sources in your paper?

3. Compare and contrast the humanities essay on pages 480–484 and the IMRAD report on pages 485–491. What similarities do they share with respect to research and research writing? What differences stand out? What do these similarities and differences suggest about research in different fields of study?

Learning-Objectives Checklist ✓

Have you achieved this chapter's learning objectives? Check your progress with the items below, revisiting topics in the chapter as needed. *I have* . . .

____ carefully examined my research findings so as to deepen my thinking on the topic and imagine my paper (470).

____ assessed my working thesis and strengthened it in light of my research (471).

____ organized my thinking by considering what I discovered through research, along with traditional methods of organization (472–473).

____ drafted my paper either systematically or freely, but have focused on respecting my sources and reasoning with the evidence (474–475).

____ smoothly integrated and carefully documented source material into my writing (476–479).

____ compared and contrasted research-writing practices in a humanities essay and a sciences IMRAD report (480–491).

Chapter 28

MLA Style

In writing research papers, it is commonly said, "You are commanded to borrow but forbidden to steal." To borrow ideas while avoiding plagiarism (see pages 459–468), you must not only mention the sources you borrow from but also document them completely and accurately. You must follow to the last dot the documentation conventions for papers written in your area of study.

If you are composing a research paper in the humanities, your instructor will most likely require you to follow the conventions established in the style manual of the Modern Language Association (MLA). This chapter provides you with explanations and examples for citing sources in MLA format.

Visually Speaking   Library shelves organize a vast amount of knowledge (Figure 28.1). In what sense does a system such as MLA style make sense of and order knowledge in research writing?

Learning **Objectives**

By working through this chapter, you will be able to

- explain and implement MLA guidelines for documenting sources.
- produce research writing that adheres to MLA guidelines for formatting.
- evaluate MLA practices at work in a sample student research-based essay.

fig. 28.1

MLA Documentation Guidelines

The MLA system involves two parts: (1) an in-text citation within your paper when you use a source and (2) a matching bibliographic entry at the end of your paper. Note these features of the MLA system:

- **It's minimalist.** In your paper, you provide the least amount of information needed for your reader to identify the source in the works-cited list.
- **It uses signal phrases and parenthetical references** to set off source material from your own thinking and discussion.
  Note: A signal phrase names the author and places the material in context (e.g., "As Margaret Atwood argues in *Survival*").
- **It's smooth, unobtrusive, and orderly.** MLA in-text citations identify borrowed material while keeping the paper readable. Moreover, alphabetized entries in the works-cited list at the end of the paper make locating source details easy.

You can see these features at work in the example below. "Anna Hutchens" and "(449)" tell the reader the following things:

- The borrowed material came from a source written by Anna Hutchens.
- The specific material can be found on page 449 of the source.
- Full source details are in the works-cited list under the author's last name.

1. In-Text Citation in Body of Paper

> As Anna Hutchens puts it, there is an "absence of a policy framework and institutional mechanisms that promote women's empowerment as a rights-based rather than a culture-based issue" (449).

2. Matching Works-Cited Entry at End of Paper

> Hutchens, Anna. "Empowering Women Through Fair Trade? Lessons from Asia." *Third World Quarterly* 31.3 (2010): 449-67. *Academic Search Premier*. Web. 18 Jan. 2012.

In-Text Citation: The Basics

In MLA, in-text citations typically follow these guidelines:

1. Refer to the author (plus the work's title, if helpful) and a page number by using one of these methods:

   Last name and page number in parentheses:

   ⌐ last name only in citation
   > Fair trade is not necessary for consumers to "exercise a moral choice" with their money (Chandler 256). ⌐ no "p." for "page"
   └ no comma between name and page number

   Name cited in sentence, page number in parentheses:

   ⌐ full name in first reference
   > As Paul Chandler admits, fair trade is not necessary for consumers to "exercise a moral choice" with their money (256). ⌐ page number only in citation

2. Present and punctuate citations according to these rules:
- Place the parenthetical reference after the source material.
- Within the parentheses, normally give the author's last name only.
- Do not put a comma between the author's last name and the page reference.
- Cite the page number as a numeral, not a word.
- Don't use *p.*, *pp.*, or *page(s)* before the page number(s).
- Place any sentence punctuation after the closed parenthesis.

 For many of these rules, exceptions exist. For example, classic literary texts could be cited by chapters, books, acts, scenes, or lines. Moreover, many electronic sources have no stated authors and/or no pagination. See pages 500–507 for complete coverage of in-text citation practices.

Works Cited: The Basics

Complete coverage of MLA works-cited issues (examples included) is offered on pages 508–524, rules for formatting the works-cited page are on page 496, and a sample works-cited page is shown on page 533. Here, however, are some templates for the most common entries:

Template for Book:

> Author's Last Name, First Name. *Title of Book*. Publication City: Publisher, year of publication. Medium. (Other publication details are integrated as needed.)
>
> Nichols, Alex, and Charlotte Opal. *Fair Trade: Market-Driven Ethical Consumption*. London: Sage, 2004. Print.

Template for Periodical Article in an Online Database:

> Author's Last Name, First Name. "Title of Article." *Journal Title* volume, issue, and/or date details: page numbers. *Title of Database*. Medium. Date of access.
>
> Chandler, Paul. "Fair Trade and Global Justice." *Globalizations* 3.2 (2006): 255-57. *Academic Search Premier*. Web. 19 Jan. 2013.

 If you read the print article, end the citation after the page numbers with "Print" as the medium.

Template for a Web Document:

> Author's or Editor's Last Name, First Name (if available). "Title of Page, Posting, or Document." *Title of Web site* (if different from document title). Version or edition used. Publisher or sponsor of site (if known; if not, use *N.p.*), Date of publication, last update, or posting (if known; if not, use *n.d.*). Medium. Date of access.
>
> "What is Fairtrade?" *Fairtrade International*. Fairtrade Labelling Organizations Intl., n.d. Web. 10 February 2013.

Web Link: For additional questions and answers about MLA format, see the MLA Q&A page at http://www.mla.org/handbook_faq.

MLA Format Guidelines

The MLA system offers guidelines not only for documentation but also for the paper's format—its parts and their presentation. Format guidelines are detailed in Figures 28.2–28.4 and on the following pages, as well as in the sample MLA paper on page 525.

MLA Format at a Glance

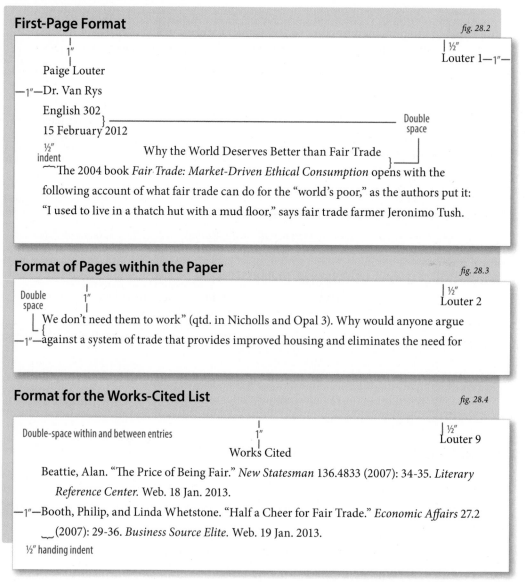

First-Page Format   *fig. 28.2*

1"

Paige Louter

—1"—Dr. Van Rys

English 302

15 February 2012

½" indent

Why the World Deserves Better than Fair Trade

Double space

The 2004 book *Fair Trade: Market-Driven Ethical Consumption* opens with the following account of what fair trade can do for the "world's poor," as the authors put it: "I used to live in a thatch hut with a mud floor," says fair trade farmer Jeronimo Tush.

½"
Louter 1—1"—

Format of Pages within the Paper   *fig. 28.3*

Double space

1"

½"
Louter 2

We don't need them to work" (qtd. in Nicholls and Opal 3). Why would anyone argue

—1"—against a system of trade that provides improved housing and eliminates the need for

Format for the Works-Cited List   *fig. 28.4*

Double-space within and between entries

1"

½"
Louter 9

Works Cited

Beattie, Alan. "The Price of Being Fair." *New Statesman* 136.4833 (2007): 34-35. *Literary Reference Center*. Web. 18 Jan. 2013.

—1"—Booth, Philip, and Linda Whetstone. "Half a Cheer for Fair Trade." *Economic Affairs* 27.2 (2007): 29-36. *Business Source Elite*. Web. 19 Jan. 2013.

½" handing indent

Whole-Paper Format and Printing Issues

The instruction below and on the next pages explain how to set up the parts of your paper and print it for submission. Page references are to the sample MLA paper later in this chapter.

Running Head and Pagination (page 525)

- Number pages consecutively in the upper-right corner, one-half inch from the top and flush with the right margin (1 inch from the edge of the page).
- Use numerals only—without *p., page, #,* or any other symbol.
- Include your last name on each page typed one space before the page number. (Your name identifies the page if it's misplaced.)

 Your word-processing program should be able to combine the running head and pagination automatically.

Heading on First Page (page 525)

MLA does not require a separate title page. On the first page of your paper, include the following details flush left and double spaced, one inch from the top:

- Your name, both first and last in regular order
- Your professor's or instructor's name (presented as he or she prefers)
- The course name and number, plus the section number if appropriate (e.g., History 100-05). Follow your instructor's directions.
- The date that you are submitting the paper: use the international format (e.g., 11 November 2013).

Paper Title (page 525)

- Double-spaced below the heading, center your paper's title.
- Do not italicize, underline, or boldface the title; put it in quotation marks or all caps; or use a period (though a question mark may be acceptable if warranted).
- Follow standard capitalization practices for titles.

Works-Cited List (page 533)

- Start the list on a new page immediately after your paper's conclusion.
- Continue the running head and pagination.
- Center the heading "Works Cited" one inch from the top of the page; don't use quotation marks, underlining, boldface, or any other typographical markers.
- Begin your list two spaces below the heading. Arrange all entries alphabetically by the authors' last names; for sources without identified authors, alphabetize using the work's title, ignoring *a, an,* or *the.*
- If you are listing two or more works by the same author, alphabetize them by the titles of the works. Use the author's name for the first entry; in later entries, replace the name with three hyphens.

(See more "Works-Cited List" formatting tips on the next page.)

- Start each entry flush left; indent second and subsequent lines for specific entries one-half inch. Use your word-processing program's hanging indent feature.
- Double-space within and between all entries, and follow standard rules for capitalization, italics, quotation marks, and punctuation.
- Do not repeat the "Works Cited" heading if your list runs longer than one page.
- Print on standard 8.5-by 11-inch paper.

Paper, Printing, and Binding

- Use quality 20 pound bond paper. Avoid both thin, erasable paper and heavy card stock. Similarly, stick with standard white or off-white paper—no neons, pastels, letterheads, or scents.
- Use a laser or inkjet printer to create a crisp, clean copy; avoid using nearly empty print cartridges.
- Avoid submitting a paper with handwritten corrections; however, if you must make a change, make a caret symbol (^), put a single clean line through words that must be dropped, and write additions above the line.
- As a first choice, use a paperclip. A single staple in the upper left corner may be acceptable. Avoid fancy covers or bindings, and never simply fold over the corners.
- Print your essay single-sided. Do double-sided printing only with your instructor's permission.

> **Electronic Submission or Posting:** If your instructor accepts or encourages electronic submission, follow his or her guidelines concerning these issues:
> - **Mode of submission:** email attachment, pdf posting, flash drive, and so on
> - **Pagination/reference markers:** If your document will not have stable page numbers, number the paragraphs. Place the paragraph number in brackets, follow with a space, and then begin the paragraph.
> - **Internet addresses:** If you have included URLs, reverse the MLA print practice of putting them in angle brackets; instead, make URLs live links.

Typographical Issues

Typeface: Choose a standard serif typeface like Times New Roman. (Serif type, for example, the type you're reading, has finishes on each letter, as opposed to sans serif, like this.) Avoid unusual, hard-to-read typefaces.

Type Size: Use a readable type size, preferably 12 points, throughout the paper.

Type Styles (underlining, italics, bold, etc.):

- Use italics (not underlining) for titles of resources and individual words requiring this feature. An exception may be an online publication or posting; consult your instructor.
- Avoid using boldface, yellow highlighting, all caps, and so on.

Page-Layout Issues

Spacing

- **Margins:** Set margins top and bottom, left and right at one inch, with the exception of the running head (one-half inch from top).
- **Line Spacing:** Double-space the entire paper—including the heading and works-cited entries, as well as tables, captions, and inset quotations.
- **Line Justification:** Use left justified throughout, except for the running head (right justified) and the title and works-cited heading (both centered). Leave the right margin ragged.
- **Word Hyphenation:** Avoid hyphenating words at the end of lines; in your word processor, turn off this tool.
- **Spacing after Punctuation:** Use one space after most forms of punctuation, including end punctuation—but not before or after a dash or a hyphen.
- **Paragraph Indenting:** Indent all paragraphs one-half inch.

Longer (Inset) Quotations (see page 527)

- Indent one inch verse quotations longer than three lines and prose quotations longer than four typed lines.
- Use no quotation marks, and place the parenthetical citation after the closing punctuation.
- With a verse quotation, make each line of the poem or play a new line; do not run the lines together. Follow the indenting and spacing in the verse itself.
- To quote two or more paragraphs, indent the first line of each paragraph one-quarter inch in addition to the one inch for the whole passage. However, if the first sentence quoted does not begin a paragraph in the source, do not make the additional indent. Indent only the first lines of subsequent paragraphs.

Tables and Illustrations

Position tables, illustrations, and other visuals near your discussion of them—ideally, immediately after your first reference to the graphic, whether pasted in after a paragraph or positioned on a separate following page. Observe these rules:

- **Tables:** Identify all tables using "Table," an Arabic numeral, and a caption (descriptive title). Both the identifying headings and captions should be flush left, appropriately capitalized. Provide source information and explanatory notes below the table. Identify notes with superscript lowercase letters, not numerals. Double-space throughout the table.
- **Illustrations:** Number and label other visuals (graphs, charts, drawings, photos, maps, etc.) using "Figure" or "Fig.," an Arabic numeral (followed by a period), and a title or caption one space after the period—all flush left below the illustration, along with source information and notes.

Guidelines for In-Text Citations

The *MLA Handbook for Writers of Research Papers,* Seventh Edition (2009), suggests giving credit for your sources of information in the body of your research paper. One way to do so is by indicating the author and/or title in the text of your essay, and then putting a page reference in parentheses after the summary, paraphrase, or quotation, as needed. The simplest way to do so is to insert the appropriate information (usually the author and page number) in parentheses after the words or ideas taken from the source.

To avoid disrupting your writing, place citations where a pause would naturally occur (usually at the end of a sentence but sometimes within a sentence, before internal punctuation such as a comma or semicolon). These in-text citations (often called "parenthetical references") refer to sources listed on the "Works Cited" page at the end of your paper. (See page 533 for a sample works-cited list.) Essentially, each in-text citation must clearly point to a source in your works cited, and every source in the works-cited list must be referred to at least once within your paper.

Citations for regular sources

As you integrate citations into your paper, follow the guidelines below, referring to the sample citation as needed.

Sample In-Text Citation

> As James Cuno, director of the Harvard University Art Museums, points out, the public, which subsidizes museums either directly through donations or indirectly via their status as tax-free nonprofit organizations, expects them to "carry out their duties professionally on its behalf" (164).

- **Make sure each in-text citation clearly points to an entry in your list of works cited.** The identifying information provided (usually the author's last name) must be the word or words by which the entry is alphabetized in that list.

- **Keep citations brief, and integrate them smoothly** into your writing.

- **When paraphrasing or summarizing rather than quoting, make it clear where your borrowing begins and ends.** Use stylistic cues to distinguish the source's thoughts ("Kalmbach points out . . . ," "Some critics argue . . .") from your own ("I believe . . . ," "It seems obvious, however"). See pages 476–479 for more on integrating sources.

- **When using a shortened title of a work, begin with the word by which the work is alphabetized** in your list of works cited (e.g., "Egyptian, Classical," not "Middle Eastern Art," for "Egyptian, Classical, and Middle Eastern Art").

- **For inclusive page numbers larger than ninety-nine, give only the last two digits of the second number** (346–48, not 346–348).

- **When including a parenthetical citation at the end of a sentence, place it before the end punctuation.** (Citations for long, indented quotations are an exception. See page 479.)

Citations for sources without traditional authorship and/or pagination

Today many sources, especially electronic ones, have no stated authors and/or no pagination. For such sources, use these in-text citation strategies:

Source Without a Stated Author

In a signal phrase or in the parenthetical reference, identify the source as precisely as possible by indicating the sponsoring agency, the type of document, or the title (shortened in the parenthetical reference). See pages 502–503.

> While the Brooklyn Museum may be best known for the recent controversy over the Sensation exhibition, it does contain a strong collection of contemporary if less controversial art, "ranging from representational to abstract to conceptual" ("Contemporary Art").

Source with No Pagination

If no pagination exists within the document, use paragraph numbers (with the abbreviation *par.*), if the document provides them. If the document includes neither page nor paragraph numbers, cite the entire work. Do not create your own numbering system.

> The Museum's *Art of the Americas* collection includes extensive holdings of works by the aboriginal peoples of North, Central, and South America, many of these gathered by archaeologist Herbert Spinden during at least seven expeditions between 1929 and 1950 (*Art of the Americas* par. 3).

Because parenthetical notations are used to signal the end of an attribution, sources with no pagination or paragraph numbers offer a special challenge. When no parenthetical notation is possible, signal a shift back to your own discussion with a source-reflective statement indicating your thinking about the source.

> . . . indicated by his recording the audio tour of the exhibit, his supporting the show financially, and his promoting *Sensation* at his Web site. As Welland's discussion of David Bowie's participation suggests, the controversy over the Brooklyn Museum of Art's *Sensation* exhibit . . .

INSIGHT Stable pagination for many electronic resources is available when you use the ".pdf" rather than the ".html" version of the source. For instruction on smoothly integrating source material into your paper, see pages 476–479. For cautions about sources without identified authors, see pages 502, 503, 510, and 516.

Ilin Sergey / Shutterstock.com

Sample In-Text Citations

The following entries illustrate the most common in-text citations.

One Author: A Complete Work

You do not need a parenthetical citation if you identify the author in your text. (See the first entry below.) However, you must give the author's last name in a parenthetical citation if it is not mentioned in the text. (See the second entry.) When a source is listed in your works-cited page with an editor, a translator, a speaker, or an artist instead of the author, use that person's name in your citation.

With Author in Text: (This is the preferred way of citing a complete work.)

> In *No Need for Hunger*, Robert Spitzer recommends that the U.S. government develop a new foreign policy to help Third World countries overcome poverty and hunger.

Without Author in Text:

> *No Need for Hunger* recommends that the U.S. government develop a new foreign policy to help Third World countries overcome poverty and hunger (Spitzer).

Note: Do not offer page numbers when citing complete works, articles in alphabetized encyclopedias, one-page articles, and unpaginated sources.

One Author: Part of a Work

List the necessary page numbers in parentheses if you borrow words or ideas from a particular source. Leave a space between the author's last name and the page reference. No abbreviation or punctuation is needed.

With Author in Text:

> Bullough writes that genetic engineering was dubbed "eugenics" by a cousin of Darwin's, Sir Francis Galton, in 1885 (5).

Without Author in Text:

> Genetic engineering was dubbed "eugenics" by a cousin of Darwin's, Sir Francis Galton, in 1885 (Bullough 5).

A Work by Two or Three Authors

Give the last names of every author in the same order that they appear in the works-cited section. (The correct order of the authors' names can be found on the title page of the book.)

> Students learned more than a full year's Spanish in ten days using the complete supermemory method (Ostrander and Schroeder 51).

A Work by Four or More Authors

Give the first author's last name as it appears in the works-cited section followed by *et al.* (meaning "and others").

> Communication on the job is more than talking; it is "inseparable from your total behavior" (Culligan et al. 111).

Note: You may instead choose to list all of the authors' last names.

Two or More Works by the Same Author(s)

In addition to the author's last name(s) and page number(s), include a shortened version of the work's title when you cite two or more works by the same author(s).

With Author in Text:

> Wallerstein and Blakeslee claim that divorce creates an enduring identity for children of the marriage (*Unexpected Legacy* 62).

Without Author in Text:

> They are intensely lonely despite active social lives (Wallerstein and Blakeslee, *Second Chances* 51).

Note: When including both author(s) and title in a parenthetical reference, separate them with a comma, as shown above, but do not put a comma between the title and the page number.

Works by Authors with the Same Last Name

When citing different sources by authors with the same last name, it is best to use the authors' full names in the text to avoid confusion. However, if circumstances call for parenthetical references, add each author's first initial. If first initials are the same, use each author's full name.

> Some critics think *Titus Andronicus* too abysmally melodramatic to be a work of Shakespeare (A. Parker 73). Others suggest that Shakespeare meant it as black comedy (D. Parker 486).

A Work Authored by an Agency, a Committee, or an Organization

If a book or other work was written by an organization such as an agency, a committee, or a task force, it is said to have a corporate author. (See also page 510.) If the corporate name is long, include it in the text (rather than in parentheses) to avoid disrupting the flow of your writing. After the full name has been used at least once, use a shortened form of the name (common abbreviations are acceptable) in subsequent references. For example, Task Force may be used for Task Force on Education for Economic Growth.

> The thesis of the Task Force's report is that economic success depends on our ability to improve large-scale education and training as quickly as possible (113–14).

An Anonymous Work

When there is no author listed, give the title or a shortened version of the title as it appears in the works-cited section. (See page 510.)

> Statistics indicate that drinking water can make up 20 percent of a person's total exposure to lead (*Information* 572).

Two or More Works Included in One Citation

To cite multiple works within a single parenthetical reference, separate the references with a semicolon.

> In Medieval Europe, Latin translations of the works of Rhazes, a Persian scholar, were a primary source of medical knowledge (Albala 22; Lewis 266).

A Series of Citations from a Single Work

If no confusion is possible, it is not necessary to name a source repeatedly when making multiple parenthetical references to that source in a single paragraph. If all references are to the same page, identify that page in a parenthetical note after the last reference. If the references are to different pages within the same work, you need identify the work only once, and then use a parenthetical note with page number alone for the subsequent references.

> Domesticating science meant not only spreading scientific knowledge, but also promoting it as a topic of public conversation (Heilbron 2). One way to enhance its charm was by depicting cherubic putti as "angelic research assistants" in book illustrations (5).

A Work Referred to in Another Work

If you must cite an indirect source—that is, information from a source that is quoted from another source—use the abbreviation *qtd. in* (quoted in) before the indirect source in your reference.

> Paton improved the conditions in Diepkloof (a prison) by "removing all the more obvious aids to detention. The dormitories [were] open at night: the great barred gate [was] gone" (qtd. in Callan xviii).

A Work Without Page Numbers

If a work has no page numbers or paragraph numbers, treat it as you would a complete work. (See page 502.) This is commonly the case with electronic resources, for example. Do not count pages to create reference numbers of your own.

> Antibiotics become ineffective against such organisms through two natural processes: first, genetic mutation; and second, the subsequent transfer of this mutated genetic material to other organisms (Davies).

A Work in an Anthology or a Collection

When citing the entirety of a work that is part of an anthology or a collection, if it is identified by author in your list of works cited, treat the citation as you would for any other complete work. (See page 502.)

> In "The Canadian Postmodern," Linda Hutcheon offers a clear analysis of the self-reflexive nature of contemporary Canadian fiction.

Similarly, if you are citing particular pages of such a work, follow the directions for citing part of a work. (See page 502.)

> According to Hutcheon, "postmodernism seems to designate cultural practices that are fundamentally self-reflexive, in other words, art that is self-consciously artifice" (18).

(To format this sort of entry in your list of works cited, see pages 510–511.)

An Item from a Reference Work

An entry from a reference work such as an encyclopedia or a dictionary should be cited similarly to a work from an anthology or a collection (see above). For a dictionary definition, include the abbreviation *def.* followed by the particular entry designation.

> This message becomes a juggernaut in the truest sense, a belief that "elicits blind devotion or sacrifice" ("Juggernaut," def. 1).

Note: While many such entries are identified only by title (as above), some reference works include an author's name for each entry (as below). Others may identify the entry author by initials, with a list of full names elsewhere in the work.

> The decisions of the International Court of Justice are "based on principles of international law and cannot be appealed" (Pranger).

(See pages 512–513 for guidelines to formatting these entries in your works-cited list.)

A Part of a Multivolume Work

When citing only one volume of a multivolume work, if you identify the volume number in the works-cited list, there is no need to include it in your in-text citation. However, if you cite more than one volume of a work, each in-text reference must identify the appropriate volume. Give the volume number followed by page number, separated by a colon and a space.

> "A human being asleep," says Spengler, ". . . is leading only a plantlike existence" (2: 4).

When citing a whole volume, however, either identify the volume number in parentheses with the abbreviation *vol.* (using a comma to separate it from the author's name) or use the full word *volume* in your text.

> The land of Wisconsin has shaped its many inhabitants more significantly than they ever shaped that land (Stephens, vol. 1).

A One-Page Work

Cite a one-page work just as you would a complete work. (See page 502.)

> As Samantha Adams argues in her editorial, it is time for NASA "to fully reevaluate the possibility of a manned mission to Mars."

A Sacred Text or Famous Literary Work

Sacred texts and famous literary works are published in many different editions. For that reason, it is helpful to identify sections, parts, chapters, and such instead of or in addition to page numbers. If using page numbers, list them first, followed by an abbreviation for the type of division and the division number.

> The more important a person's role in society—the more apparent power an individual has—the more that person is a slave to the forces of history (Tolstoy 690; bk. 9, ch. 1).

Books of the Bible and other well-known literary works may be abbreviated, if no confusion is possible.

> "A generation goes, and a generation comes, but the earth remains forever" (*The New Oxford Annotated Bible*, Eccles. 1.4).

> As Shakespeare's famous Danish prince observes, "One may smile, and smile, and be a villain" (Ham. 1.5.104).

Quoting Prose

To cite prose from fiction (novels, short stories), list more than the page number if the work is available in several editions. Give the page reference first, and then add a chapter, section, or book number in abbreviated form after a semicolon.

> In *The House of the Spirits,* Isabel Allende describes Marcos, "dressed in mechanic's overalls, with huge racer's goggles" (13; ch. 1).

When you are quoting any sort of prose that takes more than four typed lines, indent each line of the quotation one inch (ten spaces) and double-space it; do not add quotation marks. In this case, you put the parenthetical citation (the pages and chapter numbers) outside the end punctuation mark of the quotation itself.

> Allende describes the flying machine that Marcos has assembled:
>
>> The contraption lay with its stomach on terra firma, heavy and sluggish and looking more like a wounded duck than like one of those newfangled airplanes they were starting to produce in the United States. There was nothing in its appearance to suggest that it could move, much less take flight across the snowy peaks. (12; ch. 1)

Quoting Verse

Do not use page numbers when referencing classic verse plays and poems. Instead, cite them by division (act, scene, canto, book, part) and line, using Arabic numerals for the various divisions unless your instructor prefers Roman numerals. Use periods to separate the various numbers.

> In the first act, Hamlet comments, "How weary, stale, flat and unprofitable, / Seem to me all the uses of this world" (1.2.133–34).

Note: A slash, with a space on each side, shows where each new line of verse begins. If you are citing lines only, use the word *line* or *lines* in your first reference and numbers only in additional references.

> At the beginning of the sestet in Robert Frost's "Design," the speaker asks this pointed question: "What had that flower to do with being white, / The wayside blue and innocent heal-all?" (lines 9–10).

Verse quotations of more than three lines should be indented one inch and double-spaced. Do not add quotation marks. Each line of the poem or play begins a new line of the quotation; do not run the lines together. If a line or lines of poetry are dropped from the quotation, ellipses that extend the width of the stanza should be used to indicate the omission.

> Bin Ramke's poem "A Little Ovid Late in the Day" tells of reading by the last light of a summer day:
>
> > [T]ales of incest, corruption,
> >
> > any big, mythic vice
> >
> > against the color of the sun,
> >
> > the sweetness of the time of day—
> >
> > I know the story,
> >
> > it is the light I care about. (3–8)

Listing an Internet Address

The current (seventh edition) MLA Handbook discourages use of Internet addresses, or URLs, as they can so easily change with time. Ideally, you should refer to an entire Web site by its title, or to a specific article on a site by its author; then, include full reference information in your works-cited list. A URL should be listed in your document or in your works-cited list only when the reader probably cannot locate the source without it, or if your instructor requires it. If that is the case, enclose the address in brackets:

> <www.cengage.com/us/>

Because most word processors will automatically convert the URL to a live hyperlink, you can either turn off the auto-formatting option on your computer or cancel the formatting as soon as it appears. If the instructor allows it, however, you may use live links in electronic versions of your text.

Quick Guide

MLA Works Cited

The works-cited section lists only the sources you have cited in your text. Begin your list on the page after the text and continue numbering each page. Format your works-cited pages using these guidelines and page 533.

1. **Type the page number in the upper-right corner,** one-half inch from the top of the page, with your last name before it.

2. **Center the title *Works Cited*** (not in italics, in quotation marks, or underlined) one inch from the top; then double-space before the first entry.

3. **Begin each entry flush with the left margin.** If the entry runs more than one line, indent additional lines one-half inch or use the hanging indent function on your computer.

4. **End each element of the entry with a period.** (Elements are separated by periods in most cases unless only a space is sufficient.) Use a single space after all punctuation.

5. **Double-space lines within each entry and between entries.**

6. **List each entry alphabetically by the author's last name.** If there is no author, use the first word of the title (disregard *A*, *An*, or *The* as the first word). If there are multiple authors, alphabetize them according to which author is listed first in the publication.

7. **The *MLA Handbook*, Seventh Edition, requires that each source be identified as print, Web, or other** (such as television or DVD). For print sources, this information is included after the publisher and date. For Web publications, include *Web.* after the date of publication or updating of the site, and before the date you accessed the site.

8. **A basic entry for a book would be as follows:**

   > Alt, Christina. *Virginia Woolf and the Study of Nature.* New York: Cambridge UP, 2010. Print.

9. **A basic entry for a journal or magazine would be as follows:**

   > Ferguson Smith, Martin. "Virginia Woolf's Second Visit to Greece." *English Studies* 92.1 (2011): 55-83. Print.

10. **A basic entry for an online source would be as follows.** Note that the URL is included only if the reader probably cannot locate the source without it, or when your instructor requires it. (See page 518.)

    > Clarke, S. N. "Virginia Woolf (1882-1941): A Short Biography." *Virginia Woolf Society of Great Britain.* N.p. 2000. Web. 12 March 2013.

Works-Cited Entries: Nonperiodical Print Publications

Components

The entries that follow illustrate the information needed to cite books, sections of a book, pamphlets, and government publications published in print format. The possible components of these entries are listed in order below:

1. Author's name
2. Title of a part of the book (an article in the book or a foreword)
3. Title of the book, italicized
4. Name of editor or translator
5. Edition
6. Number of volume
7. Name of series
8. Place of publication, publisher, year of publication
9. Page numbers, if citation is to only a part (For page spans, use a hyphen; if clarity is maintained, for pages above 100 you may also drop a digit from the second number—for example, 234-41, 234-332.)
10. Medium of publication (Print)

> **fyi** In general, if any of these components do not apply, they are not included in the works-cited entry. However, in the rare instance that a book does not state publication information, use the following abbreviations in place of information you cannot supply:
>
> **N.p.** No place of publication given
> **N.p.** No publisher given
> **N.d.** No date of publication given
> **N. pag.** No pagination given

Additional Guidelines

- List only the city for the place of publication if the city is in the United States. For cities outside the United States, add an abbreviation for the country if necessary for clarity. If several cities are listed, give only the first.
- Publishers' names should be shortened by omitting articles (*a, an, the*), business abbreviations (*Co., Inc.*), and descriptive words (*Books, Press*). For publishing houses that consist of the names of more than one person, cite only the first of the surnames. Abbreviate University Press as UP. Also use standard abbreviations whenever possible.

A Book by One Author

> Richardson, Catherine. *Shakespeare and Material Culture.* New York: Oxford UP, 2011.
> Print.

Two or More Books by the Same Author

List the books alphabetically according to title. After the first entry, substitute three hyphens for the author's name.

> Dershowitz, Alan M. *Rights from Wrongs.* New York: Basic, 2005. - - - . Print. *Supreme
> Injustice: How the High Court Hijacked Election 2000.* Oxford: Oxford UP, 2001.
> Print.

A Work by Two or Three Authors

> Naifeh, Steven, and Gregory White Smith. *Van Gogh: The Life.* New York: Random,
> 2011. Print.

Note: List authors in title-page order. Reverse only the first author's name.

A Work by Four or More Authors

> Schulte-Peevers, Andrea, et al. *Germany.* Victoria, Austral.: Lonely Planet, 2000. Print.

A Work Authored by an Agency, a Committee, or an Organization

> Exxon Mobil Corporation. *Great Plains 2000.* Lincolnwood: Publications Intl.,
> 2001. Print.

An Anonymous Book

> *Chase's Calendar of Events 2002.* Chicago: Contemporary, 2002. Print.

A Single Work from an Anthology

> Mitchell, Joseph. "The Bottom of the Harbor." *American Sea Writing.* Ed. Peter Neill.
> New York: Lib. of America, 2000. 584–608. Print.

A Complete Anthology

If you cite a complete anthology, begin the entry with the editor(s).

> Neill, Peter, ed. *American Sea Writing.* New York: Lib. of America, 2000. Print.

> Smith, Rochelle, and Sharon L. Jones, eds. *The Prentice Hall Anthology of African
> American Literature.* Upper Saddle River: Prentice, 2000. Print.

Two or More Works from an Anthology or a Collection

To avoid unnecessary repetition when citing two or more entries from a larger collection, you may cite the collection once with complete publication information (see Rothfield, below). The individual entries (see Becker and Cuno, below) can then be cross-referenced by listing the author, title of the piece, editor of the collection, and page numbers.

> Becker, Carol. "The Brooklyn Controversy: A View from the Bridge." Rothfield 15–21.
>
> Cuno, James. "Sensation and the Ethics of Funding Exhibitions." Rothfield 162–70.
>
> Rothfield, Lawrence, ed. *Unsettling Sensation: Arts-Policy Lessons from the Brooklyn Museum of Art Controversy. Rutgers Ser. on the Public Life of the Arts.* New Brunswick: Rutgers UP, 2001. Print.

One Volume of a Multivolume Work

> Cooke, Jacob Ernest, and Milton M. Klein, eds. *North America in Colonial Times.* Vol. 2. New York: Scribner's, 1998. Print.

Note: If you cite two or more volumes in a multivolume work, give the total number of volumes after each title. Offer specific references to volume and page numbers in the parenthetical reference in your text, like this: (3: 112–114).

> Salzman, Jack, David Lionel Smith, and Cornel West, eds. *Encyclopedia of African-American Culture and History.* 5 vols. New York: Simon, 1996. Print.

An Introduction, a Preface, a Foreword, or an Afterword

To cite the introduction, preface, foreword, or afterword of a book, list the author of the part first. Then identify the part by type, with no quotation marks or italics, followed by the book title. Next, identify the author of the work, using the word *by.* (If the book's author and the part's author are the same person, give just the last name after *by.*) For a book that gives cover credit to an editor instead of an author, identify the editor as usual. List any page numbers for the part cited.

> Barry, Anne. Afterword. *Making Room for Students.* By Celia Oyler. New York: Teachers College, 1996. 139–40. Print.
>
> Proulx, Annie. Introduction. *Dance of the Happy Shades.* By Alice Munro. Toronto: Penguin Canada, 2005. Print.
>
> Atwood, Margaret. Introduction. *Alice Munro's Best: Selected Stories.* By Alice Monro. Toronto: McClelland, 2006. vii-xviii. Print.

A Republished Book (Reprint)

Give the original publication date after the title.

> Atwood, Margaret. *Surfacing*. 1972. New York: Doubleday, 1998. Print.

Note: After the original publication facts, cite new material added: Introd. C. Becker.

A Book with Multiple Publishers

When a book lists more than one publisher (not just different offices of the same publisher), include all of them in the order given on the book's title page, separated by a semicolon.

> Wells, H. G. *The Complete Short Stories of H. G. Wells*. New York: St. Martin's; London: A. & C. Black, 1987. Print.

Second and Subsequent Editions

An edition refers to the particular publication you are citing, as in the third (3rd) edition.

> Joss, Molly W. *Looking Good in Presentations*. 3rd ed. Scottsdale: Coriolis, 1999. Print.

An Edition with Author and Editor

The abbreviation *ed.* also refers to the work of one or more persons that is prepared by another person, an editor.

> Shakespeare, William. *A Midsummer Night's Dream*. Ed. Jane Bachman. Lincolnwood: NTC, 1994. Print.

A Translation

> Lebert, Stephan, and Norbert Lebert. *My Father's Keeper*. Trans. Julian Evans. Boston: Little, 2001. Print.

An Article in a Familiar Reference Book

It is not necessary to give full publication information for familiar reference works (encyclopedias and dictionaries). For these titles, list only the edition (if available), the publication year, and the medium of publication you used. If an article is initialed, check the index of authors (in the opening section of each volume) for the author's full name.

> "Technical Education." *Encyclopedia Americana*. 2001 ed. Print.

> Lum, P. Andrea. "Computed Tomography." *World Book*. 2000 ed. Print.

When citing a single definition of several listed, add the abbreviation *Def.* and the particular number or letter for that definition.

> "Macaroni." Def. 2b. *The American Heritage College Dictionary*. 4th ed. 2002. Print.

An Article in an Unfamiliar Reference Book

For citations of lesser-known reference works, give full publication information, as for any other sort of book.

> "S Corporation." *The Portable MBA Desk Reference.* Ed. Paul A. Argenti. New York: Wiley, 1994. Print.

A Government Publication

State the name of the government (country, state, and so on) followed by the name of the agency. Most U.S. federal publications are published by the Government Printing Office (GPO).

> United States. Dept. of Labor. Bureau of Labor Statistics. *Occupational Outlook Handbook 2006-2007.* Indianapolis: Jist Works, 2006. Print.

When citing the *Congressional Record,* the date, page numbers, and medium you used are all that is required for that source.

> *Cong. Rec.* 5 Feb. 2002: S311–15. Print.

A Book in a Series

Give the series name and number (if any), neither italicized nor in quotation marks, followed by a period, at the end of the listing, after the medium of publication.

> Cudworth, Erika. *Environment and Society.* London; New York: Routledge, 2003. Print. Routledge Introductions to Environment Ser.

A Book with a Title Within Its Title

If the title contains a title normally in quotation marks, keep the quotation marks and italicize the entire title.

> Stuckey-French, Elizabeth. *"The First Paper Girl in Red Oak, Iowa" and Other Stories.* New York: Doubleday, 2000. Print.

Note: If the title contains a title that is normally italicized, do not italicize that title in your entry:

> Beckwith, Charles E. *Twentieth Century Interpretations of* A Tale of Two Cities: *A Collection of Critical Essays.* Upper Saddle River: Prentice, 1972. Print.

A Sacred Text

The Bible and other such sacred texts are treated as anonymous books. Documentation should read exactly as it is printed on the title page.

> *The Jerusalem Bible.* Garden City: Doubleday, 1966. Print.

The Published Proceedings of a Conference

The published proceedings of a conference should be treated as a book. However, if the title of the publication does not identify the conference by title, date, and location, add the appropriate information immediately after the title.

> Hildy, Franklin J., ed. *New Issues in the Reconstruction of Shakespeare's Theatre: Proceedings of the Conference Held at the University of Georgia, February 16–18, 1990.* New York: Peter Lang, 1990. Print.

To cite a particular presentation from the published proceedings of a conference, treat it as a work in an anthology.

> Beckerman, Bernard. "The Uses and Management of the Elizabethan Stage." *The Third Globe: Symposium for the Reconstruction of the Globe Playhouse, Wayne State University, 1979.* Ed. C. Walter Hodges, S. Schoenbaum, and Leonard Leone. Detroit: Wayne State UP, 1981. 151-63. Print.

A Published Dissertation

An entry for a published dissertation contains the same information as a book entry, with a few added details. Add the abbreviation *Diss.* and the degree-granting institution before the publication facts and medium.

> Jansen, James Richard. *Images of Dostoevsky in German Literary Expressionism.* Diss. U of Utah, 2003. Ann Arbor: UMI, 2003. Print.

An Unpublished Dissertation

The entry for an unpublished dissertation lists author, title in quotation marks, degree-granting institution, year of acceptance, and medium. (For a master's thesis, use MA thesis or MS thesis rather than Diss.)

> Vaidhyanathan, Siva. "Unoriginal Sins: Copyright and American Culture." Diss. U Texas, 1999. Print.

A Pamphlet, Manual, or Other Workplace Document

Treat any such publication as you would a book.

> Grayson, George W. *The North American Free Trade Agreement.* New York: Foreign Policy Assn., 1993. Print.

If publication information is missing, list the country of publication in brackets if known. Use n.p. (no place) if the country or the publisher is unknown and n.d. if the date is unknown, just as you would for a book.

> *Pedestrian Safety.* [United States]: n.p., n.d. Print.

Works-Cited Entries: Print Periodical Articles

Possible Components, in Order

1. Author's name, last name first
2. Title of article, in quotation marks and headline style capitalization
3. Name of periodical, italicized
4. Series number or name, if relevant (not preceded by period or comma)
5. Volume number (for a scholarly journal)
6. Issue number, separated from volume with a period but no space
7. Date of publication (abbreviate all months but May, June, July)
8. Page numbers, preceded by a colon, without "p." or "pp." (For articles continued nonconsecutively, add a plus sign after the first page number.)
9. Medium of publication (Print)
10. Supplementary information as needed

Note: Any components that do not apply are not listed.

An Article in a Weekly or Biweekly Magazine

List the author (if identified), article title (in quotation marks), publication title (italicized), full date of publication, and page numbers for the article. Do not include volume and issue numbers.

> Dickinson, Tim. "The NRA vs. America." *Rolling Stone* 2 Feb. 2013: 43-48. Print.

An Article in a Monthly or Bimonthly Magazine

For a monthly or bimonthly magazine, list the author (if identified), article title (in quotation marks), and publication title (italicized). Then identify the month(s) and year of the issue, followed by page numbers for the article. Do not give volume and issue numbers.

> Slater, Dan. "A Million First Dates: How Online Dating Is Threatening Monogamy."
> *Atlantic Monthly* Apr. 2013: 40-46. Print.

An Article in a Scholarly Journal Paginated by Issue

List the volume number immediately after the journal title, followed by a period and the issue number, and then the year of publication (in parentheses). End with the page numbers of the article followed by the medium of publication (Print.).

> Go, Kenji. "Montaigne's 'Cannibals' and *The Tempest* Revisited." *Studies in Philology*
> 109.4 (2012): 455-73. Print.

An Article in a Scholarly Journal with Continuous Pagination

An article in a scholarly journal with continuous pagination uses the same citation format, with volume, issue, month or season, and inclusive page numbers.

> Frosch, Thomas R. "The Missing Child in *A Midsummer Night's Dream*." *American Imago* 64.2 (2007): 485–511. Print.

An Unsigned Article in a Periodical

If no author is identified for an article, list the entry alphabetically by title among your works cited (ignoring any initial *A*, *An*, or *The*).

> "Feeding the Hungry." *Economist*. 371.8374 (2004): 74. Print.

A Printed Interview

Begin with the name of the person interviewed if that's who you are quoting.

> Robinson, Marilynne. "Marilynne Robinson: The Art of Fiction No. 198." By Sarah Fay. *Paris Review* 186 (2008): 37-66. Print.

Note: If the interview is untitled, the word *Interview* (no italics) and a period follow the interviewee's name.

A Newspaper Article

> Segal, Jeff, and Lauren Silva. "Case of Art Imitating Life?" *Wall Street Journal* 3 Mar. 2008, Eastern ed.: C9. Print.

Note: Cite the edition of a major daily newspaper (if given) after the date (1 May 1995, Midwest ed.: 1). If a local paper's name does not include the city of publication, add it in brackets (not italicized) after the name.

To cite an article in a lettered section of the newspaper, list the section and the page number. (For example, A4 would refer to page 4 in section A of the newspaper.) If the sections are numbered, however, use a comma after the year (or the edition); then indicate the section and follow it with a colon, the page number (sec. 1: 20), and the medium of publication you used.

An Unsigned Newspaper Article

An unsigned newspaper article follows the same format as citing a regular newspaper article:

> "Bombs—Real and Threatened—Keep Northern Ireland Edgy." *Chicago Tribune* 6 Dec. 2001, sec. 1: 20. Print.

A Newspaper Editorial or Letter to the Editor

If an article is an unsigned editorial, put *Editorial* (no italics) and a period after the title.

> "Hospital Power." Editorial. *Bangor Daily News* 14 Sept. 2004: A6. Print.

To identify a letter to the editor, put *Letter* (no italics) and a period after the author's name.

> Sory, Forrest. Letter. *Milwaukee Journal Sentinel* July 2001: 10. Print.

A Review

Begin with the author (if identified) and title of the review. Use the notation *Rev. of* between the title of the review and that of the original work. Identify the author of the original work with the word *by*. Then follow with publication data for the review.

> Buskey, Megan. "A Wealth of Insight." Rev. of *When I Was a Child I Read Books,* by Marilynne Robinson. *Wilson Quarterly* 36.2 (2012): 98-99. Print.

Note: If you cite the review of a work by an editor, translator, or director, use *ed., trans.,* or *dir.,* instead of *by.*

An Abstract

An abstract is a summary of a work. To cite an abstract, first give the publication information for the original work (if any); then list the publication information for the abstract itself. Add the term *Abstract* and a period between these if the journal title does not include that word. If the journal identifies abstracts by item number, include the word *item* followed by the number. (Add the section identifier [A, B, or C] for those volumes of *Dissertation Abstracts* [DA] and *Dissertation Abstracts International* [DAI] that have one.) If no item number exists, list the page number(s).

> Faber, A. J. "Examining Remarried Couples Through a Bowenian Family System Lens." *Journal of Divorce and Remarriage* 40.4 (2004): 121–33. *Social Work Abstracts* 40 (2004): item 1298. Print.

An Article with a Title or Quotation Within Its Title

When an article title contains within it a title of a longer work (e.g., a novel or a film), italicize that title. If the article title contains within it a quotation or the title of a shorter work (e.g., a poem or a short story), then place that quotation or title within single quotation marks.

> Petit, Susan. "Field of Deferred Dreams: Baseball and Historical Amnesia in Marilynne Robinson's *Gilead* and *Home*." *MELUS* 37.4 (2012): 119-37. Print.

> Melczarek, Nick. "Narrative Motivation in Faulkner's 'A Rose for Emily.'" *Explicator* 67.4 (2009): 237-43. Print.

An Article Reprinted in a Loose-Leaf Collection

The entry begins with original publication information, including the medium of publication, and ends with the name of the loose-leaf volume *(Youth)*, editor, volume number, publication information including name of the information service (SIRS), and the article number. In the example below, the plus sign indicates continuing but nonconsecutive pages.

> O'Connell, Loraine. "Busy Teens Feel the Beep." *Orlando Sentinel* 7 Jan. 1993: E1+. Print. *Youth.* Ed. Eleanor Goldstein. Vol. 4. Boca Raton: SIRS, 1993. Art. 41.

Works-Cited Entries: Online Sources

Components

Citations for online sources generally follow the strategies used for print sources, including the medium of publication (Web). After the author's name and title of the work (either italicized or in quotes, depending on the type of work), include the title of the overall Web site in italics, and additional information as described below. Because URLs can change, the URL should be provided only if the reader probably cannot locate the source without it, or if your instructor requires it.

1. Author's name
2. Title of the article or work, italicized or in quotation marks
3. Title of the overall Web site, italicized (if different from item 2)
4. Version or edition used
5. Publisher or sponsor of the site; if not available, use *N.p.*
6. Date of publication, with day, month, and year if available; if nothing is available, use *n.d.*
7. Medium of publication *(Web)*
8. Date of access (day, month, and year)

Including a URL for a Site

If you must include a URL to provide guidance to a site (or because your instructor requires URLs), give it after the date of access, a period, and a space. Enclose it in angle brackets and follow it with a period.

> "Fort Frederica." *National Parks Service.* U.S. Department of the Interior, n.d. Web. 27 Feb. 2013. <http://home.nps.gov/fofr/forteachers/curriculummaterials.htm>.

If the URL must be divided between two lines, break it only after a single or double slash. Do not add a hyphen. If possible, include the complete address, including *http://* for the work you are citing.

> MacLeod, Donald. "Shake-Up for Academic Publishing." *Guardian Unlimited.* Guardian News and Media Ltd., 10 Nov. 2008. Web. 6 Jan. 2013. <http://www.guardian.co.uk/Archive/>.

A Nonperiodical Publication

Most items online are not posted on a regular schedule; they are nonperiodical. Business pages, blog entries, PDF documents, online books, audio or video posts, and a host of other postings are nonperiodical publications. This includes most Web sites sponsored by magazines and newspapers. Such items can be identified following the guidelines on the previous page. (For additional guidelines regarding scholarly journals or periodical publications in an online database, see page 521.)

Items Existing Only Online

Many publications exist only in online form. Because such publications can move unexpectedly, it is important to include enough information for your reader to locate them again regardless of their new location.

- **A Typical Online Item**

  Booth, Philip. "Robert Frost's Prime Directive." *Poets.org.* Academy of American Poets, n.d. Web. 1 Oct. 2013.

- **An Online Item, No Author Identified**

  Begin with the title of the work, in quotation marks or italics, as appropriate. Alphabetize this entry by the first significant word of the title ("NetDay" in this case).

  "NetDay AmeriCorps Bridge Program 2001-2003." *NetDay.* Project Tomorrow, n.d. Web. 25 Nov. 2013.

- **A Home Page**

  If a nonperiodical publication has no title, identify it with a descriptor such as *Home page, Introduction,* or *Online posting* (using no italics or quotation marks). You may add the name of the publication's creator or editor after the overall site title, if appropriate.

  Wheaton, Wil. Home page. *Wil Wheaton dot Net.* N.p., 31 May 2006. Web. 19 Mar. 2013.

- **An Online Item with a Compiler, an Editor, or a Translator**

  When alphabetizing an entry by its compiler, editor, or translator, treat that person's name as usual, followed by an abbreviation for her or his role. If an author is identified, however, the compiler, editor, or translator follows the item title, with the abbreviation for the role preceding the compiler, editor, or translator's name.

  Webster, Michael, comp. "Books and Articles Cited in 'Notes on the Writings of E. E. Cummings.'" *Spring.* E. E. Cummings Society, n.d. 4 Oct. 2013.

  Lao-tzu. *Tao Te Ching.* Trans. J. Legge. *Internet Sacred Text Archive.* John Bruno Hare, n.d. Web. 14 Apr. 2013.

An Entry in an Online Reference Work

Unless the author of the entry is identified, begin with the entry name in quotation marks. Follow with the usual online publication information.

> "Eakins, Thomas." *Britannica Online Encyclopedia.* Encyclopedia Britannica, 2008. Web. 26 Sept. 2013.

An Online Poem

List the poet's name, the title of the poem, and any print publication information before the electronic publication details.

> Nemerov, Howard. "Found Poem." *War Stories.* Chicago: U of Chicago P, 1987. *Poets.org.* Web. 5 Oct. 2013.

An Online Transcript of a Broadcast

Give the original publication information for the broadcast. Following the medium of publication, add *Transcript,* followed by a period.

> Lehrer, Jim. "Character Above All." *Online NewsHour.* Natl. Public Radio, 29 May 1996. PBS.org. Web. Transcript. 23 Apr. 2013.

An Online Government Publication

As with a governmental publication in print, begin with the name of the government (country, state, and so on) followed by the name of the agency. After the publication title, add the electronic publication information.

> United States. Dept. of Labor. Office of Disability Employment Policy. *Emergency Preparedness for People with Disabilities.* Disability Employment Agency. Apr. 2004. Web. 12 Sept. 2013.

Items Including Print Publication Information

In general, follow the format for printed books. Include publication information for the original print version if available. Follow the date of publication with the electronic information, including the title of the site or database, sponsor, date of electronic posting (or *n.d.* if not available), medium of publication *(Web.)*, and your date of access.

> Simon, Julian L. *The Ultimate Resource II: People, Materials, and Environment.* College Park: U of Maryland, 1996. *U of Maryland Libraries.* Web. 9 Apr. 2013.

When citing part of an online book (such as the foreword) follow the example on page 511, but end with the online source, the term *Web,* and the date of access.

> Taylor, Bayard. Preface. *Faust.* Trans. Bayard Taylor. Boston: Houghton, 1883. iii-xvii. *Google Book Search.* Web. 7 March 2013.

Items Including Nonprint Publication Information

For online postings of photographs, videos, sound recordings, works of art, and so on, follow the examples on pages 522–524. In place of the original medium of publication, however, include the title of the database or Web site (italicized), followed by the medium *(Web.)* and the date of access, as for other online entries.

- **An Artwork**

  Goya, Francisco de. *Saturn Devouring His Children.* 1819-1823. Museo Nacional del Prado, Madrid. *Museodelprado.es.* Web. 13 Dec. 2013.

- **A Photograph**

  Brumfield, William Craft. *Church of Saint Nicholas Mokryi.* 1996. Prints and Photographs Div., Lib. of Cong. *Brumfield Photograph Collection.* Web. 9 May 2013.

- **An Audio Recording**

  "Gildy Arrives in Summerfield." *The Great Gildersleeve.* NBC. 31 Aug. 1941. *EThomsen.com.* Web. 13 Apr. 2013.

- **A Video**

  Sita Sings the Blues. Prod. Nina Paley. 2008. *Internet Archive.* Web. 5 June 2013.

- **An Unpublished Manuscript**

  "The Work-for-All Plan." 1933. Mildred Hicks Papers. Manuscript, Archives, and Rare Book Lib., Emory U. *Online Manuscript Resources in Southern Women's History.* Web. 31 Jan. 2013.

Journal Published Only Online

Some journals are published only on the Web, with no print version. For such publications, follow the basic guidelines given for print periodicals, though conclude with *Web* instead of *Print*, followed by your date of access. Also, if no page numbers are given, or if each item in the journal is numbered separately, replace the normal page notation with *n. pag.*

Marsden, Steve. "Texts and Transformission: Teaching American Literature with Juxta." *Teaching American Literature: A Journal of Theory and Practice.* 2011. Web. 30 Sept. 2013.

A Periodical Publication in an Online Database

Articles from different sources may be incorporated into an online database. To cite an article from a database, begin your citation with the usual information for citing print periodicals, but drop the medium of original publication *(Print)*. Instead, include the title of the database (italicized), the medium of publication *(Web)*, and the date of access.

Klaver, Elizabeth. "Hobo Time and Marilynne Robinson's *Housekeeping.*" *Journal of the Midwest Modern Language Association* 43.1 (2010): 27-43. *Humanities International Complete.* Web. 30 Nov. 2013.

Works-Cited Entries: Other Sources (Primary, Personal, and Multimedia)

The following examples of works-cited entries illustrate how to cite sources such as television or radio programs, films, live performances, works of art, and other miscellaneous nonprint sources.

A Periodically Published Database on CD-ROM or DVD-ROM

Citations for materials published on CD-ROM or DVD-ROM are similar to those for print sources, with these added considerations: (1) The contents of a work may vary from one medium to another; therefore, the citation should always identify the medium. (2) The publisher and vendor of the publication may be different, in which case both must be identified. (3) Because of periodic updates, multiple versions of the same database may exist, which calls for citation if possible of both the date of the document cited and the date of the database itself.

> Ackley, Patricia. "Jobs of the Twenty-First Century." *New Rochelle Informer* 15 Apr. 1994: A4. CD-ROM. *New Rochelle Informer Ondisc.* Oct. 1994.

> Baker, Anthony. *The New Earth Science.* Cincinnati: Freeman's P, 1991. DVD-ROM. *New Media Inc.,* 2004.

Reference Work on CD-ROM

If you use an encyclopedia or other reference book recorded on CD-ROM, use the form below. If available, include publication information for the printed source.

> *The American Heritage Dictionary of the English Language.* 3rd ed. Boston: Houghton, 1992. CD-ROM. Cambridge, MA: Softkey Intl., 1994.

A Television or Radio Program

Include the medium (*Television* or *Radio*) at the end of the citation, followed by a period.

> "Florence and the Machine; Lykke Li." *Austin City Limits.* PBS. KDIN, Iowa, 24 April 2013. Television.

A Film

The director, distributor, and year of release follow the title. Other information may be included if pertinent. End with the medium, in this case *Film*, followed by a period.

> *Lincoln.* Dir. Steven Spielberg. Perf. Daniel Day-Lewis, Sally Field. DreamWorks, 2012. Film.

A Video Recording or an Audio Recording

Cite a filmstrip, slide program, videocassette, or DVD as you do a film; include the medium of publication last, followed by a period.

> *Monet: Shadow & Light.* Devine Productions, 1999. Videocassette.

If you are citing a specific song on a musical recording, place its title in quotation marks before the title of the recording.

> Bernstein, Leonard. "Maria." *West Side Story.* Columbia, 1995. CD.

A Performance

Treat this similarly to a film, adding the location and date of the performance.

> *Clybourne Park.* McGuire Proscenium, Guthrie Theater, Minneapolis. 4 Aug. 2013. Performance.

An Artwork on Display

> Titian. *The Entombment.* N.d. Painting. Louvre, Paris.

A Letter, Memo, or Email Received by the Author (You)

For an unpublished letter or memo, include the form of the material after the date: *TS* for a typescript or printout, and *MS* for a work written by hand.

> Thomas, Bob. "Re: Research Plan." Message to author. 10 Jan. 2013. Email.

An Interview by the Author (You)

> Brooks, Sarah. Personal interview. 15 Oct. 2013.

A Cartoon or Comic Strip (in Print)

> Chast, Roz. "Ed Revere, Spam Courier." Cartoon. *The New Yorker* 22 Apr. 2013: 67. Print.

An Advertisement (in Print)

List the subject of the advertisement (product, company, organization, or such), followed by *Advertisement* and a period. Then give the usual publication information.

> Lockheed Martin. Advertisement. *The Atlantic Monthly* Apr. 2013: 14. Print.

A Lecture, a Speech, an Address, or a Reading

Provide the speaker's name, the title of the presentation (if known) in quotation marks, the meeting and the sponsoring organization, the location, and the date. End with an appropriate descriptive label such as *Address, Lecture,* or *Reading.*

> Gopnik, Adam. "Radical Winter." CBC Massey Lectures. Dalhousie Arts Centre, Halifax, Nova Scotia. 12 Oct. 2011. Lecture.

A Legal or Historical Document

If your paper requires a number of legal citations, the MLA advises consulting the most recent edition of *The Bluebook: A Uniform System of Citation* (Cambridge: Harvard Law Rev. Assn.: Print). If you are providing only a few such citations, the MLA provides that the titles of laws, acts, and similar documents should appear in regular type (not italicized or enclosed in quotation marks), both within the text and in the list of works cited. The titles are abbreviated, and works are cited by sections, with years included if relevant. End your citation with the medium of publication followed by a period.

> 7 USC. Sec. 308a. 1928. Print.

> Do-Not-Call Implementation Act. Pub. L. 108-10. Stat. 117-557. 11 Mar. 2003. Print.

Abbreviate the names of law cases (spelling out the first important word of each party's name). Do not italicize the name in your works-cited list (although it should be italicized within the body of your paper). Follow with the case number or volume, inclusive page or reference numbers, the name of the court, the date (or year) of the decision, the medium consulted, and the date of access for a Web site.

> Missouri v. Seibert. 02-1371. Supreme Court of the U.S. 28 June 2004. FindLaw.com. Web. 4 June 2013.

A Map or Chart

Follow the format for an anonymous book, adding *Map* or *Chart* (without italics), followed by a period, the city and publisher, date, and the medium of publication.

> *Wisconsin Territory.* Map. Madison: Wisconsin Trails, 1988. Print.

Sample MLA Paper

Student writer Paige Louter wrote "Why the World Deserves Better than Fair Trade" as an argumentative research paper for her expository writing class. In her paper, she explores the limited success of the fair trade movement, documenting her research using MLA style. Strictly speaking, MLA format does not require or even recommend a title page or an outline. (For more on outlines, you can also see pages 48–53.) You can use Paige's paper in three ways:

1. To study how a well-written, major research paper develops careful thinking, builds a discussion, and orders supporting points and evidence.
2. To examine how source summaries, paraphrases, and quotations are carefully integrated into the writer's discussion to advance her thinking— a full-length example of the strategies addressed on pages 476–479.
3. To see in detail the format and documentation practices of MLA style, practices that allow the writer to share a professional-looking paper that fairly respects sources used.

Sample Paper: Format, In-Text Citation, and Works-Cited List

Note that MLA format requires that the paper be double-spaced throughout.

The writer's last name and page number are placed in the upper right corner of every page.

No separate title page is required. The heading identifies the writer, the professor, the course, and the date—in the order and format shown, flush left.

The title, indicating the paper's topic and theme, is centered, in regular typeface and type size—no special effects such as boldface.

From the start, in-text citations indicate borrowed material: summaries, paraphrases, and quotations.

Louter 1

Paige Louter

Dr. Van Rys

English 302

15 February 2012

Why the World Deserves Better than Fair Trade

The 2004 book *Fair Trade: Market-Driven Ethical Consumption* opens with the following account of what fair trade can do for the "world's poor": "I used to live in a thatch hut with a mud floor," says fair trade farmer Jeronimo Tush. "Now I have two concrete houses. And . . . my children now only go to school. We don't need them to work" (qtd. in Nicholls and Opal 3). Why would anyone argue against a system of trade that provides improved housing and eliminates the need for child labor? Fair trade is admirable in its effort to address injustice, to promote human rights all over the world, to fight poverty, and to promote ethical food-production and consumption practices. However, there is a darker side to the fair trade movement: this seemingly just-trade model is in reality falling short of its idealistic claims, and is in fact creating new problems. Though the fair trade movement is perhaps not beyond saving, it must undergo radical change to survive. Additionally, in order to demand change and perhaps even offer solutions themselves, consumers—especially those who wish to call themselves socially conscious—must educate themselves as to the harmful effects for which fair trade is responsible.

To begin with, the term "fair trade" itself is a source of confusion among many consumers. "Fair trade," not capitalized and written as two words, is the general term for the concept. However, "fairtrade" written as one word is the official name of products labeled by the Fairtrade Labelling Organizations International (FLO)—thereby making the products eligible for the Fairtrade International certification mark (see Figure 1). Here's where it gets more confusing: the American branch of fair trade product certification is called Fair Trade USA—two words, both capitalized (Figure 2 below). Anyone can claim that his or her product is fair trade, but without one of the logos below, a product cannot be Fairtrade (or Fair Trade); however,

1

2

Louter 2

companies themselves may not fully realize this. As Amarjit Sahota, the director of Organic Monitor puts it, "Companies do not always distinguish between Fairtrade and fair trade. Only the first concept is independently audited and internationally recognized . . . . Firms that use the latter term aren't necessarily trying to deceive consumers. It's simply hard to distinguish [between the two]" (qtd. in Hodge 17-18). This essay will consistently use the terms "fair trade" and "Fairtrade."

Fig. 1. This yin-yang-esque image is the official certification label of Fairtrade International (Hussey 16).

Fig. 2. Fair Trade USA's label suggests a racially-based dichotomy between producer and consumer (Hussey 16).

Considering this difference in terminology, then, what guidelines are necessary for a product to achieve Fairtrade status? "Fair trade" as a general term could potentially be applied to any product that appears to empower disadvantaged producers. "Fairtrade" as a label, however, indicates certain guarantees for those supplying the products. These guarantees are, according to the Fairtrade International Web site, "Stable prices . . . a Fairtrade Premium . . . partnership. [. . . and] empowerment of farmers and workers." ("What is [sic] Fairtrade?"). Further

unpacked, this means that Fairtrade producers have guaranteed minimum prices for their goods, an extra amount or Premium paid to the management of the producers, and a say in how their own goods are to be produced and sold. The Premium is a concept that consumers are often unfamiliar with, and in concept, it could indeed do much good for the communities of Fairtrade producers; the Premium is intended for investment in beneficial projects such as schools and healthcare facilities. None of these guarantees appear to be objectively wrong, and perhaps in a perfect world Fairtrade could operate under these principles in an entirely beneficial way. There is

a shocking gap, however, between Fairtrade ideals and reality—a concept that will be more fully addressed later in the essay.

Before criticizing the fair trade movement, one should pay attention to the

3

4

Louter acknowledges the benefits of fair trade before continuing her argument about its weaknesses.

benefits that the movement provides. Paul Chandler, the Chief Executive of Traidcraft (a fair trade organization in the UK), offers a succinct summary of the positive effects of purchasing fair trade products:

> Fair trade activity has a positive impact on the livelihoods and welfare of 5 those producers directly involved in fair trade supply chains . . . . Second, fair trade gives consumers an opportunity to exercise a moral choice in their own purchasing practices . . . . Third, fair trade offers an effective critique of business practices, showing there are practical alternative ways of trading that can be more beneficial for the poor. (Chandler 256)

A quotation longer than four typed lines is inset—indented 10 spaces (about 1 inch) and double-spaced throughout; ellipses indicate material left out of the quotation; end punctuation is placed before the parenthetical citation.

Chandler is obviously not bias-free in his analysis of the fair trade industry, yet 6 his points have merit. There are indeed many success stories generated by fair trade practices: families lifted out of poverty, farmers supported when they would have otherwise faced ruin, children freed from daily labor and allowed to go to school. In addition, fair trade does provide consumers with at least the awareness that their dollars can make a difference when it comes to social justice. Finally, the fair trade movement does deserve credit for demonstrating that the current global system of trade, which does not always have the concerns of the poor at heart, is not the only option.

The writer transitions to arguments critiquing fair trade; she quotes from and debates a source.

After taking all these benefits into account, it seems that ethically-minded 7 consumers should choose fair trade products whenever possible. These pros, however, are only a small piece of the bigger picture. In fact, each of Chandler's claims is only partially true: each declaration needs to be modified and qualified before it can accurately speak to the reality of fair trade. First, not every producer "directly involved in fair trade supply chains" benefits from the guaranteed minimum price that is a key tenant of Fairtrade products (Chandler 256). Next, as Philip Booth and Linda Whetstone argue, "those promoting fair trade should have the humility to accept that their way of doing business is not objectively better for the poor than other ways of doing business" (29). In other words, fair trade is not necessary for consumers to "exercise a moral choice" with their money (Chandler 256). Chandler's final claim is that fair trade shows that alternative ways of trading, ones that better address the needs of the poor around the world, can and do exist. Yet while most consumers would immediately agree that poverty must be addressed head-on, Chandler offers no objective reasons as to why fair trade practice is the best

One-inch margins are used left and right, top and bottom, with the exception of the header, which is one-half inch from the top.

Louter 4

avenue through which to do this. Still, the fair trade movement has demonstrated that many consumers are willing to spend more in response to the promise that their dollars are helping those in need. In addition, perhaps future ethical consumption initiatives will gain more immediate legitimacy as a result. Later in this essay, each of these responses to Chandler's claims will be unpacked in further detail, and with more support. This initial set of responses is valuable, however, because it demonstrates a key problem with the claims of many who support fair trade: the claims are often only partially true, based on feel-good rhetoric and fair trade ideals rather than on hard evidence. Further, evidence, when cited, is often very selective. Nevertheless, many fair trade proponents have legitimate, well-supported arguments that will be addressed later in this paper.

Considering that the livelihoods (and lives) of many are at stake in the failure of the fair trade movement, perhaps a less dramatic—yet serious—problem is that the quality of certified Fairtrade coffee is often significantly poorer than coffee that is not Fairtrade. However, this problem is significant when one considers that some consumers will forgo Fairtrade coffee based on its inferior taste. If the WFTO wishes to avoid charges of providing charity rather than actual trade opportunities to its producers, the organization must have some way of ensuring that its products are purchased for their quality as well as for the economic aid they offer farmers. One critic of the Fairtrade industry asserted that it is "stuck in a charity-driven, charity-supported model . . . that smacks of colonialism" (Hutchens 458). In order to address this issue, one must ask why Fairtrade coffee would taste consistently poorer than other coffee. The answer essentially comes down to a lack of quality control. There are, shockingly, no Fairtrade standards regarding the quality of the product. Because quality-control is lacking, and because there is a maximum amount of coffee beans that the Fairtrade buyers will accept from any one cooperative, the farmers can sell only part of their produce at the Fairtrade price, and they sell the remainder on the open market. In other words, because the Fairtrade market does not monitor the quality of the beans that they receive, farmers consistently sell their higher quality beans on the open market. In addition, the coffee co-ops do not keep track of which beans come from which farmers. In fact, co-ops regularly mix all purchased beans together, thereby removing any incentive for farmers to sell only their best beans as fair trade produce. David Henderson calls this a "free-ride problem" (63). In contrast

Louter 5

to the "Organic Specialty" label which assures a consumer that a product is healthier, grown with less harmful chemicals and so on, the "Fairtrade" label offers no similar assurance of quality. Therefore, Fairtrade consumers are often purchasing products out of charity, a practice that is not a sustainable business model. Furthermore, when quality standards are not enforced, the implication is that the Fairtrade system believes that the producers are incapable of creating excellent product.

Unfortunately, Fairtrade has even bigger problems than quality control, one of which is its failure to promote women's rights, a principle ostensibly championed by the World Fair Trade Organization (WFTO). However, as Anna Hutchens puts it, there is an "absence of a policy framework and institutional mechanisms that promote women's empowerment as a rights-based rather than a culture-based issue" (449). In other words, the WFTO does not intentionally seek to universalize human rights when it comes to women. Consumers are told that women in the Fairtrade system are empowered and uplifted, but in practice, the WFTO does not seek to actively include them. The best that can be said is that they are not actively excluded. In order to achieve FLO certification, producer organizations are not required to meet any standards when it comes to working to empower women, and when it came to one coffee cooperative, "only seven of the 116 . . . members . . . were female and no women had served on the cooperative board or its managerial positions" (Hutchens 452). Sadly, this particular cooperative appears to be the rule rather than the exception. A further problem, stemming from the lack of universally applied empowerment of women, is that "women are not made exempt from their existing household duties" despite their increased workload of producing Fairtrade goods (452). And even those women who manage to find time to balance their domestic and fair trade producing roles may not benefit as they should: "Fairtrade payments typically go to the assumed male head of the household and cannot be assumed to 'trickle down' to benefit all the household members" (452).

Though gender-based disparity is bad enough, women are not the only ones who do not reap the full reward that the WFTO would like consumers to believe exists. Others denied these rewards are the farmers barred from entering the Fairtrade coffee business, as well as those workers who are employed under the Fairtrade label yet work in substandard conditions and receive substandard pay. Many agree that "there are . . . significant opportunities for corruption within the

9

10

Louter 6

fair trade co-operatives [sic]" (Booth and Whetstone 33). In other words, the idea that the payment for a cup of coffee purchased in Europe or North America goes directly to the hand of an impoverished coffee bean farmer is a myth.

Beyond all these problems, many economists such as those who work at the Adam Smith Institute say that fair trade simply does not make sense in terms of the market system by which it operates. These economic arguments are potentially devastating if it is found that fair trade ultimately increases, rather than alleviates, the economic hardships in which the producers work. Fair trade operates on the principle of guaranteeing a minimum price for a product, regardless of how low the real market value for that product drops. This minimum price is called a price floor, which, when set above the market price, creates a surplus, and which in turn creates a price drop in the market price. "If there were a free market," writes Jeremy Weber, "new entrants would increase supply and decrease price. The minimum price . . . by definition prevents that outcome" (113). The result? There is just too much Fairtrade coffee being produced. Farmers are often unable to sell more than a small percentage of their coffee beans to Fairtrade buyers, and new producers who wish to enter the Fairtrade business are finding it nearly impossible: "The increased difficulty of entering the Fair Trade market threatens to exclude the marginalized coffee growers who Fair Trade supposedly supports" (Weber 113). For example, starting in 2004, Fair Trade certification cost $3200. In fact, dual-certification of Fairtrade and Organic is often now required, and the latter costs anywhere between $300 and $2000. But the difficulty doesn't end there—renewal fees too can cost thousands of dollars. As a result, even if a coffee cooperative desiring the Fairtrade mark can raise the necessary money, the waiting list is seemingly endless: thousands of co-ops await certification, hoping to get a chance to sell their products at artificially high Fairtrade prices. Essentially, the economic principles on which Fairtrade operates are inevitably leading towards increased difficulties for any coffee farmer who did not achieve Fairtrade certification in the early days of the movement. "Fair trade may be fashionable and give people a nice warm feeling," say Paul Booth and Linda Whetstone, "but only free trade backed up by the rule of law and the protection of private property have actually lifted entire populations out of poverty for the long term" (35).

Perhaps of less concern to the world at large, but of more concern to the university and college community (and indeed most North American and European

11

12

After discussing economic theory and providing some statistics, the writer concludes her point with an authoritative and well phrased quotation.

In a series of paragraphs, the writer enumerates judgment traps created by fair trade, culminating in neo-colonialism.

The right margin is ragged, not justified.

Paragraphs are indented 5 spaces, inset quotations 10 spaces.

consumers), is the illusion evoked by purchasing fair trade products. First, the purchase can lull consumers into a false sense of accomplishment, leaving them less likely to investigate the idealistic claims of the movement or to seek out alternate forms of spending ethically. "The fair trade movement . . . suggests that the production and purchase of fair trade produce somehow lies on a higher moral plane than other business activity," say Booth and Whetstone (30). However, consumers do have other options such as simply purchasing cheaper coffee and donating the difference in price between the regular and the fair trade product to a charity. Booth and Whetstone continue: "the fair trade movement may have found a successful marketing device for increasing philanthropy but that does not make their products ethical" (31).

> **Strong topic sentences offer transitions between paragraphs and move the discussion forward.**

But Fairtrade customers are also subject to a second illusion: that their   13
purchases make them more ethical than other consumers who do not actively pursue Fairtrade purchases. There are countless alternatives to certified Fairtrade in terms of ethical consumption, many of which are more sustainable in the long term and not as rife with complications and downsides. Fairtrade purchases, though, tend to have a public component; people can see and hear other consumers requesting Fairtrade coffee or chocolate at cafés or grocery stores, and these same militantly moral consumers can publically call attention to those who do not make the same choice.

Finally, Fairtrade consumers can misjudge producers. Whereas Fairtrade has   14
been rightly criticized for inadvertently spreading a sort of neo-colonial attitude, consider, for instance, the problem of quality control that was explored earlier: that Fairtrade does not press producers to develop high quality products. "Companies such as Green & Black's," on the other hand, "say they aid farmers more by helping them to improve quality and go organic rather than just guaranteeing a price" (Beattie 34). The Fairtrade model ensures that producers will never be able to grow beyond the need for a fixed minimum, while alternate models seek to empower producers. It is not hard to see which paradigm is rife with paternalistic, colonialist implications. Getting consumers in the right frame of mind is not an irrelevant need. As Ian Hussey puts it, "decolonization is not just a material process, but also a mental one" (17). Fair trade, he says, "serves to reinforce racist and colonial distinctions between the poor Global South farmer and the benevolent Global North

> **Throughout the paper, authors' names, titles of works, and page references create clear, accurate citations for borrowed material— summaries, paraphrases, and quotations.**

Louter 8

consumer" (15). In the long run, this mindset is destructive in that it denigrates Fairtrade producers as charity cases rather than potential partners.

It may at this point appear that fair trade and its proponents have not been given a fair voice. After all, as thinkers such as Andrew Walton have pointed out, fair trade needs to be understood as being an interim measure for seeking justice. The world is "non-ideal" and fair trade is only a second-best measure—not "global market justice" in and of itself (Walton 435). Indeed, critics of the movement do fair trade an injustice when they argue that it should be rejected simply because it is not a perfect and complete alternative to the current global economy. Ignoring for a moment all practical considerations, fair trade and movements such as the "Make Poverty History" campaign do the entire world a service in bringing issues of poverty and injustice to the forefront of the continuing global conversation. How consumers spend their money can make a serious difference. It is a shame that fair trade has not proven to be the solution that it originally aspired to be.

15

In this light, the future of fair trade, of ethical consuming at all, seems bleak. The claims of Fairtrade organizations do not match up with reality, and the best intentions of countless activists and socially concerned consumers appear to have ultimately done more damage than good. But it is not enough to tear down an existing structure such as fair trade. Alternatives or changes to fair trade must be sought; consumers and producers alike have a right and a responsibility to demand better. In the future, strong claims such as those of the fair trade movement must "be subject to strong tests" (Booth and Whetstone 29). Consumers must no longer praise a solution such as fair trade without being educated as to its implications and consequences. Luckily, the burden for change does not rest on the "Global North consumer" alone. By transcending the colonial mindset, North can work with South, and a united global force can share the challenges of addressing injustices from the personal to the economic. Fair trade may not have all the answers, but it has certainly taught us to ask the right questions.

16

> In her closing paragraphs, the writer consolidates her critique while offering some balance, and then points forward to possible solutions.

Louter 9

Works Cited

The paper's bibliography lists a range of scholarly books, scholarly articles, and Web sites on the topic.

Beattie, Alan. "The Price of Being Fair." *New Statesman* 136.4833 (2007): 34-35. *Literary Reference Center*. Web. 18 Jan. 2012.

Booth, Philip, and Linda Whetstone. "Half a Cheer for Fair Trade." *Economic Affairs* 27.2 (2007): 29-36. *Business Source Elite*. Web. 19 Jan. 2012.

Chandler, Paul. "Fair Trade and Global Justice." *Globalizations* 3.2 (2006): 255-57. *Academic Search Premier*. Web. 19 Jan. 2012.

Sources are listed in alphabetical order by author (or by title if no author is given).

Henderson, David R. "Fair Trade Is Counterproductive—And Unfair." *Economic Affairs* 28.3 (2008): 62-64. *Business Source Elite*. Web. 19 Jan. 2012.

Hodge, Neil. "Chocs Away." *Financial Management* (2010): 14-21. *Business Source Elite*. Web. 18 Jan. 2012.

The list is double-spaced throughout—both between and within entries.

Hussey, Ian. "Fair Trade and Empire: An Anti-Capitalist Critique of the Fair Trade Movement." *Briarpatch* 40.5 (2011): 15-18. *Canadian Reference Centre*. Web. 18 Jan. 2012.

Hutchens, Anna. "Empowering Women Through Fair Trade? Lessons from Asia." *Third World Quarterly* 31.3 (2010): 449-67. *Academic Search Premier*. Web. 18 Jan. 2012.

Second and subsequent lines of entries are indented one half inch (hanging indent).

Nichols, Alex, and Charlotte Opal. *Fair Trade: Market-Driven Ethical Consumption*. London: Sage, 2004. Print.

Walton, Andrew. "What Is Fair Trade?" *Third World Quarterly* 31.3 (2010): 431-47. *Academic Search Premier*. Web. 19 Jan. 2012.

Titles are properly italicized or placed in quotation marks.

"What is [sic] Fairtrade?" *Fairtrade International*. Fairtrade Labelling Organizations International, n.d. Web. 10 Feb. 2012.

Weber, Jeremy. "Fair Trade Coffee Enthusiasts Should Confront Reality." *CATO Journal* 27.1 (2007): 109-17. *Academic Search Premier*. Web. 19 Jan. 2012.

Correct abbreviations are used throughout.

Reading for Better Writing

Working by yourself or with a group, answer these questions:

1. How did Paige's paper impact your understanding of global justice?
2. By reviewing topic sentences and skimming the paper, outline Louter's argument. How would you characterize her logic? How does her reasoning unfold?
3. What types of evidence does Louter use? Where has she gotten her evidence? Are her sources reliable? Does she have a balanced range of sources?
4. How does Louter distinguish her own thinking from source material? Why are these strategies necessary?

Critical-Thinking and Writing Activities

As directed by your instructor, complete the following critical-thinking and writing activities by yourself or with classmates.

1. The MLA style involves many rules about format and documentation. To make some sense of these rules, answer this question by yourself or with classmates: What is the essential logic of the MLA system? In other words, what does the MLA hope to accomplish with these rules?

2. Create MLA works-cited entries for the following publications:
   - An article in the summer 2009 issue (volume 34, no. 2) of the periodical *MELUS*, by Joni Adamson and Scott Slovic: "The Shoulders We Stand On: An Introduction to Ethnicity and Ecocriticism" (pages 5-24)
   - Ernest Hemingway's novel *A Farewell to Arms*, published in 1986 by Collier Books, located in New York City
   - The Web page "Vaccines for Children Program (VCP)," part of the Vaccines and Immunizations section of the Centers for Disease Control and Prevention (CDC) Web site, sponsored by the U.S. government's Department of Health and Human Services. No author or publication date is listed. The site was last accessed April 26, 2013, at http://www.cdc.gov/vaccines/programs/vfc/index.html.

Learning-Objectives Checklist ✓

Have you achieved this chapter's learning objectives? Check your progress with the items below, revisiting topics in the chapter as needed. *I have . . .*

____ gained an overview of the MLA system of documentation—the basic logic of in-text citations in relation to works-cited entries (494–495).

____ correctly implemented MLA format guidelines for whole-paper issues (e.g., header, heading on the first page, pagination), typography, and page layout (496–499).

____ applied rules of in-text citation, whether for regular sources or for sources without traditional authorship and/or pagination (500–507).

____ developed a works-cited list that is properly formatted and that correctly and fully identifies sources, whether books or journal articles or online documents (508–524).

____ examined MLA style at work in Paige Louter's "Why the World Deserves Better Than Fair Trade," learning how the system is practiced concretely in a research-based argumentative essay (524–533).

Chapter 29

APA Style

Those who write papers in the social sciences—psychology, sociology, political science, and education, for example— usually follow the research-writing guidelines of the American Psychological Association (APA). This chapter summarizes these guidelines and helps you use APA format and documentation.

APA format is similar to MLA format in two ways: Both require (1) parenthetical citations within the text and (2) a final listing of all references cited in the paper. But in the social sciences, the date of publication is often much more crucial than it is in the humanities, so the date is highlighted in in-text citations. APA format also requires a cover page and an abstract.

Visually Speaking Figure 29.1 suggests something about humans and their societies. Consider the possibilities, and explore what social-science research and research writing in particular seek to contribute to an understanding of people and the societies they build.

Learning **Objectives**

By working through this chapter, you will be able to

- explain and implement APA guidelines for documenting sources.
- produce research writing that adheres to APA guidelines for format.
- identify and critique APA practices at work in a sample student research report.

Scott Norsworthy / Shutterstock.com

fig. 29.1

APA Documentation Guidelines

The APA system involves two parts: (1) an in-text citation within your paper when you use a source and (2) a matching bibliographic entry at the end of your paper. Note these features of the APA author-date system:

- **It uses signal phrases and parenthetical references** to set off source material from your own thinking and discussion. A signal phrase names the author and places the material in context (e.g., "As Jung described it, the collective unconscious. . .").
- **It's date-sensitive.** Because the publication dates of resources are especially important in social science research, the publication year is included in the parenthetical reference and after the authors' names in the reference entry.
- **It's smooth, unobtrusive, and orderly.** APA in-text citations identify borrowed material while keeping the paper readable. Moreover, alphabetized reference entries at the end of the paper make locating source details easy.

You can see these features at work in the example below. The parenthetical material "Pascopella, 2011, p. 32" tells the reader these things:

- The borrowed material came from a source authored by Pascopella.
- The source was published in 2011.
- The specific material can be found on page 32 of the source.
- Full source details are in the reference list under the surname Pascopella.

1. In-Text Citation in Body of Paper

> In newcomer programs, "separate, relatively self-contained educational interventions" (Pascopella, 2011, p. 32) are implemented to meet the academic and transitional needs of recent immigrants before they enter a mainstream English Language Development.

2. Matching Reference Entry at End of Paper

> Pascopella, A. (2011). Successful strategies for English language learners. *District Administration, 47*(2), 29-44.

In-Text Citation: The Basics

See pages 539–542 for complete details on in-text citation.

1. Refer to the author(s) and date of publication by using one of these methods:

Last name(s), publication date in parentheses:

> ELLs normally spend just three years in 30-minute "pull-out" English language development programs (Calderón et al., 2011).

Last name(s) cited in text with publication date in parentheses:

> In "Key Issues for Teaching English Learners in Academic Classrooms," Carrier (2005) explained that it takes an average of one to three years to reach conversational proficiency in a second language, but five to seven years to reach academic proficiency.

2. Present and punctuate citations according to these rules:

- Keep authors and publication dates as close together as possible in the sentence.
- Separate the author's last name, the date, and any locating detail with commas.
- If referencing part of a source, use an appropriate abbreviation: *p.* (page), *para.* (paragraph)—but do not abbreviate *chapter*.

Note: When citing previous research, use past tense or present perfect tense—Smith(2003) found *or* Smith(2003) has found.

References: The Basics

Complete coverage of reference issues is offered on pages 543–553, and a sample references list is shown on page 563. Here, however, are templates for the most common entries:

Template for Book:

> Author's Last Name, Initials. (Publication Year). *Title of book*. Publication City, State or Country: Publisher. [Other publication details are integrated as needed.]

┌─ author's name,   ┌─ publication year in parentheses,   ┌─ exact and full title in italics, first word and
followed by period   followed by period   proper nouns capitalized, followed by period

Pandya, J. Z. (2011). *Overtested: How high-stakes accountability fails English Language Learners*. New York, NY: Teachers College Press.

publication location from ─┘   └─ publisher name from title page,
title page, followed by colon   followed by period

fig. 29.2

Template for Periodical Article:

> Author's Last Name, Initials. (Publication Year). Title of article. *Journal Title, volume*(issue), page numbers. [Other publication details are integrated as needed. For online periodical articles, add the digital object identifier (see page 549).]

┌─ author's name,   ┌─ article title, no quotation marks, first
followed by period   word and proper nouns capitalized

Slama, R. B. (2012). A longitudinal analysis of academic English proficiency outcomes for adolescent English Language Learners in the United States. *Journal of Educational Psychology, 104*(2), 265-285. doi: 10.1037/a0025861

page numbers followed ─┘   journal title and volume ─┘
by period   number italicized

fig. 29.3

Template for Online Document:

> Author's Last Name, Initials. (Publication Date). *Title of work* OR Title of entry. DOI (digital object identifier) OR Retrieval statement including URL

┌─ author's name,   ┌─ publication date in parentheses,   ┌─ document
followed by period   followed by period   title

U.S. Department of Education. (2013, January). *Projection of education statistics to 2021.* Retrieved from http://nces.ed.gov/programs/projections/projections2021/

└─ retrieval statement

fig. 29.4

APA Format Guidelines

To submit a polished academic paper in APA format, follow the rules below and refer to the sample APA paper on pages 554–563.

- **Title Page:** On the first page, include your paper's title, your name, and your institution's name on three separate lines, double-spaced, centered, and positioned in the top half of the page. Flush left at the top, type *Running head:* (no italics) followed by your abbreviated title in all uppercase letters; and flush right at the top, type the page number 1.

- **Abstract:** On the second page, include an abstract—a 150- to 250-word paragraph summarizing your paper. Place the title *Abstract* (no italics) approximately one inch from the top of the page and center it. Place the running head and page number 2 at the top of the page.

- **Body:** Format the body (which begins on the third page) as follows:

- **Margins:** Leave a one-inch margin on all four sides of each page (one and one-half inches on the left if the paper will be bound). Do not justify lines, but rather leave a ragged right margin and do not break words at the ends of lines.

- **Line Spacing:** Double-space your entire paper, unless your instructor allows single spacing for tables and figures.

- **Page Numbers:** Place your running head and the page number flush left and flush right respectively, at the top of each page, beginning with the title page.

- **Headings:** Like an outline, headings show the organization of your paper and the importance of each topic. All topics of equal importance should have headings of the same level, or style. Below are the various levels of headings used in APA papers.

Level 1:	**Centered, Boldface, Uppercase and Lowercase Heading**
Level 2:	**Flush Left, Boldface, Uppercase and Lowercase Side Heading**
Level 3:	**Indented, boldface, lowercase paragraph heading ending with a period.**
Level 4:	***Indented, boldface, italicized, lowercase paragraph heading with a period.***
Level 5:	*Indented, italicized, lowercase paragraph heading with a period.*

Example:

> **Teaching K-12 English Language Learners in the Mainstream Classroom**
> **The English Language Learner Landscape**
> **Myths and misconceptions.**
> ***Myth 1: Exposure will lead to learning.***
> *The need for explicit morphological instruction.*

- **Appendix:** Tables and figures (graphs, charts, maps, etc.) already appear on separate pages following the reference list. If necessary, one or more appendices may also supplement your text, following any tables or figures.

Guidelines for In-Text Citations

The Form of an Entry

The APA documentation style is sometimes called the "author–date" system because both the author and the date of the publication must be mentioned in the text when citing a source. Both might appear in the flow of the sentence, like this:

> Children in India are being trafficked for adoption, organ transplants, and labor such as prostitution, according to a 2007 article by Nilanjana Ray.

If either name or date does not appear in the text, it must be mentioned within parentheses at the most convenient place, like this:

> According to an article by Nilanjana Ray (2007), children in India . . .

> According to a recent article (Ray, 2007), children in India . . .

Points to Remember

1. When paraphrasing rather than quoting, make it clear where your borrowing begins and ends. Use stylistic cues to distinguish the source's thoughts ("Kalmbach points out . . . ," "Some critics argue . . .") from your own ("I believe . . . ," "It seems obvious, however . . .").

2. When using a shortened title of a work, begin with the word by which the work is alphabetized in your references list (for example, for "Measurement of Stress in Fasting Man," use "Measurement of Stress," not "Fasting Man").

3. When including a parenthetical citation at the end of a sentence, place it before the end punctuation: (Sacks, 1964).

Sample In-Text Citations

One Author: A Complete Work

The correct form for a parenthetical reference to a single source by a single author is parenthesis, last name, comma, space, year of publication, parenthesis. Also note that final punctuation should be placed outside the parentheses.

> . . . in this way, the public began to connect certain childhood vaccinations with an autism epidemic (Baker, 2008).

One Author: Part of a Work

When you cite a specific part of a source, give the page number, chapter, or section, using the appropriate abbreviations (p. or pp., chap., or sec. For others, see page 543). Always give the page number for a direct quotation.

> . . . while a variety of political and scientific forces were at work in the developing crisis, it was parents who pressed the case "that autism had become epidemic and that vaccines were its cause" (Baker, 2008, p. 251).

One Author: Several Publications in the Same Year

If the same author has published two or more articles in the same year, avoid confusion by placing a small letter *a* after the first work listed in the references list, *b* after the next one, and so on. Determine the order alphabetically by title.

Parenthetical Citation:

> ▪ Reefs harbor life forms heretofore unknown (Milius, 2001a, 2001b).

References:

> Milius, D. (2001a). Another world hides inside coral reefs. *Science News, 160*(16), 244.
>
> Milius, D. (2001b). Unknown squids—with elbows—tease science. *Science News, 160*(24), 390.

Works by Authors with the Same Last Name

When citing different sources by authors with the same last name, add the authors' initials to avoid confusion, even if the publication dates are different.

> While J. D. Wallace (2011) argued that privatizing social security would benefit only the wealthiest citizens, others such as E. S. Wallace (2013) supported greater control for individuals.

Two to Five Authors

In APA style, all authors—up to as many as five—must be mentioned in the first text citation, like this:

> Love changes not just who we are, but who we can become, as well (Lewis, Amini, & Lannon, 2000).

Note: The last two authors' names are always separated by a comma and an ampersand (&) when enclosed in parentheses.

For works with two authors, list both in every citation. For works with three to five authors, list all only the first time; after that, use only the name of the first author followed by "et al.," like this:

> These discoveries lead to the hypothesis that love actually alters the brain's structure (Lewis et al., 2000).

Six or More Authors

If your source has six or more authors, refer to the work by the first author's name followed by "et al.," both for the first reference in the text and all references after that. However, be sure to list all the authors (up to seven) in your references list.

> According to a recent study, post-traumatic stress disorder (PTSD) continues to dominate the lives of Vietnam veterans, though in modified forms (Trembley et al., 2012).

A Work Authored by an Agency, a Committee, or Other Organization

Treat the name of the group as if it were the last name of the author. If the name is long and easily abbreviated, provide the abbreviation in square brackets. Use the abbreviation without brackets in subsequent references, as follows:

First Text Citation:

> A problem for many veterans continues to be heightened sensitivity to noise (National Institute of Mental Health [NIMH], 2012).

Subsequent Citations:

> In addition, veterans suffering from PTSD continue to have difficulty discussing their experiences (NIMH, 2012).

A Work with No Author Indicated

If your source lists no author, treat the first few words of the title (capitalized normally) as you would an author's last name. A title of an article or a chapter belongs in quotation marks; the titles of books or reports should be italicized:

> ... including a guide to low-stress postures ("How to Do It," 2013).

A Work Referred to in Another Work

If you need to cite a source that you have found referred to in another source (a "secondary" source), mention the original source in your text. Then, in your parenthetical citation, cite the secondary source, using the words "as cited in."

> ... theorem given by Ullman (as cited in Hoffman, 2008).

Note: In your references list at the end of the paper, you would write out a full citation for Hoffman (not Ullman).

A Work in an Anthology

When citing an article or a chapter in an anthology or a collection, use the authors' names for the specific article, not the names of the anthology's editors. (Similarly, the article should be listed by its authors' names in the references section. See page 544.)

> Phonological changes can be understood from a variationist perspective (Guy, 2005).

An Electronic or Other Internet Source

As with print sources, cite an electronic source by the author (or by shortened title if the author is unknown) and the publication date (not the date you accessed the source).

> One study compared and contrasted the use of Web and touch screen transaction log files in a hospital setting (Nicholas, Huntington, & Williams, 2001).

A Web site

Whenever possible, cite a Web site by its author and posting date. In addition, refer to a specific page or document rather than to a home page or a menu page. If you are referring to a specific part of a Web page that does not have page numbers, direct your reader, if possible, with a section heading and a paragraph number.

> According to the National Multiple Sclerosis Society (2009, "Complexities" section, para. 2), understanding of MS could not begin until scientists began to research nerve transmission in the 1920s.

Two or More Works in a Parenthetical Reference

Sometimes it is necessary to lump several citations into one parenthetical reference. In that case, cite the sources as you usually would, separating the citations with semicolons. Place the citations in alphabetical order, just as they would be ordered in the references list.

> Others report near-death experiences (Rommer, 2007; Sabom, 2010).

A Sacred Text or Famous Literary Work

Sacred texts and famous literary works are published in many different editions. For that reason, the original date of publication may be unavailable or not pertinent. In these cases, use your edition's year of translation (for example, *trans.* 2003) or indicate your edition's year of publication (2003 *version*). When you are referring to specific sections of the work, it is best to identify parts, chapters, or other divisions instead of your version's page numbers.

> An interesting literary case of such dysfunctional family behavior can be found in Franz Kafka's *The Metamorphosis,* where it becomes the commandment of family duty for Gregor's parents and sister to swallow their disgust and endure him (trans. 1972, part 3).

Books of the Bible and other well-known literary works may be abbreviated, if no confusion is possible.

> "Generations come and generations go, but the earth remains forever" (*The New International Version Study Bible,* 1985 version, Eccles. 1.4).

Personal Communications

If you do the kind of personal research recommended elsewhere in *The College Writer,* you may have to cite personal communications that have provided you with some of your knowledge. Personal communications may include personal letters, phone calls, emails, and so forth. Because they are not published in a permanent form, APA style does not place them among the citations in your references list. Instead, cite them only in the text of your paper in parentheses, like this:

> . . . according to M. T. Cann (personal communication, April 1, 2013).

> . . . by today (M. T. Cann, personal communication, April 1, 2013).

Quick Guide

APA References

The references section lists all the sources you have cited in your text (with the exception of personal communications such as phone calls and emails). Begin your references list on a new page after the last page of your paper. Number each references page, continuing the numbering from the text. Then format your references list by following the guidelines below.

1. Type the running head in the upper-left corner and the page number in the upper-right corner, approximately one-half inch from the top of the page.

2. Center the title, *References,* approximately one inch from the top; then double-space before the first entry.

3. Begin each entry flush with the left margin. If the entry runs more than one line, indent additional lines approximately one-half inch (five to seven spaces) using a hanging indent.

4. Adhere to the following conventions about spacing, capitalization, and italics:
   - Double-space between all lines on the references page.
   - Use one space following each word and punctuation mark.
   - With book and article titles, capitalize only the first letter of the title (and subtitle) and proper nouns. (Note that this practice differs from the presentation of titles in the body of the essay.) ***Example:*** The impact of the cold war on Asia.
   - Use italics for titles of books and periodicals, not underlining.

5. List each entry alphabetically by the last name of the author, or, if no author is given, by the title (disregarding A, An, or The). For works with multiple authors, use the first author listed in the publication.

6. Follow these conventions with respect to abbreviations:
   - With authors' names, generally shorten first and middle names to initials, leaving a space after the period. For a work with more than one author, use an ampersand (&) before the last author's name.
   - For publisher locations, use the full city name plus the two-letter U.S. Postal Service abbreviation for the state. For international publishers, include a province and country name.
   - Spell out "Press" in full, but for other publishing information, use the abbreviations below.

Comp. . . . . .compiler, compiled, compiled by	Pt. . . . . Part
	Sec. (sect.). . . . . .section(s)
Ed. . . . . editor(s)	2nd ed. . . . . Second edition
N.d. . . . . .no date given	Suppl. . . . . Supplement
N.p. . . . . .no place of publication, no publisher given	Tech. Rep. . . . . .Technical Report
	Trans. (tr.) . . . . translator, translation
p., pp. . . . . . .page(s) (if necessary for clarity)	

Reference Entries: Books and Other Documents

The general form for a book or brochure entry is this:

▌ Author, A. (year). *Title*. Location: Publisher.

The entries that follow illustrate the information needed to cite books, sections of a book, brochures, and government publications.

A Book by One Author

▌ Quinlan, J. P. (2011). *The last economic superpower: The retreat of globalization, the end of American dominance, and what we can do about it*. New York, NY: McGraw-Hill.

A Book by Two or More Authors

List up to seven authors by last name and first initial, separating them by commas, with an ampersand (&) before the last.

▌ Hooyman, N., & Kramer, B. (2006). *Living through loss: Interventions across the life span*. New York, NY: Columbia University Press.

For eight or more authors, list the first six followed by an ellipsis, and then the last.

An Anonymous Book

If an author is listed as "Anonymous," treat it as the author's name. Otherwise, follow this format:

▌ *Publication manual of the American Psychological Association* (6th ed.). (2010). Washington, DC: American Psychological Association.

A Chapter from a Book

List the chapter title after the date of publication, followed by a period or appropriate end punctuation. Use *In* before the book title, and follow the book title with the inclusive page numbers of the chapter.

▌ Tattersall, I. (2002). How did we achieve humanity? In *The monkey in the mirror* (pp. 138–168). New York, NY: Harcourt.

A Single Work from an Anthology

Start with information about the individual work, followed by details about the collection in which it appears, including the page span. For editors' names in the middle of an entry, follow the usual order: initial first, surname last. Note the placement of Eds. in parentheses.

▌ Guy, G. R. (2005). Variationist approaches to phonological change. In B. D. Joseph & R. D. Janda (Eds.), *The handbook of historical linguistics* (pp. 369–400). Malden, MA: Blackwell.

One Volume of a Multivolume Edited Work

Indicate the volume in parentheses after the work's title.

Salzman, J., Smith, D. L., & West, C. (Eds.). (1996). *Encyclopedia of African-American culture and history* (Vol. 4). New York, NY: Simon & Schuster Macmillan.

A Separately Titled Volume in a Multivolume Work

The Associated Press. (1995). *Twentieth-century America: Vol. 8. The crisis of national confidence: 1974–1980*. Danbury, CT: Grolier Educational Corp.

Note: When a work is part of a larger series or collection, as with this example, make a two-part title with the series and the particular volume you are citing.

An Edited Work, One in a Series

Start the entry with the work's author, publication date, and title. Then follow with publication details about the series.

Marshall, P. G. (2002). The impact of the cold war on Asia. In T. O'Neill (Ed.), *World history by era: Vol. 9. The nuclear age* (pp. 162–166). San Diego, CA: Greenhaven Press.

A Group Author as Publisher

When the author is also the publisher, simply put Author in the spot where you would list the publisher's name.

Amnesty International. (2007). *Maze of injustice: The failure to protect indigenous women from sexual violence in the USA*. London, England: Author.

Note: If the publication is a brochure, identify it as such in brackets after the title.

An Edition Other Than the First

Baylis, J., Smith, S., & Owens, P. (2011). *The globalization of world politics: An introduction to international relations* (5th ed.). Oxford, England: Oxford University Press.

Two or More Books by the Same Author

When you are listing multiple works by the same author, arrange them by the year of publication, earliest first.

Sacks, O. (1995). *An anthropologist on Mars: Seven paradoxical tales*. New York, NY: Alfred A. Knopf.

Sacks, O. (2007). *Musicophilia: Tales of music and the brain*. New York, NY: Alfred A. Knopf.

An English Translation

> Setha, R. (1998). *Unarmed* (R. Narasimhan, Trans.). Chennai, India: Macmillan. (Original work published 1995)

Note: If you use the original work, cite the original version; the non-English title is followed by its English translation, not italicized, in square brackets.

An Article in a Reference Book

Start the entry with the author of the article, if identified. If no author is listed, begin the entry with the title of the article.

> Lewer, N. (1999). Non-lethal weapons. In *World encyclopedia of peace* (pp. 279–280). Oxford, England: Pergamon Press.

A Reprint, Different Form

> Albanov, V. (2000). *In the land of white death: An epic story of survival in the Siberian Arctic.* New York, NY: Modern Library. (Original work published 1917)

Note: This work was originally published in Russia in 1917; the 2000 reprint is the first English version. If you are citing a reprint from another source, the parentheses would contain "Reprinted from Title, pp. xx–xx, by A. Author, year, Location: Publisher."

A Technical or Research Report

> Taylor, B. G., Fitzgerald, N., Hunt, D., Reardon, J. A., & Brownstein, H. H. (2001). *ADAM preliminary 2000 findings on drug use and drug markets: Adult male arrestees.* Washington, DC: National Institute of Justice.

A Government Publication

Generally, refer to the government agency as the author. When possible, provide an identification number for the document after the title in parentheses.

> National Institute on Drug Abuse. (2000). *Inhalant abuse* (NIH Publication No. 00–3818). Rockville, MD: National Clearinghouse on Alcohol and Drug Information.

For reports obtained from the U.S. Government Printing Office, list location and publisher as "Washington, DC: Government Printing Office."

Reference Entries: Print Periodical Articles

The general form for a periodical entry is this:

> Author, A. (year). Article title. *Periodical Title, volume number*(issue number), page numbers.

If the periodical does not use volume and issue numbers, include some other designation with the year, such as a date, a month, or a season. The entries that follow illustrate the information and arrangement needed to cite most types of print periodicals.

Note: Issue number is required only for journals that paginate each issue separately.

An Article in a Scholarly Journal

> Premdas, R. R. (2011). Identity, ethnicity, and the Caribbean homeland in an era of globalization. *Social Identities, 17*(6), 811-832.

 Pay attention to the features of this basic reference to a scholarly journal:

1. Provide the authors' last names and initials, as for a book reference.
2. Place the year of publication in parentheses, followed by a period.
3. Format the article's title in lowercase, except for the first word of the main title and of a subtitle and except for proper nouns, acronyms, or initialisms; do not italicize the article title or place it in quotation marks.
4. Capitalize the first and all main words in the journal title; italicize it.
5. Italicize the volume number but not the issue number; place the issue in parentheses, without a space after the volume number. No issue number is needed if the journal is paginated consecutively throughout a volume.
6. Provide inclusive page numbers, without "pp." or "pages."

An Abstract of a Scholarly Article (from a Secondary Source)

When referencing an abstract published separately from an article, provide publication details of the article followed by information about where the abstract was published.

> Shlipak, M. G., Simon, J. A., Grady, O., Lin, F., Wenger, N. K., & Furberg, C. D. (2001, September). Renal insufficiency and cardiovascular events in postmenopausal women with coronary heart disease. *Journal of the American College of Cardiology, 38*, 705–711. Abstract obtained from *Geriatrics, 2001, 56*(12). (Abstract No. 5645351.)

A Journal Article, More Than Seven Authors

> Yamada, A., Suzuki, M., Kato, M., Suzuki, M., Tanaka, S., Shindo, . . . Furkawa, TA. (2007). Emotional distress and its correlates among parents of children with persuasive developmental disorders. *Psychiatry & Clinical Neurosciences, 61*(6), 651–657.

Note: In the text, abbreviate the parenthetical citation: (Yamada et al., 2007).

A Review

To reference a book review or a review of another medium (film, exhibit, and so on), indicate the review and the medium in brackets, along with the title of the work being reviewed by the author listed.

> Hutcheon, L., & Hutcheon, M. (2008). Turning into the mind. [Review of the book *Musicophilia: Tales of music and the brain,* by O. Sacks]. *Canadian Medical Association Journal, 178*(4), 441.

A Magazine Article

> Weintraub, B. (2007, October). Unusual suspects. *Psychology Today, 40*(5), 80–87.

Note: If the article is unsigned, begin the entry with the title of the article.

> Tomatoes target toughest cancer. (2002, February). *Prevention, 54*(2), 53.

A Newspaper Article

For newspaper articles, include the full publication date, year first followed by a comma, the month (spelled out) and the day. Identify the article's location in the newspaper using page numbers and section letters, as appropriate. If the article is a letter to the editor, identify it as such in brackets following the title. For newspapers, use *p.* or *pp.* before the page numbers; if the article is not on continuous pages, give all the page numbers, separated by commas.

> Schmitt, E., & Shanker, T. (2008, March 18). U.S. adapts cold-war idea to fight terrorists. *The New York Times,* pp. 1A, 14A–15A.

> Knaub, M. (2013, August 12). Area men recall their time as 'braceros.' *Yuma Times,* pp. 1A, 5A.

A Newsletter Article

Newsletter article entries are similar to newspaper article entries; only a volume number is added.

> Teaching mainstreamed special education students. (2002, February). *The Council Chronicle,* 11, pp. 6–8.

Reference Entries: Online Sources

When it comes to references for online sources, follow these guidelines:

1. **Whenever possible, use the final version of an electronic resource.** Typically, this is called the archival copy or the version of record, as opposed to a prepublished version. Right now, that final version is likely the same as the printed version of an article, though there is some movement toward the online publication being the final version (complete with additional data, graphics, and so on).

2. **In the reference entry for an electronic source, start with the same elements in the same order for print or other fixed-media resources** (author, title, and so on). Then add the most reliable electronic retrieval information that will (a) clarify what version of the source you used and (b) help your reader find the source him- or herself. Determine what you need to include based on these guidelines:

   - **Whenever possible, use the electronic document's Digital Object Identifier (DOI).** More and more, electronic publishers are using this registration code for the content of journal articles and other documents so that the document can be located on the Internet, even if the URL changes. The DOI will usually be published at the beginning of the article or be available in the article's citation.

     > Author, A. A. (year). Title of article. *Title of Periodical, volume number*(issue number), pages. doi: code

   - **If a DOI is not available for the electronic document,** give the URL (without a period at the end). Generally, a database name is no longer needed, except for hard-to-find documents and those accessed through subscription-only databases. Use the home- or menu-page URL for subscription-only databases and online reference works.

     > Author, A. A. (year). Title of article. *Title of Periodical, volume number*(issue number), pages. Retrieved from URL

   - **If the content of the document is stable** (e.g., archival copy or copy of record with DOI), do not include a retrieval date in your reference entry. However, if the content is likely to change or be updated, as is the case with a lot of the material on the free Web, then offer a retrieval date. This would be the case with open-Web material with no fixed publication date, edition, or version, or material that is prepublished (in preparation, in press).

     > Author, A. A. (year). *Title of document.* Retrieved date from Web site: URL

A Journal Article with DOI

> Knowles, F. E. (2012). Toward emancipatory education: An application of Habermasian theory to Native American educational policy. *International Journal of Qualitative Studies in Education 25*(7), 885–904. doi: 10.1080/09518398.2012.720735

Note: Because the DOI references the final version of the article, the retrieval date, URL, and database name are not needed. If the online article is a preprint version, add "Advance online publication" and your retrieval date before the DOI.

A Journal Article Without DOI

> Bell, J. B., & Nye, E. C. (2007). Specific symptoms predict suicidal ideation in Vietnam combat veterans with Post-Traumatic Stress Disorder. *Military Medicine, 172*(11), 1144–1147. Retrieved from http://www.ebscohost.com

Note: Because this article has no DOI, the URL is provided for the subscription database search service. If you retrieved the article from the open Web, you would supply the exact URL. If the version of the article you access is in press and you have retrieved it from the author's personal or institutional Web site, place "in press" in parentheses after the author's name and add a retrieval date before the URL.

A Newspaper Article

> Clifford, S., & Rampell, C. (2013, April 13). Sometimes, we want prices to fool us. *The New York Times*. Retrieved from http://www.nytimes.com

An Article in an Online Magazine (Ezine) not Published in Print

> Morris, A. (2013, February). Hidden within ourselves: A psychoanalytic examination of the effects of repression in Michael Haneke's *Caché. Bright Lights Film Journal*. Retrieved April 27, 2013, from http://brightlightsfilm.com/79/79-cache-michael -haneke-psychoanalysis-interpretation_morris.php

A Book Review

> Shapiro, K. (2007). Mystic chords. [Review of the book *Musicophilia: Tales of music and the brain,* by O. Sacks]. Commentary, *124*(5), 73–77. Retrieved from http://web .ebscohost.com

An Electronic Book

> Kafka, F. (2002). *Metamorphosis*. D. Wylie (Trans.). Available from http://www .gutenberg.org/etext/5200

Note: If the URL goes directly to the ebook, use "Retrieved from."

Material from an Online Reference Work

▮ Agonism. (2008). *In Encyclopaedia Britannica*. Retrieved from http://search.eb.com

Note: See pages 452–453 for advice on using Wikipedia.

Online Course Material

▮ Roderiguez, N. Unit 3, *Lecture 3: Sociological Theories of Deviance*. Retrieved from University of Houston Web site: http://www.uh.edu/~nestor/lecturenotes /unit3lecture3.html

A Workplace Document or Other "Gray Literature"

"Gray Literature" refers to informative documents (e.g., brochures, fact sheets, white papers) produced by government agencies, corporations, and nonprofit groups. If possible, give a document number or identify the type of document in brackets.

▮ Foehr, U. G. (2006). *Media multitasking among American youth: Prevalance, predictors and pairings* (Publication No. 7592). Retrieved from the Kaiser Family Foundation: http://www.kff.org/entmedia/upload/7592.pdf

Undated Content on Web site

▮ National Institute of Allergy and Infectious Diseases. (n.d.). *Antimicrobial (drug) resistance*. Retrieved from http://www3.niaid.nih.gov/topics /AntimicrobialResistance/default.htm

A Podcast

▮ Byrd, D., & Block, J. (Producers). (2008, February 5). Antonio Rangel: This is your brain on wine. *Earth & Sky: A Clear Voice for Science* [Audio podcast]. Retrieved from http://www.earthsky.org/clear-voices/52199

Message on a Newsgroup, an Online Forum, or a Discussion Group

▮ Avnish, J. (2008, March 18). Sex education especially vital to teens nowadays. [Online forum post]. Retrieved from http://groups.google.ca/group/AIDS-Beyond -Borders/topics

A Blog Post

▮ Koyzis, D. (2007, June 27). Conservative environmentalists. [Web log post]. Retrieved from http://byzantinecalvinist.blogspot.com/2007_06_01_archive.html

Note about URLs: When necessary, break a URL before a slash or other punctuation mark or after a double slash. Do not underline or italicize the URL, place it in angle brackets, or end it with a period.

Reference Entries: Other Sources (Primary, Personal, and Multimedia)

Cite audiovisual media sources and electronic sources as follows.

Specialized Computer Software with Limited Distribution

Standard nonspecialized computer software does not require a reference entry. Treat software as an unauthored work unless an individual has property rights to it.

> Carreau, S. (2001). Champfoot (Version 3.3) [Computer software]. Saint Mandé, France: Author.

Show the software version in parentheses after the title and the medium in brackets.

A Television or Radio Broadcast

Indicate the episode by writers, if possible. Then follow with the airing date, the episode title, and the type of series in brackets. Add the producer(s) as you would the editors(s) of a print medium, and complete the entry with details about the series itself.

> Berger, C. (Writer). (2001, December 19). Feederwatch [Radio series program]. In D. Byrd & J. Block (Producers), *Earth & Sky*. Austin, TX: The Production Block.

An Audio Recording

Begin the entry with the speaker's or writer's name, not the producer. Indicate the type of recording in brackets.

> Kim, E. (Author, speaker). (2000). *Ten thousand sorrows* [CD]. New York, NY: Random House.

A Music Recording

Give the name and function of the originators or primary contributors. Indicate the recording medium in brackets immediately following the title.

> ARS Femina Ensemble. (Performers). (1998). *Musica de la puebla de Los Angeles: Music by women of baroque Mexico, Cuba, & Europe* [CD]. Louisville, KY: Nannerl Recordings.

A Motion Picture

Give the name and function of the director, producer, or both.

> Lee, A. (Director). (2012). *Life of Pi* [Motion picture]. United States: Twentieth-Century Fox.

A Published Interview, Titled, No Author

Start the entry with the interview's title, followed by publication details.

> Stephen Harper: The Report interview. (2002, January 7). *The Report* (Alberta, BC), 29, 10–11.

A Published Interview, Titled, Single Author

Start the entry with the interviewee's name, followed by the date and the title. Place the interviewer's name in brackets before other publication details.

> Fussman, C. (2002, January). What I've learned. [Interview by Robert McNamara.] Esquire, 137, 85.

An Unpublished Paper Presented at a Meeting

Indicate when the paper was presented, at what meeting, in what location.

> Sifferd, K., & Hirstein, W. (2012, June). *On the criminal culpability of successful and unsuccessful psychopaths.* Paper presented at the meeting of the Society for Philosophy and Psychology, Boulder, CO.

An Unpublished Doctoral Dissertation

Place the dissertation's title in italics, even though the work is unpublished. Indicate the school at which the writer completed the dissertation.

> Roberts, W. (2001). *Crime amidst suburban wealth* (Unpublished doctoral dissertation). Bowling Green State University, Bowling Green, OH.

Sample APA Paper

In her Writing in Education course, student writer Amanda Khoe put together a best practices anthology of articles on teaching English Language Learners (ELL—students for whom English is not their first language). Amanda wrote the following essay as the introduction to her anthology. Here, she surveys the articles (called a literature review) and synthesizes their findings as she explains the practical implications for ELL teaching. You can use Amanda's paper in three ways

1. To study how a well-written research paper uses a range of resources to build a discussion or line of reasoning that answers a research question. .
2. To examine how sources are used and integrated into social-sciences research writing—a full-length discussion of the strategies addressed on pages 476–479.
3. To see in detail the format and documentation practices of APA style.

Note: Often, a social-sciences research paper takes the form of an experiment report. For an example of such a report, see pages 485–491.

Sample Title Page

Note that APA format requires that the paper be double-spaced throughout, with a one-inch margin on all sides.

Type running head (abbreviated title in uppercase letters) flush left.

Running head: TEACHING K–12 ENGLISH LANGUAGE LEARNERS   1

Full title, author(s), and school name are centered on the page, typed in uppercase and lowercase.

Teaching K–12 English Language Learners
in the Mainstream Classroom
Amanda Khoe
University of California Davis

Sample Abstract

The abstract summarizes the paper's central issue, its main conclusion, the key reasoning and evidence presented, and the study's significance.

TEACHING K–12 ENGLISH LANGUAGE LEARNERS   2

Abstract

While ELLs are the fastest growing student subpopulation in K–12, they are more likely to perform poorly on standardized tests and to drop out of school than other students. One explanation is that teachers in the mainstream classroom are underprepared for teaching ELLs and thus need additional training. Recent studies have shown that the best approach to ELL instruction is to use an array of teaching strategies that fit varied ELL contexts. While diverse programs exist (e.g., dual language, newcomer, English Language Development), so do myths and misconceptions about ELL pedagogy: that ELLs will learn English simply through exposure, that second-language acquisition follows a universal pattern, that what works with non-ELL students will work with ELLs, and that nonverbal methods work best with ELL students. Given that ELLs need 1–3 years to gain conversational proficiency and 5–7 years to gain academic proficiency in English, teachers in the mainstream classroom need to do more than follow just good teaching (JGT) practices. They need to use (in ways that fit their classroom context) interactive teaching techniques, comprehensive vocabulary instruction, scaffolding strategies, varied modes of assessment, and cultural sensitivity to ensure greater success for ELLs.

Keywords: ELL, K–12, ELD, SIOP, JGT, scaffolding

A running
head and page
number top
each page.

The title is centered one inch
from the top,
and the paper is
double-spaced
throughout.

Using properly
referenced statistics, Amanda
raises the
challenges of
ELL students in
the mainstream
classroom.

Citing issues
that teachers
face, she offers
her thesis about
ELL education,
a thesis rooted
in her survey of
the literature.

A brief paragraph forecasts
the content of
the her essay.

A heading
identifies the
first section.

Teaching K–12 English Language Learners in the Mainstream Classroom

English Language Learners (ELLs) are the fastest growing student subpopulation in the United States. From 1979 to 1999, overall enrollment in America's K–12 public schools increased by 6 percent while the ELL population soared by 138 percent (Harper & de Jong, 2004). By the 2007–2008 school year, 5.3 million ELLs constituted 10.6 percent of K–12 public school enrollment (Calderón, Slavin, & Sánchez, 2011). Even as their population burgeons, ELL students remain more likely to perform poorly on standardized tests and to drop out of school than their non-ELL peers (Verdugo & Flores, 2007). ELLs' low academic achievement can be attributed in large part to the shortage of prepared classroom teachers. Though 42 percent of K–12 public school teachers have ELLs in their class, only 12.5 percent have received more than eight hours of professional development in ELL teaching practices (de Jong & Harper, 2005). English Language Learners require well-trained teachers and tailored instruction; unfortunately, mainstream K–12 teachers with ELL students are too often ill equipped to educate these unique students.

The size of the ELL population coupled with its disturbingly low academic achievement has spawned many studies and much heated debate on how to improve ELL pedagogy. To avoid "succumb[ing] to the allure of strategy books" (Carrier, 2005, p. 5), teachers must first understand peripheral issues affecting the ELL population. Presently, no federal guidelines exist for states regarding how to identify, assess, place, or instruct ELLs (Calderón et al., 2011). The best strategies for serving ELLs are informed by distinct, in some cases even opposing, schools of thought. As the following studies have demonstrated, effective ELL education is kaleidoscopic, with various strategies to match the array of possible contexts.

This anthology introduction begins with a report on the demographic composition and needs of ELL students, follows with basic theoretical frameworks that currently guide ELL education, and ends with a synthesis of the ELL literature that yields concrete strategies for teaching in a mainstream classroom with English Language Learners.

The English Language Learner Landscape

Though ELL students bring myriad languages, cultures, and personal histories to the classroom, they are typically classified as a single group. In "Effective Instruction for English Learners," Calderón et al. (2011) have cataloged four discrete subcategories within the ELL population: special education ELLs, ELLs

TEACHING K–12 ENGLISH LANGUAGE LEARNERS 4

inappropriately reclassified as general education after passing a district language test, migrant ELLs whose education is interrupted as their family follows the crops from one location to another, and transnational ELLs who return to their native country and attend school only to re-emigrate to the United States. Over 20 percent of ELLs are recent immigrants, and 80 percent of second-generation children (U.S.-born children whose parents were born outside the U.S.) are ELLs. Evidently, ELLs are as diverse as they are prevalent.

> When authors are identified in the sentence, only the date is required in the in-text citation.

In contrast to Calderón et al. (2011), Pascopella (2011) has explained in "Successful Strategies for English Language Learners," that there are various ELL program types to match the various types of ELL students. In dual language programs, bilingual students receive instruction in English and another language (e.g., Spanish). In newcomer programs, "separate, relatively self-contained educational interventions" (p. 32) are implemented to meet the academic and transitional needs of recent immigrants before they enter a mainstream English Language Development (ELD) program. In structured English immersion programs, students are taught entirely in English. Today, sheltered English programs are the dominant trend. The prototypical sheltered English program—Sheltered Instruction Observation Protocol (SIOP)—uses nonconventional methods to teach academic content to English Language Learners.

> In her topic sentence, the writer sets up a contrast between two sources. A direct quotation is cited by page number.

Myths and Misconceptions. In "Misconceptions about Teaching English-Language Learners," Harper and de Jong (2004) have called attention to the negative effects of ELL teaching practices based on misinformation. First, some teachers assume that mere exposure to English and interaction with English speakers will result in English-language learning. Conversely, the authors have asserted that ELLs require deliberate instruction in the grammatical, morphological, and phonological aspects of English if they are to communicate successfully in an academic context. Second, today's reductive approaches to ELL education are based on the premise that second-language acquisition follows a universal pattern. Unfortunately, such methods fail to meet ELLs' idiosyncratic language needs. Third, it is a common misconception that if a teaching practice is good for native English speakers it is also good for ELLs. De Jong and Harper (2005) have argued that teaching strategies in a classroom with non-native and native English speakers often emphasize that students must "talk to learn" but fail to address how students will "learn to talk" (p. 102). Fourth, ELL teachers tend to believe that presenting concepts using purely nonverbal techniques

> A subheading further divides this section of the essay.

> The writer enumerates misconceptions using clear transition words and references to multiple sources.

TEACHING K–12 ENGLISH LANGUAGE LEARNERS   5

is most effective. While nonverbal methods can support ELLs' English acquisition, Harper and de Jong (2004) have warned that overdependence on nonlinguistic instruction can impede students' ability to integrate language and content.

In "Effective Instruction for English-Language Learners" (2011), Protheroe has attempted to dispel myths about young ELLs. Contrary to the notion that English-only instruction produces the best second-language acquisition results, Protheroe found that high literacy in a student's first language (L1) presages high levels of reading achievement in his/her second language (L2). Accordingly, teachers should supplement their English instruction with instruction in the native language(s) of their students as much as possible. Unlike Harper and de Jong, Protheroe has asserted that instruction that works well for non-ELLs is equally effective for ELLs, so long as modifications are made to accommodate students' language "capacities, needs, and limitations" (p.28).

Linguistic Needs. English Language Learners undertake the challenge of simultaneously learning a new language and new academic content. In "Key Issues for Teaching English Learners in Academic Classrooms," Carrier (2005) has explained that it takes an average of one to three years to reach conversational proficiency in a second language, but five to seven years to reach academic proficiency. In spite of this, ELLs normally spend just three years in 30-minute "pull-out" English Language Development programs (Calderón et al., 2011). Calderón et al. have argued that this is but one example of how ELL teaching practices are unsympathetic to the considerably greater linguistic needs of English Language Learners.

Researchers in educational linguistics have found that second language learners often possess more knowledge than they can express. Nonstandard accents help illustrate this point. Underestimating their ELL students' intellectual capacity, teachers often emphasize pronunciation over other language dimensions and academic content. But ELLs are likely to be as cognitively mature as their non-ELL peers. Typically, ELLs acquire content at a faster rate than second language skills. Thus, English Language Learners often understand more than they can articulate through spoken or written language (de Jong & Harper, 2005). Educators must recognize that an ELL's accent or imprecise grammar does not necessarily indicate academic incompetence. Accordingly, second language instruction should provide non-linguistic means for students to demonstrate their learning.

Sidebar annotations:

Summarizing a source, Amanda identifies myths about ELLs.

A second subheading signals a turn to another subtopic.

When authors are not identified within the sentence, both the authors and the date, separated by a comma, are listed in the in-text citation.

Paragraph markers: 7, 8, 9

TEACHING K–12 ENGLISH LANGUAGE LEARNERS   6

Best Practices for ELL Education

A heading identifies the second main section of the essay.

The current educational climate prizes inclusive instruction. While this *10* emphasis is not inherently detrimental, it is driven by the "just good teaching (JGT), native-speaker perspective" (de Jong & Harper, 2005, p. 102), which assumes that all students possess at least rudimentary oral and literacy skills in English, and that ELLs learn at the same pace and in the same manner as non-ELLs. JGT practices include "activating knowledge, using cooperative learning, process writing, and graphic organizers" (p. 102). In "Preparing Mainstream Teachers for English-Language Learners: Is Being a Good Teacher Good Enough?" de Jong and Harper (2005) insisted that ELLs require more than generic JGT practices to fully acquire academic content and build language skills.

Multiple sources in one in-text citation are listed in alphabetical order by author and separated by semicolons.

Moving beyond JGT involves activating and strengthening background *11* knowledge in order to prime students for new content (Coleman and Goldenberg, 2011; Short & Echevarria, 2004; Verdugo & Flores, 2007). In "Promoting Literacy Development," Coleman and Goldenberg (2011) have suggested interactive and direct teaching techniques for extracting students' existing knowledge. Interactive teaching, defined as "verbal interaction that gives students opportunities to converse with the teacher and with peers" (p. 16), combined with "extended academic talk" (Short & Echevarria, 2004, p. 12) challenge ELLs both linguistically and in other cognitive domains. Calderón et al. (2011) have maintained that the consort to background content knowledge is background vocabulary knowledge. Students need long-term, explicit, and comprehensive vocabulary instruction in all subject areas to foster both word-level skills (e.g., decoding) and text-level skills (e.g., fluency). Through exposure to words in multiple forms and contexts, students develop phonological awareness and better reading comprehension. Moreover, repetition prompts students to operate on their own vocabulary (and content) background in novel ways.

"Et al." indicates a subsequent reference to a source with three or more authors.

Amanda synthesizes the findings of several studies about stressing academic language in ELL instruction.

Researchers have also found that stressing academic language can help both *12* ELLs and struggling non-ELLs retain specific subject material (Carrier, 2005; de Jong & Harper, 2005; Harper & de Jong, 2004; Protheroe, 2011). To avoid diluting the curriculum, teachers should concentrate on introducing vocabulary terms that are key to understanding the subject matter (de Jong & Harper, 2005). The Sheltered Instruction Observation Protocol Model (SIOP) recommends "emphasizing academic vocabulary development" (Short & Echevarria, 2004, p. 12). For example, academic language in a unit on earthquakes might include the words plate tectonics, magnitude, and seismoscope. Spotlighting academic vocabulary serves the dual goals of facilitating content and language acquisition.

Multiple Modes, Scaffolding, and L1 Development. Needless to say, English   *13* Language Learners benefit from extensive scaffolding strategies. When a teacher scaffolds, he or she shifts the difficulty and pace to meet the needs of the student. One way to scaffold learning is to use "multiple modes of input and output" that are not dependent on language (Carrier, 2005, p. 4; de Jong & Harper, 2005). Manipulatives, drama/role play, and graphics can be used by educators to "input" content and by ELL students to "output" their own knowledge when they cannot adequately express themselves through language (Coleman & Goldenberg, 2011). Likewise, various modes of assessment can be used to capture the full scope of learning. For instance, asking a student to draw instead of write the answer to a test question can reveal learning that goes beyond rote memorization (de Jong & Harper, 2005). In a related vein, teaching strategies such as question-generating, summarizing, and predicting can foster metacognitive skill-building and help ELLs take ownership of their own learning (Verdugo & Flores, 2007). Multiple modes of instruction and assessment should be used regularly in ELL education.

In addition, a community orientation has proven effective in ELL instruction.   *14* In "English-Language Learners: Key Issues," Verdugo and Flores found higher ELL retention rates in "supportive school environments" (2007, p. 177) where ELL families were involved in students' learning and small group instruction was a common practice. In peer groups, students gain confidence and build social skills (Mays, 2008). Additionally, students can scaffold each others' learning by offering translations between English and an ELL's primary language.

ELLs' development in their primary languages can predict and facilitate their   *15* development in English. Thus, classroom teachers with ELL students must avoid the temptation to implement English-only policies. Such policies can actually hinder rather than help ELLs' English acquisition (Coleman & Goldenberg, 2011; Mays, 2008). Teachers should use students' primary language as much as possible to "support [students]…and to make content more accessible" (Coleman & Goldenberg, 2011, p. 16). A teacher might draw a Spanish-speaking student's attention to the cognates found in English and Spanish (e.g., "activity" and "actividad"). If

---

Signaled with a subheading, the next section addresses instructional strategies discussed by several sources.

TEACHING K–12 ENGLISH LANGUAGE LEARNERS   8

the teacher cannot speak the student's primary language, he or she can opt for
the scaffolding strategies mentioned earlier. In addition to assessing students'
proficiency in their primary language, focusing on the similarities and differences
between English and students' primary language can "help students consciously
transfer the skills and knowledge from their primary language to English" (Coleman
& Goldenberg, 2011, p. 18).

Cultural Considerations. English Language Learners straddle the border between   16
the world of their heritage (native/primary) language and the English-speaking
world. Mays (2008) has emphasized the importance of cultural sensitivity in the
ELL classroom in "The Cultural Divide of Discourse: Understanding How English-
Language Learners' Primary Discourse Influences Acquisition of Literacy." While
the American classroom values active questioning and collaboration, many ELLs
are accustomed to classroom etiquette that is radically hierarchical. ELL students
may be uncomfortable expressing their own opinions and questioning the authority
of the teacher or the textbook. Some ELLs may, in fact, consciously reject the "host
[American] culture and [English] language" (de Jong & Harper, 2005, p. 117) because
acquiring English would signal assimilation and cost them social capital. Moreover,
multicultural sensitivity doesn't account for all the issues that arise in a multilingual
classroom.

Cultural incongruence between mainstream teachers and their ELL students   17
can obstruct teaching and learning. In California public schools, where 61 percent
of students are from minority backgrounds, just 21 percent of teachers identify as
minorities (Verdugo & Flores, 2007). Consciously or not, non-minority teachers
might hold lower expectations for their minority students. Thus, teachers must be
self-critical about their own attitudes towards multilingualism and vigilant about the
implicit messages sent by "English-only" classroom policies (de Jong & Harper, 2005).
To reconcile cultural differences, teachers are responsible for familiarizing themselves
with students' cultures and respecting their primary discourses (Mays, 2008).

Teachers can support the diverse cultures and languages of their students   18
through assignments, assessments, and classroom materials. For example, assigning
personal narratives for homework and facilitating multilingual book clubs mitigate
the collision of students' primary discourses and the academic discourse. In addition
to assigning tasks that encourage students to share their family and community

---

Backed up by two sources, Amanda cautions against English-only policies for ELL students.

With a new subheading, Amanda turns to cultural issues that impact ELLs in the mainstream classroom.

Changes to a direct quotation are signalled by brackets.

TEACHING K–12 ENGLISH LANGUAGE LEARNERS   9

experiences, teachers should maintain a classroom library that is representative of students' diversity. Indeed, embedding instruction and materials from different cultures forges an atmosphere of tolerance for ELL and non-ELL students alike. Finally, Mays (2008) has advocated "culturally responsive management styles and unbiased assessments" (p. 416). Teachers should vary question types and media, and they should discuss the process of arriving at an answer (whether correct or incorrect). Taking the time to "value the ELL voice" (p. 418) builds student-teacher relationships based on mutual trust and respect; in turn, these genuine bonds nurture learning.

Closing Remarks

A final main heading signals the conclusion.

In 1972, the Supreme Court ruling in Lau v. Nichols mandated that school   19
districts help students overcome language barriers so that they can participate in and benefit from mainstream schooling. Nearly forty years later, the severe disparities in academic achievement between ELLs and non-ELLs continue to hinder the nation's overall educational attainment. While policymakers, researchers, and educators have yet to reach a consensus on how to best instruct this growing subpopulation, competing theories on ELL teaching share several themes. The model for future ELL education is naturally multifaceted, refined by trial and error, and ultimately based on contextual features.

Amanda puts issues surrounding ELL education in historical and political context.

Collectively, the research articles cited in this introduction detail ELL teaching   20
practices that are effective in most circumstances. A concerted training program is needed to prepare teachers for the multilingual classroom. Broadly speaking, effective ELL teaching begins with an understanding of the second language acquisition process and an embracing of the diversity within the ELL population. In the classroom, mainstream teachers should strive to tap into students' existing knowledge and relate academic content to students' cultural backgrounds. By identifying the distinct linguistic demands inherent in different subjects, teachers can provide explicit vocabulary instruction—an essential foundation for literacy development. To encourage long-term academic literacy, teachers should capitalize on innovative scaffolding strategies, including but not limited to multiple modes of instruction and assessment, as well as using students' primary language. Given these frameworks, K–12 classroom teachers can tailor effective strategies to promote their English Language Learners' academic achievement.

The last paragraph summarizes the findings of the research surveyed and synthesizes the advice on best ELL teaching practices for the mainstream classroom.

"Teaching K-12 English Language Learners in the Mainstream Classroom" by Amanda Khoe. Used by permission of the author.

TEACHING K–12 ENGLISH LANGUAGE LEARNERS   10

References

All works referred to in the paper appear on the references page, listed alphabetically by author (or title).

Carrier, K. A. (2005). Key issues for teaching English Language Learners in academic classrooms. *Middle School Journal 37*(2), 4–9. Retrieved from www .firstsearch.org

Calderón, M., Slavin, R., & Sánchez, M. (2011). Effective instruction for English learners. *The Future of Children 21*(1), 103–127.

Coleman, R., & Goldenberg, C. (2011). Promoting literacy development. *Education Digest 76*(6), 14–18.

Each entry follows APA guidelines for listing authors, dates, titles, and publishing information.

de Jong, E. J., & Harper, C. A. (2005). Preparing mainstream teachers for English Language Learners: Is being a good teacher good enough? *Teacher Education Quarterly 32*(2), 101–118. Retrieved from www.firstsearch.org

Harper, C., & de Jong, E. (2004). Misconceptions about teaching English Language Learners. *Journal of Adolescent & Adults Literacy 48*(2), 152–162.

Mays, L. (2008). The cultural divide of discourse: Understanding how English Language Learners' primary discourse influences acquisition of literacy. *The Reading Teacher 61*(5), 415–418.

Pascopella, A. (2011). Successful strategies for English Language Learners. *District Administration 47*(2), 29–44.

Capitalization, punctuation, and hanging indentation are consistent with APA format.

Protheroe, N. (2011). Effective instruction for English Language Learners. *Principal 90*(3), 26–29.

Short, D., & Echevarria, J. (2004). *Teacher skills to support English Language Learners. Educational Leadership 62*(4), 8–13.

Verdugo, R. R., & Flores, R. (2007). *English-Language Learners: Key issues. Education and Urban Society 39*: 167–194. doi: 10.1177/00131245062948

Reading for Better Writing

Working by yourself or with a group, answer these questions:

1. Amanda Khoe's essay focuses on English Language Learners. What was your own experience of ELL in K–12? Are you an ELL yourself? If not, did you have ELLs in your classrooms? What parts of Amanda's discussion resonate with your own experience or help you better understand the ELL experience?

2. What essential question is Amanda asking? What essential answer does she give?

3. Functioning in part as a literature review, this essay summarizes and synthesizes research on the topic. Examine a paragraph in the essay's body: how do summary and synthesis work? What do they accomplish? What do these strategies tell you about writing in the social sciences?

Critical-Thinking and Writing Activities

As directed by your instructor, complete the following critical-thinking and writing activities by yourself or with classmates.

1. To make sense of APA format rules, answer these questions: What is the essential logic of the APA system? How does this logic reflect research practices and values in the Social Sciences?

2. Create references list entries in correct APA style for the following sources:

   - An article in the summer 2009 issue (volume 34, no. 2) of the periodical *MELUS*, by Joni Adamson and Scott Slovic: "The Shoulders We Stand On: An Introduction to Ethnicity and Ecocriticism" (pages 5–24)

   - The book *The Playful World: How Technology Is Transforming Our Imagination,* by Mark Pesce, published in 2000 by Ballantine Books, located in New York City

   - The Web page "Vaccines for Children Program (VCP)," part of the Vaccines and Immunizations section of the Centers for Disease Control and Prevention (CDC) Web site, sponsored by the U.S. government's Department of Health and Human Services. No author or publication date is listed. The site was last accessed April 26, 2013, at http://www.cdc.gov/vaccines /programs/vfc/index.html.

Learning-Objectives Checklist ✓

Have you achieved this chapter's learning objectives? Check your progress with the items below, revisiting topics in the chapter as needed. *I have . . .*

____ gained an overview of the APA system of documentation—the basic logic of in-text citations in relation to reference entries (536–537).

____ correctly implemented APA format guidelines (e.g., title page, abstract, running head, pagination, heading system, references page) (538).

____ applied rules of in-text citation for a whole range of sources (539–542).

____ developed a references list that is properly formatted and that correctly and fully identifies sources, whether books or journal articles or online documents (543–553).

____ examined APA style at work in Amanda Khoe's "Teaching English Language Learners in the Mainstream Classroom," learning how the system is practiced effectively in her literature review (554–563).

IV. Handbook

Chapter 30

Marking Punctuation

Period

After Sentences   567.1

Use a **period** to end a sentence that makes a statement, requests something, or gives a mild command.

Statement: By 2013, women made up 56 percent of undergraduate students and 59 percent of graduate students.

Request: Please read the instructions carefully.

Mild command: If your topic sentence isn't clear, rewrite it.

Indirect question: The professor asked if we had completed the test.

Note: It is not necessary to place a period after a statement that has parentheses around it and is part of another sentence.

Think about joining a club **(the student affairs office has a list of organizations)** for fun and for leadership experience.

After Initials and Abbreviations   567.2

Use a period after an initial and some abbreviations.

Mr.	Mrs.	B.C.E.	Ph.D.	Sen. Russ Feingold
Jr.	Sr.	D.D.S.	U.S.	Booker T. Washington
Dr.	M.A.	p.m.	B.A.	A. A. Milne

Some abbreviations (such as *pm*) also can be written without periods. Use no spacing in abbreviations except when providing a person's initials.

When an abbreviation is the last word in a sentence, use only one period at the end of the sentence.

Mikhail eyed each door until he found the name Rosa Lopez, **Ph.D.**

As Decimal Points   567.3

Use a period as a decimal point.

The government spends approximately **$15.5** million each year just to process student loan forms.

Ellipsis

568.1

To Show Omitted Words

Use an **ellipsis** (three periods) to show that one or more words have been omitted in a quotation. When typing, leave one space before and after each period.

> **(Original)** We the people of the United States, in order to form a more perfect Union, establish justice, insure domestic tranquility, provide for the common defense, promote the general welfare, and secure the blessings of liberty to ourselves and our posterity, do ordain and establish this Constitution for the United States of America.
>
> —Preamble, U.S. Constitution

> **(Quotation)** "We the people . . . in order to form a more perfect Union . . . establish this Constitution for the United States of America."

Note: Omit internal punctuation (a comma, a semicolon, a colon, or a dash) on either side of the ellipsis marks unless it is needed for clarity.

568.2

To Use After Sentences

If words from a quotation are omitted at the end of a sentence, place the ellipsis after the period or other end punctuation.

> **(Quotation)** "Five score years ago, a great American, in whose symbolic shadow we stand, signed the Emancipation Proclamation. . . . But one hundred years later, we must face the tragic fact that the Negro is still not free."
>
> —Martin Luther King, Jr., "I Have a Dream"

The first word of a sentence following a period and an ellipsis may be capitalized, even though it was not capitalized in the original.

> **(Quotation)** "Five score years ago, a great American . . . signed the Emancipation Proclamation. . . . One hundred years later, . . . the Negro is still not free."

Note: If the quoted material forms a complete sentence (even if it was not in the original), use a period, then an ellipsis.

> **(Original)** I am tired; my heart is sick and sad. From where the sun now stands I will fight no more forever.
>
> —Chief Joseph of the Nez Percé

> **(Quotation)** "I am tired. . . . I will fight no more forever."

568.3

To Show Pauses

Use an ellipsis to indicate a pause or to show unfinished thoughts.

> Listen . . . did you hear that?

> I can't figure out . . . this number doesn't . . . just how do I apply the equation in this case?

Question Mark

After Direct Questions

Use a **question mark** at the end of a direct question.

> What can I know? What ought I to do? What may I hope?   —Immanuel Kant

> Since when do you have to agree with people to defend them from injustice?
> —Lillian Hellman

Not After Indirect Questions

No question mark is used after an indirect question.

> After listening to Edgar sing, Mr. Noteworthy asked him if he had ever had formal voice training.

> **Note:** When a single-word question like *how, when,* or *why* is woven into the flow of a sentence, capitalization and special punctuation are not usually required.

> The questions we need to address at our next board meeting are not *why* or *whether,* but *how* and *when.*

After Quotations That Are Questions

When a question ends with a quotation that is also a question, use only one question mark, and place it within the quotation marks. (Also see 583.4.)

> Do you often ask yourself, "What should I be?"

To Show Uncertainty

Use a question mark within parentheses to show uncertainty about a word or phrase within a sentence.

> This July will be the 34th (?) anniversary of the first moon walk.

> **Note:** Do *not* use a question mark in this manner for formal writing.

For Questions in Parentheses or Dashes

A question within parentheses—or a question set off by dashes—is punctuated with a question mark unless the sentence ends with a question mark.

> You must consult your handbook **(what choice do you have?)** when you need to know a punctuation rule.

> Should I use your charge card (you have one, don't you), or should I pay cash?

> Maybe somewhere in the pasts of these humbled people, there were cases of bad mothering or absent fathering or emotional neglect—**what family surviving the '50s was exempt?**—but I couldn't believe these human errors brought the physical changes in Frank.
> —Mary Kay Blakely, *Wake Me When It's Over*

Punctuation Exercises:

Periods, Ellipses, Question Marks

A. End Punctuation

Indicate the correct form of end punctuation for each sentence—a period or a question mark.

1. Have you heard of the Ring of Fire
2. It is a volcanically active area
3. The Ring of Fire circles the Pacific
4. How many people has it killed
5. Over 300,000 died from one tsunami
6. Where did the tsunami take place
7. The tsunami ravaged India
8. An earthquake rocked Chile
9. The Ring of Fire is restless
10. How can we predict its catastrophes

B. Ellipses

Shorten each sentence by removing the bold words and inserting an ellipsis.

1. "Now we are engaged in a great civil war, testing whether that nation, **or any nation so conceived and so dedicated,** can long endure."
2. "We have come to dedicate a portion of that field, as a final resting place for those who here gave their lives **that that nation might live.**"
3. "But, in a larger sense, we can not dedicate—**we can not consecrate—we can not hallow**—this ground."
4. "The brave men, **living and dead,** who struggled here, have consecrated it, **far above our poor power to add or detract.**"
5. "The world will little note, **nor long remember** what we say here, but it can never forget what they did here."

C. Punctuation Practice

Indicate where periods and question marks are needed in the following paragraph by writing the word and the mark after it, and by writing any initials or abbreviations correctly.

Music is the universal language At least that's what people say But have you ever noticed how hard it is to get people to agree on music Play a song by BB King, and some people will be in heaven and others in dread Why would that be Dr Jim Fredericks indicates that the reason may be music's power to reach to our very hearts "Music is intensely personal, and the type of music that makes one person excited and happy may make another person very uncomfortable" Jill Davis, PhD, disagrees She says music is primarily cultural What does music do except make us feel "at home" or feel like a stranger When music alienates us, we dislike it, but when it makes us feel welcome, we like it So, what music makes you feel at home

Comma

Between Independent Clauses

571.1

Use a **comma** between independent clauses that are joined by a coordinating conjunction (*and, but, or, nor, for, yet, so*). (See 659.2.)

> Heath Ledger completed his brilliant portrayal as the Joker in *The Dark Knight,* **but** he died before the film was released.

Note: Do not confuse a compound verb with a compound sentence.

> Ledger's Joker became instantly iconic and won him the Oscar for best supporting actor. (compound verb)
>
> His death resulted from the abuse of prescription drugs, but it was ruled an accident. (compound sentence)

Between Items in a Series

571.2

Use commas to separate individual words, phrases, or clauses in a series. (A series contains at least three items.)

> Many college students must balance studying with **taking care of a family, working a job, getting exercise, and finding time to relax.**

Note: Do *not* use commas when all the items in a series are connected with *or, nor,* or *and.*

> Hmm . . . should I study **or** do laundry **or** go out?

To Separate Adjectives

571.3

Use commas to separate adjectives that *equally* modify the same noun. Notice in the examples below that no comma separates the last adjective from the noun.

> You should exercise regularly and follow a **sensible, healthful** diet.

> A good diet is one that includes lots of **high-protein, low-fat** foods.

To Determine Equal Modifiers

To determine whether the adjectives in a sentence modify a noun *equally*, use these two tests.

1. Reverse the order of the adjectives; if the sentence is clear, the adjectives modify equally. (In the example below, *hot* and *crowded* can be reversed, and the sentence is still clear; *short* and *coffee* cannot.)

   > Matt was tired of working in the **hot, crowded** lab and decided to take a **short coffee** break.

2. Insert *and* between the adjectives; if the sentence reads well, use a comma when *and* is omitted. (The word *and* can be inserted between *hot* and *crowded*, but *and* does not make sense between *short* and *coffee*.)

572.1 To Set Off Nonrestrictive Appositives

A specific kind of explanatory word or phrase called an **appositive** identifies or renames a preceding noun or pronoun.

> Albert Einstein, **the famous mathematician and physicist,** developed the theory of relativity.

Note: Do *not* use commas with *restrictive appositives.* A restrictive appositive is essential to the basic meaning of the sentence.

> The famous mathematician and physicist **Albert Einstein** developed the theory of relativity.

572.2 To Set Off Adverb Dependent Clauses

Use a comma after most introductory dependent clauses functioning as adverbs.

> **Although Charlemagne was a great patron of learning,** he never learned to write properly. (adverb dependent clause)

You may use a comma if the adverb dependent clause following the independent clause is not essential. Adverb clauses beginning with *even though, although, while,* or another conjunction expressing a contrast are usually not needed to complete the meaning of a sentence.

> Charlemagne never learned to write properly, **even though he continued to practice.**

Note: A comma is *not* used if the dependent clause following the independent clause is needed to complete the meaning of the sentence.

> Maybe Charlemagne didn't learn **because he had an empire to run.**

572.3 After Introductory Phrases

Use a comma after introductory phrases.

> **In spite of his practicing,** Charlemagne's handwriting remained poor.

Note: A comma is usually omitted if the phrase follows an independent clause.

> Charlemagne's handwriting remained poor **in spite of his practicing.**

Also Note: You may omit the comma after a short (four or fewer words) introductory phrase unless it is needed to ensure clarity.

> **At 6:00 a.m.** he would rise and practice his penmanship.

572.4 To Set Off Transitional Expressions

Use a comma to set off conjunctive adverbs and transitional phrases. (See 577.2–577.3.)

> Handwriting is not, **as a matter of fact,** easy to improve upon later in life; **however,** it can be done if you are determined enough.

Note: If a transitional expression blends smoothly with the rest of the sentence, it does not need to be set off. ***Example:*** If you are in fact coming, I'll see you there.

A Closer Look
Nonrestrictive and Restrictive Clauses and Phrases

Use Commas with Nonrestrictive Clauses and Phrases

573.1

Use commas to enclose **nonrestrictive** (unnecessary) phrases or dependent (adjective) clauses. A nonrestrictive phrase or dependent clause adds information that is not necessary to the basic meaning of the sentence. For example, if the clause or phrase (in **boldface**) were left out of the two examples below, the meaning of the sentences would remain clear. Therefore, commas are used to set off the nonrestrictive information.

> The locker rooms in Swain Hall, **which were painted and updated last summer**, give professors a place to shower. (nonrestrictive clause)

> Work-study programs, **offered on many campuses,** give students the opportunity to earn tuition money. (nonrestrictive phrase)

Don't Use Commas with Restrictive Clauses and Phrases

573.2

Do *not* use commas to set off **restrictive** (necessary) adjective clauses and phrases. A restrictive clause or phrase adds information that the reader needs to understand the sentence. For example, if the adjective clause and phrase (in **boldface**) were dropped from the examples below, the meaning would be unclear.

> Only the professors **who run at noon** use the locker rooms in Swain Hall to shower. (restrictive clause)

> Using tuition money **earned through work-study programs** is the only way some students can afford to go to college. (restrictive phrase)

Using "That" or "Which"

573.3

Use *that* to introduce restrictive (necessary) adjective clauses; use *which* to introduce nonrestrictive (unnecessary) adjective clauses. When the two words are used in this way, the reader can quickly distinguish the necessary information from the unnecessary.

> Campus jobs **that are funded by the university** are awarded to students only. (restrictive)

> The cafeteria, **which is run by an independent contractor**, can hire nonstudents. (nonrestrictive)

Note: Clauses beginning with who can be either restrictive or nonrestrictive.

> Students **who pay for their own education** are highly motivated. (restrictive)

> The admissions counselor, **who has studied student records,** said that many returning students earn high GPAs in spite of demanding family obligations. (nonrestrictive)

574.1

To Set Off Items in Addresses and Dates

Use commas to set off items in an address and the year in a date.

> Send your letter to **1600 Pennsylvania Avenue, Washington, DC 20006, before January 1, 2014,** or send an email to president@whitehouse.gov.

Note: No comma is placed between the state and ZIP code. Also, no comma separates the items if only the month and year are given: January 2014.

574.2

To Set Off Dialogue

Use commas to set off the words of the speaker from the rest of the sentence.

> **"Never be afraid to ask for help,"** advised Ms. Kane.

> **"With the evidence that we now have,"** Professor Thom said, **"many scientists believe there is life on Mars."**

574.3

To Separate Nouns of Direct Address

Use a comma to separate a noun of direct address from the rest of the sentence.

> **Jamie,** would you please stop whistling while I'm trying to work?

574.4

To Separate Interjections

Use a comma to separate a mild interjection from the rest of the sentence.

> **Okay,** so now what do I do?

Note: Exclamation points are used after strong interjections: Wow! You're kidding!

574.5

To Set Off Interruptions

Use commas to set off a word, phrase, or clause that interrupts the movement of a sentence. Such expressions usually can be identified through the following tests: (1) They may be omitted without changing the meaning of a sentence; and (2) they may be placed nearly anywhere in the sentence without changing its meaning.

> For me, **well,** it was just a good job gone!   —Langston Hughes, "A Good Job Gone"

> Lela, **as a general rule,** always comes to class ready for a pop quiz.

574.6

To Separate Numbers

Use commas to separate a series of numbers to distinguish hundreds, thousands, millions, and so on.

> Do you know how to write the amount **$2,025** on a check?

> **25,000   973,240   18,620,197**

To Enclose Explanatory Words

575.1

Use commas to enclose an explanatory word or phrase.

> Time management, **according to many professionals,** is such an important skill that it should be taught in college.

To Separate Contrasted Elements

575.2

Use commas to separate contrasted elements within a sentence.

> We work to become, **not to acquire.**
> —Eugene Delacroix

> Where all think alike, **no one thinks very much.**
> —Walter Lippmann

Before Tags

575.3

Use a comma before tags, which are short statements or questions at the ends of sentences.

> You studied for the test, **right?**

To Enclose Titles or Initials

575.4

Use commas to enclose a title or initials and given names that follow a surname.

> Until Martin, **Sr.,** was 15, he never had more than three months of schooling in any one year.
> —Ed Clayton, *Martin Luther King: The Peaceful Warrior*

> The genealogical files included the names Sanders, **L. H.,** and Sanders, **Lucy Hale.**

Note: Some style manuals no longer require commas around titles.

For Clarity or Emphasis

575.5

Use a comma for clarity or for emphasis. There will be times when none of the traditional rules call for a comma, but one will be needed to prevent misreading or to emphasize an important idea.

> What she does, does matter to us. (clarity)

> It may be those who do most, dream most. (emphasis)
> —Stephen Leacock

Avoid Overusing Commas

The commas (in **red**) below are used incorrectly. Do *not* use a comma between the subject and its verb or the verb and its object.

> Current periodicals on the subject of psychology, are available at nearly all bookstores.

> I think she should read, *Psychology Today.*

Do *not* use a comma before an indirect quotation.

> My roommate said, that she doesn't understand the notes I took.

Punctuation Exercises:

Commas

A. Basic Comma Use

Indicate correct comma placement in each sentence below. Some sentences have multiple commas.

1. To succeed in college you need focus dedication and hard work.
2. A compatible amiable roommate helps and you will want access to a computer.
3. To keep your sanity a balanced workable schedule is also a must.
4. You should consult with family friends and counselors about course schedules.
5. Between classes jobs and the social scene many students are stretched.
6. College prepares people for life and one way is by teaching them to juggle priorities.
7. Students also must afford books supplies and food.
8. A manageable realistic budget keeps money matters in order.
9. Students should work hard think deeply and enjoy their time in college.
10. With goals such as these students can get the most out of college.

B. Restrictive and Nonrestrictive Clauses and Phrases

For each sentence, indicate correct comma placement. If a sentence needs no commas, write "correct."

1. Author Lauren Beukes who lives in South Africa wrote *Moxyland*.
2. *Moxyland* a dystopian thriller focuses on a world overrun by governmental and corporate domination of technology.
3. Gareth L. Powell who is an author in his own right said the book "gives us a dystopia to rival 1984."
4. Another reviewer said *Moxyland* is a book that changed science fiction.
5. Lauren Beukes an avid user of social media released a *Moxyland* soundtrack and a plush doll which gave two-thirds of its proceeds to a women's charity.

C. Advanced Comma Use

For each sentence, indicate correct comma placement.

1. I live at 3415 West Kane Drive Chicago Illinois.
2. Jamar where do you live?
3. All right who turned out the lights?
4. If you think I turned them out well you're mistaken.
5. I sure would like to receive a check for $5000.

Semicolon

To Join Two Independent Clauses

577.1

Use a **semicolon** to join two or more closely related independent clauses that are not connected with a coordinating conjunction. In other words, each of the clauses could stand alone as a separate sentence.

> I was thrown out of college for cheating on the metaphysics exam; I looked into the soul of the boy next to me.
>
> —Woody Allen

Before Conjunctive Adverbs

577.2

Use a semicolon before a conjunctive adverb when the word clarifies the relationship between two independent clauses in a compound sentence. A comma often follows the conjunctive adverb. Common conjunctive adverbs include *also, besides, however, instead, meanwhile, then,* and *therefore.*

> Many college freshmen are on their own for the first time; **however,** others are already independent and even have families.

Before Transitional Phrases

577.3

Use a semicolon before a transitional phrase when the phrase clarifies the relationship between two independent clauses in a compound sentence. A comma usually follows the transitional phrase.

> Pablo was born in the Andes; **as a result,** he loves mountains.

Transitional Phrases

after all	at the same time	in addition	in the first place
as a matter of fact	even so	in conclusion	on the contrary
as a result	for example	in fact	on the other hand
at any rate	for instance	in other words	

To Separate Independent Clauses Containing Commas

577.4

Use a semicolon to separate independent clauses that contain internal commas, even when the independent clauses are connected by a coordinating conjunction.

> Your MP3 player, computer, bike, and other valuables are expensive to replace; so include these items in your homeowner's insurance policy and remember to use the locks on your door, bike, and storage area.

To Separate Items in a Series That Contains Commas

577.5

Use a semicolon to separate items in a series that already contain commas.

> My favorite foods are pizza with pepperoni, onions, and olives; peanut butter and banana sandwiches; and liver with bacon, peppers, and onions.

Colon

578.1   After Salutations

Use a **colon** after the salutation of a business letter.

     Dear Mr. Spielberg: Dear Professor Higgins: Dear Members:

578.2   Between Numbers Indicating Time or Ratios

Use a colon between the hours, minutes, and seconds of a number indicating time.

     8:30 p.m.   9:45 a.m.   10:24:55

Use a colon between two numbers in a ratio.

     The ratio of computers to students is 1:20. (one to twenty)

578.3   For Emphasis

Use a colon to emphasize a word, a phrase, a clause, or a sentence that explains or adds impact to the main clause.

     I have one goal for myself: to become the first person in my family to graduate from college.

578.4   To Distinguish Parts of Publications

Use a colon between a title and a subtitle, volume and page, and chapter and verse.

     Ron Brown: An Uncommon Life   *Britannica* 4: 211   Psalm 23:1–6

578.5   To Introduce Quotations

Use a colon to introduce a quotation following a complete sentence.

     John Locke is credited with this prescription for a good life: "A sound mind in a sound body."

     Lou Gottlieb, however, offered this version: "A sound mind or a sound body—take your pick."

578.6   To Introduce a List

Use a colon to introduce a list following a complete sentence.

     A college student needs a number of things to succeed: basic skills, creativity, and determination.

Avoid Colon Errors

Do *not* use a colon between a verb and its object or complement.

     Dave likes: comfortable space and time to think. (**Incorrect**)

     Dave likes two things: comfortable space and time to think. (**Correct**)

Hyphen

In Compound Words   579.1

Use a **hyphen** to make some compound words.

great-great-grandfather (noun)   starry-eyed (adjective)

mother-in-law (noun)   three-year-old (adjective)

Writers sometimes combine words in new and unexpected ways. Such combinations are usually hyphenated.

> And they pried pieces of **baked-too-fast** sunshine cake from the roofs of their mouths and looked once more into the boy's eyes.
>
> —Toni Morrison, *Song of Solomon*

Note: Consult a dictionary to find how it lists a particular compound word. Some compound words (*living room*) do not use a hyphen and are written separately. Some are written solid (*bedroom*). Some do not use a hyphen when the word is a noun (*ice cream*) but do use a hyphen when it is a verb or an adjective (*ice-cream sundae*).

To Join Letters and Words   579.2

Use a hyphen to join a capital letter or a lowercase letter to a noun or a participle.

T-shirt   U-turn   V-shaped   x-ray

To Join Words in Compound Numbers   579.3

Use a hyphen to join the words in compound numbers from twenty-one to ninety-nine when it is necessary to write them out. (See 598.1.)

Forty-two people found seats in the cramped classroom.

Between Numbers in Fractions   579.4

Use a hyphen between the numerator and the denominator of a fraction, but not when one or both of these elements are already hyphenated.

four-tenths   five-sixteenths   seven thirty-seconds (7/32)

In a Special Series   579.5

Use a hyphen when two or more words have a common element that is omitted in all but the last term.

We have cedar posts in **four-, six-,** and **eight-**inch widths.

To Create New Words   579.6

Use a hyphen to form new words beginning with the prefixes *self, ex, all,* and *half.* Also use a hyphen to join any prefix to a proper noun, a proper adjective, or the official name of an office.

post-Depression   mid-May   ex-mayor

580.1

To Prevent Confusion

Use a hyphen with prefixes or suffixes to avoid confusion or awkward spelling.

re-cover (not *recover*) the sofa   **shell-like** (not *shelllike*) shape

580.2

To Join Numbers

Use a hyphen to join numbers indicating a range, a score, or a vote.

Students study **30-40** hours a week.   The final score was **84-82**.

580.3

To Divide Words

Use a hyphen to divide a word between syllables at the end of a line of print.

Guidelines for Word Division

1. Leave enough of the word at the end of the line to identify the word.
2. Never divide a one-syllable word: **rained, skills, through.**
3. Avoid dividing a word of five or fewer letters: **paper, study, July.**
4. Never divide a one-letter syllable from the rest of the word: **omit-ted,** not **o-mitted.**
5. Always divide a compound word between its basic units: **sister-in-law,** not **sis-ter-in-law.**
6. Never divide abbreviations or contractions: **shouldn't,** not **should-n't.**
7. When a vowel is a syllable by itself, divide the word after the vowel: **epi-sode,** not **ep-isode.**
8. Avoid dividing a numeral: **1,000,000,** not **1,000,-000.**
9. Avoid dividing the last word in a paragraph.
10. Never divide the last word in more than two lines in a row.
11. Check a dictionary for acceptable word divisions.

580.4

To Form Adjectives

Use a hyphen to join two or more words that serve as a single-thought adjective before a noun.

In real life I am a large, **big-boned** woman with rough, **man-working** hands.

—Alice Walker, "Everyday Use"

Most single-thought adjectives are not hyphenated when they come after the noun. (Check the dictionary to be sure.)

In real life, I am large and **big boned.**

Note: When the first of these words is an adverb ending in *ly,* do not use a hyphen. Also, do not use a hyphen when a number or a letter is the final element in a single-thought adjective.

fresh**ly** painted barn   grade **A** milk (letter is the final element)

Dash

To Set Off Nonessential Elements

Use a **dash** to set off nonessential elements—explanations, examples, or definitions—when you want to emphasize them.

> Near the semester's end—**and this is not always due to poor planning**—some students may find themselves in academic trouble.

> The term *caveat emptor*—**let the buyer beware**—is especially appropriate to Internet shopping.

> **Note:** A dash is indicated by two hyphens--with no spacing before or after--in typewriter-generated material. Don't use a single hyphen when a dash (two hyphens) is required.

To Set Off an Introductory Series

Use a dash to set off an introductory series from the clause that explains the series.

> **Cereal, coffee, and Facebook**—without these I can't get going in the morning.

To Show Missing Text

Use a dash to show that words or letters are missing.

> **Mr. —** won't let us marry.
>
> —Alice Walker, *The Color Purple*

To Show Interrupted Speech

Use a dash (or an ellipsis) to show interrupted or faltering speech in dialogue. (Also see 568.3.)

> Well, **I—ah—had** this terrible case of the flu, **and—then—ah—the** library closed because of that flash flood, **and—well—the** high humidity jammed my printer.
>
> —Excuse No. 101

> "If you *think* you can—"
> "Oh, I *know*—"
> "Don't interrupt!"

For Emphasis

Use a dash in place of a colon to introduce or to emphasize a word, a series, a phrase, or a clause.

> **Jogging**—that's what he lives for.

> **Life is like a grindstone**—whether it grinds you down or polishes you up depends on what you're made of.

> **This is how the world moves**—not like an arrow, but a boomerang.
>
> —Ralph Ellison

Punctuation Exercises:

Semicolons, Colons, Hyphens, and Dashes

A. Semicolons and Colons

Indicate correct placement of semicolons or colons in each sentence.

1. Aaron Copland revolutionized music Leonard Bernstein called him "Moses."
2. Copland wrote ballets such as *Appalachian Spring, Billy the Kid,* and *Rodeo* music for films such as *Our Town* and *The Red Pony* and symphonies such as the *Organ Symphony,* the *Short Symphony,* and his *Third Symphony.*
3. Copland also founded ASCAP the American Society of Composers, Authors, and Publishers.
4. ASCAP made it possible to be a composer it set up royalty standards.
5. Copland was trained in Paris despite that fact, he was all-American.
6. Copland is well known for one piece "Fanfare for the Common Man."
7. Unlike Bernstein, Copland wrote slowly he composed at the piano.
8. At first, Copland composed atonal music he changed his style during the Great Depression.
9. In the '50s, Copland and Bernstein ran up against an antagonist McCarthy.
10. Copland showed the way for young composers he was a kind of "Moses."

B. Hyphens

For each item, insert hyphens correctly. If an item needs no hyphen, write "correct."

1. forty five
2. midMarch
3. nine thirty seconds
4. father in law
5. recreate (meaning "to create again")
6. a 36 38 score
7. hard working people
8. grade A meat
9. U shaped valley
10. two year old

C. Dashes

For each sentence, indicate correct dash placement.

1. The expression *carpe diem* seize the day was written on the classroom wall.
2. "Faith, hope, and love these three, but the greatest of these is love."
3. He stuttered, "I um well wanted to ask you on a date."
4. Performing before a live audience that's what I love.
5. I will caution you this is what I tell everyone don't give up your dreams.

Quotation Marks

To Punctuate Titles   583.1

Use **quotation marks** to punctuate some titles. (Also see 585.2.)

"Two Friends" (short story)
"New Car Designs" (newspaper article)
"Sparks" (song)
"Multiculturalism and the Language Battle" (lecture title)
"The New Admissions Game" (magazine article)
"Reflections on Advertising" (chapter in a book)
"Blink" (television episode from *Doctor Who*)
"Annabel Lee" (short poem)

For Special Words   583.2

Use quotation marks (1) to show that a word is being discussed as a word, (2) to indicate that a word or phrase is directly quoted, (3) to indicate that a word is slang, or (4) to point out that a word is being used in a humorous or ironic way.

1. A commentary on the times is that the word **"honesty"** is now preceded by **"old-fashioned."**
2. She said she was **"incensed."**
3. I drank a Dixie and ate bar peanuts and asked the bartender where I could hear **"chanky-chank,"** as Cajuns call their music.   —William Least Heat-Moon, *Blue Highways*
4. In an attempt to be popular, he works very hard at being **"cute."**

> **Note:** A word used as a word can also be set off with italics.

Placement of Periods or Commas   583.3

Always place periods and commas inside quotation marks.

"Dr. Slaughter wants you to have liquids, Will," Mama said anxiously. "He said not to give you any solid food tonight."   —Olive Ann Burns, *Cold Sassy Tree*

Placement of Exclamation Points or Question Marks   583.4

Place an exclamation point or a question mark inside quotation marks when it punctuates both the main sentence and the quotation *or* just the quotation; place it outside when it punctuates the main sentence.

Do you often ask yourself, "What should I be?"

I almost croaked when he asked, "That won't be a problem, will it?"

Did he really say, "Finish this by tomorrow"?

Placement of Semicolons or Colons   583.5

Always place semicolons or colons outside quotation marks.

I just read "Computers and Creativity"; I now have some different ideas about the role of computers in the arts.

A Closer Look
Marking Quoted Material

584.1

For Direct Quotations

Use quotation marks before and after a direct quotation—a person's exact words.

> Sitting in my one-room apartment, I remember Mom saying, **"Don't go to the party with him."**

Note: Do *not* use quotation marks for *indirect* quotations.

> I remember Mom saying **that I should not date him.** (These are not the speaker's exact words.)

584.2

For Quoted Passages

Use quotation marks before and after a quoted passage. Any word that is not part of the original quotation must be placed inside brackets.

> **(Original)** First of all, it must accept responsibility for providing shelter for the homeless.

> **(Quotation)** "First of all, it **[the federal government]** must accept responsibility for providing shelter for the homeless."

Note: If you quote only part of the original passage, be sure to construct a sentence that is both accurate and grammatically correct.

> The report goes on to say that the federal government **"must accept responsibility for providing shelter for the homeless."**

584.3

For Long Quotations

If more than one paragraph is quoted, quotation marks are placed before each paragraph and at the end of the last paragraph **(Example A).** Quotations that are five or more lines (MLA style) or forty words or more (APA style) are usually set off from the text by indenting ten spaces from the left margin (a style called "block form"). Do not use quotation marks before or after a block-form quotation **(Example B),** except in cases where quotation marks appear in the original passage **(Example C).**

Example A   *fig. 30.1*   **Example B**   *fig. 30.2*   **Example C**   *fig. 30.3*

584.4

For Quoting Quotations

Use single quotation marks to punctuate quoted material within a quotation.

> **"I was lucky,"** said Jane. **"The proctor announced, 'Put your pencils down,' just as I was filling in the last answer."**

Italics (Underlining)

In Handwritten and Printed Material   585.1

Italics is a printer's term for a style of type that is slightly slanted. In this sentence, the word *happiness* is printed in italics. In material that is handwritten or typed on a machine that cannot print in italics, underline each word or letter that should be in italics.

> In <u>The Road to Memphis</u>, racism is a contagious disease.
> (typed or handwritten)

> Mildred Taylor's *The Road to Memphis* exposes racism. (printed)

In Titles   585.2

Use italics to indicate the titles of magazines, newspapers, books, pamphlets, full-length plays, films, videos, radio and television programs, book-length poems, ballets, operas, lengthy musical compositions, CDs, paintings and sculptures, legal cases, Web sites, and the names of ships and aircraft. (Also see 583.1)

The Week (magazine)	*New York Times* (newspaper)
The Lost Symbol (book)	*Yankee Tavern* (play)
Enola Gay (airplane)	*The Fame* (album)
ACLU v. State of Ohio (legal case)	*Billy the Kid* (ballet)
Avatar (film)	*The Thinker* (sculpture)
CSI (television program)	*GeoCities* (Web site)
College Loans (pamphlet)	

When one title appears within another title, punctuate as follows:

> I read an article entitled "The Making of *Up*." (title of movie in an article title)

> He wants to watch *Inside the* New York Times on PBS tonight.
> (title of newspaper in title of TV program)

For Key Terms   585.3

Italics are often used for a key term in a discussion or for a technical term, especially when it is accompanied by its definition. Italicize the term the first time it is used. Thereafter, put the term in roman type.

> This flower has a ***zygomorphic*** (bilateral symmetry) structure.

For Foreign Words and Scientific Names   585.4

Use italics for foreign words that have not been adopted into the English language; italics are also used to denote scientific names.

> Say ***arrivederci*** to your fears and try new activities. (foreign word)

> The voyageurs discovered the shy ***Castor canadensis,*** or North American beaver.
> (scientific name)

Parentheses

586.1   To Enclose Explanatory or Supplementary Material

Use **parentheses** to enclose explanatory or supplementary material that interrupts the normal sentence structure.

> The RA **(resident assistant)** became my best friend.

586.2   To Set Off Numbers in a List

Use parentheses to set off numbers used with a series of words or phrases.

> Dr. Beck told us **(1)** plan ahead, **(2)** stay flexible, and **(3)** follow through.

586.3   For Parenthetical Sentences

When using a full "sentence" within another sentence, do not capitalize it or use a period inside the parentheses.

> Your friend doesn't have the assignment **(he was just thinking about calling you)**, so you'll have to make a few more calls.

When the parenthetical sentence comes after the main sentence, capitalize and punctuate it the same way you would any other complete sentence.

> But Mom doesn't say boo to Dad; she's always sweet to him. **(Actually she's sort of sweet to everybody.)**
> —Norma Fox Mazer, *Up on Fong Mountain*

586.4   To Set Off References

Use parentheses to set off references to authors, titles, pages, and years.

> The statistics are alarming **(see page 9)** and demand action.

> **Note:** For unavoidable parentheses within parentheses (. . . [. . .] . . .), use brackets. Avoid overuse of parentheses by using commas instead.

Diagonal

586.5   To Form Fractions or Show Choices

Use a **diagonal** (also called a *slash*) to form a fraction. Also place a diagonal between two words to indicate that either is acceptable.

> My **walking/running** shoe size is **5 1/2**; my dress shoes are **6 1/2**.

586.6   When Quoting Poetry

When quoting poetry, use a diagonal (with one space before and after) to show where each line ends in the actual poem.

> A dryness is upon the house / My father loved and tended. / Beyond his firm and sculptured door / His light and lease have ended.
> —Gwendolyn Brooks, "In Honor of David Anderson Brooks, My Father"

Brackets

With Words That Clarify

Use **brackets** before and after words that are added to clarify what another person has said or written.

> "They'd [**the sweat bees**] get into your mouth, ears, eyes, nose. You'd feel them all over you."
> —Marilyn Johnson and Sasha Nyary, "Roosevelts in the Amazon"

> **Note:** The brackets indicate that the words *the sweat bees* are not part of the original quotation but were added for clarification. (See 584.2.)

Around Comments by Someone Other Than the Author

Place brackets around comments that have been added by someone other than the author or speaker.

> "In conclusion, *docendo discimus*. Let the school year begin!" [**Huh?**]

Around Editorial Corrections

Place brackets around an editorial correction or addition.

> "Brooklyn alone has 8 percent of lead poisoning [**victims**] nationwide," said Marjorie Moore.
> —Donna Actie, student writer

Around the Word *Sic*

Brackets should be placed around the word *sic* (Latin for "so" or "thus") in quoted material; the word indicates that an error appearing in the quoted material was made by the original speaker or writer.

> "There is a higher principal [**sic**] at stake here: Is the school administration aware of the situation?"

Exclamation Point

To Express Strong Feeling

Use an **exclamation point** to express strong feeling. It may be placed at the end of a sentence (or an elliptical expression that stands for a sentence). Use exclamation points sparingly.

> "That's not the point," said Wangero. "These are all pieces of dresses Grandma used to wear. She did all this stitching by hand. **Imagine!**"
> —Alice Walker, "Everyday Use"

> Su-su-something's crawling up the back of my neck!
> —Mark Twain, Roughing It

> She was on tiptoe, stretching for an orange, when they heard, "**HEY YOU!**"
> —Beverley Naidoo, Journey to Jo'burg

Apostrophe

588.1   In Contractions

Use an **apostrophe** to show that one or more letters have been left out of two words joined to form a contraction.

don't → o is left out   **she'd** → woul is left out   **it's** → i is left out

Note: An apostrophe is also used to show that one or more numerals or letters have been left out of numbers or words.

class of **'02** → 20 is left out   good **mornin'** → g is left out

588.2   To Form Plurals

Use an apostrophe and an *s* to form the plural of a letter, a number, a sign, or a word discussed as a word.

A → **A's**   8 → **8's**   + → **+'s**
You use too many *and's* in your writing.

Note: If two apostrophes are called for in the same word, omit the second one.

Follow closely the do's and **don'ts** (not **don't's**) on the checklist.

588.3   To Form Singular Possessives

The possessive form of singular nouns is usually made by adding an apostrophe and an *s*.

Spock's ears   my **computer's** memory

Note: When a singular noun of more than one syllable ends with an *s* or a *z* sound, the possessive may be formed by adding just an apostrophe—or an apostrophe and an *s*.

When the singular noun is a one-syllable word, however, the possessive is usually formed by adding both an apostrophe and an *s*.

Dallas' sports teams *or* **Dallas's** sports teams (two-syllable word)

Kiss's last concert   my **boss's** generosity (one-syllable words)

588.4   To Form Plural Possessives

The possessive form of plural nouns ending in *s* is made by adding just an apostrophe.

the **Joneses'** great-grandfather   **bosses'** offices

Note: For plural nouns not ending in *s*, add an apostrophe and *s*.

women's health issues   **children's** program

To Determine Ownership

You will punctuate possessives correctly if you remember that the word that comes immediately before the apostrophe is the owner.

girl's guitar *(girl is the owner)*   **girls'** guitar *(girls are the owners)*
boss's office *(boss is the owner)*   **bosses'** office *(bosses are the owners)*

Titles 593.1

Capitalize the first word of a title, the last word, and every word in between except articles (*a, an, the*), short prepositions, *to* in an infinitive, and coordinating conjunctions. Follow this rule for titles of books, newspapers, magazines, poems, plays, songs, articles, films, works of art, and stories.

Going to Meet the Man	*Chicago Tribune*
"Nothing Gold Can Stay"	"Jobs in the Cyber Arena"
A Midsummer Night's Dream	*The War of the Roses*

Note: When citing titles in a bibliography, check the style manual you've been asked to follow. For example, in APA style, only the first word of a title is capitalized.

Organizations 593.2

Capitalize the name of an organization or a team and its members.

American Indian Movement	**Democratic Party**
Tampa Bay Buccaneers	**Tucson Drama Club**

Abbreviations 593.3

Capitalize abbreviations of titles and organizations. (Some other abbreviations are also capitalized. See pages 601–602.) (Also see 567.2.)

M.D.   Ph.D.   NAACP   C.E.   B.C.E.   GPA

Letters 593.4

Capitalize letters used to indicate a form or shape.

U-turn   I-beam   S-curve   V-shaped   T-shirt

Words Used as Names 593.5

Capitalize words like *father, mother, uncle, senator,* and *professor* when they are parts of titles that include a personal name or when they are substituted for proper nouns (especially in direct address). (Also see 574.3.)

Hello, **Senator** Feingold. (*Senator* is part of the name.)
Our **senator** is an environmentalist.

Who was your chemistry **professor** last quarter?
I had **Professor** Williams for Chemistry 101.

Note: To test whether a word is being substituted for a proper noun, simply read the sentence with a proper noun in place of the word. If the proper noun fits in the sentence, the word being tested should be capitalized. Usually the word is not capitalized if it follows a possessive—*my, his, our, your,* and so on.

Did **Dad (Brad)** pack the stereo in the trailer? (Brad works in this sentence.)

Did your **dad (Brad)** pack the stereo in the trailer? (*Brad* does not work in this sentence; the word *dad* follows the possessive *your.*)

594.1   **Titles of Courses**

Words such as *technology, history,* and *science* are proper nouns when they are included in the titles of specific courses; they are common nouns when they name a field of study.

> Who teaches **Art History 202?** (title of a specific course)

> Professor Bunker loves teaching **history.** (a field of study)

> **Note:** The words *freshman, sophomore, junior,* and *senior* are not capitalized unless they are part of an official title.

> > The **seniors** who maintained high GPAs were honored at the **Mount Mary Senior Honors Banquet.**

594.2   **Internet and Email**

The words *Internet* and *World Wide Web* are always capitalized because they are considered proper nouns. When your writing includes a web address (URL), capitalize any letters that the site's owner does (on printed materials or on the site itself). Not only is it respectful to reprint a web address exactly as it appears elsewhere, but, in fact, some web addresses are case-sensitive and must be entered into a browser's address bar exactly as presented.

> When doing research on the **Internet,** be sure to record each site's **web** address (**URL**) and each contact's **email** address.

> **Note:** Some people include capital letters in their email addresses to make certain features evident. Although email addresses are not case-sensitive, repeat each letter in print just as its owner uses it.

Avoid Capitalization Errors

Do not capitalize any of the following:

- A prefix attached to a proper noun
- Seasons of the year
- Words used to indicate direction or position
- Common nouns and titles that appear near, but are not part of, a proper noun

Capitalize	Do Not Capitalize
American	un-American
January, February	winter, spring
The South is quite conservative.	Turn south at the stop sign.
Duluth City College	a Duluth college
Chancellor John Bohm	John Bohm, our chancellor
President Bush	the president of the United States
Earth (the planet)	earthmover
Internet	email

Mechanics Exercises:

Capitalization

A. Capitalization Practice

For each sentence, write the correct form of any incorrectly capitalized or lowercased words.

1. Vice president Joe Biden will speak in topeka, Kansas, on thursday.
2. What Jarrod meant to say is this: the dallas cowboys have enough talent to win the Super bowl.
3. The beautiful double rainbow in Yellowstone national park seemed like an act of god.
4. Does starbucks have a wireless internet connection?
5. The vehicle in question was driving North along interstate 55 before making a u-turn.
6. are you taking introduction to mass communication 101 with professor Williams next semester?
7. I'm going to the south to visit my brother in the peach state.
8. A story in the *San Francisco chronicle* quoted the Secretary of Agriculture saying, "we are concerned with the development of our farmland."
9. Shoot me an email if you want to go with me to the civil war reenactment.
10. The french restaurant serves an amazing aged Cheese platter.

B. Using Capitalization

For each line of the following email message, write the correct form of any incorrectly capitalized or lowercased words.

> dear Dr. Cruz,   1
>
> Thank You for letting me shadow you for a day at St. Vincent Hospital. I very   2
> much enjoyed observing the arthroscopic surgery and was impressed with the   3
> expertise of the hospital's Staff! I hope we can meet up soon to discuss questions 4
> about my Human functional anatomy 410 course.   5
>
> Best Wishes,   6
>
> Kimbra Jenson   7

C. Capitalization Errors

Write the correct form of any incorrectly capitalized or lowercased words.

summer	prime minister	David Cameron	m.d.
Vice President	the bible	spanish	

Plurals

596.1   ### Nouns Ending in a Consonant

Some nouns remain unchanged when used as plurals (*species, moose, halibut,* and so on), but the plurals of most nouns are formed by adding an *s* to the singular form.

dorm—**dorms**   credit—**credits**   midterm—**midterms**

The plurals of nouns ending in *sh, ch, x, s,* and *z* are made by adding *es* to the singular form.

lunch—**lunches**   wish—**wishes**   class—**classes**

596.2   ### Nouns Ending in *y*

The plurals of common nouns that end in *y* (preceded by a consonant) are formed by changing the *y* to *i* and adding *es*.

dormitory—**dormitories**   sorority—**sororities**   duty—**duties**

The plurals of common nouns that end in *y* (preceded by a vowel) are formed by adding only an s.

attorney—**attorneys**   monkey—**monkeys**   toy—**toys**

The plurals of all proper nouns ending in *y* (whether preceded by a consonant or a vowel) are formed by adding an *s*.

the three **Kathys**   the five **Faheys**

596.3   ### Nouns Ending in *o*

The plurals of words ending in *o* (preceded by a vowel) are formed by adding an *s*.

radio—**radios**   cameo—**cameos**   studio—**studios**

The plurals of most nouns ending in *o* (preceded by a consonant) are formed by adding *es*.

echo—**echoes**   hero—**heroes**   tomato—**tomatoes**

Musical terms always form plurals by adding an *s;* check a dictionary for other words of this type.

alto—**altos**   banjo—**banjos**   solo—**solos**   piano—**pianos**

596.4   ### Nouns Ending in *f* or *fe*

The plurals of nouns that end in *f* or *fe* are formed in one of two ways: If the final *f* sound is still heard in the plural form of the word, simply add *s;* if the final sound is a *v* sound, change the *f* to *ve* and add an *s*.

Plural ends with *f* sound: roof—**roofs**   chief—**chiefs**
Plural ends with *v* sound: wife—**wives**   loaf—**loaves**

Note: The plurals of some nouns that end in *f* or *fe* can be formed by either adding *s* or changing the *f* to *ve* and adding an *s*.

Plural ends with either sound: hoof—**hoofs, hooves**

Irregular Spelling

Many foreign words (as well as some of English origin) form a plural by taking on an irregular spelling; others are now acceptable with the commonly used *s* or *es* ending. Take time to check a dictionary.

child—**children**	alumnus—**alumni**	syllabus—**syllabi, syllabuses**
goose—**geese**	datum—**data**	radius—**radii, radiuses**

Words Discussed as Words

The plurals of symbols, letters, figures, and words discussed as words are formed by adding an apostrophe and an *s*.

Many colleges have now added **A/B's** and **B/C's** as standard grades.

Note: You can choose to omit the apostrophe when the omission does not cause confusion.

YMCA's or YMCAs   CD's or CDs

Nouns Ending in *ful*

The plurals of nouns that end with *ful* are formed by adding an *s* at the end of the word.

three **teaspoonfuls**   two **tankfuls**   four **bagfuls**

Compound Nouns

The plurals of compound nouns are usually formed by adding an *s* or an *es* to the important word in the compound. (Also see 579.1.)

brothers-in-law   **maids** of honor   **secretaries** of state

Collective Nouns

Collective nouns do not change in form when they are used as plurals.

class (a unit—singular form)

class (individual members—plural form)

Because the spelling of the collective noun does not change, it is often the pronoun used in place of the collective noun that indicates whether the noun is singular or plural. Use a singular pronoun (**its**) to show that the collective noun is singular. Use a plural pronoun (**their**) to show that the collective noun is plural.

The class needs to change **its** motto.

(The writer is thinking of the group as a unit.)

The class brainstormed with **their** professor.

(The writer is thinking of the group as individuals.)

esl Note: To determine whether a plural requires the article *the,* you must first determine whether it is definite or indefinite. Definite plurals use *the,* whereas indefinite plurals do not require any article. (See 678.3–679.1.)

Numbers

Numerals or Words

Numbers from one to one hundred are usually written as words; numbers 101 and greater are usually written as numerals. (APA style uses numerals for numbers 10 and higher.) Hyphenate numbers written as two words if less than one hundred.

> **two   seven   ten   twenty-five   106   1,079**

The same rule applies to the use of ordinal numbers.

> **second   tenth   twenty-fifth   ninety-eighth   106th   333rd**

If numbers greater than 101 are used infrequently in a piece of writing, you may spell out those that can be written in one or two words.

> **two hundred   fifty thousand   six billion**

You may use a combination of numerals and words for very large numbers.

> **1.5 million   3 billion to 3.2 billion   6 trillion**

Numbers being compared or contrasted should be kept in the same style.

> **8 to 11** years old *or* **eight** to **eleven** years old

Particular decades may be spelled out or written as numerals.

> the **'80s** and **'90s** *or* the **eighties** and **nineties**

Numerals Only

Use numerals for the following forms: decimals, percentages, pages, chapters (and other parts of a book), addresses, dates, telephone numbers, identification numbers, and statistics.

> **26.2**   **8** percent   chapter **7**
> pages **287–289**   Highway **36**   **(212) 555–1234**
> **398-55-0000**   a vote of **23** to **4**   May **8, 2007**

> **Note:** Abbreviations and symbols are often used in charts, graphs, footnotes, and so forth, but typically they are not used in texts.
>
> > He is **five feet one inch** tall and **ten years old.**
> > She walked **three and one-half miles** to work through **twelve inches** of snow.

However, abbreviations and symbols may be used in scientific, mathematical, statistical, and technical texts (APA style).

> Between **20%** and **23%** of the cultures yielded positive results.
> Your **245B** model requires **220V.**

Always use numerals with abbreviations and symbols.

> **5'4"   8%   10** in.   **3** tbsp.   **6** lb. **8** oz.   **90°**F

Use numerals after the name of local branches of labor unions.

> The Office and Professional Employees International Union, Local **8**

Hyphenated Numbers

Hyphens are used to form compound modifiers indicating measurement. They are also used for inclusive numbers and written-out fractions.

a **three-mile** trip	the **2001–2005** presidential term
a **2,500-mile** road trip	**one-sixth** of the pie
a **thirteen-foot** clearance	**three-eighths** of the book

Time and Money

If time is expressed with an abbreviation, use numerals; if it is expressed in words, spell out the number.

4:00 a.m. *or* **four** o'clock (not 4 o'clock)

the **5:15** p.m. train

a **seven o'clock** wake-up call

If money is expressed with a symbol, use numerals; if the currency is expressed in words, spell out the number.

$20 or **twenty** dollars (not 20 dollars)

Abbreviations of time and of money may be used in text.

The concert begins at **7:00** p.m., and tickets cost **$30.**

Words Only

Use words to express numbers that begin a sentence.

Fourteen students "forgot" their assignments.

Three hundred contest entries were received.

Note: Change the sentence structure if this rule creates a clumsy construction.

Six hundred thirty-nine students are new to the campus this fall. (Clumsy)

This fall, **639** students are new to the campus. (Better)

Use words for numbers that precede a compound modifier that includes a numeral. (If the compound modifier uses a spelled-out number, use numerals in front of it.)

She sold **twenty 35-millimeter** cameras in one day.

The chef prepared **24 eight-ounce** filets.

Use words for the names of numbered streets of one hundred or less.

Ninth Avenue

123 Forty-fourth Street

Use words for the names of buildings if that name is also its address.

One Thousand State Street   **Two Fifty Park Avenue**

Use words for references to particular centuries.

the twenty-first century   **the fourth century B.C.E.**

Mechanics Exercises:

Plurals and Numbers

A. Plurals

For each of the following words, write the correct plural form.

1. team
2. party
3. ratio
4. shelf
5. child

6. sister-in-law
7. video
8. bucketful
9. choir
10. serf

B. Numbers

For each sentence below, write the correct form of any incorrectly used numbers.

1. 4 tiny ducklings crossed a driveway near Six Hundred and Nine Lewis Street.
2. Out of all my friends, Alex woke up 1st around 6 o'clock.
3. The 6 cheeseburgers cost 12 dollars.
4. I read only fifty % of chapter three.
5. At half past 2 the temperature was still seventy degrees Fahrenheit.
6. The recipe calls for two tsp. salt and three oz. butter.

C. Mechanics Practice

In the following paragraph, correct any number errors by writing the line number and the correct form. Also write the plural of each underlined word.

> Let me tell you how to grill some wonderful steak. First, consider buying   1
> your meat from a butcher rather than from local grocery. The ideal steak cut   2
> is between one and a half to 2 inches thick. Next, you will need to prepare the 3
> steaks for grilling. Start by trimming excess fat to about one-quarter of an   4
> inch thick and seasoning the meat with two tsp. of salt and cracked pepper.   5
> Then, when the grill has preheated, grill the steaks for 16 to twenty minutes.   6
> If you so choose, rotate the steaks forty-five degrees on both sides for nice   7
> diamond grill mark. When the steaks are done, turn off the grill and enjoy.   8
> And remember, steak goes great with potato and fresh mushroom.   9

Abbreviations

601.1

An **abbreviation** is the shortened form of a word or a phrase. These abbreviations are always acceptable in both formal and informal writing:

Mr.   Mrs.   Ms.   Dr.   Jr.   a.m. (A.M.)   p.m. (P.M.)

Note: In formal writing, do not abbreviate the names of states, countries, months, days, units of measure, or courses of study. Do not abbreviate the words *Street, Road, Avenue, Company,* and similar words when they are part of a proper name. Also, do not use signs or symbols (%, &, #, @) in place of words. (The dollar sign, however, is appropriate when numerals are used to express an amount of money. See 599.2.)

Also Note: When abbreviations are called for (in charts, lists, bibliographies, notes, and indexes, for example), standard abbreviations are preferred. Reserve the postal abbreviations for ZIP code addresses.

Correspondence Abbreviations

601.2

States/Territories

	Standard	Postal
Alabama	Ala.	AL
Alaska	Alaska	AK
Arizona	Ariz.	AZ
Arkansas	Ark.	AR
California	Cal.	CA
Colorado	Colo.	CO
Connecticut	Conn.	CT
Delaware	Del.	DE
District of Columbia	D.C.	DC
Florida	Fla.	FL
Georgia	Ga.	GA
Guam	Guam	GU
Hawaii	Hawaii	HI
Idaho	Idaho	ID
Illinois	Ill.	IL
Indiana	Ind.	IN
Iowa	Ia.	IA
Kansas	Kans.	KS
Kentucky	Ky.	KY
Louisiana	La.	LA
Maine	Me.	ME
Maryland	Md.	MD
Massachusetts	Mass.	MA
Michigan	Mich.	MI
Minnesota	Minn.	MN
Mississippi	Miss.	MS
Missouri	Mo.	MO
Montana	Mont.	MT
Nebraska	Neb.	NE
Nevada	Nev.	NV
New Hampshire	N.H.	NH
New Jersey	N.J.	NJ
New Mexico	N. Mex.	NM
New York	N.Y.	NY
North Carolina	N.C.	NC
North Dakota	N. Dak.	ND
Ohio	Ohio	OH

	Standard	Postal
Oklahoma	Okla.	OK
Oregon	Ore.	OR
Pennsylvania	Pa.	PA
Puerto Rico	P.R.	PR
Rhode Island	R.I.	RI
South Carolina	S.C.	SC
South Dakota	S. Dak.	SD
Tennessee	Tenn.	TN
Texas	Tex.	TX
Utah	Utah	UT
Vermont	Vt.	VT
Virginia	Va.	VA
Virgin Islands	V.I.	VI
Washington	Wash.	WA
West Virginia	W. Va.	WV
Wisconsin	Wis.	WI
Wyoming	Wyo.	WY

Canadian Provinces

	Standard	Postal
Alberta	Alta.	AB
British Columbia	B.C.	BC
Manitoba	Man.	MB
New Brunswick	N.B.	NB
Newfoundland and Labrador	N.F. Lab.	NL
Northwest Territories	N.W.T.	NT
Nova Scotia	N.S.	NS
Nunavut		NU
Ontario	Ont.	ON
Prince Edward Island	P.E.I.	PE
Quebec	Que.	QC
Saskatchewan	Sask.	SK
Yukon Territory	Y.T.	YT

Address Abbreviations

	Standard	Postal
Apartment	Apt.	APT
Avenue	Ave.	AVE
Boulevard	Blvd.	BLVD
Circle	Cir.	CIR
Court	Ct.	CT
Drive	Dr.	DR
East	E.	E
Expressway	Expy.	EXPY
Freeway	Frwy.	FWY
Heights	Hts.	HTS
Highway	Hwy.	HWY
Hospital	Hosp.	HOSP
Junction	Junc.	JCT
Lake	L.	LK
Lakes	Ls.	LKS
Lane	Ln.	LN
Meadows	Mdws.	MDWS
North	N.	N
Palms	Palms	PLMS
Park	Pk.	PK
Parkway	Pky.	PKY
Place	Pl.	PL
Plaza	Plaza	PLZ
Post Office Box	P.O. Box	PO BOX
Ridge	Rdg.	RDG
River	R.	RV
Road	Rd.	RD
Room	Rm.	RM
Rural	R.	R
Rural Route	R.R.	RR
Shore	Sh.	SH
South	S.	S
Square	Sq.	SQ
Station	Sta.	STA
Street	St.	ST
Suite	Ste.	STE
Terrace	Ter.	TER
Turnpike	Tpke.	TPKE
Union	Un.	UN
View	View	VW
Village	Vil.	VLG
West	W.	W

Common Abbreviations

abr. abridged, abridgment

AC, ac alternating current, air-conditioning

ack. acknowledgment

AM amplitude modulation

A.M., a.m. before noon (Latin *ante meridiem*)

AP advanced placement

ASAP as soon as possible

avg., av. average

B.A. bachelor of arts degree

BBB Better Business Bureau

B.C.E. before common era

bibliog. bibliography

biog. biographer, biographical, biography

B.S. bachelor of science degree

C 1. Celsius **2.** centigrade **3.** coulomb

c. 1. circa (about) **2.** cup(s)

cc 1. cubic centimeter **2.** carbon copy **3.** community college

CDT, C.D.T. central daylight time

C.E. common era

CEEB College Entrance Examination Board

chap. chapter(s)

cm centimeter(s)

c/o care of

COD, c.o.d. 1. cash on delivery **2.** collect on delivery

co-op cooperative

CST, C.S.T. central standard time

cu 1. cubic **2.** cumulative

D.A. district attorney

d.b.a., d/b/a doing business as

DC, dc direct current

dec. deceased

dept. department

disc. discount

DST, D.S.T. daylight saving time

dup. duplicate

ed. edition, editor

EDT, E.D.T. eastern daylight time

e.g. for example (Latin *exempli gratia*)

EST, E.S.T. eastern standard time

etc. and so forth (Latin *et cetera*)

F Fahrenheit, French, Friday

FM frequency modulation

F.O.B., f.o.b. free on board

FYI for your information

g 1. gravity **2.** gram(s)

gal. gallon(s)

gds. goods

gloss. glossary

GNP gross national product

GPA grade point average

hdqrs. headquarters

HIV human immunodeficiency virus

hp horsepower

Hz hertz

ibid. in the same place (Latin *ibidem*)

id. the same (Latin *idem*)

i.e. that is (Latin *id est*)

illus. illustration

inc. incorporated

IQ, I.Q. intelligence quotient

IRS Internal Revenue Service

ISBN International Standard Book Number

JP, J.P. justice of the peace

K 1. kelvin (temperature unit) **2.** Kelvin (temperature scale)

kc kilocycle(s)

kg kilogram(s)

km kilometer(s)

kn knot(s)

kw kilowatt(s)

L liter(s), lake

lat. latitude

l.c. lowercase

lit. literary; literature

log logarithm, logic

long. longitude

Ltd., ltd. limited

m meter(s)

M.A. master of arts degree

man. manual

Mc, mc megacycle

MC master of ceremonies

M.D. doctor of medicine (Latin *medicinae doctor*)

mdse. merchandise

MDT, M.D. T. mountain daylight time

mfg. manufacture, manufacturing

mg milligram(s)

mi. 1. mile(s) **2.** mill(s) (monetary unit)

misc. miscellaneous

mL milliliter(s)

mm millimeter(s)

mpg, m.p.g. miles per gallon

mph, m.p.h. miles per hour

MS 1. manuscript **2.** multiple sclerosis

Ms. title of courtesy for a woman

M.S. master of science degree

MST, M.S.T. mountain standard time

NE northeast

neg. negative

N.S.F., n.s.f. not sufficient funds

NW northwest

oz, oz. ounce(s)

PA public-address system

pct. percent

pd. paid

PDT, P.D.T. Pacific daylight time

PFC, Pfc. private first class

pg., p. page

Ph.D. doctor of philosophy

P.M., p.m. after noon (Latin *post meridiem*)

POW, P.O.W. prisoner of war

pp. pages

ppd. 1. postpaid **2.** prepaid

PR, P.R. public relations

PSAT Preliminary Scholastic Aptitude Test

psi, p.s.i. pounds per square inch

PST, P.S.T. Pacific standard time

PTA, P.T.A. Parent-Teacher Association

R.A. residence assistant

RF radio frequency

R.P.M., rpm revolutions per minute

R.S.V.P., r.s.v.p. please reply (French *répondez s'il vous plaît*)

SAT Scholastic Aptitude Test

SE southeast

SOS 1. international distress signal **2.** any call for help

Sr. 1. senior (after surname) **2.** sister (religious)

SRO, S.R.O. standing room only

std. standard

SW southwest

syn. synonymous, synonym

tbs., tbsp. tablespoon(s)

TM trademark

UHF, uhf ultrahigh frequency

v 1. physics: velocity **2.** volume

V electricity: volt

VA Veterans Administration

VHF, vhf very high frequency

VIP informal: very important person

vol. 1. volume **2.** volunteer

vs. versus, verse

W 1. electricity: watt(s) **2.** physics: (also **w**) work **3.** west

whse., whs. warehouse

whsle. wholesale

wkly. weekly

w/o without

wt. weight

www World Wide Web

Acronyms and Initialisms

Acronyms   603.1

An **acronym** is a word formed from the first (or first few) letters of words in a set phrase. Even though acronyms are abbreviations, they require no periods.

radar	radio detecting and ranging
CARE	Cooperative for Assistance and Relief Everywhere
NASA	National Aeronautics and Space Administration
VISTA	Volunteers in Service to America
FICA	Federal Insurance Contributions Act

Initialisms   603.2

An **initialism** is similar to an acronym except that the initials used to form this abbreviation are pronounced individually.

CIA	Central Intelligence Agency
FBI	Federal Bureau of Investigation
FHA	Federal Housing Administration

Common Acronyms and Initialisms   603.3

AIDS	acquired immune deficiency syndrome	**OSHA**	Occupational Safety and Health Administration
APR	annual percentage rate	**PAC**	political action committee
CAD	computer-aided design	**PIN**	personal identification number
CAM	computer-aided manufacturing	**POP**	point of purchase
CETA	Comprehensive Employment and Training Act	**PSA**	public service announcement
FAA	Federal Aviation Administration	**REA**	Rural Electrification Administration
FCC	Federal Communications Commission	**RICO**	Racketeer Influenced and Corrupt Organizations (Act)
FDA	Food and Drug Administration	**ROTC**	Reserve Officers' Training Corps
FDIC	Federal Deposit Insurance Corporation	**SADD**	Students Against Destructive Decisions
FEMA	Federal Emergency Management Agency	**SASE**	self-addressed stamped envelope
		SPOT	satellite positioning and tracking
FHA	Federal Housing Administration	**SSA**	Social Security Administration
FTC	Federal Trade Commission	**SUV**	sport-utility vehicle
IRS	Internal Revenue Service	**SWAT**	Special Weapons and Tactics
MADD	Mothers Against Drunk Driving	**TDD**	telecommunications device for the deaf
NAFTA	North American Free Trade Agreement	**TMJ**	temporomandibular joint
NATO	North Atlantic Treaty Organization	**TVA**	Tennessee Valley Authority
OEO	Office of Economic Opportunity	**VA**	Veterans Administration
ORV	off-road vehicle	**WHO**	World Health Organization

Mechanics Exercises:

Abbreviations, Acronyms, and Initialisms

A. Abbreviations

Indicate whether the following abbreviations would be acceptable in a formal piece of writing. Write "yes" for appropriate and "no" for inappropriate.

1. MN
2. Sask.
3. Dr.
4. R.A.
5. P.M.

6. Jr.
7. Ave.
8. Misc.
9. Mrs.
10. $5.25

B. Acronyms and Initialisms

Indicate whether each term is an acronym or an initialism.

1. PSA
2. FDA
3. MADD
4. NATO
5. NASA

6. TMJ
7. VA
8. SWAT
9. IRS
10. FAA

C. Mechanics Practice

For each sentence, write the correct abbreviation, acronym, or initialism of the underlined word or words.

1. Mister Anderson of the Federal Deposit Insurance Corporation called today regarding the bank's membership status.
2. We cruised south on Falcon Drive in our new sport-utility vehicle.
3. The student's low grade point average negated a high score on the Scholastic Aptitude Test.
4. Do you know the latitude and longitude of Key West, Florida?
5. You can add two teaspoons salt and one tablespoon basil for extra flavor.

Basic Spelling Rules

Write i Before e   605.1

Write *i* before *e* except after *c*, or when sounded like *a* as in *neighbor* and *weigh*.

believe   relief   receive   eight

> **Note:** This sentence contains eight exceptions:
> **Neither sheik dared leisurely seize either weird species of financiers.**

Words with Consonant Endings   605.2

When a one-syllable word (*bat*) ends in a consonant (*t*) preceded by one vowel (*a*), double the final consonant before adding a suffix that begins with a vowel (*batting*).

sum—**summary**   god—**goddess**

> **Note:** When a multisyllable word (*control*) ends in a consonant (*l*) preceded by one vowel (*o*), the accent is on the last syllable (*con trol´*), and the suffix begins with a vowel (*ing*)—the same rule holds true: Double the final consonant (*controlling*).
>
> prefer—**preferred**   begin—**beginning**
> forget—**forgettable**   admit—**admittance**

Words with a Final Silent e   605.3

If a word ends with a silent *e,* drop the *e* before adding a suffix that begins with a vowel. Do *not* drop the *e* when the suffix begins with a consonant.

state—**stating**—**statement**   like—**liking**—**likeness**
use—**using**—**useful**   nine—**ninety**—**nineteen**

> **Note:** Exceptions are **judgment, truly, argument, ninth.**

Words Ending in y   605.4

When *y* is the last letter in a word and the *y* is preceded by a consonant, change the *y* to *i* before adding any suffix except those beginning with *i*.

fry—**fries, frying**   hurry—**hurried, hurrying**
lady—**ladies**   ply—**pliable**
happy—**happiness**   beauty—**beautiful**

> **Note:** When forming the plural of a word that ends with a *y* that is preceded by a vowel, add *s*.
>
> toy—**toys**   play—**plays**   monkey—**monkeys**

Tip: Never trust your spelling to even the best spell checker. Carefully proofread and use a dictionary for words you know your spell checker does not cover.

Commonly Misspelled Words

The commonly misspelled words that follow are hyphenated to show where they would logically be broken at the end of a line.

A

ab-bre-vi-ate
abrupt
ab-scess
ab-sence
ab-so-lute (-ly)
ab-sorb-ent
ab-surd
abun-dance
ac-a-dem-ic
ac-cede
ac-cel-er-ate
ac-cept (-ance)
ac-ces-si-ble
ac-ces-so-ry
ac-ci-den-tal-ly
ac-com-mo-date
ac-com-pa-ny
ac-com-plice
ac-com-plish
ac-cor-dance
ac-cord-ing
ac-count
ac-crued
ac-cu-mu-late
ac-cu-rate
ac-cus-tom (-ed)
ache
achieve (-ment)
ac-knowl-edge
ac-quaint-ance
ac-qui-esce
ac-quired
ac-tu-al
adapt
ad-di-tion (-al)
ad-dress
ad-e-quate
ad-journed
ad-just-ment
ad-mi-ra-ble
ad-mis-si-ble
ad-mit-tance
ad-van-ta-geous
ad-ver-tise-ment
ad-ver-tis-ing

ad-vice (n.)
ad-vis-able
ad-vise (v.)
ad-vis-er
ae-ri-al
af-fect
af-fi-da-vit
a-gainst
ag-gra-vate
ag-gres-sion
a-gree-able
a-gree-ment
aisle
al-co-hol
a-lign-ment
al-ley
al-lot-ted
al-low-ance
all right
al-most
al-ready
al-though
al-to-geth-er
a-lu-mi-num
al-um-nus
al-ways
am-a-teur
a-mend-ment
a-mong
a-mount
a-nal-y-sis
an-a-lyze
an-cient
an-ec-dote
an-es-thet-ic
an-gle
an-ni-hi-late
an-ni-ver-sa-ry
an-nounce
an-noy-ance
an-nu-al
a-noint
a-non-y-mous
an-swer
ant-arc-tic
an-tic-i-pate

anx-i-ety
anx-ious
a-part-ment
a-pol-o-gize
ap-pa-ra-tus
ap-par-ent (-ly)
ap-peal
ap-pear-ance
ap-pe-tite
ap-pli-ance
ap-pli-ca-ble
ap-pli-ca-tion
ap-point-ment
ap-prais-al
ap-pre-ci-ate
ap-proach
ap-pro-pri-ate
ap-prov-al
ap-prox-i-mate-ly
ap-ti-tude
ar-chi-tect
arc-tic
ar-gu-ment
a-rith-me-tic
a-rouse
ar-range-ment
ar-riv-al
ar-ti-cle
ar-ti-fi-cial
as-cend
as-cer-tain
as-i-nine
as-sas-sin
as-sess (-ment)
as-sign-ment
as-sist-ance
as-so-ci-ate
as-so-ci-a-tion
as-sume
as-sur-ance
as-ter-isk
ath-lete
ath-let-ic
at-tach
at-tack (-ed)
at-tempt

at-tend-ance
at-ten-tion
at-ti-tude
at-tor-ney
at-trac-tive
au-di-ble
au-di-ence
au-dit
au-thor-i-ty
au-to-mo-bile
au-tumn
aux-il-ia-ry
a-vail-a-ble
av-er-age
aw-ful
aw-ful-ly
awk-ward

B

bac-ca-lau-re-ate
bach-e-lor
bag-gage
bal-ance
bal-loon
bal-lot
ba-nan-a
ban-dage
bank-rupt
bar-gain
bar-rel
base-ment
ba-sis
bat-tery
beau-ti-ful
beau-ty
be-com-ing
beg-gar
be-gin-ning
be-hav-ior
be-ing
be-lief
be-lieve
ben-e-fi-cial
ben-e-fit (-ed)
be-tween
bi-cy-cle

bis-cuit
bliz-zard
book-keep-er
bought
bouil-lon
bound-a-ry
break-fast
breath (n.)
breathe (v.)
brief
bril-liant
Brit-ain
bro-chure
brought
bruise
bud-get
bul-le-tin
buoy-ant
bu-reau
bur-glar
bury
busi-ness
busy

C

caf-e-te-ria
caf-feine
cal-en-dar
cam-paign
can-celed
can-di-date
can-is-ter
ca-noe
ca-pac-i-ty
cap-i-tal
cap-i-tol
cap-tain
car-bu-ret-or
ca-reer
car-i-ca-ture
car-riage
cash-ier
cas-se-role
cas-u-al-ty
cat-a-log
ca-tas-tro-phe

caught
cav-al-ry
cel-e-bra-tion
cem-e-ter-y
cen-sus
cen-tu-ry
cer-tain
cer-tif-i-cate
ces-sa-tion
chal-lenge
chan-cel-lor
change-a-ble
char-ac-ter (-is-tic)
chauf-feur
chief
chim-ney
choc-o-late
choice
choose
Chris-tian
cir-cuit
cir-cu-lar
cir-cum-stance
civ-i-li-za-tion
cli-en-tele
cli-mate
climb
clothes
coach
co-coa
co-er-cion
col-lar
col-lat-er-al
col-lege
col-le-giate
col-lo-qui-al
colo-nel
col-or
co-los-sal
col-umn
com-e-dy
com-ing
com-mence
com-mer-cial
com-mis-sion
com-mit
com-mit-ment
com-mit-ted
com-mit-tee
com-mu-ni-cate
com-mu-ni-ty
com-par-a-tive

com-par-i-son
com-pel
com-pe-tent
com-pe-ti-tion
com-pet-i-tive-ly
com-plain
com-ple-ment
com-plete-ly
com-plex-ion
com-pli-ment
com-pro-mise
con-cede
con-ceive
con-cern-ing
con-cert
con-ces-sion
con-clude
con-crete
con-curred
con-cur-rence
con-demn
con-de-scend
con-di-tion
con-fer-ence
con-ferred
con-fi-dence
con-fi-den-tial
con-grat-u-late
con-science
con-sci-en-tious
con-scious
con-sen-sus
con-se-quence
con-ser-va-tive
con-sid-er-ably
con-sign-ment
con-sis-tent
con-sti-tu-tion
con-tempt-ible
con-tin-u-al-ly
con-tin-ue
con-tin-u-ous
con-trol
con-tro-ver-sy
con-ven-ience
con-vince
cool-ly
co-op-er-ate
cor-dial
cor-po-ra-tion
cor-re-late
cor-re-spond

cor-re-spond-
  ence
cor-rob-o-rate
cough
coun-cil
coun-sel
coun-ter-feit
coun-try
cour-age
cou-ra-geous
cour-te-ous
cour-te-sy
cous-in
cov-er-age
cred-i-tor
cri-sis
crit-i-cism
crit-i-cize
cru-el
cu-ri-os-i-ty
cu-ri-ous
cur-rent
cur-ric-u-lum
cus-tom
cus-tom-ary
cus-tom-er
cyl-in-der

D

dai-ly
dair-y
dealt
debt-or
de-ceased
de-ceit-ful
de-ceive
de-cid-ed
de-ci-sion
dec-la-ra-tion
dec-o-rate
de-duct-i-ble
de-fend-ant
de-fense
de-ferred
def-i-cit
def-i-nite (-ly)
def-i-ni-tion
del-e-gate
de-li-cious
de-pend-ent
de-pos-i-tor
de-pot

de-scend
de-scribe
de-scrip-tion
de-sert
de-serve
de-sign
de-sir-able
de-sir-ous
de-spair
des-per-ate
de-spise
des-sert
de-te-ri-o-rate
de-ter-mine
de-vel-op
de-vel-op-ment
de-vice
de-vise
di-a-mond
di-a-phragm
di-ar-rhe-a
dic-tio-nary
dif-fer-ence
dif-fer-ent
dif-fi-cul-ty
di-lap-i-dat-ed
di-lem-ma
din-ing
di-plo-ma
di-rec-tor
dis-agree-able
dis-ap-pear
dis-ap-point
dis-ap-prove
dis-as-trous
dis-ci-pline
dis-cov-er
dis-crep-an-cy
dis-cuss
dis-cus-sion
dis-ease
dis-sat-is-fied
dis-si-pate
dis-tin-guish
dis-trib-ute
di-vide
di-vis-i-ble
di-vi-sion
doc-tor
doesn't
dom-i-nant
dor-mi-to-ry

doubt
drudg-ery
du-pli-cate
dye-ing
dy-ing

E

ea-ger-ly
ear-nest
eco-nom-i-cal
econ-o-my
ec-sta-sy
e-di-tion
ef-fer-ves-cent
ef-fi-ca-cy
ef-fi-cien-cy
eighth
ei-ther
e-lab-o-rate
e-lec-tric-i-ty
el-e-phant
el-i-gi-ble
e-lim-i-nate
el-lipse
em-bar-rass
e-mer-gen-cy
em-i-nent
em-pha-size
em-ploy-ee
em-ploy-ment
e-mul-sion
en-close
en-cour-age
en-deav-or
en-dorse-ment
en-gi-neer
En-glish
e-nor-mous
e-nough
en-ter-prise
en-ter-tain
en-thu-si-as-tic
en-tire-ly
en-trance
en-vel-op (v.)
en-ve-lope (n.)
en-vi-ron-ment
equip-ment
equipped
e-quiv-a-lent
es-pe-cial-ly
es-sen-tial

es-tab-lish
es-teemed
et-i-quette
ev-i-dence
ex-ag-ger-ate
ex-ceed
ex-cel-lent
ex-cept
ex-cep-tion-al-ly
ex-ces-sive
ex-cite
ex-ec-u-tive
ex-er-cise
ex-haust (-ed)
ex-hi-bi-tion
ex-hil-a-ra-tion
ex-is-tence
ex-or-bi-tant
ex-pect
ex-pe-di-tion
ex-pend-i-ture
ex-pen-sive
ex-pe-ri-ence
ex-plain
ex-pla-na-tion
ex-pres-sion
ex-qui-site
ex-ten-sion
ex-tinct
ex-traor-di-nar-y
ex-treme-ly

F

fa-cil-i-ties
fal-la-cy
fa-mil-iar
fa-mous
fas-ci-nate
fash-ion
fa-tigue (-d)
fau-cet
fa-vor-ite
fea-si-ble
fea-ture
Feb-ru-ar-y
fed-er-al
fem-i-nine
fer-tile
fic-ti-tious
field
fierce
fi-ery

fi-nal-ly
fi-nan-cial-ly
fo-li-age
for-ci-ble
for-eign
for-feit
for-go
for-mal-ly
for-mer-ly
for-tu-nate
for-ty
for-ward
foun-tain
fourth
frag-ile
fran-ti-cal-ly
freight
friend
ful-fill
fun-da-men-tal
fur-ther-more
fu-tile

G

gad-get
gan-grene
ga-rage
gas-o-line
gauge
ge-ne-al-o-gy
gen-er-al-ly
gen-er-ous
ge-nius
gen-u-ine
ge-og-ra-phy
ghet-to
ghost
glo-ri-ous
gnaw
go-ril-la
gov-ern-ment
gov-er-nor
gra-cious
grad-u-a-tion
gram-mar
grate-ful
grat-i-tude
grease
grief
griev-ous
gro-cery
grudge

grue-some
guar-an-tee
guard
guard-i-an
guer-ril-la
guess
guid-ance
guide
guilty
gym-na-si-um
gyp-sy
gy-ro-scope

H

hab-i-tat
ham-mer
hand-ker-chief
han-dle (-d)
hand-some
hap-haz-ard
hap-pen
hap-pi-ness
ha-rass
har-bor
hast-i-ly
hav-ing
haz-ard-ous
height
hem-or-rhage
hes-i-tate
hin-drance
his-to-ry
hoarse
hol-i-day
hon-or
hop-ing
hop-ping
horde
hor-ri-ble
hos-pi-tal
hu-mor-ous
hur-ried-ly
hy-drau-lic
hy-giene

I

i-am-bic
i-ci-cle
i-den-ti-cal
id-io-syn-cra-sy
il-leg-i-ble
il-lit-er-ate

il-lus-trate
im-ag-i-nary
im-ag-i-na-tive
im-ag-ine
im-i-ta-tion
im-me-di-ate-ly
im-mense
im-mi-grant
im-mor-tal
im-pa-tient
im-per-a-tive
im-por-tance
im-pos-si-ble
im-promp-tu
im-prove-ment
in-al-ien-able
in-ci-den-tal-ly
in-con-ve-nience
in-cred-i-ble
in-curred
in-def-i-nite-ly
in-del-ible
in-de-pend-ence
in-de-pend-ent
in-dict-ment
in-dis-pens-able
in-di-vid-u-al
in-duce-ment
in-dus-tri-al
in-dus-tri-ous
in-ev-i-ta-ble
in-fe-ri-or
in-ferred
in-fi-nite
in-flam-ma-ble
in-flu-en-tial
in-ge-nious
in-gen-u-ous
in-im-i-ta-ble
in-i-tial
ini-ti-a-tion
in-no-cence
in-no-cent
in-oc-u-la-tion
in-quir-y
in-stal-la-tion
in-stance
in-stead
in-sti-tute
in-struc-tor
in-sur-ance
in-tel-lec-tu-al

in-tel-li-gence
in-ten-tion
in-ter-cede
in-ter-est-ing
in-ter-fere
in-ter-mit-tent
in-ter-pret (-ed)
in-ter-rupt
in-ter-view
in-ti-mate
in-va-lid
in-ves-ti-gate
in-ves-tor
in-vi-ta-tion
ir-i-des-cent
ir-rel-e-vant
ir-re-sis-ti-ble
ir-rev-er-ent
ir-ri-gate
is-land
is-sue
i-tem-ized
i-tin-er-ar-y

J

jan-i-tor
jeal-ous (-y)
jeop-ar-dize
jew-el-ry
jour-nal
jour-ney
judg-ment
jus-tice
jus-ti-fi-able

K

kitch-en
knowl-edge
knuck-le

L

la-bel
lab-o-ra-to-ry
lac-quer
lan-guage
laugh
laun-dry
law-yer
league
lec-ture
le-gal
leg-i-ble

leg-is-la-ture
le-git-i-mate
lei-sure
length
let-ter-head
li-a-bil-i-ty
li-a-ble
li-ai-son
lib-er-al
li-brar-y
li-cense
lieu-ten-ant
light-ning
lik-able
like-ly
lin-eage
liq-ue-fy
liq-uid
lis-ten
lit-er-ary
lit-er-a-ture
live-li-hood
log-a-rithm
lone-li-ness
loose
lose
los-ing
lov-able
love-ly
lun-cheon
lux-u-ry

M

ma-chine
mag-a-zine
mag-nif-i-cent
main-tain
main-te-nance
ma-jor-i-ty
mak-ing
man-age-ment
ma-neu-ver
man-u-al
man-u-fac-ture
man-u-script
mar-riage
mar-shal
ma-te-ri-al
math-e-mat-ics
max-i-mum
may-or
mean-ness

meant
mea-sure
med-i-cine
me-di-eval
me-di-o-cre
me-di-um
mem-o-ran-dum
men-us
mer-chan-dise
mer-it
mes-sage
mile-age
mil-lion-aire
min-i-a-ture
min-i-mum
min-ute
mir-ror
mis-cel-la-neous
mis-chief
mis-chie-vous
mis-er-a-ble
mis-ery
mis-sile
mis-sion-ary
mis-spell
mois-ture
mol-e-cule
mo-men-tous
mo-not-o-nous
mon-u-ment
mort-gage
mu-nic-i-pal
mus-cle
mu-si-cian
mus-tache
mys-te-ri-ous

N

na-ive
nat-u-ral-ly
nec-es-sary
ne-ces-si-ty
neg-li-gi-ble
ne-go-ti-ate
neigh-bor-hood
nev-er-the-less
nick-el
niece
nine-teenth
nine-ty
no-tice-able
no-to-ri-ety

nu-cle-ar
nui-sance

O

o-be-di-ence
o-bey
o-blige
ob-sta-cle
oc-ca-sion
oc-ca-sion-al-ly
oc-cu-pant
oc-cur
oc-curred
oc-cur-rence
of-fense
of-fi-cial
of-ten
o-mis-sion
o-mit-ted
op-er-ate
o-pin-ion
op-po-nent
op-por-tu-ni-ty
op-po-site
op-ti-mism
or-di-nance
or-di-nar-i-ly
orig-i-nal
out-ra-geous

P

pag-eant
pam-phlet
par-a-dise
para-graph
par-al-lel
par-a-lyze
pa-ren-the-ses
pa-ren-the-sis
par-lia-ment
par-tial
par-tic-i-pant
par-tic-i-pate
par-tic-u-lar-ly
pas-time
pa-tience
pa-tron-age
pe-cu-liar
per-ceive
per-haps
per-il
per-ma-nent

per-mis-si-ble
per-pen-dic-u-lar
per-se-ver-ance
per-sis-tent
per-son-al (-ly)
per-son-nel
per-spi-ra-tion
per-suade
phase
phe-nom-e-non
phi-los-o-phy
phy-si-cian
piece
planned
pla-teau
plau-si-ble
play-wright
pleas-ant
plea-sure
pneu-mo-nia
pol-i-ti-cian
pos-sess
pos-ses-sion
pos-si-ble
prac-ti-cal-ly
prai-rie
pre-cede
pre-ce-dence
pre-ced-ing
pre-cious
pre-cise-ly
pre-ci-sion
pre-de-ces-sor
pref-er-a-ble
pref-er-ence
pre-ferred
prej-u-dice
pre-lim-i-nar-y
pre-mi-um
prep-a-ra-tion
pres-ence
prev-a-lent
pre-vi-ous
prim-i-tive
prin-ci-pal
prin-ci-ple
pri-or-i-ty
pris-on-er
priv-i-lege
prob-a-bly
pro-ce-dure
pro-ceed

pro-fes-sor
prom-i-nent
pro-nounce
pro-nun-ci-a-tion
pro-pa-gan-da
pros-e-cute
pro-tein
psy-chol-o-gy
pub-lic-ly
pump-kin
pur-chase
pur-sue
pur-su-ing
pur-suit

Q

qual-i-fied
qual-i-ty
quan-ti-ty
quar-ter
ques-tion-naire
quite
quo-tient

R

raise
rap-port
re-al-ize
re-al-ly
re-cede
re-ceipt
re-ceive
re-ceived
rec-i-pe
re-cip-i-ent
rec-og-ni-tion
rec-og-nize
rec-om-mend
re-cur-rence
ref-er-ence
re-ferred
reg-is-tra-tion
re-hearse
reign
re-im-burse
rel-e-vant
re-lieve
re-li-gious
re-mem-ber
re-mem-brance
rem-i-nisce
ren-dez-vous

re-new-al
rep-e-ti-tion
rep-re-sen-ta-tive
req-ui-si-tion
res-er-voir
re-sis-tance
re-spect-a-bly
re-spect-ful-ly
re-spec-tive-ly
re-spon-si-bil-i-ty
res-tau-rant
rheu-ma-tism
rhyme
rhythm
ri-dic-u-lous
route

S

sac-ri-le-gious
safe-ty
sal-a-ry
sand-wich
sat-is-fac-to-ry
Sat-ur-day
scarce-ly
scene
scen-er-y
sched-ule
schol-ar-ship
sci-ence
scis-sors
sec-re-tary
seize
sen-si-ble
sen-tence
sen-ti-nel
sep-a-rate
ser-geant
sev-er-al
se-vere-ly
shep-herd
sher-iff
shin-ing
siege
sig-nif-i-cance
sim-i-lar

si-mul-ta-ne-ous
since
sin-cere-ly
ski-ing
sol-dier
sol-emn
so-phis-ti-cat-ed
soph-o-more
so-ror-i-ty
source
sou-ve-nir
spa-ghet-ti
spe-cif-ic
spec-i-men
speech
sphere
spon-sor
spon-ta-ne-ous
sta-tion-ary
sta-tion-ery
sta-tis-tic
stat-ue
stat-ure
stat-ute
stom-ach
stopped
straight
strat-e-gy
strength
stretched
study-ing
sub-si-dize
sub-stan-tial
sub-sti-tute
sub-tle
suc-ceed
suc-cess
suf-fi-cient
sum-ma-rize
su-per-fi-cial
su-per-in-tend-
    ent
su-pe-ri-or-i-ty
su-per-sede
sup-ple-ment
sup-pose

sure-ly
sur-prise
sur-veil-lance
sur-vey
sus-cep-ti-ble
sus-pi-cious
sus-te-nance
syl-la-ble
sym-met-ri-cal
sym-pa-thy
sym-pho-ny
symp-tom
syn-chro-nous

T

tar-iff
tech-nique
tele-gram
tem-per-a-ment
tem-per-a-ture
tem-po-rary
ten-den-cy
ten-ta-tive
ter-res-tri-al
ter-ri-ble
ter-ri-to-ry
the-ater
their
there-fore
thief
thor-ough (-ly)
though
through-out
tired
to-bac-co
to-geth-er
to-mor-row
tongue
to-night
touch
tour-na-ment
tour-ni-quet
to-ward
trag-e-dy
trai-tor
tran-quil-iz-er

trans-ferred
trea-sur-er
tru-ly
Tues-day
tu-i-tion
typ-i-cal
typ-ing

U

unan-i-mous
un-con-scious
un-doubt-ed-ly
un-for-tu-nate-ly
unique
u-ni-son
uni-ver-si-ty
un-nec-es-sary
un-prec-e-
    dent-ed
un-til
up-per
ur-gent
us-able
use-ful
using
usu-al-ly
u-ten-sil
u-til-ize

V

va-can-cies
va-ca-tion
vac-u-um
vague
valu-able
va-ri-ety
var-i-ous
veg-e-ta-ble
ve-hi-cle
veil
ve-loc-i-ty
ven-geance
vi-cin-i-ty
view
vig-i-lance
vil-lain

vi-o-lence
vis-i-bil-i-ty
vis-i-ble
vis-i-tor
voice
vol-ume
vol-un-tary
vol-un-teer

W

wan-der
war-rant
weath-er
Wednes-day
weird
wel-come
wel-fare
where
wheth-er
which
whole
whol-ly
whose
width
wom-en
worth-while
wor-thy
wreck-age
wres-tler
writ-ing
writ-ten
wrought

Y

yel-low
yes-ter-day
yield

Steps to Becoming a Better Speller

1. **Be patient.** Becoming a good speller takes time.

2. **Check the correct pronunciation of each word you are attempting to spell.**
   Knowing the correct pronunciation of each word can help you to remember its spelling.

3. **Note the meaning and history of each word as you are checking the dictionary for the pronunciation.**
   Knowing the meaning and history of a word provides you with a better notion of how the word is properly used, and it can help you remember the word's spelling.

4. **Before you close the dictionary, practice spelling the word.**
   You can do so by looking away from the page and trying to "see" the word in your "mind's eye." Write the word on a piece of paper. Check the spelling in the dictionary and repeat the process until you are able to spell the word correctly.

5. **Learn some spelling rules.**
   The four rules in this handbook (page 605) are four of the most useful—although there are others.

6. **Make a list of the words that you misspell.**
   Select the first ten words and practice spelling them.
   First: Read each word carefully; then write it on a piece of paper. Look at the written word to see that it's spelled correctly. Repeat the process for those words that you misspelled.
   Then: Ask someone to read the words to you so you can write them again. Then check for misspellings. Repeat both steps with your next ten words.

7. **Write often.**
   As noted educator Frank Smith said,

   "There is little point in learning to spell
   if you have little intention of writing."

Mechanics Exercises:

Spelling

Correct any spelling errors in the following letter by writing the line number and the correct spelling of the word(s).

Dear Dr. Hanson: *1*

I wanted to pass along an updat regarding my project for the Undergraduate   *2*
Recearch Conference. I'm makin great progress, but I have a few questions.   *3*
I'll start with my progress: *4*

- As of Febuary 21, my primary and secondary research is in excelent   *5*
  order.   *6*
- I've completed writng, revising, and editing my literature review.   *7*
- I beleive I will finish a first draft by the end of the week.   *8*

Here are my questions for you: *9*

- Should I make a PowerPoint version for my presentation?   *10*
- Who is in charge of advertiseing for the event?   *11*
- How soon from now will room asignments be announced?   *12*

I've really enjoyed researching the relatinship between stress and eating   *13*
habits among college students. You'll find the introduction to my   *14*
presentation in the enclosed pamflet.   *15*

Thanks for takin the time to read over these materials.   *16*

Sinserely,   *17*
Jim White   *18*

Chapter 32

Using the Right Word

The following glossary contains words that are commonly confused.

a, an Use *a* as the article before words that begin with consonant sounds and before words that begin with the long vowel sound *u* (yü). Use *an* before words that begin with other vowel sounds.

> **An** older student showed Kris **an** easier way to get to class.
>
> **A** uniform is required attire for **a** cafeteria worker.

613.1

a lot, alot, allot *Alot* is not a word; *a lot* (two words) is a vague descriptive phrase that should be used sparingly, especially in formal writing. *Allot* means to give someone a share.

> Prof Dubi **allots** each of us five spelling errors per semester, and he thinks that's **a lot**.

613.2

accept, except The verb *accept* means "to receive or believe"; the preposition *except* means "other than."

> The instructor **accepted** the student's story about being late, but she wondered why no one **except** him had forgotten about the change to daylight saving time.

613.3

adapt, adopt, adept *Adapt* means "to adjust or change to fit"; *adopt* means "to choose and treat as your own" (a child, an idea). *Adept* is an adjective meaning "proficient or well trained."

> After much thought and deliberation, we agreed to **adopt** the black Lab from the shelter. Now we have to agree on how to **adapt** our lifestyle to fit our new roommate.

613.4

adverse, averse *Adverse* means "hostile, unfavorable, or harmful." *Averse* means "to have a definite feeling of distaste—disinclined."

> Groans and other **adverse** reactions were noted as the new students, **averse** to strenuous exercise, were ushered past the X-5000 pump-and-crunch machine.

613.5

advice, advise *Advice* is a noun meaning "information or recommendation"; *advise* is a verb meaning "to recommend."

> Successful people will often give you sound **advice**, so I **advise** you to listen.

613.6

affect, effect *Affect* means "to influence"; the noun *effect* means "the result."

> The employment growth in a field will **affect** your chances of getting a job. The **effect** may be a new career choice.

613.7

614.1   **aid, aide** As a verb, *aid* means "to help"; as a noun, *aid* means "the help given." An *aide* is a person who acts as an assistant.

614.2   **all, of** Of is seldom needed after all.

> **All** the reports had an error in them.
> **All** the speakers spoke English.
> **All of** us voted to reschedule the meeting.
> (Here *of* is needed for the sentence to make sense.)

614.3   **all right, alright** *Alright* is the incorrect form of *all right*. (**Note:** The following are spelled correctly: *always, altogether, already, almost*.)

614.4   **allude, elude** *Allude* means "to indirectly refer to or hint at something"; *elude* means "to escape attention or understanding altogether."

> Ravi often **alluded** to wanting a supper invitation by mentioning the "awfully good" smells from the kitchen. These hints never **eluded** Ma's good heart.

614.5   **allusion, illusion** *Allusion* is an indirect reference to something or someone, especially in literature; *illusion* is a false picture or idea.

> Did you recognize the **allusion** to David in the reading assignment? Until I read that part, I was under the **illusion** that the young boy would run away from the bully.

614.6   **already, all ready** *Already* is an adverb meaning "before this time" or "by this time." *All ready* is an adjective form meaning "fully prepared." (**Note:** Use *all ready* if you can substitute *ready* alone in the sentence.)

> By the time I was a junior in high school, I had **already** taken my SATs. That way, I was **all ready** to apply early to college.

614.7   **altogether, all together** *Altogether* means "entirely." *All together* means "in a group" or "all at once." (**Note:** Use *all together* if you can substitute *together* alone in the sentence.)

> **All together** there are 35,000 job titles to choose from. That's **altogether** too many to even think about.

614.8   **among, between** *Among* is used when emphasizing distribution throughout a body or a group of three or more; *between* is used when emphasizing distribution to two individuals.

> There was discontent **among** the relatives after learning that their aunt had divided her entire fortune **between** a canary and a favorite waitress at the local cafe.

614.9   **amoral, immoral** *Amoral* means "neither moral (right) nor immoral (wrong)"; *immoral* means "wrong, or in conflict with traditional values."

> Carnivores are **amoral** in their hunt; poachers are **immoral** in theirs.

614.10   **amount, number** *Amount* is used for bulk measurement. *Number* is used to count separate units. (See also fewer.)

> The **number** of new instructors hired next year will depend on the **amount** of revenue raised by the new sales tax.

and etc. Don't use *and* before etc. since *et cetera* means "and the rest."

> Did you remember your textbook, notebook, handout, **etc.**?

615.1

annual, biannual, semiannual, biennial, perennial An *annual* event happens once every year. A *biannual* event happens twice a year (*semiannual* is the same as *biannual*). A *biennial* event happens every two years. A *perennial* event happens throughout the year, every year.

615.2

anxious, eager Both words mean "looking forward to," but *anxious* also connotes fear or concern.

> The professor is **eager** to move into the new building, but she's a little **anxious** that students won't be able to find her new office.

615.3

anymore, any more *Anymore* (an adverb) means "any longer"; *any more* means "any additional."

> We won't use that textbook **anymore**; call if you have **any mor**e questions.

615.4

any one (of), anyone *Any one* means "any one of a number of people, places, or things"; *anyone* is a pronoun meaning "any person."

> Choose **any one** of the proposed weekend schedules. **Anyone** wishing to work on Saturday instead of Sunday may do so.

615.5

appraise, apprise *Appraise* means "to determine value." *Apprise* means "to inform."

> Because of the tax assessor's recent **appraisal** of our home, we were **apprised** of an increase in our property tax.

615.6

as Don't use *as* in place of *whether* or *if*.

> I don't know **as** I'll accept the offer. (Incorrect)
> I don't know **whether** I'll accept the offer. (Correct)

615.7

Don't use *as* when it is unclear whether it means *because* or *when*.

> We rowed toward shore **as** it started raining. (Unclear)
> We rowed toward shore **because** it started raining. (Correct)

assure, ensure, insure (See insure.)

bad, badly *Bad* is an adjective, used both before nouns and as a predicate adjective after linking verbs. *Badly* is an adverb.

> Christina felt **bad** about serving us **bad** food.
> Larisa played **badly** today.

615.8

beside, besides *Beside* means "by the side of." *Besides* means "in addition to."

> **Besides** the two suitcases you've already loaded into the trunk, remember the smaller one **beside** the van.

615.9

between, among (See among.)

bring, take *Bring* suggests the action is directed toward the speaker; *take* suggests the action is directed away from the speaker.

> If you're not going to **bring** the video to class, **take** it back to the resource center.

615.10

Using the Right Word Exercises:

Using the Right Word I

A. Selecting the Right Word

Choose the correct word from those in parentheses for each sentence.

1. Hunter was *(accepted, excepted)* into a summer internship program at an accounting firm.

2. The celebrity was unable to *(allude, elude)* the paparazzi outside of the night club.

3. Juan is quite *(adapt, adopt, adept)* at playing the electric guitar.

4. Does *(anyone, any one)* know of a scenic location for a Sunday picnic?

5. I feel *(anxious, eager)* around people who are loud and outgoing.

6. Today was a good day because it did not go as *(bad, badly)* as yesterday.

7. *(Altogether, All together)* thirty-five people waited outside of the movie theater for the premiere of the new movie.

8. Are you under the *(allusion, illusion)* that the young businesswoman will abandon her friends?

9. The new round of layoffs may *(affect, effect)* my position with the company.

10. What *(amount, number)* of money will it take to purchase a plane ticket to France?

B. Replacing Incorrect Words

For each sentence below, identify the misused words and correct them.

1. Phil appraised his buddy about the affects of pushing a car more than 3,000 miles without a oil change.

2. Do you mean to elude that I'm in need of some fashion advise?

3. A strong friendship among Cary and Nyssa helped get them through an averse situation.

can, may In formal contexts, *can* is used to mean "being able to do"; *may* is used to mean "having permission to do."   **617.1**

> **May** I borrow your bicycle to get to the library? Then I **can** start working on our group project.

capital, capitol The noun *capital* refers to a city or to money. The adjective *capital* means "major or important" or "seat of government." *Capitol* refers to a building.   **617.2**

> The **capitol** is in the **capital** city for a **capital** reason. The city government contributed **capital** for the building expense.

cent, sent, scent *Cent* is a coin; *sent* is the past tense of the verb "send"; *scent* is an odor or a smell.   **617.3**

> For forty-one **cents**, I **sent** my friend a love poem in a perfumed envelope. She adored the **scent** but hated the poem.

chord, cord *Chord* may mean "an emotion or a feeling," but it also may mean "the combination of three or more tones sounded at the same time," as with a guitar *chord*. A *cord* is a string or a rope.   **617.4**

> The guitar player strummed the opening **chord**, which struck a responsive **chord** with the audience.

chose, choose *Chose* (chōz) is the past tense of the verb *choose* (chüz). (See page 643.)   **617.5**

> For generations, people **chose** their careers based on their parents' careers; now people **choose** their careers based on the job market.

climactic, climatic *Climactic* refers to the climax, or high point, of an event; *climatic* refers to the climate, or weather conditions.   **617.6**

> Because we are using the open-air amphitheater, **climatic** conditions will just about guarantee the wind gusts we need for the **climactic** third act.

coarse, course *Coarse* means "of inferior quality, rough, or crude"; *course* means "a direction or a path taken." *Course* also means "a class or a series of studies."   **617.7**

> A basic writing **course** is required of all students.
>
> Due to years of woodworking, the instructor's hands are rather **coarse**.

compare with, compare to Things in the same category are *compared with* each other; things in different categories are *compared to* each other.   **617.8**

> **Compare** Christopher Marlowe's plays **with** William Shakespeare's plays.
>
> My brother **compared** reading *The Tempest* **to** visiting another country.

complement, compliment *Complement* means "to complete or go well with." *Compliment* means "to offer an expression of admiration or praise."   **617.9**

> We wanted to **compliment** Zach on his decorating efforts; the bright yellow walls **complement** the purple carpet.

comprehensible, comprehensive *Comprehensible* means "capable of being understood"; *comprehensive* means "covering a broad range, or inclusive."   **617.10**

> The theory is **comprehensible** only to those who have a **comprehensive** knowledge of physics.

618.1 **comprise, compose** *Comprise* means "to contain or consist of"; *compose* means "to create or form by bringing parts together."

> Fruitcake **comprises** a variety of nuts, candied fruit, and spice.
>
> Fruitcake is **composed of** (not *comprised of*) a variety of ingredients.

618.2 **conscience, conscious** A *conscience* gives one the capacity to know right from wrong. *Conscious* means "awake or alert, not sleeping or comatose."

> Your **conscience** will guide you, but you have to be **conscious** to hear what it's "saying."

618.3 **continual, continuous** *Continual* often implies that something is happening often, recurring; *continuous* usually implies that something keeps happening, uninterrupted.

> The **continuous** loud music during the night gave the building manager not only a headache but also **continual** phone calls.

618.4 **counsel, council, consul** When used as a noun, *counsel* means "advice"; when used as a verb, *counsel* means "to advise." *Council* refers to a group that advises. A *consul* is a government official appointed to reside in a foreign country.

> The city **council** was asked to **counsel** our student **council** on running an efficient meeting. Their **counsel** was very helpful.

618.5 **decent, descent, dissent** *Decent* means "good." *Descent* is the process of going or stepping downward. *Dissent* means "disagreement."

> The food was **decent**.
>
> The elevator's fast **descent** clogged my ears.
>
> Their **dissent** over the decisions was obvious in their sullen expressions.

618.6 **desert, dessert** *Desert* is barren wilderness. *Dessert* is food served at the end of a meal. The verb *desert* means "to abandon."

618.7 **different from, different than** Use *different* from in formal writing; use either form in informal or colloquial settings.

> Rafael's interpretation was **different from** Andrea's.

618.8 **discreet, discrete** *Discreet* means "showing good judgment, unobtrusive, modest"; *discrete* means "distinct, separate."

> The essay question had three **discrete** parts.
>
> Her roommate had apparently never heard of quiet, **discreet** conversation.

618.9 **disinterested, uninterested** Both words mean "not interested." However, *disinterested* is also used to mean "unbiased or impartial."

> A person chosen as an arbitrator must be a **disinterested** party.
>
> Professor Eldridge was **uninterested** in our complaints about the assignment.

effect, affect (See *affect*.)

618.10 **elicit, illicit** *Elicit* is a verb meaning "to bring out." *Illicit* is an adjective meaning "unlawful."

> It took a hand signal to **elicit** the **illicit** exchange of cash for drugs.

eminent, imminent *Eminent* means "prominent, conspicuous, or famous"; *imminent* means "ready or threatening to happen."   **619.1**

> With the island's government about to collapse, assassination attempts on several **eminent** officials seemed **imminent**.

ensure, insure, assure (See insure.)

except, accept (See accept.)

explicit, implicit *Explicit* means "expressed directly or clearly defined"; *implicit* means "implied or unstated."   **619.2**

> The professor **explicitly** asked that the experiment be wrapped up on Monday, **implicitly** demanding that her lab assistants work on the weekend.

farther, further *Farther* refers to a physical distance; *further* refers to additional time, quantity, or degree.   **619.3**

> **Further** research showed that walking **farther** rather than faster would improve his health.

fewer, less *Fewer* refers to the number of separate units; *less* refers to bulk quantity.   **619.4**

> Because of spell checkers, students can produce papers containing **fewer** errors in **less** time.

figuratively, literally *Figuratively* means "in a metaphorical or analogous way—describing something by comparing it to something else"; *literally* means "actually."   **619.5**

> The lab was **literally** filled with sulfurous gases—**figuratively** speaking, dragon's breath.

first, firstly Both words are adverbs meaning "before another in time" or "in the first place." However, do not use *firstly*, which is stiff and unnatural sounding.   **619.6**

> **Firstly** I want to see the manager. (Incorrect)
>
> **First** I want to see the manager. (Correct)

Note: When enumerating, use the forms *first, second, third, next, last*—without the *ly*.

fiscal, physical *Fiscal* means "related to financial matters"; *physical* means "related to material things."   **619.7**

> The school's **fiscal** work is handled by its accounting staff.
>
> The **physical** work is handled by its maintenance staff.

for, fore, four *For* is a conjunction meaning "because" or is a preposition used to indicate the object or recipient of something; *fore* means "earlier" or "the front"; *four* is the word for the number 4.   **619.8**

> The crew brought treats **for** the barge's **four** dogs, who always enjoy the breeze at the **fore** of the vessel.

former, latter When two things are being discussed, *former* refers to the first thing, and *latter* to the second.   **619.9**

> Our choices are going to a movie or eating at the Pizza Palace: The **former** is too expensive, and the **latter** too fattening.

Using the Right Word Exercises:

Using the Right Word II

A. Selecting the Right Word

Choose the correct word from those in parentheses for each sentence.

1. The (*capital, capitol*) building looked radiant with the fall sunshine beaming on its white dome.

2. That jacket would (*complement, compliment*) the colors of your dress.

3. The museum had three (*discreet, discrete*) levels, each with a different theme.

4. Darren took (*counsel, council, consul*) from his internship coordinator regarding his career path.

5. Would you (*comprise, compose*) an updated report on our position in the New York power and electric industry?

6. Our destination along Interstate 43 was (*farther, further*) than we expected.

7. The (*climactic, climatic*) point of the baseball game occurred when Vicki caught a foul ball.

8. The (*decent, descent, dissent*) down Pike's Peak Mountain was a scary experience.

9. I was so sleepy that I felt barely (*conscience, conscious*).

10. The (*cent, sent, scent*) coming from the garbage left us all gagging for fresh air.

B. Replacing Incorrect Words

For each sentence below, identify the misused words and correct them.

1. Our second coarse was descent, but the desert was the real winner.

2. The farther we delay restructuring our finances, the worse our physical situation will be.

3. My aunt is firstly a good judge of character and second an imminent authority on all things Milwaukee.

good, well *Good* is an adjective; *well* is nearly always an adverb. (When used to indicate state of health, *well* is an adjective.)

> A **good** job offers opportunities for advancement, especially for those who do their jobs **well**.

621.1

heal, heel *Heal* (a verb) means "to mend or restore to health"; a *heel* (noun) is the back part of a human foot.

621.2

healthful, healthy *Healthful* means "causing or improving health"; *healthy* means "possessing health."

> **Healthful** foods and regular exercise build **healthy** bodies.

621.3

I, me *I* is a subject pronoun; *me* is used as an object of a preposition, a direct object, or an indirect object. (See 636.1.) (A good way to know if *I* or *me* should be used in a compound subject is to eliminate the other subject; the sentence should make sense with the pronoun—*I* or *me*—alone.)

> My roommate and **me** went to the library last night. (Incorrect)
>
> My roommate and **I** went to the library last night. (Correct: Eliminate "my roommate and"; the sentence still makes sense.)
>
> Rasheed gave the concert tickets to Erick and **I**. (Incorrect)
>
> Rasheed gave the concert tickets to Erick and **me**. (Correct: Eliminate "Erick and"; the sentence still makes sense.)

621.4

illusion, allusion (See allusion.)

immigrate (to), emigrate (from) *Immigrate* means "to come into a new country or environment." *Emigrate* means "to go out of one country to live in another."

> **Immigrating** to a new country is a challenging experience.
>
> People **emigrating** from their homelands face unknown challenges.

621.5

imminent, eminent (See eminent.)

imply, infer *Imply* means "to suggest without saying outright"; *infer* means "to draw a conclusion from facts." (A writer or a speaker *implies*; a reader or a listener *infers*.)

> Dr. Rufus **implied** I should study more; I **inferred** he meant my grades had to improve, or I'd be repeating the class.

621.6

ingenious, ingenuous *Ingenious* means "intelligent, discerning, clever"; *ingenuous* means "unassuming, natural, showing childlike innocence and candidness."

> Gretchen devised an **ingenious** plan to work and receive college credit for it.
>
> Ramón displays an **ingenuous** quality that attracts others.

621.7

insure, ensure, assure *Insure* means "to secure from financial harm or loss," *ensure* means "to make certain of something," and *assure* means "to put someone's mind at rest."

> Plenty of studying generally **ensures** academic success.
>
> Nicole **assured** her father that she had **insured** her new car.

621.8

interstate, intrastate *Interstate* means "existing between two or more states"; *intrastate* means "existing within a state."

621.9

622.1 **irregardless, regardless** *Irregardless* is a nonstandard synonym for *regardless*.

> **Irregardless** of his circumstance, José is cheerful. (Incorrect)
>
> **Regardless** of his circumstance, José is cheerful. (Correct)

622.2 **it's, its** *It's* is the contraction of "it is." *Its* is the possessive form of "it."

> **It's** not hard to see why my husband feeds that alley cat; **its** pitiful limp and mournful mewing would melt any heart.

622.3 **later, latter** *Later* means "after a period of time." *Latter* refers to the second of two things mentioned.

> The **latter** of the two restaurants you mentioned sounds good.
>
> Let's meet there **later**.

622.4 **lay, lie** *Lay* means "to place." *Lay* is a transitive verb. (See 638.2.) Its principal parts are *lay, laid, laid*. (See 643.)

> If you **lay** another book on my table, I won't have room for anything else.
>
> Yesterday, you **laid** two books on the table.
>
> Over the last few days, you must have **laid** at least 20 books there.

Lie means "to recline." *Lie* is an intransitive verb. (See 638.2.) Its principal parts are *lie, lay, lain*.

> The cat **lies** down anywhere it pleases.
>
> It **lay** down yesterday on my tax forms.
>
> It has **lain** down many times on the kitchen table.

622.5 **learn, teach** *Learn* means "to acquire information"; *teach* means "to give information."

> Sometimes it's easier to **teach** someone else a lesson than it is to **learn** one yourself.

622.6 **leave, let** *Leave* means "to allow something to remain behind." *Let* means "to permit."

> Please **let** me help you carry that chair; otherwise, **leave** it for the movers to pick up.

622.7 **lend, borrow** *Lend* means "to give for temporary use"; *borrow* means "to receive for temporary use."

> I asked Haddad to **lend** me $15 for a CD, but he said I'd have to find someone else to **borrow** the money from.

less, fewer (See fewer.)

622.8 **liable, libel** *Liable* is an adjective meaning "responsible according to the law" or "exposed to an adverse action"; the noun *libel* is a written defamatory statement about someone, and the verb *libel* means "to publish or make such a statement."

> Supermarket tabloids, **liable** for ruining many a reputation, make a practice of **libeling** the rich and the famous.

622.9 **liable, likely** *Liable* means "responsible according to the law" or "exposed to an adverse action"; *likely* means "in all probability."

> Rain seems **likely** today, but if we cancel the game, we are still **liable** for paying the referees.

like, as *Like* should not be used in place of *as*. *Like* is a preposition, which is followed by its object (a noun, a pronoun, or a noun phrase). *As* is a subordinating conjunction, which introduces a clause. Do not use *like* as a subordinating conjunction. Use *as* instead.

623.1

> You don't know her **like** I do. (Incorrect)
>
> You don't know her **as** I do. (Correct)
>
> **Like** the others in my study group, I do my work as any serious student would—carefully and thoroughly. (Correct)

literally, figuratively (See **figuratively**.)

loose, lose, loss The adjective *loose* (lüs) means "free, untied, unrestricted"; the verb *lose* (lüz) means "to misplace or fail to find or control"; the noun *loss* (los) means "something that is misplaced and cannot be found."

623.2

> Her sadness at the **loss** of her longtime companion caused her to **lose** weight, and her clothes felt uncomfortably **loose**.

may, can (See **can**.)

maybe, may be Use *maybe* as an adverb meaning "perhaps;" use *may be* as a verb phrase.

623.3

> She **may be** the computer technician we've been looking for. **Maybe** she will upgrade the software and memory.

miner, minor A *miner* digs in the ground for ore. A *minor* is a person who is not legally an adult. The adjective *minor* means "of no great importance."

623.4

> The use of **minors** as coal **miners** is no **minor** problem.

number, amount (See **amount**.)

OK, okay This expression, spelled either way, is appropriate in informal writing; however, avoid using it in papers, reports, or formal correspondence of any kind.

623.5

> Your proposal is satisfactory [not okay] on most levels.

oral, verbal *Oral* means "uttered with the mouth"; *verbal* means "relating to or consisting of words and the comprehension of words."

623.6

> The actor's **oral** abilities were outstanding, her pronunciation and intonation impeccable, but I doubted the playwright's **verbal** skills after trying to decipher the play's meaning.

passed, past *Passed* is a verb. *Past* can be used as a noun, an adjective, or a preposition.

623.7

> That little pickup truck **passed** my 'Vette! (verb)
>
> My stepchildren hold on dearly to the **past**. (noun)
>
> I'm sorry, but my **past** life is not your business. (adjective)
>
> The officer drove **past** us, not noticing our flat tire. (preposition)

peace, piece *Peace* means "tranquility or freedom from war." A *piece* is a part or fragment.

623.8

> Someone once observed that **peace** is not a condition, but a process—a process of building goodwill one **piece** at a time.

Using the Right Word Exercises:

Using the Right Word III

A. Selecting the Right Word

Choose the correct word from those in parentheses for each sentence.

1. Raphael injured his (*heal, heel*) when he took out the trash shoeless.

2. (*Irregardless, Regardless*) of how you feel about the assignment, you have to get it done by Friday.

3. Could you (*borrow, lend*) me three quarters for laundry?

4. My car suffered (*miner, minor*) damages from last night's hailstorm.

5. You (*maybe, may be*) upset with me, but I hope you will soon forgive me.

6. Before you look to the future, you should recognize lessons from the (*passed, past*).

7. Can you (*insure, ensure, assure*) me that I will receive an annual review?

8. Andrew (*immigrated, emigrated*) from Australia.

9. The offender was found (*liable, libel*) for all medical expenses.

10. The Taj Mahal was incredible; I was most impressed by (*it's, its*) majesty.

B. Replacing Incorrect Words

For each sentence below, identify the misused words and correct them.

1. Despite feeling under the weather, Andre was good enough to give a verbal presentation at a company meeting.

2. Teresa inferred I should look for a new job, while I implied she meant I had no chance for a promotion.

3. Before you lie down another box, make sure the shelf is sturdy enough; otherwise it is liable to collapse.

people, person Use *people* to refer to human populations, races, or groups; use *person* to refer to an individual or the physical body.   625.1

> What the American **people** need is a good insect repellent.
>
> The forest ranger recommends that we check our **persons** for wood ticks when we leave the woods.

percent, percentage *Percent* means "per hundred"; for example, 60 percent of 100 jelly beans would be 60 jelly beans. *Percentage* refers to a portion of the whole. Generally, use the word *percent* when it is preceded by a number. Use *percentage* when no number is used.   625.2

> Each person's **percentage** of the reward amounted to $125—25 **percent** of the $500 offered by Crime Stoppers.

personal, personnel *Personal* (an adjective) means "private." *Personnel* (a noun) are people working at a particular job.   625.3

> Although choosing a major is a **personal** decision, it can be helpful to consult with guidance **personnel**.

perspective, prospective *Perspective* (a noun) is a point of view or the capacity to view things realistically; *prospective* is an adjective meaning "expected in or related to the future."   625.4

> From my immigrant neighbor's **perspective**, any job is a good job.
>
> **Prospective** students wandered the campus on visitors' day.

pore, pour, poor The noun *pore* is an opening in the skin; the verb *pore* means "to gaze intently." *Pour* means "to move with a continuous flow." *Poor* means "needy or pitiable."   625.5

> **Pour** hot water into a bowl, put your face over it, and let the steam open your **pores**. Your **poor** skin will thank you.

precede, proceed To *precede* means "to go or come before"; *proceed* means "to move on after having stopped" or "go ahead."   625.6

> Our biology instructor often **preceded** his lecture with these words:
>
> "OK, sponges, **proceed** to soak up more fascinating facts!"

principal, principle As an adjective, *principal* means "primary." As a noun, it can mean "a school administrator" or "a sum of money." A *principle* (noun) is an idea or a doctrine.   625.7

> His **principal** gripe is lack of freedom. (adjective)
>
> My son's **principal** expressed his concerns to the teachers. (noun)
>
> After 20 years, the amount of interest was higher than the **principal**. (noun)
>
> The **principle** of *caveat emptor* guides most consumer groups. (noun)

quiet, quit, quite *Quiet* is the opposite of noisy. *Quit* means "to stop or give up." *Quite* (an adverb) means "completely" or "to a considerable extent."   625.8

> The meeting remained **quite quiet** when the boss told us he'd **quit**.

quote, quotation *Quote* is a verb; *quotation* is a noun.   625.9

> The **quotation** I used was from Woody Allen. You may **quote** me on that.

real, very, really Do not use the adjective *real* in place of the adverbs *very* or *really*.   625.10

> My friend's cake is usually **very** [not *real*] fresh, but this cake is **really** stale.

626.1   **right, write, wright, rite** *Right* means "correct or proper"; it also refers to that which a person has a legal claim to, as in *copyright*. *Write* means "to inscribe or record." A *wright* is a person who makes or builds something. *Rite* is a ritual or ceremonial act.

> Did you **write** that it is the **right** of the **shipwright** to perform the **rite** of christening— breaking a bottle of champagne on the bow of the ship?

626.2   **scene, seen** *Scene* refers to the setting or location where something happens; it also may mean "sight or spectacle." *Seen* is the past participle of the verb "see."

> An exhibitionist likes to be **seen** making a **scene**.

626.3   **set, sit** *Set* means "to place." *Sit* means "to put the body in a seated position." *Set* is a transitive verb; *sit* is an intransitive verb (See 638.2.).

> How can you just **sit** there and watch as I **set** the table?

626.4   **sight, cite, site** *Sight* means "the act of seeing" (a verb) or "something that is seen" (a noun). *Cite* (a verb) means "to quote" or "to summon to court." *Site* means "a place or location" (noun) or "to place on a site" (verb).

> After **sighting** the faulty wiring, the inspector **cited** the building contractor for breaking two city codes at a downtown work **site**.

626.5   **some, sum** *Some* refers to an unknown thing, an unspecified number, or a part of something. *Sum* is a certain amount of money or the result of adding numbers together.

> **Some** of the students answered too quickly and came up with the wrong **sum**.

626.6   **stationary, stationery** *Stationary* means "not movable"; *stationery* refers to the paper and envelopes used to write letters.

> Odina uses **stationery** that she can feed through her portable printer. Then she drops the mail into a **stationary** mail receptacle at the mall.

take, bring (See bring.)

teach, learn (See learn.)

626.7   **than, then** *Than* is used in a comparison; *then* is an adverb that tells when.

> Study more **than** you think you need to. **Then** you will probably be satisfied with your grades.

626.8   **their, there, they're** *Their* is a possessive personal pronoun. *There* is an adverb used as a filler word or to point out location. *They're* is the contraction for "they are."

> Look over **there**. **There** is a comfortable place for students to study for **their** exams, so **they're** more likely to do a good job.

626.9   **threw, through** *Threw* is the past tense of "throw." *Through* (a preposition) means "from one side of something to the other."

> In a fit of frustration, Sachiko **threw** his cell phone right **through** the window.

626.10   **to, too, two** *To* is a preposition that can mean "in the direction of." *To* is also used to form an infinitive. *Too* (an adverb) means "also" or "very." *Two* is the number 2.

> **Two** causes of eye problems among students are lights that fail **to** illuminate properly and computer screens with **too** much glare.

vain, vane, vein *Vain* means "valueless or fruitless"; it may also mean "holding a high regard for oneself." *Vane* is a flat piece of material set up to show which way the wind blows. *Vein* refers to a blood vessel or a mineral deposit.   627.1

> The weather **vane** indicates the direction of the wind; the blood **vein** determines the direction of flowing blood; and the **vain** mind moves in no particular direction, content to think only about itself.

vary, very The verb *vary* means "to change"; the adverb *very* means "to a high degree."   627.2

> To ensure the **very** best employee relations, the workloads should not **vary** greatly from worker to worker.

verbal, oral (See oral.)

waist, waste The noun *waist* refers to the part of the body just above the hips. The verb *waste* means "to squander" or "to wear away, decay"; the noun *waste* refers to material that is unused or useless.   627.3

> His **waist** is small because he **wastes** no opportunity to exercise.

wait, weight *Wait* means "to stay somewhere expecting something." *Weight* refers to a degree or unit of heaviness.   627.4

> The **weight** of sadness eventually lessens; one must simply **wait** for the pain to dissipate.

ware, wear, where The noun *ware* refers to a product that is sold; the verb *wear* means "to have on or to carry on one's body"; the adverb *where* asks the question "In what place?" or "In what situation?"   627.5

> The designer boasted, "**Where** can one **wear** my **wares**? Anywhere."

weather, whether *Weather* refers to the condition of the atmosphere. *Whether* refers to a possibility.   627.6

> **Weather** conditions affect all of us, **whether** we are farmers or plumbers.

well, good (See good.)

which, that (See 573.3.)

who, which, that *Who* refers to people. *Which* refers to nonliving objects or to animals. (*Which* should never refer to people.) *That* may refer to animals, people, or nonliving objects. (See also 573.3.)   627.7

who, whom *Who* is used as the subject of a verb; *whom* is used as the object of a preposition or as a direct object.   627.8

> Captain Mather, to **whom** the survivors owe their lives, is the man **who** is being honored today.

who's, whose *Who's* is the contraction for "who is." *Whose* is a possessive pronoun.   627.9

> **Whose** car are we using, and **who's** going to pay for the gas?

your, you're *Your* is a possessive pronoun. *You're* is the contraction for "you are."   627.10

> If **you're** like most Americans, you will have held eight jobs by **your** fortieth birthday.

Using the Right Word Exercises:

Using the Right Word IV

A. Selecting the Right Word

Choose the correct word from those in parentheses for each sentence.

1. The (*principal, principle*) of relativity applies to any scientific investigation.

2. Vince gave an interesting (*perspective, prospective*) on the importance of workplace writing proficiency.

3. The large piece of rock that fell from the cliff face remained (*stationary, stationery*) near the entrance to the hiking trail.

4. Have you decided (*weather, whether*) to take your boyfriend to your Thanksgiving dinner?

5. If (*your, you're*) planning to begin work on Monday, we'll have the training materials ready for you.

6. Latoya tried in (*vain, vane, vein*) to find her missing car keys.

7. I think Christopher Nolan's *Inception* is even better (*than, then*) The Dark Knight.

8. The professor reminded her students to (*sight, cite, site*) any sources they use in their papers.

9. Mack and Gordon discussed (*who's, whose*) car they should take to the mall.

10. Although not recommended, pulling an all-night study session is considered a (*right, write, wright, rite*) of passage among college students.

B. Replacing Incorrect Words

For each sentence below, identify the misused words and correct them.

1. The company began making personal changes by interviewing perspective suitors.

2. Students whom wish to proceed with the medical mission trip will need to bring there applications to the volunteer office.

3. Hopefully the some of my two checks will not go to waist at the casino.

Chapter 33

Understanding Grammar

Grammar is the study of the structure and features of the language, consisting of rules and standards that are to be followed to produce acceptable writing and speaking. **Parts of speech** refers to the eight different categories that indicate how words are used in the English language—as *nouns, pronouns, verbs, adjectives, adverbs, prepositions, conjunctions,* or *interjections.*

Noun

629.1

A **noun** is a word that names something: a person, a place, a thing, or an idea.

> Toni Morrison/author   *Lone Star*/film   Renaissance/era
> UC-Davis/university   *A Congress of Wonders*/book

esl Note: See 677.1–678.2 for information on count and noncount nouns.

Classes of Nouns

All nouns are either proper nouns or common nouns. Nouns may also be classified as *individual* or *collective,* or *concrete* or *abstract.*

Proper Nouns

629.2

A **proper noun,** which is always capitalized, names a specific person, place, thing, or idea.

> Rembrandt, Bertrand Russell (people)
> Stratford-upon-Avon, Tower of London (places)
> *The Night Watch,* Rosetta stone (things)
> New Deal, Christianity (ideas)

Common Nouns

629.3

A **common noun** is a general name for a person, a place, a thing, or an idea. Common nouns are not capitalized.

> optimist, instructor (people)   cafeteria, park (places)
> computer, chair (things)   freedom, love (ideas)

630.1

Collective Nouns

A **collective noun** names a group or a unit.

> family   audience   crowd   committee   team   class

630.2

Concrete Nouns

A **concrete noun** names a thing that is tangible (can be seen, touched, heard, smelled, or tasted).

> child   The White Stripes   gym   village   microwave oven   pizza

630.3

Abstract Nouns

An **abstract noun** names an idea, a condition, or a feeling—in other words, something that cannot be seen, touched, heard, smelled, or tasted.

> beauty   Jungian psychology   anxiety   agoraphobia   trust

Forms of Nouns

Nouns are grouped according to their *number, gender,* and *case.*

630.4

Number of Nouns

Number indicates whether a noun is singular or plural.

A singular noun refers to one person, place, thing, or idea.

> student   laboratory   lecture   note   grade   result

A plural noun refers to more than one person, place, thing, or idea.

> students   laboratories   lectures   notes   grades   results

630.5

Gender of Nouns

Gender indicates whether a noun is masculine, feminine, neuter, or indefinite.

Masculine:
> father   king   brother   men   colt   rooster

Feminine:
> mother   queen   sister   women   filly   hen

Neuter (without sex):
> notebook   monitor   car   printer

Indefinite or common (masculine or feminine):
> professor   customer   children   doctor   people

Case of Nouns

The **case** of a noun tells what role the noun plays in a sentence. There are three cases: *nominative, possessive,* and *objective.*

A noun in the **nominative case** is used as a subject. The subject of a sentence tells who or what the sentence is about.

> **Dean Henning** manages the College of Arts and Communication.

> **Note:** A noun is also in the nominative case when it is used as a predicate noun (or predicate nominative). A predicate noun follows a linking verb, usually a form of the *be* verb (such as *am, is, are, was, were, be, being, been*), and repeats or renames the subject.
>
> Ms. Yokum is the **person** to talk to about the college's impact in our community.

A noun in the **possessive case** shows possession or ownership. In this form, it acts as an adjective.

> Our **president's** willingness to discuss concerns with students has boosted campus morale.

A noun in the **objective case** serves as an object of the preposition, a direct object, an indirect object, or an object complement.

> To survive, institutions of higher **learning** sometimes cut **budgets** in spite of **protests** from **students** and **instructors**. (*Learning* is the object of the preposition *of, protests* is the object of the preposition *in spite of, budgets* is the direct object of the verb *cut,* and *students* and *instructors* are the objects of the preposition *from.*)

A Closer Look
at Direct and Indirect Objects

A **direct object** is a noun (or pronoun) that identifies what or who receives the action of the verb.

> Budget cutbacks reduced class **choices.** (*Choices* is the direct object of the active verb *reduced.*)

An **indirect object** is a noun (or pronoun) that identifies the person *to whom* or *for whom* something is done, or the thing *to which or for which* something is done. An indirect object is always accompanied by a direct object.

> Recent budget cuts have given **students** fewer class choices. (*Choices* is the direct object of *have given; students* is the indirect object.)

> **esl Note:** Not every transitive verb is followed by *both* a direct object and an indirect object. Both can, however, follow *give, send, show, tell, teach, find, sell, ask, offer, pay, pass,* and *hand.*

Grammar Exercises:

Nouns

A. Classes of Nouns

Identify the class or classes that correctly describe the underlined noun in each sentence.

1. Jenna used a <u>pencil</u> to sketch a design for the new recreational center.
   - a. proper noun
   - b. common noun
   - c. concrete noun

2. My <u>team</u> won a regional debate championship.
   - a. collective noun
   - b. common noun
   - c. abstract noun

3. The end of the movie left me with deep <u>disappointment</u>.
   - a. common noun
   - b. concrete noun
   - c. abstract noun

4. Tomorrow night I'm going to the <u>Arizona Diamondbacks</u> game.
   - a. proper noun
   - b. abstract noun
   - c. common noun

5. Can someone buy me a <u>soda</u> at the store?
   - a. collective noun
   - b. concrete noun
   - c. abstract noun

6. I'm trying to work up the <u>motivation</u> to go to the gym.
   - a. proper noun
   - b. common noun
   - c. abstract noun

B. Case of Nouns

For each sentence identify the case of the underlined noun.

1. Social media Web sites have changed the way we receive <u>news</u>.
   - a. nominative case
   - b. possessive case
   - c. objective case

2. <u>Kings of Leon</u> play rock music.
   - a. nominative case
   - b. possessive case
   - c. objective case

3. <u>Justin's</u> favorite restaurant is on LaGrange Avenue.
   - a. nominative case
   - b. possessive case
   - c. objective case

C. Gender of Nouns

Write down the feminine nouns from the list below.

   desk   writer   princess   child   pilot   tree   waitress

Pronoun

A **pronoun** is a word that is used in place of a noun.

> Roger was the most interesting 10-year-old **I** ever taught. **He** was a good thinker and thus a good writer. **I** remember **his** paragraph about the cowboy hat **he** received from **his** grandparents. **It** was "too new looking." The brim was not rolled properly. But the hat's imperfections were not the main idea in Roger's writing. No, the main idea was how **he** was fixing the hat **himself** by wearing it when **he** showered.

Antecedents

An **antecedent** is the noun or pronoun that the pronoun refers to or replaces. Most pronouns have antecedents, but not all do. (See 634.4.)

> As the wellness **counselor** checked *her* chart, several **students** *who* were waiting *their* turns shifted uncomfortably. (*Counselor* is the antecedent of *her*; *students* is the antecedent of *who* and *their*.)

> **Note:** Each pronoun must agree with its antecedent in number, person, and gender. (See pages 635–636 and 665.)

Classes of Pronouns

Personal

I, me, my, mine / we, us, our, ours / you, your, yours
they, them, their, theirs / he, him, his, she, her, hers, it, its

Reflexive and Intensive

myself, yourself, himself, herself, itself, ourselves, yourselves, themselves

Relative

who, whose, whom, which, that

Indefinite

all	anything	everybody	most	no one	some
another	both	everyone	much	nothing	somebody
any	each	everything	neither	one	someone
anybody	each one	few	nobody	other	something
anyone	either	many	none	several	such

Interrogative

who, whose, whom, which, what

Demonstrative

this, that, these, those

Reciprocal

each other, one another

Classes of Pronouns

There are several classes of pronouns: *personal, reflexive and intensive, relative, indefinite, interrogative,* and *demonstrative.*

634.1   Personal Pronouns

A **personal pronoun** refers to a specific person or thing.

> *Marge* started **her** car; **she** drove the antique *convertible* to Monterey, where **she** hoped to sell **it** at an auction.

634.2   Reflexive and Intensive Pronouns

A **reflexive pronoun** is formed by adding *-self* or *-selves* to a personal pronoun. A reflexive pronoun can act as a direct object or an indirect object of a verb, an object of a preposition, or a predicate nominative.

> Charles loves **himself**. (direct object of *loves*)
> Charles gives **himself** A's for fashion sense. (indirect object of *gives*)
> Charles smiles at **himself** in store windows. (object of preposition *at*)
> Charles can be **himself** anywhere. (predicate nominative)

An **intensive pronoun** intensifies, or emphasizes, the noun or pronoun it refers to.

> Leo **himself** taught his children to invest their lives in others.
> The lesson was sometimes painful—but they learned it **themselves**.

634.3   Relative Pronouns

A **relative pronoun** relates an adjective dependent (relative) clause to the noun or pronoun it modifies. (The noun is italicized in each example below; the relative pronoun is in bold.)

> *Freshmen* **who** believe they have a lot to learn are absolutely right.
> Just navigating this *campus,* **which** is huge, can be challenging.

Make sure you know when to use the relative pronouns *who* or *whom* and *that* or *which.* (See 573.3, 627.7, 627.8, and 657.3.)

634.4   Indefinite Pronouns

An **indefinite pronoun** refers to unnamed or unknown people, places, or things.

> **Everyone** seemed amused when I was searching for my classroom in the student center. (The antecedent of *everyone* is unnamed.)
> **Nothing** is more unnerving than rushing at the last minute into the wrong room for the wrong class. (The antecedent of *nothing* is unknown.)

Most indefinite pronouns are singular, so when they are used as subjects, they should have singular verbs. (See pages 661–664.)

Interrogative Pronouns

An **interrogative pronoun** asks a question.

> So **which** will it be—highlighting and attaching a campus map to the inside of your backpack, or being lost and late for the first two weeks?

> **Note:** When an interrogative pronoun modifies a noun, it functions as an adjective.

Demonstrative Pronouns

A **demonstrative pronoun** points out people, places, or things.

> We advise **this:** Bring along as many maps and schedules as you need.
> **Those** are useful tools. **That** is the solution.

> **Note:** When a demonstrative pronoun modifies a noun, it functions as an adjective.

Forms of Personal Pronouns

The **form** of a personal pronoun indicates its *number* (singular or plural), its *person* (first, second, or third), its *case* (nominative, possessive, or objective), and its *gender* (masculine, feminine, neuter, or indefinite).

Number of Pronouns

A **personal pronoun** is either singular *(I, you, he, she, it)* or plural *(we, you, they).*

> **He** should have a budget and stick to it. (singular)
> **We** can help new students learn about budgeting. (plural)

Person of Pronouns

The **person** of a pronoun indicates whether the person is speaking (first person), is spoken to (second person), or is spoken about (third person).

First person is used to name the speaker(s).

> **I** know **I** need to handle **my** stress in a healthful way, especially during exam week; **my** usual chips-and-doughnuts binge isn't helping. (singular)
> **We** all decided to bike to the tennis court. (plural)

Second person is used to name the person(s) spoken to.

> Maria, **you** grab the rackets, okay? (singular)
> John and Tanya, can **you** find the water bottles? (plural)

Third person is used to name the person(s) or thing(s) spoken about.

> Today's students are interested in wellness issues. **They** are concerned about **their** health, fitness, and nutrition. (plural)
> Maria practices yoga and feels **she** is calmer for **her** choice. (singular)
> One of the advantages of regular exercise is that **it** raises one's energy level. (singular)

636.1   Case of Pronouns

The **case** of each pronoun tells what role it plays in a sentence. There are three cases: *nominative, possessive,* and *objective.*

A pronoun in the **nominative case** is used as a subject. The following are nominative forms: *I, you, he, she, it, we, they.*

> **He** found an old map in the trunk.

> My friend and **I** went biking. (not *me*)

A pronoun is also in the nominative case when it is used as a predicate nominative, following a linking verb *(am, is, are, was, were, seems)* and renaming the subject.

> It was **he** who discovered electricity. (not *him*)

A pronoun in the **possessive case** shows possession or ownership: *my, mine, our, ours, his, her, hers, their, theirs, its, your, yours.* A possessive pronoun before a noun acts as an adjective: *your* coat.

> That coat is **hers**.   This coat is **mine**.   **Your** coat is lost.

A pronoun in the **objective case** can be used as the direct object, indirect object, object of a preposition, or object complement: *me, you, him, her, it, us, them.*

> Professor Adler hired **her**. (*Her* is the direct object of the verb *hired*.)

> He showed Mary and **me** the language lab. (*Me* is the indirect object of the verb *showed*.)

> He introduced the three of **us**—Mary, Shavonn, and **me**—to the faculty. (*Us* is the object of the preposition *of*; *me* is part of the appositive renaming *us*.)

636.2   Gender of Pronouns

The **gender** of a pronoun indicates whether the pronoun is masculine, feminine, neuter, or indefinite. (See page 104.)

Masculine: he, him, his	**Neuter** (without sex): it, its
Feminine: she, her, hers	**Indefinite** (masculine or feminine): they, them, their

636.3

Number, Person, and Case of Personal Pronouns

	Nominative Case	Possessive Case	Objective Case
First Person Singular	I	my, mine	me
Second Person Singular	you	your, yours	you
Third Person Singular	he, she, it	his, her, hers, its	him, her, it
First Person Plural	we	our, ours	us
Second Person Plural	you	your, yours	you
Third Person Plural	they	their, theirs	them

Grammar Exercises:

Pronouns

A. Classes of Pronouns

Identify the class of the underlined pronoun in each sentence.

1. Krunal asked <u>himself</u> if he should reprioritize his responsibilities.
   - a. personal
   - b. reflexive
   - c. relative

2. <u>Who</u> is coming to the pep rally?
   - a. demonstrative
   - b. relative
   - c. interrogative

3. <u>That</u> is quite possibly the most worthless product I've ever used.
   - a. demonstrative
   - b. reflexive
   - c. interrogative

4. Victoria washed <u>her</u> car on the way home from work.
   - a. personal
   - b. intensive
   - c. indefinite

5. <u>Some</u> of the hamburgers were undercooked.
   - a. personal
   - b. intensive
   - c. indefinite

6. The new fitness center, <u>which</u> is awesome, is open until 10:00 p.m.
   - a. personal
   - b. relative
   - c. reflexive

B. Person of Pronouns

For each sentence, indicate whether the underlined pronoun is written in the first, second, or third person.

1. Russell is excited for <u>his</u> new opportunity at the sailing club.
   - a. first person
   - b. second person
   - c. third person

2. Hey Britney, can <u>you</u> pass me the salt and pepper?
   - a. first person
   - b. second person
   - c. third person

3. I was hoping I could make the start of the play, but <u>my</u> class schedule interfered with my plans.
   - a. first person
   - b. second person
   - c. third person

C. Case of Pronouns

Write down the objective-case pronouns from the list below.

his   me   your   us   he   they   them   him

638.1

Verb

A **verb** shows action (*pondered, grins*), links words (*is, seemed*), or accompanies another action verb as an auxiliary or helping verb (*can, does*).

> Harry **honked** the horn. (shows action)
> Harry **is** impatient. (links words)
> Harry **was** honking the truck's horn. (accompanies the verb *honking*)

Classes of Verbs

Verbs are classified as action, auxiliary (helping), or linking (state of being).

638.2

Action Verbs: Transitive and Intransitive

As its name implies, an **action verb** shows action. Some action verbs are *transitive*; others are *intransitive*. (The term *action* does not always refer to a physical activity.)

> Rain **splashed** the windshield. (transitive verb)
> Josie **drove** off the road. (intransitive verb)

Transitive verbs have direct objects that receive the action (625.2, 647.5).

> The health care industry **employs** more than 7 million **workers** in the United States. (*Workers* is the direct object of the action verb *employs*.)

Intransitive verbs communicate action that is complete in itself. They do not need an object to receive the action.

> My new college roommate **smiles** and **laughs** a lot.

> **Note:** Some verbs can be either transitive or intransitive.
> Ms. Hull **teaches** physiology and microbiology. (transitive)
> She **teaches** well. (intransitive)

638.3

Auxiliary (Helping) Verbs

Auxiliary verbs (helping verbs) help to form some of the *tenses* (634.1), the *mood* (635.2), and the *voice* (635.1) of the main verb. In the following example, the auxiliary verbs are in **bold**, and the main verbs are in *italics*.

> I *believe*, I **have** always *believed*, and I **will** always *believe* in private enterprise as the backbone of economic well-being in America.
> —Franklin D. Roosevelt

Common Auxiliary Verbs

am	been	could	does	have	might	should	will
are	being	did	had	is	must	shall	would
be	can	do	has	may	shall	was	were

> **esl Note:** "Be" auxiliary verbs are always followed by either a verb ending in *ing* or a past participle. Also see "Common Modal Auxiliary Verbs" (683.2).

Linking (State of Being) Verbs
639.1

A **linking verb** is a special form of intransitive verb that links the subject of a sentence to a noun, a pronoun, or an adjective in the predicate. (See the chart below.)

The streets **are** flooded. (adjective)   The streets **are** rivers! (noun)

Common Linking Verbs

am   are   be   become   been   being   is   was   were

Additional Linking Verbs

appear   feel   look   seem   sound   grow   remain   smell   taste

Note: The verbs listed as "additional linking verbs" above function as linking verbs when they do not show actual action. An adjective usually follows these linking verbs.

The thunder **sounded** ominous. (adjective)

My little brother **grew** frightened. (adjective)

Note: When these same words are used as action verbs, an adverb or a direct object may follow them.

I **looked** carefully at him. (adverb)

My little brother **grew** corn for a science project. (direct object)

Forms of Verbs

A verb's **form** differs depending on its *number* (singular, plural), *person* (first, second, third), *tense* (present, past, future, present perfect, past perfect, future perfect), *voice* (active, passive), and *mood* (indicative, imperative, subjunctive).

Number of a Verb
639.2

Number indicates whether a verb is singular or plural. The verb and its subject both must be singular, or they both must be plural. (See "Subject–Verb Agreement," pages 661–664.)

My college **enrolls** high schoolers in summer programs. (singular)

Many colleges **enroll** high schoolers in summer courses. (plural)

Person of a Verb
639.3

Person indicates whether the subject of the verb is *first, second,* or *third person.* The verb and its subject must be in the same person. Verbs usually have a different form only in **third person singular of the present tense.**

	First Person	Second Person	Third Person
Singular	I think	you think	he/she/it thinks
Plural	we think	you think	they think

640.1 Tense of a Verb

Tense indicates the time of an action or state of being. There are three basic tenses (*past, present, and future*) and three verbal aspects (*progressive, perfect, and perfect progressive*).

640.2 Present Tense

Present tense expresses action happening at the present time or regularly.

> In the United States, more than 75 percent of workers **hold** service jobs.

Present progressive tense also expresses action that is happening continually, in an ongoing fashion at the present time, but it is formed by combining *am, are,* or *is* and the present participle (ending in *ing*) of the main verb.

> More women than ever before **are working** outside the home.

Present perfect tense expresses action that began in the past and has recently been completed or that continues up to the present time.

> My sister **has taken** four years of swimming lessons.

Present perfect progressive tense also expresses an action that began in the past but stresses the continuing nature of the action. Like the present progressive tense, it is formed by combining auxiliary verbs (*have been* or *has been*) and present participles.

> She **has been taking** them since she was six years old.

640.3 Past Tense

Past tense expresses action that was completed at a particular time in the past.

> A hundred years ago, more than 75 percent of laborers **worked** in agriculture.

Past progressive tense expresses past action that continued over an interval of time. It is formed by combining *was* or *were* with the present participle of the main verb.

> A century ago, my great-grandparents **were farming**.

Past perfect tense expresses an action in the past that was completed at a specific time before another past action occurred.

> By the time we sat down for dinner, my cousins **had eaten** all the olives.

Past perfect progressive tense expresses a past action but stresses the continuing nature of the action. It is formed by using *had been* along with the present participle.

> They **had been eating** the olives all afternoon.

640.4 Future Tense

Future tense expresses action that will take place in the future.

> Next summer I **will work** as a lifeguard.

Future progressive tense expresses an action that will be continuous in the future.

> I **will be working** for the park district at North Beach.

Future perfect tense expresses future action that will be completed by a specific time.

> By 10:00 p.m., I **will have completed** my research project.

Future perfect progressive tense also expresses future action that will be completed by a specific time but (as with other perfect progressive tenses) stresses the action's continuous nature. It is formed using *will have been* along with the present participle.

> I **will have been researching** the project for three weeks by the time it's due.

Voice of a Verb

Voice indicates whether the subject is acting or being acted upon.

Active voice indicates that the subject of the verb is performing the action.

> People **update** their resumés on a regular basis. (The subject, *People*, is acting; *resumés* is the direct object.)

Passive voice indicates that the subject of the verb is being acted upon or is receiving the action. A passive verb is formed by combining a *be* verb with a past participle.

> Your resumé **should be updated** on a regular basis. (The subject, *resumé,* is receiving the action.)

Using Active Voice

Generally, use active voice rather than passive voice for more direct, energetic writing. To change your passive sentences to active ones, do the following: First, find the noun that is doing the action and make it the subject. Then find the word that had been the subject and use it as the direct object.

> **Passive:** The winning goal **was scored** by Eva. (The subject, *goal,* is not acting.)
>
> **Active:** Eva **scored** the winning goal. (The subject, *Eva,* is acting.)

Note: When you want to emphasize the receiver more than the doer—or when the doer is unknown—use the passive voice. (Much technical and scientific writing regularly uses the passive voice.)

Mood of a Verb

The mood of a verb indicates the tone or attitude with which a statement is made.

Indicative mood, the most common, is used to state a fact or to ask a question.

> **Can** any theme **capture** the essence of the complex 1960s culture? President John F. Kennedy's directive [stated below] **represents** one ideal popular during that decade.

Imperative mood is used to give a command. (The subject of an imperative sentence is *you,* which is usually understood and not stated in the sentence.)

> **Ask** not what your country can do for you—**ask** what you can do for your country. — John F. Kennedy

Subjunctive mood is used to express a wish, an impossibility or unlikely condition, or a necessity. The subjunctive mood is often used with *if* or *that.* The verb forms below create an atypical subject–verb agreement, forming the subjunctive mood.

> If I **were** rich, I would travel for the rest of my life. (a wish)
>
> If each of your brain cells **were** one person, there would be enough people to populate 25 planets. (an impossibility)
>
> The English Department requires that every student **pass** a proficiency test. (a necessity)

642.1 Verbals

A **verbal** is a word that is made from a verb, but it functions as a noun, an adjective, or an adverb. There are three types of verbals: *gerunds, infinitives,* and *participles.*

642.2 Gerunds

A **gerund** ends in *ing* and is used as a noun.

> **Waking** each morning is the first challenge. (subject)
>
> I start **moving** at about seven o'clock. (direct object)
>
> I work at **jump-starting** my weary system. (object of the preposition)
>
> As Woody Allen once said, "Eighty percent of life is **showing up**." (predicate nominative)

642.3 Infinitives

An infinitive is *to* and the base form of the verb. The infinitive may be used as a noun, an adjective, or an adverb.

> **To succeed** is not easy. (noun)
>
> That is the most important thing **to remember**. (adjective)
>
> Students are wise **to work** hard. (adverb)

> **esl Note:** It can be difficult to know whether a gerund or an infinitive should follow a verb. It's helpful to become familiar with lists of specific verbs that can be followed by one but not the other. (See 682.2–683.1.)

642.4 Participles

A **present participle** ends in *ing* and functions as an adjective. A **past participle** ends in *ed* (or another past tense form) and also functions as an adjective.

> The **studying** students were annoyed by the **partying** ones.
>
> The students **playing** loud music were **annoying**.
>
> (These participles function as adjectives: *studying* students and *partying* students. Notice, however, that *playing* has a direct object: *music*. All three types of verbals may have direct objects. See 655.3.)

Using Verbals

Make sure that you use verbals correctly; look carefully at the examples below.

Verbal: **Diving** is a popular Olympic sport.
(*Diving* is a gerund used as a subject.)

Diving gracefully, the Olympian hoped to get high marks.
(*Diving* is a participle modifying *Olympian*.)

Verb: The next competitor was **diving** in the practice pool.
(Here, *diving* is a verb, not a verbal.)

Irregular Verbs

Irregular verbs can often be confusing. That's because the past tense and past participle of irregular verbs are formed by changing the word itself, not merely by adding *d* or *ed*. The following list contains the most troublesome irregular verbs.

Common Irregular Verbs and Their Principal Parts

Present Tense	Past Tense	Past Participle	Present Tense	Past Tense	Past Participle	Present Tense	Past Tense	Past Participle
am, be	was, were	been	fly	flew	flown	see	saw	seen
arise	arose	arisen	forget	forgot	forgotten, forgot	set	set	set
awake	awoke, awaked	awoken, awaked	freeze	froze	frozen	shake	shook	shaken
beat	beat	beaten	get	got	gotten	shine (light)	shone	shone
become	became	become	give	gave	given	shine (polish)	shined	shined
begin	began	begun	go	went	gone	show	showed	shown
bite	bit	bitten, bit	grow	grew	grown	shrink	shrank	shrunk
blow	blew	blown	hang (execute)	hanged	hanged	sing	sang	sung
break	broke	broken	hang (suspend)	hung	hung	sink	sank	sunk
bring	brought	brought	have	had	had	sit	sat	sat
build	built	built	hear	heard	heard	sleep	slept	slept
burn	burnt, burned	burnt, burned	hide	hid	hidden	speak	spoke	spoken
			hit	hit	hit	spend	spent	spent
burst	burst	burst	keep	kept	kept	spring	sprang	sprung
buy	bought	bought	know	knew	known	stand	stood	stood
catch	caught	caught	lay	laid	laid	steal	stole	stolen
choose	chose	chosen	lead	led	led	strike	struck	struck, stricken
come	came	come	leave	left	left	strive	strove	striven
cost	cost	cost	lend	lent	lent	swear	swore	sworn
cut	cut	cut	let	let	let	swim	swam	swum
dig	dug	dug	lie (deceive)	lied	lied	swing	swung	swung
dive	dived, dove	dived	lie (recline)	lay	lain	take	took	taken
do	did	done	make	made	made	teach	taught	taught
draw	drew	drawn	mean	meant	meant	tear	tore	torn
dream	dreamed, dreamt	dreamed, dreamt	meet	met	met	tell	told	told
			pay	paid	paid	think	thought	thought
drink	drank	drunk	prove	proved	proved, proven	throw	threw	thrown
drive	drove	driven				wake	woke, waked	woken, waked
eat	ate	eaten	put	put	put			
fall	fell	fallen	read	read	read	wear	wore	worn
feel	felt	felt	ride	rode	ridden	weave	wove	woven
fight	fought	fought	ring	rang	rung	wind	wound	wound
find	found	found	rise	rose	risen	wring	wrung	wrung
flee	fled	fled	run	ran	run	write	wrote	written

Grammar Exercises:

Verbs

A. Classes of Verbs

Identify the class of the underlined verb in each sentence.

1. Shawn sprinted back to his apartment to retrieve his homework.

   a. action verb   b. auxiliary verb   c. linking verb

2. The streets were teeming with partygoers.

   a. action verb   b. auxiliary verb   c. linking verb

3. Niki's gaze remained fixed on the ice-cream cone.

   a. action verb   b. auxiliary verb   c. linking verb

4. I think I should take time to study the new material.

   a. action verb   b. auxiliary verb   c. linking verb

B. Forms of Verbs

For each sentence, identify the tense of the underlined verb.

1. Before we even got to the concert, the band had played my favorite song.

   a. past tense   b. past progressive tense   c. past perfect tense

2. On Sunday I will finish my manuscript.

   a. future tense   b. future progressive tense   c. future perfect tense

3. The mechanics have been working for ten straight hours.

   a. present progressive tense   b. present perfect tense
   c. past progressive tense

4. Yesterday at this time I was relaxing on the beach.

   a. past tense   b. past progressive tense   c. past perfect tense

C. Irregular Verbs

Write the past tense of the following irregular verbs.

1. buy
2. prove
3. swim
4. lead
5. pay
6. lay
7. wear
8. fly
9. give
10. sleep

Adjective

645.1

An **adjective** describes or modifies a noun or pronoun. The articles *a, an,* and *the* are adjectives.

> Advertising is **a big** and **powerful** industry. (*A, big,* and *powerful* modify the noun *industry.*)

Numbers are also adjectives.

> **Fifty-three** relatives came to my party.

645.2

> **Note:** Many demonstrative, indefinite, and interrogative forms may be used as either adjectives or pronouns (*that, these, many, some, whose,* and so on). These words are adjectives if they come before a noun and modify it; they are pronouns if they stand alone.

> **Some** advertisements are less than truthful. (*Some* modifies *advertisements* and is an adjective.)

> **Many** cause us to chuckle at their outrageous claims. (*Many* stands alone; it is a pronoun and replaces the noun *advertisements.*)

Proper Adjectives

645.3

Proper adjectives are created from proper nouns and are capitalized.

> **English** has been influenced by advertising slogans. (proper noun)

> The **English** language is constantly changing. (proper adjective)

Predicate Adjectives

645.4

A **predicate adjective** follows a form of the *be* verb (or other linking verb) and describes the subject. (See 639.1.)

> At its best, advertising is **useful**; at its worst, **deceptive**. (*Useful* and *deceptive* modify the noun *advertising.*)

Forms of Adjectives

645.5

Adjectives have three forms: *positive, comparative,* and *superlative.*

The **positive form** is the adjective in its regular form. It describes a noun or a pronoun without comparing it to anyone or anything else.

> Joysport walking shoes are **strong** and **comfortable**.

The **comparative form** (*-er, more,* or *less*) compares two things. (*More* and *less* are used generally with adjectives of two or more syllables.)

> Air soles make Mile Eaters **stronger** and **more comfortable** than Joysports.

The **superlative form** (*-est, most,* or *least*) compares three or more things. (*Most* and *least* are used most often with adjectives of two or more syllables.)

> My old Canvas Wonders are the **strongest, most comfortable** shoes of all!

> **esl Note:** Two or more adjectives before a noun should have a certain order when they do not modify the noun equally. (See 571.3.)

Adverb

646.1

An **adverb** describes or modifies a verb, an adjective, another adverb, or a whole sentence. An adverb answers questions such as *how, when, where, why, how often,* or *how much.*

> The temperature fell **sharply**. (*Sharply* modifies the verb *fell*.)
>
> The temperature was **quite** low. (*Quite* modifies the adjective *low*.)
>
> The temperature dropped **very quickly**. (*Very* modifies the adverb *quickly*, which modifies the verb *dropped*.)
>
> **Unfortunately**, the temperature stayed cool. (*Unfortunately* modifies the whole sentence.)

646.2

Types of Adverbs

Adverbs can be grouped in four ways: *time, place, manner,* and *degree.*

Time (These adverbs tell *when, how often,* and *how long.*)
> today, yesterday   daily, weekly   briefly, eternally

Place (These adverbs tell *where, to where,* and *from where.*)
> here, there   nearby, beyond   backward, forward

Manner (These adverbs often end in *ly* and tell *how* something is done.)
> precisely   regularly   regally   smoothly   well

Degree (These adverbs tell *how much* or *how little.*)
> substantially   greatly   entirely   partly   too

646.3

Forms of Adverbs

Adverbs have three forms: *positive, comparative,* and *superlative.*

The **positive form** is the adverb in its regular form. It describes a verb, an adjective, or another adverb without comparing it to anyone or anything else.

> With Joysport shoes, you'll walk **fast**. They support your feet **well**.

The **comparative form** (*-er, more,* or *less*) compares two things. (*More* and *less* are used generally with adverbs of two or more syllables.)

> Wear Jockos instead of Joysports, and you'll walk **faster**. Jockos' special soles support your feet **better** than the Joysports do.

The **superlative form** (*-est, most,* or *least*) compares three or more things. (*Most* and *least* are used most often with adverbs of two or more syllables.)

> Really, I walk **fastest** wearing my old Canvas Wonders. They seem to support my feet, my knees, and my pocketbook **best** of all.

Regular Adverbs			Irregular Adverbs		
positive	**comparative**	**superlative**	**positive**	**comparative**	**superlative**
fast	faster	fastest	well	better	best
effectively	more effectively	most effectively	badly	worse	worst

Preposition

A **preposition** is a word (or group of words) that shows the relationship between its object (a noun or pronoun following the preposition) and another word in the sentence.

> **Regarding** your reasons **for** going **to** college, do they all hinge **on** getting a good job **after** graduation? (In this sentence, *reasons, going, college, getting,* and *graduation* are objects of their preceding prepositions *regarding, for, to, on,* and *after.*)

Prepositional Phrases

A **prepositional phrase** includes the preposition, the object of the preposition, and the modifiers of the object. A prepositional phrase may function as an adverb or an adjective.

> A broader knowledge **of the world** is one benefit **of higher education.**
> (The two phrases function as adjectives modifying the nouns *knowledge* and *benefit* respectively.)
>
> He placed the flower **in the window.** (The phrase functions as an adverb modifying the verb *placed.*)

Prepositions

aboard	back of	excepting	notwithstanding	save
about	because of	for	of	since
above	before	from	off	subsequent to
according to	behind	from among	on	through
across	below	from between	on account of	throughout
across from	beneath	from under	on behalf of	'til
after	beside	in	onto	to
against	besides	in addition to	on top of	together with
along	between	in behalf of	opposite	toward
alongside	beyond	in front of	out	under
alongside of	by	in place of	out of	underneath
along with	by means of	in regard to	outside	until
amid	concerning	inside	outside of	unto
among	considering	inside of	over	up
apart from	despite	in spite of	over to	upon
around	down	instead of	owing to	up to
as far as	down from	into	past	with
aside from	during	like	prior to	within
at	except	near	regarding	without
away from	except for	near to	round	

esl Note: Prepositions often pair up with a verb and become part of an idiom, a slang expression, or a two-word verb. (See pages 684 and 699–702.)

648.1 Conjunction

A **conjunction** connects individual words or groups of words.

> **When** we came back to Paris, it was clear **and** cold **and** lovely.
>
> —Ernest Hemingway

648.2 Coordinating Conjunctions

Coordinating conjunctions usually connect a word to a word, a phrase to a phrase, or a clause to a clause. The words, phrases, or clauses joined by a coordinating conjunction are equal in importance or are of the same type.

> Civilization is a race between education **and** catastrophe.
>
> —H. G. Wells

648.3 Correlative Conjunctions

Correlative conjunctions are a type of coordinating conjunction used in pairs.

> There are two inadvisable ways to think: **either** believe everything **or** doubt everything.

648.4 Subordinating Conjunctions

Subordinating conjunctions connect two clauses that are not equally important. A subordinating conjunction connects a dependent clause to an independent clause. The conjunction is part of the dependent clause.

> Experience is the worst teacher; it gives the test **before** it presents the lesson. (The clause *before it presents the lesson* is dependent. It connects to the independent clause *it gives the test*.)

648.5

Conjunctions	
Coordinating:	and, but, or, nor, for, so, yet
Correlative:	either, or; neither, nor; not only, but (but also); both, and; whether, or
Subordinating:	after, although, as, as if, as long as, because, before, even though, if, in order that, provided that, since, so that, though, unless, until, when, whenever, where, while

Note: Relative pronouns (628.3) can also connect clauses.

648.6 Interjection

An **interjection** communicates strong emotion or surprise (*oh, ouch, hey,* and so on). Punctuation (often a comma or an exclamation point) is used to set off an interjection.

> **Hey! Wait! Well,** so much for catching the bus.

Grammar Exercises:

Adjectives, Adverbs, Prepositions, Conjunctions, and Injections

A. Forms of Adjectives

Write the correct form (positive, comparative, or superlative) of the adjective shown in parentheses for each sentence.

1. I ate the _____ chicken wings I had ever tasted in my life. (*spicy*)

2. The Internet connection at the coffeehouse is _____ than the connection at the library. (*fast*)

3. Arizona is known for its _____ and dry climate. (*hot*)

4. Online shopping is _____ than mall shopping. (*efficient*)

B. Types of Adverbs

Indicate whether the adverb reveals time, place, manner, or degree.

1. completely	3. easily	5. everywhere
2. smartly	4. briefly	6. tomorrow

C. Conjunctions

Create a three-column table and label the columns "Coordinating," "Subordinating," and "Correlative." Then sort out the conjunctions below into their appropriate columns.

after	for	though
although	if	unless
and	in order that	until
as	neither/nor	when
as if	nor	whenever
as long as	not only/but also	where
because	or	while
before	provided that	yet
both/and	since	
but	so	
either/or	so that	
even though	that	

A Closer Look
at the Parts of Speech

Noun

A **noun** is a word that names something: a person, a place, a thing, or an idea.

Toni Morrison/author	*Lone Star*/film
UC–Davis/university	Renaissance/era
A Congress of Wonders/book	

Pronoun

A **pronoun** is a word used in place of a noun.

I	my	that	themselves	which
it	ours	they	everybody	you

Verb

A **verb** is a word that expresses action, links words, or acts as an auxiliary verb to the main verb.

are	break	drag	fly	run	sit	was
bite	catch	eat	is	see	tear	were

Adjective

An **adjective** describes or modifies a noun or pronoun. (The articles *a*, *an*, and *the* are adjectives.)

The carbonated drink went down easy on **that hot, dry** day. (*The* and *carbonated* modify *drink*; *that*, *hot*, and *dry* modify *day*.)

Adverb

An **adverb** describes or modifies a verb, an adjective, another adverb, or a whole sentence. An adverb generally answers questions such as *how*, *when*, *where*, *how often*, or *how much*.

greatly	precisely	regularly	there
here	today	partly	quickly
slowly	yesterday	nearly	loudly

Preposition

A **preposition** is a word (or group of words) that shows the relationship between its object (a noun or pronoun that follows the preposition) and another word in the sentence. Prepositions introduce prepositional phrases, which are modifiers.

across   for   with   out   to   of

Conjunction

A **conjunction** connects individual words or groups of words.

and   because   but   for   or   since   so   yet

Interjection

An **interjection** is a word that communicates strong emotion or surprise. Punctuation (often a comma or an exclamation point) is used to set off an interjection from the rest of the sentence.

Stop! No! What, am I invisible?

Chapter 34

Constructing Sentences

651.1

A **sentence** is made up of at least a subject (sometimes understood) and a verb and expresses a complete thought. Sentences can make statements, ask questions, give commands, or express feelings.

> The Web delivers the universe in a box.

Using Subjects and Predicates

651.2

Sentences have two main parts: a **subject** and a **predicate**.

> Technology frustrates many people.

> **Note:** In the sentence above, *technology* is the subject—the sentence talks about technology. *Frustrates many people* is the complete predicate—it tells what the subject is doing.

The Subject

651.3

The **subject** names the person or thing either performing the action, receiving the action, or being described or renamed. The subject is most often a noun or a pronoun.

> **Technology** is an integral part of almost every business.
> **Manufacturers** need technology to compete in the world market.
> **They** could not go far without it.

A verbal phrase or a noun dependent clause may also function as a subject.

> **To survive without technology** is difficult. (infinitive phrase)
> **Downloading information from the Web** is easy. (gerund phrase)
> **That the information age would arrive** was inevitable. (noun dependent clause)

> **Note:** To determine the subject of a sentence, ask yourself *who* or *what* performs or receives the action or is described. In most sentences, the subject comes before the verb; however, in many questions and some other instances, that order is reversed. (See 658.2, 658.3, 662.1, and 692.)

> **esl Note:** Some languages permit the omission of a subject in a sentence; English does not. A subject must be included in every sentence. (The only exception is an "understood subject," which is discussed at 652.4.)

652.1

Simple Subject

A **simple subject** is the subject without the words that describe or modify it.

Thirty years ago, reasonably well-trained **mechanics** could fix any car on the road.

652.2

Complete Subject

A **complete subject** is the simple subject *and* the words that describe or modify it.

Thirty years ago, **reasonably well-trained mechanics** could fix any car on the road.

652.3

Compound Subject

A **compound subject** is composed of two or more simple subjects joined by a conjunction and sharing the same predicate(s).

Today, **mechanics** and **technicians** would need to master a half million manual pages to fix every car on the road.

Dealerships and their service **departments** must sometimes explain that situation to the customers.

652.4

Understood Subject

Sometimes a subject is **understood**. This means it is not stated in the sentence, but a reader clearly understands what the subject is. An understood subject occurs in a command (imperative sentence). (See 658.3.)

(You) Park on this side of the street. (The subject *you* is understood.)

Put the CD player in the trunk.

652.5

Delayed Subject

In sentences that begin with *There is, There was,* or *Here is,* the subject follows the verb.

There are 70,000 **fans** in the stadium. (The subject is *fans; are* is the verb. *There* is an expletive, an empty word.)

Here is a **problem** for stadium security. (*Problem* is the subject. *Here* is an adverb.)

The subject is also delayed in questions.

Where was the **event**? (*Event* is the subject.)

Was **Dave Matthews** playing? (*Dave Matthews* is the subject.)

The Predicate (Verb)

653.1

The **predicate**, which contains the verb, is the part of the sentence that either tells what the subject is doing, tells what is being done to the subject, or describes or renames the subject.

> Students **need technical skills as well as basic academic skills.**

Simple Predicate

653.2

A **simple predicate** is the complete verb without the words that describe or modify it. (The complete verb can consist of more that one word.)

> Today's workplace **requires** employees to have a range of skills.

Complete Predicate

653.3

A **complete predicate** is the verb, all the words that modify or explain it, and any objects or complements.

> Today's workplace **requires employees to have a range of skills.**

Compound Predicate

653.4

A **compound predicate** is composed of two or more verbs, all the words that modify or explain them, and any objects or complements.

> Engineers **analyze problems** and **calculate solutions.**

Direct Object

653.5

A **direct object** is the part of the predicate that receives the action of an active transitive verb. A direct object makes the meaning of the verb complete.

> Marcos visited several **campuses.** (The direct object *campuses* receives the action of the verb *visited* by answering the question "Marcos visited what?")

Note: A direct object may be compound.

> A counselor explained the academic **programs** and the application **process.**

Indirect Object

653.6

An **indirect object** is the word(s) that tells *to whom/to what* or *for whom/for what* something is done. A sentence must have a direct object before it can have an indirect object.

> I showed our **children** my new school.

Use these questions to find an indirect object:

- What is the verb?   *showed*
- *Showed* what?   *school* (direct object)
- Showed *school* to whom?   *children* (indirect object)

> I wrote **them** a note.

Note: An indirect object may be compound.

> I gave the **instructor** and a few **classmates** my email address.

Constructing Sentences Exercises:

Subjects and Predicates

A. Subjects

1. Write the complete subject of each numbered sentence in the following paragraph. Then underline the simple subjects. (You will find one compound subject.)

> (1) Every modern war seems to have its own terrible illness for soldiers. (2) In World War I, blistered skin and ravaged lungs resulted from exposure to mustard gas. (3) World War II saw the problem of "shell shock." (4) Agent Orange was blamed for causing cancer in Vietnam War veterans. (5) The Gulf War saw the rise of "post-traumatic stress disorder." (6) And many veterans of combat in Iraq and Iran return with "mild traumatic brain injury" due to improvised explosive devices.

2. Create your own sentence with an understood subject.
3. Create your own sentence with a delayed subject.

B. Predicates

1. Write the complete predicate of each numbered sentence in the following paragraph. Then underline the simple predicates. (You will find one compound predicate.)

> (1) Women today have more than one choice for professional assistance with childbirth. (2) The obstetrician of your parents' era is trained to diagnose abnormalities and is prepared to deal with emergencies. (3) Today's midwife practitioner, on the other hand, is focused upon normal deliveries. (4) This makes the two occupations quite complementary.

2. List the direct objects in the numbered sentences of the following paragraph. If a sentence also includes an indirect object, list that in parentheses after the direct object.

> (1) Different situations bring you happiness. (2) Various pursuits deliver satisfaction. (3) And many agree that parents pass along their values and goals to their children. (4) So your own offspring will also receive this intangible inheritance.

Using Phrases

A **phrase** is a group of related words that functions as a single part of speech. A phrase lacks a subject, a predicate, or both. There are three phrases in the following sentence:

> **Examples of technology can be found in ancient civilizations.**

> **of technology**
> (prepositional phrase that functions as an adjective; no subject or predicate)

> **can be found**
> (verb phrase—all of the words of the verb; no subject)

> **in ancient civilizations**
> (prepositional phrase that functions as an adverb; no subject or predicate)

Types of Phrases

There are several types of phrases: *verb, verbal, prepositional, appositive,* and *absolute.*

Verb Phrase

A **verb phrase** consists of a main verb and its helping verbs.

> Students, worried about exams, **have camped** at the library all week.

Verbal Phrase

A **verbal phrase** is a phrase that expands on one of the three types of verbals: *gerund, infinitive,* or *participle.* (See 642.)

A **gerund phrase** consists of a gerund and its modifiers and objects. The whole phrase functions as a noun. (See 642.2.)

> **Becoming a marine biologist** is Rashanda's dream. (The gerund phrase is used as the subject of the sentence.)

> She has acquainted herself with the various methods for **collecting sea-life samples.** (The gerund phrase is the object of the preposition *for.*)

An **infinitive phrase** consists of an infinitive and its modifiers and objects. The whole phrase functions as a noun, an adjective, or an adverb. (See 642.3.)

> **To dream** is the first step in any endeavor. (The infinitive phrase functions as a noun used as the subject.)

> Remember **to make a plan to realize your dream.** (The infinitive phrase *to make a plan* functions as a noun used as a direct object; *to realize your dream* functions as an adjective modifying *plan.*)

> Finally, apply all of your talents and skills **to achieve your goals.** (The infinitive phrase functions as an adverb modifying *apply.*)

A **participial phrase** consists of a present or past participle (a verb form ending in *ing* or *ed*) and its modifiers. The phrase functions as an adjective. (See 642.4.)

> **Doing poorly in biology,** Theo signed up for a tutor. (The participial phrase modifies the noun *Theo.*)

> Some students **frustrated by difficult course work** don't seek help. (The participial phrase modifies the noun *students.*)

656.1

Functions of Verbal Phrases			*fig. 34.1*
	Noun	**Adjective**	**Adverb**
Gerund	■		
Infinitive	■	■	■
Participial		■	

656.2

Prepositional Phrase

A **prepositional phrase** is a group of words beginning with a preposition and ending with its object, a noun or a pronoun. Prepositional phrases are used mainly as adjectives and adverbs. See 647.3 for a list of prepositions.

> Denying the existence **of exam week** hasn't worked **for anyone** yet.
> (The prepositional phrase *of exam week* is used as an adjective modifying the noun *existence*; *for anyone* is used as an adverb modifying the verb *has worked*.)

> Test days still dawn and GPAs still plummet **for the unprepared student**.
> (The prepositional phrase *for the unprepared student* is used as an adverb modifying the verbs *dawn* and *plummet*.)

esl Note: Do not mistake the following adverbs for nouns and incorrectly use them as objects of prepositions: *here, there, everywhere*.

656.3

Appositive Phrase

An **appositive phrase**, which follows a noun or a pronoun and renames it, consists of a noun and its modifiers. An appositive adds new information about the noun or pronoun it follows.

> The Olympic-size pool, **a prized addition to the physical education building**, gets plenty of use. (The appositive phrase renames *pool*.)

656.4

Absolute Phrase

An **absolute phrase** consists of a noun and a participle (plus the participle's object, if there is one, and any modifiers). It usually modifies the entire sentence.

> **Their enthusiasm sometimes waning**, the students who cannot swim are required to take lessons. (The noun *enthusiasm* is modified by the present participle *waning*; the entire phrase modifies *students*.)

 Phrases can add valuable information to sentences, but some phrases add nothing but "fat" to your writing. For a list of phrases to avoid, see page 101.

Using Clauses

A **clause** is a group of related words that has both a subject and a verb.

Independent/Dependent Clauses

657.1

An **independent clause** contains at least one subject and one verb, presents a complete thought, and can stand alone as a sentence; a **dependent clause** (also called a subordinate clause) does not present a complete thought and cannot stand alone (make sense) as a sentence.

> Though airplanes are twentieth-century inventions (dependent clause), people have always dreamed of flying (independent clause).

Types of Clauses

There are three basic types of dependent, or subordinate, clauses: *adverb, adjective,* and *noun*. These dependent clauses are combined with independent clauses to form complex and compound-complex sentences.

Adverb Clause

657.2

An **adverb clause** is used like an adverb to modify a verb, an adjective, or an adverb. All adverb clauses begin with subordinating conjunctions. (See 648.4.)

> **Because Orville won a coin toss,** he got to fly the power-driven air machine first. (The adverb clause modifies the verb *got.*)

Adjective Clause

657.3

An **adjective clause** is used like an adjective to modify a noun or a pronoun. Adjective clauses begin with relative pronouns *(which, that, who).* (See 634.3.)

> The men **who invented the first airplane** were brothers, Orville and Wilbur Wright. (The adjective clause modifies the noun *men. Who* is the subject of the adjective clause.)

> The first flight, **which took place December 17, 1903,** was made by Orville. (The adjective clause modifies the noun *flight. Which* is the subject of the adjective clause.)

Noun Clause

657.4

A **noun clause** is used in place of a noun. Noun clauses can appear as subjects, as direct or indirect objects, as predicate nominatives, or as objects of prepositions. Noun clauses can also play a role in the independent clause. They are introduced by subordinating words such as *what, that, when, why, how, whatever, who, whom, whoever,* and *whomever.*

> He wants to know **what made modern aviation possible.** (The noun clause functions as the object of the infinitive.)

> **Whoever invents an airplane with vertical takeoff ability** will be a hero. (The noun clause functions as the subject.)

Note: If you can replace a whole clause with the pronoun *something* or *someone,* it is a noun clause.

Using Sentence Variety

A sentence can be classified according to the kind of statement it makes and according to the way it is constructed.

Kinds of Sentences

Sentences can make five basic kinds of statements: *declarative, interrogative, imperative, exclamatory,* or *conditional.*

658.1

Declarative Sentence

Declarative sentences make statements. They tell us something about a person, a place, a thing, or an idea.

> In 1955, Rosa Parks refused to follow segregation rules on a bus in Montgomery, Alabama.

658.2

Interrogative Sentence

Interrogative sentences ask questions.

> Do you think Ms. Parks knew she was making history?
> Would you have had the courage to do what she did?

658.3

Imperative Sentence

Imperative sentences give commands. They often contain an understood subject (*you*). (See 652.4.)

> Read chapters 6 through 10 for tomorrow.

esl Note: Imperative sentences with an understood subject are the only sentences in which it is acceptable to have no subjects stated.

658.4

Exclamatory Sentence

Exclamatory sentences communicate strong emotion or surprise. They are punctuated with exclamation points.

> I simply can't keep up with these long reading assignments!
> Oh my gosh, you scared me!

658.5

Conditional Sentence

Conditional sentences express two circumstances. One of the circumstances depends on the other circumstance. The words *if, when,* or *unless* are often used in the dependent clause in conditional sentences.

> **If** you practice a few study-reading techniques, college reading loads will be manageable.
> **When** I manage my time, it seems I have more of it.
> Don't ask me to help you **unless** you are willing to do the reading first.

Structure of Sentences

A sentence may be *simple, compound, complex,* or *compound-complex,* depending on how the independent and dependent clauses are combined.

Simple Sentence
659.1

A **simple sentence** contains one independent clause. The independent clause may have compound subjects and verbs, and it may also contain phrases.

> My **back aches.**
> (single subject: *back*; single verb: *aches*)

> My **teeth** and my **eyes hurt.**
> (compound subject: *teeth* and *eyes*; single verb: *hurt*)

> My **memory** and my **logic come** and **go.**
> (compound subject: *memory* and *logic*; compound verb: *come* and *go*)

> I **must need a vacation.**
> (single subject: *I*; single verb: *must need*; direct object: *vacation*)

Compound Sentence
659.2

A **compound sentence** consists of two independent clauses. The clauses must be joined by a semicolon, by a comma and a coordinating conjunction (*and, but, or, nor, so, for, yet*), or by a semicolon followed by a conjunctive adverb (*besides, however, instead, meanwhile, then, therefore*) and a comma.

> I had eight hours of sleep, **so** why am I so exhausted?

> I take good care of myself; I get enough sleep.

> I still feel fatigued; **therefore,** I must need more exercise.

Complex Sentence
659.3

A **complex sentence** contains one independent clause (in bold) and one or more dependent clauses (underlined).

> When I can, **I get eight hours of sleep.** (dependent clause; independent clause)

> When I get up on time, and if someone hasn't used up all the milk,

> **I eat breakfast.** (two dependent clauses; independent clause)

When the dependent clause comes before the independent clause, use a comma.

Compound-Complex Sentence
659.4

A **compound-complex sentence** contains two or more independent clauses (in bold type) and one or more dependent clauses (underlined).

> If I'm not in a hurry, **I take leisurely walks,** and **I try to spot some wildlife.**
> (dependent clause; two independent clauses)

> **I saw a hawk** when I was walking, and **other smaller birds were chasing it.**
> (dependent clause, independent clause; independent clause)

Constructing Sentences Exercises:

Phrases, Clauses, and Sentence Variety

A. Phrases and Clauses

Identify the numbered phrases (gerund, infinitive, participial, prepositional, appositive, or absolute), and clauses (adverb, adjective, or noun). Note that not every type is represented.

> The marionette, (1) a type of puppet manipulated by strings or rods, has been around for millennia. Stringed puppets have been found in Egyptian tombs from around 2000 B.C. Greek philosophers such as Xenophon wrote about these articulated puppets as early as 422 B.C. (2) To control their marionettes, the ancient Romans used rods from above, and Italy retains a strong tradition of articulated puppetry from these Roman roots. (3) Employed in religious performances during ancient times, marionettes found similar use in morality plays during the Renaissance. Most likely, the term "marionette" originated as a diminutive form (4) of the Virgin Mary's name in these plays. Starting in the eighteenth century, entire operas were performed by marionettes in theaters such as the Salzburg Marionette Theatre in Austria, (5) which continues performances to this day. Of course, marionettes have also starred in television and film, and (6) since puppetry is still a valued storytelling art, chances are you've seen them perform at your local grade school.

B. Sentence Variety

Identify each sentence in the following paragraph by kind (declarative, interrogative, imperative, exclamatory, or conditional).

> (1) Do you realize how far personal computers have come since their early days? (2) Understand that the first examples were marketed to scientists and researchers. (3) After that came kits for hobbyists to build and program their own machines. (4) The introduction of the microprocessor chip allowed PCs to proliferate after 1975. (5) If blinkenlights.com is correct, the HP 9830, originally sold in 1972, qualifies as the very first personal computer, being a fully built desktop machine with a keyboard and display. (6) Other people argue that the Commodore PET in 1977 better suited that designation because it was commercially available to everyone. (7) In any case, the popular Apple II and the IBM-PC then solidified the personal computer's role in business and at home.

Chapter 35

Avoiding Sentence Errors

Subject–Verb Agreement

661.1

The subject and verb of any clause must agree in both *person* and *number*. Person indicates whether the subject of the verb is *first, second,* or *third person. Number* indicates whether the subject and verb are *singular* or *plural.* (See 639.2 and 639.3.)

	Singular	Plural
First Person	I think	we think
Second Person	you think	you think
Third Person	he/she/it thinks	they think

Agreement in Number

661.2

A verb must agree in number (singular or plural) with its subject.

> The **student was** rewarded for her hard work. (Both the subject *student* and the verb *was* are singular; they agree in number.)

Note: Do not be confused by phrases that come between the subject and the verb. Such phrases may begin with words like *in addition to, as well as,* or *together with.*

> The **instructor**, as well as the students, **is** expected to attend the orientation. (*Instructor,* not *students,* is the subject.)

Compound Subjects

661.3

Compound subjects connected with *and* usually require a plural verb.

> **Dedication and creativity are** trademarks of successful students.

Note: If a compound subject joined by *and* is thought of as a unit, use a singular verb.

> **Macaroni and cheese is** always available in the cafeteria.

(Also see 662.3 and 662.4.)

662.1   Delayed Subjects

Delayed subjects occur when the verb comes *before* the subject in a sentence. In these inverted sentences, the true (delayed) subject must still agree with the verb.

> There **are** many nontraditional **students** on our campus.
> Here **is** the **syllabus** you need.
> (*Students* and *syllabus* are the subjects of these sentences, not the adverbs *there* and *here*.)

> **Note:** Using an inverted sentence, on occasion, will lend variety to your writing style. Simply remember to make the delayed subjects agree with the verbs.

> However, included among the list's topmost items **was "revise research paper."**
> (Because the true subject here is singular—one item—the singular verb *was* is correct.)

662.2   Titles as Subjects

When the subject of a sentence is the title of a work of art, literature, or music, the verb should be singular. This is also true of a word (or phrase) being used as a word (or phrase).

> *Lyrical Ballads* **was** published in 1798 by two of England's greatest poets, Wordsworth and Coleridge. (Even though the title of the book, *Lyrical Ballads*, is plural in form, it is still a single title being used as the subject, correctly taking the singular verb *was*.)

> **"Over-the-counter drugs" is** a phrase that means nonprescription medications. (Even though the phrase is plural in form, it is still a single phrase being used as the subject, correctly taking the singular verb *is*.)

662.3   Singular Subjects with *Or* or *Nor*

Singular subjects joined by *or* or *nor* take a singular verb.

> Neither a **textbook** nor a **notebook is required** for this class.

> **Note:** When the subject nearer a present-tense verb is the singular pronoun *I* or *you*, the correct singular verb does not end in *s*. (See the chart on page 666.1.)

> Neither **Marcus** nor **I feel** (not *feels*) right about this.
> Either **Rosa** or **you have** (not *has*) to take notes for me.
> Either **you** or **Rosa has** to take notes for me.

662.4   Singular/Plural Subjects

When one of the subjects joined by *or* or *nor* is singular and one is plural, the verb must agree with the subject nearer the verb.

> Neither the **professor** nor her **students were** in the lab. (The plural subject *students* is nearer the verb; therefore, the plural verb *were* agrees with *students*.)

> Neither the **students** nor the **professor was** in the lab. (The singular subject *professor* is nearer the verb; therefore, the singular verb *was* is used to agree with *professor*.)

Collective Nouns

Generally, **collective nouns** (*faculty, pair, crew, assembly, congress, species, crowd, army, team, committee,* and so on) take a singular verb. However, if you want to emphasize differences among individuals in the group or are referring to the group as individuals, you can use a plural verb.

> My lab **team takes** its work very seriously. (*Team* refers to the group as a unit; it requires a singular verb, *takes.*)

> The **team assume** separate responsibilities for each study they undertake. (In this example, *team* refers to individuals within the group; it requires a plural verb, *assume.*)

> **Note:** Collective nouns such as (the) *police, poor, elderly,* and *young* use plural verbs.
> The police direct traffic here between 7:00 and 9:00 a.m.

Plural Nouns with Singular Meaning

Some nouns that are plural in form but singular in meaning take a singular verb: *mumps, measles, news, mathematics, economics, robotics,* and so on.

> **Economics is** sometimes called "the dismal science."

> The economic **news is** not very good.

> **Note:** The most common exceptions are *scissors, trousers, tidings,* and *pliers.*
> The **scissors are** missing again.
> **Are** these **trousers** prewashed?

With Linking Verbs

When a sentence contains a linking verb (usually a form of *be*)—and a noun or pronoun comes before and after that verb—the verb must agree with the subject, not the predicate nominative (the noun or pronoun coming after the verb).

> The cause of his problem **was** poor study habits. (*Cause* requires a singular verb, even though the predicate nominative, *habits,* is plural.)

> His poor study habits **were** the cause of his problem. (*Habits* requires a plural verb, even though the predicate nominative, *cause,* is singular.)

Nouns Showing Measurement, Time, and Money

Mathematical phrases and phrases that name a period of time, a unit of measurement, or an amount of money take a singular verb.

> Three and three **is** six.

> Eight pages **is** a long paper on this topic.

> In my opinion, two dollars **is** a high price for a cup of coffee.

664.1   Relative Pronouns

When a **relative pronoun** (*who, which, that*) is used as the subject of a dependent clause, the number of the verb is determined by that pronoun's antecedent. (The *antecedent* is the word to which the pronoun refers.)

> This is one of the **books that are** required for English class.
> (The relative pronoun *that* requires the plural verb *are* because its antecedent is *books*, not the word *one*. To test this type of sentence for agreement, read the *of* phrase first: *Of the books that are . . .*)

> **Note:** Generally, the antecedent is the nearest noun or pronoun to the relative pronoun and is often the object of a preposition. Sometimes, however, the antecedent is not the nearest noun or pronoun, especially in sentences with the phrase "the only one of."

> Dr. Graciosa wondered why Claire was the only **one** of her students **who was** not attending lectures regularly. (In this case, the addition of the modifiers *the only* changes the meaning of the sentence. The antecedent of *who* is *one*, not *students*. Only one student was not attending.)

664.2   Indefinite Pronoun with Singular Verb

Many indefinite pronouns (*someone, somebody, something; anyone, anybody, anything; no one, nobody, nothing; everyone, everybody, everything; each, either, neither, one, this*) serving as subjects require a singular verb.

> **Everybody is** welcome to attend the chancellor's reception.
>
> **No one was** sent an invitation.

> **Note:** Although it may seem to indicate more than one, *each* is a singular pronoun and requires a singular verb. Do not be confused by words or phrases that come between the indefinite pronoun and the verb.

> **Each** of the new students **is** (not *are*) **encouraged** to attend the reception.

664.3   Indefinite Pronoun with Plural Verb

Some indefinite pronouns (*both, few, many, most,* and *several*) are plural; they require a plural verb.

> **Few are** offered the opportunity to study abroad.
>
> **Most take** advantage of opportunities closer to home.

664.4   Indefinite Pronoun or Quantity Word with Singular/Plural Verb

Some indefinite pronouns or quantity words (*all, any, most, part, half, none,* and *some*) may be either singular or plural, depending on the nouns they refer to. Look inside the prepositional phrase to see what the antecedent is.

> **Some** of the students **were** missing. (*Students*, the noun that *some* refers to, is plural; therefore, the pronoun *some* is considered plural, and the plural verb *were* is used to agree with it.)

> **Most** of the lecture **was** over by the time we arrived. (Because *lecture* is singular, *most* is also singular, requiring the singular verb *was*.)

Pronoun–Antecedent Agreement

665.1

A pronoun must agree in number, person, and gender (sex) with its *antecedent*. The antecedent is the word to which the pronoun refers.

> **Yoshi** brought **his** laptop computer and e-book to school. (The pronoun *his* refers to the antecedent *Yoshi*. Both the pronoun and its antecedent are singular, third person, and masculine; therefore, the pronoun is said to agree with its antecedent.)

Singular Pronoun

665.2

Use a singular pronoun to refer to such antecedents as *each, either, neither, one, anyone, anybody, everyone, everybody, somebody, another, nobody,* and *a person.*

> **Each** of the maintenance vehicles has **their** doors locked at night. (Incorrect)
>
> **Each** of the maintenance vehicles has **its** doors locked at night. (Correct: Both *Each* and *its* are singular.)
>
> **Somebody** left **his or her** (not *their*) vehicle unlocked. (Correct)

Plural Pronoun

665.3

When a plural pronoun *(they, their)* is mistakenly used with a singular indefinite pronoun (such as *everyone* or *everybody*), you may correct the sentence by replacing *their* or *they* with optional pronouns *(her or his* or *he or she)*, or make the antecedent plural.

> **Everyone** must learn to wait **their** turn. (Incorrect)
>
> **Everyone** must learn to wait **her or his** turn. (Correct: Optional pronouns *her* or *his* are used.)
>
> **People** must learn to wait **their** turns. (Correct: The singular antecedent, *Everyone,* is changed to the plural antecedent, *People.*)

Two or More Antecedents

665.4

When two or more antecedents are joined by *and,* they are considered plural.

> **Tomas** and **Jamal** are finishing **their** assignments.

When two or more singular antecedents are joined by *or* or *nor,* they are considered singular.

> **Connie** or **Shavonn** left **her** headset in the library.

> **Note:** If one of the antecedents is masculine and one feminine, the pronouns should likewise be masculine and feminine.
>
> Is **Ahmad** or **Phyllis** bringing **his or her** laptop computer?

> **Note:** If one of the antecedents joined by *or* or *nor* is singular and one is plural, the pronoun is made to agree with the nearer antecedent.
>
> Neither **Ravi** nor **his friends** want to spend **their** time studying.
>
> Neither **his friends** nor **Ravi** wants to spend **his** time studying.

Avoiding Sentence Errors Exercises:

Agreement

A. Subject-Verb Agreement

Correct the agreement errors in the following paragraph by writing down the line number and any incorrect verb, crossed out, with the correct form beside it.

> There is in beautiful Barcelona, Spain, many surprises to be found. *1*
> Barcelona, Spain's second-largest city, and Madrid, the country's capital, *2*
> has a traditional rivalry. At one time, the population of Barcelona were *3*
> forbidden to speak the city's native tongue, Catalan, by a royal decree from *4*
> Madrid. Today, however, neither Spanish nor Catalan are discriminated *5*
> against in the region. One of the sites that belongs on every tour, the *6*
> outlandish cathedral La Sagrada Familia ("The Sacred Family"), was *7*
> designed by Antoni Gaudi. Everyone using the word "gaudy" actually has *8*
> Gaudi's name on his or her tongue. A series of thirteenth- to fifteenth- *9*
> century palaces now house the Museo Picasso, which display a history *10*
> of Picasso's work and his many years living in Barcelona. *Les Demoiselles* *11*
> *d'Avignon,* or *The Young Ladies of Avignon,* are one example of a painting *12*
> inspired by his time in Barcelona. Whether you prefer cobblestone streets *13*
> with centuries-old buildings or asphalt streets with modern shops and *14*
> taverns, each are found in Barcelona. At night, every one of the streets *15*
> seem to have a festive air, reflecting the vivacity of Spanish culture. *16*

B. Pronoun-Antecedent and Subject-Verb Agreement

Provide the correct pronoun or verb for each blank in the following sentences. Use the directions or choices in parentheses.

1. Some people _____ math with an abacus. (*do/does*)

2. This counting device has been used for thousands of years, and _____ is still very popular in Eastern nations. (pronoun for "device")

3. The earliest examples _____ employed between 2700 and 2300 B.C. in Sumeria. (*was/were*)

4. As recently as the 1990s, school children in the Soviet Union were taught to use _____ . (pronoun for "examples" in the previous sentence)

5. Pocket-sized abacuses _____ still popular in Japan, despite the availability of portable calculators. (*is/are*)

6. Expert abacus users _____ able to add, subtract, multiply, divide, and even calculate square roots and cube roots very quickly. (*is/are*)

Shifts in Sentence Construction

A shift is an improper change in structure midway through a sentence. The following examples will help you identify and fix several different kinds of shifts.

Shift in Person   667.1

Shift in person is mixing first, second, or third person within a sentence. (See 635.4 and 639.3.)

Shift: **One** may get spring fever unless **you** live in California or Florida. (The sentence shifts from third person, *one,* to second person, *you.*)

Corrected: **You** may get spring fever unless **you** live in California or Florida. (Stays in second person)

Corrected: **People** may get spring fever unless **they** live in California or Florida. (*People,* a third person plural noun, requires a third person plural pronoun, *they.*)

Shift in Tense   667.2

Shift in tense is using more than one tense in a sentence when only one is needed.

Shift: Sheila **looked** at nine apartments in one weekend before she **had chosen** one. (Tense shifts from past to past perfect for no reason.)

Corrected: Sheila **looked** at nine apartments in one weekend before she **chose** one. (Tense stays in past.)

Shift in Voice   667.3

Shift in voice is mixing active with passive voice. Usually, a sentence beginning in active voice should remain so to the end.

Shift: As you look (active voice) for just the right place, many interesting apartments **will probably be seen.** (passive voice)

Corrected: As you look (active voice) for just the right place, **you will probably see** (active voice) many interesting apartments.

Unparallel Construction   667.4

Unparallel construction occurs when the kind of words or phrases being used shifts or changes in the middle of a sentence.

Shift: In my hometown, people pass the time shooting pool, pitching horseshoes, and at softball games. (Sentence shifts from a series of general phrases, *shooting pool* and *pitching horseshoes,* to the prepositional phrase *at softball games.*)

Parallel: In my hometown, people pass the time **shooting pool, pitching horseshoes, and playing softball.** (Now all three activities are gerund phrases—they are consistent, or parallel.)

Fragments, Comma Splices, and Run-Ons

Except in a few special situations, you should use complete sentences when you write. By definition, a complete sentence expresses a complete thought. However, a sentence may actually contain several ideas, not just one. The trick is getting those ideas to work together to form a clear, interesting sentence that expresses your exact meaning. Among the most common sentence errors that writers make are fragments, comma splices, and run-ons.

668.1 Fragments

A **fragment** is a phrase or dependent clause used as a sentence. It is not a sentence, however, because a phrase lacks a subject, a verb, or some other essential part, and a dependent clause must be connected to an independent clause to complete its meaning.

Fragment: Pete gunned the engine. Forgetting that the boat was hooked to the truck. (This is a sentence followed by a fragment. This error can be corrected by combining the fragment with the sentence.)

Corrected: Pete gunned the engine, forgetting that the boat was hooked to the truck.

Fragment: Even though my best friend had a little boy last year. (This clause does not convey a complete thought. We need to know what is happening despite the birth of the little boy.)

Corrected: Even though my best friend had a little boy last year, **I do not comprehend the full meaning of "motherhood."**

668.2 Comma Splices

A **comma splice** is a mistake made when two independent clauses are connected ("spliced") with only a comma. The comma is not enough: A period, semicolon, or conjunction is needed.

Splice: People say that being a stay-at-home mom or dad is an important job, their actions tell a different story.

Corrected: People say that being a stay-at-home mom or dad is an important job, **but** their actions tell a different story. (The coordinating conjunction *but,* added after the comma, corrects the splice.)

Corrected: People say that being a stay-at-home mom or dad is an important job; their actions tell a different story. (A semicolon—rather than just a comma—makes the sentence correct.)

Corrected: People say that being a stay-at-home mom or dad is an important job. **Their** actions tell a different story. (A period creates two sentences and corrects the splice.)

Run-Ons

A run-on sentence is actually two sentences (two independent clauses) joined without adequate punctuation or a connecting word.

Run-on: The Alamo holds a special place in American history it was the site of an important battle between the United States and Mexico.

Corrected: **The Alamo holds a special place in American history because it was the site of an important battle between the United States and Mexico.** (A subordinating conjunction is added to fix the run-on by making the second clause dependent.)

Run-on: Antonio de Santa Anna, the president of Mexico who once held a funeral for his amputated leg, is the same Santa Anna who stormed the Alamo he led his troops to victory over the Texan rebels defending that fort. Two famous American frontiersmen died they were James Bowie and Davy Crockett. Santa Anna enjoyed fame, power, and respect among his followers. He died in 1876 he was poor, blind, and ignored.

Corrected: Antonio de Santa Anna, the president of Mexico who once held a funeral for his amputated leg, is the same Santa Anna who stormed the Alamo. He led his troops to victory over the Texan rebels defending that fort. Two famous American frontiersmen were killed in the battle; they were James Bowie and Davy Crockett. Santa Anna enjoyed fame, power, and respect among his followers. When he died in 1876, he was poor, blind, and ignored.

The writer corrected the run-on sentences in the paragraph above by adding punctuation and making one sentence a dependent clause. While doing so, the writer also made a few changes to improve the ideas. The writer makes further improvements in the paragraph below by revising one sentence and by combining two sets of short sentences into one stronger sentence.

Improved: Antonio de Santa Anna, the president of Mexico who once held a funeral for his amputated leg, is the same Santa Anna who stormed the Alamo. He led his troops to victory over Texan rebels defending that fort. Two famous American frontiersmen, **James Bowie and Davy Crockett, were killed in the battle.** Santa Anna enjoyed fame, power, and respect among his followers; **but when** he died in 1876, he was poor, blind, and ignored.

fyi Once you make a correction, you may see an opportunity to add, cut, or improve something else. Correcting and editing sentences can be frustrating at times, but with practice, these processes can become some of the more enjoyable parts of the writing process.

Avoiding Sentence Errors Exercises:

Shifts in Construction, Fragments, Comma Splices, and Run-Ons

A. Identifying Errors

Identify the type of sentence error illustrated by each example below. If the error is a shift in construction, tell which type. (See page 667.)

1. Much music in the Western world is based upon a "diatonic scale" of seven notes, five half steps separate all but two notes in a complete diatonic scale.

2. A quick look at the piano keyboard to understand this scale.

3. From C to B, for example, you can count seven white keys and five black keys, and one can see that each black key is a half step between the white keys on either side.

4. There is no black key between E and F, nor between B and C, so these notes were understood to be only a half step apart.

5. One advantage of this arrangement of black and white keys is that pianists can easily tell the difference between notes as they touch the keyboard imagine if there were nothing but white keys all a half step apart!

B. Correcting Errors

In the following paragraph, locate each sentence error (fragment, comma splice, run-on, and unparallel construction). Identify each with the sentence number and name of the error. Then write the sentence correctly.

(1) When you're listening to jazz, you're hearing a uniquely American style of music. (2) From the American South, a fusion of African and European traditions. (3) As Art Blakely, an originator of bebop drumming, is quoted saying, "No America, no jazz." (4) The earliest jazz bands emerged in New Orleans around the turn of the twentieth century here black gospel music and Latin American brass met, and Dixieland was spawned in the 1910s. (5) During the 1920s, many popular and influential jazz musicians found their way to Chicago clubs, recordings in the Windy City began to spread the sound to other parts of the country. (6) New York City also played an important role in jazz history by adding piano, incorporating jazz into swing music, and through sales of jazz records. (7) During the late 1920s and the 1930s, local jazz bands formed all around the country, establishing the style firmly in American culture.

Misplaced and Dangling Modifiers

Writing is thinking. Before you can write clearly, you must think clearly. Nothing is more frustrating for the reader than having to reread writing just to understand its basic meaning. Look carefully at the common errors that follow. Then use this section as a checklist when you revise. Always avoid leaving misplaced or dangling modifiers in your finished work.

Misplaced Modifiers

671.1

Misplaced modifiers are descriptive words or phrases so separated from what they are describing that the reader is confused.

Misplaced: The neighbor's dog has nearly been barking nonstop for two hours. (*Nearly* been barking?)

Corrected: The neighbor's dog has been barking nonstop **for nearly two hours.** (Watch your placement of *only, just, nearly, barely,* and so on.)

Misplaced: The commercial advertised an assortment of combs for active people with unbreakable teeth. (*People* with unbreakable teeth?)

Corrected: The commercial advertised an assortment of combs **with unbreakable teeth for active people.** (*Combs* with unbreakable teeth)

Misplaced: The pool staff gave large beach towels to the students marked with chlorine-resistant ID numbers. (*Students* marked with chlorine-resistant ID numbers?)

Corrected: The pool staff gave large beach towels **marked with chlorine-resistant ID numbers to the students.** (*Towels* marked with chlorine-resistant ID numbers)

Dangling Modifiers

671.2

Dangling modifiers are descriptive phrases that tell about a subject that isn't stated in the sentence. These often occur as participial phrases containing *ing* or *ed* words.

Dangling: After standing in line all afternoon, the manager informed us that all the tickets had been sold. (It sounds as if the manager has been *standing in line all afternoon.*)

Corrected: **After we had stood in line all afternoon,** the manager informed us that all the tickets had been sold.

Dangling: After living in the house for one month, the electrician recommended we update all the wiring. (It sounds as if the electrician has been *living in the house.*)

Corrected: After living in the house for one month, **we hired an electrician, who recommended we update all the wiring.**

Ambiguous Wording

Sloppy sentences confuse readers. No one should have to wonder, "What does this writer mean?" When you revise and edit, check for indefinite pronoun references, incomplete comparisons, and unclear wording.

672.1 Indefinite Pronoun References

An **indefinite reference** is a problem caused by careless use of pronouns. There must always be a word or phrase nearby (its antecedent) that a pronoun clearly replaces.

Indefinite: When Tonya attempted to put her dictionary on the shelf, it fell to the floor. (The pronoun *it* could refer to either the dictionary or the shelf since both are singular nouns.)

Corrected: When Tonya attempted to put her dictionary on the shelf, **the shelf** fell to the floor.

Indefinite: Juanita reminded Kerri that she needed to photocopy her resumé before going to her interview. (Who *needed to photocopy her resumé*—Juanita or Kerri?)

Corrected: Juanita reminded Kerri **to photocopy her resumé before going to her interview.**

672.2 Incomplete Comparisons

Incomplete comparisons—leaving out words that show exactly what is being compared to what—can confuse readers.

Incomplete: After completing our lab experiment, we concluded that helium is lighter. (*Lighter* than what?)

Corrected: After completing our lab experiment, we concluded that helium is lighter **than oxygen.**

672.3 Unclear Wording

One type of ambiguous writing is wording that has two or more possible meanings due to an unclear reference to something elsewhere in the sentence. (See 672.1.)

Unclear: I couldn't believe that my sister bought a cat with all those allergy problems. (Who has the *allergy problems*—the cat or the sister?)

Corrected: I couldn't believe that my sister, **who is very allergic, bought a cat.**

Unclear: Dao intended to wash the car when he finished his homework, but he never did. (It is unclear which he *never did*—wash the car or finish his homework.)

Corrected: Dao intended to wash the car when he finished his homework, **but he never did manage to wash the car.**

Avoiding Sentence Errors Exercises:

Misplaced and Dangling Modifiers and Ambiguous Wording

A. Correcting Sentences

Rewrite the following sentences to correct misplaced and dangling modifiers and ambiguous wording.

1. When it touched down on the moon in 1969, the onboard guidance computer of the *Apollo 11's Eagle* lander contained less than 80 kilobytes of memory.

2. The cheapest mp3 player today at least has 1 gigabyte.

3. That's equivalent to 14,000 *Apollo 11* computers roughly in one device.

4. Even a typical smartphone or handheld computer could theoretically control about 5,000 lunar landers at once, properly programmed!

5. Imagine using your phone or pocket game to land 5,000 *Apollo* craft in your car or bedroom.

6. Of course, you couldn't see all the lunar-lander controls at once because of their tiny screens.

7. After spending almost a day on the moon's surface, NASA had the crew launch back into orbit and return to Earth.

8. The *Eagle's* journey to the moon had made it a sensation around the world.

9. The crew were all heroes, but they certainly liked the Earth better.

10. Today the Science Museum in London displays a lunar-lander replica for visitors in full size.

B. Correcting Errors in Context

Locate a misplaced modifier and several indefinite-pronoun-reference errors in the following paragraph. For each error, write the sentence number, identify the error type, and rewrite the sentences correctly.,

(1) One famous Russian joke lampoons the *nouveau-riche* Russians, known as "New Russians," by comparing cars. (2) In this joke, unexpectedly, a New Russian and an old man wake up in an emergency room. (3) The New Russian asks the old man how he ended up there. (4) The old man replies, "I put my war-trophy Messerschmitt jet engine on my old Zaporozhets car to make it go faster. (5) But after a couple of miles I lost control and crashed into a tree. (6) How about you?" (7) He answers that when an old Zaporozhets passed his new Ferrari on the highway, he thought it had stalled. (8) So he opened the door and stepped out.

Nonstandard Language

Nonstandard language is language that does not conform to the standards set by schools, media, and public institutions. It is often acceptable in everyday conversation and in fictional writing but seldom is used in formal speech or other forms of writing.

674.1

Colloquial Language

Colloquial language is wording used in informal conversation that is unacceptable in formal writing.

> *Colloquial:* Hey, wait up! Cal wants to go with.
>
> *Standard:* **Hey, wait!** Cal wants to go with us.

674.2

Double Preposition

The use of certain **double prepositions**—*off of, off to, from off*—is unacceptable.

> *Double
> Preposition:* Pick up the dirty clothes from off the floor.
>
> *Standard:* Pick up the dirty clothes **from the floor.**

674.3

Substitution

Avoid substituting *and* for *to*.

> *Substitution:* Try and get to class on time.
>
> *Standard:* **Try to** get to class on time.

Avoid substituting *of* for *have* when combining with *could, would, should,* or *might.*

> *Substitution:* I should of studied for that exam.
>
> *Standard:* **I should have** studied for that exam.

674.4

Double Negative

A **double negative** is a sentence that contains two negative words used to express a single negative idea. Double negatives are unacceptable in academic writing.

> *Double
> Negative:* After paying for essentials, I haven't got no money left.
>
> *Standard:* **I haven't got** any money left. / **I have no** money left.

674.5

Slang

Avoid the use of **slang** or any "in" words in formal writing.

> *Slang:* The way the stadium roof opened was way cool.
>
> *Standard:* The way the stadium roof opened **was remarkable.**

Avoiding Sentence Errors Exercises:

Nonstandard Language

A. Correcting Sentences

Identify the type of error exhibited in each sentence below (colloquialism, double preposition, substitution, double negative, or slang). Then correct it.

1. Would you of guessed that soccer is the world's most popular sport?
2. The word "soccer" is Oxford slang for "association," 'cause officially the game is "Association Football."
3. In most countries the sport's called "football," or some variation like *fútbol* or *fußball*.
4. The World Cup is a wicked awesome competition played every four years.
5. Soccer rules were set up in England in 1863, and they haven't hardly changed since then.
6. The point of the game is to try and kick the ball into the other team's goal area.
7. Normally play continues until someone commits a foul or kicks a ball off of the field.
8. Most players aren't not allowed to touch the ball with their hands.
9. If you've ever watched soccer, though, you might of seen the goalie engage the ball that way.
10. The other players don't have no official titles.
11. Most times, though, there are forwards, defenders, and midfielders.
12. According to the rules, games needn't never go into overtime; they can end in a tie.
13. But some games can just keep agoin' in overtime till somebody scores.
14. The U.S. team did pretty good for itself in the 2010 games.
15. Some folks say that Europeans feel closer to us since our team rocked big time and stayed in the competition so long.
16. I wonder what they would of thought if the U.S. had won!
17. Personally, though, I was rooting for Spain from the get go.
18. If you're interested, it doesn't hardly take much equipment to play soccer.
19. All's you really need's a ball and maybe some markers for the goals.
20. Well, you also gotta have two teams with eleven players each.

B. Correcting Your Own Writing

Spend 5 minutes writing freely about a sport you find interesting. Imagine describing that sport to someone unfamiliar with it, or simply explain your own interest in it. When you have finished, review your writing for nonstandard language and make any necessary corrections.

Quick Guide

Avoiding Sentence Problems

Does every subject agree with its verb? (See pages 661–664.)
- In person and number?
- When a word or phrase comes between the subject and the verb?
- When the subject is delayed?
- When the subject is a title?
- When a compound subject is connected with o*r*?
- When the subject is a collective noun (*faculty, team,* or *crowd*)?
- When the subject is a relative pronoun (*who, which, that*)?
- When the subject is an indefinite pronoun (*everyone, anybody,* or *many*)?

Does every pronoun agree with its antecedent? (See page 665.)
- When the pronoun is a singular indefinite pronoun such as *each, either,* or *another?*
- When two antecedents are joined with *and?*
- When two antecedents are joined with *or?*

Did you unintentionally create inappropriate shifts? (See page 667.)
- In person?
- In tense?
- From active voice to passive voice?
- In another unparallel construction?

Are all your sentences complete? (See pages 668–670.)
- Have you used sentence fragments?
- Are some sentences "spliced" or run together?

Did you use any misplaced modifiers or ambiguous wording? (See pages 671–673.)
- Have you used misplaced or dangling modifiers?
- Have you used incomplete comparisons or indefinite references?

Did you use any nonstandard language? (See pages 674–675.)
- Have you used slang or colloquial language?
- Have you used double negatives or double prepositions?

Chapter 36

Multilingual and ESL Guidelines

English may be your second, third, or fifth language. As a multilingual learner, you bring to your writing the culture and knowledge of the languages you use. This broader perspective enables you to draw on many experiences and greater knowledge as you write and speak. Whether you are an international student or someone who has lived in North America a long time and is now learning more about English, this chapter provides you with important information about writing in English.

Five Parts of Speech

Noun

Count Nouns

Count nouns refer to things that can be counted. They can have *a*, *an*, *the*, or *one* in front of them. One or more adjectives can come between the articles *a*, *an*, *the*, or *one* and the singular count noun.

> **an apple, one orange, a plum, a purple plum**

Count nouns can be singular, as in the examples above, or plural, as in the examples below.

> **plums, apples, oranges**

> **Note:** When count nouns are plural, they can have the article *the*, a number, or a demonstrative adjective in front of them. (See 679.1 and 679.3.)
> I used **the** plums to make a pie.
> He placed **five** apples on my desk.
> **These** oranges are so juicy!

The *number* of a noun refers to whether it names a single thing (*book*), in which case its number is *singular*, or whether it names more than one thing (*books*), in which case the number of the noun is *plural*.

> **Note:** There are different ways in which the plural form of nouns is created. For more information, see pages 596–597.

678.1   Noncount Nouns

Noncount nouns refer to things that cannot be counted. Do not use *a, an,* or *one* in front of them. They have no plural form, so they always take a singular verb. Some nouns that end in *s* are not plural; they are noncount nouns.

> **fruit, furniture, rain, thunder, advice, mathematics, news**

Abstract nouns name ideas or conditions rather than people, places, or objects. Many abstract nouns are noncount nouns.

> The students had **fun** at the party. Good **health** is a wonderful gift.

Collective nouns name a whole category or group and are often noncount nouns.

> **homework, furniture, money**

Note: The parts or components of a group or category named by a noncount noun are often count nouns. For example, *report* and *assignment* are count nouns that are parts of the collective, noncount noun *homework*.

678.2   Two-Way Nouns

Some nouns can be used as either count or noncount nouns, depending on what they refer to.

> I would like a **glass** of water. (count noun)
>
> **Glass** is used to make windows. (noncount noun)

Articles and Other Noun Markers

678.3   Specific Articles

Use articles and other noun markers or modifiers to give more information about nouns. The **specific** (or **definite**) **article** *the* is used to refer to a specific noun.

> I found **the** book I misplaced yesterday.

678.4   Indefinite Articles and Indefinite Adjectives

Use the **indefinite article** *a* or *an* to refer to a nonspecific noun. Use *an* before singular nouns beginning with the vowels *a, e, i, o,* and *u*. Use *a* before nouns beginning with all other letters of the alphabet, the consonants. Exceptions do occur: *a* unit; *a* university.

> I always take **an** apple to work.
>
> It is good to have **a** book with you when you travel.

Indefinite adjectives can also mark nonspecific nouns—*all, any, each, either, every, few, many, more, most, neither, several, some* (for singular and plural count nouns); *all, any, more, most, much, some* (for noncount nouns).

> **Every** student is encouraged to register early.
>
> **Most** classes fill quickly.

Determining Whether to Use Articles

Listed below are a number of guidelines to help you determine whether to use an article and which one to use.

Use *a* or *an* with singular count nouns that do not refer to one specific item.

> **A zebra** has black and white stripes. **An apple** is good for you.

Do not use *a* or *an* with plural count nouns.

> **Zebras** have black and white stripes. **Apples** are good for you.

Do not use *a* or *an* with noncount nouns.

> **Homework** needs to be done promptly.

Use *the* with singular count nouns that refer to one specific item.

> **The apple** you gave me was delicious.

Use *the* with plural count nouns.

> **The zebras** at Brookfield Zoo were healthy.

Use *the* with noncount nouns.

> **The money** from my uncle is a gift.

Do not use *the* with most singular proper nouns.

> **Mother Theresa** loved the poor and downcast.

> **Note:** There are many exceptions: *the* Sahara Desert, *the* University of Minnesota, *the* Fourth of July

Use *the* with plural nouns.

> **the Joneses** (both Mr. and Mrs. Jones), **the Rocky Mountains, the United States**

Possessive Adjectives

The possessive case of nouns and pronouns can be used as adjectives to mark nouns.

possessive nouns: *Tanya's, father's, store's*

> The car is **Tanya's,** not her **father's.**

possessive pronouns: *my, your, his, her, its, our*

> **My** hat is purple.

Demonstrative Adjectives

Demonstrative pronouns can be used as adjectives to mark nouns.

Demonstrative adjectives: *this, that, these, those* (for singular and plural count nouns); *this, that* (for noncount nouns)

> **Those** chairs are lovely. Where did you buy **that** furniture?

Multilingual/ESL Exercises:

Nouns, Articles, and Other Noun Markers

A. Count and Noncount Nouns

Make a list of count nouns from the following paragraph. Next make a list of noncount nouns.

> We live in a time of confusing economics. On the one hand, it is 1
> necessary to spend money to keep the economy stimulated. Manufacturers 2
> use every psychological trick they can identify to coax consumers to buy 3
> more products. As a matter of fact, advertisers work to make the public want 4
> things it doesn't actually need. On the other hand, citizens are expected to 5
> invest and save for emergencies and for their retirement. Shame is used as a 6
> motivator to accomplish this. Unfortunately, in a world where citizens have 7
> been relabeled as consumers, the psychology of sales too often outweighs the 8
> shadow of shame. 9

B. Articles and Other Noun Markers

For each numbered blank, write an appropriate article or noun marker as needed. (If none is needed, write "none needed.") Then identify each added article or adjective by type (specific article, indefinite article, indefinite adjective, possessive adjective, demonstrative adjective, or quantifier).

> Does (1)_____ family own a dog? If so, what made you choose (2)_____ breed instead of a different one? In (3)_____ house, we have (4) _____ dogs. (5)_____ dog is a Chihuahua and (6)_____ other is (7)_____ Bichon Frise. The Chihuahua barks at (8)_____ people but not at others. Well, to be truthful, he always barks at (9)_____ strangers, but seldom at a family member or (10)_____ friend. (11)_____ Bichon Frise is too friendly and excited to bark. He jumps on each and (12)_____ person who visits us. Scientists say that (13)_____ dogs originally descended from (14)_____ wolf. From my observation of (15)_____ Chihuaha and Bichon Frise, it is obvious that different dogs descended differently.

Quantifiers

Expressions of quantity and measure are often used with nouns. Below are some of these expressions and guidelines for using them.

The following expressions of quantity can be used with count nouns: *each, every, both, a couple of, a few, several, many, a number of.*

> We enjoyed **both** concerts we attended. **A couple of** songs performed were familiar to us.

Use a number to indicate a specific quantity of a continuum.

> I saw **fifteen** cardinals in the park.

To indicate a specific quantity of a noncount noun, use *a* + quantity (such as *bag, bottle, bowl, carton, glass,* or *piece*) + *of* + noun.

> I bought **a carton of milk, a head of lettuce, a piece of cheese,** and **a bag of flour** at the grocery store.

The following expressions can be used with noncount nouns: *a little, much, a great deal of.*

> We had **much** wind and **a little** rain as the storm passed through yesterday.

The following expressions of quantity can be used with both count and noncount nouns: *no/not any, some, a lot of, lots of, plenty of, most, all, this, that.*

> I would like **some** apples *(count noun)* and **some** rice *(noncount noun)*, please.

Verb

As the main part of the predicate, a verb conveys much of a sentence's meaning. Using verb tenses and forms correctly ensures that your readers will understand your sentences as you intend them to. For a more thorough review of verbs, see pages 638–644.

Progressive (Continuous) Tenses

Progressive or continuous tense verbs express action in progress (see page 640).

To form the **present progressive** tense, use the helping verb *am, is,* or *are* with the *ing* form of the main verb.

> He **is washing** the car right now.
> Kent and Chen **are studying** for a test.

To form the **past progressive** tense, use the helping verb *was* or *were* with the *ing* form of the main verb.

> Yesterday he **was working** in the garden all day.
> Julia and Juan **were watching** a movie.

To form the future progressive tense, use *will* or a phrase that indicates the future, the helping verb *be*, and the *ing* form of the main verb.

> Next week he **will be painting** the house.
> He **plans to be painting** the house soon.

682.1

Note that some verbs are generally not used in the progressive tenses, such as the following groups of frequently used verbs:

- Verbs that express thoughts, attitudes, and desires: *know, understand, want, prefer*
- Verbs that describe appearances: *seem, resemble*
- Verbs that indicate possession: *belong, have, own, possess*
- Verbs that signify inclusion: *contain, hold*

Kala **knows** how to ride a motorcycle.

NOT THIS: Kala is **knowing** how to ride a motorcycle.

682.2

Objects and Complements of Verbs

Active transitive verbs take objects. These can be direct objects, indirect objects, or object complements. Linking verbs take subject complements—predicate nominatives or predicate adjectives—that rename or describe the subject.

682.3

Infinitives as Objects

Infinitives can follow many verbs, including these: *agree, appear, attempt, consent, decide, demand, deserve, endeavor, fail, hesitate, hope, intend, need, offer, plan, prepare, promise, refuse, seem, tend, volunteer, wish.* (See 642.3 for more on infinitives.)

He **promised to bring** some samples.

The following verbs are among those that can be followed by a noun or pronoun plus the infinitive: *ask, beg, choose, expect, intend, need, prepare, promise, want.*

I **expect you to be** there on time.

> **Note:** Except in the passive voice, the following verbs must have a noun or pronoun before the infinitive: *advise, allow, appoint, authorize, cause, challenge, command, convince, encourage, forbid, force, hire, instruct, invite, order, permit, remind, require, select, teach, tell, tempt, trust.*
>
> I will **authorize Emily to use** my credit card.

Unmarked infinitives (no *to*) can follow these verbs: *have, help, let, make.*

These glasses **help me see** the board.

682.4

Gerunds as Objects

Gerunds can follow these verbs: *admit, avoid, consider, deny, discuss, dislike, enjoy, finish, imagine, miss, postpone, quit, recall, recommend, regret.* (Also see 642.2.)

I **recommended hiring** Ian for the job.

Here *hiring* is the direct object of the active verb *recommended*, and *Ian* is the object of the gerund.

Infinitives or Gerunds as Objects

Either **gerunds** or **infinitives** can follow these verbs: *begin, continue, hate, like, love, prefer, remember, start, stop, try.*

> I **hate having** cold feet. I **hate to have** cold feet. (In either form, the verbal phrase is the direct object of the verb hate.)

Note: Sometimes the meaning of a sentence will change depending on whether you use a gerund or an infinitive.

> I stopped to smoke. (I *stopped* weeding the garden *to smoke* a cigarette.)

> I stopped smoking. (I no longer smoke.)

Common Modal Auxiliary Verbs

Modal auxiliary verbs are a kind of auxiliary verb. (See 638.3.) They help the main verb express meaning. Modals are sometimes grouped with other helping or auxiliary verbs.

Modal verbs must be followed by the base form of a verb without *to* (not by a gerund or an infinitive). Also, modal verbs do not change form; they are always used as they appear in the following chart.

Modal	Expresses	Sample Sentence
can	ability	I *can* make tamales.
could	ability	I *could* babysit Tuesday.
	possibility	He *could* be sick.
might	possibility	I *might* be early.
may, might	possibility	I *may* sleep late Saturday.
	request	*May* I be excused?
must	strong need	I *must* study more.
have to	strong need	I *have to* (have got to) exercise.
ought to	feeling of duty	I *ought to* (should) help Dad.
should	advisability	She *should* retire.
	expectation	I *should* have caught that train.
shall	intent	*Shall* I stay longer?
will	intent	I *will* visit my grandma soon.
would	intent	I *would* live to regret my offer.
	repeated action	He *would* walk in the meadow.
would + you	polite request	*Would you* help me?
could + you	polite request	*Could you* type this letter?
will + you	polite request	*Will you* give me a ride?
can + you	polite request	*Can you* make supper tonight?

Common Two-Word Verbs

This chart lists some common verbs in which two words—a verb and a preposition—work together to express a specific action. A noun or pronoun is often inserted between the parts of the two-word verb when it is used in a sentence: *break it down, call it off.*

break down	to take apart or fall apart
call off	cancel
call up	make a phone call
clear out	leave a place quickly
cross out	draw a line through
do over	repeat
figure out	find a solution
fill in/out	complete a form or an application
fill up	fill a container or tank
* **find out**	discover
* **get in**	enter a vehicle or building
* **get out of**	leave a car, a house, or a situation
* **get over**	recover from a sickness or a problem
give back	return something
give in/up	surrender or quit
hand in	give homework to a teacher
hand out	give someone something
hang up	put down a phone receiver
leave out	omit or don't use
let in/out	allow someone or something to enter or go out
look up	find information
mix up	confuse
pay back	return money or a favor
pick out	choose
point out	call attention to
put away	return something to its proper place
put down	place something on a table, the floor, and so on.
put off	delay doing something
shut off	turn off a machine or light
* **take part**	participate
talk over	discuss
think over	consider carefully
try on	put on clothing to see if it fits
turn down	lower the volume
turn up	raise the volume
write down	write on a piece of paper

* These two-word verbs should not have a noun or pronoun inserted between their parts.

Spelling Guidelines for Verb Forms

The same spelling rules that apply when adding a suffix to other words apply to verbs as well. Most verbs need a suffix to indicate tense or form. The third-person singular form of a verb, for example, usually ends in *s,* but it can also end in *es.* Formation of *ing* and *ed* forms of verbs and verbals needs careful attention, too. Consult the rules below to determine which spelling is correct for each verb. (For general spelling guidelines, see page 605.)

 There may be exceptions to these rules when forming the past tense of irregular verbs because the verbs are formed by changing the word itself, not merely by adding *d* or *ed.* (See the chart of irregular verbs on page 643.)

Past Tense: Adding *ed*

685.1

Add *ed* . . .

- When a verb ends with two consonants:
  touch—**touched** ask—**asked** pass—**passed**

- When a verb ends with a consonant preceded by two vowels:
  heal—**healed** gain—**gained**

- When a verb ends in *y* preceded by a vowel:
  annoy—**annoyed** flay—**flayed**

- When a multisyllable verb's last syllable is not stressed (even when the last syllable ends with a consonant preceded by a vowel):
  budget—**budgeted** enter—**entered** interpret—**interpreted**

Change *y* to *i* and add *ed* when a verb ends in a consonant followed by *y:*
  liquefy—**liquefied** worry—**worried**

Double the final consonant and add *ed* . . .

- When a verb has one syllable and ends with a consonant preceded by a vowel:
  wrap—**wrapped** drop—**dropped**

- When a multisyllable verb's last syllable (ending in a consonant preceded by a vowel) is stressed:
  admit—**admitted** confer—**conferred** abut—**abutted**

Past Tense: Adding *d*

685.2

Add *d* . . .

- When a verb ends with *e:*
  chime—**chimed** tape—**taped**

- When a verb ends with *ie:*
  tie—**tied** die—**died** lie—**lied**

686.1

Present Tense: Adding *s* or *es*

Add *es* . . .

- When a verb ends in *ch, sh, s, x,* or *z:*
  watch—**watches**   fix—**fixes**

- To *do* and *go:*
  do—**does**   go—**goes**

Change *y* to *i* and add *es* when the verb ends in a consonant followed by *y:*
  liquefy—**liquefies**   quantify—**quantifies**

Add *s* to most other verbs, including those already ending in *e* and those that end in a vowel followed by *y:*
  write—**writes**   buy—**buys**

686.2

Present Tense: Adding *ing*

Drop the *e* and add *ing* when the verb ends in *e:*
  drive—**driving**   rise—**rising**

Double the final consonant and add *ing* . . .

- When a verb has one syllable and ends with a consonant preceded by a single vowel:
  wrap—**wrapping**   sit—**sitting**

- When a multisyllable verb's last syllable (ending in a consonant preceded by a single vowel) is stressed:
  forget—**forgetting**   begin—**beginning**   abut—**abutting**

Change *ie* to *y* and add *ing* when a verb ends with *ie:*
  tie—**tying**   die—**dying**   lie—**lying**

Add *ing* . . .

- When a verb ends with two consonants:
  touch—**touching**   ask—**asking**   pass—**passing**

- When a verb ends with a consonant preceded by two vowels:
  heal—**healing**   gain—**gaining**

- When a verb ends in *y:*
  buy—**buying**   study—**studying**   cry—**crying**

- When a multisyllable verb's last syllable is not stressed (even when the last syllable ends with a consonant preceded by a vowel):
  budget—**budgeting**   enter—**entering**   interpret—**interpreting**

Note: Never trust your spelling to even the best computer spell checker. Carefully proofread. Use a dictionary for questionable words your spell checker may miss.

Multilingual/ESL Exercises:

Verbs, Objects, and Complements

A. Errors in Context

Correct any verb, object, and complement errors in the sentences below. Write down the error, crossed out, with the correction beside it.

> (1) Evolutionary psychologist Robert Dunbar suggest that brain size directly affects behavior in terms of how many individuals a mammal can to care about. (2) A chimpanzee is possessing an emotional connection with about 50 other chimpanzees. (3) If a tribe's size grow beyond that, the group tends fighting. (4) Studies of human brain size predict that humans are having the ability to care for roughly 150 other people, and Dunbar says research bears that out. (5) Fortunately, humans decide building hierarchies to support larger societies. (6) Also, people can conceiving of a universal family of humanity. (7) Can you to think that way?

B. Forming Tenses

Write the correct past tense for each of the verbs listed below. (Note that some of these verbs have irregular past-tense forms.)

1. say _____   5. parrot _____
2. go _____   6. make _____
3. derive _____   7. lift _____
4. maintain _____   8. offer _____

Write the correct present tense form (adding *s* or *es*) for each of these verbs.

1. will _____   5. speak _____
2. come _____   6. display _____
3. wonder _____   7. propagate _____
4. verify _____   8. go _____

Write the correct present tense form (adding *ing*) for each of these verbs.

1. activate _____   5. manage _____
2. portray _____   6. travel _____
3. begin _____   7. monopolize _____
4. start _____   8. fly _____

Adjective

688.1

Placing Adjectives

You probably know that an adjective often comes before the noun it modifies. When several adjectives are used in a row to modify a single noun, it is important to arrange the adjectives in the well-established sequence used in English writing and speaking. The following list shows the usual order of adjectives. (Also see 571.3.)

First, place . . .

1. articles . . . . **a, an, the**
   demonstrative adjectives . . . . **that, those**
   possessives. . . . . **my, her, Misha's**

Then place words that . . .

2. indicate time. . . . . **first, next, final**
3. tell how many. . . . .**one, few, some**
4. evaluate . . . . **beautiful, dignified, graceful**
5. tell what size. . . . .**big, small, short, tall**
6. tell what shape . . . . **round, square**
7. describe a condition . . . . **messy, clean, dark**
8. tell what age . . . . **old, young, new, antique**
9. tell what color. . . . . **blue, red, yellow**
10. tell what nationality . . . . **English, Chinese, Mexican**
11. tell what religion . . . . **Buddhist, Jewish, Protestant**
12. tell what material. . . . .**satin, velvet, wooden**

Finally, place nouns . . .

13. used as adjectives. . . . . **computer [monitor], spice [rack]**
    my second try (1 + 2 + noun)
    gorgeous young white swans (4 + 8 + 9 + noun)

688.2

Present and Past Participles as Adjectives

Both the **present participle** and the **past participle** can be used as adjectives. (Also see 642.4.) Exercise care in choosing whether to use the present participle or the past participle. A participle can come either before a noun or after a linking verb.

A **present participle** used as an adjective should describe a person or thing that is causing a feeling or situation.

    His **annoying** comments made me angry.

A **past participle** should describe a person or thing that experiences a feeling or situation.

    He was **annoyed** because he had to wait so long.

Note: Within each of the following pairs, the present (*ing* form) and past (*ed* form) participles have different meanings.

annoying/annoyed	depressing/depressed	fascinating/fascinated
boring/bored	exciting/excited	surprising/surprised
confusing/confused	exhausting/exhausted	

Nouns as Adjectives

Nouns sometimes function as adjectives by modifying another noun. When a noun is used as an adjective, it is always singular.

> Many European cities have **rose** gardens.
>
> Marta recently joined a **book** club.

TIP: Try to avoid using more than two nouns as adjectives for another noun. These "noun compounds" can get confusing. Prepositional phrases may get the meaning across better than long noun strings.

> **Correct:** Omar is a **crew** member in the **restaurant** kitchen during **second** shift.
>
> *Not correct:* Omar is a **second-shift restaurant kitchen crew** member.

Adverb

Placing Adverbs

Consider the following guidelines for placing adverbs correctly. See page 646 for more information about adverbs.

Place adverbs that tell how often (*frequently, seldom, never, always, sometimes*) after a helping (auxiliary) verb and before the main verb. In a sentence without a helping verb, adverbs that tell *how often* are placed before an action verb but after a linking verb.

> The salesclerk will **usually** help me.

Place adverbs that tell when (*yesterday, now, at five o'clock*) at the end of a sentence.

> Auntie El came home **yesterday.**

Adverbs that tell where (*upside-down, around, downstairs*) usually follow the verb they modify. Many prepositional phrases (*at the beach, under the stairs, below the water*) function as adverbs that tell where.

> We waited **on the porch.**

Adverbs that tell how (*quickly, slowly, loudly*) can be placed either at the beginning, in the middle, or at the end of a sentence—but not between a verb and its direct object.

> **Softly** he called my name. He **softly** called my name. He called my name **softly.**

Place adverbs that modify adjectives directly before the adjective.

> That is a **most** unusual dress.

Adverbs that modify clauses are most often placed in front of the clause, but they can also go inside or at the end of the clause.

> **Fortunately,** we were not involved in the accident.
> We were not involved, **fortunately,** in the accident.
> We were not involved in the accident, **fortunately.**

> **Note:** Adverbs that are used with verbs that have direct objects must *not* be placed between the verb and its object.

> **Correct:** Luis **usually** catches the most fish. **Usually,** Luis catches the most fish.
>
> *Not correct:* Luis catches **usually** the most fish.

Preposition

A **preposition** combines with a noun to form a prepositional phrase, which acts as a modifier—an adverb or an adjective. See pages 647 and 650 for a list of common prepositions and for more information about prepositions.

690.1

Using *in, on, at,* and *by*

In, on, at, and *by* are four common prepositions that refer to time and place. Here are some examples of how these prepositions are used in each case.

To show time

    on a specific day or date: *on* June 7, *on* Wednesday

    in part of a day: *in* the afternoon

    in a year or month: *in* 2008, *in* April

    in a period of time: completed *in* an hour

    by a specific time or date: *by* noon, *by* the fifth of May

    at a specific time of day or night: *at* 3:30 this afternoon

To show place

    at a meeting place or location: *at* school, *at* the park

    at the edge of something: standing *at* the bar

    at the corner of something: turning *at* the intersection

    at a target: throwing a dart *at* the target

    on a surface: left *on* the floor

    on an electronic medium: *on* the Internet, *on* television

    in an enclosed space: *in* the box, *in* the room

    in a geographic location: *in* New York City, *in* Germany

    in a print medium: *in* a journal

    by a landmark: *by* the fountain

TIP: Do not insert a preposition between a transitive verb and its direct object. Intransitive verbs, however, are often followed by a prepositional phrase (a phrase that begins with a preposition).

    I **cooked** hot dogs on the grill. (transitive verb)

    I **ate** in the park. (intransitive verb)

690.2

Phrasal Prepositions

Some prepositional phrases begin with more than one preposition. These **phrasal prepositions** are commonly used in both written and spoken communication. A list of common phrasal prepositions follows:

according to	because of	in case of	on the side of
across from	by way of	in spite of	up to
along with	except for	instead of	with respect to

Multilingual/ESL Exercises:

Adjectives, Adverbs, Prepositions

A. Adjective Order

Rewrite the following phrases to place the adjectives in the proper order.

1. sandstone first square several red gigantic the blocks

2. a sticky brown few last delicious figs

3. rough-barked old some round huge trees

B. Present and Past Participles

Choose the correct adjective form (present or past participle) in each case below.

1. Deborah was annoying/annoyed that her wedding dress was not finished.

2. The exciting/excited day was quickly approaching, but the preparation was making her exhausting/exhausted.

3. Then surprising/surprised news arrived: An old high school friend was coming to help!

4. Her fiancé Trevor was confusing/confused at first that her old friend, Michael, was willing to be a "bridesmaid."

5. Trevor figured that Michael must be a fascinating/fascinated fellow.

C. At, By, In, or On

Write the best preposition—*at, by, in,* or *on*—for each blank in the sentences below.

1. _____ what time do you get up most mornings?

2. Do you come to school _____ car, _____ bike, _____ bus, or do you walk?

3. After school, I have to work _____ a pizza parlor most evenings.

4. The pizza restaurant is _____ the downtown area, _____ the public library.

5. I like pizza with mushrooms _____ it.

6. The place I work posts free coupons _____ its Web site.

7. The current coupon expires _____ June 8.

8. We have tables, so you can eat _____ the store if you like.

9. Our pizzas are cooked _____ a wood-burning oven.

10. Once, I cooked a pizza _____ my grill at home, over charcoal.

Understanding Sentence Basics

Simple sentences in the English language follow the five basic patterns shown below. (See pages 651–660 for more information.)

Subject + Verb

```
 ┌─S─┐┌─V─┐
```
Naomie winked.

Some verbs like *winked* are intransitive. Intransitive verbs do not need a direct object to express a complete thought. (See 638.2.)

Subject + Verb + Direct Object

```
 ┌─S─┐┌─V─┐┌─DO─┐
```
Harris grinds his teeth.

Some verbs like *grinds* are transitive. Transitive verbs *do* need a direct object to express a complete thought. (See 638.2.)

Subject + Verb + Indirect Object + Direct Object

```
 ┌─S─┐┌─V─┐┌─IO─┐┌─DO─┐
```
Elena offered her friend an anchovy.

The direct object names who or what receives the action; the indirect object names to whom or for whom the action was done.

Subject + Verb + Direct Object + Object Complement

```
 ┌──────S──────┐┌─V─┐ DO ┌──────OC──────┐
```
The chancellor named Ravi the outstanding student of 2010.

The object complement renames or describes the direct object.

Subject + Linking Verb + Predicate Nominative (or Predicate Adjective)

```
 ┌─S─┐LV ┌──────PN──────┐        ┌─S─┐LV┌──PA──┐
```
Paula is a computer programmer.   **Paula is very intelligent.**

A linking verb connects the subject to the predicate noun or predicate adjective. The predicate noun renames the subject; the predicate adjective describes the subject.

Inverted Order

In the sentence patterns above, the subject comes before the verb. In a few types of sentences, such as those below, the subject comes *after* the verb.

```
 LV┌─S─┐ ┌─PN─┐              LV ┌──S──┐
```
Is Larisa a poet?   **There was a meeting.**
(A question)   (A sentence beginning with "there")

Sentence Problems

This section looks at potential trouble spots and sentence problems. For more information about English sentences, their parts, and how to construct them, see pages 651 through 660 in the handbook. Pages 661 through 676 cover the types of problems and errors found in English writing. The guide to avoiding sentence problems found on page 676 is an excellent editing tool.

Double Negatives 693.1

When making a sentence negative, use *not* or another negative adverb (*never, rarely, hardly, seldom,* and so on), but not both. Using both results in a double negative (see 674.4).

Subject–Verb Agreement 693.2

Be sure the subject and verb in every clause agree in person and number. (See pages 661–664.)

The **student was** rewarded for her hard work.

The **students were** rewarded for their hard work.

The **instructor,** as well as the students, **is** expected to attend the orientation.

The **students,** as well as the instructor, **are** expected to attend the orientation.

Omitted Words 693.3

Do not omit subjects or the expletives *there* or *here*. In all English clauses and sentences (except imperatives in which the subject *you* is understood), there must be a subject.

    Correct: Your mother was very quiet; **she** seemed to be upset.
  Not correct: Your mother was very quiet; seemed to be upset.

    Correct: **There** is not much time left.
  Not correct: Not much time left.

Repeated Words 693.4

Do not repeat the subject of a clause or sentence.

    Correct: The doctor prescribed an antibiotic.
  Not correct: The doctor, **she** prescribed an antibiotic.

Do not repeat an object in an adjective dependent clause.

    Correct: I forgot the flowers that I intended to give to my hosts.
  Not correct: I forgot the flowers that I intended to give **them** to my hosts.

Note: Sometimes the relative pronoun that begins the adjective dependent clause is omitted but understood.

I forgot the flowers I intended to give to my hosts.
(The relative pronoun *that* is omitted.)

694.1 Conditional Sentences

Conditional sentences express a situation requiring that a condition be met in order to be true. Selecting the correct verb tense for use in the two clauses of a conditional sentence can be problematic. Below you will find an explanation of the three types of conditional sentences and the verb tenses that are needed to form them.

1. **Factual conditionals:** The conditional clause begins with *if, when, whenever,* or a similar expression. Furthermore, the verbs in the conditional clause and the main clause should be in the same tense.

   Whenever we **had** time, we **took** a break and **went** for a swim.

2. **Predictive conditionals** express future conditions and possible results. The conditional clause begins with *if* or *unless* and has a present tense verb. The main clause uses a modal (*will, can, should, may, might*) plus the base form of the verb.

   Unless we **find** a better deal, we **will buy** this sound system.

3. **Hypothetical past conditionals** describe a situation that is unlikely to happen or that is contrary to fact. To describe situations in the past, the verb in the conditional clause is in the past perfect tense, and the verb in the main clause is formed from *would have, could have,* or *might have* plus the past participle.

   If we **had started out** earlier, we **would have arrived** on time.

Note: If the hypothetical situation is a present or future one, the verb in the conditional clause is in the past tense, and the verb in the main clause is formed from *would, could,* or *might* plus the base form of the verb.

   If we **bought** groceries once a week, we **would** not **have** to go to the store so often.

694.2 Quoted and Reported Speech

Quoted speech is the use of exact words from another source in your own writing; you must enclose these words in quotation marks. It is also possible to report nearly exact words without quotation marks. This is called **reported speech,** or indirect quotation. (See pages 583–584 for a review of the use of quotation marks.)

   Direct quotation: Felicia said, "Don't worry about tomorrow."

   Indirect quotation: Felicia said that you don't have to worry about tomorrow.

In the case of a question, when a direct quotation is changed to an indirect quotation, the question mark is not needed.

   Direct quotation: Ahmad asked, "Which of you will give me a hand?"

   Indirect quotation: Ahmad asked which of us would give him a hand.

Notice how pronouns are often changed in indirect quotations.

   Direct quotation: My friends said, "**You're** crazy."

   Indirect quotation: My friends said that **I** was crazy.

Note: In academic writing, the use of another source's spoken or written words in one's own writing without proper acknowledgment is called *plagiarism*. Plagiarism is severely penalized in academic situations. (See pages 459–468.)

Multilingual/ESL Exercises:

Sentence Problems

A. Errors in Context

Correct the error(s) in each sentence below. Write down the error, crossed out, with the correction beside it.

---

(1) Flying by commercial jet can be a great way to travel if you have a long way to go and needs to get there quickly. (2) You can't never ignore, however, that the convenience comes with a price. (3) Security checks is becoming more intrusive every year. (4) Also, airlines they are reducing flights, crowding planes, and charging for services like meals. (5) If you wanted a leisurely vacation, you do better to choose different transportation. (6) An ocean voyage it takes longer but doesn't cause no jet lag. (7) People makes the same mistake with their road trips. (8) They gets in a car and rushes down the highway to a destination. (9) If they took a train instead, they relax and watch the countryside. (10) A jeep or a motorcycle are another great way to make a road trip. (11) Because these vehicles are open to the air, can feel in touch with the terrain. (12) If you were to travel back roads, you enjoy the journey as much as the arrival.

B. Quoted and Reported Speech

Rewrite direct quotations as indirect quotations and vice versa.

1. Kimi told Hal, "I pay my bills with income from my online writing."
2. "How did you get started?" he asked.
3. She answered that their friend Toi had introduced her to a site for essayists.
4. She told him, "I had to fill out an application and submit a sample of work."
5. She said they made her revise her biography several times before accepting it.

C. Defining Problems

In your own words, define each of the following sentence problems or types.

1. Double negatives
2. Omitted words
3. Repeated words
4. Conditional sentences
5. Quoted speech
6. Reported speech

Numbers, Word Parts, and Idioms

Numbers

As a multilingual/ESL learner, you may be accustomed to a way of writing numbers that is different than the way it is done in North America. Become familiar with the North American conventions for writing numbers. Pages 598–599 show you how numbers are written and punctuated in both word and numeral form.

696.1

Using Punctuation with Numerals

Note that the **period** is used to express percentages (5.5%, 75.9%) and the **comma** is used to organize large numbers into units (7,000; 23,100; 231,990,000). Commas are not used, however, in writing the year (2011). (Also see 574.1 and 574.6.)

696.2

Cardinal Numbers

Cardinal numbers are used when counting a number of parts or objects. Cardinal numbers can be used as nouns (she counted to **ten**), pronouns (I invited many guests, but only **three** came), or adjectives (there are **ten** boys here).

Write out in words the numbers one through one hundred. Numbers 101 and greater are often written as numerals. (See 598.1.)

696.3

Ordinal Numbers

Ordinal numbers show place or succession in a series: the fourth row, the twenty-first century, the tenth time, and so on. Ordinal numbers are used to talk about the parts into which a whole can be divided, such as a fourth or a tenth, and as the denominator in fractions, such as one-fourth or three-fifths. Written fractions can also be used as nouns (I gave him **four-fifths**) or as adjectives (a **four-fifths** majority).

Note: See the list below for names and symbols of the first twenty-five ordinal numbers. Consult a college dictionary for a complete list of cardinal and ordinal numbers.

First	1st	Tenth	10th	Nineteenth	19th
Second	2nd	Eleventh	11th	Twentieth	20th
Third	3rd	Twelfth	12th	Twenty-first	21st
Fourth	4th	Thirteenth	13th	Twenty-second	22nd
Fifth	5th	Fourteenth	14th	Twenty-third	23rd
Sixth	6th	Fifteenth	15th	Twenty-fourth	24th
Seventh	7th	Sixteenth	16th	Twenty-fifth	25th
Eighth	8th	Seventeenth	17th		
Ninth	9th	Eighteenth	18th		

Prefixes, Suffixes, and Roots

Following is a list of many common word parts and their meanings. Learning them can help you determine the meaning of unfamiliar words as you come across them in your reading. For instance, if you know that *hemi* means "half," you can conclude that *hemisphere* means "half of a sphere."

Prefixes	Meaning	Suffixes	Meaning
a, an	not, without	able, ible	able, can do
anti, ant	against	age	act of, state of
co, con, com	together, with	al	relating to
di	two, twice	ate	cause, make
dis, dif	apart, away	en	made of
ex, e, ec, ef	out	ence, ency	action, quality
hemi, semi	half	esis, osis	action, process
il, ir, in, im	not	ice	condition, quality
inter	between	ile	relating to
intra	within	ish	resembling
multi	many	ment	act of, state of
non	not	ology	study, theory
ob, of, op, oc	toward, against	ous	full of, having
per	throughout	sion, tion	act of, state of
post	after	some	like, tending to
super, supr	above, more	tude	state of
trans, tra	across, beyond	ward	in the direction of
tri	three		
uni	one		

Roots	Meaning	Roots	Meaning
acu	sharp	ject	throw
am, amor	love, liking	log, ology	word, study, speech
anthrop	man	man	hand
aster, astr	star	micro	small
auto	self	mit, miss	send
biblio	book	nom	law, order
bio	life	onym	name
capit, capt	head	path, pathy	feeling, suffering
chron	time	rupt	break
cit	to call, start	scrib, script	write
cred	believe	spec, spect, spic	look
dem	people	tele	far
dict	say, speak	tempo	time
erg	work	tox	poison
fid, feder	faith, trust	vac	empty
fract, frag	break	ver, veri	true
graph, gram	write, written	zo	animal

Multilingual/ESL Exercises:

Numbers and Word Parts

A. Punctuating Numerals

For the following numbers, add or correct punctuation as necessary to suit North American style. (Some of the numbers are already correct, and two items need to be punctuated correctly as percentages.)

A. 3000

B. 44

C. 9.400.207,33

D. 200,000,01

E. 600000009

F. 23,7%

G. Dec. 21 2012

H. 100

I. 1.877,14

J. 17,7%

B. Numbers in Text

Write each number below as it should appear in text.

A. 900

B. 4/5

C. 99

D. 24

E. 101

F. 42

G. 17

H. 1/3

I. 70

J. 1,001

C. Prefixes, Suffixes, and Roots

Break each of the following terms into its component parts (prefix, root, and/or suffix) and define it in your own words.

1. semiserious

2. pseudonym

3. toxicology

4. bibliography

5. verified

6. coauthor

7. westward

8. microfinance

9. antipathy

10. international

11. infantile

12. postponement

13. astrophysics

14. ticklish

15. multihued

16. incredulous

Idioms

Idioms are phrases that are used in a special way. An idiom can't be understood just by knowing the meaning of each word in the phrase. It must be learned as a whole. For example, the idiom to *bury the hatchet* means to "settle an argument," even though the individual words in the phrase mean something much different. These pages list some of the common idioms in American English.

a bad apple	• One troublemaker on a team may be called **a bad apple.** *(a bad influence)*
an axe to grind	• Mom has **an axe to grind** with the owners of the dog that dug up her flower garden. *(a problem to settle)*
as the crow flies	• She lives only two miles from here **as the crow flies.** *(in a straight line)*
beat around the bush	• Dad said, "Where were you? Don't **beat around the bush.**" *(avoid getting to the point)*
benefit of the doubt	• Ms. Hy gave Henri the **benefit of the doubt** when he explained why he fell asleep in class. *(another chance)*
beyond the shadow of a doubt	• Salvatore won the 50-yard dash **beyond the shadow of a doubt.** *(for certain)*
blew my top	• When my money got stolen, I **blew my top.** *(showed great anger)*
bone to pick	• Nick had a **bone to pick** with Adrian when he learned they both liked the same girl. *(problem to settle)*
break the ice	• Shanta was the first to **break the ice** in the room full of new students. *(start a conversation)*
burn the midnight oil	• Carmen had to **burn the midnight oil** the day before the big test. *(work late into the night)*
chomping at the bit	• Dwayne was **chomping at the bit** when it was his turn to bat. *(eager, excited)*
cold shoulder	• Alicia always gives me the **cold shoulder** after our disagreements. *(ignores me)*
cry wolf	• If you **cry wolf** too often, no one will come when you really need help. *(say you are in trouble when you aren't)*
drop in the bucket	• My donation was a **drop in the bucket.** *(a small amount compared with what's needed)*
face the music	• José had to **face the music** when he got caught cheating on the test. *(deal with the punishment)*
flew off the handle	• Tramayne **flew off the handle** when he saw his little brother playing with matches. *(became very angry)*
floating on air	• Teresa was **floating on air** when she read the letter. *(feeling very happy)*

food for thought	• The coach gave us some **food for thought** when she said that winning isn't everything. *(something to think about)*
get down to business	• In five minutes you need to **get down to business** on this assignment. *(start working)*
get the upper hand	• The other team will **get the upper hand** if we don't play better in the second half. *(probably win)*
go overboard	• The teacher told us not **to go overboard** with fancy lettering on our posters. *(do too much)*
hit the ceiling	• Rosa **hit the ceiling** when she saw her sister painting the television. *(was very angry)*
hit the hay	• Patrice **hit the hay** early because she was tired. *(went to bed)*
in a nutshell	• **In a nutshell,** Coach Roby told us to play our best. *(to summarize)*
in the nick of time	• Zong grabbed his little brother's hand **in the nick of time** before he touched the hot pan. *(just in time)*
in the same boat	• My friend and I are **in the same boat** when it comes to doing Saturday chores. *(have the same problem)*
iron out	• Jamil and his brother were told to **iron out** their differences about cleaning their room. *(solve, work out)*
it stands to reason	• **It stands to reason** that if you keep lifting weights, you will get stronger. *(it makes sense)*
knuckle down	• Grandpa told me to **knuckle down** at school if I want to be a doctor. *(work hard)*
learn the ropes	• Being new in school, I knew it would take some time to **learn the ropes.** *(get to know how things are done)*
let's face it	• "**Let's face it!**" said Mr. Sills. "You're a better long distance runner than you are a sprinter." *(let's admit it)*
let the cat out of the bag	• Tia **let the cat out of the bag** and got her sister in trouble. *(told a secret)*
lose face	• If I strike out again, I will **lose face.** *(be embarrassed)*
nose to the grindstone	• If I keep my **nose to the grindstone,** I will finish my homework in one hour. *(working hard)*
on cloud nine	• Walking home from the party, I was **on cloud nine.** *(feeling very happy)*
on pins and needles	• I was **on pins and needles** as I waited to see the doctor. *(feeling nervous)*
over and above	• **Over and above** the assigned reading, I read two library books. *(in addition to)*

put his foot in his mouth	• Chivas **put his foot in his mouth** when he called his teacher by the wrong name. *(said something embarrassing)*
put your best foot forward	• Grandpa said that whenever you do something, you should **put your best foot forward.** *(do the best that you can do)*
rock the boat	• The coach said, "Don't **rock the boat** if you want to stay on the team." *(cause trouble)*
rude awakening	• I had a **rude awakening** when I saw the letter *F* at the top of my Spanish quiz. *(sudden, unpleasant surprise)*
save face	• Grant tried to **save face** when he said he was sorry for making fun of me in class. *(fix an embarrassing situation)*
see eye to eye	• My sister and I finally **see eye to eye** about who gets to use the phone first after school. *(are in agreement)*
sight unseen	• Grandma bought the television **sight unseen.** *(without seeing it first)*
take a dim view	• My brother will **take a dim view** if I don't help him at the store. *(disapprove)*
take it with a grain of salt	• If my sister tells you she has no homework, **take it with a grain of salt.** *(don't believe everything you're told)*
take the bull by the horns	• This team needs to **take the bull by the horns** to win the game. *(take control)*
through thick and thin	• Max and I will be friends **through thick and thin.** *(in good times and in bad times)*
time flies	• When you're having fun, **time flies.** *(time passes quickly)*
time to kill	• We had **time to kill** before the ballpark gates would open. *(extra time)*
under the weather	• I was feeling **under the weather,** so I didn't go to school. *(sick)*
word of mouth	• We found out who the new teacher was by **word of mouth.** *(talking to other people)*

Note: Like idioms, collocations are groups of words that often appear together. They may help you identify different senses of a word; for example, *old* means slightly different things in these collocations: *old man, old friends.* You will find sentence construction easier if you check for collocations.

Multilingual/ESL Exercises:

Idioms

A. Using Idioms

Replace the underlined words with appropriate idioms.

> Here's (1) <u>something to think about</u>. In order for a democracy to succeed, its citizens must participate. That just (2) <u>makes sense</u>. But (3) <u>let's admit it</u>, far too many U.S. citizens just don't vote. What excuse do they give? Many say, "My vote doesn't matter; it's just (4) <u>a small amount compared to what's needed</u>." I (5) <u>disapprove</u> of this excuse. It's time for these people to (6) <u>deal with the negative effects</u> concerning this abdication of responsibility. Notice that word "abdication." In a democracy, every person is a king. We are all (7) <u>facing the same problem</u>. I'm not saying we need (8) <u>to do too much</u> with our political involvement. However, we should at least vote, and that means researching the issues to avoid (9) <u>being embarrassed</u> because of our choices.

B. Defining Idioms

Using your own words, define the following idioms.

1. benefit of the doubt
2. burn the midnight oil
3. floating on air
4. get down to business
5. let's face it
6. over and above
7. see eye to eye
8. a bad apple
9. flew off the handle
10. break the ice
11. food for thought
12. iron out
13. lose face
14. hit the ceiling
15. on cloud nine
16. learn the ropes
17. bone to pick
18. cold shoulder
19. as the crow flies
20. in a nutshell

Targeting Trouble Spots

A sentence that is perfectly acceptable in one language may be unacceptable when directly translated into English. For example, many East Asian languages do not use articles, so using these words can be a challenge to learners of English. The following pages will help you target trouble spots for your general language group.

Help for Speakers of Latin Languages

Advice	DO NOT Write . . .	DO Write . . .
Study the use of count and noncount nouns (671.1–672.2).	I have three homeworks.	I have three homework assignments. *or* I have three types of homework.
Do not omit the subject, *it* as subject, or *there* with delayed subjects (646.5, 687.3).	Is hot sitting in this room. Are going to the theater.	It is hot sitting in this room. We are going to the theater.
Place most subjects before the verb (686).	Gave I the tutor my thanks.	I gave the tutor my thanks.
Avoid using *the* with certain generalizations (673.1).	The business is a difficult major.	Business is a difficult major.
Avoid using *the* with singular proper nouns (673.1).	The April is the cruelest month.	April is the cruelest month.
Avoid double subjects (687.4).	My mother she is a nurse.	My mother is a nurse.
Learn whether to use a gerund or an infinitive after a verb (676.2–677.1).	The professor wants finishing the paperwork. She regrets to wait until the last minute.	The professor wants to finish the paperwork. She regrets waiting until the last minute.
Do not use *which* to refer to people (621.7).	The professors which teach English are here.	The professors who teach English are here. *or* The professors that teach English are here.
Avoid double negatives (687.1).	I never got no assignment.	I never got the assignment. *or* I got no assignment.

Help for Speakers of European Languages

Advice	DO NOT Write . . .	DO Write . . .
Do not omit the subject, *it* as a subject, or *there* with delayed subjects (646.5, 687.3).	Are thousands of books in the library. Is okay to talk.	There are thousands of books in the library. It is okay to talk.
Avoid using *the* with certain generalizations and singular proper nouns (673.1).	I excel at the physics. The Professor Smith marks grammar errors.	I excel at physics. Professor Smith marks grammar errors.
Learn to use progressive verb tenses (676.1).	I still work on my term paper.	I am working on my term paper.
Learn whether to use a gerund or an infinitive after a verb (676.2–677.1).	The students need finishing their projects. The professors finished to grade the papers.	The students need to finish their projects. The professors finished grading the papers.
Avoid placing adverbs between verbs and direct objects (683.2).	I wrote very quickly the first draft.	I wrote the first draft very quickly.
Do not use *which* to refer to people (621.7).	I am one of the students which sing in the choir.	I am one of the students who sing in the choir.

Help for Speakers of African and Caribbean Languages

Advice	DO NOT Write . . .	DO Write . . .
Avoid double subjects (687.4).	The professor she gave us an assignment.	The professor gave us an assignment.
Use plural nouns after plural numbers (675.1).	The class has two professor.	The class has two professors.
Use the correct form of the *be* verb (633.1).	The union be having a blood drive. We be going.	The union is having a blood drive. We are going.
Make subjects and verbs agree in number (655.2).	She have her own notes. They finishes on time.	She has her own notes. They finish on time.
Use past tense verbs correctly (634).	When the semester began, I study hard.	When the semester began, I studied hard.
Study the rules for article use (672.3–673.1).	I need to buy computer. Entrance exam is required.	I need to buy a computer. An entrance exam is required.

Help for Speakers of East Asian Languages

Advice	DO NOT Write . . .	DO Write . . .
Use plural forms of nouns (675.1).	I have three difficult class.	I have three difficult classes.
Learn to use adjectival forms (682.1–683.1).	He is a very intelligence professor.	He is a very intelligent professor.
Use the objective case of pronouns (630.1).	The tutor helps I with homework.	The tutor helps me with homework.
Include a subject (or *there*) (646.5, 687.3).	Is good to be here. Are many parts.	It is good to be here. There are many parts.
Study subject–verb agreement (655.2).	The course have a long reading list.	The course has a long reading list.
Study past tenses (634).	We study yesterday. At first, I don't get it.	We studied yesterday. At first, I didn't get it.
Use articles—*a, an,* and *the* (672.3–673.1).	I want to be nurse.	I want to be a nurse.
Study conjunction use (642.1–642.5).	Though she studies, but she struggles.	Though she studies, she struggles.
Learn whether to use a gerund or an infinitive (676.2–677.1).	The students need helping each other study.	The students need to help each other study.

Help for Speakers of Middle Eastern Languages

Advice	DO NOT Write . . .	DO Write . . .
Study pronoun gender and case (630).	My mother works hard at his job. Give she credit.	My mother works hard at her job. Give her credit.
Don't include a pronoun after a relative clause (651.3, 687.4).	The study space that I share with two others it is too small.	The study space that I share with two others is too small.
Place most subjects before the verb (686).	Received the freshmen the assignment.	The freshmen received the assignment.
Don't overuse progressive verb tenses (676.1).	I am needing a nap. I am wanting food.	I need a nap. I want food.
Use the definite article *the* correctly (673.1).	Union is closed during the July.	The union is closed during July.

Handbook: Mixed Review

A. Period, Comma, Quotation Marks, Question Mark, Apostrophe

Rewrite each of the following sentences, inserting punctuation where needed.

1. I asked Could I have an extension on my paper Professor Rubel
2. He responded Well Rob all the other papers have been turned in
3. Yes thats true I replied but no one elses paper will be as good as mine
4. Youd better be right said Professor Rubel How many days better will it be
5. I cringed and asked How about five days better
6. Professor Rubels eyebrows shot up Five days better will have to be phenomenal
7. Three days I asked sheepishly
8. Thats still very much better than everyone else Professor Rubel pointed out.
9. Okay what about one day better I responded
10. I think thats the level of better that you can do Rob One day it is

B. Title Capitalization, Quotation Marks, Italics

For each sentence, rewrite titles, correctly capitalizing them and using quotation marks or italics (underlining) as needed.

1. In the New york times, I read the article, Four representatives Charged In ethics Probe.
2. The music album Sea of cowards by the band The Dead Weather includes the song I'm mad.
3. I read the chapter An empire Crumbles in the novel The shadow of Reichenbach falls, which was reviewed well in the library journal.
4. Have you read the poem the Fiddler Of Dooney in the collection W.b. Yeats: selected Poems?
5. In John Steinbeck's book The acts of King Arthur And his noble Knights, I most enjoyed the chapter the Noble tale of Sir Lancelot Of The Lake.
6. A chapter entitled Management writing has been added to the second edition of the handbook Write For Business.
7. We went to the Riverside Theater to see Adam Lambert sing his song For your entertainment.
8. The radio show Performance today stars Fred Child.
9. The song Joyful, Joyful comes from Beethoven's symphony Ode to joy.
10. We'll sail to Mexico aboard a boat called The lark Of The sea.

Handbook: Mixed Review

A. Capitalization, Plurals

Correct the capitalization and plural errors in each sentence by writing the correct word or words.

1. Some Holidays fall on different daies of the week.
2. A holiday like the fourth of july or halloween can fall on only one Date but on any day.
3. Holidaies such as Memorial day or Labor day always fall on a Monday.
4. In the badger state, christmas is often white, but in the aloha state, it never is.
5. Festivals such as taste of chicago or milwaukee's summerfest stretch out over weekes.
6. In that way, these celebrationes are similar to chinese new year, which lasts for many daies.
7. On new year's eve in the west, husbands dance with their wifes and leave their childs with babysitters.
8. Reveleres often have a few glassesful of wine or champagne to celebrate New year's eve.
9. It's funny how most Americanes don't know when columbus day is, which celebrates Columbus's discovery of the new world.
10. It's also strange how many earthlings don't know if earth day is in march, april, or may.

B. Numbers and Spelling

Correct the number and spelling errors in each sentence by writing the correct form or words.

1. Do monkies and other great aps like to eat French frys?
2. 300 million Americans seem to like frys, as do many of the 6,000,000,000 others in the world.
3. Fries and a 4- or eight-ounce burger is a common meal for Americans.
4. If you drive through before eleven a.m., you'll get hashes brown instead of frys at most fast-food places.
5. One eight-ounce burger can pack a whopping four hundred fifty calories.
6. The local fast-food restaurant employs 43 people, with 2 Steve's and 3 Jacob's.
7. They cut about three hundred tomatos every day.
8. In addition to 11 fry cooks, they employ 3 cheves.
9. They advertise over 1,000,000,000 served.
10. On each burger, they squirt one teaspoon of ketchup and one half teaspoon of mustard.

Handbook: Mixed Review

Spelling

Write the correct spelling of each word below.

1. abundence
2. acommodate
3. aquiesce
4. advize
5. althrough
6. annoint
7. biscut
8. celibration
9. comission
10. concieve
11. confidencial
12. consientous
13. deseased
14. dependant
15. disipline
16. eficeincy
17. essencial
18. exhorbitant
19. extreem
20. Feberary
21. freind
22. harrass
23. interupt
24. irigate
25. judgement
26. laundary
27. licence
28. ofen
29. opperate
30. parlament
31. personell
32. preferrance
33. previlant
34. procede
35. pumkin
36. questionaire
37. reccurrence
38. rehersal
39. restaraunt
40. reumatism
41. sceen
42. seperate
43. simmilar
44. speciman
45. stomache
46. sumerize
47. surveylance
48. unneccessary
49. useable
50. vegtable
51. villian
52. volunter
53. wether
54. wholely
55. writen
56. yeild

Handbook: Mixed Review

Usage

Correct the usage in the following document by writing down the line number and the usage errors, crossed out, with the correct words beside them.

When I sat down to eat at Leon's Texas Grill, I remembered a friend's advise: *1*

"Alright, get ready for allot of food." His prediction was all together accurate.   *2*

When I smelled the delicious aroma of beef brisket on the barbecue, I was anxious   *3*

to get some of my own. I wanted it bad. But the brisket was complimented by   *4*

beans, potato salad, and other sides. Leon's also offered spicy sausage, steaks,   *5*

and more meats than I could chose from. I decided that the first coarse would   *6*

be brisket with beans. I had a guilty conscious as I ate fore hunks of brisket and   *7*

went back for more. Everything tasted so well. I was under no allusion that I   *8*

would be loosing wait tonight.   *9*

Brisket would normally be vary tough, but slow grilling assures its tenderness.   *10*

Brisket often cooks for hours and is only latter served to customers. What an   *11*

ingenuous way to make tough meat flavorful and delicious! I was liable to   *12*

literally eat everything in the restaurant, and then loose conscienceness.   *13*

I was in the midst of my third helping when one of the restaurant's personal past   *14*

me with a cart that had peaces of cake and pie and other types of desert. My pour   *15*

stomach was already quiet full, and I felt real sleepy, but from my prospective,   *16*

I wasn't going to be getting back here anytime soon. Those were sum of the   *17*

most delicious sweets I'd ever scene. I looked threw all the options their and   *18*

picked too cupcakes. I was being vary gluttonous, and my waste would reveal   *19*

my indiscretions.   *20*

After my meal, I wished I could meet the man whom established this restaurant.   *21*

I would have told him, "Leon, your my hero." Then, a second latter, I would've   *22*

past out.   *23*

Handbook: Mixed Review

A. Noun, Pronoun, Verb, Adjective, Adverb

Identify each underlined word as a noun (n), a pronoun (pron), a verb (v), an adjective (adj), or an adverb (adv).

> (1) You may not (2) think much about that (3) green stuff under your feet—yes, (4) grass—but it has conquered the world. Grass didn't exist at all until the (5) late Cretaceous period, but once it (6) arrived on the scene, (7) it took over. Whole animal (8) species grew up to graze upon this (9) hardy plant, eating both the leaves and the (10) heads of grain. Some types of grass, such as barley, (11) produce grains that humans (12) also eat. Farm kids (13) often pluck a long stalk of grass and chew on (14) it, but you wouldn't be able to chew on the (15) largest stalks from the grass family—the giant bamboo. Unlike its (16) tiny cousins, bamboo plants grow (17) so rapidly that they have been purported to be used to torture people. (18) Maybe they are just getting back at (19) us for (20) always walking on top of them.

B. Coordinating, Correlative, and Subordinating Conjunctions

Create a three-column table, labeling the columns "Coordinating," "Correlative," and "Subordinating." Then sort the following conjunctions, writing them in their correct columns.

as long as	although	since
after	so that	unless
yet	so	whenever
both/and	or	as
when	even though	whereas
because	for	until
either/or	where	nor
though	as if	not only/but also
before	in order that	and
neither/nor	whether/or	provided that
while	but	

Handbook: Mixed Review

A. Fragments

Turn each fragment into a sentence by adding what is missing (a subject, a verb, a subject and a verb, or a complete thought).

1. During the big game.
2. When we scored the winning goal.
3. Shouted our fight song.
4. Just before the whistle blew.
5. Smiling from ear to ear.
6. The scoreboard overhead.
7. With looks of amazement.
8. In order to commemorate the win.
9. The college newspaper.
10. Whenever we win a big game.

B. Other Sentence Errors

Rewrite each sentence, fixing the comma splice, run-on, agreement error, or nonstandard language.

1. The team fought like never before they won in overtime.
2. Each team member gave their all.
3. Three touchdowns, three extra points, and a field goal sets the score at 24-21.
4. Tim, Jake, and Kurt, they played their best games ever.
5. Tim broke his passing record, Jake beat his rushing yards.
6. Kurt been kicking the ball through the goalposts every time.
7. You should of been there.
8. I'm gonna watch every game this year.
9. Coach Carlson say he's never had such a good team.
10. I is planning to try out next year.

C. Dangling/Misplaced Modifiers

Rewrite each sentence to correct the dangling or misplaced modifiers.

1. After watching from the stands for the whole game, the team scored the winning field goal.
2. I congratulated the linebacker for tackling the quarterback on his way to the locker room.
3. A kicker once punted the ball from our second string.
4. A cheerleader climbed to the top of the pyramid with red hair.
5. After kicking the winning field goal, the other team left looking dejected.

Images:

Model Credits

Page 4: Dan Heath. "Why Change is So Hard: Self Control is Exhaustible" from Fast Company 6/2/2010

Page 31: "The Gullible Family" by Mary Bruins. Used by permission of the author.

Page 144: "The Entomology of Village Life" by Robert Minto. Used by permission of the author.

Page 148: "Spare Change" by Teresa Zsuffa. Used by permission of the author.

Page 151: "When Dreams Take Flight" by Elizabeth Fuller, From The New York Times, November 25, 2009. © 2009 The New York Times. All rights reserved. Used by permission and protected by the Copyright Laws of the United States. The printing, copying, redistribution, or retransmission of the Material without express written permission is prohibited.

Page 153: "Call Me Crazy, But I Have to Be Myself" by Mary Seymour. From Newsweek, July 29, 2002 © 2002 Newsweek, Inc. All rights reserved. Used by permission and protected by the Copyright Laws of the United States. The printing, copying, redistribution, or retransmission of the Material without express written permission is prohibited.

Page 155: "The Muscle Mystique" from HIGH TIDE IN TUCSON: ESSAYS FROM NOW OR NEVER by Barbara Kingsolver, pages 80-84. HarperCollins, 1995. Copyright (c) 1995 by Barbara Kingsolver. Reprinted by permission of HarperCollins Publishers Inc. and The Frances Goldin Literary Agency.

Page 164: "The Slender Trap" by Trina Piscitelli. Used by permission of the author.

Page 167: "Dutch Discord" by Brittany Korver. Used by permission of the author.

Page 171: Mary Brophy Marcus, "If You Let Me Play..." from U.S. NEWS & WORLD REPORT, October 27, 1997. Copyright 1997 U.S. News & World Report, L.P. Reprinted with permission.

Page 174: "Mind Over Mass Media" by Steven Pinker, From The New York Times, June 10, 2010. © 2010 The New York Times. All rights reserved. Used by permission and protected by the Copyright Laws of the United States. The printing, copying, redistribution, or retransmission of the Material without express written permission is prohibited.

Page 184: "Seth in Beloved and Orleanna in Poisonwood Bible: Isolation, Children, and Getting Out" by Rachel De Smith. Used by permission of the author.

Page 187: Gelareh Asayesh, "Shrouded in Contradiction." Copyright 2001 Gelareh Asayesh. First appeared in The New York Times Magazine, November 2, 2001. Reprinted by permission of the author.

Page 190: "Shades of Prejudice" by Shankar Vedantam from January 18, 2010, The New York Times. Reprinted by permission of SLL/Sterling Lord Literistic, Inc. Copyright (c) January 18, 2010 by Shankar Vedantam

Amy Johansson / Shutterstock.com

Malota / Shutterstock.com

image100/Corbis

Stefan Schurr / Shutterstock.com

Index

Application, 23
Checklist, 24
Evaluation, 14–16, 22
Modes of, 19–23
Reading, 4–9
Reasoning, inductive and
   deductive, 18
Synthesis, 21
Viewing, 10–15
Writing, 16–23
Cross-curricular research,
   APA style for, 535–564
   Drafting, 68
   MLA style for, 493–434
   Planning, 54
   Process, 127
   Publishing, 110
   Revising, 90

D

Dactylic foot, 289
Dagger, 589.5
Dangling modifiers, 671.2
Dash, 581
   Questions with, 569.5
Databases, 409, 411,
   442–445
   citing, 495, 521
Dates, punctuation of, 574.1
Decent/descent/dissent, 618.5
Decimal points, 567.3, 598
Declarative sentence, 658.1
   Punctuation of, 567.1
Deductive reasoning, 18,
   300
Define, key word, 365
Definition,
   Activities, 252
   Checklist, 252
   Essays of, 238–249
   Graphic organizer, 53
   Guidelines, 250–251
   Paragraph, 62, 237
   Thesis, 47

Delayed subject, 652.5,
   652.1
Demonstrative pronoun,
   633.3, 635.2
Denouement, 286
Dependent clause, 657.1
Describe, key word, 366
Description and narration,
   137–160
   Activities, 160
   Checklist, 160
   Essays of 144–152
   Guidelines, 158–159
Description and reflection,
   137–160
   Activities, 160
   Checklist, 160
   Essays of 153–157
   Guidelines, 158–159
Desert/dessert, 618.6
Details,
   Connecting, 84
   Five W's, 114
   Organizing, 115
   Specific, 85, 114
   Supporting, 62–64, 85
   Types of, 85
Development,
   Of an essay, 114–126
   Methods of, 46–47, 112–
   113, 386
   Middle, 60–61
   Subject, 34–35
Dewey decimal system, 439
Diagonal, 589.5
Diagram, key word, 366
   Venn, 52
Dialogue,
   Punctuation of, 574.2,
   583.3–4
Diction, 286
Dieresis, 589.5
Different from/different than,
   618.7
Dimeter, 289
Direct address, 574.3

Direct object, 631.2, 653.5
Direct quotation, 539, 584.1
Directed free writing,
   36–37, 113
Directories, 441, 448
Disabilities, acceptable
   terms, 103
Discreet/discrete, 618.8
Discuss, key word, 366
Disinterested/uninterested,
   618.9
Dissent/decent/descent, 618.5
Dividing words, 580.3
Documentation in research
   paper, 398, 478–479
   APA references, 543–553
   MLA works cited, 508–
   524
Domain name, Internet, 446
Double-entry notebook, 421
Double negative, 674.4,
   691.1
Double preposition, 674.2
Double subject, 693.4
Drafting, 55–68, 116–117
   Activities, 68
   Analogy, 63
   Cause/effect, 63
   Checklist, 68
   Climax, 69
   Coherent structure, 61
   Compare/contrast, 69
   Definition, 62
   Ending, 65–67
   Final, 124–126
   First, 58–67, 116–117
   Illustration, 62
   Middle, 60–64
   Openings, 58–59
   Research paper, 469–484
   Support, 62–64
   Unifying, 66